Mustafa Barzani and the Kurdish Liberation
Movement (1931–1961)

Mustafa Barzani and the Kurdish Liberation Movement (1931–1961)

Massoud Barzani

*Edited, with a General Introduction,
by Ahmed Ferhadi*

MUSTAFA BARZANI AND THE KURDISH LIBERATION MOVEMENT
© Ahmed Ferhadi, 2003

First published 2003 by
PALGRAVE MACMILLAN™
175 Fifth Avenue, New York, N.Y. 10010 and
Houndmills, Basingstoke, Hampshire, England RG21 6XS
Companies and representatives throughout the world

PALGRAVE MACMILLAN is the global academic imprint of the Palgrave Macmillan division of St. Martin's Press, LLC and of Palgrave Macmillan Ltd. Macmillan® is a registered trademark in the United States, United Kingdom and other countries. Palgrave is a registered trademark in the European Union and other countries.

ISBN 0–312–29316–X hardback

Cataloging-in-Publication Data is available from the Library of Congress.

A catalogue record for this book is available from the British Library.

Design by Newgen Imaging Systems (P) Ltd., Chennai, India.

First edition: September, 2003
10 9 8 7 6 5 4 3 2 1

Printed in the United States of America.

Dedicated to Martyrs for Freedom Everywhere

Contents

Abbreviations

CENTO	Central Treaty Organization, which was known as the Baghdad Pact (member countries: Britain, Iran, Iraq, Pakistan, and Turkey)
HP	Hiwa [Hope] Party
ICP	Iraqi Communist Party
IP	Istiqlal [Independence] Party
IPC	Iraqi Petroleum Company
KDP	Kurdistan Democratic Party (founded on August 16, 1946)
KDPI	Kurdistan Democratic Party of Iran (founded on August 16, 1945)
NDP	National Democratic Party
NUF	National Unity Front
PRM	Popular Resistance Militia
PUK	Patriotic Union of Kurdistan
RAF	(British) Royal Air Force
RCC	Revolutionary Command Council (of the Ba'thist government)
UAR	United Arab Republic (comprising Egypt and Syria from 1958 to 1961 under President Nasser)
USSR	Union of the Soviet Socialist Republic

General Introduction

K nown for his Spartan *modus vivendi* and widely admired, Mustafa Barzani (March 3, 1914 March 1, 1979) was the leader of the Kurdish national movement for half of the twentieth century. The frequent incidence of wholesale sellout of Kurds by regional as well as Western powers throughout his lifetime corroborated the credence of his incisive and oft-quoted dictum, "The Kurds have no friends but their mountains."

"Barzani's life was the stuff of legend," and was "intertwined with the vicissitudes of Kurdish nationalism for half a century," writes Jonathan C. Randal (*After Such Knowledge What Forgiveness?*, 1997). "His battlefield spoils, told and retold hundreds of times wherever Kurds live, are a rare cause for pride and kept the very notion of Kurdish nationalism alive for decades. He possessed that essential ingredient of leadership, the gift of commanding emotional loyalty, which moved men and women to drop everything and follow him despite impossible odds."[1]

Barzani spent most of his life fighting various governments partitioning Kurdistan. The life-long odyssey of his struggle began in 1907 when he was barely three years old. At that age, he and his mother were incarcerated at Mosul Prison in the aftermath of a raid on their region by the Ottoman Turkish forces led by Muhamed Fadil Pasha Daghistani.[2] His father was subsequently brought to the same city to face the gallows. Not only did he fight successive Iraqi regimes, be they under Ottoman or British rule or independent, but he also pursued the struggle inside Iranian Kurdistan, where he participated in the founding of the ephemeral Kurdish Republic of Mahabad by Qazi Muhammed in 1946. In the wake of the collapse of the nascent republic, Barzani and his men set out on a daring march into the Soviet Union on foot for a sojourn of a dozen years before they returned to Iraqi Kurdistan in 1959. A bloody coup in Baghdad brought the Ba'thist regime to power in 1963, and Barzani had to fight back collaborating combatant units of Iraqi and Syrian armies in Iraqi Kurdistan. The concluding episode of this odyssey was the collapse of the hitherto most formidable and momentous Kurdish liberation movement when, in 1975, reconciled Iran and Iraq joined forces in fighting it after the shah of Iran and then Iraqi vice president Saddam Hussein personally signed the Accord of Algiers. Mustafa Barzani had to bid another farewell, which unbeknownst to him would be his last, to his cherished land and made for the United States this time. He died in Washington several years later after a bout with cancer on March 1, 1979. Interment in Iraqi Kurdistan precluded, Barzani's remains were flown to Hallaj, a northwestern village of Iranian Kurdistan, to be buried there. Wrapped in the Kurdish flag, his body was subsequently moved to his birthplace, Barzan, where he was laid to rest on October 8, 1993.

Pride

Such was Mustafa Barzani's pride that he did not set foot in Baghdad again after his estrangement with the Iraqi ruler Abd al-Karim Qasim in 1960. In subsequent years and regimes, then Vice President Saddam Hussein and, prior to that, President Abd al-Rahman Arif had to go to Kurdistan to meet him.[3]

In a meeting in Soviet Azerbaijan, Communist leader Baqirov threatened Barzani, telling him to accept his recommendations or bear responsibility for the consequences. Baqirov was an assistant to and close friend of Stalin's Interior Minister, Lavrenti Beria, through whom he enjoyed special privileges with Stalin himself. Barzani replied,

> Comrade Baqirov, we did not come here for you to threaten us. If we were to yield to threats, you would not see us here. We came here to put the cause of the oppressed people of Kurdistan before the peoples of the Soviet Union, to defend our honor and the dignity of our people. Please understand that we will not submit to threats. We emphatically will not accept to be appended to a people who is [sic] no better than ours, even if it is the people of Azerbaijan, whom we consider a friend and a brother. We are an independent people and not a part of Azerbaijan. We will not accept the obliteration of the identity of the Kurdish people.

Memoirs

Mustafa Barzani did not write his memoirs, nor did he publish. He was not very keen on narrating the circumstances that he had encountered in his life. His son, Massoud, has put together a dossier of documents, stories, and letters, as well as rare photos, and pieced them into a narrative with his reflections and analyses of historic events during the period 1931–1961.

Discussing various aspects of this specific three-decade-long period of Kurdish history with Massoud Barzani in an exclusive interview, he stated that he considers these years to be "the formative years of the Kurdish nationalist movement." Although he has appended, analyzed, and commented on subsequent events and provided updates up to the early 1990s, Mr. Barzani told me that he would like to have the time to write a sequel to the book before long to cover the ensuing events up to this time.[4]

Massoud Barzani was born on August 16, 1946 in the Kurdish Republic of Mahabad, the same day his father, Mustafa Barzani, and others founded the Kurdistan Democratic Party (KDP), of which he is currently president.[5] In the ensuing 12 years, he did not see his father, who was living in exile in the Soviet Union. Fortuitously, Massoud arrived in Iran from the United States on the day his father passed away in Washington D.C. in 1979.

Massoud Barzani admits his limitations in writing at the outset. In his introduction to Part I of this book, he relates, "Admittedly, I am neither a writer, nor a specialized researcher, nor a historian. I have fought hard to set aside my biases to command objectivity and fairness in meeting this challenging project, and to bring to readers and those interested in the Kurdish cause the fruits of this labor."

He underscores honesty in narrating facts and equates skewing them with treason. "[W]riting history is a trust that must be kept for those who decide to take it on. No objection ought to be raised for expressing views or for commenting on events that do not correspond to an author's persuasion. However, to distort facts and history is an unequivocal treason," states Barzani in his introduction to Part IV.

Of the late Sheikh Rashid of Lolan, the archenemy of the Barzanis, writes Massoud Barzani, "Sheikh Rashid was known to have continued to abhor the Barzanis to his dying day. In spite of this hatred, I must point out some facts about him. Of all the Sheikhs in Kurdistan, he was the firmest and the most unshakable in his beliefs. Unlike other chiefs who vacillated, he upheld his values, especially those germane to issues of honor." On the other hand, Barzani has no such savory remarks for his own political party, the KDP, when he thinks it has erred. For instance, in 1959, "When al-Shawwaf was killed and officers loyal to Prime Minister Abdul-Karim Qasim regained control over the Fifth Brigade and the city of Mosul, Popular Resistance Militia squads under the Iraqi Communist Party's command committed atrocious retaliatory crimes against the population of Mosul, with the complicity and at times the help of the KDP branch in Mosul, which led armed men from Kurdish tribes to march on the city." Barzani's conclusion is that "from the beginning to the end, the Mosul events ushered in a new era of bloody struggle in Iraq, and no one escapes blame and responsibility. Nationalists, Communists, and Kurds all committed sins and errors against themselves, their country, and people. They sinned against Iraq."

This book sheds light on confidential telegrams of the British government that reveal what may not be realized by many observers, i.e., the intention that Central Treaty Organization (CENTO) member states, Turkey and Iran, harbored to expropriate Iraqi Kurdistan in the wake of the July 14 revolution of 1958.

In the Documents section are some "documents from 1943 [to] 1945 which [Mustafa] Barzani had kept in a special valise," writes Massoud Barzani. "He told me that he had kept all the documents from that period henceforth. However, some of them were lost in the Araxes River when [the Barzanis] crossed into Soviet territory. I have tried to shed as much light as possible on the ambiguous aspects in these documents."

Of interest in the same section is a protracted letter to Mustafa Barzani, handwritten on October 5, 1959 by (then KDP member) Jalal Talabani, who was attending the International Youth Festival in Peking, China, at the time (Document no. 21). He signed off using his *nom de guerre*, "Pivot." Talabani wrote another letter to Barzani on July 30, 1957 (Document no. 22) before the two men would meet. Mr. Talabani is currently the chairman of the Patriotic Union of Kurdistan (PUK).

Bearing the Brunt

Massoud Barzani and his immediate family, as well as his Barzani tribe, have sacrificed beyond description. Iraqi government agents have assassinated three of his brothers. He, himself, was the target of an assassination attempt in Vienna, Austria, on January 8, 1979. His six children grew up as refugees in Iran. Iraq has destroyed his hometown of Barzan 16 times. Thirty-two of his family members were among the 8,000 Barzanis of the Quashtappa camp, whom Iraq eliminated in one instance in 1983.

The Barzanis had been forcibly relocated to a camp adjacent to and closely monitored by the military camp in the town of Quashtappa, in the plains about 20 kilometers (km) south of Arbil. There, they first came under aerial bombardment from Iranian Air Force fighters at the beginning of the Iraq–Iran war, which lasted from 1980 until 1988. Accused of collaboration with the Iranians this time, the Iraqi army extracted all the male Barzanis between the ages of 10 and 80 from the camp in July 1983, paraded them in Baghdad as Iranian prisoners of war (POWs), and then propelled them into oblivion. They have not been heard from since.

A decade after the incident, when London-based author, journalist, and film-maker from New Zealand, Sheri Laizer, went to Iraqi Kurdistan, she talked to bereaved Barzani women.

> The women spoke in short anguished sentences, searching their memories for words which could begin to describe what had happened ... 'We don't know anything about what happened to our men," she explained. "They were all taken away by the government ... I had four sons. At the time they were captured, the youngest was 10 years old, the next 15, the third about 20 years old, married with two children, and the eldest was 25 years old. He was also married and had four children. We don't know why they were taken. It happened very early at about five one morning. Those who were awake had already got up to pray. Others were still in bed. The army came and surrounded our village. Saddam's soldiers commanded everyone to come outside and then they rounded us up and took all the men. Whoever was awake was taken first, then those still sleeping were sought and taken from their beds ... One time they came to the camp we'd been moved to by night, and surrounded us as before. They rounded up any men who were there, even those who were sick or injured, even those who were mad, even those whose two eyes were blind. The soldiers tied their feet with animal tethers and dragged them off. No one was left, not at all. By God, there was not an adult male left in the village old enough to slaughter the chickens. They took everyone and just dumped them into lorries and went away. Year after year, we women were left to wash the bodies of our dead and guard the camp ourselves." Tears filled her eyes. She didn't try to wipe them away. She looked far into the distance, not seeing us any more (*Martyrs, Traitors, and Patriots: Kurdustan after the War*, Lazier 1996).[6] Flimsy hopes that had lingered for half a decade about the possible survival of the disappeared Barzanis were dashed. In 1988, when asked about the missing Barzanis, Saddam made a television announcement in which he declared they had been sent to the "engravers" (in other words, the cemetery). But the bodies have still to be located.[7]

The Book

This book comprises a biography of sorts of the late Mustafa Barzani by his son, Massoud, who sporadically blends it with his own memories of the legendary leader and provides a veritable mine of photos, documents and correspondence in Kurdish, Arabic, Persian, and Russian. Much of this material has rarely been seen before. Massoud Barzani narrates events in the first person, analyzes them, and updates some of them up to the early 1990s, when he finished writing the manuscript in Arabic. The work first appeared in the form of a series of four rudimentary booklets in Arabic. They were printed at the local KDP Press with very limited circulation between December 1986 and December 1990. Mr. Nemat Sharif had diligently attempted the laborious first-draft translation of the book into English before the task was passed on.

This version of the work is the first book by Massoud Barzani available in English to date. To preserve the original format, the book comprises four parts, each corresponding to one of the original Arabic booklets and each prefaced by an introduction by Mr. Barzani.

To facilitate the reading of each part independently, transition from one part to the next occasionally may entail some repetition of background events. To preserve the narrative and convey it verbatim in the English translation, all necessary additions have been inserted within brackets. Consequently, any item found between brackets, i.e. [...], be it within the body of the text, in the footnotes, or elsewhere in the book, has been added to the original work for the purpose of elucidation.

Barzan and Barzani

The namesake of Mustafa Barzani, the Barzani tribe, and the other Barzanis is the region of Barzan, from where they come.

Barzan is located in the northernmost part of Iraqi Kurdistan, 158 kilometers/ 95 miles (80 *air* kilometers/48 *air* miles) to the north of Arbil City. Administratively, it is in the Mergasur District within the jurisdiction of Arbil Province.

Orthography of Names

An attempt has been made to bring some uniformity to the disparate English spellings of the same names transcribed from Middle Eastern languages. Nonetheless, direct quotations have retained their original method of spelling. The following observations are intended to elucidate the orthography of names.

Personal Names. Throughout the book, Barzani, The Barzani, Mulla(h) Mustafa, or Mulla(h) Mustafa Barzani all refer to Mustafa Barzani unless stated otherwise.

The spelling of the word Mulla(h) as in Mulla(h) Mustafa Barzani, reflects its Arabic pronunciation. In Kurdish it sounds like Mala (with the second vowel being long and accented). It means clergyman. However, when prefixed to male names among the Kurds, this word does not always imply that the person is a man of religion.

The definite article *al*, which means "the" in Arabic, is prefixed to one of the names of God to form compound proper nouns beginning with the word *abd* (servant) like Abd al-Qadir (the Servant of the Omnipotent). Its pronunciation is contingent upon the nature of the following letter: Abd al-Qadir is pronounced Abdul Qadir, but Abd al-Rahman is pronounced Abdur Rahman (the Servant of the Compassionate). The letter l of the definite article is pronounced in the former but assimilated in the latter. The prefix has been invariably spelled *al* in such names regardless of its pronunciation.

Although its Arabic spelling is identical, the late Egyptian President Abd al-Nasser's first name could be found spelled in English as Gamal (the way the Egyptians pronounced it) or Jamal (as pronounced by others). To maintain consistency in this work, the full name has been spelled Jamal Abd al-Nasser rather than Gamal Abdel Nasser, which is often found in pertinent English literature.

When the word martyr precedes a name, it does not necessarily have a religious connotation or undertone as it once did. Kurds often use the Arabic word *shaheed* (martyr) to refer to a fallen comrade in battle.

Geographical Names. Like personal names, albeit to a lesser extent, geographical names of many loci in Kurdistan lack a harmonious orthographical representation in English. For example, Kurdistan has been spelled Kordestan (based on its Persian pronunciation) and Koordistan, among other spelling forms. The regional capital city of Iraqi Kurdistan, Arbil, is also spelled Erbil and Irbil almost as frequently. As if that were not confusing enough, Arbili Kurds themselves, including yours truly, call their city *Hawler*. Founded before 2300 B.C. by the Sumerians, who called it Urbillum, this thriving city of about one million inhabitants today is one of the world's oldest continuously inhabited communities. In the Battle of Gaugamela, also known as the Battle of Arbela, fought near the town in 331 B.C., Alexander the Great decisively defeated the Persian king, Darius III, opening the way for his conquest of Persia (*cf. The New Encyclopedia Britannica* 1987, p. 378).[8]

Province, District, and Subdistrict

Since antiquity, the Kurds, as a homogeneous community, have occupied a vast, cohesive region called Kurdistan, which means the land of the Kurds or Kurdland. It comprises northwestern parts of present-day Iran, northern Iraq, parts of northern Syria, and southeastern Turkey, with overlaps into the Republic of Armenia. According to David McDowall (*Modern History of the Kurds*, 1997), "The term 'Kurdistan' was first used in the twelfth century as a geographical term by the Saljuqs."[9] According to G. Chaliand (*People without a Country*, 1980). the geographical term Kurdistan, "covers a part of the regions peopled by Kurds. There are Kurds from the Taurus mountains to the Western plateaus of Iran and from Mount Ararat to the foothills adjoining the Mesopotamia plain."[10]

However, Kurdistan[11] is more than just a geographical term. "Although the term Kurdistan appears on few maps, it is clearly more than a geographical term since it refers also to a human culture which exists in that land. To this extent, Kurdistan is a social and political concept," says McDowall (*The Kurds*, 1989).[12]

Under the British mandate (1920–1932), three former *vilayets* (provinces) of the Ottoman Empire, which were known as Mesopotamia in the West, were renamed Iraq. They were Mousul, Baghdad, and Basrah. Administratively, the new country consisted of 14 (now 18) provinces, called *liwas* (later renamed *muhafazas*). Within the jurisdiction of each *muhafaza*, there are a number of districts called *qazas*, within the boundaries of which there exist some *nahiyas*, or subdistricts. Within the administrative boundaries of each *nahiya* are some villages. The Kurds were concentrated in the provinces of Mousul, Arbil, Kirkuk, Sulaymaniya, and Diyala.

The Kurdish areas of Iraq cover roughly 74,000 km^2 (17 percent) of the total territory of the country's 438,446 km^2 according to Ismet Sherif Vanly (*Kurdistan in Iraq*, 1980)[13] In March 1975 about *half* of Iraqi Kurdistan was granted a form of autonomy and officially named the Autonomous Region comprising three *muhafazas*: Arbil, Sulaymaniya, and Duhok, which was upgraded to a *muhafaza*. It used to be a *qaza* within the jurisdiction of Mousul *liwa*.

Barzan is a *nahiya* (subdistrict), and its villages are within the *qaza* (district) of Mergasur, which in turn is within the administrative jurisdiction of Arbil *muhafaza* (province). The province is named after Arbil City, the regional capital of Iraqi Kurdistan.

On the Issues

Although the book narrates events up to 1961, the author provides comparisons and analyses that encompass the situation in subsequent years and offers his insight when this becomes relevant in Part IV of the book, especially in his preface to it. For instance, on successive Iraqi regimes since the formation of the Iraqi State and the perpetual suffering of all the Iraqi people, Massoud Barzani says,

> The Iraqis have suffered tremendous agony. They have never tasted true liberty and independence. Historically, they have found themselves either ruled by a Turkish Governor, a British Commissioner or a small band that leaped to power through a bloody coup d'état. They have never elected a Parliament or a President freely, not even once. They have never willingly pledged allegiance to a ruler. The Iraqis are a people whose freedom has been usurped. However, their rulers have ruled in their name, killed in their name, destroyed in their name, waged wars and compromised their sovereignty and independence all in their name. The Iraqi people [has] never had the right to express [its] opinion. All this happens while Iraq is being ruled by a political party claiming to be "the bearer of the banner of unity, freedom, and social-ism"[14] and accusing its predecessors of treason, dictatorship, and being agents [to foreigners].

He depicts as "black" the coups d'état in Baghdad that have brought the Ba'th Party to power twice, first for a brief period in the wake of the bloody coup of 1963 and then in 1968. (The full name of the Ba'th Party is the Arab Socialist Ba'th

Party. The word ba'th means "resurrection" in Arabic.) Its grip on power has not been dislodged ever since. He argues that a power struggle in the government of Republican Iraq's first ruler, Abd al-Karim Qasim, paved the way for deviation from the revolutionary path and for

a loss of values that led to the incident of the black coup of February 8, 1963, and the ensuing black coups d'état. Owing to the crimes committed against them and against the national sovereignty of Iraq since the February 8, 1963 coup and especially since the coup d'état of July 17, 1968, the Iraqis have forgotten the ills of their erstwhile leaders. The number of all those executed during the periods when Nuri al-Sa'id [the perennial prime minister under monarchy] and Abd al-Karim Qasim reigned is less than half the number of those executed in a single day by the present regime. Even leaders of the Ba'th Party did not escape the collective purges that occurred in the 1979 massacre, which cost the Ba'th Party some of its best and most principled leaders, including the honorable fighter, Abd al-Khaliq al-Samarra'i.[15]

The Ba'th Party's stance on the issue of national minorities in the Arab World was discussed in the booklet that was printed by the Dar al-Thawra Press in Baghdad in 1979. The thesis had been deliberated on and approved at the party's Eleventh National Congress:

... [T]he condition the Party provided for affiliation with the Arab nation as the Constitution states in its General Principles is as follows:
An Arab is anyone whose language is Arabic, who lives or aspires to live on Arab land, and who believes in his affiliation with the Arab nation.
This definition means that Arab identity extends to all individuals and groups who meet this condition, without regard to race. This leaves the door wide open to absorb minorities and smaller ethnic groups into the Arab nation. As for nationalities with relatively larger populations within the Arab homeland, which have languages and ethnic traits that are fairly different from the Arabic language and traits like the Kurdish nationality, we must recognize their specific local ethnicity and resolve any contradiction between their characteristics and those of the Arab national movement. These nationalities possess languages and traits which are different from those of the Arab nation but at the same time it is erroneous to consider them as different from Arabs as the Persian, Indian, and other nationalities are.
Nationalities with languages and traits different from those of the Arab nation that have lived within the Arab homeland for a long time, such as the Kurdish nationality, have established deep-rooted ties with the Arab nation. In fact they have lived, ever since they emerged and over this long period of time, in what is historically known as the Arab Homeland regardless of different names of its parts, and of the different names taken by states founded on it. This is an important issue, since the land these nationalities live on was a part of the Arab states which emerged thousands of years ago, the last one being the greater Abbasid State. This land was, therefore, home to other nationalities at the same time. Accordingly, the Arab identity of the land, home to these nationalities, was not acquired through coercion, imperialism, or usurpation. It was acquired through a historical reality extending for thousands of years. Over that, there was not any dispute or discord over all that long period.
These nationalities were, throughout various historical eras, a living component of the Arab entity, tied to and interacting with it. They were not foreign bodies [within the Arab entity] and did not contradict it. Ties between these and the Arab nation

have thus become profound and inclusive within the framework of the Islamic creed for many centuries.

In his rebuttal, Massoud Barzani discredits this claim, saying, "This document claims that the Kurds are a nation inhabiting Arab land. This is a falsification of history and of reality. It is a position stemming from blind racism. The Kurds are the most ancient of all the nations that have inhabited Kurdistan, their homeland. They have never conceded, either in the Abbasid era or at any other time, that Kurdistan is a part of the Arab homeland, and they will not do so ever." He emphasizes that "The fact that the Kurds are a nation and that Kurdistan is their land cannot be erased by merely issuing a 'yellow document.' This is a chauvinistic mentality whose time has passed," and calls on scholars to address the issue: "Indeed, this is an extremely dangerous document and represents the culmination of the despicable racist thought. I hope that Arab and Kurdish writers, researchers, and historians will give it the attention it deserves, study it scientifically, and respond to it according to the rationale of history and reality which are supported by the facts that repudiate these misleading allegations."

Massoud Barzani exhorts the Kurds to undo what has befallen the oil-rich city of Kirkuk, which used to have a Kurdish majority. The Ba'thist government altered its ethnic makeup by expelling most of its Kurdish and Turkoman inhabitants and replacing them with Arab tribes.

A word of advice to every Kurd and to future generations: Remember that the Ba'thist regime is the one which arabized Kirkuk and many other areas of Kurdistan for no reason other than its blindly racist outlook. It behooves the Kurds to strive with might and main to erase all effects of arabization from Kurdistan.

Whither Kurdistan?

At the end of the twentieth century, the number of the member states of the United Nations (UN) rose to 188 when the tiny island state of Nauru joined the world organization on September 14, 1999. Nauru has a population of 9,300.[16] On the other hand, Kurdistan, which is almost the size of France[17] and has a population of about 30 million, remained *terra incognita*. The Kurds had to walk alone throughout the twentieth century. "From Sheikh Sa'id's rebellion against the Turks in 1925 to the legendary Mulla Mustafa Barzani and his son Massoud, Kurds have grabbed the occasional headline and challenged central authorities more or less continually throughout the 20th century," writes Nicole Watts of the University of Washington (*Expanding Kurdish Studies: A Review Essay*, 1998).[18] They have had to walk long and hard into the new century, and, unless their call is heeded, their arduous march is bound to continue. "If they heed not thy call; walk alone," said the Indian poet and Nobel laureate, Rabindranath Tagore.

Ahmed Ferhadi, Ph.D.
New York University
September 1999

Part I

The First Barzan Uprising (1931–1932)

Introduction to Part I

The idea of writing this book has arisen from my sense of the importance of studying the history of the struggle of the Kurdish people and shedding light on the patriotic role of the Barzanis, who have taken part in formulating and forging numerous vicissitudes of this history.

Admittedly, I am neither a writer, nor a specialized researcher, nor a historian. I have fought hard to set aside my biases to command objectivity and fairness in meeting this challenging project, and to bring to readers and those interested in the Kurdish cause the fruits of this labor.

I must point out that despite a life full of heroism, sacrifice, and challenge devoted to the liberation and advancement of the Kurdish people, a life that reflects, in its transformations and demands, a significant share in the political history of the Kurdish people, the immortal Barzani never liked the idea of writing his memoirs and telling of the circumstances he faced in his life.

In this study, I wish to shed light on the first Barzan uprising in some detail, and to record information and facts I heard from participants in those events.

As the Kurdish struggle continued, detailed accounts of the first Barzan uprising remained unknown to many Kurds and to the outside world. Accounts of Iraqi officers who participated in military campaigns and accounts of British employees in Iraq are not objective and fair. They were not, I must stress, written to be objective.

It is wrong to expect the British or officers trained by and serving under British commanders to impart the truth. They expressed official points of view, according to their own interests. Their accounts do not correspond to events on the ground or with the legitimacy of the national uprising.

From my position in the modern Kurdish national liberation movement, I find that it is imperative and a sacred duty to at least attempt to elucidate the vague or hidden aspects of this uprising and its role in paving the way for subsequent revolts and uprisings in Barzan.

No patriot, I believe, can effectively contribute to the struggle of his nation unless he mindfully studies its history. A nation's present is the rebirth of its past, and a nation's future is the progeny of its present.

Massoud Barzani
Kurdistan
January 1986

Chapter I

The Kurdish National Movement during and after World War I

It is inconceivable that any nation has been and continues to be suffering as much injustice and oppression as the Kurds have. Nonetheless, they have yet to learn and extrapolate from past experience. Over the centuries, the Kurdish cause has remained captive to powers vying for control of the Middle East. Foreign powers, especially imperialists, have favored their own interests over the principle of legitimate Kurdish aspirations. They have made compromises and concluded deals at the expense of the hopes, sufferings, and great sacrifices of the Kurdish people.

As World War I ended and the Ottoman Empire collapsed, peoples of the region rose to gain liberty and independence. Naturally, the Kurds demanded their full rights, no less than other peoples of the region.

The Treaty of Svres[1] (1920) fired Kurdish hopes, as its Article 64 stated:

> If within one year from the coming into force of the present Treaty the Kurdish peoples within the areas defined in Article 62 shall address themselves to the Council of the League of Nations in such a manner as to show that a majority of the population of these areas desires independence from Turkey, and if the Council then considers that these peoples are capable of such independence and recommends that it should be granted to them, Turkey hereby agrees to execute such a recommendation, and to renounce all rights and title over these areas.
>
> The detailed provisions for such renunciation will form the subject of a separate agreement between the Principal Allied Powers and Turkey.
>
> If and when such renunciation takes place, no objection will be raised by the Principle Allied Powers to the voluntary adhesion to such an independent Kurdish State of the Kurds inhabiting that part of Kurdistan which has been hitherto been [sic] included in the Mosul Vilayet.

All Iraqi Kurdistan was a part of the Mosul Vilayet. The discovery of huge quantities of oil in the Baba Gurgur fields in Kirkuk multiplied the value of this region and further deepened the struggle between Britain and Turkey. Oil gushed for the first time from Baba Gurgur on October 10, 1927.

Britain successfully used the Kurdish cause as a bargaining chip against Turkey's unyielding demand for the Vilayet of Mosul as an indivisible part of

Turkish territory. Evidently insincere in their promises to Sheikh Mahmud al-Hafeed to grant Kurdistan independence, the British introduced evasive steps toward the independence of Kurdistan, followed by ambivalent policy as to whether to include Kirkuk and its oil fields in the state of Kurdistan!

In the Treaty of Lausanne[2] in 1923, the Allied powers reneged on the Treaty of Sèvres and Kemalist Turkey hardened its stance vis-à-vis the Kurds more than before. This infamous treaty killed all Kurdish hopes of attaining their rights as promised.

Paragraph 2 of Article 3 of the Treaty of Lausanne stated that the Iraqi–Turkish border and Mosul Vilayet disputes would be referred to the League of Nations for arbitration should the governments of Turkey and Britain fail to reach an adequate settlement within nine months of signing the treaty.

The Vilayet of Mosul was within the French sphere of influence in accordance with prior secret treaties between the British and French colonial powers. France, however, ceded Mosul to its ally, Britain, in 1919; the deal was finalized in the San Remo Pact[3] in 1920. Turkey continued to claim Mosul.

After Turkey and Britain failed to reach a solution, the League of Nations undertook the task on September 30, 1924. It appointed an international committee (consisting of Count Teleki, a former Hungarian premier; Colonel Paulus of Belgium, and Fersen, a Swedish charge d'affaires) assisted by a number of experts to study the Mosul problem thoroughly from all aspects and present its recommendations to the League of Nations, which in turn would render its decision accordingly.

The committee arrived in Baghdad on December 16, 1924, and in Mosul the following day. After two months of surveying the region and gathering the views of its residents, it delivered a report stressing the pertinence of the Brussels Line[4] and recommending the annexation of the whole area south of the Brussels Line to Iraq provided that (1) Iraq would remain under British mandate for 25 years; and (2) Kurdish interests as to administrative matters were to be safeguarded, and Kurdish was to be adopted as the official language used in communication and schools in the designated area. Otherwise, it would be preferable to keep the region under Turkish sovereignty.

Although the League of Nations approved the committee's recommendations, Kurdish interests were never protected. In fact, Britain and the governments of Turkey and Iraq worked against these interests. The carving up of Kurdistan was maintained in the manner we see it today.

Initially, the Turks did not recognize the resolution of the League of Nations and the Brussels Line. However, they reluctantly yielded to British pressure and signed the Turko-Iraqi-British Treaty on June 5, 1926. Henceforth, Turkey recognized the Brussels Line and affirmed the partition of Kurdistan. Cooperation and collaboration began among the signatories, especially in establishing contact with the Kurdish national liberation movement. By extension, the CENTO[5] alliance emerged as the embodiment of the anti-Kurdish policy. It is worth noting that cooperation among them against any rise in the Kurdish national movement continues to this day.

Therefore, in conclusion, the Treaty of Lausanne and its consequent developments, especially with regard to what has become known as the Mosul question, worked against Kurdish interests. Disputes were resolved at the expense of legitimate Kurdish rights.

By resolving the Mosul issue, the British imperialist policy mission in the Middle East was decided upon and implemented. Ever since, Britain has supported the oppressors of the Kurdish people. In his book, *Kurd wa Turk wa Arab*, Edmonds (1971), the [British] political advisor to the Iraqi Ministry of the Interior, said that the Kurds rescued the Iraqi government when the League of Nations Committee traveled to Kurdistan to conduct the Mosul referendum. He wrote:

> The Kurds in general were of course well pleased with the conditions to which the award had been made subject. In a letter to Sir Henry Dobbs, written at the time, describing the splendid way in which Sulaimani had risen to the occasion, I had concluded:
> "The visit of the Commission has given a new impetus to Kurdish nationalism which has swept into the anti-Turkish camp many disgruntled persons whom even the most optimistic among us had at first expected to declare in favour of Turkey. The longer interviews were almost invariably strongly nationalist but not generally separatist in tone.... The Kurds of Sulaimani have struck what may prove to have been the decisive blow in the fight for the preservation of Iraq, and know it. Can the Iraqi government rise to the occasion and adopt a far-sighted and generous policy towards the Kurds?"

The report of the Special Commission appointed by the League of Nations had now come to confirm their own feeling that, after having saved Iraq at a moment of perilous crisis by carrying the resolutions approving the Anglo-Iraqi Treaty on that historic night of 10 June 1924, now, by their stand at Sulaimani, they had once again saved the country from a fatal dismemberment. The leaders of Kurdish opinion were thus in good conceit both with themselves and with the State of which they felt they had shown themselves no mean citizens [(*Kurds, Turks, and Arabs: Politics, Travel, and Research in Northern Iraq 1919–1925*, Edmonds 1957, p. 434)].

The Kurds, of course, did not accept the unjust resolutions that resulted in the loss of their rights and partitioned their homeland. This position suited neither British, nor Turkish, nor Iraqi interests. Time and again, the Kurds challenged the will of imperialists and occupiers. Unhappily, their revolts were ruthlessly crushed. In Turkey, Kemal Ataturk committed atrocities against the Kurds while he established the Turkish Republic. He expelled the Greeks and compelled the Allies' recognition with Kurdish help. Initially, Ataturk made generous pledges only to renounce them after securing his position. Of that dark period, the Indian leader Jawaharlal Nehru wrote succinctly and movingly in a letter to his daughter Indira Gandhi:

> Kemal Pasha mercilessly crushed the Kurds, set up special independence courts to try them by the thousands and executed the two Kurdish leaders, Sheikh Sa'id and Doctor Fuad, among others. They died for their hope of an independent

Kurdista... thus, we saw the Turks, who only recently fought for their freedom, crush the Kurds for asking for their own. Strange as such to see the transformation of nationalism from defending one's country to usurping the freedom of others. In 1929 the Kurds rebelled again but they were crushed only for a while. How could the struggle of a nation for freedom be crushed forever when they are willing to pay the price?!

In Iran, the Kurdish movement was simmering, too. It was crushed as well at the hands of Reza Shah Pahlavi's forces. There too, the atrocities of Turkey and Iraq were repeated.

In Iraq, a Kurdish state was founded for the first time in [modern] history, and Sheikh Mahmud al-Hafeed was crowned King of Kurdistan.[6] Soon the British turned against him and commissioned Major [Ely Bannister] Soane to govern Suleimaniyya to restrict Sheikh Mahmud's authority and conspire against him. Sheikh Mahmud rebelled and arrested all British employees on May 20, 1919. After a month, he was wounded and captured by British forces in the battle of Darbandi Baziyan. Later, he was exiled to India. As a result of Turkish inflexibility and the rise of public pressure, British officials were obliged to return Sheikh Mahmud to Suleimaniyya and to crown him King of Kurdistan on September 14, 1922.

Sheikh Mahmud's revolution continued in ebb and flow until 1931. He was viewed as the leader of the Kurdish national movement. Indeed, he was the leader and symbol of the nation immortalized in the history of the Kurdish people by his struggle and patriotic stance.

Extremely angered by anyone who exhibited loyalty to Sheikh Mahmud, or who was willing to support him, the British administration first identified Sheikh Ahmad Barzani and his followers and moved to suppress them because of Barzani's honorable stand and his refusal to submit to Britain.

Barzan was unjustly attacked on December 9, 1931, by troops of the Bileh garrison. It was unjustified aggression that led to the Barzan Revolt.

Chapter 2

A Brief History of the Barzan Tribe

The Barzan tribe was named after the village of Barzan, center of the sheikhdom. The sheikhs of Barzan are descendants of Imadia princes. Their grandfather, Massoud, moved to the village of Hafneka, near Barzan, where he settled and married. His son Sa'id stayed on. His grandson, Taj al-Din, a talented religious scholar, or 'alim, who attracted a great number of followers, eventually founded his own tekkeyeh[1] of Barzan. His son, Sheikh Abd al-Rahman, inherited the sheikhdom, and he passed it on to his son Sheikh Abdullah, who was known for his asceticism and piety. [Sheikh Abdullah] sent his son Sheikh Abd al-Salam to the Nahriya Seminary to be taught by the eminent Sheikh Sayyed Taha Nahri. After the death of his father, Sheikh Abd al-Salam ran the Barzan Tekkeyeh, and the number of his followers grew immensely. He founded a seminary in Barzan, which became so famous throughout the region that students flocked to it. At the same time, he maintained his cordial ties to Sayyed Taha Nahri. During one of his visits to the tekkeyehs, Mawlana Khalid Naqshibandi visited the Barzan Tekkeyeh and appointed Sheikh Abd al-Salam his heir. He took Sheikh Abd al-Salam along to visit Sayyed Taha, who became another heir of Mawlana Khalid Naqishbandi.

Three years before his death in 1872, Sheikh Abd al-Salam wrote a valuable book on *Fiqh* [Islamic jurisprudence]. After him, his son Mohammad administered the Barzan Tekkeyeh. He had studied under the tutelage of his father and become exemplary for his asceticism and piety. The Barzan Tekkeyeh became an asylum for the oppressed and the aggrieved of the tribes adjacent to Barzan. Thus, tribal chiefs complained to the Ottoman government, and Sheikh Mohammad was ostracized to Bitlis in Turkish Kurdistan and imprisoned there for a year. After his return to Barzan, he did not live much longer. He died in 1903. He was survived by five sons: Sheikh Abd al-Salam, Sheikh Ahmad, Mohammad Siddique, Babo, and Mulla Mustafa.[2]

Geographical Location of the Barzan Region

The region of Barzan is located in the northernmost part of Iraqi Kurdistan [158 km/95 miles to the north of Arbil City]. Administratively, it is in the Mergasur District within the jurisdiction of Arbil Province.

Mergasur District consists of three subdistricts: Mergasur, Shirwan, and Barzan. It is bordered by the Rewanduz District in the east, the Imadia District in the west, the Aqra District in the south, and the Turkish frontier in the north.

This community of 400 villages earns its livelihood mainly from farming and raising cattle and sheep. The inhabitants number some 35,000 to 40,000 according to a census conducted [by Kurdish authorities] during the September Revolution[3] in the late 1960s. Barzan is rough, mountainous terrain, and almost impassable. Southward, the Great Zab cuts across west Barzan and passes through Baikhma Canyon to flow into the Tigris River south of Mosul. The Rou Kochek rivulet flows from the north through the midsection of this region where it meets the Great Zab near Rezan. Mount Shirin overlooks the village of Barzan; the Botin, Piran, Qalandar, Bradost, Zardana, and Kori Hori mountains are all located within the Barzan subdistrict.

Barzan under the Leadership of Sheikh Abd al-Salam

The Barzan tribe became a force to be reckoned with under the leadership of Abd al-Salam, who emerged as a religious and patriotic leader. He marked the advent of a new breed of leadership and enacted significant social reforms in his region. Until then, not all Barzanis recognized the Barzan Sheikhdom. After his reforms, all proclaimed their allegiance and support for Sheikh Abd al-Salam. The following tribes recognized his leadership and supported his reforms: Shirwani, Dolamari, Mizzori, Barozhi, Nizari, Gardi, and Harki Binajé[4]; these tribes were incorporated into the Barzani confederacy.

Sheikh Abd al-Salam's reforms are worth mentioning here, for they signify his broadmindedness. They were as follows:

1. Nullification of land ownership.
2. Redistribution of land among the peasants.
3. Abolition of dowries and compulsory marriages.
4. Reassertion of justice and equality as the bases for social organization.
5. Building of a mosque in each village for worship, discussion, and hearings to resolve village problems.
6. Establishment of a committee in every village to oversee all aspects of local affairs.
7. Organizing the armed members of each tribe and appointing their leaders.

Ahmad Agha Birsiyavi, Barzani's maternal uncle, played a major role in supporting and preserving these reforms. With his tribe, he was considered Sheikh Abd al-Salam's main supporter. Therefore, we conclude that the history of the struggle of Barzan began at the turn of the twentieth century. In a more precise, realistic, and objective sense, it began with the era of the martyr Sheikh Abd al-Salam Barzani. During his brief rule, the Sheikh proved to be an astute religious and political leader. In addition to his revolutionary reforms, he strengthened the ties among most Kurdish tribes and gained the respect of all Kurdistan.

Sheikh Abd al-Salam's profound sense of oppression by the Ottoman rulers inspired his active search for deliverance from that oppression. Time and again, he visited his compatriots and regional and tribal leaders in search of a more effective way of dealing with the Ottoman government. He played a principal role in spreading the idea of political reform among the Kurds and established strong ties with the Kurdish organizations which were active at the time, such as the Ta'ali wa Taraqqi al-Kurd [Ascendance and Advancement of the Kurds] Society, the Hevi[5] Society, and Istiqlal al-Kurd [Kurdish Independence] Society. He also culti-vated good relations with Sheikh Mahmud al-Hafeed, Sheikh Abd al-Qadir Nahri, and Ismail Agha Shikak (Simko).

In the spring of 1907, Sheikh Abd al-Salam attended an important meeting at the house of Sheikh Nur Mohammed Brivkani, leader of the Qadiri Tekkeyeh in Brivkan Village. This meeting was attended by many Kurdish tribal chiefs. They decided to send a telegram to the Sublime Porte in Istanbul containing the following Kurdish demands:

1. To make Kurdish the official language in Kurdish areas.
2. To make Kurdish the language of education in Kurdish areas.
3. To appoint Kurdish-speaking governors and other employees of districts and subdistricts.
4. To apply Islamic jurisprudence in the courts, since Islam is the state religion.
5. To keep the compulsory draft relief tax[6] as it was, provided funds were used to build roads and schools in Kurdish areas.

In his book *Imarat Bahdinan al-Kurdiyya Aw Imarat al-Imadiyya* (The Kurdish Bahdinan Principality or the Imadiyya Principality), Damalouji (1952) stated that copies of the telegram were sent to Sheikh Abd al-Qadir Nahri, Amin Ali Badrkhan and Sharif Pasha bin Sa'id Pasha. This proved contrary to the opinion of the signatories, who intended the telegram for the officials alone, but Sheikh Abd al-Salam wanted it that way. All present at the meeting solemnly swore to uphold and defend those demands. The telegram was sent under Sheikh Abd al-Salam's signature representing all participants.

When the telegram was received, the Sublime Porte considered it an act of insubordination against the state and a separatist demand; therefore, it declared a general mobilization. Before the end of 1907, an army under the command of Mohammed Fadhil Pasha al-Daghistani moved on Barzan, unchallenged by tribal leaders in his path. Despite the desperately short notice, Sheikh Abd al-Salam called for self-defense. Whereas the Barzanis resisted for two months, others col-laborated with the invaders at worst or did nothing at best. Eventually Sheikh Abd al-Salam was driven out of his region. He retreated to Tiyari,[7] where the [Christian] Assyrian leader Mar Shimon received him honorably and gave him shelter. At that time, strong ties of friendship were forged between the Barzanis and Assyrians, which have lasted ever since. We Barzanis are eternally grateful for Mar Shimon's honorable stand.

Daghistani's forces burned villages, pillaged and looted. They arrested women and children. It was during this confrontation that Mulla Mustafa, then three years old, was taken prisoner by the Ottoman forces, together with his mother. They were imprisoned in Mosul. Meanwhile, a great number of armed men took to remote mountains and awaited orders from the Sheikh.

Sheikh Abd al-Salam returned to Barzan in 1908 and met with his men in Walati Zheri[8] behind Mount Shirin, north of Barzan. The Kurdish forces staged a concerted ambush on Ottoman units in the area. Sustaining great losses, they cleared the area of the Ottoman army. This overwhelming victory forced the government to negotiate a peace settlement. Prisoners were released and the region compensated for damages sustained. Major General As'ad Pasha, commander of the Twelfth Army and *Wali* [governor] of Mosul, took charge. He administered the region in a just and rational manner. Life returned to normal without enmity and terror. However, when Sulayman Nadhif was appointed the Governor of Mosul, he returned to a policy of oppression and terror as never before. In 1913 he sent a large army to apprehend Sheikh Abd al-Salam, who once again left the area. He visited Sayyed Taha bin. Mohammed Siddique Nahri in the village of Rajhan, near Urmia in Iranian Kurdistan. The Sublime Porte put a high price on his head, dead or alive. During this time, the Sheikh went to visit Ismail Agha Shikak. Together, they went to Tiblisi, where they met the representative of the Russian czar, who pledged support for the Kurdish liberation struggle against the Ottomans.

After an affable farewell by Ismail Agha Shikak in Selmas, Sheikh Abd al-Salam passed through the village of Gangachin[9] on his way back, where the village chief, Sofi Abdullah, begged the sheikh to spend the night in his company. When the sheikh consented, Sofi Abdullah committed his hideous crime. He arrested the sheikh and his three guards while they were asleep and turned them over to the Turks in Siro. He received a reward for his treachery. Sheikh Abd al-Salam and his three companions were quickly moved to Mosul. After a summary trial, Sulayman Nadhif ordered their execution on December 14, 1914 (another account puts the execution in January 1915).

With his death, the Kurds lost a leader who, if he had lived to the end of World War I, might have steered the Kurdish situation to a different end.

After Sheikh Abd al-Salam was martyred, Ahmad Agha Birsiyavi moved with 100 of his armed men to the village of Barzan to protect Sheikh Ahmad and his brothers from the hostile neighboring tribes. In his martyred brother's footsteps, Sheikh Ahmad [1896–1969] took charge at the age of 18. He upheld Sheikh Abd al-Salam's principles with courage and enthusiasm, and he preserved and further advanced his social reforms. He rose to the religious and patriotic role expected of him. Championing his brother's principles, Sheikh Ahmad was the first to support Sheikh Mahmud al-Hafeed in his revolt against the British in 1919.

Cognizant of the pivotal role played by Sheikh Abd al-Salam, Sheikh Abd al-Qadir Nahri sent a letter, carried by Sheikh Abd al-Rahman Sharnakhi, to Sheikh Ahmad, urging him to lead the Kurdish national movement. Sheikh Ahmad insisted that it was the role of Sheikh Abd al-Qadir. Thus, as requested, Sheikh Ahmad sent his brother Mustafa Barzani to Turkish Kurdistan, along with Abd al-Rahman Sharnakhi. As I recall, he met with Sheikh Abd al-Qadir and Sheikh Sa'id of Piran in the Mush area sometime between 1917 and 1919.

Chapter 3

Barzan and the Revolution of Sheikh Mahmud al-Hafeed

While advocating the 1919 revolution of Sheikh Mahmud against British imperialism, Sheikh Ahmad Barzani sent letters to Kurdish tribal chiefs and sheikhs in the Bahdinan region urging them to support Sheikh Mahmud. In addition, he sent his brother Mulla Mustafa, who was in command of a number of Barzani fighters, through the Piyaw Valley,[1] and another group of fighters through the Balek[2] region to join the revolution. Both forces were ambushed several times by British agents along the way, and several of the Kurdish troops were killed before reaching Suleimaniyya. By the time the Barzanis arrived, the revolt had already been brought to an end. Sheikh Mahmud was wounded in Darbandi Bazian and captured by the British.

Sheikh Ahmad's stand, of course, directly challenged the interests and desires of British imperialism. A few tribal chiefs showed Sheikh Ahmad's letters to the British commander in Mosul, thereby enraging him; as a result, the British decided to direct a lethal blow at Barzan by driving out the local tribes and repopulating the region with Assyrians. The Assyrians, though but a tiny minority, rejected this repulsive plan. They refused to injure their historically good ties with the Barzanis. The British, preoccupied with more urgent matters, postponed the plan to a more favorable time.

The Slaying of Colonel Bill and Captain Scott

In November 1919, Colonel Bill, the British commissioner in Mosul, accompanied by Captain Scott, the governor of the Aqra District, toured the Surchi, Zebar, and Barzan regions. Bill threatened to punish Sheikh Ahmad and levy large fines on the tribal chiefs of the region on a variety of grounds. When Colonel Bill arrived in Barzan, Sheikh Ahmad did not receive him because of his reckless behavior and unjustified threats. Nevertheless, Bill believed that this was the way to instill fear and impose his authority.

During this period, the tribal chiefs of Zebar and Surchi agreed to ambush Colonel Bill and his company on their way back, near the village of Bira Kapra. Faris Agha Zebari sent his relative Babaker Agha Zebari to Barzan asking for Sheikh Ahmad's approval and support of their plan. Aware of what might transpire, the plan was approved with the stipulation that they would uphold their pledges. This dangerous act would undoubtedly incite Britain to take strict measures. Sheikh Ahmed sent his own brother, Mohammed Siddique Barzani, to Bira

Kapra[3] to join the attack. Indeed, both Bill and Scott were killed in the ambush on November 4, 1919.

On November 14, 1919, the tribal forces of the area carried out a concerted attack and took over Aqra and its treasury. Discord surfaced among the tribes on how to divide the wealth. Disappointed, Sheikh Ahmad recognized a peril that had to be dealt with immediately. The Sheikh gathered all the tribal chiefs and told them, "If you were ready to fight over a trivial amount such as the Aqra treasury, then what will happen if you get the wealth of Mosul?" Distressed, he returned to Barzan with all of his fighters. Other tribes followed suit and returned to their homes.

Provoking the Assyrians

Closely watching events and developments, in the spring of 1920 the British authorities provoked the Assyrians against the Kurds. Faris Agha Zebari fled to Iran with his family and tribe. They were taken in by Ismail Agha Shikak. In Barzan, fierce fighting ensued between the Barzanis and Assyrians under the command of Agha Butrus. In this bloody battle, Sa'id Wali Beg,[4] a renowned Barzani leader, was martyred. Both parties soon became aware of the malicious British plan, and the fray came to an end. The relations between Barzan and the Assyrians had not been bad on any given day. The favor Mar Shimon did in protecting Sheikh Abd al-Salam, Sheikh Ahmad's older brother, could never be forgotten. That was when he left Barzan after fierce fighting against the Ottoman army in 1907 and went to Tiyari, Mar Shimon's center.

In addition to the Assyrians, Barzan enjoyed good relations with the Armenians as well. Because it is germane to our Armenian ties, I will relate what I heard from [Mustafa] Barzani:

> As Armenians were being slaughtered in 1920–1921, Andranik Pasha sent a letter to Sheikh Ahmad Barzani asking for his help. He ordered Wali Beg to head a force of 200 men to back up the Armenians. I was among them. As we crossed Rekani, Horamari, and others areas along the way, we told them that we were going to beat the Armenians because the Turkish government had, unfortunately, misled many people into believing that the war was between Muslims and Christians, and that Turkey was fighting for Islam. We brought the Armenians safely to Syria. Among them was the family of Andranik Pasha. We returned to Barzan via Zakho after we lost 14 martyrs in clashes with the Turkish army.

The British tried to placate Sheikh Ahmad Barzani and win him over to their side at any cost. Despite a carrot-and-stick ploy used to sway him, Sheikh Ahmad held his ground and never knuckled under to the imperialists. In 1931 military operations were halted, and the situation grew far calmer. When the Commissioner of Mosul demanded that Sheikh Ahmad not obstruct the administrative authorities, the Sheikh agreed to comply as long as they provided the region with the necessary services. Then they requested that a British army regiment be dispatched to Bilah.[5] This duly took place, and Mosul pledged noninterference on the part of the regiment.

As British officials visited him, Sheikh Ahmad repeated that he sought neither power nor wealth, that he wanted only peace and freedom in his land, that the Barzanis were thankful for God-given wealth and sustenance, and that they neither wished to subjugate anyone nor be subjugated themselves.

The British were cognizant that Barzan was a revolutionary hotbed bound to explode at any moment and a latent force not to be slighted. They discovered the strong ties of the Barzanis to their sheikh. They failed in their endeavors to plant moles or seeds of discord among the Barzanis, who refused even to speak to soldiers or police.

The British seized the earliest opportunity to crush Barzan and remove what they perceived as a barrier to implementing their policies. Furthermore, they learned of Sheikh Ahmad Barzani's contacts with Kurdish leaders of Turkish Kurdistan, i.e., Sheikh Sa'id of Piran, Sheikh Abd al-Qadir b. Sayyed Ubaidallah Nahri, and others. Despite the British silence, they were furtively planning aggression. I heard [Mustafa] Barzani speak several times of his meeting with the Governor of Mosul in 1929–1930. The sheikh had sent him to request the removal, or at least the replacement, of the British regiment in Bilah with an Iraqi one. He said,

> The governor was happy to hear this proposal and promised to do his best to secure approval. A few days after the government had approved the proposal, I headed back to Barzan. I stopped in Bilah, and I was well received by the regiment commander, who told me, "I am aware of your mission. I've received orders to prepare to turn the region over to an Iraqi regiment as per your request. I wish you a happy life with your Muslim brethren. We infidel Englishmen will leave you, and you will see the situation."

Barzani added that as he related to Sheikh Ahmad what he had heard, Sheikh Ahmad immediately realized what the British officer meant. He foresaw increased tension and that the British would soon retaliate against Barzan. After a while, the British regiment was replaced by an Iraqi regiment under the command of Colonel Barqi, the brother of Bakr Sidqi. As soon as he arrived in Bilah he began to stir up trouble, provoke incidents, and plan harassment.

The Attack by the Bradostis

The authorities resorted to the provocation of Kurdish tribes against Barzan. During the summer of 1931, the Bradostis[6] raided Barzani villages of the Shirwani tribe. They burned houses and looted the villages of Girkal, Kolak, and Babiki.[7]

During this raid, Barzani was visiting the area. He gathered a number of men and pursued the Bradostis into the Hirat steppe. In a swift encounter, all the wealth and cattle of the villages were recovered. The Bradostis raided the same villages again on November 25, 1931. Again, the Barzanis had to fend off attackers. Thus, Sheikh Ahmad sent Wali Beg on November 27, 1931. Commanding a large force, he defeated the Bradostis in the first clash and recovered the stolen property. Wali Beg had decided to teach the attackers a lesson. He pursued them to their home region. For the Bradostis, this was a bitter defeat.

The Plan to Attack Barzan

Once the Bradostis were defeated, the Prefect of Zebar in Bilah expressed to Sheikh Ahmad Barzani the desire of the Iraqi government to end the strife between the Barzanis and the Bradostis. Sheikh Ahmad welcomed any unbiased government-proposed solution. The prefect replied that he was prepared to act as go-between and investigate if Sheikh Ahmad sent one of his envoys along. The sheikh delegated his brother Mohammed Siddique. They traveled to the area on December 3, 1931, while Mulla Mustafa was away from Barzan on another assignment. Colonel Barqi learned that Sheikh Ahmad was in Barzan with only few guards and relayed the information to his superiors. He was ordered at once to exploit this golden opportunity to lead an all-out assault on Barzan to capture Sheikh Ahmad. Indeed, most of the Barzani forces were either with Wali Beg or with Mohammed Siddique.

The Iraqi plan was to surround Barzan and demand Sheikh Ahmad's unconditional surrender. Hence, the government would impose its conditions on the Barzanis while they were unable to fight and their sheikh was in custody.

The Battle of Barqi Beg

Unaware of Mulla Mustafa's return to Barzan the evening before, Colonel Barqi surrounded Barzan the night of December 9, 1931. At dawn, he captured the first shepherd to leave the village for nearby pastures. Colonel Barqi sent the shepherd with a letter to Sheikh Ahmad demanding his unconditional surrender. The shepherd, an eyewitness, confirmed the siege of Barzan when he gave the letter to the Sheikh.

Sheikh Ahmad called Mulla Mustafa and the villagers for a meeting in the village mosque. They discussed the Barqi affair and what should be done. They decided to resist the aggressors and fight to the last man. Thus, Sheikh Ahmad responded to Barqi's letter, saying, "You have brought your forces to our home. Self-defense is our legitimate right. We will defend ourselves, do what you can."

With his men positioned to fight, Sheikh Ahmad moved to the nearby hills of Garowa Bani overlooking Barzan. At sunrise, a plane sent down a barrage of fire, initiating a day-long assault on Barzan from all directions. The Barzanis daringly fought an unequal battle, defending their homes, women, and children. At night, the Barzanis took the offensive despite their small force, which did not exceed 80 men. It was a fierce battle, at times including hand-to-hand combat. The aggressors were defeated and Barzani pursued Colonel Barqi as far as his regiment's headquarters. Barqi escaped with only a few of his men.

The aggressors left behind 126 dead, as well as a number of wounded, and large quantities of arms and ammunition. Contrary to government expectations, the Barzanis achieved a great victory and secured much-needed armaments. They lost five martyrs: Mahmud Zubair Barzani; Haji Babakr Hafnaki; Tayyib Shiro Hafnaki; Jijok Hafnaki; and Aziz Mustafa Bibani.

When the news reached Mohammed Siddique, he arrested the governor of Zebar and his eight police escorts. Siddique returned quickly to Barzan but left a smaller force, headed by Hasso Mohammed Amin Birsiyavi in that area, to defend the border village in case the Bradostis returned. Near the village of Bedaroon, a policeman from the governor's guards attempted to escape. He was shot and killed. Unfortunately, he was the only Christian among the guards. The British government accused Khalil Khoshavi of killing him because of his religion and demanded his unconditional surrender in all negotiations that followed, as will be reported in more detail later.

Mohammed Siddique and his force arrived in Barzan on December 11, 1931. On December 12, 1931, Sheikh Ahmad ordered the release of the governor of Zebar, his guards, and all prisoners taken in the Battle of Barzan. They were transferred safely to Bilah. Sheikh Ahmad sent a letter with the governor expressing his regrets for the bloodshed and the victims and his desire to restore peace and tranquility to the region.

The government pretended to approve the Sheikh's request for several reasons. Chief among them was the preoccupation of government forces with suppressing Sheikh Mahmud's revolt in Suleimaniyya. Other reasons included the inability of government forces to maneuver as well in winter and the lesson they learned from the Barzanis' fight against Colonel Barqi on December 9. Aware of Bilah's inability to lead another campaign, the government urgently wanted to bring in more and better-trained forces. For these reasons, the government compromised with the Sheikh of Barzan.

Tranquility reigned until the spring of 1932, when news reached Sheikh Ahmad that the government was taking measures and amassing troops in Rewanduz, Aqra, and Imadia in preparation for a grand assault on Barzan. The government should have reconsidered the plan, if for no other reason than the fierce Barzani resistance on December 9, 1931. On the contrary, they felt that a larger force and better planning were needed.

Government Intentions Toward Barzan

In his book *A Road through Kurdistan*, A. M. Hamilton (1937) stressed the nefarious intention of the Iraqi government toward Barzan, and its resolve to deal Barzan a death blow regardless of the cost. He wrote,

> When the government campaigned in 1931 against Sheikh Ahmad Barzani, I was faced once with the following opinion:
> "Well, what should we do with the Iraqi army which we have spent so much to build and equip if we do not send it to your road, Rewanduz Road, to learn the art of war, and get trained in the fight against the Kurds?" Here was my answer, which was laughed at:
> "Closer than that area to Baghdad, there is between Baghdad and Mosul a vast empty desert, [which] only a few other countries possess in addition to Iraq. It is good to try out guns and artillery, move tanks and fly planes. Let artillery roar there

where it can hit no one. Do not send it to Kurdistan. There are southern Arabs there too and they could be hit as well."

Therefore, the government had decided to crush Barzan. With this hateful, chauvinistic and reactionary outlook, the government wanted to test and train its army by thrusting it into an unjust war against innocent citizens who had done nothing but reject a policy of subjugation and racism directed against them.

Chapter 4

The Uprising

As of March 1932, the government had amassed troops in all three prefectures of Aqra, Imadia, and Rewanduz in preparation for the offensive. In his book *Harakat Barzan al-Ula: 1932 (The First Revolts of Barzan in 1932)*, Abd al-Aziz al-Uqaili (1955) described these preparations accurately: They were intended to rout the Barzanis. In its session on January 12, 1932, the Iraqi cabinet decided to launch a massive offensive on Barzan, ostensibly to establish a system of civil administration in the Barzan region.

This justification is without any foundation because there was already a civilian administration in the Barzan region, and Sheikh Ahmad was not in opposition to it. As A. M. Hamilton remarked, "the government had to put to use an army on which it had splurged so much" (1937). The goal was to vanquish Barzan because of its firm patriotic stand. I find it necessary to quote verbatim from al-Uqaili's book (1955) with regards to the [government's] amassment of the troops to defeat the Barzanis so that we get a true picture of the numbers and armament of the forces prepared for this offensive.

Amassment of Troops to Rout the Barzanis

Resolution of the Iraqi Cabinet: Whereas Sheikh Ahmad has persisted in his rebellion, continued to attack the villages of the tribes refusing to submit to his authority, refrained from paying taxes, and in order to establish an orderly civilian administration in the Barzan region, therefore, the Cabinet, in its session of January 12, 1932, has resolved that (1) subdistrict government centers shall be formed in the regions of Shirwan, Barozh (Barzan), and Mizuri Bala, and that (2) in each of these regions a center of the subdistrict shall be erected along with two police barracks. The operations against Sheikh Ahmad Barzani shall take place at a time mutually agreed upon by the Ministries of the Interior and Defense.

13—The military plan:

A. To implement the above resolution, the Chief of Staff has drawn up the following plan for the army's move on Sheikh Ahmad Barzani. The Chief of Staff and the Ministry of the Interior jointly decided to execute the plan on March 15, 1932. Troops were amassed as follows:

1. In the Balakyan Region: The Dai Force, commanded by Colonel Khalil Zaki, at its Headquarters, comprised the following: the Third Cavalry Battalion (minus a squad of sabers and a machine-gun company), the Second Mountain Detachment,

the Second, Third, and Ninth Infantry Regiments, a field hospital, a machine-gun platoon, a mechanized transport platoon, three animal transport platoons, an Iraqi cooperative squadron, a British Attack Squadron, and a police force numbering 100 infantry and 200 mounted men.

2. In Aqra: The Aqra Squad, the Fifth Infantry Regiment, an artillery platoon (from the Third Mountain Detachment), a squad of sabers, and a machine-gun company (from the Third Battalion).

3. In Kirkuk: the Seventh Infantry Regiment.

The mission was to be carried out in three phases:

Phase one: to occupy the Shirwan region, build a road, establish a subdistrict government center near Goratoo and two police stations in Birsiyav and Rezan.

Phase two: to cross the Rou Kochek rivulet near Chami, occupy the region of Mizuri Bala, establish a subdistrict government center and two police stations, and construct a bridge over the Rou Kochek near Chami.

Phase three: to occupy the Barzan region, establish a subdistrict government center and two police stations.

B. Thus, we learn that the plan aimed to impede rebels from Bilah and Imadia, and gradually move deeper into the rebels' turf from Bapishtiyan in order to surround Sheikh Ahmad with his followers and force them to either surrender or to flee westward to Imadia or northward to Turkish territories. To close expected paths in both directions, it was decided to employ the Paul Squad, while a police force led by Officer Izra was already in place, to close the front line from Suri Police station to the edge of the Rekan frontier. On December 11, 1932, the Republic of Iraq formally requested that the Republic of Turkey deny Sheikh Ahmad and his followers asylum and deter border officials from assisting them in any way.

14—The Amassment

On March 13, 1932 the units listed above in Article 13 gathered at their designated sites. The units converging on Balikiyan were named the Dai Force, headed by Col. Khalil Zaki, commander of the Eastern Region. He moved with his force from Kirkuk on March 11 and arrived in Diyana at 8:30 on March 12. He set up an Operations Center and prepared to execute his part of the plan. He was asked to draw a plan for a formation which came to be known as the Dai Squad to spearhead the campaign. The Dai Squad was derived from the Dai Force. Commanded by Haj Sirri Ahmad, the Dai Squad consisted of the following: an operations center, a cavalry company, a machine-gun unit from the Third Cavalry Battalion, an artillery detachment from the Second Mountain Battalion, the Second and Third Infantry Regiments, and a police force of 100 infantry and 100 mounted men.

The Interior Ministry's Ultimatum to Sheikh Ahmad

On March 10, 1932, the Ministry of the Interior presented Sheikh Ahmad Barzani with an ultimatum, telling him that it was imperative that he come before the prefect of Zebar and swear his allegiance and obedience no later than March 14. The British administrator sent a similar letter to the sheikh. The sheikh rejected the ultimatum because he knew full well that he would be arrested. He had solid information concerning the government's intentions. For their part, the Barzanis started to take precautions and make the necessary preparations to repel the aggression. They divided their forces into three, as follows:

1. The main force, commanded by Mulla Mustafa Barzani, responsible for defending the Mergasur–Shirwan axis against the Dai Force.
2. A second force, commanded by Mohammed Siddique Barzani, assisted by Haji Taha Imadi, responsible for defending Balinda-Imadia against the Paul Squad.
3. Sheikh Ahmad kept a force under his own supervision facing the semibesieged Bilah Regiment in order to block the Peris road and intercept the [government] reinforcements coming from Aqra.

The Barzani force did not exceed 1,000 combatants. Their weapons consisted of a variety of rifles (Mausers, Jambaizaris, and English ones), as well as some Lewis machine guns that they had captured from government forces at the Battle of December 9, 1931. They complained about the shortage of ammunition, as their only source was whatever they had captured in battle.

The Barzanis formed supply committees to provide bread to fighters from villages behind the front lines. Populations near the front were relocated to secure villages away from the action. The troop strength and arms capability of the government forces as documented by al-Uqaili have been described in detail.

Beginning of the Onslaught

Having left Balikiyan for Mazna on March 15, 1932, the Dai Force reached Mergasur the following evening. The first battle broke out on March 18, near the village of Korki, east of Mergasur. Advancing units of the Dai Force clashed with a Barzani force commanded by Ahmad Nadir, and a fierce battle ensued. Defeated, the Dai Force retreated to Mergasur, leaving behind a number of dead and arms. To avenge this defeat and to boost morale, the [British] Royal Air Force (RAF) entered the conflict on March 19, and began saturation bombing of most of the villages in the Barzan region, particularly the village of Barzan itself.

Unchallenged, the fierce bombardment continued day and night with severe brutality. Land operations were limited to a few indecisive and insignificant skirmishes during the day. The bombing continued to the end of March.

The Battle of Dola Vazhé

In the beginning of April, 1932, the Dai Squad, commanded by Colonel Haj Sirri Ahmad, began a major all-out offensive on the area—which included the villages of Mamisk, Zhazhok, Vazhé, Birsiyav, Bani Biya, Korki, and Bani—located between Mergasur and Shirwan.

Providing full backup to the infantry, the RAF also dropped supplies and food. On April 3, something unexpected took place: The Barzanis left the valley completely deserted before the advancing Dai Squad all the way to Birsiyav. They dug in at the higher elevations. The Dai Squad believed that they had occupied the target areas with no resistance, but soon all was changed, and their jubilation and arrogance were lost in catastrophe and defeat.

Often, Mustafa Barzani proudly related his memories of this battle, stressing that it was an onerous test, especially as the cruel and accurate aerial bombardment continued. On the night of April 3, Barzani gathered all of his forces on this front and waged a concerted assault on the Dai Squad, which had reached Birsiyav. The squad was isolated from the rest of the government forces, and fierce hand-to-hand combat ensued. The squad was completely crushed: Only a few escaped; 253 were killed, and many were wounded and taken prisoner. Barzani seized all of the squad's armaments and supplies. The Battle of Dola Vazhé, which became known as a Barzani legend, has been immortalized in ballads and poems.

The British General Robinson personally oversaw this battle. He was in the rear, and while the Barzanis pursued his retreating forces, he was wounded without being recognized as the general. The Barzanis took over his headquarters and seized all of its arms and supplies. The Barzanis allowed all of the wounded to return to Mergasur, the headquarters of the Dai Force. Furthermore, they provided transport for those who were unable to reach Mergasur.

The British and their agents received the news as if they had been struck by lightning. They brought in forces from Kirkuk and Baghdad but failed to conduct another campaign on this front. Instead, they focused on brutal aerial bombing day and night.

Gains and Losses

The Barzanis gained large quantities of weapons, munitions, and foodstuffs. They seized a supply convoy of 300 mules. It raised their morale and toughened their resolve to continue to resist. They lost 12 martyrs in this battle: Abdullah Mirkhan Mergasuri, Chawshin Goran, Hussein Mohammed Hostani, Babakir Bekhshashi, Sharif Kani Dairi, Azzo Espindari, Mohammed Kori Mamiski, Mustafa Haidari Dolamari, Khidir Kharay, Mulla Salim Korkay, Ibrahim Shawali Korkayn, and Sheikh Wasman Dolamari. Another 34 fell to various injuries. In this battle, a shining star was rising over Barzan: Mulla Mustafa on the war front, who was proving his exceptional defensive and offensive military superiority. Encouraged by his brother Sheikh Ahmad Barzani, his outstanding abilities raised the morale of his fighters and their trust in his leadership.

On the other two fronts, the situation was as follows:

1. The Barzan–Aqra Front: The Aqra Company failed to occupy Mount Peris, which they attempted in late March and again in April. The Bilah regiment remained inactive and partially surrounded. On April 18, an airplane attacking Barzan was downed near the village of Hasnaka, 5 km [3 miles] east of Barzan, killing its pilot. Despite the cooperation of some mercenaries, such as Ahmad Zebari and a few Surchi sheikhs, all attempts to reinforce the Bileh garrison failed. On this front, Mahmud Faqui Smayil Hasini and Younis Abd al-Rahman Barzani were martyred.

2. The Balinda–Imadia Front: The threat to this front was substantial because of the unlimited cooperation with the Paul Squad, on the part of Kalhi Rekani, chief of the Rekani tribe. Nonetheless, the force failed in its attempts to cross the Zab River, but an unfortunate event occurred. The ungrateful Siddique Agha Horamari, who had

sought refuge in Barzan and was protected by Sheikh Ahmad from the Rekanis' transgressions, captured 25 Barzanis of the Walati Zheri region and turned them over to the government in Imadia for a worthless recompense. Thus, yesterday's foe, Kalhi Rekani, was now his friend. This crime shocked the entire population of the region.

A Temporary Truce

After the Barzanis' major victory in Dola Vazhé, all land operations were halted. Defeated and humiliated, the government discontinued all other planned phases of the operation but vowed to erase at any cost the shame it had suffered. Government forces were faced with formidable men fighting in difficult mountainous terrain. Believing in the justice of their cause, the Barzanis completely trusted their leader and guide Sheikh Ahmad.

On April 27, 1932, a British airplane was downed near Shirwan, and both pilots were captured with slight injuries. Barzani retold this story as follows:

> While we were bathing in the Rou Kochek river near the village of Kaniya Linja, a group of planes attacked us; one was bombing from very low altitude. We fired at it from all directions. It was hit and smoke arose. We saw its two pilots parachute down between Shirwan and Chami. We sent a group of men and captured them.

Sheikh Ahmad asked the government to send an interpreter and a physician to treat the pilots. Captain Holt arrived on May 3 with a physician and an interpreter. Sheikh Ahmad met with him and explained his point of view regarding the injustice and brutality to which Barzan had been subjected. At last, Sheikh Ahmad agreed to free the two pilots in return for Holt's pledge on behalf of the British government to release the 25 Barzanis who had been turned in by Siddique Agha Horamari through treachery and betrayal. On May 5, 1932, Holt returned to Arbil and fulfilled his promise of releasing the Barzanis, whom he respectfully and safely sent back to Sheikh Ahmad.

At this meeting, they also had agreed in principle to end the fighting and to begin negotiations to normalize conditions, return the army to its original garrisons, rebuild the region, retain police stations and civil administration, and issue a general amnesty. Indeed, the fighting stopped for about two weeks. However, the government did not honor Captain Holt's commitment and pressed for the unconditional surrender of Sheikh Ahmad and all Barzanis. Thus, after two weeks of truce, the RAF resumed its fierce and savage bombardment.

Preparing to Seek Asylum Abroad

In a series of meetings with the chiefs of the Barzan tribes, Sheikh Ahmad studied the situation. The tribes decided to explore other options if it became necessary and resistance could no longer be continued. Obviously, one small tribe could not defy British imperialism alone. Arrogant with victory in the war, Britain was the biggest colonial power in the world. Unfortunately, the powerless rulers in

Baghdad were mere pawns in the hands of the British. Many saw the defiance of Britain as sheer madness.

It was decided to contact both the Turkish and the Iranian governments to accept the entry of the Barzanis. The response was positive, provided they turn in their weapons upon entry.

The Barzanis finally agreed to take the following steps:

1. Led by Mulla Mustafa Barzani, the Mergasur Force was to withdraw to the west of the Rou Kochek rivulet while retaining the peaks of Mount Halbat between Mergasur and Shirwan, and was to establish a strong line of defense west of the rivulet.
2. Withdraw the Balinda Force and establish a line of defense in Walati Zheri.
3. Withdraw the Barzan Force and establish a line of defense on Mount Shirin.

Families from the villages of Barozh, Nizar, Shirwani, and Dolemari flocked to the Shirwani, region. Along with the Gardis and the Mizuris, they converged west of the Rou Kochek rivulet and behind Mount Shirin at the Turkish border. For the first time, the people in the region saw the night flares dropped by the bombers, which inflicted heavy losses on families and their livestock. The casualties of the families exceeded even those of the fighters at the front.

After completing the withdrawal and setting up new lines of defense, it was decided to send two forces of 50 fighters each, one, led by Wali Beg, behind the enemy lines between Mergasur and Rewanduz; the other, led by Khalil Khoshavi, to the Aqra–Barzan Axis.

The army exploited this retreat and advanced to the new positions abandoned by the Barzanis. The two forces infiltrated the enemy lines and inflicted heavy casualties on them. Some army units even sent distress signals to the RAF to drop supplies because convoys were subject to constant ambush by the two forces along the treacherous roads. These conditions agitated the government greatly, perhaps even more than the fighting at the front.

The Negotiations Stall

The authorities sought Sheikh Nur al-Din Brivkani's intervention. They asked him to meet with Sheikh Ahmad Barzani and convince him to return to Barzan and obey government orders as the rest of the Iraqi tribes were doing.

Sheikh Nur al-Din reached Sheikh Ahmad's headquarters in late May. He was welcomed and received with honor. In a long meeting, Sheikh Nur al-Din stated the government's position and its desire to negotiate. Sheikh Ahmad agreed to negotiate and affirmed his earnest desire for normalization and cooperation. Sheikh Nur al-Din returned to Bilah and was transported on a special plane to Mosul. There, he conveyed Sheikh Ahmad's views and desires to the British commissioner and the governor.

Sheikh Nur al-Din returned to Sheikh Ahmad and informed him of the government's approval of a meeting with him in Hostan Village,[1] provided Sheikh

Ahmad would be escorted by no more than three of his personal guards. Although a whole regiment was evidently stationed there at the time, Sheikh Nur al-Din was certain that the British would not waive this condition.

Sheikh Ahmad's response was that he did not trust the British and could never accept their conditions. He suggested that Sheikh Nur al-Din convey his views to them: They must either meet away from the army or allow him to bring as many guards as he wished to ensure his safety and avert possible betrayal. Let it be clear that there was to be no meeting if both suggestions were rejected. He reaffirmed the Barzanis' readiness to fight as long as possible and to leave Iraq if necessary. They would not submit to Britain.

Saddened and distressed, Sheikh Nur al-Din replied, "Our heartfelt emotions are with you, Your Eminence. I fail to grasp how we can defy Britain, which occupies half the globe. It will destroy us; eradicate us. Let us be realistic and accept God's will."

Sheikh Ahmad replied, "I am grateful for your noble feelings, and I do not doubt your good and sincere intentions. Nonetheless, even if we return to Barzan, give up our arms and retire to make our living, the British will not be satisfied. They want us without rights and any say. They occupy our land and are enemies of our religion. I realize that a small tribe like ours cannot defeat Britain, but life is an honorable stand. I want to please Allah and satisfy my conscience. It is important that history records that we fought British imperialism and its agents despite our scarce resources; that we did not succumb. They can scorch our earth and destroy our villages; they can expel or kill us but they cannot get our allegiance. We will remain enemies. This is our resolve and we will not regret it. You may convey this to the British verbatim."

Saddened and sobbing, Sheikh Nur al-Din left, saying, "I ask God with all my heart that He bless you and help you to succeed. I wish I were able to endure what you are enduring, but each of us must follow his own destiny." It was agreed that Sheikh Nur al-Din would return only if the British Commissioner agreed to either one of Sheikh Ahmad's suggestions. Sheikh Nur al-Din was certain of rejection.

Two days after the return of Sheikh Nur al-Din, a number of British aircraft appeared in successive waves, bombing whatever they saw on the ground. For the first time, they dropped delayed-action bombs on the region, claiming the lives of many children as they played around them.

With the advent of June, Sheikh Ahmad called all chiefs of the Barzan tribes, i.e., Wali Beg,[2] Khalil Khoshavi, Ahmad Nadir,[3] Abdullah Karkamoy, and Hassan Mohammed Amin, and they decided to retreat in good order and enter Turkey while continuing to fight in order to cover their retreat. As they vacated their positions, the army moved in. Hence, a final decision was reached to seek asylum in Turkey. Preparing to cross into Turkey, they gathered on the border in the Zeit Valley[4] and began contacts with Turkish authorities to arrange for their entrance.

Chapter 5

Asylum in Turkey

Early in June, preparations were under way to leave Iraqi territory and cross into Turkey. On June 10, 1932, all families, including those from nearby villages, gathered in Zeit and were ready to cross the border. In consultation with Barzani leaders, the following terms were agreed upon:

1. The least possible number of families were to enter Turkey.
2. Families not in harm's way were to return home and resume their normal life. They were to turn in a few old guns to the government.
3. Only families at risk would cross into Turkey.
4. A force of 200–300 fighters, commanded by Khalil Khoshavi, Ahmad Nadir, Abdullah Karkamoy, and Hassan Mohammed Amin were to remain in Gardi villages near the border, and all excess weapons were to be left with them to use if needed.

On June 20, Sheikh Ahmad sent a delegation, consisting of Mohammed Siddique Barzani and Haji Taha Imadi, to the village of Grana in Turkey to arrange for the families to cross the border. Asylum was granted on the condition that they lay down their arms in Grana. In fact, some weapons were turned in to avoid trouble with the Turks. As designated, families crossed the border and gathered in Grana, where a Turkish force was stationed.

The news of the Barzanis seeking asylum in Turkey delighted the Iraqi authorities, who believed that they had at last eliminated their most treacherous problem. To prove that their military pressure had forced the Barzanis to leave Iraq, army units began exercises to demonstrate their martial prowess.

The Battle of Zeit

On June 12, the Paul Squad, with mercenaries of Kalhi Rekani, tried to cross the Greater Zab to the Barzan area to loot Mizuri villages. Barzani forces on that front challenged them, caused many losses, and brought the incursion to an end.

Certain that the Barzanis had left for the neighborhood of Hoba and Zeit villages to protect the caravan of families crossing into Turkey, on June 15, the Iraqi army deployed units in the subdistrict of Greater Shirwan. The air force brutally pounded the Zeit Gorge, which was crowded with families at the time. On June 19 and 20, the Dai Squad tested its bad luck again. They were set to occupy the elevations overlooking the Zeit Gorge to capture as many families as possible. Ahmad Nadir was to defend the strait and he, indeed, performed astoundingly. With only 15 of his comrades, he gained the initiative and won the attack. Again, they defeated and pursued the Dai Squad to Shirwan. Seventy-five enemy corpses were left on the battlefield. Barzani would often tell this story:

> The army tried to occupy the eastern stretch of the Zeit Valley. This would have put them in control of the valley and the families in it. They advanced until they nearly reached their target. Then we heard the roar of guns and automatic weapons. We knew that the fight had just begun. We hurried to reinforce our comrades, but by the time we arrived the battle had been decisively won. As we climbed to the mountain top, we saw defeated enemy bands racing in all directions as Ahmad Nadir and his comrades chased them. We realized that we would not have caught up with them. Thus, we waited for the battle to subside. By the grace of God, Ahmad Nadir and all his men returned unharmed. We then went to search for enemy losses. We found 75 killed in action, and we collected 75 weapons.

Trying at last to achieve a small victory, the Dai Squad's bad luck had led to yet another defeat.

Crossing into Turkey—the Isolation of Sheikh Ahmad

On June 21, the last family had left Zeit Village and crossed to Grana. In all, 400 families had gathered in Grana that day. On June 22, Sheikh Ahmad, his brothers, Wali Beg, and a number of men crossed into Turkey. Approximately 250 men remained in Gardi villages; extra weapons were hidden away in caves with assistance from many Gardi loyalists.

The Gardis are part of the Barzan confederacy, which consists of seven tribes: Shirwani, Dolamari, Mizuri, Barozhi, Nizari, Gardi, and settled Harkis (Binajé). Most Gardi villages came under Turkish control when borders were drawn.

When Sheikh Ahmad arrived in Grana, the Turkish authorities transferred him and his men to Erzurum through Gavar and Van.[1] From Van, they took Sheikh Ahmad, Taha Imadi, and Ali Muho Barzani to Ankara while continuing to bring families to Erzurum. On their way, families were separated. Only Sheikh Ahmad and his brothers' families (Mohammed Siddique, Babo, Mulla Mustafa, and the children of the martyr Sheikh Abd al-Salam, their oldest brother), Wali Beg's and ten other families, among them the family of Haji Taha Imadi, reached Erzurum. The rest of the families were gathered and, contrary to the initial Turkish pledge, were sent back to Iraq. Once in Iraq, families were allowed to return to their villages without much difficulty. Families in Erzurum remained there for a month and were then taken to Erzinjan. Haji Taha was allowed to return, but Sheikh Ahmad and Ali Muho were detained in Ankara.

The Return to Shamdinan

Barzani recalled the history of this period, saying,

I tried to convince the Turks to let us join Sheikh Ahmad or to return him to us. Repeatedly they rejected our request. But at last they agreed to our return to Shamdinan without assistance; not even in the transporting of families. I had to sell my horse, which I loved, and women's jewelry to pay for transportation from Erzinjan to Gavar. I will never forget the love and support rendered by our Kurdish brethren of Turkey. However, they were in a worse position than we were. They still suffered from the atrocities and savagery to which they had been subjected. Their fear and shock were clearly written on their faces. Despite their own miseries, they never withheld assistance from us. Often they would listen to our experiences and cry; and often I sympathized with their agony despite our own affliction. I was very distressed at their condition. Having inquired sufficiently about roads, we left Gavar after only two days' respite. We continued our journey to Shamdinan.[2] In the severe cold of late November 1932, we travelled the distance between Gavar and Shamdinan on foot and on animals. We faced death many times because of the severe weather. Children could not walk, and we had to carry them. Then, indeed, several children died. At any rate, after much difficulty and hardship, we reached Shamdinan. There we were in a much better position. We were among people we knew, and they greatly lessened our travail. We split among the Gardi villages; the villagers deluged us with love and regard. I will always remember their stand, especially Samad Granaee[3] who assisted me when I needed him most. I had exhausted all my money and possessions. There still remained payment for the animals which had brought us from Gavar. I pondered what to do and whom to ask while the caravan chief, unaware of my dilemma, waited for his wages!

I asked Samad and he promptly responded, "How could I not! I will sell all I have and do all I can not to let you down or embarrass you." He, indeed, came to my rescue. Every time I tried to repay him, he refused, and I still owe him the sum.

Gardi villages were in remote and difficult terrain, far from government interference. Conditions improved for the Barzanis, to some extent, once they were reunited. At least it was possible for them to communicate with each other. The force they had left in the region was devoutly loyal. They had kept their organization and weapons, and no one had defected, either to Turkey or Iraq. Mulla Mustafa's return boosted their confidence. They stayed in the Gardi region until the spring of 1933. With the Barzani fighters away, the [Iraqi] government had seized the opportunity to build police stations in most villages of the Barzan region, and they kept four army regiments in the area; two in Bilah and Barzan, and two in Mergasur and Shirwan, to support the police if need be.

Chapter 6

The Return to Barzan

In the spring of 1933, the Turkish authorities handed Sheikh Ahmad Barzani over to the Iraqi government at the border at the Cizre-Zakho. When his brothers and followers heard the news, they decided to leave Turkey and return to Barzan. They knew that if the Turks did not coordinate with Iraq to crush them militarily, they would, at best, be asked to leave Turkish territory.

They quietly dispersed their families into the villages. Men were to fortify Mount Shirin and other difficult terrain which the army could not reach or maneuver in easily. Thus, fighters split into three groups and infiltrated the region. They had agreed to avoid clashes except in self-defense. In fact, nothing significant occurred. But the return of organized and sizable Barzani forces to the area worried the [Iraqi] government greatly. Thus, the government pressured Sheikh Ahmad and sent messages in his name to the Barzanis to return home; they said a general amnesty would be issued for all except Khalil Khoshavi, whose surrender the British persisted in demanding, presumably for having killed a Christian policeman near the village of Bedaroon.[1]

Every time the government tried to convince the Barzanis to return to their villages, they failed because Mulla Mustafa Barzani refused to return as long as Sheikh Ahmad was in government custody in Mosul.

Sheikh Ahmad's Return to Barzan

At last the government, which was loath to resume military operations because it was unsure of the outcome, was compelled to return Sheikh Ahmad to Barzan in late August of 1933. He took the Arbil–Mergasur route to Barzan.

Mustafa Barzani Goes to Mosul

Barzani said, "When we heard the news of Sheikh Ahmad's return to Barzan, we went to a place near Shirwan to meet him. We were all indescribably delighted to see him safe and well. After we rested awhile and exchanged the news, Sheikh Ahmad ordered me to go to Shirwan to arrange for my trip to Mosul. I carried out his order, but pleaded with him not to come to Mosul or go to any government center where they might arrest him because dirty trickery is their middle name. I besought him to be circumspect, even if they threatened to execute me. He simply said, 'Go now, and let's see how things unfold.'"

Sheikh Ahmad had promised the government to send his brother Mustafa Barzani to Mosul as soon as he reached Barzan. Regardless of the cost, it was not in his nature to break a promise. The British commissioner and the governor of Mosul had both pledged on behalf of their respective governments to issue a general amnesty, return the army to its garrisons, establish peace and security in the region, and begin reconstruction. Indeed, a general amnesty was issued, and the army withdrew, but the civil administration remained. Again, Khalil Khoshavi was excluded from the amnesty. With his relatives, he retreated to a remote area to avoid the authorities. Others returned to their villages, but no one turned in their weapons.

Barzani added, "When I arrived in Shirwan, I went to the regimental headquarters, escorted by one guard. Neither of us carried a weapon. Surprised, the regiment commander received us, not believing that I was Mulla Mustafa. He sent for the village head to confirm my identity. The following day, with all due honor and respect, I was taken to Mergasur, Arbil, and finally to Mosul. I was warmly received by the administrator and governor, both of whom stressed their respective governments' resolve to fulfill their pledges to Sheikh Ahmad. After ten days in Mosul, I returned to Barzan."

Broken Promises and Forced Exile

Before long, the government invited Sheikh Ahmad to Mosul. He accepted and was cordially received. After two weeks in Mosul, he sent a close aide to Barzan and asked Mustafa Barzani to go to Mosul. Through a special code agreed upon previously, Mulla Mustafa Barzani verified the authenticity of the message and went to Mosul. He was immediately taken to where Sheikh Ahmad was staying.

I remember when I asked Barzani why he went to Mosul while Sheikh Ahmad was there, he replied: "I was sure the government would not allow us to return to Barzan if we were both captured, so I was always against any such move. However, obeying Sheikh Ahmad's orders was more important than anything else. When I arrived at the house where he was staying, I asked him, 'Why did you ask me to come here when you are here?' He said that the officials had given him their word of honor and promised that they would not betray us, and that they are living up to their promises. 'If they go back on their word, God is greater than they are. Let the chips fall where they may.'"

The government did indeed go back on its word, and did not allow the Sheikh and [Mulla] Mustafa to return [to Barzan]. Furthermore, they sent for their other two brothers, Mohammed Siddique and Babo, and for Sheikh Abd al-Salam's children and all of their families. They were transported to Mosul, thus marking the beginning of a period of exile and detention.

An Attempt to Poison Barzani

In mid-1936, the governor of Mosul summoned Mustafa Barzani to his office, where they mixed poison in his coffee. Miraculously, he escaped death. After two weeks in a coma and a struggle with death, he began to convalesce. A grateful man, he always acknowledged the help he received from [the Arab notables] Sheikh Ajil al-Yawer of the Shammar tribe and from the houses of Kashmoolah and Abbawi.

From Mosul to Baghdad and Nasiriyya

In late 1936, the Barzanis were transferred to Baghdad. Sheikh Mahmud [al-Hafeed of Suleimaniyya] was also in exile in Baghdad and took the opportunity to exchange visits with Sheikh Ahmad. Suspicious, the government ordered the Barzanis' transfer to Nasiriyya.

The Imposition of Martial Law—Chaotic Conditions

By and large, the situation in the Barzan region was calm. As Sheikh Ahmad, his brothers, and their families were held in Mosul, Khalil Khoshavi, Ahmad Nadir, and Abdullah Karkamoy retreated to the mountains and resisted police attempts to arrest and try them in military court. These special courts were established on August 5, 1935, to seek revenge on Barzani leaders, in contradiction to the government-issued general amnesty.

Headed by Major Ismail al-Agha, the military court consisted of Lt. Colonel Fakhri Amin, Colonel Abd al-Qadir Yasin, and two Kurdish judges, Mohammed Siddique Abdullah and Siddique Tahir. This court issued death sentences to a number of Barzanis (Aziz Hostani, Omer Korani, Faris Ali, Mohammed Mahmud, and Mulla Zadah Isama'il), and sentenced many others to imprisonment and exile. After these trials, a large number of Barzanis withdrew to the mountains, which eventually curbed the execution campaign. Wali Beg was deported to Kirkuk. Khalil Khoshavi retreated to Mount Govend, and his family was deported to southern Iraq.

In September 1935, the irreplaceable Ahmad Nadir was martyred in a clash with a Turkish force that was collaborating with an Iraqi force attempting to arrest or eliminate the Barzanis. Consequently, rebel morale plummeted to its lowest. Abdullah Karkamoy was wounded and forced to surrender to Iraqi forces. Khalil Khoshavi and 30 of his relatives escaped the siege laid by Iraqi and Turkish forces. Through the Rekani region, they moved toward Syria, which was under French mandate at the time. Pressured by Britain, Iraq amassed a large number of mercenary and police squads to pursue Khalil Khoshavi. They set a price of 5,000 dinars on his head, dead or alive. Khalil did not reach the Syrian border. He returned to the region of Doski Zhuri[2] (Upper Doski) and decided to remain there in seclusion until the following spring.

On the one hand, the region of Upper Doski was so poor that they could not provide for 30 additional men in their villages, especially during the severe winter months, which would virtually isolate villages from each other. On the other hand, Khalil Khoshavi had defended Kalhi Rekani against Sito Agha Horamari in 1923 while delivering a message to him from Sheikh Ahmad. Indeed, during that Horamari raid, Khalil Khoshavi had rescued him from certain death. Therefore, remembering this honorable stand, he believed that Kalhi Rekani would return the favor and help him through the winter.

Having been contacted and having assured them of his help, Kalhi Rekani allowed them to go to a secluded cave and supplied them with about two weeks' worth of foodstuffs. At the same time, he went to Imadia and informed on them to the government. He returned with two army companies and a police company and guided them to the cave. Surrounded and caught by surprise, Khalil and his companions were asked to surrender. They refused and fought to the last bullet. All were martyred. Kalhi Rekani paid dearly for his treason in 1961.

The Valor of Women during the Uprising

Khalil was martyred in February of 1936. His severed head was taken to Shirwan. His mother and wife were brought in to identify it. They say that an officer pointed at Khalil's head and asked his mother, "Do you know whose head this is?" She replied, "Yes, it is the head of my son Khalil, whom you murdered treacher- ously and in cold blood, and I am proud of him." Khalil's wife almost fainted, and she wept. Her mother-in-law rebuked her, saying, "Don't cry in front of these cowards, because they will taunt us!"

Indeed, the taunts and mockery of one's enemies are among the greatest of misfortunes. I cherish these [Arabic] verses by al-Shafi'i:[3]

> Never show ill-wishers your humiliation;
> The enemies' taunts are an adversity.
> Hope not for compassion from a miser;
> For from fire comes no water for the thirsty.

After the martyrdom of Khalil Khoshavi and his comrades, the armed struggle in Barzan came to a complete standstill. The government was greatly relieved. There was no one left to defy its orders, as Sheikh Ahmad and his brothers were under arrest in southern Iraq, Wali Beg was deported to Kirkuk, and Abdullah Karkamoy had died. Ahmad Nadir and Khalil Khoshavi had been martyred. So there was no one left to take charge of the region.

From Nasiriyya to Kifri and Altin Kopru

In 1939, the authorities transferred Sheikh Ahmad, his fellows, and their families to Altin Kopru and Kifri for a short while and from there to Suleimaniyya.

A New Period

In Suleimaniyya, conditions improved for the Barzanis, because the climate suited them better, although Barzani was praising the hospitality of the Arab families among whom they had resided in the South. During this period, the World War II broke out and preoccupied British officials. A good while had elapsed since deportation, and the authorities almost forgot the question of the Barzanis, who were now enjoying considerable freedom. Once more, contact with the Barzan region was possible, and the government permitted many of their families to join or visit them in Suleimaniyya. Contacts were firmly established with the Hiwa (Hope) Party (HP) and with patriotic notables.

Barzani told me the following:

> When Rashid Ali al-Gailani launched his anti-British movement, a high-ranking British officer hastened to meet me in Suleimaniyya, and he made me a generous offer in the name of the British government. In return, he asked me to go to Arbil in order to contact Kurdish [army] officers there, urge them to rebel against the government of Rashid Ali al-Gailani and coordinate with them and then go to Barzan. He promised the British government would be prepared to transport thousands of rifles, ammunitions, and supplies, either by land or by air, and he asked me to proclaim an independent Kurdistan there, and urge Kurdish officers and soldiers to join in. He promised that the British government would recognize this state, and would commit itself to supporting and protecting it.
>
> When I heard his statements, I did not promise a thing. I asked him to allow me a short respite. I immediately went to Sheikh Ahmad and presented the offer to him. He replied, "The British need such a move today. They will keep their promises only for a while, and will leave us in the lurch as always. Therefore, you must inform him that we will make no such move." When I did so, the British officer was astounded and tried to convince me to accept the offer. I persistently refused.

Barzani's Return to Barzan

The Barzanis remained in Suleimaniyya until 1943. In May of 1943, assisted by the HP and other patriotic elements, Mustafa Barzani took the opportunity to return to Barzan. He left Suleimaniyya on July 12, 1943, for the Iranian border, accompanied by only two men: Mustafa Abdullah Aqrawi and Sulayman Soorah.[4]

Barzani said, "I requested the Sheikh's permission [to leave]; I also asked him to give me the necessary guidance and instructions. He enjoined me always to be just in dealing with the people, to not let arrogance seep into my soul, to avoid any confrontation with the government forces unless I was sure of success, and not to compromise just because we were in their hands."

Barzani entered Iran disguised in the garb of a Muslim cleric and arrived in Shino [Oshnoviyeh], where a good number of Barzanis had resettled after leaving Iraq because of police and military campaigns. Mamand Agha Gaich, chief of the Qadiri sect and of the Mamesh tribe, had helped them resettle in the villages around Shino. An earnest patriot, Mamand Agha welcomed Barzani and gave him all of his help.

A High Price on Barzani's Head

Barzani told a cheerful story of an incident in Mamand Agha's divan. He said, "As I was sitting in his divan, Qarani Agha Mamesh[5] arrived to inform Mamand

Agha of my flight from Suleimaniyya and told him that both the Iranian and Iraqi governments were offering 50,000 dinars each for my capture, dead or alive. He advised Mamand Agha to watch his territory closely and not to miss out on this valuable opportunity if I should pass through. Qarani Agha did not know me, of course. 'It is a shame to speak in such a manner; the man who would capture Barzani has not been born yet!' Mamand Agha replied."

At last, the Barzanis united again behind Mulla Mustafa [Barzani]. Of them, I recall Mamand, Mirza Agha, Hassan Ahmad Nadir, and their relatives. They numbered about 30, a fair number with which to start. While Barzani was among his countrymen in the Shino area, he learned from a nomad that the regent[6] was in Mergasur in the company of Mahmud Beg Khalifah Samad.[7] He moved swiftly through Kele Shin,[8] and, as I recall, it was in late July. He arrived in Mergasur in the evening. Unfortunately, the regent had left only two hours earlier. He missed a valuable conquest. I heard Barzani say several times: "I was delighted when I heard that the Regent was in Mergasur, and decided to take him hostage and shorten my task. But I was appalled to learn that he had left only two hours before I arrived."

Preparing to Attack

Barzani and his companions headed for Barzan, the news spread among the people in the region, and every house rejoiced! Young men lined up to join him until the number of armed and unarmed men reached 750 in only two weeks. Initially, Barzani avoided challenging government forces until he had organized and armed his men well. He executed his plan, and in successive surprise attacks he took over all police stations in the region except the stations of Barzan, Bilah, Mergasur, and Shirwan. The strategy was to target smaller and more accessible forces first and avoid larger forces in the above-mentioned locations.

Within two months, the number of those under arms grew to more than 2,000. There was joy in every house because of Barzani's return and his swift victories over the government forces. In the autumn of the same year, the government sent one delegation after another to Barzani, seeking negotiations and a ceasefire. Barzani stipulated the repatriation to Barzan of Sheikh Ahmad and all the exiled deportees as a *sine qua non* for such negotiations. The government fulfilled this condition, and Sheikh Ahmad returned to Barzan in glory and triumph with his comrades, their families, and all who accompanied them. This courageous move was a significant turning point in the history of the struggle of Barzan. It gained the respect and support of all Kurdish patriots. Barzan became the national beacon of the Kurdish liberation movement.

A ceasefire agreement was reached. Negotiations resulted in a significant accord in which the government of Nuri al-Sa'id agreed to Barzani's demands:

1. Dismiss/transfer corrupt employees who were known to accept bribes and abuse power.

2. Establish a Kurdistan region that would include the provinces of Kirkuk, Suleimaniyya, Arbil, and the Kurdish districts of Dohuk, Aqra, Shaikhan, Sinjar, Zakho, and Imadia in Mosul Province; and the two districts of Khanaqin and Mandali in Diyala Province.
3. Make Kurdish an official language.
4. Appoint a Kurdish vice minister in every ministry.
5. Appoint a Kurdish minister in charge of the region of Kurdistan.
6. Compensate all losses resulting from military campaigns.
7. Build schools, a hospital, roads, and reconstruct the region.
8. Leave military, financial, and foreign affairs under the control of the central government.

Nuri al-Sa'id's cabinet resigned on June 3, 1944. al-Pachachi formed a new cabinet that did not honor the accord under the pretext that it had been signed by the previous cabinet. All of these maneuvers were orchestrated by British imperialists and led to the outbreak of the 1945 revolution.

Extrapolation

Studying the history of the struggle of our people during this and prior uprisings, it becomes clear that there were great leaders and ardent men who struggled for the legitimate rights of the Kurdish people. In spite of their lofty sacrifices, Kurdish rights remained unrecognized and usurped. The reasons, in my opinion, are as follows:

1. Lack of coordination among revolutions or uprisings. For example, when an uprising broke out in one location, people in other areas were not aware of it.
2. The enemies' choice of times to aim blows at the Kurdish movements. I do not believe that the Kurds selected the appropriate time for a revolution, even once.
3. Misjudging the subjective and objective conditions: When they should have resorted to armed struggle, they negotiated, and when they should have searched for peaceful means, they fought.
4. Enemies were richer, mightier, and more shrewd, especially the British imperialists who always opposed Kurdish aspirations.

Although the Kurds have not yet attained their rights, by their enormous sacrifices they have proved to the world that they are a nation with wherewithal and ethos. Each generation has proved to the next that there are legitimate rights, which have been usurped, and that the struggle to retrieve them must continue.

Part II

The Barzan Revolt (1943–1945)
Introduction to Part II

As the world eagerly followed the course of World War II and awaited its conclusion, the hopes of oppressed peoples rekindled with the receding of Nazi power. Patriotic and democratic organizations and societies around the world mobilized their masses and escalated their struggles for their peoples' rights. Naturally, Kurdish organizations, like their counterparts elsewhere in the world, began searching for an opportunity for the Kurds—an opportunity that might transpire through the changes brought on by the war.

As the political center of Kurdish activism at both organizational and individual levels, Suleimaniyya embraced Barzani in 1940, when he returned from exile during the war. In Suleimaniyya, Barzani used the opportunity to contact Kurdish organizations and patriotic notables to exchange views about the Kurdish movement and the future of Kurdistan. At the same time, he established contact with the Barzan region. He learned that a fair number of armed men had already fortified themselves in the mountains, another number had joined the police forces and were assigned to police stations and yet another group had escaped government harassment by going to Iran.

In a series of contacts that lasted until 1943, Barzani decided that the time was right to assert the Kurdish position. People were ready, for they were weary of the government and police forces. Agitated, they were awaiting deliverance. The British were focused on the war; the Kurdish issue was small by comparison. The region needed a leader.

After sufficiently studying the subject with the HP and a number of Kurdish nationalist personalities, a coordinated agreement was reached regarding a plan for a revolution. Barzani secured an unequivocal pledge of support from them. Hence, on July 12, 1943, Barzani decided to return to Barzan.

Accompanied by two of his friends, Mustafa Abdullah and Sulayman Soora, Barzani left Suleimaniyya for Iran disguised as a Muslim cleric. It is worth noting here that Sheikh Latif gave him invaluable help, with the consent and support of his father, the eminent leader Sheikh Mahmud al-Hafeed.

Circumstances had changed greatly since earlier times. Whereas the uprising of 1931–1932 was limited to the Barzan region, this time it would include vast areas of Kurdistan as a ground-breaking step toward a total revolution, in which the intelligentsia, the peasants, and nationalist tribes would participate. Barzani realized the great tasks and responsibilities that lay ahead and what ramifications were involved in light of recent developments.

Barzani's return to Barzan and subsequent events proved to come at a very critical period. Because of Iraq's strategic location for the Allied forces as World War II reached its peak, Iraq's internal affairs captured much of the Allies' attention, notably that of the British imperialists.

When Rashid 'Ali al-Gailani rebelled in May 1941, the British tried to convince Barzani to return to Arbil and persuade Kurdish officers to rebel and resist Rashid 'Ali. In exchange, they promised to arm and finance the revolution, and to recognize independent Kurdistan at a later date. After consulting his older brother Sheikh Ahmad Barzani, Mulla Mustafa Barzani rejected the British offer. Since the British were concerned mainly with their own interests, he doubted their veracity.

British interests were congruent with neither the Kurdish struggle nor with Arab aspirations. Essentially, the British ruled Iraq. They directed the Iraqi government to allow the emergence of a feudalist class in Kurdistan and in the Arab Middle East as well. British imperialism presented the Kurdish movement as anti-Arab and continues to do so even today. The authenticity of the Kurdish national movement and the legitimacy of its goals thwarted all such attempts. Although Arab nationalism was hitherto immature and relations between the two movements [of Arabs and Kurds] were not what they should have been, Barzani recognized the significance of distinguishing between imperialism and its acolytes and his Arab brethren. The first thing he did was to issue the following call to the Iraqi people:

> I do not and will not fight the Iraqi people, to whom I belong. Our struggle is against imperialism and its agents; against those who suck the blood of our Iraqi people and who have trodden on the sovereignty and interests of the people.

This message was well received in Iraq and abroad. Abd al-Rahman Azzam Pasha, the former secretary general of the League of Arab Nations, wrote in the [Egyptian] magazine *Hilal* (October 1943):

> We must pay more attention to our Kurdish brothers of Iraq. I love and appreciate Iraqi Kurds as much as I love and appreciate my own people. The Kurds are sincere and straightforward people. They will not harm us and they must not think that Arab unity will harm them.
>
> The future and progress of Iraq are closely tied to solving the Kurdish problem. The Arab nation must afford them the ability and freedom to decide their fate with us. We must not leave the Kurdish problem in Iraq without a solution.

The Kurdish cause has come a long way, but it is still without a solution. The plight of a nation cannot remain without a solution forever. Security and stability in the Middle East are inextricably intertwined with the cause of the Kurdish nation. We, the Kurds, must distinguish between friend and foe and choose our natural position in the trenches against imperialism and revisionism. Regardless of the cost, we must continue our struggle.

Kurdistan
August 1986

Chapter 7

Return from Exile

Barzani's Return

On July 12, 1943, Barzani left the city of Suleimaniyya and reached the region of Mahabad in a week. He was hosted by Haji Baba Sheikh.[1] Then, he continued with his two companions, Mustafa and Sulayman, from the village of Akhcha Zaiwa, near Naghadeh, where Mamand Maseeh resided after he had left Iraq.

On the outskirts of the village, he saw a group of children swimming in the Gadar River. He found out that one of them was the son of Mamand Maseeh. He asked the child to lead him to Mamand's house. Although Mamand's wife did not know them, she received them with honor and offered them food in accordance with the laws of Kurdish hospitality. Upon his return home, Mamand received Barzani with tears of joy in his eyes. He praised the Lord and said, "This is the day I have been eagerly awaiting." The next day, they went to the village of Koolij,[2] where they visited the house of Mamand Agha of Koolij, chief of the Qadiri sect, of the Mamesh tribe. They were warmly received by Mamand Agha and his relatives, especially by Abdullah Agha Jildiyan, who offered them all possible assistance.

Another group of Barzanis lived in the village of Kani Rash, near Shino. Among them were Ahmad Naz, Mirza Agha Rasho, Mohammed Isa, Khan Avdal Mohammed, Abdullah Korayi, Salih Korayi, Mohammed Mamand, and Mohammed Agha Boker. Barzani sent word to them of his arrival and invited them over to see him. They accepted the invitation at once, while vacillating between doubt and certainty. They welcomed him with tears of joy. I had the good fortune to meet a few of them and listen to their memories of that period.

After a night in Mamand Agha's company, Barzani and his two companions moved to Iraqi Kurdistan. On this subject, I heard the following from Mustafa Barzani:

> While sitting in the divan, Qarani Agha Mamesh[3] arrived to inform Mamand Agha Koolij of a rumor about the flight of Mustafa Barzani from Suleimaniyya and the Iraqi government's offer of 50,000 dinars to anyone who captured him dead or alive. He asked Mamand Agha not to miss this opportunity. Mamand Agha replied that the person who would capture Barzani had not been born yet!

Of course, Qarani Agha did not know Barzani, but at last he recognized him. He did not utter a word and left.

Mamand Agha encouraged the Barzanis to go with Barzani. He promised to provide for their families, and he did. As a present, he gave Barzani a "Birno" rifle, an expensive gun at the time. Barzani kept it until he crossed the Araxes river.

Barzani and his comrades crossed into Iraq on July 28, 1945. Mamand Agha sent one of his men, Khidr-a Qita, to guide them all the way to the border. Their first stop was the Khailanis' summer resort in Dol and Maydan, near Mount Halgord. He visited Mamek Khailani[4] in his tent. There he learned that the regent was in Mergamir[5] in Mahmud Beg Khalifah Samad's resort. He moved swiftly, with every intention of taking the regent hostage, which would have expedited his task and ensured his success with a minimum of effort. He arrived in the evening, but unfortunately the regent had left Mergamir for Rewanduz in the company of Mahmud Beg during the day. Barzani missed the opportunity.

After a short recess with Mahmud Beg, Barzani continued on to Barzan. He reached the village of Bebil and went to the house of Mohammed Mulla who was well respected in the area. He learned about recent developments in the region. In addition, Mohammed Mulla gave him word about a group of men who had refused to surrender. Among them were Omer Abdullah Khalanayi, Rasho Khal Hamza, Mohammed Amin Mirkhan, and Qadir Bavayi. They had gone to Mount Bradost with about 30 men.

At the Mamandan summer resort, Barzani was warmly received by his comrades-in-arms and loyal friends. As they reminisced about their past, Barzani asked them about the region. He arranged their first meeting to organize their affairs. They reached several important decisions regarding their new role and the reorganization of their forces. Barzani explained the significant developments in the movement, its expansion, and prospects. He stressed the need to follow Sheikh Ahmad's counsel to (1) be just in all practices and affairs, (2) avoid arrogance, and (3) avoid confrontation with government forces unless certain of a major victory; especially in the first clash.

At this time, news arrived from Mergasur that the police force stationed in Bilah had left for Mergasur to conduct a joint operation with the police force stationed there, with the assistance of local guides led by Mohammed Agha Mergasuri. The operation was against the group fortified in Mount Bradost before Barzani was to join it. The authorities did not know of Barzani's arrival, primarily because people did not stoop to cooperate with the government. Consequently, the authorities seldom received accurate information.

Mohammed Kakshar Mergasuri carried Barzani's letter to the authorities in Mergasur informing them of his arrival in the region and warning them against taking any action against the local population. The contents of the letter were telegraphed to Arbil, and the authorities therefore learned of Barzani's safe arrival in the region. They hurried to reinforce their barracks with additional troops and to give them enough food and supplies to last a long time as a precaution against an attack or a long siege.

Government Reaction

Being a Kurd and known for his absolute loyalty to Britain, the governor of Suleimaniyya, the power-hungry Sheikh Mustafa Qaradaghi, went out of his way to prove his loyalty to the government. He felt inferior toward his superiors. We have often seen this attitude from some Kurdish government employees, who received important positions at their people's expense and appeared to be "more royalist than the king."

Sheikh Qaradaghi often took excessive measures against the Barzanis even before Barzani left Suleimaniyya. He stopped paying them the allowances the government earmarked for those affected by forced relocation. He also forbade Suleimaniyya patriots to assist them.

The government issued orders to exile Sheikh Ahmad Barzani to Hillah, together with all of the Barzanis and their families in his party. The governor executed the order immediately, as a direct reaction to learning of Mustafa Barzani's return to his region. It was a reaction consistent with the government's insistence on oppressive measures. The events that followed are detailed below.

Touring the Region

Barzani decided to tour the villages of the Barzan region to meet the people, talk with them, and learn about local conditions at first hand, as well as to camouflage his plan and avoid clashes with government forces. During his tour, which lasted until the end of September of 1943, a large number of fighters joined him—some armed and others unarmed. Among them were Aziz Agha Zrari, Salih Kania Lanji, 'Aris Khano Bidaroni, Taha Rashk Birokhi, Mohammed Sa'id Birokhi, Haji Birokhi, Mulla Shini Bidaroni, Shimad Dizoyi, Hasso Mirkhan, Hasso Yousif, Salim Abdullah Seilki, and other young men. They added significantly to the number of Barzani's forces, as he had a sufficient number of young people who later became leaders.

This tour continued during the months of August and September of 1943. Barzani formed a clear impression of the area as he learned more of the circumstances. Also, he explained his new program and the important developments in the new movement, which was widely supported by the masses and patriotic organizations of Kurdistan.

A number of local dignitaries had been ostracized to remote regions, but others were still in the area and played a positive role in encouraging the young to learn the principles for which Sheikh Abd al-Salam and Sheikh Ahmad struggled. The dignitaries explained the reasons and motives that made them targets of enemies in any location. Regular meetings were held in every village. In this manner, the Barzanis preserved their traditions, vitality, and social ties as best they could. Thus, they were able to challenge government carnage and injustice against them. Barzani's tour reached all the way to the borders of Iran. He established contact with the J.K. Society.[6] He sent several letters to the heads of Kurdish tribes in Iraqi Kurdistan, calling on them to refuse to take up arms on behalf of the government, to keep national unity, and to end tribal discord.

Chapter 8

The Armed Revolt of 1943

Organization of Forces

Having completed his tour and satisfied with conditions, Barzani decided to organize his forces in groups, with 15–30 fighters to a group. He appointed three commanders for his forces: Mohammed Amin Mirkhan, Mamand Maseeh, and Saleh Kaniya Lanji. Rasho Khal Hamza was put in charge of administration. Barzani gathered all of his forces and set clear and well-defined rules of operation. Briefly, they were as follows:

1. Fighters must obey their commanders and carry out their orders.
2. Commanders must stand together with their fighters and treat them as brothers, on an equal footing.
3. Force must never be used to procure anything from citizens.
4. The spoils of war must be distributed fairly and on the basis of need.
5. Prisoners of war must be treated humanely, and their personal belongings were not to be confiscated.
6. Instructions must be adhered to completely.

Many *peshmergas*,[1] who were with Barzani and took part in these events, told me that that period was the best time of their lives, and that it was the best organized because of their common feeling of trust and fairness, as well as the bonds of mutual affection and sympathy, equality, and commitment.

Barzani lived with his forces and shared their duties. He refused privileges and often took turns mounting guard. He enjoyed a caring and trusting camaraderie with his forces that deepened day after day. They loved him, persevered with him in their darkest days, and chose death with him over life without him.

Contacting the Government

Certain of the people's unlimited support and the ability of his forces to endure and fight, Barzani decided to execute his plan. He sent a letter to the government for the station chief of Shitna, Petty Officer Qadir Beg Rewanduzi, to pass on to his superiors. In his letter, he said that he was prepared to communicate and to find a peaceful solution to the problem, and that he had avoided clashes over the past two months to avoid complicating the issue further. He agreed with Qadir Beg to receive a response three days later at a place near Mazna on Mount Bradost. The government forces tried to surround the place, thus revealing the government's nefarious intentions.

The Decision to Initiate Operations

Despairing of a positive government response to his peace initiative, Barzani realized that the situation necessitated a strong presence in order for the government to comply with his demands, so he gathered his forces and addressed them:

> We have avoided clashes with government forces during the past two months in the hope that we would succeed in reaching a peaceful settlement. However, the government does not care for the blood of its forces. We cannot wait any longer. Therefore, I am consulting you about beginning to hit and occupy police stations in the region.

They all supported the plan with alacrity and proclaimed their utter readiness. As mentioned earlier, a number of Barzanis were employed in the police force and appointed at local police stations. The government had carefully planned to eschew excessive measures and let people live in peace and security. Indeed, it was a wise strategy that produced significant positive results. Otherwise, the situation would have undergone a hazardous change.

The First Operation

The first operation began with the seizure of the Shanader police station on October 2, 1943. Mohammed Amin Mirkhan, Mamand Maseeh and Aziz Agha Zrari, along with their forces, were assigned to carry out this operation. Omer Shanaderi, who had gone there earlier on Barzani's orders, was waiting there for them. As planned, they took over the station and seized all weapons, ammunition, and food. More importantly, all police were taken prisoners without a single shot being fired. Ali Khan Shirwani played a large role in the takeover of the station. He was a policeman there. Mission accomplished, they returned to Bira Sal; Barzani was awaiting their arrival. Immediately, he ordered the release of all prisoners. He distributed the captured weapons and ammunition among those who did not have any. He put Omer in command of a group of fighters in recognition of his fighting capabilities and courage.

After occupying the Shanader police station, Barzani decided to go to the Mizuri region for a while. There he was joined by Hussain Charkis Bindori, Sulayman Dizoy, Yasin Bindori, and Rashid Moki. They were men of valor, and a number of young men accompanied them. Barzani contacted Nuri Shirwani, who was there, and put him in charge of running the Shirwan station, to which Nuri agreed. However, hours before his return to Shirwan, a mobile police force nearly the size of a regiment had arrived. Their presence precluded the execution of the plan. The commander of that force requested a meeting with Barzani. It was naïve to expect Barzani to go to Shirwan just on his say-so. The meeting did not take place, and Barzani moved to Birsiyav and planned to take over the station at Khairzok.

The Battle of Khairzok

On October 12, 1943, Barzani's forces surrounded Khairzok station. The police resisted, refused to surrender, and asked for reinforcements from Mergasur and Shirwan. The mobile police force left Shirwan only two days after they had arrived. Barzani was aware of their activities.

Fortified at strategic points, the partisans awaited the arrival of the mobile battalion to render it a lethal blow. Barzani instructed his forces not to strike until the enemy had reached the Halonar steppe between Birsiyav and Khairzok. There, the famous, most successful battle of the uprising took place. In fact, it was a decisive battle. Barzani personally took part, and the fighting continued until dark. For the government forces, it was a catastrophe. They lost 120 men, including the battalion commander. He was of the prominent al-Omeri family in Mosul (the narrator did not recall his name). Sixty-five were taken prisoner, most of them wounded.

Battle gains: 130 rifles, 8 Bren machine guns, and a large amount of ammunition, foodstuffs, and other military equipment and supplies.

Battle losses: Ahmad Afandi was martyred and four were wounded, including Barzani, who was slightly injured. Fate had it that the person who had wounded Barzani was captured after he was injured himself. Not only did Barzani not allow anyone to harm him, but he afforded him with special care. The following day, Barzani sent him to Mergasur with the rest of the prisoners. They were accompanied by Nabi Hassan, a trustworthy man, to ensure their safe return. This battle cleared the region of government forces and brought it under full control of the partisans. Once the region had been put in order, Barzani went to the village of Bidaron on October 15, 1943, where he was joined by As'ad Khoshavi after his seizure of the Bira Kapra station. As'ad Khoshavi, the family of his brother, Khalil Khoshavi, along with a few of their relatives, had been deported to Bira Kapra earlier.

Barzani was happy to see As'ad return safely, for he was more liable to be arrested than others. Barzani had asked him to be careful and to be prepared to join the revolution as soon as armed operations began. This operation coincided with and was similar to the one against the Shanadar station. As'ad and his group seized all weapons and other supplies in the station. With him were two sons of his brother Khalil, Ali and Khoshavi, in addition to Mohammed Shukr Seilki and Ahmad Goran. It is worth noting that As'ad was very close to Barzani until he died. He was a capable, reasonable, and an intelligent administrator as we will come to see in more detail later.

After the great victory of Khairzok, the partisans' morale and the people's confidence in them rose. Favorable conditions permitted more strikes against government centers. Commanding one of his forces, Barzani personally moved to the areas surrounding Shirwan. He dispatched three groups, one led by Mohammed Amin Mirkhan to Chami, another led by Haji Birokhi to Zeit, and a third group led by Salim Abdullah to Seilki. In a concerted attack, fighting broke out on all three fronts, forcing the government for the first time since the beginning of the uprising to use the air force to break the siege and rescue their troops.

In Shirwan, the enemy resisted fiercely. Other stations were seized, and police were taken prisoner. In Chami, the station commander Mohammed Amin Kakhor was killed. After a week-long siege, the Shirwan station surrendered. Thus, the government was cleared out of the eastern side of the Rou Kochek rivulet. The remaining stations of Argosh, Mirozotil, and Shangeel lost hope of getting any reinforcements. They surrendered without resistance. Rihana Shlaymoon, commander of the Beidal station, changed sides. He is an Assyrian from Diyana who went with Barzani to the Soviet Union and has remained a loyal ally ever since. Having no choice, the commander of the Kani Bot station fled to Barzan before the forces of the uprising reached him. This cleared the west side of the Rou Kochek rivulet. Barzani wanted to drive the government forces out of the region. Thus, he dispatched Nuri Shirwani to Rezan station and Salim Abdullah Seilki, who was in command of another force, to the Barzan station. After fierce resistance, the Rezan station surrendered, and its commander, the wounded Ali Beg Qamchi Rash [the Black Whip], fled to the house of Wali Beg in Rezan, where he was given sanctuary.

In Barzan, as a military force from the Bileh garrison advanced to rescue the Barzan station, a savage battle took place on the Mela Heights, situated between Rezan and Bilah. Salim Abdullah was martyred, and his death had an enormous effect on ending the siege on the Barzan police station and the failure of the partisans' offensive. The partisans failed to take the Barzan station. Barzani appointed As'ad Khoshavi to command that front. He assigned Mamand Maseeh to attack the Shitna station and Mohammed Mirkhan to secure Sari Bardi, as he had received information confirming the move of a police force from Sidakan to Rewanduz.

After heavy fighting, the Shitna station surrendered, and the station commander, Petty Officer Qadir Beg Rewanduzi, was captured. In Sari Bardi, the partisans won a great victory, which astounded the enemy. They did not expect the partisans there. The government force advancing from Sidakan was caught in an ambush, and in a swift battle all but three men were wiped out. The commander of the force, Adjutant Hamdi Afandi was killed, and Adjutant Zorab was captured. The air force tried to support the troops but was too late to save them. The partisans returned safely and triumphantly. They had seized 54 rifles, two machine guns, four pistols and 15 mules.

New Victories

October 1943 was a month of victories. The entire region was cleared of government forces except for three locations, Mergasur, Barzan, and Bilah, which remained under siege until a truce went into effect. The following police stations were taken: Shanader, Khairzok, Bira Kapr, Zet, Chami, Seilki, Miroz, Argosh, Teel, Shangeel, Kani Bot, Bidiyal, Shirwan, Rezan, Shitna, Bidron, and Kaniya Rash. The partisans seized 680 rifles and 24 machine guns, in addition to large quantities of ammunition and foodstuffs. Food was distributed among the populace, the principal base supporting the revolt, and the number of partisans doubled. These victories were achieved owing to superb planning, the fighters' zeal, unlimited popular support, and the local people's earnest desire for freedom after the sufferings they had endured when their region was occupied in 1932.

Choosing Command Headquarters

Barzani decided to set up his command and control headquarters in the village of Bistri, near Mergasur, midway between his forces on the Rewanduz and Barzan fronts. He expected the army to take part in the upcoming battles. The government needed to raise the sunken morale of its forces, especially in the light of the crushing defeat of the mobile police force. The army was its only recourse.

Indeed, an army brigade reached Mergasur on October 28, 1943. Other military forces were amassed in Rewanduz and Balekiyan. Barzani appointed Saleh Kaniya Lenji as commander of the front between Mergasur and Shirwan, as well as Aris Khano as deputy commander. He personally went to Shitna and Hawidyan to ensure a strong line of defense on that front and to devise a strategy to confront any offensive by military units in Rewanduz.

The Battle of Gora Tu

The news of Barzani's absence and of the inadequacy of his forces in that sector reached the commander of the Mergasur garrison. He believed that it was a good opportunity and waged an attack on November 6, 1943, to retake the villages between Mergasur and Shirwan. Barzani's forces, led by Saleh Kaniya Lanji and Aris Khano Bidaroni, engaged them in a fierce battle around Gora Tu Village that lasted until dark and ended in the defeat and retreat of the army to Mergasur after sustaining heavy casualties.

Mohammed Amin Mirkhan rendered valuable assistance in this battle. He was commanding another force on his way to Khalifan to strike the enemy from behind near the Strait of Gali Ali Beg. He heard the artillery and machine guns raging on Mount Bradost, overlooking Mergasur, and quickly came to help his comrades. Despite having been assigned elsewhere, he decided to intervene and played a vital role in defeating the enemy. He attacked the Brigade Command Center in Mergasur, which confused Commander Ahmad Hamdi and flustered the fighting units. The Brigade Command Center lost control, and unit commanders acted without waiting for orders.

The impact of this [military] defeat on the government was severe because it had struck the Iraqi army this time. An armored vehicle and two automobiles were destroyed. The partisans gained four machine guns, 50 rifles, and a large quantity of ammunition. They captured 11 soldiers. Saleh Kaniya Lanji and Nabi Hassan were wounded.

Another Attempt by the Government Foiled

After the defeat of November 6, the army decided to wage another offensive on November 8 to remove the revolutionaries from the positions overlooking the garrison. A ferocious battle lasted until evening and ended in a more crushing defeat than that of November 6. The army fled, leaving behind its dead and its equipment on the battlefield. Forty rifles, three machine guns, and a good quantity of ammunition were captured. Abd al-Raham Qazi, commander of an artillery battery in Mergasur and a patriotic Kurdish officer who had established contact with Barzani, told me the following story:

> I was trying to shell distant targets, away from partisan positions. However, that day the brigade commander accompanied me and ordered me to shell positions I was sure contained revolutionaries. Against my will, I was obliged to shell them. I was very anxious and worried about casualties in Barzani's forces. Next morning, I received a message from Barzani reassuring me that there had only been two injured. I took a deep breath and wrote back to him explaining my agonizing position.

One of the two wounded was Mohammed Amin Mirkhan, who had fought courageously and admirably. After these two defeats, Barzani clearly knew that government forces stationed in Mergasur would be unable to launch another attack alone. Therefore, he left an adequate force stationed there to maintain the siege on Mergasur Brigade headquarters. He personally led a large force to the Rewanduz front to reinforce and devise a strong defensive plan to counter any assault by army units amassed in Rewanduz.

The Battle of Mazna

The situation at the Mergasur camp was ominous. It was under a tight siege that precluded the soldiers from leaving their barracks. To break the siege, the government decided to attack on two fronts. From Rewanduz, a brigade legion supported by a brigade of mobile police was to move simultaneously with the Mergasur brigade. Both forces were to meet in Mazna.

The plan was executed on November 10, 1943, in the largest battle of that period. All forces on both sides were active on fronts extending from Balekiyan to Mergasur. The air force supported government troops extensively on the ground. The fighting continued all day with no victor in sight. However, by dusk Barzani's forces waged an all-out assault, forcing government forces of both prongs to retreat to their barracks in Balekiyan and Mergasur. Defeated, the army left a large number of its dead along the road between Hawediyan and Mergasur. Mergasur Brigade Commander Colonel Ahmad Hamdi's car was attacked. A number of his escorts were killed, and he had a nervous breakdown, a condition that lasted the rest of his life.

Women played a heroic role in providing water and food to the partisans while the heavy shelling and gunfire continued. It is difficult to favor one's role over another's because all fought earnestly and carried out their functions diligently, regardless of the cost. Partisans wounded were Haji Haider Argoshi, Sa'id Abd al-Wahab Argoshi, and Hussein Birokhi. There was no loss of life.

With higher morale and in triumph, the partisans brought the region under their full control. Reassured, Barzani returned to his command center in Bistri. On November 12, he received a letter from the military commander of Rewanduz pleading for permission to transfer the bodies of his men to Rewanduz. For humanitarian reasons, he responded positively and sent a letter with his messenger, Sa'id Sari, stressing his desire for peace and for an end to the bloodshed.

An unarmed battalion came to pick up the army corpses. Barzani instructed his forces and the citizens to assist in picking up and transporting their dead.

Chapter 9

Negotiations with the Government

The Beginning of Negotiations

B arzani's victories and his partisans' liberation of the region on the one hand, and the failure of government forces to end the uprising or at least to limit its influence on the other, forced government policy makers to negotiate with Barzani and ask Wahab Mohammed Ali Agha Jundiyan,[1] a patriot and Barzani loyalist, to explore Barzani's willingness to receive a government representative.

Barzani welcomed the government initiative and its willingness to come to terms. On November 29, 1943, the government sent Nuri Baweel Agha Rewanduzi to Barzani's command center in Bistri and officially informed him of the government's desire to negotiate and find a peaceful solution to the problem. Barzani, in turn, stressed his readiness and his sincere desire to come to terms. He also expressed his regret for the loss of lives because of the government's obdurate rejection of his peace initiative in the first place. He emphasized that the issue was one of Kurdish national rights and that there was nothing personal involved. Nuri Baweel Agha carried Barzani's response back to Baghdad. A week later, he returned with Pisho Sayyed Taha[2] to relay the government's request to Barzani to end the siege against the Mergasur garrison and demonstrate his good intentions.

Barzani refused, replying that it was up to the government to demonstrate its good intentions. The oppressor, not the oppressed, should prove this point. Both government representatives returned empty-handed, and government planes began a resupply operation, parachuting food and supplies, most of which fell into the hands of the partisans encircling the garrison. Their attempt at resupply had failed.

The Role of the Hiwa Party in the Uprising

The HP[3] played a vital role in reinvigorating popular support for Barzani's uprising, while their own victories encouraged and inspired HP members and other Kurdish patriots.

Among HP activities was the distribution in Baghdad and other Iraqi cities of leaflets supporting the uprising and denouncing the government's repressive measures and its anti-Kurdish and specifically anti-Barzani intentions. Both the British and Iraqi governments took note of those leaflets and sensed a new and significant development in the Kurdish nationalist movement. They realized that events in Kurdistan were not a tribal rebellion, limited to a few mountains, that they could suppress easily. This was an armed national revolution supported by the Kurdish people in Iraqi Kurdistan—especially the educated—and it was a symbol of Kurdish aspirations.

Faced with this new reality, the British ambassador informed Barzani of his government's desire to end hostilities and negotiate with the Iraqi government. He pointed out the strategic importance of Iraq for Britain and its allies, since supply lines to the Soviet Union passed through Iraq, specifically through Kurdistan. He stressed that continuing the revolt meant fighting Britain and the Allies. He concluded his letter with pledges that if Barzani respected this request, his government would use its influence with the Iraqi government to secure Kurdish national rights.

The Iraqi forces failed to quell Barzani's uprising. Preoccupied by World War II on many fronts that required all of its efforts and energy, Britain could not afford to be sidetracked. On the other hand, Turkey had not yet taken a position regarding the war. Furthermore, an armed Kurdish revolt in Iraqi Kurdistan would unnerve the Turks. Britain exerted tremendous pressure on the Iraqi government to come to terms with Barzani on tactical grounds before his uprising expanded to the other parts of Kurdistan and the Soviets intervened to support it; particularly because the Soviet army was stationed along the Iran–Iraq border. Therefore, strategically, British policy was to end the revolt by yielding to a few Kurdish demands until the War ended and the international situation was cleared up. Then Britain would be able to intervene militarily on Iraq's behalf and vanquish Barzani.

Nuri al-Sa'id Forms a New Cabinet

On December 25, 1943, Nuri al-Sa'id included three Kurdish ministers in his new cabinet. They were Ahmad Mukhtar Baban (justice), Umar Nadhmi (interior), and Majid Mustafa, a Minister Without Portfolio—especially appointed to resolve the Kurdish question.

Majid Mustafa informed Barzani of his mission and asked for his assistance in accomplishing this task. As a first step toward peace, they agreed to a ceasefire. Majid Mustafa visited Sheikh Ahmad Barzani, exiled in Hillah, and asked him to send one of his sons to Barzani to urge him to [adopt] a peace agreement. At first, Sheikh Ahmad Barzani declined. Majid Mustafa persisted until he agreed to send his son, Mohammed Khalid, who reached Mergasur on December 29, 1943, accompanied by Adjutant Fadhil Ali Afandi. Barzani received him in Lower Mergasur after a long period of forced separation.

Two hours earlier, army units had violated the ceasefire and martyred Mohammed Kakshar, a close associate of Barzani and a notable in the region. As a result, Barzani ordered Mohammed Amin Mirkhan to launch a surprise attack on the brigade barracks. He wiped out the garrison that had violated the truce and killed Mohammed Kakshar. This was the last military operation.

Mohammed Khalid spent a few days with his uncle, conveyed his father's orders and advice, and returned to Baghdad. The government waited eagerly for Barzani's response, and as soon as Mohammed Khalid returned, Majid Mustafa visited the area to discuss the elements of the agreement with Barzani.

The First Meeting between Barzani and Majid

On January 7, 1944, Majid Mustafa, who officially represented the Iraqi government, arrived in Mergasur. He was authorized to discuss all of Barzani's demands and to draw up a plan for the agreement. Before his arrival, Barzani had cooperated and agreed with the HP on Kurdish demands. Barzani received Majid Mustafa and a group of officers, in Espindar Village, near Mergasur. Once they had discussed the situation and exchanged views, Barzani presented the following Kurdish demands:

1. Expulsion or transfer of government employees known for bribery and abuse of power.
2. Establishment of the Kurdistan Vilayat, comprised of the provinces of Kirkuk, Suleimaniyya, Arbil, and the Kurdish prefectures of the Mosul Province: i.e., Zakho, Imadiyya, Duhok, Aqra, Shaikhan, and Sinjar, as well as the districts of Khanaqin and Mandali in Diyala Province.
3. Recognition of Kurdish as the official language of the state of Kurdistan.
4. Appointment of a Kurdish deputy for each minister.
5. Establishment of a ministry headed by a Kurdish minister to govern the proposed state of Kurdistan.
6. Compensation for damages sustained.
7. Establishment of schools and hospitals, building of roads, and reconstruction of the region.
8. In the Kurdistan Vilayat, military, financial, and foreign affairs were to remain under the control of the central government.
9. Repatriation of the deportees and the release of prisoners.

After dinner in Espindar, the conversation became unofficial and light. Majid Mustafa asked Barzani, "How did you choose the name *Jash* Police[4] for the government's Kurdish militia?" Barzani replied, "If you don't serve your Kurdish people, then we'll call you '*Jash* Minister' as well." Majid Mustafa: "Please, please don't call me that, sir!" They all burst out laughing. For the first time, Barzani used the term "*Jash* police" to describe Kurds who collaborate with the government against the revolt. After that, the term blended into the Kurdish culture to denote all those who betray the cause of their people.

Later, Majid [Mustafa] invited Barzani to visit the brigade headquarters. Barzani spoke of events of that visit as follows:

When Majid suggested I visit the Mergasur garrison, I agreed, provided a number of our forces would be deployed in sensitive areas inside the barracks. Majid wrote to the commander. He replied that he would collect all weapons from the soldiers and put them under guard by Barzani's men.

Accordingly, we sent some of our men to the camp, and we followed. We were received by the commander and a group of officers at Gora Mirza, a point between Espindar and Mergasur. The meeting turned to a visit of hugs and kisses between the revolutionary partisans and the soldiers. An unbelievable scene. Enemies a week earlier, they hugged and disavowed all feelings of hatred. They turned the camp grounds into a Kurdish dance floor all night long.

This fraternal meeting led me to order the opening of the Rewanduz-Mergasur road to allow food and other supplies into the barracks, which had been surrounded until that moment. Indeed, the meeting of partisans and soldiers had a great effect on me.

Barzani took this opportunity to meet Kurdish officers in Mergasur who were known to be sympathetic and had cooperated with him as best they could. Among them, we mention Abd al-Rahman Qazi, Nuri Mulla Maroof, Nuri Mulla Hakim, Nuri Ahmad Taha, Rafiq Koyi, and Mohammed Saleh.[5]

Majid Returns to Baghdad

On the morning of January 8, Majid Mustafa returned to Baghdad and Barzani returned to Espindar. He invited the brigade commander and his officers for lunch. One of the officers, Amin Rewanduzi, wanted to test Barzani's sharpshooting skills. He walked off a good distance and set his cigarette pack up as a target for Barzani. With his own rifle, Barzani hit the target on the first try. The officer picked up his pierced pack again, tucked it in his pocket and said, "This is something to remember for life."

After lunch, all of the officers returned to Mergasur, and relations moved toward normalization. They continued to visit each other.

The Army's Withdrawal

Majid Mustafa returned to Baghdad, and orders were issued to army units stationed in the area to return to their barracks. Amin Rewanduzi was appointed liaison officer to oversee the withdrawal. The army withdrew from Mergasur to Rewanduz and from Bilah to Aqra, and the area was cleared of government authority. This was a significant victory both for the Barzanis and for the Kurdish movement in general.

Chapter 10

A Temporary Response to the Demands of the Revolutionaries

The Government's Positive Steps

After Majid [Mustafa] returned to Baghdad, the Iraqi cabinet met on January 25 and decided on the following:

1. To appoint new employees to administer the districts of Imadia, Rewanduz, Mergasur, and Aqra; and to appoint liaison officers in all of these district centers.
2. To reopen police stations in the Barzan region.
3. To open the road between the stations.
4. To deport Mulla Mustafa Barzani from the Barzan region.
5. To return Sheikh Ahmad Barzani and his relatives to their place of birth.
6. To return the weapons to the government.
7. In principle, the government agreed to issue a general amnesty but left out government employees and members of the armed forces who had joined Barzani. The amnesty was to be announced when the government deemed it appropriate.
8. The Minister of the Interior and a Minister at Large were authorized to implement Articles 4 and 5 at a time they deemed appropriate.

I am not certain if Majid [Mustafa] honestly conveyed these decisions to Barzani and the HP or not, because they do not correspond to Barzani's demands which had been given to Majid [Mustafa]. It appears that the government devised two policies—one strategic and the other tactical.

In a positive move, the government appointed the following Kurdish liaison officers to the areas next to their names below:

1. Brigadier Baha' ad-Din Sheikh Nuri, Suleimaniyya.
2. Colonel Amin Rewanduzi, Rewanduz.
3. Captain Sayyed Aziz Sayyed Abdullah, Mergasur.
4. Captain Mir Haj Ahmad, Aqra.

5. Captain Mustafa Khoshnaw, Barzan.
6. Major Izzat Abd al-Aziz, Bilah.
7. Captain Majeed Ali, Imadia.
8. Captain Fuad Arif, Pishdar.

These officers were to report directly to the Minister Without Portfolio. Food was sent to the region and distributed under their supervision. The appointment of liaison officers was well received in Barzan and other regions of Kurdistan. It was generally considered a step in the right direction, a step toward a peaceful resolution.

Sheikh Ahmad's Return to Barzan

On December 12, 1944, the government permitted Sheikh Ahmad Barzani, his companions, and their families to return to Barzan. He reached the village of Sreshma and was hosted by Ahmad Shabaz,[1] who generously provided all of the assistance he could offer. A Barzani force, commanded by As'ad Khoshavi, had just arrived in Sreshma to receive the returnees and protect them. Barzani was waiting in Shanader. He said that he considered that day the happiest of his life.

Sheikh Ahmad settled in. With the exception of Kalhi Rekani and Sheikh Rashid of Lolan, the tribal chiefs visited and welcomed him back and renewed their solidarity with Barzan.[2]

Barzani's Visit to Baghdad

Majid [Mustafa] was active at this time and often traveled between Baghdad and Kurdistan. He accompanied Barzani to Baghdad on February 22, as a confidence-building measure and to sign the agreement. It was a good opportunity for Barzani, the HP leaders, and other Kurdish patriots to meet and exchange views.

Barzani stayed at the Shatt al-Arab Hotel. Warmly received in Baghdad, he met with the regent, Nuri al-Sa'id, and concerned ministers. The government pledged to implement the points agreed upon with Majid [Mustafa]. After a week in Baghdad, Barzani returned to Barzan.

Among the steps Majid [Mustafa] took was to extend invitations to many Kurdish tribal leaders to come to Kirkuk in March. He requested that Nuri al-Sa'id attend that meeting and speak there. Nuri al-Sa'id did address this meeting, praising the Kurdish people and promising to implement the agreement and abide by it. This, however, was belied by the fact that the majority of the administration was strongly opposed to what it termed Nuri al-Sa'id's compromise. In a government ploy characteristic of Iraqi politics at the time, Nuri al-Sa'id was dismissed, and Hamdi al-Pachachi formed a new cabinet, which turned its back on the agreement and openly antagonized the Kurdish national movement, as will be discussed in more detail later.

In its last few days, Nuri al-Sa'id's administration had given Majid [Mustafa] limited authority to deal with a few minor problems. After a few months, the liaison officer Amin Rewanduzi was ordered to return to his base unit and, according to Sayyed Aziz's own letter to Izzat Abd al-Aziz, dated April 2, 1944, ordered to attend military training. After this recall, all operational steps to implement the agreement were practically frozen; the government's undeclared intentions were suspect, and the situation began to deteriorate.

Nuri al-Sa'id's Resignation and the Beginning of the Game

On June 3, 1944, Nuri al-Sa'id's cabinet resigned and Hamdi al-Pachachi formed a new cabinet which included two Kurdish ministers, Ahmad Mukhtar (justice) and Tawfiq Wahbi (economy), but not Majid [Mustafa]. Britain, the real power behind Iraq's politics, orchestrated this show. As World War II came to a conclusion, Britain was able to use its military power, if necessary, to deal with the problems.

At that time, the Kurdish question was one of the most critical issues that pre-occupied the British government and seriously threatened its interests in the Middle East. The Kurds of Iran were active again and the Soviet army was in Kurdistan and Azerbaijan. Britain feared the Soviet army's intervention in support of the Iraqi Kurds. Soon, through the deception and cheap schemes for which they were known, the British decided to quell the Kurdish revolt. They conspired to shelve Nuri al-Sa'id temporarily and replaced him with someone else who was not bound by his pledges. Thus, the new cabinet felt free of all obligations.

Confirming the discussion above, in his letter of resignation, Nuri al-Sa'id wrote regarding the Kurdish Question:

> Since I have briefly spoken of the Kurdish issue in modern times, especially in Iraq, I must speak of some of the Iraqi Kurds and their proclivities in general, as they are citizens; and of the plan that must be followed in the administration of their affairs in these complicated circumstances through which we are now going. In my view, Iraqi Kurds fall into three classes:
>
> 1. Chiefs of Tribes: They live a life closer to feudalism than that of a civilian's. They have no specific political goals. Their main concern is to keep what power and influence they have inherited within their regions and tribes.
> 2. Merchants: They always want full government control for order and peace in order to advance and protect their commercial interests.
> 3. Intelligentsia: They are growing and their wishes are no greater than those of the rest of the educated Iraqis. They want to increase the number of schools and expand education, as well as to add to the benefits of civilian life in areas such as construction and health. They also wish to be in charge of local administration and to end the influence of the first class.
>
> As for their political goals in an independent Greater Kurdistan, the wise among them do not believe this idea can be realized unless it is supported by the super-powers, because over 80 percent of the Kurdish area lies outside Iraq.
>
> If we take a closer look at events and news throughout this grueling War, from time to time we find initiatives indicating that some of the superpowers wish to exploit the Kurdish cause to advance their own interests, although this exploitation

has not yet come to an end, no one knows how much truth there is in these promises, how much time is needed to fulfill them or the extent to which they will be fulfilled.

In a murky world such as our present one, and until stability prevails and hidden facts and intentions are revealed, Iraq must be careful in managing the northern Kurdish region, particularly in [the] light of the turbulence in Iran. The Iranian government is flirting with Kurdish tribal chiefs who are controlling their own areas. I have learned that Kurdish councils have been established to organize and run their own affairs in Iranian Kurdistan, near the Turkish border, under Soviet control. In Turkey, a larger-than-normal army has been amassed to maintain law and order in the areas near Iran and Iraq. It is reported that communications among the various classes of Kurds have noticeably increased of late. These contacts are organized and run by the countries concerned to gauge events in all Kurdish areas.

Obviously, we are going through unusual times that require officials to be extra prudent and avoid anything which will give covetous countries an excuse to exploit this abnormal situation during the war; especially when we know that Iraqi Kurds do not have any goal which contradicts the aspirations of the rest of Iraq. Kurds, like the rest, demand reform of the Administration and attention to education, health, construction and other vital issues that must be addressed all over Iraq sooner or later so as to raise the standard of living, increase production and develop resources. These remain the objectives of the officials, and we must not allow a delay of reforms to be exploited and cause us much difficulty, or upset the good relations between the Kurds and their Arab brothers.

When I ask for special consideration for the northern regions, and taking the initiative to repair whatever can be repaired there before anywhere else, I do not mean fixing the northern region at the expense of other regions. I mean preference necessitated by the extraordinary circumstances at the present time. We must see Iraq as one complete unit and introduce comprehensive reforms for the good of the whole society.

Nuri al-Sa'id,
Prime Minister

Rejecting solutions to the Kurdish question promised by the previous administration, al-Pachachi's cabinet issued a strict policy ordering all liaison officers to return to their original units immediately. When they returned to their units, the Ministry of Defense treated them with caution and suspicion. In consultation between Barzani and the HP leadership, it was decided that both Izzat Mustafa and Mir Haj would request two months leave and let the rest return to their units.

Contacting Kurdish Political Organizations

Izzat [Mustafa] went to Syria to approach the Khoyboon Society. Mustafa Khoshnaw and Mir Haj went to Mahabad to approach the J.K. [*Jianaway Kurd* (Kurdish Resurrection)] Society for the same purpose, i.e., to strengthen ties with Kurdish patriotic and revolutionary parties and organizations, and exchange views about how best to serve the goals of the nation.

The government was growing increasingly suspicious of these two visits. Upon their return, it was decided that Mir Haj should return to his unit and then send a letter to Mustafa Khoshnaw in which he would give his impressions and views and recount what sort of treatment he had received from his superiors in the army. Mir Haj did so, and said that he found nothing out of the ordinary. Hence, Mustafa Khoshnaw returned as well.

However, shortly thereafter, both were discharged from the army and court-martialed. Mir Haj was arrested and sent to Imarah Prison. Mustafa Khoshnaw, who was in Mosul at the time, heard the news and escaped to Betwata, where he was joined by Bakr Abd al-Karim; both then went to Barzan. After returning from his visit to Syria and Egypt, Izzat [Mustafa] was harassed in Baghdad and did not stay there long. He returned to Arbil with the help of some friends, and then went to Barzan.

With actions against Kurdish officers having come to a halt, the government released Mir Haj and reinstated him in an administrative position in the Defense Ministry. However, he left Baghdad and joined his other companions in Barzan at the first opportunity.

It was evident from government practices and from trustworthy reports from Kurdish patriots in sensitive government centers that the government was moving toward ignoring the rights of the Kurdish people and preparing to wage a military offensive on a broad scale, this time with the direct support of British imperialism.

Barzani accordingly put his forces on alert. He realized that he needed to close ranks, secure national unity, end all old tribal discord, and bridge all gaps to prevent enemies from exploiting them. Therefore, he began a tour to mobilize the masses and secure tribal loyalties.

Barzani trusted the position of the political organizations and the masses of Kurdistani peasants, but he was skeptical of the stance of the tribal chiefs. Tribal loyalties were strong, as dictated by tribal traditions at that time. Hence, it was of paramount importance to do whatever was necessary to secure the allegiance of tribal chiefs, or at least to neutralize them.

Barzani's Tour among the Tribes

In the second half of 1944, Barzani began his tour with the Zebaris and Surchis. He asked them to end their tribal hatred and friction, reconcile with each other, and put national interests first. They promised to support him in his national quest. He reminded them not to succumb to government blandishments and promises. He returned to Barzan. His second visit was to the Arbil region. He met with the chiefs of the Khoshnaw tribe in the house of Salih Beg Miran[3] in Shaqlawa. He was promised support and solidarity. Then he continued his tour to the plains of Arbil, where he met tribal chiefs in the house of Mulla Afandi,[4] followed by a second meeting in the house of Fattah Agha Harki[5] in Miran Khor Village. Everyone promised that they would support him and not cooperate with the government and would do their patriotic duty if Kurdistan was attacked. They vowed support by all they held sacred.

Barzani paid a courtesy visit to governor Sa'id Qazzaz of Arbil. He returned to Barzan hoping to continue his tour of Kurdistan in the following spring of 1945. Conditions moved from bad to worse. Barzani wrote a memorandum to the Interior Minister in late November of 1944, in which he cited government short-comings and disregard for the agreement. The memorandum was not answered.

Chapter 11

The Freedom Committee and Coordination with the Hiwa Party

The Founding of the Freedom Committee

In his meetings and correspondence with government officials, Barzani worked ceaselessly to compel the government to implement the agreement and to avoid confrontation. Unconcerned, the government continued military preparations. Barzani received ample information about government plans and intentions. Based on his experience and the lessons he had learned in the 1943 uprising, Barzani decided to hasten the process with a new move that matched the new developments.

Having obtained Sheikh Ahmad Barzani's guidance and approval, he met with all of the patriotic officers in Barzan at the time. They reached a historic decision. On January 15, 1945, after a series of extensive meetings, they studied all aspects of the situation and decided to form the Freedom Committee under Barzani's chairmanship. The following program was approved:

1. Liberation of Kurdistan from oppression and injustice.
2. Formation of armed units to defend Kurdistan.
3. Working toward total national reconciliation.
4. Establishment of fraternal ties with all Kurdish patriotic and progressive parties and organizations throughout Kurdistan.
5. Declaration of Kurdish grievances through appeals to Iraqi and international public opinion via the foreign embassies in Baghdad.
6. Exposure of the government's anti-Kurdish policies through the mass media and calling for the implementation of the 1943 agreement, the base of the ceasefire.

The Kurds were overjoyed at the news, and the committee was widely supported by the masses of Kurdistan, especially by the students and the youth. The first accomplishment of the committee was the presentation of a memorandum to the Iraqi government demanding Kurdish rights and a halt to military preparations. Copies were distributed to all foreign embassies, the Arab and Kurdish intelligentsia, and college students.

On October 2, the Kurdish youth in Baghdad issued and widely distributed a communiqué strongly supporting the Freedom Committee. A copy of the committee's memorandum reinvigorated the HP, which began working enthusiastically again. The following is an excerpt from the letter by the president of the HP to Barzani:

Number: 9
Date: January 30, 1945

Dear Mr. Barzani:

On January 18, 1945, we sent a short letter to you by two of our Party members, Broska and Hindirin. Unfortunately, the government suspected the nature of their mission and they returned to Arbil. Our purpose in contacting you is that you seriously consider the HP's program for the future. Obviously, any national movement which does not have clarity of vision and a clear platform will end in failure. As you know, a strong movement needs a bold leader with two strong arms, one political and one military.

The political arm secures the necessities of defense, communicates with friends, and sets a political agenda. The military arm defends the rights of the people by force of arms and wrests these rights from the usurper. The whole world follows this model. We propose the following:

1. That we be cognizant of each other's condition and movements, and that we exchange information.
2. [That] we work to unite both organizations (the HP and the Freedom Committee). The headquarters are to be in Barzan.

Signed
Chairman, the Hiwa Party

The Freedom Committee's response to the HP:

Number: 1
Date: February 15, 1945

1. We are in receipt of your letter Ref. No. 9, dated January 30, 1945. We have understood its contents.
2. We do not think that it is appropriate to move HP headquarters to Barzan at this time.
3. Undoubtedly, the liberation of Kurdistan requires sacrifice and preparation. I thank God for the belief and trust He has given us in the legitimacy of our cause and in the need to make sacrifices.
4. My comrades on the Committee and I have decided to tour Kurdistan to introduce our program to the people.
5. We ask the Society's branches to send us views and information from HP Headquarters quickly.
6. I ask all brothers who have decided to join the revolution to join now. The time has come.
7. With the beginning of the revolution, we ask you to distribute its communiqués and bulletins in the villages and towns of Kurdistan and throughout all Iraq. We will keep you informed of our conditions.

8. Please designate a contact person in each city to secure communications with us.
9. We ask the KHK Center[1] to send us a typewriter and we have asked "D"[2] to send a stamp under the name of "Freedom Committee". Please send them quickly.
10. It has come to our attention that some individuals are coming to you in our name. This is on the orders and with the knowledge of the government. We ask that you not admit any person who does not carry our emblem.
11. Routes of communication with us will be as follows:
    a. Arbil, Shaqlawa, Rewanduz, Mazna, Shitna, Barzan.
    b. Arbil, Shaqlawa, Khalifan, Srishma, Rezan, Barzan.
    c. Mosul, Aqra, Bilah, Barzan.
    d. Mosul, Duhok, Imadia, Barzan.
12. We are well aware that the government tries through deception to trivialize our cause and to isolate Barzan from the rest of Kurdistan. Our cause is one. We do not have two causes. Our goal is the liberation of Kurdistan and nothing else. We must be aware of this attempt.
13. To foil government plans, please mobilize your members to refute government propaganda. Please continue to send us newspapers and magazines.
14. Please send us a radio so that we can stay informed about world news.
15. We will send you our news via Branch "B."[3] Contact them from now on.
16. Please distribute the memorandum directed to Iraqi dignitaries and intellectuals. Do not distribute the other one.
17. As you know, a great number of comrades have joined us. The Freedom Committee is obligated to provide for them. To prove our people's ability and achieve self-sufficiency, I call upon every sincere Kurd to help us. I hope that the HP can play a large role in collecting contributions.
18. I noticed some slacking in Branch "S,"[4] after it was the most active one, appreciated and admired by all. Please tell them to return to the level of activity expected of them. We hope to stay in touch.

Mustafa Barzani, President
The Freedom Committee

Barzani's Tour to the Bradost and Balek Regions

In mid-February, Barzani visited the regions of Bradost and Balek and resolved an old dispute between Mahmud Beg and the sons of Sayyed Taha. He continued his tour to the region of Balek and visited the villages of Beshe, Roust, Rizdor, and Dargala. He called a meeting in the house of Mohammed Agha in the village of Walash, which was attended by all of the tribal chiefs of Balek. They assured him of their support and solidarity.

He then returned to the village of Shitna and stayed two days at the house of his nephew, Sadiq Babo, whom he had sent to Shitna at the request of the local people to be the liaison with the Rewanduz, Balek, and Bradost regions. Despite his youth, Sadiq possessed all of the qualities of leadership and gained everyone's respect.

According to Mohammed Isa, who accompanied Barzani on this tour, it was in mid-February and not in mid-March as stated in Ala'uddin Sajjadi's book (1959) *Shorishakani Kurd (Kurds' Revolts)*. I believe that Mohammed Isa's version is correct in light of Mustafa Khoshnaw's letter dated March 18 to Barzani, which confirms that he was in Barzan at the time.

A Critical Meeting of the Freedom Committee

Having returned from his tour, Barzani met with members of the Freedom Committee in late February. Mohammed Mahmud Qudsi and Jalal Amin had joined the committee on February 10 and carried a letter from the HP to Barzani (contents unknown). In this meeting, the following decisions were reached:

1. Mustafa Khoshnaw was appointed commander of the Mergasur–Rewanduz front. He was to be assisted by Mohammed Qudsi.
2. Izzat Abd al-Aziz was appointed commander of the Imadia front. He was to be assisted by Abd al-Hamid Baqir.
3. Sheikh Sulayman Barzani was appointed commander of the Aqra front. He was to be assisted by an officer.
4. These commanders were to report directly to the commander in chief of the revolution, Mulla Mustafa Barzani.

Commanders reported to their areas to study conditions and make necessary preparations for defense and to send their reports to the general command. Absolute orders were issued not to initiate any military action and only to exercise the right of self-defense.

In early March, the leadership received a letter from the HP stating that military units were to occupy strategic positions on the Rewanduz Front such as the Qalandar and Bradost mountains, under the pretext of conducting ordinary maneuvers from March 5 through 14.

As soon as Barzani received the letter, he issued clear orders to Mustafa Khoshnaw. What follows is the exact text:

To: Mustafa Khoshnaw and the Commander of the Eastern Front

1. We have learned for certain that military units stationed in Rewanduz will occupy strategic positions in your area under the pretext of conducting normal maneuvers, beginning on March 4 and lasting through March 15. The following units will participate in this operation: The Fourth Brigade, an armored force, a mountain artillery battalion of 3.7 mm guns, an engineering unit, a field unit, and most likely a brigade of mobile police.
2. They must be prevented from implementing this plan under whatever name. You are authorized to take all necessary measures to defend the region. We prefer that you warn the military commander of the Rewanduz region of the grave consequences of this action.
3. In the case of the military making a move, you must occupy Mergasur immediately.
4. To avoid high casualties in case of artillery and aerial bombardment, you should not assemble a large number of your forces in one location.
5. Evacuate villages and distribute the population in the areas around their villages. Form village committees to protect their possessions.

6. Do not fire at enemy aircraft unless they fly low.
7. Form a committee responsible for prisoners of war and for their transfer to General Command Headquarters.
8. Inform us of any new developments. We await confirmation of your receipt of this letter.

Signed
Mustafa Barzani
Commander in Chief of the Revolutionary Forces
March 3, 1945

Mustafa Khoshnaw carried out Barzani's orders and warned Rafiq Arif, the military commander of the Rewanduz region, of grave consequences if he were to take action. Koshnaw received a reply reassuring him that the government had no intention of conducting any operations or maneuvers at all. Thus, the government lost the initiative.

Another Letter to the Hiwa Party

Partial contents of letter number 4, dated March 3, 1945, from the Freedom Committee to the HP:

1. The HP is authorized to issue press releases as appropriate.
2. Send representatives of HP branches to the Freedom Committee's headquarters in Barzan for coordination.
3. Contact representatives of foreign countries and explain our cause.
4. Tell those who wish to join us to go to Pileng,[5] who will arrange for their safe transfer to Barzan.
5. With the breakout of the revolution, distribute the committee's communiqués throughout Iraq.
6. Spread the word about the revolution to all, especially the students.
7. Prepare to organize a protest demonstration.
8. Cut telephone lines and sabotage the roads.
9. Aim strong blows at the interests of the companies which cooperate with the government.
10. Plan to occupy K,[6] and to organize the running of its affairs. Do not harm foreign representatives there.

Early precautions and preparations for defense thwarted the government plan and forced it to contact the revolutionaries and calm the situation. The revolutionaries' program did not aim to escalate the situation to a war. It was only intended to strengthen the lines of defense and to frustrate any surprise attack by the enemy.

Once strong defenses in Mergasur and Rewanduz were secured, the commander of the front and his aide toured the fronts of Bradost and Balek. It appears from Mustafa Khoshnaw's letter to Barzani dated March 18, 1945, that he visited the two fronts personally with his aide. The accounts in *Asrar Barzan* (*The Secrets of Barzan*, Ardalan 1958) and other sources that Mohammed Qudsi toured the two fronts alone are incorrect. After he returned to Shitna, Mustafa Khoshnaw wrote to Barzani, suggesting that he personally visit the eastern front.

Barzani reached Shitna on March 22, 1945, and stayed at Sadiq's [Babo]'s house, where he received a telegram from the governor of Arbil on March 24, requesting designation of a place to meet with a representative of the British Embassy. Barzani chose the village of Shawraw and not Hawidiyan, as mentioned by Sajjadi and Ardalan.

According to what Mohammed Isa and others who accompanied Barzani told me, they met on March 25 at Mulla Yousif Shawrawi's house. Captain Stocks represented the British Embassy and both Mohammed Qudsi and Mustafa Khoshnaw were with Barzani. Stocks told Barzani, "On behalf of Great Britain's Ambassador, I ask you (1) not to challenge the Iraqi army, which will conduct training exercises on mountain warfare in the Barzan area, supervised by British officers and British military units training the Iraqi army in the art of modern warfare. (2) There is no other political or military purpose to the training and you should not suspect any. (3) The Ambassador specifically advises [you] to come to an understanding with and obey the orders of the Iraqi government. (4) Officers must return to their units."

Barzani replied, "(1) We will not initiate fighting. (2) We will come to an understanding and obey government orders, if they implement what we have agreed upon. (3) Return of officers will depend on the Defense Ministry's position. (4) We began to have our suspicions since army units in Rewanduz prepared to occupy the region under the pretext of maneuvers. (5) We have two choices: either to liberate Kurdistan or die. We are tired of promises. Why do you choose the Barzan area for training and not some other location in Iraq when you are aware of the tension and sensitivity because of past events? We have the right to be suspicious, and to be prepared to defend ourselves."

The meeting ended without agreement, and they all left the village. A few days later, the Governor of Arbil, Sa'id Qazzaz, asked to meet with Barzani. This time they met in Mazna. The police chief of the province was with the governor and raised the same points that Stocks had discussed. He received the same answers and returned without reaching an agreement.

Chapter 12

British Intervention to Quell the Revolt

Contacts Resume

On April 20, 1945, the Governor of Arbil cabled Barzani asking him to send Izzat Abd al-Aziz to Harir to meet Major Moore. After discussion by the Freedom Committee, it was decided to send Izzat Abd al-Aziz and Mohammed Qudsi to Harir. When they arrived, Moore had left for Arbil. They were told that Chief of Staff Ismail Namiq was waiting for them in Birman, where they went and met with him. After a long meeting, of which Mohammed Qudsi attended only a part, Izzat Abd al-Aziz left in an optimistic mood. He emphasized that the political conditions were most favorable and that the government had decided to come to terms with the Freedom Committee.

Abdul and Qudsi went to Arbil to consult with HP leaders, and there they met Major Wilson, the assistant to the political advisor in Kirkuk. He also stressed that the time was right and the opportunity must not be lost. Accompanied by Major Moore, Aziz and Qudsi returned to Barzan to meet Sheikh Ahmad and Mulla Mustafa on April 25. Arrogant and reckless, Moore began the meeting with Sheikh Ahmad with the statement, "On behalf of the Ambassador of the Government of Britain, I ask you to lay down your arms and comply with the orders of the Iraqi Government."

Sheikh Ahmad's response expressed his resentment. He said, "We do not take orders from the British Ambassador. When we see that neighboring tribes have laid down their arms, then we will follow suit without hesitation," and he left the meeting.

Regretting his words, Moore apologized, but Sheikh Ahmad refused to see him again. Hopes for a peaceful settlement were dashed. Returning to Arbil, he promised on behalf of his government to do all possible to prod the Iraqi government into implementing the 1943 agreement. He also suggested that officers who had joined the revolt return to Baghdad to reassure the Iraqi government and dispel its doubts, and that Barzani call off his tours.

British officers were trying hard to drive a wedge between Barzan and the patriotic officers to strip Barzan of its educated men, their abilities and experience, and to isolate Barzan from its nationalist character, which had taken root and solidified after 1943. Thus, Barzan would be an easy target for a severe blow, and the revolution could easily be presented as a rebellion by tribesmen who were accustomed to disobedience and breaching the laws. The British were well aware of the developing national consciousness among the masses of Kurdistan, and they knew that broad segments of the society, especially the Kurdish intelligentsia, peasants, and students, sincerely and eagerly supported Barzani. They suspected the pledges of tribal chiefs, but that impelled them to create a rift in the national unity.

The Officers' Return to Baghdad

The Freedom Committee met on April 30 and decided to prevent a clash and to cut short all excuses. As a last resort, it decided that all officers would return to Baghdad, with the exception of Mustafa Khoshnaw and Mir Haj Ahmad, whose circumstances were different, as they had traveled to Mahabad.

The officers reached Kirkuk on May 2, and were received by Major Wilson, who arranged for their transfer to Baghdad. They were sent to the Ministry of Defense. Waiting at the ministry, orders were issued to court-martial them, and a trial date was set for May 20. The ministry claimed that this was a routine measure to close their files. They were not arraigned. They were suspicious of this speedy action, which revealed the government's ill intentions, and they were compelled to leave Baghdad and return to Barzan at the first opportunity. I believe that the Freedom Committee reached this decision because of their earnest desire for a peaceful solution and to avoid bloodshed. Committee members were not so naïve as to be easily deluded. In any case, the British were able to perpetuate the situation with their maneuvering, at least for a while.

The Freedom Committee's last attempt yielded nothing. It was clear that the Iraqi government, directly supported by Britain, was preparing for an all-out attack on Kurdistan. In despairing over the situation, Barzani decided to explore the Soviet position. On May 7, 1945, he sent Mamand Maseeh to Iranian Kurdistan to invite a Soviet representative to visit him. The Soviets responded by sending two officers to Barzan with Mamand Maseeh. After several meetings, they reached a common understanding and pledged to support the Kurdish revolt against any aggression. They also decided to collaborate better with the *Jhiyanaway Kurd* (Kurds' Revival) party and designated the Khiraina-Dashti-Hirat-Mergasur Road for the transportation of aid. If and when resistance became impossible, partisans would cross into Iranian Kurdistan. After the return of the Soviet officers, Barzani personally went to the Khiraina area and was hosted by Fattah Agha Harki. There, he met General Siyamandov and sent Mustafa Khoshnaw to Mahabad to learn the latest developments. He returned to Barzan on June 10, 1945.

Another Meeting with the Governor of Arbil

As requested by Sa'id Qazzaz and Captain Jackson, Barzani met with them in Mergasur on June 17, 1945. Wali Beg was also present. A quarrel developed between Barzani and Sa'id Qazzaz. Had it not been for Captain Jackson's intervention, it might have ended in disaster. The pompous Qazzaz was downright rude, and he openly referred to Barzani's visit to the Iraq–Iran border areas and his meeting with the Soviet officers.

Barzani tried to keep the discussions calm and unemotional. However, Sa'id Qazzaz's excesses angered him, and he said, "You have broken promises and accords, and closed all doors. Therefore, I have no choice but to knock on other doors for the just cause of the Kurdish people. Your masters' threats did not frighten me; how could yours when you are their abject slave?" Wali Beg rose to strike Sa'id Qazzaz, but Barzani stopped him.

Of course, no one can achieve anything at such a meeting. On the contrary, it complicated issues further. Qazzaz felt that he had been humiliated in the presence of a British officer. He ordered the Mergasur police adjutant to assassinate Wali Beg. This meeting ended all hopes for another meeting, and each side began preparing for war.

Barzani's Visit to Kurdish Districts in Mosul Province

In late June, Barzani decided to continue his tour and visited the Kurdish districts in Mosul Province. Escorted by Mohammed Qudsi and Jalal Amin, Barzani took along another 250 armed Barzanis. During his visit, he tried to end the ongoing strife between the family of Haji Malo and the sheikhs of Brivkan, which had brought about many killings.[1] They were on the brink of a wider tribal conflict and more bloodshed. The problem remained unsolved because Barzani was compelled to curtail his tour. Barzani's grand reception in every village he visited proved his immense popularity to Britain and Iraq. Thus, they requested that he curtail his tour and meet the governor of Arbil or some other official in Shirwan, Mergasur, or Bilah. The main purpose of this request was to have Barzani end his tour and return to Barzan, but Barzani did not comply and continued his trip. He realized that the time for an all-out revolution had not come yet. He knew that he needed more time and effort to organize armed units countrywide and to mobilize the masses. He had decided to go on similar trips to the regions of Suleimaniyya and Kirkuk.

In the company of many tribal chiefs in the village of Bilan, hosted by Hassan Arab Agha,[2] Barzani learned of events in Barzan. He was to go to Mireiba on August 10, and on to Ba'udreh,[3] the center of the Yazidis, and then to Sinjar. In Mireiba, he ended his tour when he received a letter from Sheikh Ahmad Barzani, confirming the martyrdom of Wali Beg inside the Mergasur police station on August 8 and the clashes that ensued between Barzanis and government forces in Mergasur, Bilah, and Barzan, and ordering him to return immediately.

Barzani gathered all tribal chiefs and informed them of the events which necessitated his urgent return to Barzan. He told them that he would try to contain and control the situation and asked them to go to their areas and await further instructions.

Undoubtedly, Barzani came a long way in uniting the people and instilling the idea that national interests are above and beyond tribalism. If he had had the opportunity to complete his program, he would have mobilized all of the masses of Kurdistan to confront the British and Iraqi rulers. In Bilan, a peasant stepped up waving his sickle and shouted at the top of his lungs, "Barzani, we will sacrifice our lives for you. With our own hands, we will secure bread and fight in defense of our land and honor." This peasant's words excited all present, and they began singing the familiar Kurdish national anthem "Ay Kurdina, Ay Mardina" (O Kurds! O noble men!).

The British recognized Barzani's popularity and realized that they were up against a revolution by the entire people. Thus, they struck using the rulers of Iraq, who blindly obeyed their orders. At the time the British desired, the fire was ignited.

After he returned to Barzan on August 18, Barzani met with the Freedom Committee. On Sheikh Ahmad's advice, it was decided to keep the situation calm and under control and to avoid clashes with government forces. Among the steps taken, a memorandum was presented to the governments of Iraq and Britain, with copies distributed to foreign embassies. Excerpts from that memorandum follow:

1. In its session on January 25, 1944, Nuri al-Sa'id's cabinet had agreed to implement necessary reforms in the region. We have waited long and to no avail.
2. Hamdi al-Pachachi's Cabinet affirmed the agreement, but in reality began to prepare to launch a large-scale military attack on us. Instead of schools and hospitals, police stations and army garrisons were built. Military units were brought in to occupy strategic points under the pretext of conducting military exercises.
3. When I [Barzani] returned visits to chiefs of Kurdish tribes, government authorities gave us warning and asked us to end our visits despite the fact that there was no legal restriction to prohibit us.
4. The Governor of Arbil issued orders to all government offices to hamper all Barzanis' transactions and to arrest them when they show up to pursue them.
5. While Wali Beg was tending to a citizen's business at the Mergasur police station he was shot inside the station.
6. An attempt was made to arrest As'ad Khoshavi in Bilah with no reason given.
7. Military units have been assembled in Rewanduz, Aqra, and Imadia in preparation for a massive assault on the Barzan region.
8. Airplanes are conducting ongoing raids on peaceful villages and have killed many women and children.
9. We [the Freedom Committee] ask the Iraqi government to halt military operations and implore all people of good will to intervene in order to bring operations to an end.
10. We [the Freedom Committee] request all ambassadors to assist our oppressed people and protect them from genocide.

On August 8, 1945, Wali Beg was martyred inside the Mergasur police station, where he had gone almost every day to solve citizens' problems. He was accompanied by four men, and all, like him, were unarmed. The station's adjutant took the opportunity, as Sa'id Qazzaz had advised. The adjutant fabricated a problem with one of Wali Beg's escorts, and as he stood up to intervene, the adjutant shot him and his escort, Hado Babok, dead. The other three, Hassan Shaina, Hado Bariya, and Hassan Gardi, courageously resisted and killed the adjutant and a number of policemen. As the news spread, people, both men and women, took over the station and took the rest of the police captive. The same thing took place in Barzan, unplanned and without orders from the leadership, because Wali Beg occupied a special place in the hearts of Barzanis; and, indeed, he was a great leader and a fine example to all. Despite the great loss, Barzani tried to contain the event without success because of the Iraqi government's arrogance and encouragement by Great Britain to use this incident as the grounds to declare war.

Chapter 13

The Revolt of 1945

Outbreak of the Revolt

On August 8, 1945, the al-Pachachi cabinet issued the following resolution:

Aware of public reports of disturbances in the region of Barzan and its surroundings because of the crimes committed by Mulla Mustafa Barzani and his followers that disturb peace and security, and because duty requires us to bring order and organization and to prevent crime, let it be resolved to militarily occupy the Barzan region, capture the criminals, and bring them to justice. The Defense Minister is authorized to take necessary measures to execute this resolution.

Governor Sa'id Qazzaz of Arbil gave Barzani notice and demanded that he surrender to the authorities. He warned all tribal chiefs to stay out or they would be severely punished. On August 19, martial law was declared in both Arbil and Mosul. The commander of operations declared the law effective immediately in the Barzan area and in the following prefectures: Rewanduz, Aqra, Imadia, and Duhok.

With martial law in effect, the army was ordered to occupy the region. The units described below were called up to begin an all-out offensive on Barzan.

The Army's Position at the Beginning of Operations

1. Legions of the Second Division Brigade were at the following training camps:
   a. Legion of the Third Brigade in Rayat, with a regiment in Rewanduz.
   b. Legion of the Fourth Brigade in Panjwin, at the easternmost frontiers of Suleimaniyya, with a regiment in Suleimaniyya.
   c. Legion of the Fifth Brigade in Zawita (near Duhok), with a regiment in Aqra.

Legions of the First Division were stationed at their permanent camps in Musayyab, Nasiriyya, and Basra. The army's mechanized force was permanently stationed in Jalawla.

The above indicates that the army units, especially the Second Division, were not in a good position at the start of the operations. To amass enough troops, ammunition, and other supplies, the army would need at least 20 days.

2. Army units, the Second Division in particular, were well-trained for mountain operations. In addition to their normal summer mountain training, the legions of the Second Division Brigade had spent all winter in training camps in the mountains and become accustomed to the severe cold of Kurdistani winter. The unit commanders were among the best Iraqi officers.

3. Short of soldiers, ammunition, supplies, animals, and vehicles, the army had to meet these deficiencies before launching the operation. Therefore, it was decided not to start until the beginning of September 1945.

4. Several decisions were made before they began:

   a. A special operations command was formed, and Staff Major General Mustafa Raghib, commander of the Second Division, was appointed commander in chief of operations.

   b. In addition to the legions of the Second Division, legions of another brigade from the First Division and a mechanized force were to be assembled in the region of operations before September.

   c. Khalifan and Bapishtiyan were to be controlled with sufficient forces to defend the Gorge of Gali Ali Beg. The Aqra garrison was to be augmented and the mountain overlooking Aqra was to be occupied before the operation began.

   d. Two supply depots were to be established, one in Bapishtiyan and another in Aqra, with sufficient provisions and forage for two months for 6,000 soldiers and 3,000 animals in Bapishtiyan, and 3,000 soldiers and 1,500 animals in Aqra.

   e. Martial law was declared in both Arbil and Mosul provinces.

   f. Makeshift camps outside operation areas were prepared to resettle and support those who left these areas.

   g. All financial support and food supplies from the Barzanis and their followers were to be stopped.

   h. Police stations were to be reinforced and supplies were to be stored to ensure long-term self-sufficiency.

   i. Both police regiments of Dohuk and Imadia were to be placed under the operations command, provided both were augmented with another police regiment and a battalion of police cavalries.

   j. A request was made to return the Mosul airfield from the British to the Iraqis for use by the Iraqi Air Force against the Barzan region. Two squadrons of the Iraqi Air Force were to be set aside for this purpose.

The Plan of Operations

The military plan can be summarized as follows:

1. Purpose: to destroy the forces of rebellious tribes and bring peace to the whole region of Zebar.

2. To accomplish this, the military must move into two sectors:

   a. Bapishtiyan, Mergasur, Khairazok, Chameh, Laira Bir, Rezan.

   b. Aqra, Dinarta, Bira Kapra, Bilah, Barzan.

3. The amassment of the units of the two sectors must occur before the date of S-1 [sic], as follows:
   a. In the Bapishtiyan region, legions of the Third, Fourth, and Fifteenth brigades.
   b. In the Aqra region, legions of the First and Fifth brigades, as well as a police force. The command center of operations was to be in Arbil.
4. Formation of forces and their assignments:
   a. The Rewanduz Force to be formed of the legions of the Third and Fourth brigades under the command of Staff Brigadier Ismail Safwat. For its initial objective, the Rewanduz Force was assigned to occupy Mergasur.
   b. The Bapishtiyan Force was to be formed of the legions of the Fifteenth Brigade, a regiment of the Fourth Brigade, a police force, and two artillery batteries under the command of Colonel Tahir Mohammed. It was assigned to defend the Strait of Gali Ali Beg, the Khalifan barracks, and the Rewanduz garrison to form a second force to back up the Rewanduz Force.
   c. The Aqra Force, assembled from the legions of the First and Fifth brigades, a police regiment, a mechanized artillery battalion (minus a battery) under the command of Brigadier Yasin Hassan. As its first objective, it was assigned to occupy Upper Aqra and Dinarta.
   d. A reserve mechanized force under the command of Staff Colonel Nuri Khairi reported directly to the operational command.
   e. A police brigade assembled from the Third and Fourth police regiments under the command of Police Commissioner Muzahim Mahir. It was assigned to advance from Imadia to Soori and clear the area of rebels.

In addition, a logistics command center was established to control transportation lines between Kirkuk, Arbil, and Mosul on the one hand, and the region of operations on the other.

The Partisans' Status

Although the revolution erupted at a time that the partisans had not chosen, fighting was imposed on them once again. It appeared that there was no way out, and they had to confront aggression and defy the harsh reality of the situation. Barzani moved to the summer resort of Hori[1] to meet Sheikh Ahmad Barzani and listen to his advice. The following decisions were reached:

1. Mohammed Siddique Barzani[2] was to be commander of the Mergasur–Rewanduz Front.
2. Haji Taha Imadi was to be commander of the Balenda–Imadia Front.
3. Mustafa Barzani would personally command the Aqra Force, in addition to overseeing all other fronts and administering the affairs of the revolution, assisted by members of the Freedom Committee.
4. As'ad Khoshavi was charged with surrounding the Bilah garrison. In addition, he was assigned to supply the forces at the Aqra Front.

5. Letters were to be sent to all tribal chiefs who had taken the oath, to ask for their help in defending Kurdistan.
6. Patriotic organizations and the urban intelligentsia were to be contacted to support the revolt and condemn the military campaign against Barzan.

Of the tribal chiefs, only a few kept their pledges and [did that] only for a short time. Most became government mercenaries and fought against the revolt. Some were arrested before they could accomplish anything.

The army had to fight a larger revolutionary force on a much wider front that extended from Balek in the east to Imadia in the west. For the first time, Kurds from outside the Barzan region actively fought alongside Barzanis. With Barzani were also capable officers who had studied modern warfare in the Iraqi army, which the British trained and supplied with modern weapons.

The revolutionary forces were estimated at 5,000 fighters, of which 3,000 were Barzanis and 2,000 were from Baradost, Balek, and Zebar regions. The revolt was widely supported, especially by students and the intelligentsia, who appreciated it more than others.

The Position of the Tribes

Because the revolt broke out before the time set for it to begin, it was impossible to control events according to plan. The government arrested those it suspected, and others quickly changed sides contrary to their promises. Others joined the revolt for a short time and then went over to the government. Of the latter group,

1. Bradostis and Sayyed Taha's sons sent their force to the front at Sari Bardi.[3]
2. Zebaris sent their forces to the Aqra Front.
3. Some Balek tribal chiefs supported the Rewanduz Front.
4. All of Haji Taha Imadi's relatives joined the revolt and moved their families to the Barzan region.
5. The Rekanis and Surchis joined the government from the very first.

A number of other tribal chiefs initially stood neutral and then went over to the government.

The Outbreak of Hostilities

Supported to the end by the RAF, the Iraqi Air Force began bombardment of the region soon after the cabinet's declaration on August 8. The status of the Rewanduz Front was as follows: There were about 10,000 fighters who held their defensive positions, which extended from Mount Qalandar to Mount Bradost and the main highway near Hawidyan. A command center was set up in the village of Shitna. They fought against the Third, Fourth, and Fifth brigades and a police force.

Their first battle began on August 25, 1945, as the Third Brigade, commanded by Staff Colonel Hasib al-Rubayi and supported by the police force, advanced to the Badliyan Heights to encircle and occupy the eastern slopes of Mount Qalandar. A fierce battle continued all day and forced the enemy to retreat to the Gali Ali Beg Gorge. Hundreds of enemy corpses littered the theater of operations, including that of Lt. Colonel Hurmz Qaisar, commander of the Second Regiment. Aerial and artillery bombardment prevented large numbers of soldiers from being taken prisoner.

Mohammed Siddique was seriously injured by artillery shrapnel; Mulla Abd al-Hadi Liri was martyred; and Mulla Sulayman Shaikhani, Mohammed Isa Seilki, and Abdullah Salih Mergasuri were wounded.

Positions initially seized by the army were all recaptured, and the partisans seized many guns and other military supplies. Mohammed Khalid and Sadiq joined the front when they learned of Mohammed Siddique's injury. The army did not attempt another assault until September 5. During this time, aerial and artillery bombardment of villages and partisan positions continued.

The Battle of Maidan Morik

In the immortal Battle of Maidan Morik,[4] fighters etched glowing examples of heroism, sacrifice, and courage into the luminous history of the Kurds. Between Mazna and Hawidyan, the Iraqi army was defeated as never before, and Maidan Morik became the aggressors' burial ground.

The Iraqi Rewanduz Force, under the command of Ismail Safwat, led a three-pronged attack in an attempt to occupy Mount Qalander and Bradost. The main force advanced with mechanized and artillery batteries along the Hawidyan–Mazna Road.

On both sides of the gorge, the partisans resisted, halting any move forward, while they systematically retreated before the main force in the gorge itself to draw the force to a suitable location and destroy it. That location was Maidan Morik. Feeling elated and triumphant, and supported by the air force, the enemy pushed their mechanized and artillery batteries along with the main force to Maidan Morik and immediately began to set up a strong base. Only an hour before dark, the partisans began an all-out attack simultaneously from the hills, the gorge, and the rear. The ferocious fighting came to hand-to-hand combat. Confused and unable to maintain command, the enemy began to lose its positions, one after another. Uncoordinated, the army units retreated in disorder, ending in their devastating defeat. The partisans captured an artillery battery in Maidan Morik and destroyed many military vehicles and hardware. They also seized hundreds of guns and automatic rifles, and huge quantities of ammunition and military supplies, as well as capturing 80 troops. The enemy casualties were 480 killed, with their corpses left in the theater of operations. The partisan forces lost five martyrs: Hassan Beg Mir Mohammed Birsiyavi, Yousif Guirgamoi, Mulla Swar Omer Swari, Ali Jojek Khardini, and Mustafa Omer Bavayi.

A number of others were wounded; except for Rasool Mohammed Rasha Komi, the narrator did not recall their names. This was nearly a mortal blow to the army. Enemy morale sank. The pool of absconders and malingerers was growing, which forced army leaders to cancel all military leaves and evacuate those whose injuries were not serious. Checkpoints were set up to capture deserters.

Having tasted a bitter defeat on September 5, the government failed to dislodge the partisans despite its savage aerial and artillery bombardment. Perhaps certain of failure, the government resorted to deception and enticement, contacting Sheikh Rashid [of] Lolan. Through him, Mahmud Beg Khalifa Samad and Sayyed Taha's sons were lured into changing sides and betraying the revolution.

During a ceasefire in April 1964, while on my way to Suleimaniyya, I was invited to lunch with the regiment commander in Dokan, Colonel Sa'b al-Hardan. He welcomed me and my companions warmly, and during his conversation he spoke of the Battle of Maidan Morik, in which he had taken part as a lieutenant. He praised the courage of the Barzanis and told us of the attack on his detachment, the grave losses sustained, and the injury to his leg. He readily admitted the serious defeat of the army in that battle. Then he told us of another incident that had occurred in July of 1963, when he was leading a group of mercenaries to occupy Shush and Shermin in the Aqra region. They were defeated in a counterattack and were forced to flee to the Aqra garrison. Then he said playfully that the Barzanis were bolder in the 1945 battles than now. "The Barzanis have not changed since 1945, and unfortunately, neither have their weapons; while you have modern weapons, aircraft, artillery, and tanks," I replied. In a rare incident, both Hasso Yousif, one of the Maidan Morik heroes, and Omer Agha, the hero of the Battle of Shush and Shermin, were sitting with us. I introduced them to the Colonel. To his credit, he stood up and kissed them both and said nobly, "I respect courageous men even if they are my enemies." We thanked him and continued on our way to Suleimaniyya.

The Balendah–Imadia Front

The revolutionary forces only numbered about 500 fighters under the command of Haji Taha Imadi, a noted Kurdish patriot. The government forces consisted of a police force and Rekani mercenaries under the command of Police Commissioner Muzahim Mahir al-Kanani. There were no fierce battles as on other fronts; however, the enemy tried several times to cross the Zab River to advance on Barzan. The partisans thwarted their attempts but sustained two martyrdoms and a number of injuries.

The Aqra Front

Barzani personally commanded this front in addition to overseeing other fronts. He moved the revolution's command center to the village of Gribish in the Nahla Valley. An officer of the Freedom Committee went with him to assist in running the affairs of the revolution.

Revolutionary fighters numbering 1,200 confronted the legions of the First and Fifth brigades and a police force under the command of Colonel Yasin Hassan. The first battle broke out on September 4 as the enemy tried to occupy the Nahla Valley in a two-pronged attack. The First Brigade attacked from Mount

Sari Aqra and the Fifth Brigade from Dinarta. A bloody battle raged from dawn to dusk; the Fifth Brigade sustained most of the losses. As the partisans encircled the enemy forces near the village of Gozka and Shive Hirch, the air force tried to break the siege by unsuccessfully bombing partisan positions all day long.

The day ended with the defeat of the enemy and the Fifth Brigade under siege. That night, most of them escaped to Dinarta, which caused the partisans to surround Dinarta the following morning. This writer has repeatedly heard from participants that enemy losses exceeded 500, with two-thirds from the Fifth Brigade of the Second Division stationed in Kirkuk. The partisans achieved another victory tantamount to the victory of Maidan Morik. They captured a usable cannon and hundreds of rifles, machine guns, and military supplies.

The partisans' losses were Mohammed Gouch Mergasuri and Mustafa Hassan Bavayi, who were martyred. Two of the best, they had destroyed or captured enemy artillery, but they paid for victory with their lives. The wounded were counted and numbered only five. The Battle of September 4 astounded army leaders. To change their reputation for the better, they believed that they must take immediate measures. They pushed fresh forces into the combat, and on September 8 transferred the Fifteenth Brigade from Rewanduz to Aqra.

The Fifth Brigade was in dire straits and was expected to surrender at any moment. They were under constant fire and had exhausted their food supplies. The air force tried unsuccessfully to parachute food to them. Most of the food ended up in partisan hands. Finally, the brigade commander asked Barzani to pledge the safety of his troops if they surrendered. Surchi traitors supplied food which prolonged their resistance, while the army's operational command was exploring swift measures to rescue the brigade.

The British General Renton was brought in to oversee the next attack. With the usable cannon captured at the battle of September 4, Barzani ordered Izzat Abd al-Aziz to take the cannon and level the Bilah garrison. He did, and the garrison surrendered, including all soldiers and police.

A New Attack under the Command of General Renton

Renton's plan of attack was for the Fifteenth Brigade to advance from Aqra to the Strait of Zanta-Dinarta; the Fifth Brigade to advance from Dinarta to Zanta and meet the Fifteenth Brigade; and the First Brigade to advance from Sar-i Aqra to Nahla Valley to press the partisans from the side. As told to me, the events of the Battle of September 12 were awe-inspiring. This battle was truly an epic of hero-ism and sacrifice. Neither Renton, the legions of the brigades, nor the air force were able to triumph. In fact, this time their defeat was more bitter and painful than any before it. Barely saving himself, General Renton escaped and chaos ensued. Commanders fled, and soldiers followed nonstop.

The partisans had completely crushed the attack by all three legions. The theater of operations was littered with bodies, 50 were taken prisoner, and losses were greater than in any other government defeat. Hundreds of guns and pieces of military equipment were left behind. Residents of nearby villages were called in to transport the spoils to liberated areas. Although small in number, the partisan losses were qualitatively great. The courageous Aziz Agha Zrari and two other revolutionaries, Ahmad Goran and Yasin Isa Bindori, were martyred. Mohammed Amin Mirkhan, Sharif Lashkiri, and Mohammed Isomari were wounded.

The deaths of Aziz Agha and his comrades distressed Barzani, for they truly were exceptional men. Despite his young age at the time, Mulla Shini Bidaroni, with his proven abilities and experience, replaced Aziz Agha. The morale of government forces plummeted, and they were unable to conduct another operation. As usual, they intensified their concerted air raids on civilians and on front lines. The RAF conducted most of the sorties. Desertion from the ranks became a common phenomenon. Furthermore, many front-line soldiers inflicted self-injuries just to be transferred to hospitals and escape from the front lines.

The Treason of Tribal Chiefs

Revolutions everywhere need men who understand them. Revolution is neither a business deal nor a contract. It is a tough struggle that not everyone can endure. The revolutionary must sacrifice himself for the good of the people; he must be tolerant and persistent. Tribal chiefs, with their "turf" mentality and narrow interests, do not preserve these traits. This is a fact well recognized by experienced British politicians. Despite the partisans' tremendous victories, achieved with bloodshed and immense sacrifices, the tribal chiefs, with their sense of inferiority, would obey a policeman but defy one another.

Using a variety of means, the government enticed and goaded tribal chiefs into taking up arms against the revolt, usually through a carrot-and-stick policy. British officers approved of such methods and took part in their implementation. The Surchis were the first to respond to the government's enticement, and became mercenaries under the commander of the Aqra Force. Soon, their treason caught on with other tribes.

Chapter 14

Barzani's Flight to Iranian Kurdistan

The Decision to Retreat to Iranian Kurdistan

Barzani's goal was to secure the legitimate rights of the Kurdish people. He did all he could to unite Kurdish ranks, yet he saw Kurdish tribal chiefs switching sides and leading government forces. Not long before, some of them had been either neutral or on the side of the revolt but they disregarded all oaths and promises. Under these conditions, it was very difficult to continue fighting. High and rugged mountains at the Iranian border are impassable in the winter. Before the Barzan region was encircled by the forces of nature and by enemies, Barzani, in quick consultations with the Freedom Committee and Sheikh Ahmad Barzani, decided to retreat to Iranian Kurdistan before rain and snow closed the roads.

Barzani issued orders to front-line commanders to alert all fighters to withdraw systematically toward the Iranian borders and to ensure that families were evacuated first. I strongly suspect that the J.K.[1] and the Soviets were consulted, since both agreed to keep this experienced force intact and to support the patriotic Kurdish political coup in Iranian Kurdistan. At the end of September 1945, the revolutionaries began to retreat according to a careful plan, carried out as follows:

1. A sufficient force moved to Kani Rash on the Iranian border to secure the road through Khuakork Valley against Bradosti mercenaries. The Rewanduz Force was to maintain a strong line of defense from Mount Qalandar to Mount Piran to prevent enemy advances.
2. Another force moved to the Piyaw lowlands to guard the families from the rear and keep the Surchi mercenaries from chasing them.
3. The Balenda Force moved to Mount Shirin and Walati Zheri to guard the families from that region from the rear and protect them from Rekani mercenaries.
4. The Peris–Bilah Road was secured from Zebari mercenaries.

As the retreat continued, families began to gather in the Kani Rash area before crossing into Iran.

Battles during the Retreat

1. *At the Aqra Front*: The Surchis committed historic treason before all of the other tribes and prevented the surrender of the Fifth Brigade, which would have changed the course of the war. On September 14, they led a force from Aqra through the road of Mount Sari Sada to Dinarta from the west and broke the siege. The treason of the Surchi chiefs tipped the balance of power in favor of the army, because they encouraged other tribes to follow suit, beginning with the Zebaris. The Bradostis, the Sharafanis, some of the Mizoris, Doskies, and Brivkanis also changed sides.

Barzani moved to Mount Peris, and a fierce battle ensued as mercenaries and government forces attempted to occupy Peris but failed. Mohammed Abdullah Gawar Shanaderi and Ali Bazi Barozhi were martyred, and Timaz Arib Seilki, Saleh Kaniya Lanji, Shino Mohammed Zhazhoki, and Mulla Shawali Korkayi were wounded.

Barzani left Mount Peris for Bira Kapra on September 30. Surchi and Zebari mercenaries attacked him in a ferocious two-pronged ambush, killing Khaled Zubair Barzani and Mulla Sheikho Shanadari. The mercenaries fled, and Barzani pushed on with his forces, reaching Barzan on October 2. The families of the Nizar and Barozh regions had already crossed Mount Shirin on their way to Kani Rash, where they were to converge.

2. *At the Rewanduz Front*: On September 26, enemy forces waged an all-out attack on the Qalandar and Bradost Mountains with the Bradostis leading the army to Qalandar, where they surprised the partisans. The army was defeated in an arduous battle, and Mount Qalandar was recaptured. The army was taught a lesson that it would not forget in a hurry. They had left tens of corpses on top of Mount Qalandar and fled all the way to the Diyana barracks. Hassan Mohammed Amin Birsiyavi, a capable and courageous leader, and Mar'an Sheikho Shaikhanayi were martyred, and Haji Birokhi, Ahmad Mustafa Kania Lanji, and Hassan Shaina were wounded.

3. *In the Piyaw lowlands*: A detachment of Surchi mercenaries tried to loot a village while the residents were still there. A partisan force challenged them in a fight that killed the chief of the mercenaries, Shoro Mustafa. Of the partisans, commander Sulayman Faqi Dairishki, Arib Qatran, and Mohammed Seilki were martyred.

At the Balenda Front, the enemy did not attempt to cross the Zab River until after the partisans had retreated. Therefore, no fighting took place.

While families were on their way to Kani Rash, the air force continued the bombing to satisfy the rulers of the Baghdad regime and their British masters. A number of pregnant women and children died along the way, either from the bombardment or from severe cold and hunger. The families crossed into Iran, and the Iraqi government announced the end of military operations. The commander general of military operations summoned the tribal chiefs, demanding that they turn in their weapons within 48 hours, established checkpoints on roads that were mainly used by the mercenaries, and ordered the arrest of anyone carrying so much as a single bullet. The mercenaries, which the government referred to as irregular forces, were discharged once the operations were over. Such were the rewards given by the commander of operations to the traitors who, in order to curry favor with him and prove their fealty to the government, had burned the villages of the deserted Barzan region.

Into Iranian Kurdistan

The revolt had ended with the crossing of the Barzanis into Iranian Kurdistan on October 11, 1945, through Kele Shin, Margavar (Dalanpar)[2] while Iraqi aircraft pursued the families to the last point at the borders.

All partisan forces and families systematically withdrew into Iranian Kurdistan. Not a single family was left behind or fell into enemy hands. Sheikh Ahmad moved along with the families, sharing their fatigue and anguish and giving them support and guidance. The partisans crossed the border shortly afterward. The families and partisans were well received by their brothers of Iranian Kurdistan, who came to their assistance, dividing them among their 49 villages to share sustenance and shelter with them.

Barzani went to the village of Nairgei where the Soviet military commander was staying and agreed with him to spread the families into villages of the Margavar, Targavar, Shino, Naghadeh, and Mahabad regions. He requested a medical group to treat the ill and the injured, among whom was Mohammed Siddique. Families split up; Sheikh Ahmad Barzani resided in Mahabad, while Mulla Mustafa Barzani, his brother Babo, and his nephew Ibrahim went to Shino. Sheikh Sulayman and the family of Mohammed Siddique went to Naghadeh. Mohammed Khalid went to the village of Koki, and As'ad Khoshavi resided in the region of Targavar.

In the spring of 1946, once the families were resettled, forces were reorganized into regiments and were given new weapons. Regimental commanders were appointed from the loyal officers who had come with Barzani from Iraq. They were Izzat Abd al-Aziz, Sayyed Aziz Sayyed Abdullah, Mustafa Khoshnaw, Mir Haj Ahmad, Mohammed Mahmud Qudsi, Abd al-Rahman Mufti, and Petty Officer Shawkat Afandi.

In Iran, they were joined by Bakr Abd al-Karim, Khairullah Abd al-Karim, Nuri Ahmad Taha, Mohammed Saleh, and Petty Officer Ahmad Afandi Koyi. From the tribes, they were joined by Mohammed Agha Jundiyan and Sulayman Beg Dargala, along with their relatives.[3]

Surely the Barzanis became the main force of the Mahabad Republic, defended it, sacrificed themselves for it, and served it as well as they could.

Part III

The Barzan Revolt (1945–1958)

Introduction to Part III

In Parts I and II of this book, I shed some light on [Mustafa] Barzani and the Barzanis' role in the first uprising of Barzan in 1931–1932. Then, as large numbers of patriotic Kurdish officers, intellectuals, and tribes joined them, the Barzan Revolt of 1943–1945 gave the leading role of the Barzanis a national dimension.

The victory that Barzani achieved over Iraqi forces, despite support by British imperialists in the 1943 battles, consolidated his position and leadership in all Kurdistan. Having proved his prowess as a leader, Barzani won much of the Kurdish hopes and confidence. It also afforded him an opportunity to contact leaders of the Kurdish liberation movement in other parts of Kurdistan, especially the leaders in Iranian Kurdistan, which was undergoing major developments as a consequence of the advancing armies of the Soviet Union and other allies into Iran.

There was total coordination between Barzani and the Freedom Committee, which led the 1945 revolt, on the one hand, and the J.K. (Kurds' Revival) Society in Iranian Kurdistan, on the other.

The J.K. letter to Barzani, calling him the "leader of the liberation of Kurdistan" and listing nine points laying out the foundations of cooperation and how to support the revolution, clearly confirms the great hopes he embodied.

In Iranian Kurdistan in 1945, Barzani and the Barzanis did not disappoint our brothers as their responsibilities multiplied. Barzani was appointed chief of staff of the republic's armed forces, became the strong military arm of the republic, and sacrificed much to defend it. His role gained national and international significance, as well as an added nationalist dimension.

In Part III I will focus on the historic developments during a critical period—the period of Barzani's stay in Iranian Kurdistan, and his great contributions to the founding and supporting of the republic from 1945 to 1947. Then I will describe in some measure his escape and march to the Soviet Union, his contacts with Soviet leaders, and his stay there until after the July 14, 1958 revolution in Iraq, which opened new horizons to the Kurdish liberation movement.

Kurdistan
January 1987

Chapter 15

The Barzanis in Iranian Kurdistan

B ased on his contacts with leaders of the Kurdish movement in Iranian Kurdistan and with Soviet officials after obtaining Sheikh Ahmad's approval, Barzani and his comrades in the Freedom Committee decided to move to Iranian Kurdistan because of the new opportunities for the Kurdish liberation movement there, and to keep his experienced force intact to stabilize the new situation in Iranian Kurdistan.

I heard from Barzani that there was direct communication with Soviet officials. His emissaries had traveled to Iran for that purpose, and Soviet officers visited him. Both Sayyed Abdullah Afandi al-Gailani and Sheikh Ubaidullah Zino had actively facilitated these contacts.

The 1943–1945 revolution ended with Barzani's crossing into Iranian Kurdistan on October 11, 1945, at the Kele Shin–Margavar (Dalanpar) point, where the borders of Iran, Iraq, and Turkey meet. British and Iraqi jets pursued the Barzani families all the way to the border.

Warmly welcomed, the Barzanis crossed the borders and were given all possible assistance. Qazi Mohammed issued a directive to all party ranks to provide all possible help (see Document no. 15). Once the situation had stabilized, the Soviets asked Barzani to remain out of the public eye for a while because of the strong protests and pressure from both the British and the Iraqi governments. Barzani moved to Sardasht and stayed in the village of Mirawa until the end of 1945. He then moved to Shino and settled there with his family, his brother Babo, and a few other relatives while Sheikh Ahmad's family was transferred to Mahabad.

Proclamation of the Republic

On January 22, 1946, the founding of the first Kurdistan Republic was declared in Mahabad, and Barzani was invited to attend the celebrations on this historic occasion. He returned to Shino and remained there until March, when he was called to Mahabad, and it was decided that the Barzanis would play a role in supporting and solidifying the republic. By virtue of their valor and high sense of commitment, the Barzanis proved to be extremely efficient and gained the trust of the leader of the republic and of the masses at large. They became a force to rely on.

Indeed, the Barzanis bore the brunt of all battles and military confrontations in the face of all attempts by the military government of Tehran to circumvent the revolution and vanquish the republic, as will be shown in more detail later.

A number of Iraqi Kurdish military officers who had joined the Barzan Revolt accompanied them to Iran: Izzat Abd al-Aziz, Sayyed Aziz Sayyed Abdullah, Mustafa Khoshnaw, Mir Haj Ahmad, Mohammed Mahmud Qudsi, Abd al-Rahman Mufti, and Petty Officer Shawkat Afandi.

In Iran, they were joined by Bakr Abd al-Karim, Khairullah Abd al-Karim, Nuri Ahmad Taha, Mohammed Salih, and the Petty Officer Ahmad Afandi Koyi. From the tribes, they were joined by Wahab Mohammed Ali Agha Jundiyan, Sulayman Beg Dergala, and their relatives.

Distribution of New Arms

Barzani was called to Mahabad again for the *Nawroz*[1] festivities of 1946. There, they discussed supplying the Barzanis with new arms. They agreed to call every male from the ages of 15 to 60 to Mahabad, and they were sent to the mosques of the city. Early in April, new weapons (Birno rifles, machine guns, and grenades) were issued to 1,500 Barzanis. They were organized into three regiments with modern training programs, in line with the training of modern armies. There was a reserve force of 700 armed Barzanis. Commanders were appointed for the three regiments as follows:

1. Major Bakr Abd al-Karim, commander of the First Regiment. Mohammed Amin Badr Khan, Mamand Maseeh, and Faris Kani Boti were appointed company commanders.
2. Captain Mustafa Khoshnaw, commander of the Second Regiment. Sa'id Wali Beg, Khoshavi Khalil, and Mustafa Jangeer were appointed company commanders.
3. Captain Mir Haj Ahmad, commander of the Third Regiment. Salih Kani Lanji, Haider Beg Arif Beg, and Wahab Agha Rewanduzi were appointed company commanders.

Once the regiments were organized and training was completed, Barzani attended a graduation ceremony with a number of the republic's officials, where he gave a speech congratulating them for a job well done and for the superb skills they had acquired. He stressed the importance of being well organized and following orders, and he stated emphatically that to defy orders of any of the three commanders was in effect to disobey his [Barzani's] orders. All three regiments were ordered to move and set up camp on the Saqqiz Front, as the threat there was greater than anywhere else, as they faced the Iranian army. Other officers remained with Barzani and served as his staff. Presidential decrees were issued to promote them to higher ranks: Staff Major Izzat Abd al-Aziz was promoted to staff colonel, and Major Bakr Abd al-Karim was promoted to Colonel. Captains Mustafa Khoshnaw, Mir Haj Ahmad, and Sayyed Aziz Sayyed Abdullah were promoted to colonels; or perhaps to lieutenant colonels. Lieutenants Khairullah Abd al-Karim and Mohammed Mahmud Qudsi were promoted to majors, Lieutenants Nuri Ahmad Taha, Jalal Amin, and Mohammed Salih were promoted to captains. Honorary ranks were bestowed on a few Barzani leaders: among them, As'ad Khoshavi and Mohammed Agha Mergasuri were made honorary colonels. Company commanders were given the rank of lieutenant, and Sayyed Ahmad Sayyed Taha Nahri was given the rank of major.

Tribal Forces

Initially, many Kurdish tribes in Iranian Kurdistan hesitated to pledge allegiance to the republic's flag; however, most of them did by the end of May. Barzani again played a leading role in bringing them under the rule of the republic. These tribes were as follows:

1. Jalali and Ilani, 400 horsemen.
2. Shikak, commanded by Omer Khan, 800 horsemen.
3. Shikak, commanded by Tahir Khan Simko, 500 horsemen.
4. Harki, commanded by Rashid Beg, 500.
5. Begzadeh, commanded by Nuri Beg, 500.
6. Harki, commanded by Zairo, 700.
7. Family of Nahri chiefs, commanded by Fahim, 200.
8. Zarza, commanded by Musa Khan, 300.
9. Qara Papagh (Turkomans), commanded by Pasha Khan and Khosrowi Khan, 500.
10. Mamash (Qadiri), commanded by Kaka Abdullah, 400.
11. Mamash, commanded by Kaka Hamza Naloosi, 500.
12. Piran, commanded by Mohammed Amin Agha and Qarani Agha, 300.
13. Mangor, commanded by Abdullah Bayazidi, 300.
14. Mangor, commanded by Salim Agha, 200.
15. Mangor, commanded by Ali Khan and Ibrahim Salari, 400.
16. Sardasht, commanded by Kaka Ala', 300 horsemen.
17. Mahabad Gawrk, commanded by Bayazid Aziz Agha, 300.
18. Saqqiz Gawrk, commanded by Ali Jwan Mardi, 400.
19. Various tribes from Sardasht, 500 horsemen.
20. Sosani tribe, 100 horsemen.
21. Mahabad and Dibokari, commanded by Jafar Karimi, 400.
22. Bokan Dibokari, commanded by the Aghas of Ilkhani Zadeh, 500.
23. Faidh Allah Begi of Saqqiz and Bokan, 800.
24. The family of Beda'e of Saqqiz, 200.
25. Various tribes of Mahabad and Shahin Diz, 300.
26. The followers of Hama Rashid Khan, 300.

The total number of these forces was 8,800 infantry and 1,700 horsemen.

Chapter 16

The First Battle: Qarawa

At dawn, on April 29, 1946, two Iranian army regiments advanced on the garrison of Saqqiz, in the territory of the First Kurdish Regiment, occupied it, moved ahead with their heavy artillery and trained several machine guns on the elevations of Qarawa, covering the whole area with firepower.

Before they settled in, the First Barzani Regiment carried out a concerted attack led by the regiment commander, Major Abd al-Karim. According to Eagleton in *The Kurdish Republic of Mahabad of 1946* (1972), in a fierce day-long battle in which all three companies took part, they captured Qarawa Peak and badly defeated the Iranian army. However, Mohammed Isa, a participant in this battle, puts the Qarawa battle four days later, that is, on May 3, 1946. The Iranian army expended great efforts to apply their air force, tanks, and heavy artillery to retake positions they had lost, all to no avail. The Qarawa River prevented the Barzanis from capturing an artillery battery in a forward position northeast of Saqqiz. Eighty soldiers, including several officers, were killed, and their bodies left on the battlefield; 120 were captured; many spoils, equipment, and arms were seized. Captured arms included 17 heavy machine guns, two cannons, and 200 rifles. There were no Barzani casualties.

The prisoners of war were transferred to Mahabad by the Hamamiyan Road while villagers looked on. The people of Mahabad came to see the prisoners of war. While they took pride in the achievement, to them it was a miraculous act; one hard to believe. This unexpected victory raised their morale, renewed their resolve, and proved their military ability and experience to the masses of Iranian Kurdistan. It brought them much respect. The following day, Qazi Mohammed and Mulla Mustafa Barzani toured the front and visited the First Battalion, which had won this momentous victory. They thanked the rank and file, and Qazi Mohammed awarded them 14,000 tomans.[1]

Regimental commander Colonel Bakr Abd al-Karim spoke in the presence of both leaders: "For the record, I say that these are heroes who do not fear death. They make little of life to defend the mission assigned them. The Kurdish nation should be proud of them and will not be disappointed."

He asked that medals for courage be awarded to the three company commanders and to Mirza Agha Rasho, Aziz Mohammed Dolarmery, Malko Zhazhoki, Ibrahim Yousif, Nabi Sar Asin, Lawoko Mamand, Malko Zairo, Hassan Sulayman, and Omer Hostani for their heroic leadership.

Until then, the populace was not aware of what the Barzanis could achieve on the battlefield. The battle of Qarawa raised their status throughout the nation of Kurdistan.

The Second Battle: Mil Qarani or Mameh Shah

In addition to the one at Saqqiz, the Iranian army maintained two additional garrisons, one in Baneh and the other in Sardasht. The Kurds controlled the supply lines to both of these garrisons. On May 3, 1946, General Razmara arrived in Saqqiz. Ostensibly, he had come to negotiate with the Kurds to keep the supply lines open. However, his real objective was to draw up a plan to attack the republic's forces and expunge the shame the Iranian army had suffered at the battle of Qarawa. He augmented the Saqqiz garrison with fresh forces after the army was defeated and forced to retreat to garrison headquarters in Saqqiz.

To negotiate borders, Razmara met with a joint Kurdish–Azerbaijani delegation headed by the Kurdish Chief of Staff Jafar Karimi, and accompanied by Kurdish members Staff Colonel Izzat Abd al-Aziz and Major Ibrahim Salih. The Azerbaijani members of the delegation were Ibrahim Ali Zadeh, Khalil Arzidakan, and Hassan Jowdat. It was agreed to keep supply routes to both garrisons open. Kurdish forces fulfilled this obligation while concentrating on fortifying their positions until June 15, the deadline for carrying out Razmara's plan. Standing before his ready troops, he told them that the honor of the Iranian army rested on that day's battle.

At five o'clock in the morning, an army brigade began a fierce attack on the positions of the Second Regiment at Mil Qarani, west of Saqqiz. This was a ferocious and bloody battle in which the Iranian army demonstrated unyielding tenacity, using every type of weapon more precisely and efficiently than [it had] in the previous battle. The air force effectively supported the infantry as well as the tank and artillery units. Initially, the Iranian army gained the upper hand.

The First Regiment, commanded by Mohammed Amin Mirkhan, moved in from the east to support the Second Regiment, which had absorbed much of the attack. Suppressing enemy artillery fire, they advanced all the way to the vicinity of Saqqiz, threatening the garrison with direct fire. In fierce resistance, the Second Regiment broke the Iranian attack and swiftly moved from defense to offense. In the early afternoon, the Iranian forces were defeated with heavy casualties while the Kurdish forces captured much of their weapons and ammunition.

Several Barzanis were wounded or martyred: Khoshavi, son of Khalil Khoshavi,[2] was one of the leaders of the counterattack. A young man, he was barely 19 when martyred. The Barzanis and others in the region mourned him deeply, for he had demonstrated capable leadership and utmost courage.

After this defeat, the Iranian leaders concluded that the Barzanis had fortified their positions and would not stir. Hopeless, they could not call in any more troops in addition to the ones they already had. The Barzanis tightened their siege on Saqqiz, considered their earlier agreement with General Razmara null and void, and cut off supplies from the garrisons of Baneh and Sardasht.

In Mahabad, a fourth regiment of Barzanis was being formed and sent to the front under the command of Colonel Bakr Abd al-Karim, commander of the First Regiment, which now was commanded by Captain Mohammed Salih and dispatched to Sardasht.

Disease Afflicts the Barzanis

The Barzanis suffered much indeed during their first few months in Iranian Kurdistan. They had left all of their possessions behind and were weakened despite all of the assistance from their Iranian Kurdish brothers. "God tries no soul past its capacity,"[3] and, as the saying goes, one may feel awkward even in his brother's house.

Despite selfless and generous assistance, the Barzanis were in an environment lacking the sanitary conditions in which precautionary measures could be taken. Since they were unable to protect themselves, a typhoid epidemic killed more than 1,500 Barzanis in the first half of 1946. Barzani losses due to a dearth of physicians were far greater than their losses in battle.

The epidemic subsided only in 1947, when a Soviet doctor arrived with some medicine. The total number of victims of the epidemic was more than 2,000 Barzani men, women, and children. Their graves were scattered throughout the villages of the Mahabad, Oshnoviyeh, and Bokan regions. Despite the epidemic, the Barzanis were assigned the task of defending the fledgling republic. They met the challenge in the manner expected of them as they became the strong right arm of the Republic of Mahabad. Their role expanded, especially when the local tribal forces were derelict in their duties and wandered off, withdrawing from the positions they had been assigned to hold because they were not used to staying at the front for long periods of time. In addition, there was intratribal and intertribal discord. Disharmony often prevented them from uniting against the enemy. Quarrels often occurred at the front because of land, property, and other personal issues, without regard to the common interest or the call of national duty. To the Barzanis' surprise, chieftains and sheikhs unscrupulously oppressed their own tribes and firmly controlled their destinies. The Barzanis could not comprehend this behavior because they had not experienced such treatment on the part of their own sheikhs. Often they intervened to protect people from the oppression of chieftains, who in turn retaliated by withholding food rations and other forms of aid from the Barzani families.

The Barzanis' loyalty and their sharing of responsibility won them respect equally from the Republic's officials and from the populace with whom they dealt and whom they treated well. For this reason, Soviet officers preferred to deal with Barzani directly; he impressed everyone with his courteous and modest behavior. They came to him for advice, especially in military matters, whereas there had been no contact between the Soviets and Barzani before the battles of Qarawa and Mil Qarani.

Chapter 17

The Founding of the Kurdistan Democratic Party

The conditions and profound developments in Iranian Kurdistan did not preclude the Freedom Committee's pondering the fate and evolution of the Kurdish national movement in Iraqi Kurdistan. In light of the successful founding of the Kurdistan Democratic Party of Iran (KDPI)[1] and the lessons of the Barzan Revolt of 1943–1945, the Kurdish struggle clearly required the founding of the KDP of Iraq, named after its Iranian counterpart. Barzani and his comrades, the patriotic officers of the Freedom Committee, studied the situation and possible developments carefully and thoroughly and decided to establish a party that would shoulder the current demands of the national struggle and adapt to new circumstances as they occurred—a party with goals expressing the aspirations of the Kurdish masses. The idea crystallized in late February of 1946. Thus, Barzani met with the patriots: attorney Hamza Abdullah, Captain Mustafa Khoshnaw, Captain Khairullah Abd al-Karim, and Lieutenants Mohammed Mahmud Qudsi and Nuri Ahmad Taha.

They laid the foundation for what came to be known as the KDP and they then moved to set down the platform and bylaws for the new party. Real barriers impeded the party's open organizational and educational objectives in the Republic of Mahabad. Barzani and other party leaders felt that the republic's warning against the party's local activities, despite its approval of the idea and the achievement, emanated from the prevalent political situation, as this would give the enemies of the fledgling republic, notably Iraq and Turkey, which were supported and protected by the Western Allies, a pretext to intensify their declared animosity. It would have been easy to suppose that the new republic, though only a few months old, harbored the ambition of carving out parts of Turkey and Iraq for a sovereign greater Kurdistan. This was the last thing the leaders of the Mahabad Republic wanted to sanction with their shaky political position, which was fraught with peril. Furthermore, the new party was only designed for Iraqi Kurdistan and the Kurdish masses in Iraq. Thus, its ideas and activities were to be limited to Iraq. Hence, attorney Hamza Abdullah was dispatched to Iraqi Kurdistan to initiate contacts with the *Shoresh* (Revolution) and *Rizgari* (Deliverance) parties, and with Mahabad's KDP branch in Suleimaniyya. Barzani and the Founding Committee fully authorized Hamza Abdullah to conduct business on their behalf. Among the recommendations he was to convey were the following:

1. To select Sheikh Latif b. Sheikh Mahmud to be the first deputy to the chairman.
2. To select Kaka Mohammed Ziyad to be the second deputy.

3. Not to introduce any changes into the party's charter, platform, or bylaws for a while.
4. To deny the imperialists the opportunity of retaliation and refrain from attacking British interests until the party's base was firmly established in order to avoid a campaign of suppression and persecution.

Furthermore, the aging British imperialism was about to depart the scene, thus allowing for a patriotic regime to emerge before the Americans filled the vacuum. America had emerged victorious from World War II and at the height of its power.

In late spring of 1946, Hamza Abdullah returned to Iraqi Kurdistan. When the Kurdish parties and notables were contacted, both the *Shoresh* and *Rizgari* party leaders agreed in principle to dissolve their organizations and join the new party, provided that they held special conferences to inform their party delegates of the new development. Conferences were held early in August of 1946. With a few minor objections and reservations, the vast majority of delegates of both parties welcomed the founding of a new party.

The First Congress

The new party held its first Congress on August 16, 1946, in Baghdad, and adopted the name The Kurdistan Democratic Party of Iraq. It was a turning point in the history of the Kurdish nation. Since then, it has been known as "the party." Delegates studied the party charter, platform, and bylaws that had been prepared in Mahabad. The final version was adopted with minor changes. Having considered the recommendations by Barzani and his colleagues, the delegates elected the party's first central committee, which consisted of the following people: Mustafa Barzani, president; Sheikh Latif bin Sheikh Mahmud, first deputy; Kaka Hama Ziyad, second deputy; Hamza Abdullah; Mir Haj Ahmad; Dr. Jafar Karim; Ali Abdullah; Salih al-Yousifi; Abd al-Karim Tawfiq; Rashid Abd al-Qadir; Rashid Bajelan; Mulla Sayyed Hakim Khanaqini; Awni Yousif; Taha Muhyeddin, and Abd al-Samad Mohammed, first alternate.

The Central Committee then held its first meeting and elected a general secretary and members of the politburo. They were Hamza Abdullah, general secretary; Ali Abdullah, member; Dr. Jafar Mohammed Karim, member; Abd al-Karim Tawfiq, member; and Rashid Abd al-Qadir, member.

The party has since led the struggle of the Kurdish masses in triumphs and setbacks. It has become synonymous with the Kurdish struggle and outlook. Despite all of its ups and downs, the party has remained credible and kept faith with the hope and aspirations of the Kurdish nation.[2]

As this critical phase concluded, communication between Barzani and the party improved. Contacts and consultations continued. The party actively raised funds in Iraq to help the Barzanis in Iranian Kurdistan, where they were suffering from disease and malnutrition.

Chapter 18

◆

Discord between Tabriz and Mahabad

The leaders of the Democratic Republics of Azerbaijan and Kurdistan were not in agreement. The Azerbaijanis wanted to contain Mahabad and bring it into their sphere of influence. To his discredit, Baqirov [the secretary general of the Communist (Bolshevik) Party of Azerbaijan] pressured Kurdish leaders to submit to the will of Tabriz. Generous Soviet aid went to Tabriz, whereas little reached Mahabad, and that with much difficulty. It was obvious early on that the two republics were moving in different directions. Emulating Baqirov's policy, Azerbaijan was clearly leftist, while Mahabad was nationalistic and independent, a position it never compromised.

Uninvolved in these purely political issues, including ties to the Soviet Union, Barzani concentrated on military matters such as organizing forces and strengthening the fronts. Ominous armed clashes between the two fledgling republics escalated, forcing the Soviets to invite both sides to a meeting in Tabriz in mid-April of 1946. An agreement between Azerbaijan and Kurdistan was reached and set down in the following articles:

Article 1: As needed, parties shall exchange representatives.
Article 2: In areas where ethnic populations are mixed, Kurdish officials shall be appointed to government offices where the majority of the inhabitants are Kurds, and vice versa.
Article 3: The two governments shall establish a joint economic committee to deal with economic problems. Both heads of state shall abide by the committee's decisions.
Article 4: When necessary, parties shall enter into a military alliance.
Article 5: Neither Republic shall enter negotiations with the Iranian government without the consent of the other.
Article 6: The government of Azerbaijan shall take necessary measures to contribute to the educational and linguistic advancement of the Kurds who live within its territory, and vice versa.
Article 7: Whoever attempts to breach the historic friendship and alliance between the two peoples or whoever tries to end their national unity shall be punished by both peoples.

It finally became evident that the fundamental discord was not about what was mentioned above, i.e., the ideological domination that Azerbaijan aspired to have. It was a border dispute, which was completely neglected in the talks, a fact that is inexplicable until one recognizes that both sides attending the meeting as observers and negotiators realized the necessity of postponing the issue until the Kurds of Iraq and Turkey were united with the Kurds of Iran. It is virtually certain that because of the conditions after the World War II, the creation of a greater unified and independent Kurdistan was not on the Soviet political agenda. It was never mentioned in talks, meetings, or conferences among the victorious countries before and after the war ended. Perhaps the Soviet political agenda for Iran was to keep their forces in Iran, where they had already been for six years, as the events of 1947 and 1948 later proved.

Qazi Mohammed's Visit to Tehran

In August of 1946, Qazi Mohammed went to Tehran on an official visit. He met with Prime Minister [Ahmad] Qavam al-Saltana and the army's chief of staff, [Ali] Razmara. Qavam al-Saltana proposed that Qazi Mohammed unify all Iranian Kurdistan in one region under one governor to be appointed by the central government and that Qazi Mohammed assume the governorship of that region.

Qazi Mohammed rejected the proposal since it would have severed all of his ties with Tabriz. The Soviets were also opposed to it. Qazi Mohammed personally favored the proposal, but he realized that Soviet approval was necessary for any project that would alter the relationship between Mahabad and Tabriz.

At the Soviet Embassy, Qazi Mohammed's reception was not what he had anticipated. He was told that accepting Qavam's proposal meant the betrayal of Azerbaijan and, therefore, the Soviets would not approve of it. At that time preparations were under way to attack Sanandaj. Eagleton (1972, p. 174, Arabic translation)[1] asserts that Soviet officers advised the Kurds against the attack. However, the facts indicate that the Soviets and Azerbaijanis ardently supported it, as Mohammed Isa and others recall Soviet officers' repeated visits to Barzani in preparation for the offensive. The Soviets sent four tanks to Saqqiz to support the attackers. The Kurdish government did not possess such weapons. Two high-ranking officers, Azimi and Kabiri, came from Tabriz to Saqqiz and prepared for the attack with Barzani and his officers. Extensive preparations continued.

Unfortunately, events took a sudden turn as international politics once again drowned in blood Kurdish hopes and brought to an end the nascent republic.

Chapter 19

Approaching the End

After the occupation of Iran by the Soviet and British armies in August of 1941, the British Foreign Ministry drafted a treaty to which the Soviets agreed. This treaty stressed that the presence of the Allied forces in Iran was neither military occupation nor a hindrance to internal security forces, economic life, citizens' freedom of movement, or the application of Iranian law and order. However, the Soviet Union backed the creation of both Azerbaijan and Kurdistan. The United States and Britain viewed this as a violation of the treaty. As pressure mounted on the Soviets to withdraw from Iran, the Iranians intensified their diplomacy at the United Nations, using the terms of this treaty. Also, Qavam al-Saltana promised the Soviets the drilling rights for oil as well as the protection of the rights of the Azerbaijanis and the Kurds and a peaceful solution to their problems.

I do not wish to go into detail, because much has already been written about this period. But I must say that the Soviet Union had pledged to withdraw its forces from Iran. Its ambassador to the UN, Mr. Andrei Gromyko, in his report of March 26, 1946, had said that the Soviets would withdraw all their forces within six weeks. Therefore, it was clear that the Soviet forces would withdraw and that Tehran would send its forces to retake Azerbaijan and Kurdistan. I am not sure what the leaders of Kurdistan and Azerbaijan thought of the fates of their peoples after Soviet withdrawal. Could they rely on Qavam's promises? Qavam proved his clever diplomacy and duplicity. To put it bluntly, the Kurdish cause was the victim of competing international interests.

Qavam al-Saltana traveled to Moscow and put his desires before Stalin: the right to drill for and exploit oil fields and natural gas in northern Iran. In return, the Soviets would withdraw their forces from northern Iran. Upon the completion of the withdrawal, as dictated by the Iranian Constitution, the Iranian Parliament began deliberating the Qavam–Stalin Treaty.

With a majority behind him in the council, Qavam al-Saltana orchestrated an attack on the treaty, describing it as perfidy and a breach of the constitution, which forbade the signing of an accord conceding rights to a foreign country without prior approval by the council. As planned, an overwhelming majority rejected the treaty. Stalin was duped as never before since rejection of the treaty came after the Soviet withdrawal had been completed.

The Fall of Azerbaijan

In Tehran, the Soviet ambassador warned Iran that his government could not remain silent concerning the events near its borders in Azerbaijan. This was the most the Soviets could do to delay the inevitable. As stated earlier, their forces had been completely withdrawn from the occupied territories from Tehran northward to the Iranian border. Discussing the advancing Iranian forces, Hashimov, the Soviet consul in Urmia, told a Kurdish delegation that the Iranian government intended to send a token force to oversee the elections and then withdraw.

Did the Kurdish delegation believe Hashimov? Although supported by the United States, Britain, a United Nations resolution, and Soviet compliance, events on the ground indicated that the Iranian government fully intended to return the geopolitics of northern Iran to prewar status. A spurious hope kept the Kurdish and Azerbaijani leaders believing that matters were as they should be. Thus, the plan to attack Sanandaj remained unchanged. The four tanks remained on the Kurdish front near Saqqiz to support the attacking Kurdish troops. The two Azerbaijani officers, Kabiri and Azimi, did not leave and remained with the troops.

As Mohammed Isa Barzani, one of the fighters, told it:

> On the night of December 10, 1946, a jeep arrived at Mustafa Barzani's headquarters carrying an urgent letter to the two Azerbaijani officers. Having read the letter, they asked to see Barzani immediately. They informed him that the Iranian army was advancing on Tabriz, that fierce fighting was taking place between Tabriz and Miyaneh, and that they had been ordered to return with their four tanks. Furthermore, Azerbaijan was requesting reinforcements from the Republic of Kurdistan. Barzani had to agree, and the tanks were returned. At the same time, an order was issued to Mohammed Amin Mirkhan to go to Miyandoab, where he would meet Barzani.

Barzani and the two officers, Kabiri and Azimi, reached Miyandoab on December 11, 1946, and learned that Iranian forces were entering Tabriz and crushing all resistance. Barzani ordered Mohammed Amin Mirkhan to wait while they looked into the situation. In the morning, they learned that Iranian forces had entered Tabriz. Many Azerbaijani officials had escaped to Baku, others surrendered, and many more had been killed in the chaos and demonstrations.

In reality, there was neither fighting in Miyaneh, as mentioned above, nor any resistance to the Iranian march. In fact, the bands of men raised by the Azerbaijan government fled and never dared to challenge the Iranian forces, moving forward more as though in a parade than in preparation for battle. Azerbaijan's immediate collapse astounded the world. Obviously, Mahabad was next.

The Retreat of the Barzanis to Mahabad

Returning from Miyandoab, Barzani stayed at the Saray, where the first regiment on the Saqqiz front was camping. He immediately ordered Mohammed Amin Mirkhan to move to Mahabad to protect the families there. He offered Azimi and

Kabiri a choice, and both preferred to return to Tabriz. They fell to government supporters in Maragheh, and their escorts died with them. The collapse of Azerbaijan encouraged the tribal chiefs to proclaim their allegiance to Tehran and their animosity toward the leaders of the republic. They not only welcomed the Iranian forces but made use of the chaos to plunder and kill Azerbaijani officials. Those who escaped death were turned over to the Tehran forces. A number of tribal chiefs challenged the Barzanis on their way to Mahabad; however, the chiefs were taught a lesson. Having failed, they fled, never to return.

Barzani ordered his forces in Saqqiz to resist any Iranian advance while awaiting further instructions. A segment of this force was assigned to gather the Barzani families living between Mahabad and Bokan in Mahabad. They had been ambushed and had fought robbers along the way. Fortunately, they all arrived, and not a single family member was left behind except in Miyandoab, where a young man, Ali Hassan Shaina, was killed, and another, Ahmad Abd al-Latif, was wounded.

The Last Meeting between the Two Leaders

After orders had been issued to the forces on the front and families had been evacuated from danger zones, Barzani went to Mahabad. He met with Qazi Mohammed and other officials to decide what was to be done about the sudden events. He learned that there was no intention to resist the Iranian forces. They would surrender, and the fall of Mahabad was only a matter of time.

There was no one left to defend the capital except the Barzanis. The tribal chiefs had changed sides and were in open conflict with the republic. They had sent emissaries rendering their allegiance to the Tehran forces and were awaiting their entry into Mahabad.

Barzani ordered his forces on the Saqqiz and Sardasht fronts to return to Mahabad immediately. All families were to move to the areas of Naghadeh and Oshnoviyeh. Barzani told me of his last meeting with Qazi Mohammed on the eve of December 16, 1946:

> I went to Qazi Mohammed and asked him what he personally intended to do. He said that he intended to sacrifice his life to prevent bloodshed in Mahabad, that he would surrender to the Iranian forces, and that he had sent an emissary to General Hamayoni in Miyandoab informing him of his decision. He broke down in tears as he continued: "Never rely on anyone but your own group. All those who took the oath of allegiance have betrayed us and are rushing to prove their loyalty to the Iranian forces. Beware of the tribal chiefs who would target you if they could. I hope that you will leave Mahabad as soon as you can to avoid confronting the Iranian forces."
>
> Then he asked me what I was going to do. I told him that we would gather our families and forces in the Oshnoviyeh and Margavar areas and avoid clashing with the Iranian forces until spring. We would try to convince the Iraqi government to issue a general amnesty, at least to include our families. If we failed, then we would all head for the Soviet Union. We would surrender neither to Iran nor Iraq. I insisted

that he go with us, and pledged my word of honor that I would sacrifice my life and the lives of all who were with me to defend him, because he was the symbol of our nation. I told him that my advice to him was not to trust Iranian promises. It would be painful to see the first president of the Republic of Kurdistan fall into enemy hands.

In tears, Qazi Mohammed rose and hugged me, saying, "I pray God will give you strength and protect you. May my sacrifice spare the citizens some of their affliction and mitigate the terror and vengeance." Then, he pulled a flag of Kurdistan from his pocket and gave it to me and said: "This is the symbol of Kurdistan. I give it to you as a token of trust in your honor, for I think you are the best man to keep it." In an atmosphere of grief and sorrow, I wished him well and left for Naghadeh.

Barzani reached Naghadeh on December 17 and, at the house of Haji Ilkhani, he heard on the radio the news of Iranian forces taking Mahabad. In fact, they entered it only when certain that the Barzanis had left. Mahabad fell, and with it fell the hopes of millions of Kurds throughout all Kurdistan. A cloak shrouded the fledgling republic.

Chapter 20

A Difficult Period

Families flocked together from the regions of Mahabad and Bokan to Naghadeh and Oshnoviyeh and the surrounding villages. Barzani residents of Margaver were still there. Sheikh Ahmad had reached Oshnoviyeh, and he met with Barzani, who then called a meeting for his commanders and chiefs to consider what to do. With few options left, they decided to establish a line of defense between Naghadeh and Mahabad, in the Barandiz Valley[1] and another in the Qasimlu Valley,[2] to avoid the Iranian forces and wait for the spring thaw. Then they would be able to return to Iraq or to go to the Soviet Union.

The Iranian army also avoided the Barzanis. Beyond Mahabad, they did not advance toward Naghadeh and did not leave the neighborhood of Urmia City. In other words, they excluded from their operations areas occupied by the Barzanis. Soon, General Hamayoni[3] contacted the two brothers, Sheikh Ahmad and Mulla Mustafa Barzani, and requested a meeting. They agreed to meet in Naghadeh at the house of Quoli Khan Qarapapagh.[4] Representing the Iranian side were General Hamayoni and Colonel Ghafari. Hamayoni asked Sheikh Ahmad what the Barzanis intended to do. He answered that they did not wish to fight the Iranian army. All they wanted was for Iran to allow them time until spring to leave Iranian territory, be it with or without the approval of the Iraqi government.

Hamayoni replied that he was not authorized to decide such matters and that he preferred to consult Tehran. He suggested that Mustafa Barzani travel with him to Tehran for this purpose. Sheikh Ahmad agreed and ordered Mulla Mustafa to go to Tehran. It was very risky, but Mulla Mustafa Barzani never disobeyed an order from Sheikh Ahmad. No one expected him to return. Iranian monarchs are historically known for breaking promises they make to their enemies; they trap and kill them. Sheikh Ahmad never lost faith that Mulla Mustafa would return unharmed.

Along with Izzat Abd al-Aziz, Nuri Ahmad Taha, Mir Haj Ahmad, Mohammed Amin Mirkhan, Jameel Tawfiq Bamerni, and Khalid Zrari, Barzani traveled to Tehran on December 21, 1946. They were accompanied by Colonel Ghafari.

Sheikh Ahmad personally oversaw the affairs of the tribe until Mulla Mustafa returned. The Barzani forces were arranged into three divisions to be stationed on three defensive fronts: Naghadeh, Piranshahr, and Margavar. In Tehran, Barzani was welcomed at the officers' club, where he met the shah, the prime minister, the chief of staff, and other officials. The shah proposed that the Barzanis either be resettled in Hamadan and given agricultural land or that they leave the Iranian territory immediately. Barzani answered that he could not decide such matters without Sheikh Ahmad, who alone could make such a decision.

During his stay in Tehran, rumors spread that Barzani and his team had been court-martialed and were soon to be executed. Barzani told me this story:

> Once Nuri Ahmad Taha came to me in tears, and I asked him what had happened. He said that he had been told by an employee of the officers' club that, "the court had issued a verdict to execute you all." I calmed him down by saying death is inevitable; today or tomorrow, it does not really matter. No need to cry. He replied, "By God, I'm not crying because of us. I am crying for those who remain after you." Then he begged me to ask the Iranians to execute him before me.

The Iranian regime believed that Barzani was their prize and the means to coerce Sheikh Ahmad to surrender and accept their conditions, thereby solving the problem of the Barzanis without much effort. Hence, they sent a delegation to Naghadeh to inform Sheikh Ahmad of the government's decision—that they must lay down arms and prepare to be relocated to Mahabad. Otherwise, Barzani's life was in danger. Sheikh Ahmad replied, "We do not succumb to perils and extortion. Each one of the Barzani tribe is Mustafa Barzani. Do whatever you wish, but we will not give up our arms, and we will fight to the last man." This stern response confounded the Tehran officials, and they resorted to a more amiable policy toward the Barzanis.

Authors who wrote the history of that period attributed to General Hamayoni a statement that Barzani's absence enabled him to disarm the Iranian Kurdish tribes without much difficulty; this would not have been feasible with Barzani in the region.

Once Qazi Mohammed and most of his cabinet members and party officials were captured and the tribes disarmed, the Iranian government was certain of its control of the area except for the Barzanis. They were the only threat to the army, and were certain to fight with or without Mulla Mustafa so long as Sheikh Ahmad was among them. Therefore, the Iranian government was forced to let Barzani and his comrades return to present the issue to Sheikh Ahmad and reach a final decision.

Barzani's Return from Tehran

Barzani and his comrades returned to Mahabad on January 29, 1947, accompanied by Colonel Ghafari. Without delay, he was received by Hamayoni, who was instructed to begin transferring the Barzanis to Hamadan immediately. He fancied that he would do that at once, but Barzani told him that the final decision was Sheikh Ahmad's. In disbelief, everyone in Oshnoviyeh was delighted to see Barzani again. They considered it a miracle for him to escape the grip of the Iranian government and return unharmed.

Barzani presented the Iranian proposal to Sheikh Ahmad and others. It was rejected unanimously. The Barzanis could not move to Hamadan to live a totally different way of life. They were in a critical position: the Iranian army had gained control of much of the area, the tribes had proclaimed their loyalty to the central government, and the Barzanis were in a foreign land where the government had stunned everyone with its swift and easy victories over the Republics of Azerbaijan and Mahabad. Despite these difficult circumstances, Sheikh Ahmad sent his reply to Hamayoni, rejecting the Iranian proposal altogether, but assuring him that they would leave Iran as soon as the snow melted and the roads were clear.

Chapter 21

An Attempt to Persuade the Tribes not to Interfere with the Barzanis

In the first week of February, Barzani visited the tribes of Mamesh, Piran, and Mangor in the Piranshahr area. He explained what had happened and informed the tribes that the Barzanis had decided to leave Iranian territory in the spring. He appealed to them not to interfere and cut off the Barzanis' escape route if the Iranian forces requested it. All promised, but only a few kept their promise. They bore arms and were inducted into the Iranian armed forces as mercenaries.

A New Meeting

In mid-February, Hamayoni and Ghafari came to Naghadeh and put three options before Sheikh Ahmad and Mulla Mustafa Barzani. The Barzanis were to (1) leave Iran immediately, (2) lay down their arms and relocate to Hamadan immediately, or (3) be prepared to confront the Iranian army.

Sheikh Ahmad replied that the first option was only acceptable after the snows melted since all roads were currently closed; the second option was also unacceptable; and as far as the third option was concerned, his fighters were not to initiate hostilities but would defend themselves if attacked. The meeting ended in failure. It dawned on everyone that fighting was inevitable and there was no way to avert or delay it. The last Barzanis in Naghadeh were relocated to Oshnoviyeh, where they established a new line of defense in the villages of Albeh, Koyek, and Tel Qalatan, overlooking the main road. Both sides were fortifying their positions and preparing for war. Iranian reinforcements lined up from Tehran and other cities.

The Silweh Incident

Confirmed sources indicated that a few of the Mamesh chiefs had received weapons and pledged to occupy strategic points in the Sabriz mountain range and all the way to the Gadir Valley, which would gravely threaten the Barzanis. To foil their plan, on February 23, 1947, a unit was ordered to capture the chiefs of Mamesh—followers of Qarani Agha—who were meeting in Silweh,[1] and bring them to Oshnoviyeh as hostages. The Barzani commander ordered them to lay down their arms. As one chief drew his handgun—whether to fight or to turn it in remains unknown—shots were heard outside and chaos ensued. Twelve of the chiefs were killed; others were captured. Of the Barzanis, Mohammed Mirza Kakshar and Baqi Kaniboti were martyred and Hali Kaloki and Darwish Khano Bidodi were wounded. Others in the villages of Shawileh, Nalos, and Bisweh[2] were arrested, and all were transferred to Oshnoviyeh. Sheikh Ahmad Barzani was outraged and ordered the release of the hostages at once. Shocked, other chiefs were also daunted by this truly unfortunate incident.

Exploring the Somay Route

On March 1, Barzani moved north to explore the Somay route[3] and meet the tribal chiefs in the region, pursuant to the second option, i.e., the departure of the Barzanis and their families to the Soviet Union.

Chiefs of the Harki, Begzadeh, Dari, Shikak, and other tribes attended the meeting. They promised Barzani to render all the assistance they possibly could. Some even encouraged [the Barzanis] to resettle in the Shabiran area, and even in the area of Jalalis, north of Mako, because they are difficult mountainous terrains that would allow the revolution to start up again. The chiefs said that an anti-shah revolution was possible because they had already contacted the Soviets, who had promised their support. I doubt if their claims were true. Tahir Khan, Simko's son, warned Barzani not to rely on their promises. He stressed that they would betray him because they were in touch with the Iranian government. Barzani returned to Oshnoviyeh and discussed and assessed the situation with his comrades.

Chapter 22

Resumption of Hostilities

The last meeting between Sheikh Ahmad Barzani and General Hamayoni ended all negotiations and made clear to the Iranian commander that the Barzanis would not lay down their arms or accept resettlement in Hamadan. The meeting confirmed that the Barzanis were determined to defend themselves and use force if attacked.

Both sides prepared for war. Additional government reinforcements reached Mahabad and Urmia. General Fazlallah Hamayoni personally led the operations, assisted by Brigadiers Beglari, Nishapuri, and Zangana, and Colonels Ansari, Foladunad, Sardadwar, Mozaffari, Majidi, and Partovi. In Naghadeh, the Barzanis divided their forces along the following lines of defense:

The Nalos–Sofiyan Front, commanded by Ali Khalil, Salih Kaniya Lanji, and Kako Mulla Ali.

The Qalatan Front, commanded by Hassan Ali Sulayman Kakshar, Sultan Mar'an Agha, and Mahmud Mira.

The Albeh–Koyek Front, commanded by Aris Khano and Mahmud Ahmad Babkayi.

The Margaver Front, commanded by Asad Khoshavi, Mohammed Amin Mirkhan, and Sheikhomer Shandari.

Barzani kept a reserve strike force under his personal command.

When the Barzanis withdrew from Saqqiz, they brought along two 75-mm cannons, which a number of young Barzanis were trained to use. An Iranian officer named Tafrashiyan[1] supervised the artillery with six other officers. He had been serving in the forces of Azerbaijan until its collapse and then joined the Barzanis. During the month of March and through the first week of April, until the Barzanis left Iran, clashes took place almost daily, as did several fierce battles.

The Battle of Nalos

An Iranian army regiment moved toward Oshnoviyeh and camped in the village of Nalos[2] preparing to attack. In the first week of March, fierce fighting broke out between this regiment and the Barzanis, who used their artillery capably with the help of Tafrashiyan, the Azeri officer. The Iranian force was badly beaten; the regimental commander, Colonel Kalashi, along with a number of his officers, was killed.

The Barzanis took over the regimental headquarters and captured all of the equipment, ammunition, and supplies. Eighty soldiers and officers were taken prisoner. Among them were Captain Khodadost, First Lieutenants Yaqubi, Baseerat, and Kamali, and Second Lieutenant Fatimi. All of the prisoners were taken to Oshnoviyeh; there the soldiers were released, but the officers were held. The following six Barzanis were martyred: Sulayman Mulla Zhazhoki, Salih Mustafa Binbiyayi, Ibrahim Mulla Hamid Binbiyayi, Omer Ahmad Wasman Barzani, Ibrahim Nafkhosh Safti, and Hal Bayazdin Kaniboti.

The Barzanis' astounding victory forced the Iranian leadership to review its plans and calculations. It also jolted the tribal chiefs into refraining from actual cooperation in the field with the Iranian forces. Their challenges to the Barzanis were only feints and flights before the Barzanis' rapid advance.

The Battle of Gojar

The possibility that the Barzanis would take refuge in the Soviet Union became more viable than ever, especially after the Iraqi government refused to let them return to Iraq under the terms they had proposed. So on March 11, Barzani went north once more to ensure the safety of the roads and meet again with the tribal chiefs. He met them at the house of Nuri Beg Begzadeh in the village of Anbi. The chiefs promised to help as the Barzanis crossed the border. However, a traitor named Hoirko went to General Hamayoni and informed him of the details of the meeting. On the night of March 13, he returned with an army regiment and surrounded the village of Gojar,[3] where Barzani was staying.

In the morning, Barzani learned that they were surrounded. He described what happened next in the following manner:

> I tried hard to avoid clashes since I had not come there to fight, and I did not have a large force. Our forces were at the line of defense we had established. I tried to leave the village and return to Margavar without fighting. As we left the village, on all sides they opened fire from the nearby hills, while Hoirko,[4] on his horse, followed us shouting, "Don't run away!" I had decided that we had to force our way out to break the siege. Thus, fighting broke out and in few hours we broke through the siege. Hoirko and a number of his men were killed and the rest fled. We returned to Margavar.

Two Barzanis were martyred—Haji Mohammed Hostani and Shawali Shando Shanadari—and three were wounded—Haso Mirkhan Khardini, Hali Mohammed Khalani, and Mustafa Rasho Lailoki.

Supported by a few tribal chiefs, the Iranian army prepared to advance from Urmia to Margavar through Barandiz. Therefore, it was necessary to establish new lines of defense at strategic points such as Bari Zar, the Havris Heights, and Kawi Zar.[5] A tenacious defense of these points would be the only way to halt the Iranian army should it advance into villages packed with Barzani families ready to leave Iran.

A New Iranian Attack on the Oshnoviyeh Front

Crushed and having lost a whole regiment at the battle of Nalos, the Iranian commander called in fresh units, including cavalry units from Luristan, and Kurdish tribes such as the Mangor, Mamesh, and others. On March 18, they waged a full-scale attack on all three axes of the Oshnoviyeh–Naghadeh Front, using tanks, heavy artillery, and concerted aerial bombardments.

In a fierce and bloody fight, Iranian forces captured the Barzanis' strategic positions. The Barzanis were tired, hungry, and out of ammunition. It was impossible to supply even bread to the fighters. However, the Iranian victory was also costly; they lost 200 men. Nevertheless, it boosted their morale considerably. The Barzanis' morale plummeted, as some of their best leaders were killed or wounded. Among them were Sultan Mar'an Agha Birsiyavi, Ali Omer Birsiyavi, Sulayman Faqi Derishki, Hassan Sulayman Mirgsuri, and Ahmad Othman Asquili. The latter two resisted and did not leave their positions in Qalatan until tanks crushed them both. Among those wounded were Ghazali Mirkhan Zhazhoki, Sulayman Dino, and Ahmad Musa Mergasuri.

The Barzanis retreated to the village of Gundawaila and to the vicinity of Shaikhan and Poshava. After the battle, Hamayoni went to Haj Omran on March 24, 1947, and met with Ali Hijazi, director general of the Iraqi police, who offered to send Iraqi forces to assist him in fighting the Barzanis. However, Hamayoni thanked him and informed him that there was no need for Iraqi help. I believe, if this meeting had occurred before the March 18 battle, Hamayoni would have welcomed the offer.

Before long, the Barzanis would be obliged to aim a blow at the Iranian army to spoil its euphoria. Sulayman Beg Dargala led a bold operation. He ambushed an army column near Qarina, between Naghadeh and Piranshahr, killing 50 soldiers and capturing 40 others that were transferred to Oshnoviyeh. This operation was, in effect, redress for the March 18, 1947 loss. Then the Iranian government began to use its air force to attack the families in all villages of which they were aware.

The Last Two Battles

The Iranian army tried to achieve a measure of victory on the Margaver Front as they had on the Oshnoviyeh Front. Thus, they began their first attack on March 25, 1947, on the Havris-Halaj Heights. A company seized one of the peaks.

Before long, the Barzani forces waged a two-pronged counterattack led by Mohammed Amin Mirkhan and Sheikhomer Shanaderi. Within an hour, they retook the peak, annihilated the company, and captured a number of the enemy, including Lieutenant Jihaniyani, whose father was an army general. They went on to pound the regiment near Havris with their artillery, forcing it to retreat after sustaining many losses, which were primarily equipment and animals. In this battle, Tabor, who had come to avenge his brother Hoirko, was killed. The air force bombarded the villages and battle zones extensively that day. An airplane was downed and its pilot was killed, as he was unable to use his parachute to escape.

Seven Barzanis were martyred: Ahmad Kakal Birsiyavi, Abdullah Shaqlawayi, Khalil Aqrawi, Hamo Nabi Rezani, Khaja Khal Mulla Rizabi, Shawkat Nu'man Imadi, and Mirkhan Dori. They were all buried in the cemetery of Halij Village. Sheikhomer Shanaderi, Omer Agha Khalanayi, Mir Sultan, Khidhir Ramo, and Wajdi Beg were wounded.

Barzani warned the Iranian commander that the life of Lieutenant Jihaniyani could not be guaranteed if the air force continued to attack Barzani civilians. The aerial bombardment stopped. It seemed that the life of Lieutenant Jihaniyani, son of General Jihaniyani, was more important than the lives of other officers captured in previous battles, for whom such warnings had been ineffective.

The second battle occurred on April 3, when an Iranian brigade attempted to advance from Urmia to occupy the Nerki (Bari Zar) Heights. Barzani said that this battle was the most violent of all and that the Barzanis resisted as never before. The fighting continued from dawn to dusk, as the Iranian forces suffered tremendous casualties and retreated. Barzani himself was wounded slightly, and Haso Yousif was critically wounded. Pir Hassan Seilki, Sa'id Mohammed Seilki, Ismail Khan Barzani, and Ali Bedaroni were martyred. This was the Barzanis' last battle against the Iranian army. They succeeded in preventing it from reaching the border and closing the road to Iraq. Mohammed Khalid Barzani assisted his uncle, Mustafa Barzani, in these battles. It is worth mentioning here that the residents of Margavar, Doshtabil, and Oshnoviyeh provided all of the assistance they could to the Barzanis up to the last minute.

The Martyrdom of Qazi Mohammed

Qazi Mohammed, Sayf Qazi, and Sadr Qazi were tried before a military court established in Mahabad and were sentenced to death. They were executed on the morning of March 31, 1947.

The Iranians carried out the sentences, when it seemed to them that they had eliminated all danger. With the tribes having surrendered and having proclaimed their allegiance, and the Barzanis on their way to Iraq, there was no deterrence to stop them from committing this horrible crime, which left every Kurd injured forever, an affront carved into the national psyche of the striving Kurds and of Kurdistan.

Barzani recorded the following words in his diary on April 2, 1947, in Arabic: "I received the news of the martyrdom of the *Peshawa*,[6] Mohammed Husain, and Sadr Qazi. 'To God we belong and to Him we shall return.' "[7]

Chapter 23

The Return to Iraq

With the roads closed, the Barzanis had to abandon their plan of escape to the Soviet Union. They were certain that they could not walk the long and dangerous road ahead. The tribal chiefs were ambivalent in their support, and the Iraqi government had insisted on their unconditional surrender. They had no choice but to submit to God's will and wait for their fate to unfold. Barzani families moved first toward the Gader River on the border. By April 10, all civilians had converged on one designated point protected from the rear by their fighters.

Ali Hijazi, the director general of the Iraqi police, was waiting on the Iraqi side of the Gader River. Sheikh Ahmed met him to arrange the reception of the families, while Hijazi insisted that Sheikh Ahmad and Barzani surrender together before the families crossed into Iraq. Sheikh Ahmad insisted that Mulla Mustafa Barzani be with the fighters at the end. Families began streaming into Iraq. There, captured Iranian officers were released, and both 75-mm cannons were destroyed.

On April 15, in an emotional farewell, Mulla Mustafa left his brother Sheikh Ahmad, his family, and friends. With 560 of his elite fighters, he left for an unknown future, expecting the worst of fate, even death. This was his last farewell because the majority of civilians, women, and children crossed into Iraq with Sheikh Ahmad. Barzani and his men split off from the rest in a separation that was to last for more than 11 years.

Barzani maintained that he had tried to persuade the Iraqi Kurdish officers to stay with him, since their situation was completely different from that of the rest. Only Mir Haj Ahmad and Abd al-Rahman Mufti agreed, whereas Izzat Abd al-Aziz, Mustafa Khoshnaw, Mohammed Mahmud Qudsi, and Khairullah Abd al-Karim insisted on returning to Iraq. Bakr Abd al-Karim, Nuri Ahmad Taha, Jalal Amin, and Mohammed Salih chose a different course, i.e., to return home secretly. They escaped death, whereas the other four officers were martyred when the regent broke his pledge to pardon them, or at least not to execute them. There are some who believe that the regent yielded to pressure from Salih Jabr's cabinet, which insisted on their execution.

The four officers, Izzat Abd al-Aziz, Mustafa Khoshnaw, Khairullah Abd al-Karim, and Mohammed Mahmud Qudsi, were executed on June 19, 1947, a day etched into the Kurdish conscience and the history of Kurdistan as Martyrs' Day. Today, the four martyrs are the eternal symbol of faith and sacrifice for the Kurds and Kurdistan.

In his book, *Ma'sat Barzan al-Mazluma* (The Tragedy of Oppressed Barzan), the late Maruf Chiawuk (1954, p. 200) states the following:

After the four officers were executed and the Barzanis sent to southern Iraq, I met the British Advisor to the [Iraqi] Ministry of the Interior, Mr. Dejiron, or as he was called, Chief of Administrative Inspectors, who asked me what I thought about the hanging of the four officers. "Why ask me after their death? People are still mourning for their young lives!" I answered him. He paused, then said, "By executing them, Salih Jabr's Cabinet committed two grave miscalculations: First, our laws and traditions preclude the execution of the penitent who pleads for mercy once he has avowed contrition and pledged allegiance. Second, it has intensely embittered and agitated the Kurds, a feeling that will never die."

He then asked me: "Do you know why the Regent was upset with Mulla Mustafa [Barzani]?" "No," I replied. "Because he wore the uniform of a Russian general," he said. I answered, "Perhaps the British themselves were upset more than the Regent. What else could he have done? He was chased out of his country, Iran hunted him, and Turkey did not accept him. Could he have returned Stalin's present? If he had done this, where could he have gone? He neither had wings to fly, nor was he a fish to disappear in the sea." I continued, "Believe me, if the government had pardoned him, he would have preferred, despite all its injustice, to return and wear a simple soldier's uniform." The British man justly said, "This man is a hero whose name will be recorded in history in letters of gold along with the names of world heroes." I rose and left.

Chapter 24

Barzani's Speech at the Crossing

Barzani and his comrades remained close to the border until the last family had crossed into Diyana. He crossed the border and entered Iraq on April 19, 1947, heading for Khwakork by way of Nazdari Daghi. He gathered his men and told them:

> We will enter Iraq and move to the northern part of Barzan. Certainly, the Iraqi regime will put together all it can to fight us: regular troops, mercenaries, and supplies. Furthermore, Iraq may seek the assistance of Iran and Turkey to eradicate us. We must avoid confrontation as much as possible because we do not have the strategic depth we need to resist; we have neither the place nor the capacity to care for our wounded, or to meet our own needs. The only ammunition we have is what each of you carries on your back. Therefore, we must be extremely cautious, and I will try to contact the Iraqi government. Perhaps we can come to an acceptable solution, although I doubt it. If we do not, then we will think of another solution.
>
> Brothers, I am moving towards an unknown fate. I do not know if I will die of hunger, cold, or an enemy bullet. In our situation, death is the likely fate. However, God is mightier than all our enemies. I rely on Him, and thus, I am resolved on defiance. You may remain with me if you feel you can endure the hardship and fate. If you are unsure, you may return and surrender. I will always be thankful for all the sacrifices you have generously given.

No one broke ranks. They all answered with one voice, saying that they would stand with him, preferring death to life without him. Later, on April 19, 1947, Barzani crossed into Iraq and through Nazdari Daghi to Khwakork.

Barzani Reorganizes His Forces

Barzani divided his force into five groups and appointed five commanders: Sheikh Sulayman, As'ad Khoshavi, Mamand Maseeh, Mohammed Amin Mirkhan, and Mustafa Mirozi. They moved toward the Mizori region and arrived on April 25, 1947. The day before they arrived, they were ambushed by a police and a *jash* (mercenary) force near the village of Zeit, where a policeman was killed and a *jash* was captured. Teili Abd al-Karim Kiliti was martyred in this ambush.

Negotiating with the Government

Having assigned his forces among the nearby villages, Barzani personally went to the village of Argosh, where he initiated contact with the Iraqi government.

On April 23, the latter sent Police Adjutant Ali Beg Wali and Wali Ibrahim Hasini, informing Barzani of the government's response, namely, that Iraq had agreed to Barzani's unconditional return. However, the government promised not to execute him based on the verdict of 1945.[1] Otherwise, the government would take all necessary measures. At the same time, they informed him of the condition of the returnees. They told him that Sheikh Ahmad, the rest of his men, and their families were in a makeshift camp in Diyana, surrounded by barbed wire and guarded by a huge force. No one was allowed to leave or enter the camp without a government permit.

Ali Beg told Barzani of government preparations to wage an all-out attack on the region if he failed to surrender. He also told him that he was sad because, "I am afraid that you and your men may face a fate similar to that of Khalil Khoshavi at the hands of Kurdish traitors." Barzani replied, "God willing, thousands of traitors will be killed before a single one of my men gets killed." Ali Beg returned with Barzani's reply: He would never surrender, and he would never return unconditionally.

I found the following letter written in Arabic among Barzani's papers. The writer is unknown, but the contents indicate that it was from one of the tribal chiefs:

> Greetings and regards: If all Kurdish tribal chiefs were to gather in one place and you, with your men, were to meet them there; that is, if you were to give yourself and your men up to those whom you trust among the Kurdish chiefs, then they would all go with you to the government and say, "We are all with Mustafa Barzani; if you punish him, you are punishing us all." According to the government, you will only be exiled for a while, as Sa'id Agha[2] says, and he has just returned from Baghdad after meeting the Arabs and others.[3]

The Mobilization of Troops

After Ali Beg returned with Barzani's firm response, the government began mobilizing troops, assisted by tribal chiefs as usual. It was like a general mobilization. In a three-pronged advance, forces moved from Shirwan in the east, from the Rekan region to Royi Shin[4] in the west, and from Aqra toward Barzan and Mount Shirin in the south.

Coordination was under way with Iran and Turkey to support the Iraqi forces. Small clashes occurred on the Shirwan Front; there Corporal Abd al-Rahman Khoshnaw and Aziz Zrari were martyred, and Wasman Mergasuri was wounded. A number of troops and mercenaries were killed, and the traitor Mohammed Amin Shivi was blinded in one eye.

The government issued warrants against Sheikh Ahmad Barzani, his brothers Mohammed Siddique and Babo, his sons Mohammed Khalid and Jamal, and his nephews. They were taken from Diyana camp and jailed in Arbil to await court-martial.

Chapter 25

The Historic Final Decision

Barzani told me that when he left Sheikh Ahmad on April 15, 1947, he had gotten his approval to escape to the Soviet Union if he could no longer sustain resistance inside Iraq. Thus, his historic final decision came on May 6, 1947, when he gathered his forces in Argosh. He told them of his decision to depart for the Soviet Union and the reason that compelled him to make the decision.

Although some felt that reaching the Soviet Union was more of an imaginary goal than a realistic one, no more than 50 partisans decided to split off and surrender to the government.

Chronology of the March

The Iraqi forces were ordered to gradually move toward Harki Binajé. On May 22, 1947, all forces had converged on the villages of Dari, Basiya, Stoni, and others. Spies had informed the Iraqi government that Barzani was in the village of Dari. Two squadrons of airplanes pounded Dari on May 23, 1947; some said that it was the most intense bombing they had ever sustained. Tamu Mustafa Binavi and Taha Aziz Espindari were martyred; 14 others were wounded.

On May 24, 1947, the forces reached the village of Bedaw, the last Iraqi village on the Turkish border. The two wounded men, Salih Husain Gozi and Hamo Hizani, were in critical condition. Unable to carry them along, Barzani asked the village chief, Khwasti, to transport them to Shirwan and turn them in to the government. At the moment of farewell, the injured Salih held the hand of his brother, Salim, and hugged him, and they both cried. As'ad Khoshavi signaled to Salim to move. Salim replied, "How could I leave my brother behind?" As'ad told him, "All these are your brothers; trust in God and get up." Salim stood up, and they all burst into tears.

Before leaving Bedaw, Barzani explained his plan to his men and assigned the group led by Misto Mirozi to spearhead their forces, followed by the group led by Mamand Maseeh, then that led by Mohammed Amin Mirkhan, then that led by Sheikh Sulayman, and finally, As'ad Khoshavi's group, which was assigned the task of assisting and carrying along anyone who might stay behind for one reason or another.

They left Bedaw Village on May 25, 1947, along the rough terrain and snow-covered mountain road of Tasta-Bedaw. The first group climbed their way up mountains as high as 3,000 meters above sea level by creating snow steps using the butts of their rifles. This allowed the groups following to carry the sick and wounded on their backs and on rudimentary stretchers. That evening, they reached the village of Bye in Turkish Kurdistan. The villagers received them with the utmost warmth and generosity. The village—no more than 20 houses— offered them all it possibly could. Having learned the shortest and safest road to the Iranian border from the village chief, Barzani, assisted by guides from Bye, took the Zinya Asingara Road, through the districts of Gavar and Shamdinan. On their way, a Barzani vanguard found Turkish troops fortifying in their positions to prevent the partisans from crossing the border. The Barzanis hid in a thicket of the forest near the headspring of the Great Zab, known as Nahaila Gavari. Turkish reconnaissance planes surveyed the area but could not find a trace of them, as they were so well covered.

Barzani narrated this story about misleading the Turkish troops when they crossed the border:

> We moved across from the Turkish troops and let them feel our presence there. As they prepared to ambush us, I ordered our forces to move eastward but to halt at dusk. Under the cover of darkness, they moved back to the same location they had left during the day. I moved back with a small force, leading the Turks to believe that we changed our direction, and that we would be crossing at a point to the east of that location. When we observed the Turkish movements, we saw they were confused, and two hours later, they packed up and moved swiftly to ambush us at the eastern crossing point. I knew that they vacated their initial position. On May 27, 1947, we crossed Ziniya Asingara at dawn, leaving the Turkish troops behind. By the time they found out, we were already at the top of Mount Spiraiz. They fired aimlessly and by the time Turkish planes arrived, we had already crossed into Iran. They returned disappointed.

On the evening of May 27, our entire force entered Jarme, the first Iranian village on the border. After having a meal, the force moved to the region of Begzadeh in Targavar in the morning and went to the villages of Anbi, Darband, and Tiloy. The tribal chiefs had fled to Urmia for fear of retribution because of their earlier behavior. The Barzani forces were strictly instructed not to disturb anyone or take anything by force, not even a loaf of bread.

The Barzanis spent May 29–31 at the summer resorts of the Harkis, where they were met with a generous reception. The Iranian government had called on the tribal chiefs for consultation about Barzani's intentions and ways to eradicate him, and asked for a volunteer to relay a letter from the Iranian government to him. Rashid Beg, chief of the Harki tribe, volunteered. The letter basically wanted to know Barzani's intentions and the reason for his return to Iran and to warn him to leave Iran immediately. Barzani told them that he would reply in writing in a few days. He never did.

Barzani often told us the story of meeting Mulla Bedr and Mulla Haider from the village of Khangei (Khanaqah), about their love and sympathy, and above all about the assistance the Barzanis received from them and their villages. He remembered the pair of socks that Mulla Haider had given him, which came in very handy during his trip.

I did not know anything about Mulla Haider or his identity until 1979, when a few Khangei residents, along with the imam of their village mosque, chanced to come visit me. After I welcomed them, the imam told me the story of Barzani's going through their village and that he had given him a pair of socks. I remembered Barzani's story and immediately confirmed that he was Mulla Haider, now an old man in his seventies.

In the Harki region, Muhyeddin Babazadeh from the village of Balanish and Lafko (Dawood Youkhana), an Iranian, joined the Barzanis. The former died in the Soviet Union and the latter remained loyal and returned with them.

On May 31, the Barzanis left the Harki region. Passing through Basiro village, they moved to the Shikak area, where they spent the next two days. The warmth and generosity exhibited by the villagers are worth mentioning here. Misty-eyed, the villagers lined up along the roadside, outside every village, welcoming the Barzanis and offering them water, yogurt, and food. The expression of these sincere feelings by simple Kurdish villagers was the source of much relief and comfort to the Barzanis. In dire need, they were able to bathe and rest. Simko Agha's uncle, known as Uncle Mirzi, volunteered ample information about the road, the tribal and village chiefs, and their loyalties and connections, as he knew them well. Grateful members of the Barzani force remembered the favors done them by the Shikaks, especially by Mr. Ado, a relative of Ismail Agha (Simko) in the village of Dostan.

On June 3, 1947, they left the village of Dostan, passing through the villages of Dilzi, Haji Jifan, and Goza Rash. In Haji Jifan, a young man named Sayyed Kamal offered them the warmest hospitality, contrary to the position taken by the village chief, Qurtas Agha, who had fled to Selmas. In Goza Rash, a man named Sartip offered them all that they needed. Living members of the Barzani force still remember the young man, whose overwhelming care and sincerity captivated all as he moved from house to house, checking and making sure that their needs were met. Among the Shikaks who joined the march were Bejan Jundi, Timor Musa, Kamil Dhulumat, Omer Husain, and Ibrahim Jalal. That same day, Iranian planes began reconnaissance sorties.

On the way, someone from the force took some canned dates from a village store without paying for them. In tears, the store owner waited for Barzani and told him about it. Barzani paid him 18 dinars, which exceeded the price of the dates. He then assembled the force and warned them that he would severely punish anyone who committed such crimes.

After a short rest in Goza Rash, they went on to the village of Filaran. Their reception in this village is well remembered. They praised the villagers for their caring, love, and concern. Of them, they especially remembered Timor Rash Teili and his son, Siddique. At midnight, they reached the village of Brosh Khoran, where the regional judge, Khalifa Sadiq, quickly came to meet Barzani. An agent of the Iranian government, he plotted against Barzani. Treacherously, he expressed his sincerity for the Kurds and Kurdistan, and said that he had accepted the Iranian offer because of his concern for Barzani. He came to inform him that the Iranian government had sent large forces and closed all roads. Sadiq added that although Iran had the resources, it was, for humanitarian reasons, willing to treat the wounded, send food and other necessities, and agreed to let Barzani stay in the area. Therefore, he wanted Barzani to designate a location where he could receive assistance and a medical team to treat the wounded.

With Khalifa Sadiq was a man named Ali, who approached one of Barzani's aides and told him the truth about Khalifa Sadiq. He wanted the aide to inform Barzani immediately that the Iranian force was not ready, and the government wanted to delay them at any cost; that there were no Iranian forces on the road except for a few armed Ajams [sic] in the valley of Qatoor, and it was better not to wait. Barzani learned the story and continued to behave as if he believed Khalifa Sadiq. Barzani thanked Khalifa and asked him to pick a suitable location where he could stay in the village and wait for him to return.

Believing that his plot had worked, Khalifa Sadiq quickly returned to the city of Khoy and informed the Iranians. The shah was touring Azerbaijan at the time and pressured his military commanders to close all roads and exterminate the Barzanis.

As soon as Khalifa Sadiq had left, Barzani called his commanders and asked them to carry along enough bread and supplies, as they had a long and difficult road ahead, and he told them that they had to cross the Qatoor Valley during the night of June 4, before dawn. Barzani was familiar with the geography of the area and knew that they had to ambush the force in Qatoor Valley because there was no room for maneuvering. Gaining the initiative in a surprise attack, he decided to remove the Iranian force in the valley. To avoid a point between Brosh Khoran and the valley, they had to take a detour into Turkish territory for several hours and return to Iran. They crossed the Qatoor Valley without incident because the Iranian force assigned to guard the valley had fled to avoid a clash with the Barzanis.

In reality, crossing the Qatoor Valley was, in effect, a brilliant military victory because it was the most dangerous point on their way. The Barzanis could have sustained heavy losses if they had been ambushed, and perhaps it would have changed the whole march as we know it today.

On the morning of June 5, 1947, they entered the region of the Arusi tribe, which rendered all the assistance and fulfilled their national duty. The grateful Barzanis recalled the residents of the Galati, Todan, and Nada villages, especially Kocho Agha Ali Beg, Bali Beg, and Bahri Beg of Nada. On June 6, they left Nada and reached the villages of Bala Soor and Bala Rash, where they were warmly welcomed, notably by Mulla Ma'mi, the head of the two villages. After a meal and short respite, they continued to the summer resort of Haji Beg Jameel, which was described by a visitor as heavenly. In the evening, they reached the village of Malhami, within the region of the Millali tribe, and spent the night there.

On June 7, they reached the village of Ambari, where they found a very honest and loyal man who knew the area all the way to the Soviet border. His name was Mirza Abdi. Despite his age, (he was then 70), he was strong and vigorous. Barzani asked him about the best road to the Araxes River. Mirza Abdi recommended the Mako–Hason Road. It would have been difficult to walk any other road, especially when in Turkey, where roads were rugged and fraught with peril. Barzani thought well of his recommendation and followed it. The next stage was decisive and risky; therefore, they had to plan carefully. On June 8, they left Ambari and reached the villages of Kilis Kand and Agh Dash near Mako. Both villages were deserted because the residents had fled to Mako, leaving behind all of their food and furniture.

The Decisive Phase

Large Iranian forces reached Mako, supported by tanks and artillery. They controlled all of the roads. Undoubtedly, the fate of the Barzanis depended on the results of the battle that awaited them. Hence, they fought their best to win.

Barzani divided his men into two forces, reconnoitered the area, and confirmed the Iranian positions. He decided to lead a suicide charge. Assisted by Mohammed Amin Mirkhan, Mamand Maseeh, and Misto Jadir Mirozi, he personally led a strike force from Kilis Gand. Assisted by Salih Kaniya Lanji and Sa'id Wali Beg, As'ad Khoshavi led the other force from Agh Dash. The attack on Iranian forces in Mako plain and Mount Sousoz on June 9, 1947, continued nonstop until June 11. Despite the ferocity and brutality of the battle, it seemed that nothing could get in the way of strong will and earnest faith. By virtue of their heroism, the Barzanis went down in history as defeating the much larger and better-equipped Iranian forces. Iranian military commanders had gathered their best forces to prevent Barzani and his men from reaching the Soviet Union and to exterminate them. They had selected the battlefield for its suitability for aerial and tank bombardment. They believed that they had Barzani in their grip and that this time he would not be able to escape.

At last the Barzanis shook the Iranian forces and moved them from the Mako bridge; then they crossed the Zangi River on June 11, 1947 at night. They reached the village of Hasoon on the morning of June 12, believing that they were out of danger, at least for a few days. The Iranian forces lost hundreds on the battlefield, and 271 were captured but were released as soon as the fighting ended. Several tanks were disabled, an airplane was downed, and an artillery battery was destroyed. Hundreds of guns and 50 mules loaded with food and supplies were seized. The animals were very useful in transporting the wounded. Mil Liri, Haji Guazi, Mohammed Mulla Mohammed Mergasuri, and Salih Liri were martyred; 14 others were injured.

Omer Agha Jalali, chief of the Kurdish Jalali tribe, received Barzani in the village of Hasoon, north of Mako and within the domain of the Jalali tribe. He promised to provide all the help he could, but he did not keep his pledge. He betrayed them and brought the Iranian forces to surprise them. This traitor was so full of antipathy that he ordered his men to return from their summer resorts so as not to provide for the Barzanis. Of all the tribes that the Barzanis came across in their march to the Soviet Union, it is worth stating here that this tribe and its chief were the only ones who compromised their patriotic duty.

Crossing the Araxes River

On June 16, 1947, Mir Haj Ahmad went to the Soviet Sarachilo[1] police station to inform the Soviet authorities that Barzani and his comrades had arrived at the village of Soketli, that they were seeking asylum, and wanted permission to cross the Araxes River.[2] Permission was granted, and Sheikh Sulayman crossed with a group on June 17, 1947. Barzani and another group crossed on June 18, 1947. The name Araxes entered the Kurdish culture, and to this day Kurds name their boys Araxes after it.

In his work *Diwani Paramerd*, the immortal Kurdish poet and philosopher, Piramerd, wrote his famous poem "Ashrat Hawara" ("Alas, ye people!") on this occasion.[3] News agencies and radio stations carried the news of Barzani's arrival with his comrades to the Soviet Union. A London radio broadcast reported it in the following manner:

London—*June 17, 1947*—In a great battle, the Iranian army clashed with the Kurds near the Russian border, and the Kurdish leader Mulla Mustafa Barzani and his followers of 2,000 fighters were able to cross to the Russian border.

London—*June 19, 1947*—The four officers were executed in Baghdad, while Mulla Mustafa Barzani miraculously escaped the trap and reached Russia unharmed.

Chapter 26

In the Soviet Union

When he entered the Soviet Union, Mulla Mustafa Barzani was taken to a place in Nakhchevan, Soviet Armenia. The rest of his group were packed in an open camp, surrounded by barbed wire and soldiers. They were not permitted to leave the camp and were each given a daily ration of 500 grams of bread and a bowl of soup. They were treated exactly like prisoners of war; each one was interrogated singly. The wounded were to be taken to a hospital for treatment.

The group did not know of Barzani's fate until July 3, when a Russian officer took Mir Haj Ahmad out in his car and returned him in the evening; this was repeated for three days. During the first two days, Mir Haj did not speak to anyone, appearing to be sad and distressed. On the third day, he seemed to be relaxed and happier. He told the group that he had been taken to where Barzani stayed, as he was very ill. Barzani was convalescing and would be visiting the camp soon, Mir Haj told his comrades.

On July 12, 1947, Barzani visited the camp, accompanied by a number of Soviet officials. They learned firsthand of the miserable conditions at the camp. Officials ordered the barbed wire to be removed, better meals to be served, and other camp conditions to be improved.

The Transfer to Azerbaijan

The Barzanis stayed in the camp for about 40 days. They were then transferred to the Soviet Republic of Azerbaijan.[1] They were assigned to Aghdam, Lachin, and Ayolagh. Barzani, Sheikh Sulayman, Ali Mohammed Siddique, Sa'id Mulla Abdullah, and Ziyab Dari were sent to the city of Shush. All endured this separation until the end of that year.

On September 29, 1947, Barzani was transferred to Baku, where Azeri officials met with him several times. It appeared that up until that time the issue of asylum had been under consideration in Moscow. Barzani sent several letters and memoranda to officials in Moscow and Baku, including Stalin and Baqirov (see Document no. 16). He stated the reasons why he and his companions had come to the Soviet Union and set down his observations and requests.

The Meeting of Barzani and Baqirov

Baqirov received Barzani for the first time in late November of 1947. More meetings followed. Barzani described the meetings in his diary:

> When Baqirov received me, I told him, "We are an extremely oppressed people. We put our hopes in the peoples of the Soviet Union. We need military knowledge and training. On behalf of the Kurdish people, I appeal to you to support and assist us, to espouse the cause of the people of Kurdistan. I hope that you relay this message to the higher command in Moscow."

The Barzanis first learned that Barzani was in Baku when the authorities arranged for Mir Haj Ahmad and Sulayman Beg to visit him in October. It seems that Moscow had instructed Baku to respect the Barzanis as freedom fighters, to reunite them, and to further their education and training. Under Moscow's orders, the government of Azerbaijan sent Sheikh Sulayman with Asadov, an Azeri official, on December 12, 1947, to visit the Barzanis and notify them to prepare to move to Baku.

The Barzanis in Baku

On December 9, 1947, Barzani inspected the camp designated for the Barzanis in Baku. On December 10, all the Barzanis were brought to Baku, as the camp was furnished and complete. Accompanied by General Atakshiyouv, Barzani visited the camp on December 22, 1947. After a few days of rest, the Barzanis were organized into a regiment under the command of As'ad Khoshavi. Sa'id Wali Beg, Mohammed Amin Mirkhan, Mamand Maseeh, and Misto Mirozi were appointed company commanders. The government of Azerbaijan appointed Lt. Colonel Kazimov, who was in Mahabad and was known as Kaka Agha, to take charge of training. He was assisted by the following officers: Abdullah Quliyov, Karimov, Mirmanov, Zainalov, Mohammedov, and Sharinov.

The Barzanis were given military uniforms and weapons, and training began for eight hours a day, in addition to four hours for learning to read and write Kurdish. Literate Barzanis were appointed to teach Kurdish to the rest. In addition to their vast experience in guerilla warfare, they acquired regular military training. They also learned to read and write Kurdish, and everything went well.

That the Soviets paid the Barzanis such attention and gave them this opportunity was of great significance. This was within the framework of a more comprehensive strategy to support the Kurdish liberation movement and to prepare these men to meet the opportune moment. Very important political measures ensued.

The Political Step: Forming a Political Leadership

On January 19, 1948, Kurds from Iraq and Iran held a conference in Baku. In a historic speech, Barzani outlined a program for struggle (for the full text of the speech, see Document no. 18). A political leadership for the Kurdish national movement was elected from among Iraqi and Iranian Kurds. Of the Iraqi Kurds were Mustafa Barzani, President; Sheikh Sulayman Barzani; Ali Mohammed Siddique; Mir Haj Ahmad Aqrawi; Sulayman Beg Dargala; Abd al-Rahman Mufti al-Imadi; and Mohammed Najib Barwari.

And of the Iranian Kurds were Sayyed Aziz Sayyed Abdullah; Rahim Qazi; Mustafa Selmasi; Hassan Husami; Rahman Garmiyani; Sayyed Karim; and Kak Murad.

It was also decided to broadcast a Kurdish program from Radio Baku and to publish a Kurdish newspaper. This initiative revived hopes of continuing the Kurdish national struggle, which had suffered a devastating blow with the collapse of the Mahabad Republic. It steeled the resolve of the refugees who felt that they had not languished and endured all of those hardships in vain and that the Soviet Union would adhere to its principles of supporting the struggles of oppressed peoples for their legitimate rights. These measures inspired them to work enthusiastically and tirelessly in anticipation of the moment when they would be called on to return to liberate the Kurdish homeland.

Terrified, the Iranian regime strongly protested the Soviet's having allowed Barzani and his comrades into the Soviet Union and demanded their surrender. The Soviet government rejected the Iranian demands. The protest was documented in a letter from the Iranian prime minister to the Soviet ambassador to Iran, dated 14 *Behman* 1326 (January 13, 1949), Document no. 12-3 in the archives of the Iranian Foreign Ministry (see Document no. 17).

Racist and arrogant, Baqirov tried to dominate the Kurdish political leadership by appending it to an Azeri leadership established in a similar manner. He employed the same tactics used with Qazi Mohammed and his delegation and the Kurdish Republic in their relations with the Iranian Republic of Azerbaijan. Barzani resisted Baqirov's pressure and refused to yield, which angered Baqirov. He read it as a challenge to his authority.

Baqirov enjoyed special privileges with Stalin, through his friend, the Interior Minister Lavrenti Beria,[2] as Baqirov was a close assistant to the latter. In a meeting, Baqirov threatened Barzani, telling him to accept his recommendations, or he would bear the responsibility for the consequences. Barzani replied,

> Comrade Baqirov, we did not come here for you to threaten us. If we were to yield to threats, you would not see us here. We came here to put the cause of the oppressed people of Kurdistan before the peoples of the Soviet Union, to defend our honor and the dignity of our people. Please understand that we will not submit to threats. We emphatically will not accept to be appended to a people who [is] no better than ours, even if it is the people of Azerbaijan, whom we consider a friend and a brother. We are an independent people and not a part of Azerbaijan. We will not accept the obliteration of the identity of the Kurdish people.

It is worthwhile to point out that members of the political leadership of the Iranian Kurds betrayed their duty to the nation and played a shameful role. They became agents of Baqirov and his secret apparatus. He used them as he wished and prodded them into causing subversion, strife, and discord. This stormy meeting between Barzani and Baqirov marked the beginning of a new tragedy for Barzani and his comrades and put an end to the political leadership, which disintegrated after those opportunists withdrew from it, declaring their allegiance to the Azeris and their blind obedience to Baqirov.

Chapter 27

The Move to the Republic of Uzbekistan: New Suffering

B aqirov's vendetta with Barzani did not end. Unable to bear it, Barzani asked Soviet authorities to transfer him and all the Barzanis to another republic to escape Baqirov's malice. Hence, they were transferred to the camp of Charchok near Tashkent, the capital of Uzbekistan, on August 29, 1948. Their training continued as planned. Barzani was given a house near the camp and a teacher to teach him Russian. In this stable environment, Barzani learned to read and write Russian fluently. On September 24, 1948, Barzani met both Yenazov, the secretary general of the Uzbek Communist Party, and Yousipov, the Uzbek prime minister. Both promised him their regard and support. Close to Stalin, Beria and his gang, Baqirov's rancor ended only when he had swayed Moscow to follow his anti-Barzani scheme.

The Agonizing Trip

On March 13, 1949, a Soviet general arrived in Tashkent and informed Barzani that he would be flown on a special plane to Moscow to meet Stalin and other Soviet leaders. The general asked Barzani to designate two individuals to accompany him on the trip. He chose Sa'id Mulla Abdullah and Ziyab Dori. They were taken to the airport that evening and were full of anticipation and optimism, which unfortunately soon turned to great sadness and sorrow. What awaited them was far more harsh and more bitter than what they had already undergone.

The plane did not go to Moscow. Instead, it went to Chambai, a town on Lake Ural. It was more of a forced deportation and exile than anything else. The following day, Sheikh Sulayman, Ali Mohammed Siddique, Sulayman Beg Dargala, Mohammed Najib, and Abd al-Rahman Mufti were to join Barzani. Instead, they were taken to Samarkand. Soviet authorities did the same with the rest of the Barzani leaders and scattered them around the vast Soviet land under the pretext of transferring them to new training camps. As'ad Khoshavi, Mohammed Amin Mirkhan, Mamand Maseeh, Misto Mirozi, Sheikhomer Shanadari, Ali Khalil, Mohammed Mahmud, Murad Sheikho, Sa'id Wali Beg, Haji Haider, Sa'id Balani, Isa Swar, and Faqi Hassan Idilbi[1] were taken on a plane to Moynak Island, in the middle of Lake Ural. Once their leaders had been relocated, the rest of the Barzanis were transported by train, in which a precise order was used to distribute them among the cars. In that order, a car was detached from the engine and left at a designated station until the last one stopped where no group knew what had happened to the rest of their comrades.

Later, they learned that each group had been assigned to a village or a town where they were under surveillance in collective factories and farms, better known as kolkhozes. They were treated as prisoners and sentenced to hard labor. They were not allowed to contact one another or to know one another's whereabouts or addresses. Their treatment was harsh and cruel, without any regard to humanitarian principles or to the obligations of a host.

These heroes were so isolated from the outside world and subjected to such a total news blackout that some of the world's most prominent newspapers could only speculate as to their fate. For example, at the time when Barzani and his companions were suffering the agony of deportation and exile, the *New York Times* reported that he had been awarded the rank of general in the Soviet army and that he was commanding a division amassed on the Iranian–Soviet border.

Chapter 28

Strikes and Protests

Despite strict surveillance, numerous incidents of harassment, and attempts to instill pessimism and hopelessness among Barzanis, they remained united, loyal to their leader, and faithful to their principles. Keeping faith led them to undertake protests and sit-ins, and to defy police suppression. Officials in Uzbekistan were astounded at the Barzanis' defiance, protests, and resistance to the secret police, all acts that were considered unforgivable crimes, punishable by death, in Stalin's time. Other than the Barzanis, none had defied the Communist authorities. The Uzbek officials were captivated by the idea that all acts of defiance centered on one demand: "We want Barzani." This tenacious conflict continued until 1951. There is nothing that can portray Barzani's state of mind and his concern about his companions better than the two lines of Persian poetry that he jotted down in his diary on November 4, 1949:

Had I once dreamed of the sorrow
  of the day when we would part
I would not have let one dream
  of a friendship enter my heart.

Facts are facts, despite attempts to nullify or obscure them. Baqirov's villainy in Azerbaijan and Yousipov's in Uzbekistan vis-à-vis the Barzanis remain worse than the villainy committed by the British occupiers and the native agents in Iraq, and perhaps their conduct toward the Soviet Union itself was the worst. Their inhuman treatment of the Barzanis harmed the reputation of the great Soviet Union, which declared itself the defender of oppressed peoples languishing under the yoke of imperialism. According to its constitution, the country's doors are open to welcome refugees struggling for liberation and for principles.

In modern history, the Barzani asylum-seekers were undeniably the first test of the Soviet treatment of refugees after the October Revolution. Friends and foes around the world had their eye on how the Soviets would treat these 500 freedom fighters who had endured severe hardship to reach their promised land, as they imagined the Soviet land. Yet, the frantic endeavors of Baqirov and Yousipov dispersed these heroes and dealt with them as undesirable intruders. They were coerced into hard-labor camps, prevented from seeing each other and driven into exile in a manner that brings to mind the Nazi trains that carried prisoners to hard labor and death camps.

Barzani was harassed in his new exile, Chambai, and barred from contacting officials. However, he never despaired. His sense of responsibility never allowed for fatalism. He asked an acquaintance who was traveling to Moscow to mail a detailed letter he had written to Stalin directly, elaborating on their condition. This was the only letter that reached the Kremlin, of the many that he had mailed in town and were confiscated by the local authorities.

Moscow Intervenes

The letter was effective, and a committee was established in Moscow to investigate the conditions of the Barzani refugees. The committee began investigations in March 1951, visiting almost all of the groups and questioning them about their repeated strikes, which often coincided, and how they had organized despite strict measures barring them from communication. The common answer was that they had come with Barzani to defend Kurdish national rights, and they wanted their leader with them.

The committee returned to Moscow with its findings. It appears that they learned how the officials of Azerbaijan and Uzbekistan were, in reality, mistreating the Barzanis and subjecting them to harsh measures. Perhaps, a report was submitted to the highest levels at the Kremlin. As a result, late in August of 1951, Mr. Vinogradov was dispatched to Tashkent with clear instructions to gather the Barzanis from their various places of exile, improve their conditions, and open a new chapter in dealing with them.

Chapter 29

The Barzanis Reunited

Upon his arrival in Tashkent, the first thing that Mr. Vinogradov did was to send a private plane to bring Barzani back from exile on September 1, 1951. Vinogradov received Barzani warmly, apologized, and said that Moscow regretted what had happened and had decided to review the Barzanis' circumstances. He enumerated the strikes Barzani's companions had staged there and how the authorities had ignored them, although in the eyes of the law this was considered a criminal offense. The deportation and suffering they had endured had been taken into consideration. He asked Barzani to write reassuring letters to the deportees and to inform them that decisive measures would be taken shortly to reunite them and to improve their appallingly wretched living conditions, which they had not anticipated.

Special planes transported Sheikh Sulayman and his comrades from Samarkand, and As'ad Khoshavi and his friends from the Moynak Island to Tashkent. Other groups continued to be brought in until all arrived in late November of 1951.

Barzani was given a residence in a Tashkent suburb while the rest were given comfortable residential units in the town of Vrivisky, which is about 50 km [30 miles] from Tashkent. A government cooperative center was established to provide all necessities, the elderly were allotted monthly stipends, and the younger people were allowed to attend schools and colleges.

The Barzanis were reunited with their leader, Mulla Mustafa Barzani, after two long years. Reunification was completed, and an era of tremendous suffering was brought to an end. After years of turmoil and migration, for the first time they enjoyed a taste of stability and peace. They exchanged stories of their good and bad days. Students went to school, peasants returned to agricultural jobs, and some Barzani men married Soviet women.

Chapter 30

Barzani's Trip to Moscow

Stalin's death in May of 1953 ushered in a new era of détente in the Soviet Union. Heavy police surveillance was lifted somewhat, and police powers and horrible suppressive measures were curtailed. Soon after these political changes, Barzani decided to travel to Moscow in an attempt to meet with the new Soviet leadership and present the cause of his people to expand it beyond the confines of Azerbaijan and Uzbekistan. A complex and important liberation cause such as that of the liberation of a people of great numbers like the Kurds was too big to be adopted by one or two of the republics in the Soviet Union alone. Known for his courage, spontaneity, and forthright manner, Barzani headed straight for the Kremlin as soon as he arrived in Moscow. At the Kremlin information desk, he revealed his identity, saying, "I am Mulla Mustafa Barzani, and I am here to present the cause of my oppressed people to Lenin's great people and Party, which has committed itself to the principle of supporting the causes of the peoples' liberation." No doubt, the official in charge was astonished; certainly he was confronted with an unprecedented commission. At once, Barzani underwent a thorough investigation by officials who specialized in such matters. Then he was moved to a Moscow hotel and called in for questioning several times. Finally, he was admitted to the Kremlin to meet the leaders of the party and the state.

There is no doubt that Barzani was amazingly successful in presenting the cause of his people and in describing the hounding and oppression they had undergone in Azerbaijan and Uzbekistan, as Soviet officials gave him a hearing and met with him again.

At one of his meetings with [Nikita Sergeyevich] Khrushchev, the Soviet leader asked Barzani to relate everything that had happened to him and his companions from the time they had crossed into Soviet territory until his arrival in Moscow. Barzani recounted the story in detail and concluded by saying, "My comrades and I fought seven states until I managed to arrive in Moscow." Quick on the draw, Khrushchev asked him to tell him the names of those countries. Barzani answered, "America, Britain, Iraq, Turkey, Iran, Azerbaijan, and Uzbekistan." Laughing, Khrushchev asked, "How did you manage to fathom Baqirov's true character?" Barzani replied,

> We know that the Soviet Union's principles call for the support of oppressed peoples and our people head the list. Therefore, we came to the Soviet Union to present our cause to the leaders. As we entered Soviet territory in Azerbaijan and Uzbekistan we were treated in a manner atypical of Soviet values and contradictory to what Lenin

had established. Anyone upholding the reputation of a great country such as the Soviet Union would never behave as Baqirov did toward a group who had fought imperialism for the rights and liberty of their people and had sought shelter in the Soviet Union to present their cause.

Then Khrushchev said, "We are aware of the many letters you sent that were confiscated by [Lavrenti] Beria. Do not think that you alone suffered the evil of this clique. All the peoples of the Soviet Union did, and even more so." After these meetings in Moscow and Barzani's successful campaign to attract attention to the Kurdish cause, close ties based on understanding and candor developed between Barzani and officials of the state and the party.

Barzani's initiative gained him the respect of all who listened to him. The Soviets recommended that he stay in Moscow, be given a house and car, and enter the Political Academy. He was treated in a manner commensurate with his status, both in the Soviet Union and as the leader of a nation. Barzani contacted his comrades in Tashkent and assured them that he was successful in his efforts and that their conditions would soon improve further.

In fact, the Barzanis were not alone in being ill-treated and oppressed. International news reports and Khrushchev's speech before the Twentieth Congress of the Soviet Communist Party demonstrated that violations of the rights and liberties of Soviet citizens were common. Daily violations no longer surprised the Soviet citizen. Subsequently, Lavrenti Beria and his chief henchman, Baqirov, received just punishment for their crimes.[1] Therefore, it is unfair to brand the generous Soviet people because of the wrongdoings of a tyrannical, corrupt gang that oppressed them as much as they oppressed the Barzanis for a period of time.

The Soviet people gave Barzani and his companions hospitality for 12 years at a time when no other country in the world was willing to open its borders to them. The Barzanis and the Kurdish people would remain indebted to the peoples and government of the Soviet Union.

Chapter 31

Conditions of the Barzanis in Iraq

Since the conditions and sufferings of the Barzanis in the Soviet Union have been detailed, it would be useful to return briefly to the conditions of the Barzanis in Iraq. They did not escape the police and persecution, despite banishment and destitution, and all attempts by patriotic Iraqi Arab and Kurdish notables to persuade the cabinet of Salih Jabr to avert the execution of the four officers and stop deporting Barzanis to various areas of Iraq.

The British, the de facto rulers of Iraq at the time, had the last word. The Iraqi government's administration and the councils of representatives and notables were mere figureheads acting according to the dictates of the British officials. The Barzanis' defense of the Mahabad Republic outraged them, and their final escape to the Soviet Union was considered unforgivable. The British pressed the Iraqis to issue strict measures to quell the Barzanis.

After Barzani and his comrades left Kurdistan for the Soviet Union, the Iraqi regime began implementing what it had intended against the Barzanis. Sheikh Ahmad, his brothers and nephews, and other relatives were transferred to the Basra Prison. They were informed of the death-penalty verdicts of the military court of 1945 in Arbil, which had tried them in absentia. Males 18 years and older were arrested and sent to Mosul and Kirkuk prisons. The families of Sheikh Ahmad and his relatives were deported to Karbala, and the families of other Barzanis were dispersed to Arbil, Kirkuk, and Mosul provinces. Women were forced to work because their men were in prison. Sheikh Ahmad remained in prison until the July 14 Revolution.

Nuri al-Sa'id sent one of his confidants to Sheikh Ahmad to write to the Regent Abd al-Ilah, expressing his regrets and allegiance to the government and the crown, promising on behalf of the Barzani tribe to remain loyal, and asking for general amnesty. Sheikh Ahmad proudly and resolutely refused, saying, "I know that I am condemned to death, and I am ready to welcome death at this time or at any moment. I do not regret what I have done because what I have done was my religious and patriotic duty. I will not ask an agent of Britain to pardon me. I do not ask forgiveness except from God." Sheikh Ahmad never feared death a day in his life, and he was not the kind of man to fear threats or compromise a cause in which he believed.

Indeed, he viewed life as a stand for honor and dignity. It is said that [Prime Minister] Nuri al-Sa'id commented on his response, saying, "Tell him, then, to enjoy the comfort of his cell until he meets his end." Sheikh Ahmad replied, "I am just here until the end of Nuri al-Sa'id," and that is precisely what happened. Sheikh Ahmad's family and relatives remained in exile until 1958, when they returned to Barzan after the July 14 Revolution. The other Barzanis, except for a few who were suspected of having influence or significant leadership roles, were released in 1950 after spending more than eight years in Mosul, Basra, and Baghdad prisons. They were allowed to return to the Barzan region in 1953.

Chapter 32

Barzani's Visit to Tashkent

Barzani's ties to the Soviet leadership gained strength and took on an official and organizational character. The Central Committee of the Soviet Communist Party appointed Mr. Voloshin[1] as a liaison officer with Barzani. Together, both returned to Tashkent in March 1954. This visit was different in the sense that both Barzani and Voloshin were officially received by Uzbek officials. Barzani visited his comrades and spent a week in their company, informing them of the results of his visit to Moscow and letting them know that the Soviet leadership had decided to pay closer attention to their conditions.

On his return to Moscow, he took along As'ad Khoshavi, who was very ill and was treated in the Soviet capital. Also accompanying him were Ali Mohammed Siddique, Ali Khalil, Sayyed Aziz Sayyed Abdullah, and Mohammed Amin Mirkhan, who were to pursue higher education in Moscow. Barzani prepared a list of 104 young men to study in the schools of the Republic of Byelorussia [renamed Belarus in 1991]. They were divided into four groups to study in Sratov, Gorki, Itanov, and Tambov. Another group was sent to the University of Tashkent. Thus, all restrictions on the Barzanis were lifted, and they were free to move about and travel. They were, in fact, treated appropriately, after all they had been put through. Barzani continued to visit the remaining Barzanis, who were mostly middle-aged men, in Tashkent, now and then.

Barzani's Visit to the Republic of Armenia

A visit to the Republic of Armenia was arranged for Barzani in 1956 so he could see for himself the conditions of the Kurds there. He stayed there for a while and learned about their activities and the numerous opportunities available to them. He established strong ties with them, and his visit remains one of the fine memories Armenian Kurds pass on from one generation to another.

Barzani and the Tripartite Aggression on Egypt

Following in the footsteps of his predecessor, the Kurdish national hero Sultan Salah al-Din al-Ayyubi [Saladin], Barzani expressed his readiness and that of his companions to volunteer to go to Egypt and defend it against the Tripartite Aggression in 1956. Cognizant of the significance of this initiative in the history of the common struggle of the Kurds and Arabs, president Jamal Abd al-Nasser[2] of Egypt appreciated this position.

The Period of 1956–1958

A number of Kurdish students in Europe were allowed to communicate with Barzani. Among them was Ismet Cherif and the Kurdish Committee in Europe (see Document nos. 19 and 20). Jalal Talabani was also able to contact Barzani during his participation in the International Youth Festival in Peking in 1955. He wrote him an extended letter explaining the conditions of the Barzani family. After writing him a second letter in 1957, they were able to meet (see Document nos. 21 and 22).

Once, Jalal Talabani told me the story of his first meeting with Barzani in Moscow in 1957, and how he almost collapsed as the two met face to face for the first time. He was the first Iraqi to meet Barzani since 1947. Visits were exchanged with many leaders of democratic and Communist parties of the Arab World. Among them was Khalid Begdash and the well-known Kurdish poet Qadri Jan, who wrote the poem "Barzani." (His handwritten copy is reproduced in Document no. 23.) The great Kurdish poet Hajar, who was residing in Syria at the time, also visited Barzani when he went to Moscow for medical treatment.

A Remarkable Period

The Barzani asylum-seekers enjoyed relative peace and comfort during the period from 1952 to 1958, after more than half a century of turmoil and hardship in their struggle against Iraq's oppressive rule. The Barzani youth benefited greatly from the Soviet Union's educational policy and the privileges and facilities the state made available to students. They attended educational institutions at every level as if to quench their thirst for knowledge because the schoolhouse door had been shut in their faces in their homeland. Here they blossomed, and their talents became manifest. A number of them received master's and doctoral degrees and specialized in various scientific disciplines. Barzani always encouraged education and led by example to motivate his followers. Thus, at age 45 he returned to school to further his own education. He continued in school, despite his leadership role, which took up much of his time, until the July 14 Revolution ushered in a new era. It heralded a qualitative change in the fate of the Barzanis and a greater responsibility for their leader, Mulla Mustafa Barzani, whose talents were no longer limited by tribalism and the Kurdish homeland in Iraq. His ascendance to a much broader realm proved the brilliance of this Kurdish leader.

Part IV

The Kurds and the July 14, 1958 Revolution (July 14, 1958– September 11, 1961)

Introduction to Part IV

The July 14 Revolution was the fruition of the tenacious struggle of the Iraqi people—Arabs, Kurds, and minorities—for their freedom, dignity, and independence from foreign domination. It was, of course, neither spontaneous nor unplanned. Planning and preparation had gone on for a long time. It was, indeed, the revolution of the Iraqi people and army together, which enjoyed a level of popular support rarely matched in history. The broad popular backing of the army and leaders of the revolution guarded against any intention of opposing the revolution early on or of conspiring against it later. Its swift success and welcoming embrace by the people once again proved its authenticity and demonstrated the gap that existed between the monarchy, on the one hand, and the people and the army on the other.

The July 14 Revolution opened new horizons for the peoples of Iraq and laid a solid foundation for the solidarity of the two principal nationalities (Arab and Kurdish) and other ethnic and religious minorities in Iraq. It advanced with great strides in both the domestic and foreign arenas.

The leadership of the July 14 Revolution attached great importance to the Kurdish cause. This is manifest in the principles established by the organization of free officers for their movement during preparations for the revolution. After the revolution succeeded, this importance was embodied in Article 3 of the [Provisional] Constitution, which stated that, "The Arabs and Kurds are partners in the Iraqi homeland." This resulted from the influence and cooperation of the National Unity Front (NUF), especially that of Mr. Kamil Chadirchi[1] and Hussein Jamil, the chairman of the Committee to Draft the Constitution.

The significance of this recognition of Kurdish rights lies in the fact that it was the fruit of faith and conviction, not of pressure or threat. The leaders of the revolution recognized the prime importance of the Kurdish question on Iraq and in the region. This single step brought them the love, respect, and backing of the whole Kurdish nation, which became a pillar of support and an army ready to sacrifice for the July 14 Revolution. When I say that the significance of recognizing the partnership and national rights of the Kurds emanated from conviction and not from exerting pressure, I mean that both parties, the Kurds and the government, were not, at that time, in a state of fighting so that one would impose conditions on the other. Aware of the practicality of the Arab–Kurdish brotherhood in the new Iraq, they agreed to join in partnership.

In my experience and according to my conviction, relations that are not built on trust will not develop and last. They will crash into an unavoidable impasse. Trust, therefore, is the foundation of the relationship between the government and the people, just as it is the basis of personal relationships among people. Trust was the basis of government–Kurdish ties early on. However, this changed as all strayed from the path of revolution, not only Abd al-Karim Qasim, as some allege. They blame him unfairly for their own mistakes and blunders.

The Kurds at the time of the July 14 Revolution of 1958 were not in an anti-government revolt. Barzani was in the Soviet Union, and the KDP did not hitherto attract so many followers or enjoy the power to intimidate leaders of the revolution into recognizing Kurdish rights in any form. Contrary to those circumstances of 1958, on March 11, 1970, the Ba'th Party was forced to recognize Kurdish autonomy in Kurdistan under increasing pressure from the revolution being led by the KDP under the command of Mustafa Barzani. Then, most of Kurdistan was liberated and beyond the central government's control. Threatened with collapse and loss of power, the Ba'th Party had only one choice, to recognize a de facto condition and submit to legitimacy and justice. Coerced but not convinced, except for a few Ba'th leaders like Abd al-Khaliq al-Samarra'i, the Ba'th Party needed time to establish itself, before it turned against what it had agreed to with the Kurdish leaders. And this is precisely what the Ba'th Party subsequently did later.

Although the leadership of the July 14 Revolution did not in fact implement Article 3 of the Constitution and did not have a clear agenda to grant the Kurdish people their rights, the trust that had developed between the two sides at the outset obscured many deficiencies in the relationship. The March 11 Manifesto puts forth a clear and comprehensive agenda, truly considered a great historic achievement on which the KDP, leader of the September 1960 Revolution, can pride itself forever. On the other hand, it must be said that the manifesto lacked the necessary element of trust. Consequently, an incident, no matter how insignificant, here or there, was subject to malicious misinterpretation by the two signatories. The March 11 Manifesto could not prevail in the face of this lack of confidence. I see that we, the Kurds, must draw lessons from the two previous experiments: July 14, 1958, and March 11, 1970.

I have permitted myself the liberty of expressing my views in the hope that all of the KDP affiliates and other Kurdish patriots who played their roles during those periods would accept my apology for stating outright that it was a grave miscalculation to allow negatives to take over the positive in assessing ties to Abd al-Karim Qasim. This helped the conspiracy of the CENTO alliance[2] and its domestic agents, along with the chauvinists, to come to pass and also created a wide gap between the KDP and Abd al-Karim Qasim. Whatever may have been said about this man, he remains a superb leader, whose favors we, the Kurds, ought never to forget. Undoubtedly, he sided with the toilers and the poor and loved and respected the Kurdish people. He was a patriot who loved Iraq and the Iraqis, and it would have been possible to deal with him if only the circumstances had been better assessed.

Abd al-Karim Qasim is often accused of deviating from the path of the Revolution and of dictatorship. Is it fair to bypass the truth? This man led a giant revolution that changed the balance of power in the Middle East and rekindled the spirit of the eager masses to break free and become independent. He formed the first cabinet in the republican era. It was composed of leaders and representatives of parties of the NUF, which opposed the monarchy. The political parties conducted their activities freely. In all fairness, let us ask, Who turned against whom?

Soon after the revolution, some political parties began concentrating on their own narrow interests at the expense of others. Instead of preserving unity and cohesion, which would have been sufficient to keep Abd al-Karim Qasim in line, the parties of the front began an intense power struggle. Each tried to take over the government and oust Abd al-Karim Qasim. They forgot their priorities and the greater duties that they owed the nation.

In my view, the parties bear more responsibility than Abd al-Karim Qasim for the derailment of the July 14 Revolution. If they had kept their unity and cohesion and had devoted all of their efforts to the whole of Iraq and its true national unity, neither Abd al-Karim Qasim nor anyone else would have been able to digress from the path of the revolution.

Abd al-Karim Qasim has long since gone to the other world. It is to his honor and credit that his enemies who callously murdered him [in the coup of February 1963] have failed to find a single document proving that he was a foreign agent, or that he was corrupt or perfidious. They were compelled to bear witness to his integrity and patriotism. May Allah bless his soul.

I never disliked Abd al-Karim Qasim, even when he sent squadrons of his planes to bombard us, because as a nation and as a family, I was convinced that he had offered us much. He alone does not bear the total responsibility for what happened. I still believe that of those who have ruled Iraq to date, he was the best.

Divisions, infighting, and power struggles among the parties opened the door for the opportunists and chauvinists to beset Abd al-Karim Qasim and isolate him from the principled forces. The patriotic forces and faithful political parties should never have allowed this to happen. This power struggle paved the way for deviation [from the revolutionary path] and a loss of values that led to the incident of the black coup of February 8, 1963, and the ensuing black coups d'état. Owing to the crimes committed against them and against the national sovereignty of Iraq since the February 8, 1963 coup, and especially since the coup d'état of July 17, 1968, the Iraqis have forgotten the ills of their former leaders. The number of all those executed during the periods when Nuri al-Sa'id and Abd al-Karim Qasim reigned is less than half the number of those executed in a single day by the present regime. Even leaders of the Ba'th Party did not escape collective purges as happened in the 1979 massacre,[3] which cost the Ba'th Party some of its best and most principled leaders, including the honorable fighter, Abd al-Khaliq al-Samarra'i.

The Iraqis have suffered tremendous agony and have never tasted true liberty and independence. Historically, they have found themselves either ruled by a Turkish governor, a British commissioner, or a small band that leaped to power through a bloody coup d'état. They have never elected a parliament or a president freely, not even once. They have never willingly pledged allegiance to a monarch. The Iraqis are a people whose freedom has been usurped. However, their rulers have ruled in their name, killed in their name, destroyed in their name, and waged wars and compromised their sovereignty and independence, all in their name. The Iraqi people have never had the right to express their opinion. All this happens while Iraq is being ruled by a political party claiming to be "the bearer of the banner of unity, freedom, and socialism"[4] and accusing its predecessors of treason, dictatorship, and being agents.

Finally, it should be pointed out that writing history is a trust that must be kept for those who decide to take it on. No objection should be raised for expressing views or for commenting on events that do not correspond to an author's persuasion. However, to distort history and facts is an unequivocal act of treason.

In the last few years, a number of books have been published in Iraq. It is obvious that Iraqi security and intelligence apparatuses have dictated to authors many of the topics. Furthermore, some security and intelligence officers have themselves written books and maliciously distorted the history of Iraq and that of its patriotic forces. It appears that the aim of a good number of these vindictive authors is to distort the history of the Kurdish liberation movement and its great leaders, brand the Kurds as tied to foreigners, and show that Kurdish revolts are driven by imperialism. They omit or overlook the fact that it is imperialism that has stifled the legitimate right of the Kurds to establish an independent state. It is the same imperialism that has established states for these chauvinists who manipulate their people's destinies.

They consider Barzani's correspondence with British officials an indication of a suspicious liaison and of his being a foreign tool. Although I do not want to discuss what has been and will be written by those who are blinded by bigotry and feelings of national superiority, I am confident that the struggle of the Kurdish people and the sacrifices of their leaders are too sublime to be stained by those vile scribblers. The truth these ill-wishers choose to ignore is that the British were the *de facto* rulers of Iraq when Barzani was corresponding with them. What was the use of sending letters to any minister, prime minister, or the king when none of them had the power to make a decision without the approval of the British ambassador? Direct correspondence with the British, as stated earlier, was a natural thing to do and it saved time.

There is another question to ask these rancorous chauvinists: What did your ancestors do when the British RAF planes were bombarding Barzan and Suleimaniyya and firing upon the women and children of Kurdistan? Where were they during the outbreak of the great *Thawrat al-Ishrin* (the 1920 Revolution) [in Southern Iraq]?

Undoubtedly, those vengeful individuals are the descendants of those who were servile minions of the British officers and officials who quelled the revolution of the people of Kurdistan as well as the 1920 Revolution. These chauvinists should read history more closely, review the files of the British intelligence and foreign ministry, and scrutinize the facts about Lawrence Pasha's[5] ties to their ancestors in order to ascertain who defied British imperialism and rejected its domination and who served it with absolute loyalty at the expense of their honor and patriotic principles.

What I find most worrisome is that the rising Kurdish generation may break the tradition and accuse its earlier leaders because they did not demonstrate "sufficient flexibility" in dealing with triumphant Britain after World War I and did not quite fathom the circumstances. Otherwise, Kurdistan would have been an independent sovereign state.

In Part IV, I have tried to shed light on a critical and sensitive period in the life of the Kurdish people in general and of the KDP in particular, i.e., the period from 1958 to 1961. I am publishing available documents regarding this period. I have endeavored to express what I think is necessary. For my observations and views, I am personally responsible. I would be grateful to anyone who will elucidate any ambiguity or rectify any errors.

Kurdistan
December 15, 1990

Chapter 33

Kurdistan under the Monarchy

In the aftermath of World War I (1914–1918), the Ottoman Empire crumbled, and the powers apportioned the Ottoman properties. The map of the region was redrawn once more to serve the interests of the imperialists and not those of the local peoples. The partition affected the Arab and Kurdish nations; however, the difference between the two is that a number of states were established in the Arab homeland, but no Kurdish state was established in any part of Kurdistan. The imperialists ceded each part of Kurdistan to one of the countries in the region against the will of the people of Kurdistan.

This unjust second partition of Kurdistan after World War I has caused much agony for the Kurdish people. It is the root cause of this region's problems and strife, which will continue until a just solution is found.

Iraq was among the weakest of the entities created by British imperialism. To rule the Iraqi people, Britain installed a government of individuals tied to it in thought and spirit, notably Nuri al-Sa'id. The era of monarchy has often been described as his. Britain imported Faisal bin al-Hussain, sharif of Mecca, and enthroned him as king of Iraq, a step that further humiliated the Iraqi people.[1]

As British forces expelled the defeated Turks and established control, British officials and politicians prepared the means and the grounds for founding the State of Iraq. When a referendum was held to decide the form of government, the vast majority of Kurds boycotted it.

The Anglo–Turkish problem did not end with World War I. A new issue surfaced. The impasse of the Mosul Vilayet [province] defied solution until it was referred to the League of Nations, which decided to form an international committee on September 30, 1924, to investigate and provide recommendations to the League of Nations. This committee arrived in Baghdad on January 1, 1925, and toured Kurdistan to learn the people's views. This time, in a referendum, the Kurds clearly expressed their desire to be independent. Britain opposed their desire because it contradicted imperialist interests. Southern Kurdistan was annexed to Iraq with British guarantees that the Kurds would enjoy their administrative and cultural rights. It must be pointed out that the Kurds' misreading of their own as well as international circumstances contributed a great deal to their inability to become independent, which is essentially a Kurdish responsibility.

In his letter to Sir Henry Dobbs, the [British] political officer C. G. Edmonds recognized that the Kurds had rescued the Iraqi entity. He wrote

The visit of the Commission has given a new impetus to Kurdish nationalism, which has swept into the anti-Turkish camp many disgruntled persons whom even the most optimistic among us had at first expected to declare in favour of Turkey. The longer interviews were almost invariably strongly nationalist but not generally separatist in tone. ... The Kurds of Suleimani[2] have struck what may prove to have been the decisive blow in the fight for the preservation of Iraq, and know it. Can the Iraqi government rise to the occasion and adopt a far-sighted and generous policy towards the Kurds?

After quoting that excerpt from his letter to Dobbs, Edmonds stated that:

The report of the special Commission appointed by the League of Nations had now come to confirm their own feeling that, after having saved Iraq at a moment of perilous crisis by carrying the resolutions approving the Anglo–Iraqi Treaty on that historic night of the 10th June 1924, now, by their stand at Suleimani, they had once again saved the country from a fatal dismemberment. The leaders of Kurdish opinion were thus in good conceit both with themselves and with the State of which they felt they had shown themselves no mean citizens. (Edmonds 1957, p. 434)

The League of Nations' committee recommended annexation of the area south of the Brussels Line[3] to Iraq, provided the following two conditions were observed: (1) Iraq was to remain under British mandate for 25 years, and (2) Kurdish rights were to be observed, and Kurdish was to be the official language in the Kurdish region. Otherwise, it would be better for the region to remain under Turkish sovereignty.

The Iraqi Constitution of 1925

The Iraqi Constitution was drafted in London and legislated by the Iraqi Founding Council without amendment. It was drawn up so as not to contradict the articles of the 1922 treaty that tied Iraq to Britain and preserved the interests of the ruling class.

Despite some democratic features in the government's principal law, the Iraqi people could not exercise their democratic freedoms, and the Kurds were not treated as the second largest nationality in Iraq after the Arabs. No care was given to include any article regarding Kurdish national rights.

Representatives were imposed by Britain and the palace. No representative from the peasants and workers who form the majority of the Iraqi people entered the National Assembly from the day it was founded until the July 14 Revolution of 1958. The assembly was reserved for the rich and feudalists among the regime's adherents.

The Iraqi people expressed their disgust at the political situation and voiced their denunciations through demonstrations and uprisings, as in the insurrection of 1948 and the uprising of 1952. In reality, Britain ruled Iraq during and after the period of the mandate. Under the monarchy, 59 cabinets were formed between October 25, 1920 and July 14, 1958. Sixteen assemblies were formed, and martial law was declared 16 times. Pretending to fight Communism, the King fought Iraqi political opposition. On August 22, 1954, a decree was issued to strip of Iraqi citizenship anyone who was accused of being a Communist.

Iraq's Population According to the 1957 Census

Iraq's population was 6.5 million according to the 1957 census, with Muslims comprising the vast majority. The Kurds came second after the Arabs. In addition to these two main Arab and Kurdish nationalities, there are minorities such as Turkomans and [Christian] Assyrians[4] in Iraq.

Of the social conditions in Iraq, Laith Abd al-Hassan al-Zubaidi wrote, "Iraq's population was 6.5 million according to the 1957 census. The majority are of Arab descent with a population of 5, 018,962 distributed among all 14 provinces of the country. The Kurdish population is 1,042,774 million distributed among the four northern provinces ..." (al-Zubaidi 1979, p. 29). The population of minorities was 236,806.

Iraq never had an honest census. The 1957 census remains the best-conducted one until now. It was fundamentally used to resolve differences between the leadership of the Kurdish revolution and the government of Iraq regarding Kirkuk and areas of mixed population when the March 11, 1970 agreement was signed.

I suspect that Laith al-Zubaidi did not consult the original registers of the 1957 census. He saw the registers that the Iraqi regime had forged after the March agreement in order to alter the ethnic and historical authenticity of Kirkuk and other Kurdish areas in the provinces of Mosul and Diyala.

The Kurds now comprise 27 percent of the total of Iraq's population. If, under normal conditions, a proper and sound census is conducted, I am certain that the Kurdish percentage will be higher.

In addition to almost completely neglecting Kurdistan, the monarchy hindered the development of the people of Kurdistan through its oppressive and racist policies and its suppression of Kurdish revolts. Furthermore, to curb Kurdish aspirations, it joined the 1937 Sa'ad Abad Pact, the 1946 Turko-Iraqi Treaty, and finally the infamous Baghdad Pact.[5] Undoubtedly these pacts and treaties were designed first and foremost to tighten the noose around the Kurdish liberation movement on every side and to collectively finish it off.

Besides using military means, the monarchy implemented a more menacing policy deliberately aimed at depriving the Kurdish people of education. Illiteracy rates soared, disease plagued the nation, and the region was neglected in the areas of health services and economic, agricultural, and other projects. The regime embraced a clique of feudalists, afforded them privileges, and allowed them to exploit peasants in the worst possible way.

Except in a few limited places, the monarchy did not implement the laws concerning local languages. It prohibited the use of Kurdish as an official language in government offices, restricted admission of Kurdish students into colleges, and proceeded down the path of ethnic discrimination with regard to government employment, especially when it came to military and cabinet positions. It banned the publication of any Kurdish political newspaper, regardless of its tendencies. This intentionally racist policy caused the Kurds to lag behind.

True, a few Kurds attained high positions in the government, but they did so as individuals loyal to Britain and the court, and not because they represented the Kurdish people. They were more royalist than the king, and they did not serve their people in any way.

The Kurds did not enjoy national rights under the monarchy. However, I must point out that they have suffered agony, deportation, arabization, and mass killings in the republican era many times more than they suffered under monarchy.

Chapter 34

Preparing for the July 14 Revolution of 1958

Lacking popular support, the monarchy relied primarily on imperialist protection and pursued a policy of complete servility. By entering into alliances against the will of the Iraqi people, the monarchy tied Iraq economically and militarily to the West. Hence, it took a hostile position against liberation movements in the Middle East and around the world. Domestically, it relied on the feudalists and the rich, allowing them to freely exploit peasants and toilers. Thus, the monarchy enabled the bourgeois class to exploit peasants, workers, and revolutionary intelligentsia. Its only concern was with the military commanders loyal to the regime.

Political, economic, and social conditions plummeted; domestic conditions were ready to explode. People rallied around the patriotic, national, and democratic parties and heroically struggled with much sacrifice for full national independence. In addition to domestic conditions, external factors also helped accelerate the pace of revolution. Among the factors were the following:

1. The rapid rise and expansion of the Arab liberation movement, the Palestinian cause, Egypt's July [23, 1952] Revolution, and the Tripartite Aggression against Egypt in 1956.
2. The founding of the Baghdad Pact and the founding of the Hashimite Union between Iraq and Jordan.
3. The Cold War between the superpowers, the Anglo-American competition in the region, the growth of liberation movements in the Third World, and the rapprochement between socialist countries and some Arab countries.

Domestically, the political map ran counter to the interests of the regime. On the political stage were decoy parties linked to Britain and its schemes that lacked a popular base. Among them were the Constitutional Unity Party led by Nuri al-Sa'id, the Nation's Socialist Party [al-Ummah] led by Salih Jabr, and the al-Ahrar [Liberal] Party led by Tawfiq al-Swedi.

Despite discord among these parties, essentially the reactionary views that they held were much the same; they espoused similar programs and operated under the umbrella of imperialism. Neither in leadership nor in their ranks were there patriotic elements acceptable to the people. Their organizations relied heavily on the rich, the feudalists and the tribal chiefs. All of these groups in essence became the power base of the regime that the people opposed.

Opposition Parties

Patriotic, nationalist, and democratic opposition parties led the struggle of the Iraqi people against imperialism and monarchy and contributed to preparation for the revolution. These parties were: the NDP, the Independence Party (IP), the Iraqi Communist Party (ICP), the Arab Socialist Ba'th Party (Ba'th), and the KDP.

At the time of the revolution, these parties enjoyed broad popular support as well as interparty ties of cooperation and understanding. Suppression by the monarchist regime differed from one party to another, as ICP and KDP members were constantly pursued and arrested, perhaps because the regime believed that the other three parties enjoyed some protection inside and outside Iraq.

The National Unity Front

After the United National Front, formed in 1954, became stagnant, the patriotic parties resumed contact with each other to form a new national front to lead the struggle of the masses. They were successful in establishing the NUF in February of 1957. The NUF consisted of the following parties: the ICP, the IP, the NDP, and the Ba'th Party and was founded for the following reasons:

1. The deteriorating internal political, social, and economic conditions and the inability to reform the status quo and to bring about progress.
2. The nationalist feelings of the leaders of the Iraqi patriotic movement, who felt that they were lagging behind the rest of the Arab countries in light of the July [23, 1952] Revolution in Egypt, the Algerian Revolution, and the situation in Syria, Lebanon, and Jordan.
3. Iraq's entrance into bilateral and multilateral alliances in the Baghdad Pact, which served the interests of imperialism.

The first communiqué issued by the NUF on March 9, 1957, contained the following patriotic demands:

1. Oust Nuri al-Sa'id's cabinet and dissolve the Council of Representatives in the parliament.
2. Withdraw from the Baghdad Pact and develop a common policy for the liberated Arab countries.
3. Resist all forms of interference by imperialists and follow an independent Arab policy based on positive neutrality.
4. Implement constitutional democratic freedoms.
5. End martial law and free political prisoners and detainees; reinstate all teachers, employees, workers, and students who were discharged for political reasons.

The NUF was a catalyst to the formation of the High Committee of Free Officers. Early in 1958, this committee asked the NUF parties about their readiness to participate in governing the country if the revolution were to succeed.

The mere founding of the NUF was a great accomplishment by the Iraqi people; it raised the army's morale, since the forces of the national movement had never united, organized, or coordinated efforts as they did once they established the NUF. Experience showed the benefits of such fronts, since no single party could represent all segments of the society, no matter how much they struggled and sacrificed. Loyalties were divided among a number of parties, and no single party could undertake all tasks.

At first, the KDP did not join the NUF because the Ba'th Party was opposed and the ICP was not encouraging either. When the KDP was asked to join the NUF before the July Revolution, the KDP, especially its secretary general, preferred caution until he consulted President Jamal Abd al-Nasser. Despite all this, the KDP maintained collaborative ties with the NUF.[1]

The Free Officers

The military personnel in Iraq were not apolitical and were involved while on the job. They often intervened in the making of political decisions, against the will of the politicians. Children of wealthy families were seldom seen in the army for they were sent abroad to specialize in civilian fields. Thus, the vast majority of the army came from the lower and middle classes and identified with the sufferings of the people.

Most Iraqis were disgruntled, including those in the military. A number of officers formed groups and organizations in preparation for the revolution until at last they succeeded in forming the High Committee of Free Officers. The formation of the NUF greatly influenced the establishment of this Committee.

Staff Brigadier Abd al-Karim Qasim was elected chairman of the committee because he was the highest-ranking officer involved. There were 15 officers on the committee. The total number of free officers reached 200, including a number of Kurdish officers such as Colonel Abdullah Aziz, Colonel Fattah Shali, and Staff Major Mustafa Aziz. With few exceptions, most free officers were not affiliated with any political party, but all agreed on their need for political cover, which was to be provided by the NUF. The NUF also realized that it could not succeed without the army. Therefore, these realizations led to a successful marriage between the two.

The Revolution's Goals and Principles as Envisioned by the Free Officers

1. Replace the monarchy with a republican regime.
2. End feudalism and redistribute land among peasants.
3. Restore Iraq's petroleum rights, restrict exploitation by foreign companies and develop an oil industry.
4. Terminate the linkage with the pound sterling and free the Iraqi economy from subordination to Britain.

5. Realize national unity among all Iraqis on the grounds that Arabs and Kurds are associates in one homeland, and safeguard the rights of minorities.
6. Establish a Revolutionary Command Council (RCC) from among the members of the high committee. The RCC would be the legislative authority until elections are held.
7. Realize social equity and bridge the social gaps between Iraqis.
8. Release all political prisoners and implement general freedom.
9. Form a civilian government of politicians known for their capabilities and patriotism.
10. Withdraw from the Baghdad Pact.
11. Withdraw from the Hashemite Union [with Jordan].
12. National liberation, the removal of British military bases, and the rescinding of all military agreements that compromise Iraq's sovereignty.
13. Arab unity is a predestined goal, the attainment of which must be worked for, unless Iraq is exposed to outside invasions aimed at the restoration of the monarchy. In that case, an immediate merger with the United Arab Republic (UAR)[2] may be called for.
14. Help the Palestinian people in every way possible to regain their land and freedom.
15. Pursue a policy of positive neutrality.
16. Establish full diplomatic relations with the socialist countries.

Chapter 35

The July 14 Revolution of 1958

On the morning of July 14 of 1958, the sun of freedom shone on Iraq, and Baghdad radio carried the good news of the replacement of the monarchy with a republican government in Iraq. It is a day of glory in the history of Iraq. Iraqis had not known a happier day until that morning of July 14.

In Kurdistan, the masses proclaimed their support and joy for the revolution. July 14 once again gave them hope, recognized their partnership with the Arab masses in Iraq, laid down the best foundation for national brotherhood, and strengthened Arab–Kurdish fraternity.

The Iraqis welcomed the revolution, in which they saw all of their hopes realized and a prosperous, happy future. Who could have predicted that their joy would not last long? The tyranny, suppression, and terror that awaited them under republican regimes would go far beyond what they had suffered under the monarchy.

Proclamation No. 1 of the Revolution

Noble people of Iraq,
Trusting in God and with the aid of the sons of the people and the national forces, we have undertaken to liberate the beloved homeland from the domination of the corrupt crew that imperialism installed to rule our people and manipulate prospects for their interests and personal gains.

Brethren,
The army is of you and for you, and has carried out what you desired by removing the tyrannical class which abused the people's rights. Your duty is to support it in its bullets, bombs, and its lion-like roars pouring on the Rihab Palace and Nuri al-Sa'id's mansion.

Remember that only by fortifying it and preserving it from the plots of imperialism and its stooges can victory be brought to completion. We appeal to you, therefore, to report to the authorities all despoilers, offenders, and traitors so that they could be uprooted. We ask that you all act as one to put an end to them and eradicate their evil.

Citizens,
While admiring your fervent patriotic spirit and your noble deeds, we call upon you to remain calm and maintain order and unity and to cooperate in positive work for the interest of the homeland.

O People,

We have taken oath to sacrifice our blood and everything we hold dear for your sake. Rest assured that we will continue to work on your behalf. Power shall be entrusted to a government emanating from you and inspired by you. This can only be realized by the creation of a people's republic, which will uphold complete Iraqi unity, tie itself in bonds of fraternity with the Arab and Islamic states, act in keeping with the principles of the United Nations and the resolutions of the Bandung Conference,[1] and honor all pledges and treaties in conformity with the interests of the homeland. Accordingly, the national government shall henceforth be called the Republic of Iraq. Responsive to the people's will, we have temporarily entrusted its presidency to a Sovereignty Council which will enjoy the authority of the president of the Republic until a popular plebiscite is held to elect one. May God grant us success in what we do to serve our beloved homeland, for it is He who hears and responds.

[Issued in] Baghdad, on this 26th day of Dhul Hijja in the year of 1377 Hijrah [Islamic Calendar], corresponding to the 14th of July of 1958.

Commander-in-Chief of the National Armed Forces (*al-Iraq fi A'hd Qasim; Ara' wa Khawatir: 1958–1988*, Fathullah 1989, p. 582)

As soon as this communiqué was released, people rushed into the streets proclaiming their unequivocal support for the revolution, expressing their joy for this great triumph, and repeating "Long live the solidarity of the people and the army." The monarchy was ended, and Iraq began a new phase in its life.

Radio Baghdad continued to broadcast proclamations and decrees. It announced the formation of the Sovereignty Council, consisting of the following: (1) Mohammed Najib al-Rubay'i, Sunni Arab; (2) Mohammed Mahdi Kubba, Shi'i Arab; and (3) Khalid al-Naqishbandi, Kurd.

Iraq's ethnic and religious composition was taken into consideration when this council was formed. The first cabinet comprised 13 ministers, including three officers: Abd al-Karim Qasim, Abd al-Salam Arif, and Naji Talib. Two Kurds were also included in this cabinet: Baba Ali Sheikh Mahmud and Dr. Mohammed Salih. The rest were leaders of NUF parties and independent patriotic dignitaries.

Lists of names of army commanders forced into retirement and of those appointed anew were issued.

The International Position Regarding the Revolution

President Jamal Abd al-Nasser supported the revolution as soon as it was announced. This was a significant position in the Arab World. In contact with the NUF, and with the free officers therefrom, Nasser was aware of the aspirations of the Iraqi people. Siddique Shanshal and Hussein Jamil had visited Cairo and informed him of the revolution to explore the possibility of providing the necessary support, especially in its early days.

Nasser not only supported the July 14 Revolution, but he immediately traveled to Moscow in order to gain the support of the Soviet Union and the Socialist bloc for it, which he did. Moscow issued orders to the Soviet army to send units to the borders with Turkey and Iran to conduct military exercises. This [action] sent a clear message to both countries not to move against the revolution of the Iraqi people.

After recognition by the UAR and the Soviet Union, other countries followed suit, recognizing the revolution and the new government in Baghdad.

Abd al-Salam Arif Heads a Delegation to Damascus

On July 18, 1958, the leaders of the revolution decided to send a delegation to Damascus. Headed by Abd al-Salam Arif, the delegations consisted of Siddique Shanshal, minister of guidance, Abd al-Jabbar al-Jomerd, foreign minister, Mohammed Hadid, minister of finance, and a number of officers.

The delegation was received with extreme warmth and generosity by President Jamal Abd al-Nasser, both officially and unofficially.[2] The trip culminated in the signing of an agreement between the two countries which stated the following:

1. Confirmation of the treaties and pacts that tied both countries together, first and foremost the Charter of the Arab League and the Joint Defense Pact among the Arab countries.
2. Confirmation of the announcement of a strong bond between the two countries with respect to the international position and affirmation of their resolve to stand as one in defending against any aggression on either or both of them and to immediately begin taking all practical measures required.
3. Full cooperation in the international arena to protect the rights of both countries, to uphold the UN charter, and to support peace in the Middle East and worldwide.
4. Taking swift steps to ensure economic and educational cooperation between the two countries.
5. Continued cooperation and consultation regarding all issues of concern to both countries.

Undoubtedly, this agreement reinforced the position of the revolution in Iraq and the world at that critical time.

The American, British, Turkish, and Iranian positions stood against the revolution. Telegrams exchanged among these countries show how they planned to abort the Revolution during its first few days. Among those countries, it appears that Turkey was the most enthusiastic to act, that she closely monitored Kurdish attitude in Iraqi Kurdistan and prepared to abort any Kurdish move by occupying the northern region of Iraq along its borders. In this regard, the British ambassador in Turkey wrote:

SECRET

The British Embassy [sic]
Istanbul
18 July, 1958

1. A possibility exists, if any of the rumors are correct, that the Kurds of Iraq are opposing the revolutionary government in Baghdad. They may attempt to secede and set up an autonomous state in the region that is called now Iraqi Kurdistan.
2. If this should happen, the Turkish government (and perhaps the Iranian government as well) will certainly be annoyed and concerned for the possible impact on

Turkish and Iranian Kurdistan and the re-emergence of the old idea of independent Kurdistan.

Their fears will be deepened further if Nasser and the Russians, who are responsible for broadcasting the pernicious news about the Kurds, exploit this movement and benefit from it.

3. It is not unlikely that the Turkish government will study the question of occupying the northern Iraqi region along its border to prevent any move toward Kurdish independence. This may lead the Turks to bring up the subject of Mosul, which they have not at all forgotten, and to take advantage of the unstable situation and redraw the border by annexing Mosul. They may look into broadening their demands to expropriate Kirkuk with its oil fields and its Turkish-speaking population.

4. These ideas are all totally unclear and at this stage they are contingent. We do not have any indication that the Turks are trying to implement any of the steps mentioned above. Also, there is no mention of these issues in the press. The only reference until now is that of Mr. Zorlu to the Ambassador on July 16 regarding the necessity of protecting minorities in Iraq from ferocious attacks. Mr. Zorlu explained that by minorities he particularly meant the 200,000 people of Turkish descent residing in Iraq.

5. Clearly we had hoped that the situation in Iraq could have been reversed since such developments as we mentioned will have disquieting consequences. If conditions worsen, there is much that can be said to ensure that oil fields in the north go to Turkey and at least prevent Nasser from seizing Iraq's valuable assets (al-A'dhami 1989, p. 48).

The British Foreign Ministry sent the following cable to its ambassador in Tehran:

From Foreign Office to Tehran   Limited
7:15 (A.M.) on 8 August, 1958
Addressed to Tehran under No. 1148 and to Ankara under No. 2399

Repeated to Amman, Beirut, Washington, Headquarters of the Middle East Forces
        My preceding telegram.

General Bakhtiyar was speaking of the possibility of the United Arab Republic establishing a Kurdish state under its influence in order to establish a land bridge to the Soviet Union. In view of Paragraph 3 of the Embassy's message in Istanbul dated July 18 which was directed to the Eastern Office, we are surprised that the Turks and Iranians are not preparing to move toward Iraqi Kurdistan with an eventual goal of dividing it between the two of them. I would appreciate your comments (al-A'Dhami 1989, p. 49).

The British Ambassador in Ankara responded to the British Foreign Office's cable in the following manner:

SECRET[3]
FROM ANKARA TO FOREIGN OFFICE

Cypher/OTP

FOREIGN OFFICE SECRET AND WHITEHALL SECRET DISTRIBUTION

Sir J. Bowker
No. 1286   D.12.15 P.M. August 13, 1958.
August 12, 1958   R.1.41 P.M. August 13, 1958.

SECRET

Addressed to Foreign Office telegram No. 1286 of August 12.
Repeated for information to: Tehran
And saving to: Amman—Beirut—Washington—P.O.M.E.F.

Your telegram No. [grp. undec.] to Tehran: Kurdistan.

In view of your prompt and discouraging response to the original idea of Turkish intervention in Iraq (paragraph 3 of my dispatch No. 85 of July 25),[4] I doubt very much if the Turks are considering further such adventures at this stage.

2. On the other [? grp. omitted], if there appeared to be a real danger of the emergence of a Kurdish satellite state or if Iraq were to join the U.A.R., a new situation might arise. The idea of an independent Kurdistan, whatever its political alignment, is of course, anathema to the Turks and equally they would be unlikely to allow the predominantly Turkish[5] provinces of northern Iraq to become part of the U.A.R. without reacting in some way.

3. In such circumstances, I think it possible that the Turks would revert to the idea of direct intervention in Iraq, perhaps in conjunction with the Iranians. But they would still be very unlikely to act without assurances of American support. It is possible that they might consider partitioning what is now Northern Iraq between Turkey and Iran, taking the (Turkish and oil bearing) provinces of Mosul and Kirkuk for themselves and leaving the (Kurdish) province to Iran.

4. Incidentally Mr. Zorlu said to the Prime Minister on August 10 that for Turkey one of the main problems in Iraq was the big Turkish community in the North. Complaints had been made by the Turkish Government about one or two incidents involving this Turkish community to which a friendly reply had been received; but the situation was still disquieting.

Foreign Office pass Tehran 75, and Saving Amman 6, Beirut 17, Washington 84, P.O.M.E.F. 34.

[Repeated to Tehran and Saving Amman, Beirut, Washington. P.O.M.]

As for the American stance regarding the Turkish intervention in Iraq, the British ambassador in Washington informed his foreign office about the true American position in the following cable:

TOP SECRET[6]
FROM WASHINGTON TO FOREIGN OFFICE

Cypher/OTP
FOREIGN OFFICE (SECRET) AND WHITEHALL (SECRET) (CABINET) DISTRIBUTION

Lord Hood
No. 1962   D: 5.10 A.M. July 19, 1958
July 19, 1958   R: 6.37 A.M. July 19, 1958

IMMEDIATE
TOP SECRET

Your telegram No. 475: Turkey and Iraq.
Following from Secretary of State

The instructions which the Americans have sent to their Ambassador in Ankara are summarized in my immediately following telegram. They did not send them off until I had signified my general agreement.

2. The Americans were extremely reluctant to use any agreement with the Turks suggesting that fear of Russian intervention was the reason for refraining from action in Iraq. Their two reasons were that it would be contrary to the whole deterrent policy to admit this, and also that everything of this kind said to the Turks would, owing to Turkish insecurity, certainly leak back to the Russians.

3. The Americans are confident that the Turks will not take any action in Iraq on their own without promises of United States support.

This is another cable from the British Ambassador in Washington D.C. to the British Foreign Office:

TOP SECRET[7]
FROM WASHINGTON TO FOREIGN OFFICE

Cypher/OTP

FOREIGN OFFICE (SECRET) AND WHITEHALL (SECRET) (CABINET) DISTRIBUTION

The Viscount Hood
No. 1963   D: 7.01 A.M. July 19, 1958
July 19, 1958   R: 7.31 A.M. July 19, 1958

IMMEDIATE
TOP SECRET
    My immediately preceding telegram

The United States Ambassador is instructed to ask for further information on Turkish plans and estimates of the situation in Iraq. The United States Government know of no organized opposition to the new régime In Iraq. They think it most likely that Turkish forces would be opposed by Iraqi population and by Iraqi military forces. They are doubtful of the feasibility from a military point of view of the proposed Turkish action, given the nature of the terrain on the Turco-Iraqi frontier. Until they have further details on Turkish plans and capabilities and in the absence of information that Turkish Intervention would be welcome in Iraq, the United States Government think it would be premature for them to encourage Turkish action.

It had been decided that the Council of the Baghdad Pact would meet in Istanbul on July 14, 1958, at the level of prime ministers of the member nations. However, the revolution prevented the meeting, and the member nations of the pact issued a statement denouncing the events of the revolution and characterizing it as "a foreign destructive influence," and asserting that "The leaders of the revolution take their cues from foreign countries" (*Thawrat 14 Tammuz 1958 fil Iraq*, al-Zubaidi 1979, p. 240).

On the same day, the Turkish government issued a statement, stating that "[T]he adventurous politicians in Iraq think that the Revolution will end the

Baghdad Pact, which is considered the source of peace in the Middle East, and choosing the day of the Pact's meeting to carry out this Revolution is the best indicator of that idea" (al-Zubaidi 1979, p. 240).

Units of the Turkish army moved toward the Iraqi border. This move resulted in a warning from the Soviet Union to Turkey on July 18, 1958, that the Turkish government would bear responsibility for any hostility against the new regime in Iraq.

In principle, the Baghdad Pact was directed against the liberation movements in the region in general, and the Kurdish liberation movement in particular. Therefore, Turkish anxiety about and fear of the July 14 Revolution were rooted in its recognition of the far-reaching impact of this revolution on the conditions of the Kurdish people, notably those under Turkish domination whom chauvinist Turks describe as "mountain Turks." Turkey did not risk a military action at that time out of fear of Kurdish resistance to any invasion and because other countries did not approve it.

In Iran, the shah announced eight days of mourning for members of the Iraqi monarchy who had been killed in the events of the July 14 Revolution. Iranian intelligence hastened to send agents to Iraq to conduct terrorist activities and assassinations.

The Kurdish people in Iraq were doing everything possible to defend their republic and to stand against any foreign attempt at invasion, regardless of its source.

Chapter 36

The Kurdistan Democratic Party (KDP)

The KDP was founded on August 16, 1946,[1] at a very critical time. World War II was over. With the defeat of the Nazis, new and glowing horizons beckoned people eager to be free and live in dignity. For the people of Kurdistan, a broader outlook seemed possible, especially after the founding of the Republic of Mahabad.

To unify the ranks of the Kurdish movement in southern Kurdistan (Iraqi Kurdistan), [Mustafa] Barzani and his companions[2] in Mahabad actively discussed the situation; as a result, Hamza Abdullah was delegated to Iraqi Kurdistan. He carried letters from Barzani to the leaders of the *Shoresh* (Revolution) and *Rizgari* (Deliverance) parties, to patriotic dignitaries, and to tribal chiefs known for their patriotism, telling them of the need to take a major national step commensurate with the demands of the era. He proposed the founding of a democratic party for Kurdistan to lead the Kurdish national liberation struggle.

Having discussed the matter thoroughly, the party leaders of *Shoresh* and *Rizgari* decided to dissolve both parties and establish the party, which announced its founding at its first congress, held on August 16, 1946. [Mustafa] Barzani was elected president.

The Kurdish people hold British imperialism directly responsible for the historic injustice of partitioning Kurdistan against the will of the Kurds. Therefore, at that time it was absolutely natural for the people of Kurdistan to view the Soviet Union as their liberating friend, as it was the rival of Western imperialism. This compelled Kurdistani organizations either to adopt Marxism-Leninism in their programs or to move along those lines. For some, this could be considered more a matter of spite against Britain than one of ideology; for others, it was a matter of genuine political belief.

The KDP joined other patriotic parties of Iraq in the struggle against imperialism and the monarchy. It led the struggle of the Kurdish people capably and actively participated in the uprisings and demonstrations of the Iraqi people that expressed the people's anger at the monarchy and their rejection of it. Hand in hand, Arabs and Kurds sacrificed their lives in their patriotic struggle.

Party objectives were clear in that their goal was to struggle to overthrow the monarchy; to liberate Iraq from imperialism, unjust alliances, and treaties; and to establish a democratic regime. The party continuously stressed the importance of an alliance of the Kurdish and Arab liberation movements and actively worked to strengthen brotherhood among the Kurds, Arabs, and minorities in Iraq.

The KDP struggled against illiteracy and for compulsory elementary education, and worked to establish more schools, institutes, and colleges in Kurdistan. It also embarked on a program to liberate women from backward conditions and strove for equality between the sexes, the rights of workers and improvement in their living conditions, and the establishment of labor unions, as well as the promotion of the peasant movement in Kurdistan and the establishment of cooperatives, to play a role on both agricultural and patriotic levels. Under KDP leadership, democratic organizations were founded.

The KDP was clearly defined in Article 2 of its program: "...our Party is a democratic revolutionary vanguard party representing the interests of workers, peasants, laborers and artisans, and the revolutionary intelligentsia in Iraqi Kurdistan."

The KDP was successful in spreading and raising the national democratic and patriotic consciousness in Kurdistan. In my view, the most important of its accomplishments was its preservation of the Kurdish national identity through its struggle and its cohesion with the masses of Kurdistan. Thousands of capable cadres rose from the KDP ranks and assumed leadership positions in the KDP and in other parties that were established later. The KDP is credited with the foiling of the Arab and Kurdish chauvinistic reactionary schemes [that aimed] to drag the September Revolution into an Arab–Kurdish war.

The KDP believed in a coalition struggle and therefore worked hard to contribute to the NUF. Although not a member, the KDP coordinated its activities with that of the NUF through the ICP and played a major role in preparing the masses of Kurdistan to support the July 14 Revolution in its early days.

This is a summary of the history of the KDP, which led the great patriotic September Revolution headed by Mustafa Barzani and extracted Baghdad's recognition of Kurdish autonomy on March 11, 1970. With all due credit for its achievements and successes, the KDP bears primary responsibility for the mistakes and setbacks that occurred during the struggle of the people of Kurdistan by virtue of its being the parent party.

The Kurdistan Democratic Party and the July 14 Revolution

Immediately after the revolution, the KDP declared its endorsement, and the Central Committee sent a cable of support and mobilized the people of Kurdistan to defend the revolution against domestic and foreign threats. On July 16, 1958, the KDP issued the following press release:

A Declaration to the Kurdish People

The KDP, the vanguard of the Kurdish liberation movement, seriously considers its historic mission to strengthen the Arab people's liberation movement so as to achieve its victory and to liberate Iraq from the hated corrupt monarchy, to establish a free republican regime, and to ensure Iraq's withdrawal from the Baghdad Pact which is aimed at the heart of the Kurdish nation. All these form the foundations for establishing a new life full of happiness, freedom, and equality for both the Arab and Kurdish peoples. Therefore, the Party has decided to struggle with all its might and abilities to defend the Republic of Iraq, its stability, and prosperity. For this purpose, the KDP considers all its members and supporters as freedom fighters for the Republic of Iraq to combat imperialism, its schemes, and agents.

After his return from the Soviet Union, KDP President Mustafa Barzani declared repeatedly that he was a soldier of the July 14 Revolution and that he put himself under the command of Abd al-Karim Qasim. The KDP organized delegations from all regions of Kurdistan to travel to Baghdad to congratulate the leaders of the revolution and to express the strong support of the people of Kurdistan. Baghdad witnessed the biggest Kurdish presence on July 27, when the leaders of the revolution received the delegation of Kurdistan, headed by Ibrahim Ahmad, Ali Abdullah, and Nuri Ahmad Taha.[3] Ibrahim Ahmad, the general secretary of the KDP, delivered an important speech. He expressed the sufferings of the Kurdish people under the monarchy and the supportive position of the party and the people of Kurdistan. The following is the text of his speech:

Your Excellency, President of the Sovereignty Council
Your Excellency, the Prime Minister and Commander in Chief of the Armed Forces:

A glance at Kurdish–Arab relations ever since the Kurds became Muslims clearly demonstrates that the two neighboring peoples have continued to co-exist on the basis of friendly, peaceful, and cooperative ties. In the Islamic era, the grounds for these ties were the Islamic principles which call for equality among all Muslims and state that there is no difference between an Arab and a non-Arab except in piety and good deed. Under Ottoman rule, both peoples experienced much oppression and injustice, hunger and hardship from a common enemy who turned the land into a supply depot and the people into a military encampment to provide for their endless wars. After the First World War, the victorious imperialist countries partitioned the lands of Arabs and Kurds among themselves as plunder. After the truce was proclaimed, Britain occupied what was called the Mosul Vilayet, of which the vast majority of the inhabitants are Kurds. This led to what is known as the Mosul Question, which was then resolved by a plebiscite in which some of the Kurds who took part voted in favor of forming a Kurdish state and others voted in favor of coexistence with the Arabs, provided they enjoyed a measure of decentralized administration. Thereafter, the Mosul Vilayet, including southern Kurdistan, was officially annexed to Iraq in 1926.

Because the old Iraqi Constitution was promulgated prior to the annexation, it contained nothing pertaining to the national rights of the Kurds. This special administration favored by those Kurds who wanted to live within Iraq was limited to guaranteeing the rights of the Kurds in speeches delivered on ceremonial occasions by the British and Iraqi officials, to some promises Britain made at the League of Nations in 1932, and to the "Local Languages Act." However, despite the trivial nature of these rights, the British and the few Iraqi rulers who took their cues from them did not allow the Kurds to enjoy them. During the long years of monarchic rule, the Kurds were subjected to oppression of two kinds. First, they shared with the Iraqi people poverty, ignorance, disease and heavy-handed tyranny; second, they underwent ethnic discrimination and deprivation of national rights.

These conditions bred the Kurdish revolts of which you know, and which imperialists and their agents at times described as separatist, British-instigated, or the other extreme, as a Communist movement. At no time were they anything other than a national liberation movement with the goal of rescuing the country from imperialists and their treasonous agents, and recasting Arab–Kurdish ties on a stronger basis for both peoples without interference from the imperialists applying their "divide and rule" axiom. The imperialists knew better than anyone that these revolutions were not separatist because the Kurds know that cessation is detrimental to their cause and enfeebles their position just as much [as] it harms the cause of the Arab people and enfeebles their position. Knowing better than anybody else that these revolutions were not of their making, the imperialists brutally and forcefully suppressed them and provided all they could to their Iraqi lackeys to maintain this suppression. What would Britain gain by instigating the Kurds against their obedient minions who provided conditions they never even imagined to satisfy their greedy, imperialistic cravings? If these movements were supported by the imperialists, why did they not succeed?

After all, weren't the imperialists responsible for partitioning the Kurdish homeland? The imperialists and their stooges knew that these movements were not Communist because the economic, social, and political development of the Kurdish people was not at the level to become a Communist movement. They made these unjust assertions in order to justify their vicious attacks on the Kurdish revolution and to distort their reputation, misdirecting Arab anger against the Kurds in accordance with their imperialistic "divide and rule" policy. Not only did the Kurds rise up on their own behalf but they also took part in every Iraqi liberation movement as well. For this, they suffered imprisonment, deportation, forced exile and killings over and above the mass killings, deportations, and exiles which they suffered because of their own revolts; the most hideous example of which was done to the valorous Barzan tribe and their beautiful country because they engaged in a liberation movement against repressive imperialism, corrupt conditions, and the decadent ruling clique. The ruling clique under the monarchy resorted to other means to fight these movements in addition to its criminal suppression of the movements of the Kurdish people. First, it joined the Sa'ad Abad Accord, then it signed the Turco–Iraqi Agreement of 1946, and finally it joined the Baghdad Pact.

Among the objectives of these pacts and agreements was the tightening of the noose around the Kurdish liberation movement from every side and collectively finishing it off. Another objective was to hinder Kurdish progress by applying an oppressive racist policy, of which the following are only a few examples:

First, the embracing appeasement of a small group of Kurdish traitors and renegades and neglect of the Kurdish people. Second, the attempt to wipe out the Kurdish language by not using it as an official language in government offices and by not applying the Local Languages Act, except in a few places, and by obstructing and limiting its applications. Third, the reference to Kurdistan as the North and Kurds as the Northerners on all occasions. Fourth, the granting of only a few scholarships to Kurdish students to study abroad and admitting fewer Kurds into Iraqi colleges and universities, without regard to the Kurdish percentage of the total Iraqi population. This resulted in a paucity of educated Kurds to occupy government positions. Fifth, the application of a policy of ethnic discrimination in hiring for government jobs. Sixth, the application of a policy of discrimination in promotions to certain army ranks and the restriction of admission into the Staff Military Academy to a very small number of Kurds. Seventh, the provision of no opportunity to the Kurds to exercise any political rights, even to put out a Kurdish political paper, irrespective of complexion or tendency.

This deliberately wrong, racist policy resulted in keeping the Kurds backward. The Kurds under the monarchy were under a double oppression. Therefore, they struggled to achieve two goals: one, to liberate Iraq from imperialism and the corrupt regime, and the other, to achieve and secure their national rights.

Free Kurds struggled hand in hand with free Arabs in all fields and in all battles. They were imprisoned, killed, or exiled with all their hopes and faith that putting a stop to imperialism and its agents would be enough to prepare the ground for the strongest of ties between the Arab and Kurdish nationalities on the foundations of brotherhood and equality that were predominant in their long history together. Free Kurds fully believed that a victory achieved by the Kurdish people in their liberation struggle was a victory for Arab nationalism in general, and that putting a stop to imperialism and its agents in Iraq was a victory for the cause of both Kurdish and Arab peoples in particular.

Accordingly, and with this faith, the Kurds participated in the blessed revolution carried out by the Iraqi army in solidarity with the Iraqi people to end the reign of the corrupt tyrannical gang.

On these grounds and with this faith, they are prepared to defend their fledgling freedom with their blood and souls. The recognition of the Kurdish national rights by the Provisional Constitution and its consideration of Kurd[s] and Arab[s] [as] partners in this homeland are the fruit of our joint struggle and confirm the belief of the free Kurds and free Arabs that the struggle of peoples is an interconnected movement. We look forward to this happy inauguration of the new republican era and we hope that new necessary laws will be legislated to implement the Constitutional guarantee. We hope and believe that steps by our nascent republic to enhance ties with the liberated Arab countries will inevitably be accompanied by a gradual broadening of the Kurdish national rights. Thus, any step taken by the Arab people toward its goals will be a step simultaneously moving the Kurdish people closer to its goals. [If we did that,] we would seal every crevice and fissure in the face of the imperialists and their agents and set an example to be followed for the co-existence of two fraternal peoples under a democratic free system.

While I extend the utmost appreciation of the Kurdish people who are represented by delegations here for the statement in our Provisional Constitution, I wish to express the sincerest of feelings from the Kurdish people toward the nascent Republic, its free leaders, and brave army. The Kurds are ready to defend their Republic and the national rights they have won with their life's blood, their wealth, and their very souls. Long live the Iraqi Republic, the republic of Arabs and Kurds.

The KDP's supportive position of the revolution from the first moments of the declaration, the expression of thousands of Kurds in various cities and towns of Kurdistan led by party cells, and their readiness to defend it played a large role in stabilizing the situation in Kurdistan to the benefit of the revolution. Many of the officers, soldiers, and policemen were Kurds, either affiliated with or supportive of the KDP; this played an effective role in controlling units stationed in Kurdistan and prevented them from staging a rebellion.

The Barzanis and the July 14 Revolution

The Barzanis had never felt settled or secure under the monarchy. The July 14 Revolution embodied their hopes and aspirations. Barzan was subjected to three large-scale military campaigns in 1932, 1943, and 1945, triggered by the Barzanis' revolt against the monarchy and its British masters. British officers led the Iraqi army's campaigns against Barzan—General Robinson in 1932 and General Renton in 1945. The RAF joined in the attacks and mercilessly bombarded peaceful villages and innocent women and children.

Military offensives also heralded campaigns of arrests and deportation of the Barzan population. The Iraqi government halted all educational, health, and agricultural services to the area. It is known that Abd al-Ilah, Nuri al-Sa'id, and Chancellor Edmonds hated the Barzanis and accused them of Communism and of having ties to the Soviet Union.

The July 14 Revolution rescued them from injustice, deportation, and dispersion and came to rehabilitate them. Sheikh Ahmad Barzani[4] was in Baghdad Prison when the revolution broke out. His brother Mustafa Barzani and 500 of his comrades were refugees in the Soviet Union. Some of their families were under house arrest in Baghdad and others in Arbil.

Because of their fierce struggle against Ottoman rule, British imperialism, and monarchy, the Barzanis won the appreciation and sympathy of Iraq's people as well as its patriotic political leaders. The leadership of the July 14 Revolution intended, from day one, to undo the oppression and injustices that had befallen this brave tribe. To implement this intention, practical measures were taken, the first of which was to release Sheikh Ahmad Barzani form jail. The Barzanis considered this a very significant step. Upon leaving the prison for his residence in the al-'Iwadhiyya [quarter in Baghdad], the Sheikh was received very warmly by crowds of Kurds who had come from various parts of Kurdistan to participate in the joy of this jubilant occasion.

Sheikh Ahmad Barzani left the prison on July 21, 1958 and paid a visit to the Ministry of Defense the following day to offer his gratitude and support to the leadership of the revolution. There, Brigadier Abd al-Karim Qasim received him most respectfully. For the first time, Sheikh Ahmad Barzani pledged his allegiance to the revolutionary government and to its leader. Abd al-Salam Arif did not attend the meeting. Reportedly, he commented that had he been present at the meeting, he would have said to Sheikh Ahmad Barzani, "Go away, Kurd, go away."[5]

Sheikh Ahmad Barzani spent 12 years in the prisons of the monarchy refusing to capitulate or even to submit a petition to the king or to Nuri al-Sa'id.

At the end of July [1958], the Sheikh and his brethren were allowed to return with their families to Barzan. Means of transportation were made available for them. The magnificent popular reception of the sheikh and his companions by the masses of Kirkuk and Arbil was indescribable.

For the first time, the Barzanis felt that they were Iraqi citizens, enjoying the right to live in their homeland. In those eternal moments, they were certain that their many sacrifices in fighting the British imperialists and their hand-picked puppets had not been in vain. They felt that the time had come to enjoy the fruits of their struggle.

To their credit, the leaders of the July 14 Revolution treated the Barzanis fairly and provided them with much assistance to compensate, at least partially, for their losses under the monarchy. They planned various projects to develop the region. The Barzanis, for their part, became loyal soldiers in defense of the July 14 Revolution, and they often defended it with their lives. Great trust developed between Barzani and Abd al-Karim Qasim until the end of 1959, after which it began to fade for reasons I will detail in the coming chapters.

Mustafa Barzani's Return from Moscow to Baghdad

Barzani told us that he heard the news of the outbreak of the Iraqi Revolution when Voloshin, a cadre at the secretariat of the Central Committee of the Communist Party of the Soviet Union and a relative of Khrushchev, called and gave him the news. Barzani was in Moscow at the time and he in turn informed his comrades, who were dispersed throughout in other Soviet cities. Undoubtedly they were overwhelmed with joy and hope to return to their beloved home after 12 years of exile.

On August 21, 1958, Barzani left Moscow for Romania with his two comrades, Mir Haj Ahmad and As'ad Khoshavi. They were received by the Romanian president. From the UAR Embassy in Bucharest, Barzani cabled Abd al-Karim Qasim, congratulating him on his victorious revolution and asking that he and his comrades be allowed to return to Iraq. From Bucharest, Barzani traveled to Prague and was received by Antonin Novotny, the president of Czechoslovakia, who kept up his friendship with Barzani until his last days. From Prague, Barzani sent the following letter to Abd al-Karim Qasim:

> To His Excellency, our beloved leader, Staff Brigadier Abd al-Karim Qasim, hero of the glorious Iraqi Revolution:
>
> On behalf of my Kurdish brothers in the Socialist diaspora, I salute you. Blessed be the Revolution which you and your hero comrades have carried out ending the evil of imperialism and corrupt monarchy, and liberating the whole Iraqi people, Arabs and Kurds alike, from submission, oppression, and servitude. You have inscribed an everlasting page in the glorious history of the struggle of the Iraqi people in particular and the history of world liberation movements in this era in general. In proclaiming the Republic, you have realized a goal long struggled for by the valiant Iraqi people since the renowned Iraqi revolution of 1920. You have achieved a striking victory. The free Kurds in Iraq have struggled along with their Arab brothers to reach this noble goal.
>
> The Barzanis' revolts were only one link in the chain of the long and fierce Iraqi struggle against imperialism and corrupt monarchy in our beloved country. Because of this ardent protracted struggle, under conditions in which the imperialists held sway thanks to their lackeys and treasonous agents, we were compelled to leave our homeland and carry on our struggle against them abroad in the free socialist countries. We firmly believed that the imperialists and their stooges would be defeated and expelled from our country, just as they were expelled from other fraternal countries such as Egypt, Syria, Yemen, etc. July 14 was a new dawn that fulfilled our hopes and longing to return to our beloved homeland to serve our people and defend our fledgling Republic. We contacted the Ambassadors of the UAR in the People's

Republic of Rumania and the People's Republic of Czechoslovakia in the first few days of the Revolution in order to obtain passports to return home. However, we have not received an answer yet.

Your Excellency, we present this application for assistance to return to our beloved homeland and to serve our Republic together with the rest of the loyal citizens.

In conclusion, may God afford you victory to completely rid the country of the agents of imperialism, to reform all that the monarchy has corrupted in the conditions of the courageous Iraqi people, and to bring the country to the peak of progress and civilization. I wish you and your comrades the best of health and vigor.

Long live the enduring Republic of Iraq, and long live the leaders and heroes of the glorious Iraqi Revolution, Staff Brigadier Abd al-Karim Qasim and his fellow Free Officers.

Long live the Arab-Kurdish fraternity under the auspices of Iraqi Unity.

Please note that at this time I am in the city of Lidice in the Republic of Czechoslovakia with my comrades, Mir Haj Ahmad and As'ad Khoshavi (*Masu'at 14 Tammuz*, Husayn 1988, vol. 2, p. 184).

Truly yours,
The Servant of the Iraqi people
Mustafa Barzani
Prague, August 29, 1958

Abd al-Karim Qasim responded to Barzani's cable and letter as follows:

We have received your cable and letter with joy. You are all welcome to return to our beloved Iraq. We have taken all measures to issue an amnesty and facilitate your trip home and that of Mir Haj and As'ad Khoshavi and all fellow citizens who are with you. Contact the Embassy of the UAR in Prague, Czechoslovakia, to secure your return.

Staff Brigadier Abd al-Karim Qasim
Prime Minister
September 2, 1958 (*Husayn* 1988, p. 186)

On the same day, the Foreign Ministry cabled the Embassy of the UAR in Prague to secure the return of Barzani and his comrades.

Among Barzani's papers, I found a copy of the last cable he sent to Abd al-Karim Qasim thanking him for his decision to allow him and his comrades to return home. The following is the text of that cable:

To His Excellency, great leader of the people, Staff Brigadier Abd al-Karim Qasim,

On behalf of all my Kurdish brothers who have long struggled, once again I congratulate you and the Iraqi people, Kurds and Arabs, for the glorious Revolution putting an end to imperialism and the reactionary and corrupt monarchist gang. This Revolution has opened the road before our people to move toward freedom, democracy, and peace.

On behalf of the Kurdish people, my comrades and I pledge to continue the struggle to shore up the foundations of this Republic and to protect it in solidarity with our Arab brothers against all attempts by imperialism and its agents. I consider myself and my comrades soldiers in the vanguard of those who struggle to defend our new Republic, the republic of Arabs and Kurds under your leadership.

Your Excellency, leader of the people: I take this opportunity to tender my sincere appreciation and that of my fellow Kurdish refugees in the Socialist countries for allowing us to return to our beloved homeland, and to join in the honor of defending the great cause of our people, the cause of defending the republic and its progress.

Long live the leader and rescuer, Abd al-Karim Qasim.

May the brotherhood between the Arabs and Kurds live forever.

Long live the Republic of Iraq, the Republic of Arabs and Kurds.

Mustafa Barzani
September 10, 1958

The KDP formed a delegation in the persons of Ibrahim Ahmad, Nuri Ahmad Taha, Sadiq Barzani, and Ubaidullah Barzani to travel to Prague and accompany Barzani on his triumphant return home. Salih Miran joined the delegation in Cairo. Abd al-Karim Qasim was inundated with cables from patriotic Arabic and Kurdish political parties supporting his decision to allow Barzani and his companions to return to Iraq.

It was later discovered that Abd al-Salam Arif had withheld Barzani's telegram and letter from Abd al-Karim Qasim and the cabinet, in consequence of which Barzani was kept waiting about a month in Romania and Czechoslovakia for a response from the revolutionary government.

At the end of September 1958, Barzani left Prague for Cairo, where he was received most warmly by President Nasser at his house; this began the historic relationship between Barzani and the pioneer of the Arab Nationalist Movement.

At long last, after 12 years of absence, Barzani arrived in Baghdad on the evening of October 6, 1958, to a popular and official reception. Tens of thousands of Iraqi Arabs, Kurds, and minorities packed al-Muthanna Airport to welcome Barzani home as a hero. They repeated over and over: "Barzani, we greet you/the Iraqi people salute you."

All of the political parties took part in this magnificent reception. It is to the ICP's credit that they assembled the largest number of their members and supporters for this reception. Barzani stayed at the Samir Amis Hotel as the guest of the Iraqi government. On the morning of September 7, 1958, he visited Brigadier Abd al-Karim Qasim and expressed his appreciation and gratitude. He stated that he "considered himself a soldier of the July 14 Revolution and under the command of the leader."

Barzani's return was no small matter. As the embodiment of the struggle of the Kurdish nation, Barzani's return fused the power of the Kurds and that of the Arabs for the defense of the republic. His homecoming enhanced the trust between the Kurdish people and the new government and reinforced Arab–Kurdish fraternal relations. He returned to Iraq symbolizing the Kurdish struggle and bearing the love and loyalty of the Kurds from all parts of Kurdistan to the July 14 Revolution and its leader.

People's delegations from all regions of Iraq—from Kurdistan, the center, and the south—continued to arrive in Baghdad to welcome Barzani and to congratulate him on his triumphant return to his beloved country. Barzani spoke briefly to the delegations congregated on the lawn of Samir Amis. The following is the text of that speech:

> Dear compatriots:
>
> As you know, my comrades and I had to leave the country because of our armed struggle against the corrupt ruling gang of the monarchy and their imperialist masters. Dearest to our hearts in the past eleven years in which we continued our struggle against imperialism and its agents were the aspirations of our Iraqi people for independence, freedom, and peace.
>
> We tried to come home as soon as we heard the news of the glorious Iraqi Revolution, from the very first day, to join in the honor of defending the Republic from its birth. While I thank the leaders of the Revolution for giving us this opportunity, I promise you before our people to be, along with my comrades, in the vanguard of defending our new Republic for its progress and prosperity; to stand together, Kurds and Arabs, under the command of the true son of Iraq, the leader Abd al-Karim Qasim.
>
> Long live the Republic of Iraq.
>
> Long live Arab-Kurdish brotherhood.[6]

The well-known Soviet journalist, Dimchenko, was in Baghdad at the time of Barzani's return. He described the splendid reception:

> ...on that morning, I was awakened by the loud noise in the streets, columns of the taxis carrying delegations from Iraqi Kurdistan decorated with Iraqi flags and white banners with writing in Kurdish and Arabic inching their way through the enormous crowds. They came to salute their national hero. They began their trip at night to arrive when his plane would land. They chanted "Long live Arab-Kurdish friendship." Thousands of people on sidewalks, on bridges, and in their bay windows repeated the same chant.
>
> They were carrying signs with simple drawings depicting a soldier, an Arab peasant, and a Kurd shaking hands warmly. This symbolized the unity of the Iraqi people. Such slogans adorned many buildings in honor of Mustafa Barzani's arrival... (*The Blazing Iraqi Kurdistan*, Dimchenko, p. 8).

Domestic and Foreign Reactions to Barzani's Return to Iraq

Barzani's splendid reception at the Baghdad Airport by thousands of Iraqi Kurds, Arabs, and minorities was the best response to all of the demagoguery by chauvinists and reactionaries who have been trying, to this day, to discount the significance of that great reception. They ascribe it to efforts by the KDP and the ICP, unaware that in so doing, they are testifying to the size and influence of both parties.

That day, the Iraqi people spoke. Those who try to falsify history will remain frustrated. Truth will not be effaced. Even if at times it is dimmed under the cloak of terror and tyranny, in the end, it will undoubtedly shine again.

Leaders of patriotic parties welcomed Barzani. Friendly and cooperative ties developed between them and Barzani, notably with Mr. Kamil Chadirchi. Those who doubted Barzani's return were a small rancorous minority of feudalists and

Kurds who served Nuri al-Sa'id and the British all of their lives and desisted not from perfidy. It is not by sheer coincidence that their positions suited those of Arab chauvinists, Britain, Turkey, and Iran.

A number of Iraqi lawyers sent a cable to Abd al-Karim Qasim, supporting his decision to approve the return of Barzani and his comrades to Iraq. The following is the text of that cable:

> To His Excellency, Staff Brigadier Abd al-Karim Qasim, Esq.
>
> Your decision to welcome the return of the great patriot Mulla Mustafa Barzani, who revolted against the imperialist decadent monarchist regime, resonated greatly with all Iraqis, Kurds as well as Arabs, and delighted them.
>
> The return of the great revolutionary Mulla Mustafa Barzani, his brethren in the struggle, and all those who were driven from their homes along with him owing to their patriotic struggle, greatly enhances the spirit of the joint struggle between the Arab and Kurdish peoples. It advances the support of our new Republic, protects it from all manipulation and evil, affords new horizons of freedom, independence, and dignified life to our people.
>
> On behalf of the lawyers, we hail your giant step to welcome this great citizen home.
>
> Long live our new Republic and the hero Abd al-Karim Qasim.
>
> Long live the Kurdish-Arab brotherhood (Husayn 1988, vol. 2, p. 187).

Fifty-two lawyers signed this cable, among them Tawfiq Munir, Kamil Qazanchi, Amir Abdullah, Abd al-Rahim Sharif, Abd al-Sattar Naji, Badi' Omer Nadhmi, Dawood Khammas, Dawood al-Sayigh, Qusai al-Qadhi, Wurya Ali Kani Marani, and Nuri Talabani.

Numerous cables and letters were sent to Barzani congratulating him on his return home (see samples in Document nos. 25, 26, 27, 28, and 29).[7]

Foreign Reactions

Barzani's visit to Cairo and his meeting with Nasser on his way home confirmed the UAR's welcome of Barzani and approval of his return. The Soviet Union and Socialist countries were pleased with his return on the grounds that a friend of theirs who had stayed with them for 11 years had returned home after a successful patriotic and democratic revolution in his country.

As was to be expected, Britain, Turkey, and Iran were against Barzani's return. Their position can be seen much more clearly in the reports that British diplomats sent to their Foreign Ministry, in statements by General Timor Bakhtiyar, and in commentaries from the Iranian press during that period. In a statement, General Timor Bakhtiyar, the Iranian deputy prime minister and chief of intelligence (SAVAK) said, "The situation in Kurdistan is unstable, and the Iranian government is watching Mulla Mustafa Barzani, who visited Cairo and is currently in Baghdad, and who was assisted by the Soviets to incite the Kurds" (Husayn 1988, vol. 2, p. 187).

In issue No. 831 dated December 15, 1958, the magazine *Taraqqi* published an article titled "Iraq, Center of Conspiracy against Iran," which vociferously attacked

Barzani and the Iraqi government for allowing him to return. The British Ambassador, Michael Wright, circulated a report dated September 22, 1958 to October 7, 1958, stating the following in the second paragraph:

> On the evening of 6 October 1958 Mulla Mustafa Barzani returned to Iraq after his visit to President Nasser in Cairo. There was a huge crowd to welcome him and his group at the airport.
>
> Obviously, many intelligent Iraqis view Mulla Mustafa's return with caution and believe that the Foreign Minister's decision to allow him to return was an unwise move. Thus, the caller for an independent Kurdistan who enjoys strong ties with the Soviet Union has re-emerged once more, [and] despite his unctuous promises and guarantees to support the Arab–Kurdish unity within Iraq. Many have interpreted his return as direct encouragement to the ICP. It appears likely that a number of [asylees] from among Mulla Mustafa's tribal followers will join him. He said at the airport on October 6 that 500 of them live in the countries of the Soviet Bloc (*Thawrat 14 Tammuz wa Abdul Karim Qasim fil Watha'iq al-Britanniya*, al-A'dhami 1989, p. 96).

British Consul Sam Foel cabled regarding his meeting with Iraqi Minister of Information Siddique Shanshal, at his house:

> Baghdad, 7 October 1958, number: 16658/1013
>
> [The tenth paragraph of the cable stated]:
> [A]nd regarding the subject of Kurds, he did not express his concern and believes that they will cooperate with the government, and he defended the decision to allow Mulla Mustafa's return; believed that he will not create problems; again he believed that it was difficult not to permit such an [asylee] to return to his home country, and that such a decision would have created much dissatisfaction among the Kurds, more than his presence would (*al-A'dhami* 1989, p. 102).

Paragraph five of the British Embassy's report in Baghdad, dated October 16, 1958, number 58/180/1013, stated:

> Now Mulla Mustafa has returned to Baghdad, and he holds many festivities for large numbers of Kurds at his quarters in a hotel. This is what makes matters worse even when there is no direct danger from the Kurds at this time. At any rate, it is a risky situation which increases the Communist danger. The government relied on them to a large degree in removing Arif. The future is uncertain, and I do not like to speculate what direction it will take (*al-A'dhami* 1989, p. 103).

In Cairo, Barzani Meets President Jamal Abd al-Nasser

The American Embassy in Cairo described Barzani's meeting with President Nasser in its cable to Washington in the following manner:

> October 7, 1958
> Mulla Mustafa Barzani and six other Kurds arrived in Cairo on October 3, 1958, from Prague on their way to Iraq. They were received by Nasser the following day.

Barzani had not remained in Russia. He had traveled to Rumania, Poland, and Czechoslovakia to spread propaganda against the despotic (monarchic) regime. Barzani said that when the Kurdish [asylees] learned of the Egyptian Revolution, it was as though new life had been breathed into them. Barzani said, "We feel, like any Arab, that our problem with imperialism and corruption is the same. We considered the Egyptian Revolution a glorious victory for all the Arab people in the Near and Middle East. Revolutionary Cairo is a guidepost for all the peoples of the Middle East. Every word Nasser has said is engraved in our hearts; his voice has been the signal of victory. Our hopes were realized when the Iraqi Revolution broke out."

Barzani is due to arrive in Baghdad to meet with the leader of the revolution Abd al-Karim Qasim. One hundred and forty-seven Kurds who had been sentenced to death will also arrive (al-A'dhami 1989, p. 51).

Homecoming of the Companions on the Historic March

Of Barzani's companions in the historic march that he led in 1947, crossing the borders of Iraq, Iran, and Turkey and eluding their armies, 500 remained behind in the Soviet Union. As soon as Barzani returned to Baghdad, he worked to secure the return of his companions. The Iraqi government took all the necessary legal and technical steps to bring them home as soon as possible. Barzani sent both Mir Haj Ahmad and As'ad Khoshavi to Moscow to coordinate and supervise the operation. The Soviet Union also facilitated their return by assigning the ship *Grozia* to transport them. The *Grozia* left the port of Odessa in the beginning of April 1959, carrying 784 people, including women and children. It docked at the port of Basra on April 16, 1959. The returning partisans were received by a huge crowd of people, mainly the generous residents of Basra. They were transported in a train to Baghdad and then to Arbil. Returnees and their families were welcomed magnificently by the Iraqi populace wherever they stopped.

Sheikh Ahmad personally came to Arbil to welcome the returning heroes, who were eager to see him. The revolutionary government fully attended to the needs of these freedom fighters, appointed their graduates to government offices, and provided their elderly with the means necessary for a dignified life. They were respected in a manner befitting their struggle and sacrifices. The government also issued a general amnesty for all Barzanis who had been sentenced to death or to varying terms of imprisonment under the monarchy. The following is the text of the resolution germane to the rehabilitation of the martyrs of the Barzan Revolt:

The General Amnesty Committee's Resolution to Rehabilitate the Martyrs of the Barzan Revolt

In the Joint Case No. 98/1945 sentence of death was passed by the military court in Arbil on Maj. Izzat Abd al-Aziz (Ret.), Capt. Mustafa Khoshnow, Capt. Khairullah Abd al-Karim, Second Lt. Mahmud Qudsi, in accordance with Article 11 of Court-Martial Decree No. 18 of 1935, and all movable and immovable assets were to be confiscated and sold, and the funds paid to the Government as compensation for the damages caused by their actions in accordance with Articles 3 and 4 of the Supplement to the Court-Martial Decree No. 60 of 1941. They were secretly sent to the gallows inside the prison on June 19, 1947.

Nazima b. Abbas, the mother of the martyr Mohammed Mahmud Qudsi, submitted to this committee an application dated September 21, 1958, requesting an award to her son's legal heirs. Attorney Hamza Abdullah representing Saliha Mirza Manaf, the wife of martyr Khairullah Abd al-Karim, asked this Committee to assess compensation due to the martyr's family, as well as the amount of the military award and the monthly retirement sum.

On investigation, Maj. Izzat Abd al-Aziz, Capt. Mustafa Khoshnaw, Capt. Khairullah Abd al-Karim, and Second Lt. Mohammed Mahmud Qudsi were sentenced to death, and they were executed by hanging under Article 1 of Law No. 23 of 1958. Therefore, they and their comrades in the aforementioned case have been included in the comprehensive General Amnesty, which also requires that their awards be conferred on their legal heirs, who have the right as well to recover their movable and immovable assets which were confiscated according to the said verdict in accordance with Articles 3 and 7, and Paragraph (a) of Article 10 of the said law; and to notify the Cabinet according to Article 11 of the same law. This ruling was issued by consensus on February 25, 1959, according to amendment No. 19 of 1959.[8]

Chairman: Abd al-Amir al-Uqaili

Member: Fakhri al-Souz, Judge
Member: Abd al-Khaliq al-Durubi, Legal Consultant, Defense Ministry
Member: Ibrahim Hamudi, Legal Director, Ministry of Interior

The General Amnesty included 101 patriots who had participated in the Barzan revolt.

On the occasion of his comrades' returning home with honor and respect, Barzani sent the following letter of thanks to Abd al-Karim Qasim:

To Your Excellency, our sole leader Abd al-Karim Qasim,
   Prime Minister and Commander in Chief of the Armed Forces

The generous reception of my Barzani brothers whom the monarchy and their imperialist masters had forced to leave their homeland has proved to the world that the Arab–Kurdish brotherhood is an invincible material force. It was not the result of chance for it has evolved and developed over many years.

Reality proved the malicious propaganda which preceded the return of these citizens and which was intended to mislead world public opinion and distort reality to be sheer mendacity. The thousands of Iraqi citizens who crowded into Basra proved that they were welcoming [Barzani] citizens who had been long missed. They were not as portrayed in propaganda and lies woven by the imperialist forces about the returnees from the USSR to Iraq.

On behalf of the Barzanis who have returned home, and on behalf of all honorable Kurds, I wish to express my gratitude and appreciation to you and to the noble Iraqi people. Our appreciation cannot be expressed in words. Instead, I promise you on behalf of my brothers who have just returned home that we will defend our independent Republic and the honor of our homeland with all our power and with utmost sincerity. Under your righteous leadership, we will foil the plots of the covetous and dash all conspiracies and intrigues. In full solidarity with our brave Arab brothers, we will reinforce the foundations of our eternal Republic and move it forward.

In conclusion, please accept our utmost appreciation and highest regards for all that you and the Iraqi people have done for the return of the Barzanis and for their comfort.

Long live our free and democratic Iraqi Republic.

May the strong Arab-Kurdish fraternity live forever.

Long live the sole leader of all Iraqis, Abd al-Karim Qasim, supporter of peace and democracy.[9]

Sincerely,
Mustafa Barzani

Because of his participation in the battles of the Barzan Revolt in 1945, Abd al-Karim Qasim knew the Barzanis and their valor well. They left a good impression on him, and he appreciated their spirit of sacrifice and resistance. A trusting relationship developed between Abd al-Karim Qasim and Mustafa Barzani. Unfortunately, chauvinists and reactionaries succeeded in piercing and penetrating the wall of this trust and caused the events that were to follow.

Chapter 37

The Struggle among the Leaders of the Revolution

There was discord among the members of the High Committee of Free Officers before the outbreak of the revolution, and it began to surface from the very first day because of Abd al-Karim Qasim and Abd al-Salam Arif's high-handedness in decision-making and appointments. They pushed aside the most important decision the committee had agreed upon, i.e., the resolution to form the RCC. This dereliction left the door wide open for the struggle to emerge. Furthermore, the cabinet that was formed after the revolution lacked harmony and a minimum of ideological coherence.

Discord among the free officers spiraled to the point where it overshadowed the cabinet and, subsequently, the political parties and the ordinary citizens. The struggle began first among the military because of differences in their views regarding several internal and external issues, as well as the shape of the new leadership of the country.

On the first day, Abd al-Karim Qasim and Abd al-Salam Arif decided on several issues that effactually banished their comrades among the free officers from Baghdad. They were appointed to secondary posts, as in the case of Abd al-Wahhab al-Shawwaf. He was first appointed the military governor general. Pressured by Abd al-Salam Arif because of an old dispute, this decision was rescinded on July 15, 1958, and al-Shawwaf was appointed commander of the Mosul garrison.

Abd al-Salam Arif's public statements and speeches, including those in Damascus on July 18, when he met with President Nasser and those he made as he toured the provinces of the country, greatly agitated Abd al-Karim Qasim. Moreover, Arif's chauvinistic attitude toward the Kurdish people made them view him with suspicion and circumspection.

Abd al-Salam Arif tried to appear as if he was the one who had carried out the July 14 Revolution and that the roles of others were subsidiary to his own. Undeniably, Abd al-Salam Arif did play a major role in carrying out the revolution, but the fact remains that it was the collective work of the free officers, each in his own capacity, and the solidarity of the people. It would have been impossible for anyone alone to bring about a great revolution such as that of July 14. It would never have been able to stand fast in the face of all the internal and external threats and challenges.

Abd al-Salam Arif tried to negate Abd al-Karim Qasim's role and neglected to mention his name in his speeches. He made a point of bringing up [the Egyptian president] Nasser's name as often as possible, which angered Abd al-Karim Qasim. A glance at his speech in the provinces during his tour of the country clearly demonstrates Arif's backwardness and ignorance of the most basic principles of politics and leadership. The following are excerpts from his speeches:

> Our republic is socialist, patriotic, godly, khaki [referring to the army by the color of their uniforms], complete and faultless, no governor or governed, no parties or cliques. One nation and one party. Neither eastern nor western. Not northern or southern. No Johnny or John Paul, only Hamad and Hammoud. No more feudalism, no more palaces or refrigerators or televisions. No disparity, no classes. No majesties or excellencies. Only freedom, justice, and equality (*Abdussalam Mohamed Arif*, Fawzi 1989, p. 80).

If anything, these incoherent sentences indicate the speaker's ignorance of the reality he lived in as well as the backwardness that makes every conscientious person pity the Iraqi people for being governed by such an individual.

In his book *Sanawat al-Ghalayan* (*The Years of Simmering*), Mohamed Hasaneyn Heikal (1988) wrote regarding the meeting specifically arranged for Siddique Shanshal with President Nasser in Damascus on July 18, 1958,

> ... [W]hen the meeting was arranged, President Nasser began by telling Siddique Shanshal that "To him, what had happened in Baghdad was like a dream that would never come true." Nasser was taken by surprise when he heard Siddique Shanshal tell him, "At the national [Pan-Arab] level, yes, Mr. President, but at the Iraqi level, it can turn into a big nightmare." Astounded, and despite all that he had heard from Abd al-Hamid al-Sarraj, Nasser realized that things were worse than he had imagined. Siddique Shanshal continued, "Now heading the Iraqi Revolution are two men; one is half insane, and the other is half sane!" In Shanshal's judgement, the half-insane man was Brigadier Abd al-Karim Qasim, chairman of the Revolutionary Command Council (RCC), and the half-sane man was Colonel Abd al-Salam Arif (Heikal 1988, p. 375).

Siddique Shanshal was the minister of guidance in the cabinet, which he described as having a half-insane president and a half-sane vice president. From Shanshal's conversation, you can imagine the depth of discord and disharmony among ministers in the same cabinet. Obviously, judging by his comments, Shanshal was not in agreement with Abd al-Salam Arif.

As time passed, the gap between the free officers grew wider, notably between Abd al-Karim Qasim and Abd al-Salam Arif. The struggle ended when Abd al-Salam Arif was forced to resign from all of his posts, accused of conspiracy, and tried before the People's Court, which sentenced him to death. Abd al-Karim Qasim commuted his sentence to a prison term. He was pardoned at the end of 1961.

This intense struggle started the July 14 Revolution on bad terms. Discord pervaded the parties' rank and file, which also split into pro- and anti-Qasim factions. The ordeal left the door wide open for the opportunists and reactionaries who toyed with the people's future and paved the way for chauvinists to take over the government and usurp the people's freedoms.

What we find in Iraq in the way of dictatorship, terror, and oppression are the harvest of that strife.

The Struggle among the Parties and the Collapse of the National Unity Front

The NUF parties preserved their unity in the first five months of the revolutionary era. They worked together to defend the republic against internal and external dangers. However, in reality, the NUF collapsed after the first five months, especially as the conflict between Abd al-Karim Qasim and Abd al-Salam Arif and his Arab nationalist trend escalated.

Foremost among their differences was the subject of immediate unification with the UAR. Callers for Arab unity used unification to symbolize their strife against Abd al-Karim Qasim, whereas the patriotic and democratic trend allied with Abd al-Karim Qasim called for a federation. Events later proved that those who called for immediate unification were not sincere in calling for any form of Arab unity. Abd al-Salam Arif came to power and ruled Iraq almost single-handedly. Then the Ba'th Party took over in a military coup d'état on July 17, 1968, and has been ruling Iraq with an iron fist ever since. What have these leaders done for Arab unity?

Initially, the differences were slight, and the parties tried to revive the NUF. Each party submitted a draft accord for discussion. Eventually the Joint Action Accord was signed in November 1958 by five parties: the NDP, the *Istiqlal* [Independence] Party (IP), the Ba'th, Party, the ICP, and the KDP. The charter of this accord contained the following items:

1. Iraq is an integral part of the Arab nation, and it will strive to achieve the best and strongest ties with the UAR to realize total Arab unity in the future.
2. The front will work to implement the articles concerning Kurdish national rights as stated in the provisional constitution issued on July 27, 1958.
3. It is necessary that the government pursue a patriotic policy and realize people's demands by achieving political and economic freedoms from imperialism.
4. The charter stresses its support for the revolution and the republic and the necessity of establishing a sound democratic life which will give political parties the right of political activity legally and openly (*Thawrat 14 Tammuz 1958 fil Iraq*, al-Zubaidi 1979, p. 462).

This charter was ineffectual. Troubles emerged in a far more acute manner, dominating inter-party relations. In February 1959, the nationalist cabinet members resigned, and Abd al-Karim Qasim controlled the government with the support of the NDP, the ICP, and the KDP. The Ba'th Party began to work against Abd al-Karim Qasim underground, and the IP remained wary, with many reservations. The conflict between the ICP and the Ba'th Party was intense and at times bloody. Each tried to control the populace and secure more privileges. From the contention two political currents emerged: one nationalist, led by the Ba'th Party, and the other democratic, led by the ICP.

Arab unity is a vast goal and demands much clearly defined struggle and effort by the Arabs. It is in the best interests of the Arabs and their friends and cannot be realized by a slogan or by issuing a declaration. Events have shown that all attempts at unification failed because they were not based on sound and scientific foundations—they were brought about by sentiments and ephemera. Those who called for unification were numerous when in opposition, but they reversed course when they came to power!

It appears that the pioneer of Arab nationalism, President Jamal Abd al-Nasser, realized that conditions were not right for immediate unification. About this he was not enthusiastic, as may be seen from his conversation with Siddique Shanshal in Damascus on July 18, 1958, as recounted by Mohamed Hasaneyn Heikal, who wrote that President Nasser told Shanshal,

> "I accepted unification with Syria for reasons of which you are aware. I thought we could take a big step forward, and then take time to fortify our lines and close the gaps. But this did not happen. To date, our lines are still long and exposed. Gaps are still open and exposed. Despite my attempts, I must admit that we have not succeeded to the extent I thought or hoped we would. I do not wish to burden the unification experiment between Egypt and Syria with all the contradictions at work in Baghdad today. Therefore, you will see me prepared to do everything possible to reinforce the Iraqi Revolution and whatever will open new horizons for all possible cooperation between our two countries. However, please do not request any unification step now." Siddique Shanshal replied that this was exactly his view, that he came to Damascus to speak frankly to Nasser about it from a nationalist perspective, and that if he had found him to be leaning in another direction, he would have advised otherwise because despite his firm belief in the validity of Arab unity, unification between Egypt and Syria was liable to be drowned beneath the powerful waves engulfing Baghdad.
>
> Nasser told the Iraqi delegation headed by Abd al-Salam Arif that he was prepared to sign any agreement with the revolutionary government in Iraq but that he was not enthusiastically in favor of any steps towards unification under the current conditions (Heikal 1988, p. 378).

The gist of the discord between the political parties did not stem from immediate unification or a federation. The Ba'th Party and the nationalist elements rallied around Abd al-Salam Arif to gain more power and influence, and each tried to exploit the other for its own purposes and to gain control of the government. Conversely, the other political parties allied themselves with Abd al-Karim Qasim to gain more privileges while Abd al-Karim Qasim exploited their alliance to stymie attempts to reduce his power or to oust him.

Thus, the conflict between the parties can be described as a tug-of-war for narrow party interests. As time passed, Abd al-Karim Qasim became suspicious of the political parties and their intentions toward him and his rule. He resorted to a policy of evasion and circumvention with the parties and encouraged discord among them. He considered himself above and beyond party politics. He thought that he did not need the parties and that he had given them more than they deserved. The parties, on the other hand, saw him as having broken his pledge to grant them freedom and participation in the government.

Abd al-Karim Qasim did not settle into a relationship with any party. He tried to exploit each as he saw fit for his own ends. He exerted great efforts to split party alliances and ranks, and he succeeded in splitting the ICP and the NDP, but he failed to split the KDP.

At any rate, the struggle among parties helped to derail Abd al-Karim Qasim and intensified his suspicions. He had seen these parties praise him early on, ascribing to him all of the traits of heroism, greatness, and virtue. These same parties began to make demands that he considered acts of defiance and abrogation of earlier positions.

In my opinion, the political parties bear historical responsibility for the atrocities and tribulations which befell Iraq. If the parties had remained united in the NUF and set aside their narrow party interests, they would have saved themselves and the Iraqi people all of the horrors and tragedies that followed. The political parties should have considered Iraq's interests before asking Abd al-Karim Qasim to do so.

Chapter 38

The Kurdistan Democratic Party after the July 14 Revolution

After the July 14 Revolution, the KDP was able, for the first time since its founding, to conduct its activities openly without being hounded by the police and the secret service. The masses of Kurdistan rallied around the KDP, whose influence multiplied now that its president had returned from the Soviet Union.

Under the monarchy, the KDP, a clandestine party, held three congresses but was never legalized. Conscious of its vital role in defending the republic, the leaders of the revolution paid special attention to the KDP and close ties developed between the KDP's president and Abd al-Karim Qasim. Under the monarchy, in addition to raids by the police and the secret service that had curbed its growth and progress, the KDP had suffered from internal problems and factionalism.

In its third congress, the KDP almost split apart when it was decided that Hamza Abdullah's membership be suspended, as he was leading one faction and Ibrahim Ahmad was leading another. Despite these difficulties, the KDP succeeded in preserving its unity and in carrying on its struggle.

Ali Abdullah says that owing to Barzani's recommendation, which was conveyed by Jalal Talabani after a visit to Moscow, Hamza Abdullah was again contacted and the KDP leaders adopted a more flexible approach toward him. And in 1957, several leaders and cadres of the ICP's Kurdistan branch changed their affiliation to the KDP.[1] To protect KDP unity and prevent factionalism, it was decided to change the KDP's name to the United Democratic Party of Kuridstan. At its Fourth Congress, it returned to its original name, the KDP.

After the July 14 Revolution and the return of the KDP's president from the USSR, it was obvious that lingering vestiges of old disputes continued to hinder the KDP's progress and its adaptation to the new era. Hamza Abdullah's faction followed Communist policies, as if the KDP was a branch of the ICP, and accused others of rightism and of following the Arab bourgeoisie. Barzani held the middle ground, hoping to resolve differences between the wings by conciliatory means. However, Hamza Abdullah's faction continued unchanged while the ICP leaders, particularly the Kurds among them, clearly interfered in KDP affairs through Hamza and his comrades, who were in control. They expelled or suspended a number of the opposing faction, including Ibrahim Ahmad and Jalal Talabani.

The discord reached a level whereby it threatened to split the party. It was not confined to the Central Committee, as it permeated the party rank and file as well. Barzani intervened directly to end this detrimental state of affairs. Decisive actions were taken at the Central Committee meeting on June 30, 1959. Hamza Abdullah and his comrades, Khasrow Tawfiq, Nejad Ahmad, Salih Rushdi, Hamid Othman, and Salih al-Haidari, were suspended. The following day, a team of KDP cadres and Barzani guards took over party headquarters and expelled the rest of Hamza Abdullah's faction.

Whatever reasons and justifications might have been behind this decision, the KDP as a whole was the chief loser, as it lost some of its most able cadres. Despite several attempts to convince Hamza and his comrades to attend the Central Committee meeting, they refused. Hamza wrote a letter to Barzani, warning him about Ibrahim Ahmad and his faction and accusing them of rightism and disloyalty to the party and Barzani. He ended his letter with the phrase: "I am steering you right." That letter ended all hope of resolving differences, and it angered Barzani. I am sure if Hamza Abdullah and his comrades had been present, the decision would have been different.

True, Hamza Abdullah and his comrades moved the KDP toward complete subordination to the ICP. If the situation had continued as in the first few months of 1959, the KDP would have lost its independence and become a branch of the ICP. It is also true that Barzani's intervention ended the discord to the benefit of the KDP, its independence and integrity, but the manner in which the discord was resolved was, in my view, not the best way to resolve such differences. I consider it to have been very harsh. Any dissension should have been resolved in a more flexible and organized manner, which would have been in the best interests of the KDP, as well as being the best way of dealing with things in general. Then the crisis should have been waited out until the KDP's Fourth Congress, which had been slated for early October 1959, or the date should have been advanced.

Barzani respected Hamza Abdullah and preferred him over others. Initially, Barzani humored him, but Hamza did not act in his interests or in the interests of the KDP during that sensitive period as he should have. What happened then became a part of KDP's history, and I think it is necessary to point out that the position Hamza Abdullah took after his expulsion was a very responsible one. He did not take any action that would cause a split in the party, and he deserves credit for that. For his position, he regained Barzani's respect and appreciation, as well as that of the KDP cadres. I recall that when he came to visit Barzani after March 11, 1970, he was received well and with respect (see Document nos. 30–43).[2]

The Attitude of the Kurdish Tribal Chiefs vis-à-vis
the July 14 Revolution and the Kurdistan Democratic Party

The July 14 Revolution opened new horizons to the Iraqi people. Among its accomplishments was the legislation of the Agrarian Reform Law of September 30, 1958. On that day, Abd al-Karim Qasim announced law no. 30 of 1958. According to the new law, maximum agricultural land ownership was limited to 1,000 donums of irrigated land and 2,000 donums of rain-fed [dry farming] land.[3] Excess land was to be distributed among peasants with the minimum ownership of land: 30 donums irrigated or 60 donums rainfed. Before the revolution, there was no limit to the land a person could own. Some feudalists owned a million donums.

Kurdish feudalists were no different from Arab ones in that both exploited the peasants. However, they did not have the means of production that their Arab counterparts had. The majority of Arab feudalists owned irrigated land and were not affected by changes in the weather. The government offered them much assistance in terms of agricultural technology, which reduced the number of small farmers and rapidly concentrated land in the hands of large landowners (*al-Haraka al-Wataniyya al-Dimuqratiyya fi Kurdistan al-Iraq: 1961–1968*, Ashirian 1978, p. 39).

The Agrarian Reform Law did not take the special circumstances of Kurdistan into consideration. In central and southern Iraq, 1,000 donums of irrigated land is considered a middle-sized fief, whereas in Kurdistan the same amount of land is considered a very large one. Initially, land reform struck very heavily at feudalism but failed to introduce any radical change in the conditions of peasants in Kurdistan. The government neglected to implement the law in the hope of winning over tribal chiefs and using them against the Kurdish movement. The chiefs were granted broad privileges over peasants.

After the July 14 Revolution, the position of the tribal chiefs varied from one region to another. Some pledged allegiance to the revolution and supported the KDP and Barzani. Others opposed it, and some even became affiliated with the Ba'th Party in order to provoke Abd al-Karim Qasim, the KDP, and Barzani. Still others were enticed by foreigners and began preparations for rebellion against the revolutionary government in Iraq, as happened in the case of Sheikh Rashid of Lolan.

The feudalists lost influence. They could no longer exploit peasants from the advent of the revolution until the end of 1959 and were psychologically prepared to undertake any action against the republic. Nonetheless, the conduct of some extremists in the PRM and that of some peasants, who saw a chance to take revenge on the feudalists, who had oppressed them for decades and had become rich from the sweat of their brows, went beyond all rational limits most of the time. The provocations grew to a degree that some feudalists could not tolerate.

Whenever there are no rules governing the interaction between social classes or defining their rights and when law does not govern or arbitrate, truth will not prevail and anarchy will take over. This is what happened in the first year of the revolution. In my view, the reason was that the new state and the parties lacked the necessary expertise and experience.

Many Pishdar tribal chiefs escaped to Iran, and many more chiefs from other regions escaped to Turkey. Tribal ties were very strong then, and the tribal chiefs did not leave alone. Typically, a number of men of the tribe would accompany their chief to an unknown fate without having given much thought to what would happen to their families and children. Both Iran and Turkey were ready to receive, arm, and return these feudalists to carry out raids on Iraqi police and border stations. This was a serious threat to the security of the revolution and the new republic.

Abd al-Karim Qasim asked Sheikh Ahmad Barzani to use his considerable influence to mediate with tribal chiefs who had fled to Iran and persuade them to return to Iraq, with the pledge that their rights would be protected according to the law. The competent state apparatus would carry out the law, and the PRM would not be allowed to interfere in their affairs if they remained loyal to the state, went about with their private lives, and severed all ties to Iran and Turkey. Sheikh Ahmad's mediation succeeded to a large extent, and a good number of the fleeing tribal chiefs did return to Iraq.

Strangely enough, a double standard was maintained from that time on. A tribal chief who pledged allegiance to the ICP would be considered democratic and progressive, one who sympathized with the KDP would be accused of being "a reactionary and a foreign agent," and the few who supported the Ba'th Party were characterized as "[Pan-Arab] Unionists."

In the midst of political struggle among the forces themselves and between them and the government, the Agrarian Reform Law was practically frozen. It was not implemented equally in all areas. In the end, land reform became a problem for the peasants. If a feudalist maligned a peasant and said that he was affiliated with the KDP or provided food to the peshmergas[4] after the September Revolution, the authorities would readily evict him from his land. Often a peasant would be killed on orders from the tribal chief, while the government took no action of any kind. In the 1960s, tribal chiefs ferociously took revenge on peasants in areas under the government's control.

Rare were those tribal chiefs who remained patriotic and sacrificed their own interests for the good of the people. In most tribes, a group took the side of the Kurdish revolution and another group took the government's side (see Document nos. 44–46).[5]

Chapter 39

The Kurdistan Democratic Party and Other Parties in Kurdistan

K urdish masses in all parts of Kurdistan welcomed the July 14 Revolution. The KDP and Iraqi Kurdistan became a strong prop for other sister parties. At that time, there was not such a large number of parties in any part of Kurdistan (as there is today). There was a Democratic Party in each of the Iranian and Syrian parts, and in Turkey the KDP was founded in 1965. Prior to that it was an organization affiliated with the KDP of Iraq.

Mustafa Barzani symbolized the Kurdish struggle for all parts of Kurdistan, and his was the last word for them all. After his return, Kurdish patriots from other parts of Kurdistan came to him and received all the support they needed from him and the KDP. The Iraq of the July 14 Revolution was the sought-after refuge for all of them.

Article 3 of the Iraqi Constitution, which recognized Kurdish national rights in Iraq, encouraged the Kurds in other parts of Kurdistan and inculcated new hope and spirit in them.

The state of organization of the Kurdistan Democratic Party of Iran (KDPI) was better than that of similar parties in Turkey and Syria because of its accumulated experience and skill. In addition to having a good number of seasoned chief cadres, the memory of the Republic of Mahabad was still fresh in their minds. A number of KDPI leaders came to Iraq after the July 14 Revolution and effectively built up their organization with support from the KDP. For the record, the active and distinguished role of the martyr Abdullah Ishaqi, better known as Ahmad Tawfiq, the general secretary of the KDPI, must be pointed out. He actively established strong ties with other Kurdish parties. As one of his serious contributions to the revolution, he was the first to travel to Beirut, accompanied by Dana Adams Schmidt,[1] the first foreign journalist to visit Kurdistan in 1962 and cover the news of the September Revolution. A great number of KDPI members joined the September Revolution.

In the remaining chapters [of this book], the discord among these parties will be discussed. Interested readers will find more details about the relationships among the fraternal parties and the support they received from the KDP in Document nos. 47–56.[2]

Chapter 39

Chapter 40

The Kurdistan Democratic Party and the Iraqi Communist Party (ICP)

K DP and ICP relations vacillated, but positive ties were the norm. The ICP was the only Iraqi party with an organizational base in Kurdistan aside from the KDP. Therefore, it was only natural that the two would cooperate and simultaneously compete, which led to a myriad of problems.

From its inception in 1946, the ICP viewed the KDP as a superfluous organization that had no raison d'être as long as the ICP existed in Kurdistan. At the same time the reality of the conflict called for the founding of a democratic nationalist party to lead the struggle of the Kurdish people. Among the Communists who recognized this reality was the martyr Salman Yousif Salman (Fahd), ICP's secretary general. In an article published in *al-Qa'ideh* newspaper in April 1945, he called on Kurdish patriots to establish such a party:

> Conscientious citizens of all classes of the Kurdish people, the cause of your people is a trust in your custody. Fulfill your duties toward your people; lead them to deliverance out of these poor conditions, establish a Kurdish popular organization befitting the reality of the Kurdish people—an organization that will serve Kurdish interests. I want you to know that you will find our Party to be most supportive and helpful (Talabani 1981:152).

However, other ICP leaders did not translate this call into reality. One of the most important points of discord between the KDP and the ICP was the ICP's position regarding the cause of the Kurdish nation. The ICP continued to deny the existence of the Kurdish nation until a new charter known as the Basim Charter was issued. The Basim Charter strongly criticized the ICP's position vis-à-vis the Kurdish nation, especially Article 10 of the ICP's charter, which considered all Kurds, Turkomans, Assyrians, Yazidis, and Armenians, as ethnic minorities. This was a grave error since the Kurds constitute the second largest nationality in Iraq; and, in terms of their ethnicity, the Yazidis are quintessential Kurds.

The KDP reaffirmed that the Kurds are of a nation on equal footing with other nations and, as such, possess the same rights including the right to self-determination. A second point of contention between the KDP and the ICP was the ICP's position regarding the establishment of democratic organizations under KDP leadership. The ICP considered the KDP to be the party of the nation's bourgeoisie and worked continuously to limit its influence.

After many bitter experiences, after the KDP put down roots among the populace in Kurdistan, and after the ICP retracted its hard-line policies regarding the points of contention cited above at its 1956 conference, the two parties agreed on the following significant points:

1. ICP recognition of the Kurdish nation and its right to self-determination.
2. The right to have a national democratic and progressive party in Kurdistan.
3. That Arab and Kurdish nations must join their struggle against imperialism.
4. Mutual recognition of the right to self-determination and the legitimacy of both peoples' aspirations to liberty and national unity.

At their conference in 1956, the Communists recognized that autonomy based on a voluntary fraternal union is a measure tied to prevalent circumstances and necessitated by the interests of both Arab and Kurdish peoples—clearly by the interest of the latter. In this context, this meant that it was not the ultimate solution for the Kurdish national cause and could not in any way replace the right to self-determination for the Kurdish nation.[1]

After the July 14 Revolution, the ICP's influence grew, and the party became the dominant popular force in the first few months after the revolution. Trusted elements from the ICP were appointed to sensitive state positions where they could have taken over the government at any moment. I am not sure how the ICP lost this opportunity, which will never come its way again.

Before the revolution, most ICP leaders were either in prison or in hiding and they never had the experience of overt political activity. They were astounded, as were others, by the soaring popular revolutionary tide after the revolution. Their blunders testified to their lack of experience.

The PRM, which often infringed on people's rights, was in fact under ICP command. This undermined the reputation of the ICP. Furthermore, under the new circumstances, the ICP imposed its hegemony on the other parties and tried to coerce them into recognizing its leadership role. This led to intractable problems between the ICP and the KDP in Kurdistan. Discussion among the cadres of both parties would often end in fights that would bring PRM intervention on behalf of the Communists. What complicated the relations between the two parties most was the ICP's interference in the internal affairs of the KDP when the dispute arose between what was called the Hamza Abdullah and Ibrahim Ahmad factions.

The KDP sent a memorandum to the ICP on October 18, 1958, complaining of the ICP positions.[2] This opened the door for a dialogue between the leaders of both parties, which culminated in the signing of the bipartisan Accord of Cooperation on November 10, 1958, intended to translate Article 3 of the Constitution into reality. The High Committee for National Cooperation was formed. It issued its first press release on February 5, 1959:

> Heroes of the peoples of Kurdistan,
> ICP and KDP Patriots, and all independents:
>
> Reinforce your unity; mobilize your forces, form your National Cooperation Committees everywhere. Do not leave room for division, and do not let your enemies come between your ranks. Multiply your alertness, and stand ready against traitors, enemies of the people (*Thawrat 14 Tammuz*, Khairi 1980, p. 180).

The Accord of Cooperation emphasized preserving the Republic, reinforcing its democratic platform, purging the state system of foreign agents and the corrupt, strengthening and arming the military, expelling French advisors, striving for realizing Arab–Kurdish brotherhood, as well as solidarity between the military and the people, renouncing the Baghdad Pact, working to achieve maximum cooperation with the UAR, building solidarity among the Arab peoples, strengthening ties to socialist and liberated countries, and staying the patriotic course in foreign policy. The accord also called for supporting the government in the implementation of the Agrarian Reform Law, the liquidation of feudalism, and the elevation of the peasants' standard of living.

Regarding the Kurdish people, the accord emphasized the following:

1. Recognition in principle of the rights of the Kurdish people, including the right to self-determination.
2. Fighting separatist thought and movements, and striving to solidify solidarity between the Arab and Kurdish nationalities.
3. Upholding Article 3 of the Provisional Constitution of the Republic of Iraq and working to implement it by legislating laws guaranteeing Kurdish national rights.
4. Caring for the interests of the Kurdish people with regard to industrialization and raising agricultural production and living standards, as well as social, educational, and health standards.
5. Strengthening fraternity between the Kurdish people and the minorities living in Kurdistan, and guaranteeing their ability to exercise their rights.

Cooperation subcommittees were formed in the provinces. After this bilateral accord, the KDP joined the NUF. Both parties issued a joint statement on February 24, 1959 with regard to the democratic organizations, the text of which follows.

Resolution of the High Committee for National Cooperation

Since our parties promulgated the National Cooperation Accord, new avenues have opened in our joint struggle. The High Committee and other Cooperation Subcommittees have been formed in some cities. It was decided to establish Investigative Committees to resolve differences so as to strengthen national cooperation. Jointly, our organizations have accomplished several fruitful activities that prove the existence of vast opportunities for cooperation. Specific obstacles confronting our parties have been identified as well. Most of these obstacles emanate from the conflict between the activities of democratic organizations that are of the same social nature, such as the existence of two youth organizations in Kurdistan.

The High Committee has studied these obstacles in a sincere and brotherly manner. Guided by the principles of the National Cooperation Accord, it has reviewed the valuable experience of the student movement and has found it necessary to arrive at the following positive resolution:

Struggle to support democracy, enhance unified action among the masses, unify joint struggle to uphold the democratic entity of the Republic, and avert the peril of forming a faction opposed to the authority of the national government in these sensitive times. All these necessitate that an illegal organization must not be allowed, during joint functions, to carry out a special activity that runs counter to the activity of a legal organization of the same social nature. The legal democratic organization has the right to illustrate its character among the masses in as conspicuous a manner as possible, because this is an aspect of guided democracy in which both our parties believe.

After reviewing the last student experience, the High Committee felt that the High Committee of the Kurdistan Student Union (KSU) had made a sound decision to suspend its activities and work within the General Student Union (GSU), a democratically established organization. While the KSU maintained the necessity of having a special entity for students in Kurdistan in the future, its decision was dictated by its sincere desire to struggle for the triumph of democracy, the only way to realize the legitimate demands of Kurdistan students.

The High Committee for National Cooperation believes in the right of each democratic organization to conduct its own activities. However, in the case of joint activities, it allows only legal social and labor organizations to exhibit their character and promote their goals. This does not mean barring the activities of other illegal organizations from specified joint activities, provided they do not violate the principles proclaimed in the National Cooperation Accord.

The High Committee for National Cooperation has found that submission of the minutes of the meetings of the [sub]committees benefits their progression. Therefore they should be submitted to the High Committee upon the conclusion of each meeting.[3]

> The High Committee for National Cooperation
> Between the ICP and the KDP
> *February 24, 1959*

Despite difficulties and ideological competition that stymied KDP and ICP relations, the ICP remained the closest of the Iraqi parties to the KDP and the Kurdish people. The ICP never opposed Kurdish revolts and uprisings, and it was better informed and more attentive to conditions in Kurdistan than the Iraqi Arab parties. From 1963 until 1973, the ICP participated in the Kurdish revolution led by Barzani.

In my view, the colossal mistake that both parties made was that the KDP trusted what the Ba'th Party kept reiterating, namely that the KDP was an extension of the Ba'th Party in Kurdistan and that the Ba'th was an extension of the KDP in the Arab regions of Iraq. The Ba'th stated emphatically that there was no need for other parties to join in building peace and security, and that they should not be allowed to do so. It is highly likely that Barzani relayed to the ICP the Ba'th Party's vehement opposition to ICP participation in the negotiations that took place between the Kurdish revolution and the Ba'th Party in 1970. The ICP accepted nonparticipation, believing that peace was more important than anything else. The KDP should not have given this opportunity to the Ba'th Party, and the ICP should have been involved in the negotiations.

In 1973, the ICP erroneously let the KDP conclude the National Action Charter with the Ba'th Party alone. In a word, the Ba'th Party succeeded in driving a wedge between the KDP and the ICP. Both paid a hefty price. The worst yet, Ba'th successfully played the two parties against each other, which led to violent armed clashes between their forces in most areas of Kurdistan, with the Ba'th Party reaping the benefits. This was the first time that relations between the KDP and the ICP gave way to fighting and bloodshed. The ICP left Kurdistan, and its armed forces joined the government. The total estrangement of the two parties persisted until 1979.

It is worth mentioning here that the ICP never attacked Barzani personally, despite its turbulent relations with the KDP. The ICP press continually spoke of Barzani's humane attitude in the worst of times toward the IPC.

Undoubtedly, the discord between the KDP and the ICP harmed them both, as well as harming the Iraqi people and the July 14 Revolution. It created many fissures through which Arab and Kurdish reactionaries and chauvinists lay in wait and set the stage for the black coup of February 8, 1963. For more details regarding the discord between the KDP and the ICP during the Qasim era, see Document nos. 57–63.[4]

The Popular Resistance Militia

The PRM was formed to train the people to use arms, along with the army, to defend the republic against foreign threats. However, it became a state within a state and exceeded its role and original purpose. Were it not for the crimes committed by the National Guard founded after the coup of February 8, 1963, the Iraqi people would have been unable to forget the PRM's excesses.

The PRM gave itself the right to act above the law, exercising functions which were properly restricted to the government. The PRM was founded in accordance with Military Operations Directive no. 989, dated July 22, 1958. Colonel Taha Bamerni was appointed PRM commander. Three regional commands were established: northern, central, and southern. The PRM's reign and its influence over Iraq reached into every aspect of life. Then the PRM committed unimaginable atrocities, particularly after the failure of the al-Shawwaf uprising in Mosul and the bloody events in Kirkuk. Abd al-Karim Qasim had to disband the PRM in July 1959, immediately after the lamentable events in Kirkuk. In Kurdistan, the PRM's conduct was a significant factor in fanning the flames of discord between the KDP and the ICP.

The People's Court

Hassan al-Alawi's magnum opus, *Abdul Karim Qasim, Ru'ya Ba'd al-Ishrin*, giving his precise description of People's Court, better known as Mahdawi's Court, is the best book on the subject. At least it is the best I have seen until now. He wrote,

The Revolutionary Government established a special military tribunal to try the corrupt in the government system from the days of the monarchy. Headed by

Colonel Fadhil Abbas al-Mahdawi, commander of the Musayyab Garrison, a Free Officer and a close relative of Abd al-Karim Qasim's . . .

Court sessions were broadcast live on radio and television. We believe that this is proof that Mahdawi had the utmost courage, self-confidence, and willingness to accept the consequences. Besides their clearly democratic character, the sessions verged on absurdity in their overindulgent use of microphones and cameras placed at the disposal of defendants accused of conspiracy against the state or of government corruption!

Broadcasting the court sessions live was a just and fair move although it caused ample headache for the July 14 Revolution and for Abd al-Karim Qasim.

Twenty years later, this appears to have been the first and last Revolutionary Tribunal to grant the accused the right to defend himself as much as he wanted to and for as long as he wanted, brought to the world in the same manner as the prosecutor's presentation and the judge's discourse. It may have been the last political court in Iraq and in the region to function in this manner (al-Alawi 1983, p. 43).

Such was Mahdawi's Court, attested to by an anti-Mahdawi-ite and a high ranking member of the Ba'th Party, which participated in the ouster and execution of Mahdawi and Abd al-Karim Qasim [in February 1963].

How are the courts in Iraq today? Is there anyone who hears anything about trials of the political opposition, be they covert or overt? How many are missing whose relatives know nothing about their fates, which were decided arbitrarily? Innumerable families wish to know where their sons are buried, let alone how they died!

I wish that Mahdawi's Court had not been the last political trial in Iraq. Indeed, I hope the courageous Iraqi people will rise, regain their dignity and pride, and their right to live, prosper, and build democratic constitutional establishments in which law will reign supreme. Then we will learn the extent of the catastrophe that befell Iraq after the July 17, 1968 coup d'état that brought the Ba'th Party to power. Only then will Nu'man Mahir al-Kan'ani's book about the crimes of the Ba'thists in Iraq after the February coup be a drop in the ocean.

Chapter 41

Freedom of Political Assembly

After the July 14 Revolution, the NUF parties worked freely for several months. Leaders of the revolution were determined to end the transitional period and grant parties legal status. However, the Law of Political Parties was not legislated until January 1960. This law defined a political party as "an association with political goals." It stipulated that only Iraqi citizens could become members. It barred members of the armed forces, state employees in the diplomatic corps, and primary- and secondary-school students from affiliation with parties. It required the founders of a party to submit to the Minister of the Interior a statement of support for the said party, signed by 50 people who qualified for membership.

By the time this law was promulgated, Abd al-Karim Qasim's relationship with the political parties had changed. Some supported him, others opposed him, while the Ba'th Party called for ousting him and made an assassination attempt on October 7, 1959. Other parties maintained their ties to him somewhat. Except for the Ba'th Party, at that time no other party had gone so far as calling for Qasim's overthrow. For his part, Abd al-Karim Qasim tried to break up the parties. He was successful with the NDP, as Mohammed Hadid had broken with Kamil Cahdirchi and formed a new party, and Dawood al-Sa'igh split off from the ICP and formed a decoy Communist Party. He failed to break up the KDP, despite his attempts to persuade Barzani to expel Ibrahim Ahmad and several other party leaders. He also attempted to convince Ibrahim Ahmad to break with his party, especially at the Fifth KDP Congress.

Among the parties that submitted requests for permits to the Ministry of the Interior was the KDP, which became legal for the first time in the history of Iraq and published its party organ, the journal *Khabat* (The Struggle).[1]

Figure 1 Sheik Abd as-Salam Barzani with the Representative of the Czar in Tiblisi in 1912.

Figure 2 Mullah Mustafa Barzani in 1944.

Figure 3 Barzani in his military uniform. Behind him, from right to left, Mohammed Mahmud Qudsi, Izzat Abdul Aziz, Khairullah Abdul Karim, and Abd ar-Rahman Mufti in Mahabad, 1946.

Figure 4 Mullah Mustafa Barzani, photo taken in 1946.

Figure 5 January 22, 1946: The day the Republic proclaimed in Mahabad. At the podium: Qadhi Mohammed declaring independence and in front of him, Mustafa Barzani with a number of other officials and dignitaries.

Figure 6 Mustafa Barzani and Qadhi Mohammed in 1946.

Figure 7   Mustafa Barzani during school time, Moscow, 1957.

Figure 8   Iraqi masses received Barzani at al-Muthanna airport in Baghdad on October 6, 1958.

Figure 9   Barzani visiting A. K. Qasim on the morning of October 7, 1958.

Figure 10   En route from USSR to Iraq, Mustafa Barzani and his comrades received by Nasser in Cairo.

Figure 11 A scene of Barzan village and behind it appears Mount Shirin.

Figure 12 Mullah Mustafa Barzani and Shaykh Latif Hafeed in Qala Diza, 1964.

Figure 13 Right to left: Barzani, As'ad Khoshavi, Shaykh Sulayman, and Saleh Kani Lanji, Soviet Union, 1955.

Figure 14 Barzani in his military uniform in 1946.

Figure 15   Tashqand: 1952. Sitting (left to right): Gorgo Babkayi, Hakim Piyand, Mustafa Barzani, and Mullah Rash. Standing (left to right): Mohammed Agha Dolamari, Nimiz, Mohammed Amin Mirkhan, and Omer Mohammed Amin Liri.

Figure 16   Barzani and Jamal Abd an-Nasir in Cairo, President Nasir's Residence, October 1958.

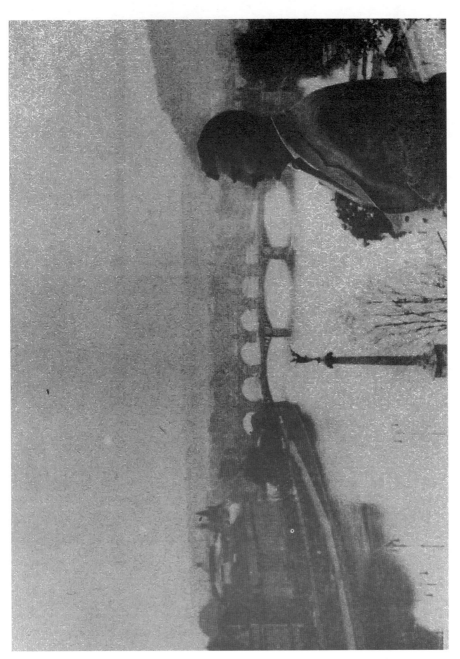

Figure 17   Mustafa Barzani during preparation to return home from exile in the USSR after the July revolution in 1958.

Chapter 42

The Kurdistan Democratic Party, Democracy, and National Unity

Conscious of the importance of democracy, the KDP's motto, "Democracy for Iraq and Autonomy for Kurdistan" signified its central role in the party's thought. The KDP believes that Kurdish rights cannot and will not be realized under dictatorship. We have learned this lesson through experience with successive regimes in Baghdad. The Kurdish people can enjoy their rights only within the framework of a democratic system in Iraq. The KDP should be proud of the fact that liberated Kurdistan has always been a haven for all Iraqi patriots who sought refuge in search of the freedom and democracy that they missed in Baghdad. I need not go into detail. Many eyewitnesses from among the Arabs and the ethnic and religious minorities are still alive.

The KDP strove for democracy before and after the fall of the monarchy in Iraq, and will continue to struggle for democracy for all of Iraq until it is realized. The KDP's clear-eyed and informed struggle for democracy is not new. It began with this party's inception. *Khabat*, the KDP's central organ, exemplified this notion in its statement in issue no. 147, dated January 17, 1960 (*Kurdistan wa al-Haraka al-Qawmiyya al-Kurdiyya*, Talabani 1981, p. 298):

> The tenacious struggle of the bi-national Iraqi people of Arabs and Kurds against imperialism and the extirpated ruling clique was intended to establish a society democratic in its political, economic, and educational systems.
>
> Democracy, which has been described as government of the people and for the people, is not a specific commodity that we import into our country. It is a concept which differs according to the country and the historical circumstances that surround it. Hence, it is futile to attempt to import a specific type of government from a specific country. Furthermore, a social system results from material needs required for development, and it is connected to the will of the people, their capabilities, and the struggle of social forces as well as the objective domestic and international conditions.
>
> In [the] light of the preceding facts, and after studying the conditions of our homeland and its special circumstances, the KDP has come to the conclusion that guided democracy with its Iraqi character, derived from our Iraqi circumstances and reality, is the best form of democracy which can fulfill the goal and wishes of our bi-national people of Arabs and Kurds. Therefore, Article 4 of the KDP Platform states: "We are fighting to protect the democratic Republic, to augment, broaden, and deepen its democratic character on the foundations of guided democracy, which guarantees individual and public freedoms for all citizens. These freedoms include the right to express one's views and beliefs; freedom of the press; freedom of

political association and the right to organize trade unions and legislate a Permanent Constitution, while guaranteeing direct democratic elections in which all males and females eighteen years of age or older will be eligible to vote." As the aforementioned Article indicates, the KDP is clearly calling for a guided democratic system that guarantees freedom for our people and withholds it from enemies; this is essential to safeguarding the Republic and protecting the people's achievements as exemplified in the glorious Revolution. Furthermore, it is a necessary requisite to ensure the economic, political, and educational development of our society, and to ensure peace and security for all citizens. Among this system's components are the founding of sound parliamentary practice, the ensuring of the people's freedom to elect their representatives to the Parliament and the forming of a Cabinet derived from the majority in the Parliament, which would be accountable to a popular Parliamentarian monitoring.

The people's interests require the unity of all patriotic and faithful forces and their participation in governing the country through a coalition Cabinet or, should it not be possible to form a unified national front incorporating everyone in the government, through a Consultative Council of representatives of the patriotic forces. Undoubtedly, respecting individual and public freedoms, guaranteeing them for all citizens, and establishing a political and parliamentary practice to be guaranteed by the Constitution are pillars of a guided democratic government.

Khabat published another article in issue no. 389 (December 21, 1960) in which it stated the following:

... [W]e cannot claim that democracy and freedom exist in any country where millions of its inhabitants are deprived of their national rights. These people must not forget the truth that shines through the eternal word. A people cannot be free while oppressing other peoples. It is the duty of the Arab, Turkish, and Persian peoples to grasp this fact and to help the Kurdish people in the struggle for their legitimate national rights. Their own freedom is not complete as long as there is a fellow nation being oppressed in their names and under the guise of their interests.

This is what was written in *Khabat* in 1960. Three decades later, we reiterate it verbatim without adding or deleting one single word. The response rests with the conscientious Arabs, Turks, and Persians.

Throughout its long struggle, the KDP has participated in building the pillars of national unity. Had the KDP not adhered to this unity and recognized its significance for the future of Arab–Kurdish relations, the party would have seized numerous favorable opportunities that have emerged over the past 40 years. The KDP's principled stance vis-à-vis democracy for Iraq has preserved Iraq's national unity.

The truth continues to shine on no matter how hard chauvinists and racists endeavor to mask it. Unless the Kurdish people enjoy their legitimate national rights and unless national unity is the common goal for all Iraqis, there will be no guarantee for independence, prosperity, stability, or well-being.

The Kurdistan Democratic Party Position vis-à-vis Arab Unity

Under the Ottomans, both the Arab and Kurdish nations suffered from the policy of "turkification" and subsequently from forced partitioning after World War I at the hands of the imperialist forces. Forcible partition served the interests of imperialist forces and contravened the interests of both nations. I have no doubt that Arab unity is in the interest of the Kurds, because if it is realized, it will remove many impediments which stand in the way of the Kurdish nation's retrieval of its unity. As we know, the Arabs are now divided into more than 20 countries, and the rulers of these countries have divided the land, peoples, and wealth of the Arab nation and control the destinies of their people as they like. Arab public opinion has no say whatsoever in the decisions made by their rulers, whether decisions concern them or other people of the region.

Arab unity is the goal of the Arab masses, not of Arab governments. When Arab unity is realized, it will mean that the will of the people has triumphed. Without a doubt, the Arab masses do not harbor bad intentions toward the Kurdish nation. On the contrary, they are ready to help the Kurds gain their rights. The masses realize that the Kurdish nation is an ancient one inhabiting its own territory, not occupying anyone else's, and is not foreign to the region. Others have usurped Kurdish rights. It is in the interest of the Arab nation to have the Kurdish nation, with its population of more than 25 million, as a friend and not an enemy. This is troubling to Iraqi rulers who oppress the Kurds of Iraqi Kurdistan under the guise of defending Arabism and preserving Arab unity. Meanwhile, these rulers find pretexts for their failure and waver in the face of their well-equipped enemies.

When peacefully realized and with the will of the masses, Arab unity will be in the interests of both the Arab and Kurdish nations, and the Kurds should welcome and support it. However, if it is a unity of rulers, it will definitely be exploited to buffet the aspirations of both the Arab and Kurdish masses. It will curtail their freedoms, dignity, and their rights.

The Kurds are by no means opposed to Arab unity, but Arab chauvinists delight in disbelieving this Kurdish position. Arab unity is first of all an Arab duty. Do the Arab masses and their friends not have the right to ask what the Arab rulers have done for the sake of unity? The Kurds sincerely wish for Arab unity to be realized on sound and democratic bases. As talk on unity abounded in Baghdad after the July 14 Revolution, and discord intensified among various Arab forces regarding a merger or federated union [with the UAR], the KDP presented a memorandum on September 11, 1958 to Abd al-Karim Qasim and Abd al-Salam Arif stating its position as follows:

> The issues of union or unification affect us in two ways: First, the degree to which they realize and protect the short- and long-term goals that the whole Iraqi people have struggled for and continue to do so. Second, the degree to which they protect and realize the principle of partnership in the country, and the degree to which they expand Kurdish national rights which are recognized in the Constitution of the Republic of Iraq. Aside from these two concomitant aspects, in principle we believe that the issues concerning union or unification are issues concerning the Arab people in the first place because they are part of this brotherly people's right to self-determination. Self-determination is the great and absolute right which the Human Rights charter has affirmed for all the peoples of the globe, and which has been re-affirmed by the Afro-Asian peoples at the Bandung Conference,[1] which the Kurdish people consider[s] a legal basis for its liberation struggle.

On these grounds, we support whatever the Arab people decide[s] as regards [its] right to self-determination in whatever form [it] chooses to organize its relationships throughout the divided Arab homeland. This is an absolute matter of principle. Regarding the situation in Iraqi Kurdistan, we have explained the two aspects that are important to us, and we cannot overlook them. To accomplish the first aspect, which is to protect the short-term and long-term goals for which the Iraqi people have struggled, and to accelerate the struggle to fulfill them, the correct way, in our view, is to not carry out either union or unification hastily. Prior to that, study and scrutiny as well as a gradual completion of numerous initial steps are necessary and the issue must be taken to the Iraqi people. The international, Arab, and Iraqi scenes especially favor this unhurried, gradual approach in making and completing the necessary preparations sensibly and with no elements of improvisation or surprise.

... The formation that would emerge would, of course, be one that would dominate the whole Arab nation. The numerical percentage of the Kurds living in the country would plummet because of the vast Arab majority. This would make the Kurds adhere to their national rights more than ever, and cause them to become more sensitive and emotional about anything pertaining to these rights, no matter how remote the connection. They would interpret the conduct and actions of the new formation in this state of mind and in this light, because their experience with the Turks in the Kemalist movement and with the Persians on numerous occasions has taught them hard lessons. This is a situation where any simple error by authorities regarding Kurdish national rights will bring about the worst of consequences.

... Any step that the Arab nation accomplishes toward achieving its goals must be accompanied by an incremental broadening of the rights of the Kurdish nation and moving it toward achieving its goals as well. It does not matter if the step to be taken by each of these two nationalities is commensurate with its own status and condition. To implement this principle, we recommend the following:

First, if Iraq wishes to enter a federated union with the liberated Arab countries, there must be recognition of a form of autonomy for Kurdistan within Iraq. Second, if Iraq wishes to enter a union with the United Arab Republic, recognition of the Kurdish nation is necessary, and Kurdistan must be recognized as a federated member in the new configuration (Talabani 1981, p. 315).

In recognition of the strategic importance of unity for the future of both nations, the KDP has spoken of Arab unity at all its Congresses. The KDP will be looking at Arab unity, solidarity, and joint struggle in [the] light of its concern for the interests of both fraternal nations. Article 6 of the KDP Platform, approved by the Tenth KDP Congress in December 1989 stated the following:

"Because of the close ties between the Kurdish and Arab national movements, their rights to self-determination, and the requirements of their common struggle for national liberation and social progress, the realization of any progress or advancement in the Arab national movement in Iraq must be accompanied by progress and advancement in the national rights of the Kurdish people."

Chapter 43

The al-Shawwaf Movement

It is known that Staff Colonel Abd al-Wahab al-Shawwaf was one of the most prominent free officers with democratic leanings. He was from a distinguished family. Before the July 14 Revolution, he had differences with Abd al-Salaam Arif. Upon the advent of the revolution, an order was issued appointing al-Shawwaf military governor general, but the order was rescinded on July 15, 1958, under pressure from Abd al-Salam Arif, and he was appointed commander of Mosul garrison instead. He considered this unjust and a way to distance him from Baghdad, which was in fact the case.

Seething with anger, al-Shawwaf reported to his new position, but like the rest of his fellow free officers, he suppressed his pain and bitterness. One must appreciate what members of the High Committee of Free Officers, to their credit, tolerated from Abd al-Karim Qasim and Abd al-Salam Arif for the sake of putting the interests of the country above their own. Colonel al-Shawwaf never resolved this enigma and watched for an opportunity to retaliate against Abd al-Karim Qasim and Abd al-Salam Arif. Before long, Abd al-Salam Arif too was dismissed from his position. Abd al-Karim Qasim, however, did not retract his position regarding Colonel al-Shawwaf, who was not recalled to Baghdad for a leadership role. I believe that this was a mistake on the part of Qasim, who should have indemnified al-Shawwaf for the wrongs of Arif, of which he was cognizant.

As the struggle intensified between Arab nationalists and Abd al-Karim Qasim, the Ba'thists and other Arab nationalists exploited al-Shawwaf's position, rallied around him, and enticed him into moving against Abd al-Karim Qasim. Ultimately, al-Shawwaf was persuaded, and he began to plan his rebellion, relying on the Ba'thists, other nationalist forces, and a few Kurdish and Arab tribal chiefs. The only common denominator among them was their animosity toward Abd al-Karim Qasim. Furthermore, the tribal chiefs were hoping to rescind the Agrarian Reform Law, which restricted their feudal authority and their exploitation of the peasants.

After its relations with Iraq deteriorated, the UAR worked actively against Abd al-Karim Qasim and gave Abd al-Hamid al-Sarraj of Syria free rein to funnel all essential aid to Colonel al-Shawwaf and assist him in his rebellion. In effect, this was blatant interference in the internal affairs of Iraq. Exploiting the opportunity of holding the Conference of Partisans of Peace in Mosul on March 5, 1959, al-Shawwaf provoked the nationalist and religious feelings of broad segments of the Mosul population. He proclaimed his coup on March 3, 1959, with the open support of Abd al-Hamid al-Sarraj, interior minister of the northern [Syrian] region of the UAR. On the first day, he arrested all of the officers in his brigade whom he suspected of loyalty to Abd al-Karim Qasim, as well as civilians who were opposed to him. His officers killed many prisoners in their custody, including Kamil Qazanchi. The al-Shawwaf Movement did not last more than 24 hours. al-Shawwaf himself was killed in his headquarters the following day, and as many of his officers who could escaped to Syria.

When al-Shawwaf was killed and officers loyal to Abd al-Karim Qasim regained control over the Fifth Brigade and the city of Mosul, PRM squads under the ICP's command committed horrendous retaliatory crimes against the population of Mosul, with the complicity and, at times, the help of the KDP branch in Mosul, which led armed men from Kurdish tribes to march on the city. Arab chauvinists continued to accuse Barzani and the KDP of the inhuman deeds in Mosul after quelling the al-Shawwaf Movement, as if what had happened was deliberately planned. Therefore, some light must be shed on the facts.

al-Shawwaf's group did not refrain from killing, torturing, and assaulting anyone who opposed them. The Kurdish officers and soldiers in the Fifth Brigade experienced all types of misery. It was known that Barzani, the KDP, and the entire Kurdish people had taken the side of Abd al-Karim Qasim. Of course, it was neither in the interests of the Kurdish people nor the Iraqi people to bring down Abd al-Karim Qasim at that time. The Kurds defended Abd al-Karim Qasim and the July 14 Revolution, a correct position, and they did well to do so. Kurdish officers and soldiers played a large part in quelling the al-Shawwaf Movement inside the garrison of the Fifth Brigade (see Document no. 64).[1]

The events in Mosul after al-Shawwaf was crushed, such as killings and dragging people through the streets, were not known to all KDP leaders. Barzani strongly condemned the crimes committed in Mosul. What happened then has become part of Iraq's history. Scores were settled! I do not need to declare anyone innocent, condemn anyone, or appease anyone. However, this is the truth. There is no justification at all either for the acts of murder and torture committed by al-Shawwaf and his officers or for the acts of revenge that followed the collapse of his movement, which were even more savage and brutal. Undoubtedly, those acts of retaliation were an important reason for the chilly relations between Abd al-Karim Qasim and the ICP, which shouldered the blame for the actions of adolescents in the PRM under the command of Abd al-Rahman al-Qassab and Adnan Chilmiran, especially the shameful massacre of Damlumaja.

In the wake of the events in Mosul, a series of critical developments fed the animosity that existed among the Iraqi political parties and between the nationalists and Abd al-Karim Qasim. Among the grave errors Abd al-Karim Qasim committed was his approval of the executions of Nazim al-Tabaqchali and Rif'at al-Haj Sirri. Despite their collusion with al-Shawwaf, they never in fact took part in the movement, and they were both brilliant free officers. Both enjoyed the respect and esteem of the army and the people. Barzani had intervened and advised Abd al-Karim Qasim not to ratify the orders for their executions. He was visiting his brother Sheikh Ahmad Barzani in the Horei resort at the time. He sent his nephew Sadiq to Baghdad especially to convey his message to Abd al-Karim Qasim concerning this issue.

From beginning to end, the Mosul events ushered in a new era of bloody struggle in Iraq, and no one escapes blame and responsibility. Nationalists, Communists, and Kurds all committed sins and errors against themselves, their country, and people. They sinned against Iraq.

The Rebellion of Sheikh Rashid of Lolan

The first whose interests were hit the hardest after the July 14 Revolution were the tribal chiefs and feudalists in Kurdistan. Under the monarchy, they had exploited the peasants without deterrence. However, their authority was virtually abolished, especially in the first year after the July 14 Revolution. Therefore, feudalists, as a class, opposed agrarian reform by any and all means at their disposal.

Sheikh Rashid resided in the village of Lolan, within the jurisdiction of the Sidakan subdistrict. He was the spiritual leader of the Baradost tribe in Iraq. He had many followers in the Iranian and Turkish parts of Kurdistan as well. The Baradost region stretches along the Iranian and Turkish borders. Thus, direct contacts with either government were easily made. Both governments provided weapons to the followers of Sheikh Rashid and induced them to rebel against the July 14 Revolution. They promised the sheikh support and protection.

Sheikh Rashid was known to have continued to abhor the Barzanis to his dying day. In spite of this hatred, I must point out some facts about him. Of all the sheikhs in Kurdistan, he was the firmest and the most unshakable in his beliefs. Unlike other chiefs who vacillated, he upheld his values, especially those germane to issues of honor. In addition to his and his followers' (the Sufis) readiness to rise against the republic, the PRM's activities and provocations accelerated his rebellion.

In early May of 1959, in a swift move, Sheikh Rashid of Lolan surrounded the Sidakan police station and arrested all PRM members there. They controlled the Sari Berdi Road to prevent reinforcements from reaching the besieged force in Sidakan. Abd al-Karim Qasim asked Barzani to deal with this development without delay. Barzani quickly moved to Rewanduz and in two days assembled a force of 1,000 Barzanis and a second force of similar numbers of the KDP's armed men from various parts of Kurdistan. In another two days he brought the situation under control and Sheikh Rashid of Lolan and his followers fled to Iran. The Iranian government gave them a warm welcome in Oshnoviyeh, provided them with all that they needed, and supplied them with more arms. Three Barzanis were martyred in these battles, and several were wounded. One of the martyrs was Omer Sulayman, who had just returned from the Soviet Union and had not seen all of his relatives yet.

The PRM was sent a congratulatory cable for the victory it had achieved! As documented by his cables to Abd al-Karim Qasim, Dawood aj-Janabi, commander of the Second Division, deliberately concealed the role that Barzani and the KDP had played, without which a victory would have been impossible. He emphasized the role of the PRM, which had done nothing at all. The insurgents remained in Iran until the fall of 1959, when Abd al-Karim Qasim declared an amnesty, upon which they returned to Iraq. In the spring of 1960, Sadiq Barzani visited

Sheikh Rashid of Lolan to dissipate the enmity and bad feelings that existed between him and Barzan. He was largely successful.

The Events in Kirkuk

Kirkuk has acquired special significance owing to sundry reasons, the most important of which is its huge oil reserves. Its economic stature has made it more prone to [the government policy of] arabization than any other Kurdish city. Kirkuk's geographical location further increases its importance.

Before the starkly racist policies that prevailed after 1975, Kirkuk's population was 80 percent Kurdish; the rest was a mix of Arabs, Turkomans, and Assyrians. It could have been the city of brotherhood if the policies of successive Iraqi regimes had only been honest. Now, Kirkuk is the symbol of arabization, deportation, oppression, and demographic distortion.

Kirkuk is considered the heart of Kurdistan. Therefore, chauvinists and vicious enemies are bent on despoiling and altering its Kurdish character. Even when Britain agreed to the establishment of the State of Kurdistan after World War I under Sheikh Mahmud al-Hafeed, it did not include Kirkuk in Kurdistan. The dividend that the people of Kurdistan have received from Kirkuk's oil has been atrocities and horrors. The Baghdad regime has used oil revenues to purchase and use weapons of destruction against the women and children of Kurdistan, while at the same time establishing universities, hospitals, and factories and building roads in the other parts of Iraq. It is not farfetched to state that the oil of Kurdistan has turned into a tragedy for the people of Kurdistan.

The arabization of Kirkuk is by no means new. However, the acts that the Ba'thist regime has committed so flagrantly and overtly have surpassed all that was done by previous regimes in Iraq. During the first period of the Ba'thist rule in 1963, residents of 23 Kurdish villages in the vicinity of Kirkuk were expelled under the pretext of security arrangements. Arab families with Sheikh Hawwas al-Sadid were settled in these villages. This was a strong point of contention during the 1966 negotiations with [Prime Minister Abd al-Rhaman] al-Bazzaz. [The next prime minister] Tahir Yahya promised to relocate these families, provided the area remain unpopulated by either Arabs or Kurds because of its proximity to the main offices of the Iraqi Petroleum Company.

Kirkuk was the main point of contention in the 1970 negotiations with the Ba'th Party as well.[2] At last, Kurdish leaders reached an agreement with the Ba'thist government to rely on the 1957 census to resolve differences with regard to Kirkuk. However, the Ba'th Party resorted to deceit and falsification of the census records. In one of the negotiation sessions before the signing of the March 11 [1970] Manifesto, [cabinet member] Abdullah Sallum al-Samarra'i made the following statement in the form of a question: "I say that Kirkuk is not Kurdish; who can prove otherwise?" After this statement, tension reigned, and Barzani snapped back:

> Kirkuk has been Kurdish for all eternity. Your statement has no basis in history; the city will remain Kurdish whether you like it or not. You can occupy it for a while, but you will never extract our recognition to legitimize what you do. Kirkuk is not

negotiable. I do not want to hear another word of this again. We shall pay whatever price it takes for Kirkuk.

After the March 11 Manifesto, the Ba'thist regime plotted to transfer Kurdish workers from the Iraqi Petroleum Company (IPC), railway and Coca Cola companies, and other government offices and establishments and replace them with Arab workers based on census records falsified by the regime, giving them various privileges. At the same time, the regime pressured Kurds and expelled them from the city of Kirkuk. Undoubtedly, that each side [the government and the Kurds] clung fast to its position regarding Kirkuk was among the most important reasons that led to the floundering of the March 11 Manifesto, 1970, and the resumption of hostilities in 1974.

In the aftermath of the collapse of the September Revolution in 1975, the regime felt freer and more at ease in multiplying its chauvinistic and racist measures, which were not only aimed at altering the ethnographic reality in Kirkuk but were also expanded to include other regions of Kurdistan. Perhaps the regime believes that it has succeeded in its evil measures, which have harmed the lasting ties between the Kurds and Arabs. I hereby stress for the regime that its success is transitory and will dissipate along with the regime sooner or later. History has proved that rulers are ephemeral and peoples are forever, especially when the rulers are racist oppressors.

A word of advice to every Kurd and to future generations: Remember that the Ba'thist regime is the one that arabized Kirkuk and many other areas of Kurdistan for no reason other than its blindly racist outlook. It behooves the Kurds to strive with might and main to erase all effects of arabization from Kurdistan.

The existence of a Turkish minority in Kirkuk is a fact that must not be denied; there is the Assyrian minority as well, and some Arabs also live in the Hawija area. They came to settle there during Madhat Pasha's era in the mid-nineteenth century. Often we hear or read that Turkomans constitute the majority in Kirkuk and the districts around it. I do not wish to discuss this point because it is as far from the truth as the heavens are from the earth. Even if this were true, it ought to be made clear that Kirkuk is on Kurdish soil, not Turkish soil. The rights of our Turkoman brothers must be fully recognized as an ethnic minority. Their rights and those of the other minorities must never be denied.

The influence of both the IPC and the Turkish Consulate in Kirkuk was substantial, notably among prominent Turkomans. Both were the root causes of many difficulties between the Kurds and Turkomans in Kirkuk. The Turanis played a big role in fanning the flames of sensitivities and provoking the Kurds, following instructions from the IPC and from Turkey, and relying on Turani elements in sensitive positions in the army and elsewhere.

In spite of their weakening influence after the July 14 Revolution, the Turanis remained visible enough to provoke the Kurds. For example, when Barzani visited the headquarters of the Second Division in November of 1958 and stayed in the officers clubhouse, a Turani officer, Hidayat Arsalan, tried to plant a time bomb in Barzani's helicopter. The plot was foiled when a Kurdish officer learned of the conspiracy. Soon after, the Turani officer suffered cardiac arrest and died with his hatred intact. The news spread in Kirkuk quickly and almost led to a bloody massacre. Fortunately, the situation was brought under control without incident.

On the first anniversary of the July 14 Revolution, Kirkuk, like the rest of the country, prepared to celebrate this happy occasion. Unfortunately, the cheering carnivals and festivities in Kirkuk turned into tragic bloody marches and recorded a dark page in the history of Kurdish–Turcoman brotherhood. Everyone lost control, and the city turned into a war zone. The commander of the Second Division encouraged the conspiracy instead of suppressing it, as his official duty required of him. He let his troops and the members of the PRM behave as they wished. The KDP's Third Branch was slow to suppress the conspiracy and so were Turkoman officials and notables. They all allowed the tragedy to happen. The only thing left to say is that chauvinism and racism must be fought everywhere and always, and the Kurdish people ought to be the vanguard, for they know better than anybody else the damage such ideas can inflict upon societies. Democracy and brotherly coexistence with other nationalities are to be cultivated in Kurdish society.

The bloody events in Kirkuk shocked Abd al-Karim Qasim and prompted him to issue a directive dissolving the PRM. Each tried to blame the other, but I believe that all share the blame without exception.

On July 20, 1959, I visited Barzan with my father. I recall that a delegation of Turkoman notables had come to Shaqlawa and met with my father in Saleh Beg Miran's residence. He spoke to them in the spirit of brotherhood, strongly condemned the events in Kirkuk, and stressed his concern for Kurdish–Turkoman relations. For more details regarding the events in Kirkuk, see Document nos. 65–69.[3]

An Attempt on Abd al-Karim Qasim's Life

The failed assassination attempt on Abd al-Karim Qasim's life occurred on October 7, 1959 on al-Rashid Street. It was planned and executed by the Ba'th Party; perhaps it is one of the operations of which the Ba'thists are most proud. The Ba'th Party had moved to a position of open animosity toward Abd al-Karim Qasim after the al-Shawwaf Movement in March of 1959. The real aim behind the attempt was to seize power. It was not because of the stance on immediate unification, to which the Ba'th Party ascribed its contention with Qasim and other forces. [Subsequent] events have proved this because the Ba'th Party has come to power twice since, once in February of 1963 and again in July of 1968, and continued to rule Iraq to date, but it has done nothing for the sake of unification. No other Arab party or government has harmed Arab unity as has the Ba'th Party and government. Unionists and Nasserists suffered under the Ba'th regime more than under any other government.

As Abd al-Karim Qasim would drive along a street in Baghdad, people would line up on both sides, clap, and chant long life to him. Usually he would be escorted by a second car. I heard Aziz Sharif say,[4] "Abd al-Karim Qasim decided to travel in one car, without his guards, after he had heard a commentator on the Voice of the Arabs Radio describing him as a coward, fearful of the revenge of the Iraqi masses because of the cavalcade of cars escorting him."

Aziz Sharif believed that Abd al-Karim Qasim's secretary, Jasim al-Azzawi, had suggested that commentary to the Voice of the Arabs Radio because he was against Qasim. Aziz Sharif added, "I advised Abd al-Karim Qasim to ignore the radio commentaries on the Voice of the Arabs, but he did not heed the advice and he was lured into going where his enemies wanted him to be."

As the assassination attempt was being carried out, votes were being counted for a new KDP Central Committee in the aftermath of the successful conclusion of the party's Fourth Congress. Barzani, the KDP leaders and cadres, and the masses of Kurdistan did everything possible to defend the July 14 Revolution at that critical moment. A number of conspirators were arrested. Others escaped to Syria and Egypt, among them was Saddam Hussein al-Tikriti.

During the negotiations of March 11, 1970, Samir Aziz al-Najim retold the details of the assassination attempt on Abd al-Karim Qasim's life. He was one of the participants, and he and Saddam Hussein were injured. Their comrade, Abd al-Wahab al-Ghrairi, was killed by friendly fire.

Although the assassination attempt failed to accomplish its goal of ending the rule of Abd al-Karim Qasim, it brought the Ba'th Party the support of nationalist forces and enemies of Abd al-Karim Qasim of all orientations. The behavior of the indicted during trial sessions by People's Court, on December 26, 1959, was extremely courageous and was admired by friend and foe.

The vast majority of the Iraqi people, parties, and patriotic and democratic forces condemned the assassination attempt and renewed their allegiance to Abd al-Karim Qasim and the July 14 Revolution. However, incongruously, Abd al-Karim Qasim refused to ratify the death sentences passed by the People's Court against the conspirators in the attempt on his life, while prior to that he had confirmed the executions of Nazim al-Tabaqchali and Rif'at al-Haj Sirri [for their involvement in the al-Shawwaf Movement].

Chapter 44

The Beginning of Tension between Barzani and Qasim

The support of the KDP and the Barzan tribe for the July 14 Revolution and for Abd al-Karim Qasim personally had great impact on the masses and patriotic tribes of Kurdistan, which turned into a bastion for the revolution. Therefore, anyone who contemplated conspiring against the revolution had to reckon with the position of the Kurdish people. Conspirators had consistently worked hard to plant the seeds of division and distrust between Abd al-Karim Qasim and his allies in the Arab and Kurdish patriotic forces.

Initially, Abd al-Karim Qasim shrugged off these attempts but he eventually came under their influence. The ideas and propositions of the chauvinists who feigned allegiance began to impact him. They wanted to separate him from one of his strongest and most loyal allies, an experienced force ready to sacrifice itself for the July 14 Revolution. Active British, Turkish, and Iranian intelligence contact was afoot with a few Kurdish tribal chiefs who had served Nuri al-Sa'id, through the coordination and full cooperation of government officials holding sensitive positions like the governor of Arbil, Badr al-Din Ali, the chief of the Mosul Police Department, Ismail Abbawi, and some others within Abd al-Karim Qasim's circle.

When Barzani returned from the Soviet Union in 1958, Abd al-Karim Qasim suggested that he open a new page with all tribes that had carried Nuri al-Sa'id's weapons against the Barzan Revolt of 1945. Barzani thought well of this suggestion, and Abd al-Karim Qasim asked the commander of the Second Division and the governor of Arbil to arrange a meeting in Arbil. Most Kurdish tribal chiefs attended the meeting, except for Kalhi Rekani and Ahmad Zebari, who were cognizant, more than others, of the crimes that they had both perpetrated against the poor.

The meeting ended on a positive note and removed many of the residual sensitivities. Many problems were solved with those whose intentions were sincere. Barzani tried, along with Abd al-Karim Qasim, to issue an order to bring both Kalhi Rekani and Ahmad Zebari before the People's Court on confirmed charges of murder. Qasim promised to do so, but he did not follow through. Fatefully, four Barzanis saw Ahmad Zebari in Mosul near the al-Sharqiya High School and shot him dead on November 4, 1959. Thus, they avenged their relatives and another 30 victims whom this tyrant had killed in cold blood. Reactionaries and spiteful chauvinistic government employees were outraged. They used this incident to justify their conspiracy against the July 14 Revolution, beginning with keeping patriots at arm's length from Abd al-Karim Qasim.

In late 1959 and early 1960, Barzani's relationship with Abd al-Karim Qasim began to cool. Abd al-Karim Qasim allowed Badr ad-Din Ali, governor of Arbil, and Ismail Abbawi, the chief of police of Mosul, extraordinary powers under the pretext of establishing security and peace in the two provinces. Obviously, both men were totally biased against the Barzanis. The government began arming Barzan's neighboring tribes such as the Zebaris, Surchis, Bradostis, and Rekanis. In the spring of 1960, the Zebaris attacked villages in the Nizar region in the Barzani subdistrict. When the Barzanis retaliated, reports were sent to Baghdad that it was they who had begun the hostilities. Such provocations continued unabated, without any serious government measures to bring them to an end. Sheikh Ahmad Barzani asked Abd al-Karim Qasim to form a neutral committee to investigate the armed provocations, and he approved the request. A special investigative committee traveled to Barzan. Representing the Barzanis on this committee was Sadiq Barzani, who, while en route to Rewanduz to accompany the committee to the region of the plains of Hirat, was killed in a car accident on June 23, 1960. On its return to Baghdad, the committee presented its independent report, which refuted earlier reports, and tensions eased. Abd al-Karim Qasim sent two of his nephews—Hamid's sons—to Barzan bearing his condolences to Sheikh Ahmad for the death of Sadiq.

Despite the risks, Sheikh Ahmad visited Baghdad on October 29, 1960. A month earlier, Barzani had returned to Baghdad. Both met Abd al-Karim Qasim and expressed Barzan's full readiness to defend the July 14 Revolution. They emphasized the Barzanis' loyalty to the person of Abd al-Karim Qasim and asked him to put an end to any factor that might, as a matter of course, alienate the Barzanis from him. Abd al-Karim Qasim promised positively to do so. However, it seems that matters had reached the point of no return (see Document nos. 70–76).[1]

Chapter 45

Calls to Assimilate the Kurdish Nation

Before Kurdish ties with the Iraqi government were completely severed in September 1961, a number of critical events accelerated the pace toward an impasse and the eventual flare-up of hostilities. The Iraqi government consistently retracted its positive measures in Kurdistan, notably those related to the rights of the Kurdish people [requiring] implementation of Article 3 of the Provisional Constitution.

In the spring of 1960, armed tribal provocations against the Barzanis coincided with both police and intelligence forces stalking KDP cadres. Influenced by a clique of opportunists and chauvinists and unable to distinguish friend from foe, Abd al-Karim Qasim was clearly moving to sever ties with the Kurdish people in the last months of 1960. He held democrats and Communists at arm's length and began flirting with the Ba'thists and those conspiring against him to appease them. In Kurdistan, he encouraged and armed feudalists. He would only see and hear reports from two malicious employees, namely, Badr ad-Din Ali in Arbil and Ismail Abbawi in Mosul. Meanwhile, the KDP and Barzani did not take these provocations seriously and hoped that they would be resolved in cooperation with the government. However, the greatest danger that threatened the Kurdish people came in the form of an article published by the newspaper *al-Thawra*, a government organ closely tied to Abd al-Karim Qasim. It called for the necessity of assimilating the Kurdish nationality and dissolving it in the crucible of the Arab nation even if it required the use of force to accomplish this goal.

As duty dictated, the KDP lucidly and courageously defied the call to assimilate the Kurdish nationality. The journal *Khabat* published a series of articles exposing this racist, reactionary call and explaining its harmful effects on the Kurdish–Arab fraternity and on national unity. An article published in *Khabat* on October 9, 1960, entitled "The Kurdish Nation and Article 2 of the Iraqi Provisional Constitution" stated the following:

> Article 2 of the Provisional Constitution asserts that Iraq is a part of the Arab nation. This is of course a sentimental statement more than a scientific and rational one. The term "Iraq," as we all know, is now used to describe one of two concepts: It either means (1) a land much smaller than today's Iraq, historically and geographically speaking, or it is used as (2) a political term meaning a country formed after World War I by adjoining a large portion of historical Iraq to southern Kurdistan which is sometimes referred to as Shahrazoor or as the Mosul Vilayet according to the administrative divisions of the Ottoman State, on some of the remnants of

which today's Iraqi state was established . . . thereby fulfilling the goals and intentions of British imperialism. The latter wanted to control the sources of wealth in the country, notably the oil fields . . . and to control the route to India. Therefore, Iraq cannot be considered a part of the Arab nation according to either the political concept of the word meaning the state, or the geographical concept.

Kurdistan was never considered part of the Arab land, either in part or as a geographical unit, including the part annexed to the Iraqi State, which is part of Kurdistan.

At specific periods in history, Kurdistan chanced to find itself in whole or part within the framework of an Islamic state, as was the case for many other Islamic countries. Even then, it was not considered one of the Arab countries.

Undoubtedly, Kurdistan cannot be considered part of the Arab homeland. Therefore, it is necessary to rewrite the Article in the Permanent Constitution concerning this issue in a more precise form which will defy misinterpretation or a potential conflict. An acceptable form would be, "The everlasting Republic of Iraq consists of a Kurdish part (Iraqi Kurdistan) and an Arab part (Mesopotamia)."

Only the Arab part of Iraq is part of the greater Arab homeland. Meanwhile, the Kurdish part is a part of the Kurds' homeland and of their country, Kurdistan. The true interests of the Arab and Kurdish nationalists must be taken into consideration as well by stating them in a suitable paragraph underlining Iraqi unity . . .

We find the clear contradiction between this Article and Article 3 of the Constitution which states ". . . Arabs and Kurds are considered partners in the homeland," which is by and large a sound statement and renders Article 2 null and void unless we consider the Kurds occupiers of the land on which they live in today's Iraq and that it was originally an Arab land. This was never the case at any period of time in history (*Al-Iraq fi A'hD Qasim; Ara' wa Khawatir: 1958–1988*, Fathullah 1989, p. 841).

After this article appeared, the military governor general interrogated and court-martialed the KDP secretary, Ibrahim Ahmad, according to Article 31 of the law amending the Appendix of the Penal Code and Article 13 of the Decrees of Martial Administration and Publications.

Khabat published several other articles discussing the reactionary and chauvinist concept of assimilation and fusion. In issue no. 440 of February 22, 1961, *Khabat* published an article entitled "Attempts to Assimilate the Kurdish Nationality and their Inevitable Results," which stated:

The Kurdish nationality is a solid historical fact which will destroy all criminal measures of fusion and annexation and all attempts of imperialists in the past and of chauvinists at present against it. Futile attempts aimed at assimilating or fusing nationalities have failed and will fail, regardless of the degree of their force and brutality.

The article in *Khabat* listed the results of the assimilation and fusion policy, as follows:

1. A policy of assimilation and fusion invokes hostility and hatred and undermines national unity. Therefore, the Kurds cannot strive to preserve a unity that brings them only servitude, deprivation of rights, and denial of their ethnicity. Furthermore, it brings war, an iron fist policy, chains, and prisons.

2. In spite of its failure to achieve assimilation and fusion, such a policy brings atrocities, catastrophes, and civil wars to the state which practices it, thereby inflicting the worst of material and moral damages on it.
3. The foundation of a state which exercises such a policy remains frail and exposed to turmoil and strife that it cannot withstand. Such a state will disintegrate as soon as circumstances permit change.
4. The people of such a state will remain under the yoke of servility and will be burdened with exorbitant taxes, and will continue to be deprived of democratic rights. A people that oppresses another cannot be free.

Loyalty to national unity and Arab–Kurdish brotherhood lies in condemning seditious attempts to wipe out the Kurdish nation and in denouncing the denial of Kurdish national rights (*Kurdistan wa al-Haraka al-Qawiyya al-Kurdiyya*, Talabani 1981, p. 310).

The call to assimilate the Kurdish nation was met with denunciation and contempt by patriotic and democratic parties. The ICP repudiated it in its press.

Let us see how the Ba'th Party deals with the issue of national minorities in the Arab World as it was discussed in the booklet printed by the Dar al-Thawra Press in Baghdad in 1979. The thesis had been deliberated on and approved at the [Ba'th Party's] Eleventh National Congress:

... [T]he condition the Party provided for affiliation with the Arab nation as the Constitution states in its General Principles is as follows:
An Arab is anyone whose language is Arabic, who lives or aspires to live on Arab land, and who believes in his affiliation with the Arab nation.
This definition means that Arab identity extends to all individuals and groups who meet this condition, without regard to race. This leaves the door wide open to absorb minorities and smaller ethnic groups into the Arab nation. As for nationalities with relatively larger populations within the Arab homeland, which have languages and ethnic traits that are fairly different from the Arabic language and traits like the Kurdish nationality, we must recognize their specific local ethnicity and resolve any contradiction between their characteristics and those of the Arab national movement. These nationalities possess languages and traits which are different from those of the Arab nation but at the same time it is erroneous to consider them as different from Arabs as the Persian, Indian, and other nationalities are.
Nationalities with languages and traits different from those of the Arab nation that have lived within the Arab homeland for a long time, such as the Kurdish nationality, have established deep-rooted ties with the Arab nation. In fact they have lived, ever since they emerged and over this long period of time, in what is historically known as the Arab Homeland regardless of different names of its parts, and of the different names taken by states founded on it. This is an important issue, since the land these nationalities live on was a part of the Arab states which emerged thousands of years ago, the last one being the greater Abbasid State. This land was, therefore, home to other nationalities at the same time. Accordingly, the Arab identity of the land, home to these nationalities, was not acquired through coercion, imperialism, or usurpation. It was acquired through a historical reality extending for thousands of years. Over that, there was not any dispute or discord over all that long period.

These nationalities were, throughout various historical eras, a living component of the Arab entity, tied to and interacting with it. They were not foreign bodies [within the Arab entity] and did not contradict it. Ties between these and the Arab nation have thus become profound and inclusive within the framework of the Islamic creed for many centuries.

Indeed, this is an extremely dangerous document and represents the culmination of the abominable racist thought. I hope that Arab and Kurdish writers, researchers, and historians will give it the attention it deserves, study it scientifically, and respond to it according to the rationale of history and reality which is supported by the facts that repudiate these misleading allegations.

I am compelled to point out that when the Kurds accepted Islam,[1] they did so willingly. They did not hold back from being assimilated into the Islamic crucible. Because Arabs ruled in the name of Islam, the Kurds played the most important roles in establishing and augmenting Islamic rule. Salah al-Din al-Ayyubi, the renowned Kurdish hero, is a perfect example of this. However, when Arabs and others called for their national rights, the Kurds also demanded theirs, as was only just.

This document claims that the Kurds are a nation inhabiting Arab land. This is a falsification of history and of reality. It is a position stemming from blind racism. The Kurds are the most ancient of all the nations that have inhabited Kurdistan, their homeland. They have never conceded, either in the Abbasid era or at any other time, that Kurdistan is a part of the Arab homeland, and they will never do so.

The fact that the Kurds are a nation and that Kurdistan is their land cannot be erased by merely issuing a "yellow document." This is a chauvinistic mentality whose time has passed. This is not the era of printing malignant ideas that will never come to fruition. However, it will cause more bloodshed and tragedies equally for Arabs and Kurds. It must be clear that these racist ideas are not representative of the views of honorable Arabs who read history and have learned its lessons.

For example, the late President Jamal Abd al-Nasser's position vis-à-vis the Kurdish cause was always supportive of legitimate Kurdish national rights. He recognized the right to self-determination for the Kurdish nation and considered it in the interests of the Arab nation, and he was absolutely correct. Most democratic forces and nationalist parties in Iraq, i.e., the Nasserists, Unionists, independents, and others, have recognized the right of the Kurdish nation to self-determination; none of them has claimed that Kurdistan is a part of the Arab homeland. Communist parties, as well as enlightened and open-minded dignitaries in the Arab countries, have recognized the Kurdish right to self-determination.

Moreover, reference can be made to statements by [the Libyan leader] Mu'ammar Gaddafi regarding the Kurdish nation, the last one of which I personally heard in March of 1986 when he spoke before the Second Conference of the international assembly. He stressed the origins of the Kurdish nation, denounced endeavors to exterminate the Kurds, called for the founding of an independent Kurdish state, and emphasized that his position stemmed from the interests of the Arab nation.

Below, excerpts are documented from the writings of some Arab intellectuals regarding the relationship between the Kurdish and Arab nations so that Kurds concerned with their nation and its relationship with the Arab nation will know what honorable Arabs say in this regard.

Dr. Shakir Khasbak[2] writes,

In our opinion, the Arab–Kurdish union must come to grips with an important truth, namely recognizing the Kurdish nation truly and completely; not just a fake recognition as past governments have done. The unity of the Kurds with Arabs does not mean assimilating the Kurds within the Arab nation. It is wrong to alter facts and laud the Arab stock at the expense of their [Kurds'] nationality and stock. Their volatile unity with the Arabs naturally makes them the strongest of allies to the liberated Arab nation. In this case, the Arabs must respond in the same manner and become the true support of the liberated Kurdish nation. The relationship between the two is then one of interest and spirit. This is the law that governs the relationship between any two nationalities anywhere in the world. Relationships between nations can be steeled when based on the principles of fraternity and mutual interests, not on exploitation. Recognizing the Kurdish nationality undoubtedly results in solidifying the Arab-Kurdish unity" (*al-Kurd wa al-Mas'ala al-Kurdiyya fil Iraq*, Khasbak 1959, p. 84).

Dr. Khasbak continues,

It ought to be stressed that past mistakes must not be allowed to recur. This requires us to fully consider a historical fact: that the Kurds are not one of the ethnic minorities that came to Iraq. They are the original inhabitants of these areas for thousands of years and their rights in Iraq are fully equal to the rights of Arabs. And as long as we have agreed on partnership in the homeland, we must try to find the best ways to buttress this partnership, and we have clear examples of systems of multinational federated states that have surpassed us in the realms of administrative progress. It is best for us to try to benefit from their experiences in the light of our own circumstances if we want to build our country on strong foundations, unshakable by desires and personal ambitions and able to withstand the test of time (Khasbak 1959, p. 86).

Aziz Sharif,[3] a prominent democratic patriot and friend of the Kurdish people, presented a valuable research paper in 1950, entitled "The Kurdish Question in Iraq," in which he stated,

The Kurdish people [has] the right to self-determination as does any other of the peoples of the world. This right does not stem from any racial considerations. The Kurds have glories unrelated to any racial descent, but earned by their contributions to the advancement of human civilization and by their glorious struggle for freedom. When the Kurdish question is discussed, the freedom of the Kurdish people to self-determination is attacked under the pretext of unity.... Between the Arabs and Kurds there exists a psychological proximity produced by their joint history over long centuries. An Arab who knows something about history prides himself on being a descendent of [the Kurdish] Salah al-Din Ayyubi. In the same manner, a Kurd holds the same views with regard to the good forefathers of Arab notables in

Islamic history. Intermarriages between Arabs and Kurds are more common than among Shiite and Sunni Arabs; and yet the Arabs are shamefully ignorant of the nature of the Kurdish question. The prevailing view in the Kurdish national movement, or at least the view which has prevailed until recently, is the official view, that is, that the Kurds are "Iraqis" and those who think from the point of view of Kurdish nationalism are separatists and enemies of Iraqi unity. At times they are described as agents of British imperialism, which itself fights Kurdish nationalism and considers it dangerous to the reactionary regimes in the three neighboring countries.

The three primary reasons contributing to the long-term misleading of the Arab masses on this issue are as follows: (1) Hostilities of Arab chauvinism toward the Kurds; (2) government propaganda; and (3) co-optation of the Kurdish movement by some agents of the British.

Aziz Sharif summed up his research by saying that the solution of the Kurdish question in Iraq includes the following:

1. The struggle of the toiling Arab masses for the right to self-determination for the Kurdish nation including secession and the founding of an independent state.
2. The absolute struggle of Kurdish progressives against isolationist tendencies among the Kurdish masses and the invitation to them to unite voluntarily with Iraq under the current circumstances.

Regarding the Kurds, Abd al-Rahman al-Bazzaz[4] states the following:

The Kurds of Iraq are a part of the Kurdish nation which inhabits a vast region including a part of Anatolia, northwestern and southwestern Iran, part of northeastern Iraq, a smaller portion of southern Soviet Armenia, and a still smaller portion of northern and northeastern Syria. ... [T]he conscientious among Iraqi Kurds, like the rest of the Kurds, feel their nationalism today and sense the sentiment of that nation one way or another, especially after the growth of nationalist feelings in the whole region.

For example, when Arabs, Turks, and Iranians, who are Kurds' neighbors and fellow citizens in their three countries, have the right to feel their nationalism and herald its slogans, or work to achieve its goals, it would be ignorant and unconscionable to deny the same to the Kurds (al-Iraq min al-Ihtilal Hatta al Istiqlal, al-Bazzaz 1967, p. 283).

Perhaps what is presented in these excerpts from the works of some Arab thinkers is the best rebuttal of the claims of those Arab chauvinists whose blind racism has insulated them from comprehending the reality of life and history.

I would like to stress here that the Kurdish nation is a nation in existence and it is one of the large nations that inhabit the Middle East in a dynamic way. It is a nation that has been historically shortchanged and unjustly partitioned, just like the Arab nation. The Kurds ought to fight isolationist ideas among their ranks; at the same time, they must resist all attempts at assimilation regardless of their source and seriously endeavor to effect the best means for fraternity with the neighboring nations of Arabs, Persians, and Turks.

The population of the Kurdish nation exceeds 25 million. At present, the Kurds are the largest nation without a political entity. The struggle of the Kurdish nation will continue, regardless of cost and time, for its rights—those rights that the UN has set down for all nations—and which can be summed up as follows:

> The right to choose and establish the nations' political systems.
> The right to define their social circumstances.
> The right to determine their cultural circumstances.
> The right to [preserve] their national territorial integrity.
> The peoples' absolute sovereignty over their natural resources (*al-Usus al Qawmiyya li Haq al Sha'b al-Kurdi fi Taqrir al Masir*, Sako 1987, p. 68).

The practices of assimilation and suppression will yield nothing. Brotherly cooperation and coexistence among nations, mutual respect, and positive contributions in building a bright, prosperous future for the people is the right path. Otherwise, the future will only bring more tragedies and failures. Finally, we the Kurds tell our Arab brothers, in rebuttal of those claims propagated in the Ba'th booklet that I pointed out earlier,

> We are your brothers. We share your destiny for good or ill. However, the Kurdish nation is not a part of the Arab nation, nor is Kurdistan a part of the Arab homeland. We implore all honorable Arabs to confront such chauvinistic ideas that do not serve their strategic interests in any way.

Chapter 46

The Estrangement

The situation in Kurdistan reached a sensitive stage at the end of 1960, and the government's positive measures after the revolution regarding the implementation of Article 3 of the Provisional Constitution were gradually abated. The lack of a clear program to translate Article 3 into reality and define the national rights of the Kurdish people constituted a major shortcoming in the relations of the Kurdish people with the Iraqi government.

The government began to dismiss Kurdish officers and employees from the army and civil establishments, respectively, especially in the Kurdish provinces. The government publicly favored feudalists in Kurdistan and ignored the KDP, the legitimate representative of the Kurdish people. Feudalists on their part exploited the tension between the KDP and Abd al-Karim Qasim, swindling the government and retaliating against the peasants with a vengeance. Reactionary and chauvinist circles also exploited the tension, shutting down Kurdish schools in numerous areas and banning Kurdish political and literary publications in Kurdistan, while the government almost totally ignored the needs of the Kurdish people.

What added to Abd al-Karim Qasim's sensitivity was Barzani's official visit to the Soviet Union on November 5, 1960, when he was invited by the Soviet government to participate in the October festivities. In Moscow, he was warmly welcomed, conducted high-level talks with Soviet officials, and was received by the Soviet leader, Nikita Khrushchev.

Barzani mentioned to the Soviets the deterioration of conditions in Kurdistan and the likelihood of their explosion due to the government's negative stance. He called for Soviet mediation to restore the situation to normalcy and improve relations between the KDP and Qasim. Many a problem between the KDP and the ICP had been resolved with Soviet mediation, personally conducted by Suslov.[1]

The Soviet views were close to those of Barzani's in that both felt it imperative to work diligently to normalize conditions in Kurdistan and to preclude more serious events. The Soviets pledged to support Barzani and the just struggle of the Kurdish people for its legitimate rights. They promised to back the KDP with support of every kind should the Kurdish people come under attack by government forces.

Barzani returned to Baghdad on January 13, 1961, and asked to meet Abd al-Karim Qasim the following day. Qasim deliberately put off the meeting for more than a week until Barzani finally saw him. From what he heard, Barzani inferred that Qasim's doubts were irreversible. Qasim had concluded that Barzani was vying with him for leadership!

Barzani left Baghdad for the last time and headed for Barzan in early March of 1961. Abd al-Karim Qasim ordered *Khabat* [the KDP's central organ] to be shut down and a number of KDP cadres of the Central Committee to be arrested, accusing them of collaboration in the assassination of Siddique Miran. Thus, the KDP was practically forced to go underground.

The KDP worked to raise the consciousness of the Kurdish masses and organize them to confront any government attack on Kurdistan. Barzani put forth great efforts to purchase arms in preparation for self-defense. Meanwhile, the government armed those perfidious tribes who were accustomed to a mercenary *modus vivendi* and had served successive regimes without thinking of their national affiliation. In addition to military preparedness, the KDP actively worked with the patriotic, national, and democratic Arab forces inside Iraq and abroad and requested their intervention to prevent war in Kurdistan. Aziz Sharif worked exceptionally hard and visited Barzan several times during the summer of 1961. He endeavored to dissuade Abd al-Karim Qasim from moving toward war but in vain.

In July of 1961, the KDP's Central Committee sent Jalal Talabani to Barzan to present the KDP's views regarding new developments and future plans. Barzani suggested that the time was not right to take any military action or to proclaim revolution. All measures, he suggested, must be restricted to preparations to confront hostilities on the part of the government. The timing was not right for the Kurdish side, and preparations were not yet complete. Therefore, the KDP politburo sent a comprehensive memorandum to Abd al-Karim Qasim on July 30, 1961, entreating him to put an end to the deterioration of conditions and to settle all disputes in a brotherly spirit. Abd al-Karim Qasim ignored the memorandum, and tensions continued unabated until the great national September Revolution erupted on September 11, 1961.

Documents

[Some of] the following are documents from 1943–1945 which [Mustafa] Barzani had kept in a special valise. He told me that he had kept all the documents from that period henceforth. However, some of them were lost in the Araxes River when [the Barzanis] crossed into Soviet territory.

I have tried to shed as much light as possible on the ambiguous aspects in these documents. Unfortunately, some ambiguity still remains, because most of those who might have known [the attendant circumstances] have passed away, and at this time it is impossible to contact the few who are left.

I would be grateful for any assistance in this regard.

Massoud Barzani

Translation from Kurdish of Document No. 1

This letter dates back to early 1944.

Massoud Barzani

To His Eminence Mulla Mustafa

Dear as my eyesight:

Today I met Younis Afandi, Supervisor of [Public] Works, in Mergasur. He came to begin the [police] stations (construction of stations): a police station in Mazina and a garrison behind the Director's residence. Two other police stations, one in Chami, and the other in Rezan. Two more police stations, one in Shanader, and the other at the bridgehead of Khallan with the Barzan school and the Mergasur dispensary. I had received your instructions about four police stations.

The police stations of Shirwan and Mergasur are now under the jurisdiction of 'Works' (under construction).

Wali Beg Sa'id Beg

Translation from Kurdish of Document No. 2

Rewanduz: April 2, 1944

My dear brother Izzat,

Good day;
A kiss and a hug. I wish you good health. A few days ago, I wrote you a letter. Of course you have received it.

My brother Izzat: Several days ago, meaning after the return of the Interior Minister, they ordered Amin Rewanduzi to go back, thus he has moved.

Today, I received a letter which states: Since Amin Rewanduzi and Sayyed Aziz's tasks (duties) have ended, they must now return: Amin Rewanduzi to his unit and Sayyed Aziz to the unified training. Therefore, I may be going to Mergasur today or tomorrow to bring essentials I need in order to go to Baghdad.

I had come to Rewanduz to go to Sidakan and bring Mahmud Beg along to Barzan. It appears that I cannot go. They have asked me to go to the unified training immediately.

I do not know your circumstances now, but, God willing, you will succeed.

My brother, please keep me informed of your situation and as soon as possible.... My best regards to brother Mustafa. I do not know if he has returned yet?! Write to me at the address for unified training in 'light weaponry'.

Your brother

Sayyid Aziz

Translation from Kurdish of Document No. 3

The writer of this letter was Lt. Col. Amin Rewanduzi. No doubt he wrote it after he was removed from his position as liaison officer for the Rewanduz region. According to Sayyed

Aziz's letter to Izzat dated April 2, 1944, both Sayyed Aziz himself and Amin Zaki Rewanduzi were removed on this date.

Massoud Barzani

Dear All:

I pray to God that all of you are fine. We parted, but our hearts dance as butterflies around you. I become stronger as I envision your love and recall all the wonderful hours we spent together. As luck would have it, those hours were all we had. It would have been beautiful to have spent more time together! God is generous.

My dear great Brother: Since our return, we are doing all we can. We have never bowed and we hope that we will always go forward. Our current news: Nuri Pasha and Majid toured Kurdistan. Everywhere they went, Cowardice nobility and citizens submitted their memoranda of Cowardice demands. I think our issues will be resolved soon. However, they were opposed in Baghdad. To reject Cowardice demands, some vicious Arabs along with the Regent, forced Nuri Pasha to resign. A new Cabinet was formed by Hamdi al-Pachachi. Leading the opposition to the Cowardice cause are Tahsin Ali, Saleh Jabr and Mustafa al-Omari. But these are transient measures to lull the opposition. I believe that the Cowardice cause must not be neglected. If it is neglected, we must not allow it. The Regent is going on vacation in America, and the kingdom will be run by a Council of Regents consisting of Nuri [Sa'id] Pasha and the Senators.

My dear: please keep us informed. We are ready to carry out your orders. Letters are half the meeting. You must not forget us. The time to forget each other has passed. You must spare no efforts in the support of Cowardice demands. Honor us by issuing a written or verbal command. Friends do not hold back. No time. Major Esbank visited here for a day, and went to Egypt for a 15-day vacation. Please resolve Mahmud Beg and Pisho's issue so no such stupid incident will happen again. All your comrades respectfully send their greetings. Our special regards to our dear brothers. God bless you, always.

Amin Rewanduzi

Before ending this letter, we received from Baghdad the following:

1. Kurdish demands are to be presented everywhere telegraphically, with copies to the Regent's Council, the Prime Minister and the British Ambassador.
2. Do all necessary to implement this request.

Translation from Kurdish of Document No. 4

I could not ascertain who the writer of this letter was. However, it is obvious that it was one of the patriotic officers. The letter contains accurate information and its contents indicate that it dates back to early 1945.

Massoud Barzani

The news here is [as follows]:

1. The decision has been confirmed to move against you on March 31, at the beginning of Spring, and to eradicate you this time. This is a definite decision with no hesitation. If any person or government has informed you otherwise, do not believe them. They will deceive you and want to keep you occupied and comfortable in the winter without preparation until the beginning of spring, when they will attack and exterminate you all.

The attack will come from three directions. The assault on your region will be three-pronged: from Bradost, they will attack Mahmud Beg Khalifa Samad; from Aqra, Imadia and Duhok, they will attack Mahmud Beg Zebari, Saeed Agha Doski and all your possible loyalists; then, they will attack you from the Rewanduz, Baradost, Ima-dia and Mosul routes. This time, they have come to a very serious decision: they will spare no effort. They will never look the other way or pardon you.

2. They have reduced the Iraqi army to two divisions: one Mountain Division, and one Desert Division. The purpose of the reduction of the army is to fill the gaps in the Mountain Division currently close to you, mend its deficiencies and prepare it for spring. They are not paying much attention to the Desert Division stationed in the south. On the contrary, they are transferring troops as reinforcements from there to the Mountain Division near you. The southern Division is almost without personnel. Troop morale is very low, and large numbers are deserting. The troops don't wish to fight. Even Arab soldiers, when transferred to the Mountain Division, are transported in handcuffs and under close surveillance from officers and guards.

3. According to a strictly top secret order, the legions of the Fourth Brigade from the Division designated to attack you in the spring will remain in Kawlus in Suleimaniyya province until January 15 to train for mountain combat. After January 15, it is to move gradually toward your area, under cover of training, and reach its designated point on schedule.

Another Brigade called the Third Legion will remain in Haji Omran, behind Rayat and near Zaini Sheikh, to train for mountain combat as well. Yet another Brigade, the Fifth Legion, is to stay in Swaratuga and train in the vicinities of Duhok, Imadia and Aqra, and will attack you at a specified time.

4. During this period, they are sending many spies to areas near you: e.g., Hakim b. Mulla Tahir Rewanduzi, Pisho (I mean Mohammed Siddique b. Sayyed Taha), Nuri Baweel and many others. They always send them to your area and environments. Beware of these spies, and treat them as they deserve.

5. If you want to teach the Iraqi army (Iraqi government) a good lesson, you must take the initiative, meaning, you must strike in the snow during the severe weather. Each time, you take over one front. For example, attack and eliminate the units around Haji Omran and Rayat. Then attack the Swaratuga units, and then move on to the vicinities of Rewanduz. I mean that you should [not] attack on three fronts simultaneously, because your forces will be weaker when divided on three fronts. But if you could eliminate a unit each time, you will be one hundred percent victorious and give the Iraqi military a crushing defeat so that it will never think of returning for another assault because of low morale. It is a neglected army and does not wish to fight. It is the same army that you tested before and it will be in worse condition this winter. So if you wish, you will be able to hunt the army as you hunt partridges. They do not have more reserves to bring in.

6. They arrested and transported Mir Haj to Imarah three days ago because he had visited you. Now Mir Haj is a prisoner and Mustafa Khoshnaw is a deserter. Police squads are after him. Mustafa and Bakr Abd al-Karim are in the vicinities of Koy Sanjaq and Rania. You may recall them in order to benefit from their knowledge and military expertise. And if you need to, command us. Many of us are ready any time you wish.

7. They are now transferring suspect Kurdish officers to the south and replacing them with Arab officers. Lately, secret and swift orders were issued to transfer Kurdish soldiers to the south en masse and replace them with Arabs. This is being carried out now.

At any rate, all I wish to stress is that you must not believe any person or government informing you that there are no military preparations underway to attack you. They will be lying.

8. It is said that The King's report about Mustafa and Mir Haj was very negative. Therefore, the government took extra measures to arrest them. It is a strong rumor.

9. Please be extra careful not to let my letter fall in the hands of Pisho, Nuri Baweel, Hakim and the like because I will be in danger and will not be able to escape.

Translation from Kurdish of Document No. 5

This is Captain Sayyid Aziz Sayyed Abdullah Afandi's letter, sent to Barzani. Apparently Govan is Barzani's alias; and Jihangeer is Sayyed Aziz's alias.
Massoud Barzani

al-Simawah: March 12, 1945

Dear beloved brother Govan:

Good day, and always wishing you abundant health, success and distinction, with my warmest regards, I remain [yours].

My brother Govan: I haven't heard your news for some time because I was away, and God willing, we will meet soon.

1. Brother Govan: I don't know your circumstances now. But I've heard that your conditions are improving day after day. You are the stronger.

2. My brother, if you wish to know our situation: the team is still as you know it. You have asked for men in your letter and everyone has heard about it. Of course, no honorable, proud human being will slack his sacred duty.

My brother, you know how much I wish to quit this life of (...) which I'm living, to join you or go to the other side. However, you are aware, and last year we came to stay, at least to not move for now. If you want more details, brother Mustafa may explain further.

There are some friends, I'm not sure if they say the truth or if it's just an excuse, who say why is so and so not going while we have to go? Or they say, why doesn't Jihangeer go? They do not go until he goes. These clichés are being repeated often. And because I can't explain in detail why I can't go, I am in a critical position.

Brother, since it is my desire and thought not to stay here: but to go to one of two places, I entreat you, after receiving my letter (as the saying goes: in light of Mustafa's information) and in consultation with him regarding the specific information about my staying or not staying here, please write to me immediately so I can reach a decision. I will consult with brother Mustafa. Because of his travels, he might know the reasons for my staying or not staying here. Therefore, please reply after being informed. I wish to leave this place and go somewhere else. I hope that you will write soon because it is very important to me.

3. My brother: If you wish to know the general situation here, there are two conflicting rumors:

One rumor says that the government is soon to issue a general amnesty to bring things to an end. The other says that the government insists on moving against you after a while, and that the following arrangements are being made:

1. Two leaflets are to be issued in the name of the Commander of Operations and distributed in your areas. The first leaflet will accuse His Eminence the Sheikh and you of rebellion, disobedience, religious infraction and atheism. And it will threaten you. The second leaflet will threaten to bomb your areas. It calls upon the citizens to stay clear of the area, as the leaflet put it "Because the government has exhausted all means to resolve the

situation in the region, and has been unable to lead them to the proper course of action, the government is obliged to discipline them by force."

2. At the same time, the government, with all its capabilities, is secretly preparing for an assault.

3. The government is preparing to conduct exercises in your areas to draw you into clashes. They will try to have British units participate in these exercises.

Rumor has it that exercises will be conducted under the name of (Great Alliance and Small Alliance Exercises). The Mountain Division, that is Mustafa Raghib's, is stationed in Kirkuk and around you, and will participate in these exercises, in addition to two British brigades. No British units are in the area except a brigade in Khanaqin and another one in Kirkuk. Both brigades have mechanized transport. I don't know if the brigade has in fact joined the division in Kirkuk. How will they secure transportation and animals? At any rate, the talk is that these exercises are to be conducted. In short, rumors indicate that units will get close to harass you and force you to confront them.

4. I know that all of you think more clearly than I do, and more accurately, but I believe that it is better that you try to avoid any confrontation as much as you can and to stay as you are. You had better prepare yourselves for the chance which may come at any time.

Please give my warm greetings and high regards to His Eminence the Mulla and to the great Sheikh and all the brothers. Finally, Long Live the Kurds and Greater Kurdistan.

5. I think it is wrong to write open letters like this. We had better prepare a code: you prepare it or we do, to use in our correspondence.

6. What I heard today, March 17, 1945:

a. They are preparing 3 ammunition and supply depots in Khilaifan, in a cave and a police station, in Arbil, in Rawadoz, and in Bilah. They will quickly fill them with ammunition and food-stuffs within 15 days.

b. The exercise is under the name of 'Summer Exercise'. The two previous ones, the Exercises 'Alliance "and" Friendship' failed because of budgetary constraints. The so-called Summer Exercise is to begin on April 7 or 8 and to end on the 17th. All three legions of the Kirkuk Division (Legions 3,4,5) and, according to rumors, two British companies will participate, and the above-mentioned legions will move: one to Rewanduz, another to Khilaifan and the third to Bilah, to a target which hasn't been designated yet.

It is said that the "First Division" from the south may also participate in these exercises.

Your Brother

Jihangeer

Translation from Kurdish of Document No. 6

March 18, 1945

Long live the Kurds and Kurdistan
Lord of the Kurds, I bow and render you my fealty.

My Lord and Commander,

1. We went to Bradost, with Sheikh Ubaidullah, visited Mahmud Beg Khalifa and understood his circumstances. The following day, we visited the son of Sayyed Taha Afandi.

2. Mahmud Beg promised to pay cordial visits to the sons of Sayyed Taha, from now on, and to prevent the government from driving a wedge between them.

3. Our visit in government circles. They ordered the Sidakan police station to transfer police families... but we will not do anything the government might use against us in its propaganda war.

4. I do not know why you didn't go. Did Izzat finish his trip?

5. I received your great letter containing photos and letters from Majid and his siblings. In Sidakan, Mahmud Beg and I reached an understanding to work accordingly.

6. Recently I heard that Sheikh Rashid called the Governor asking if the government would pardon Mahmud Beg if he took him along, and turned in his weapons. The Governor said he would now but not after the start of military operations. Hussein Agha heard this in Diyana, and Lt. Mohammed heard it from the sons of Sayyed Taha. I'm not sure if it is true, and I did not gather as much from Mahmud Beg.

7. I am sending brother Younis's letter (nom de guerre: Kotek). He sent it to me along with 200 dinars that we are keeping to cover our expenses. He sent 400 dinars to Barzan. Please let me know if you have received it, so I can let him know.

8. It is said that the government wants to come to Mazina, but that is not confirmed.

9. I am sending you Wahab Agha's letter.

10. We have a flag sent to us from Syria. We keep it here in Sheikh Sadiq's house.

11. We received another typewriter, which is also unusable.

12. Please send us Lt. Mohammed's essentials.

13. At this time, I brought Lt. Mohammed to Shitna because Mahmud was unhappy.

14. Ubaidallah will tell you the rest of the news.

Mustafa Khoshnaw

Translation from Kurdish of Document No. 7

The signatories of this letter were Dizayee chieftains, but I could not ascertain the identity of the one who wrote the postscript and chose to sign his note with [the English letters] M. H.

Massoud Barzani

Praised be His name. Long live the Kurds and Kurdistan. Long live the Kurdish people.

To our dear brother, respectfully His Eminence Mulla Mustafa

Rendering our highest regards. If you wish to know our news, with God's grace, we are all fine. We pray to HIM for your well-being and success.

Dear brother: We received the letter of our great Lord His Eminence Sheikh Ahmad. We understood its contents, and we were delighted.

Dear brother: You know that the Kurdish people are unjustly oppressed. Therefore, we ought to struggle by all means for the motherland. Your struggle is obvious, and we are ready to struggle by all means and to the best of our abilities.

We warmly greet His Eminence the Sheikh with our ample prayers for his [well being]. Our high regards to brothers (M), ('A), (H) and others. Farewell.

Your Brother	Your Brother	Your Brother	Your Brother	Your Brother
Sulayman	Mohammed Kaka Khan	Ali Khorshid Agha	Khidhir Ahmad Pasha	Sulayman Haji

March 10, 1945

My Lord and Great Leader, I kiss your hands:

I would like very much to visit you but I could not because ...

We are ready to do any service. I would kiss the ground on which His Eminence, the Sheikh walks. Our utmost regards and prayers for brother(s) M. 'A. H.

Our beloved one, be careful, very careful. Lately, I have visited Baghdad twice and saw them all. In your service, I remain

M. H.

Translation from Arabic of Document No. 8

Copy of the Telephone message

Number: 257

Date: April 21, 1945

Governor of the Zebar District

Law of general amnesty pardoning Barzanis No. 18 for the year of 1945 was issued as follows:

Article One: The king may issue general amnesty pardoning Barzanis and others who joined them in the crimes they committed before February 22, 1944, except crimes committed by members of the armed forces and employees punishable according to their special laws.
Article Two: The amnesty does not include personal rights violated in the crimes mentioned in Article One above.
Article Three: This law is effective from the date of publication in the official gazette.
Article Four: Ministers of Interior, Justice and Defense are to carry out this law.

[signed]
Copy as Original
Deputy Governor of Subdistrict [?]
April 28, 1945

Translation from Arabic of Document No. 9

Mahir: Barwari Bala, June 22, 1945

To His Highness, Esteemed Leader Revered Sheikh Mustafa Barzani

After rendering due respect, may Allah grant you joy and glory. Earlier, a letter was written to you which I sent with a young man from Imadia; I hope you have received it. To confirm, I am repeating its contents.

My lord, Lady Mayan, Guardian of the Emir of Yazidi sect and its highest chief, asked me to personally visit you. Also on behalf of Abdi Agha Sharafani, who is to be the agent of contact and introduction between you and them. Because of strict surveillance by government gangs, I did not think it appropriate to visit Your Highness at this time. I hope this letter will suffice in my stead, and to present their requests.

1. Because of her age and sex, Lady Mayan cannot personally contact you. But she wishes you to send a trustee to establish an understanding. If you wish, she will send one for the said mission.
2. Abdi Agha also wishes to continue contact with you. He personally says that you can rely on him as a special trustee and a vassal. He wants me to be aware of his views, and stressed

Lady Mayan's wishes to establish contact and communicate because of her vital position among her sect, the largest loyal Kurdish sect. If you send anyone to Princess Mayan, please do so through relatives of Abdi Agha, or directly to 'Lalash,' the place of Sheikh 'Adi's tomb, or through Baba Chawish, who is always in Lalash. Wishing you continued success, my lord.

Your Servant

Anwar Sheikh Tahir

My personal view
I think it is necessary to respond to Princess Mayan's wish because of her strong religious and social influence among the Yazidi Kurds. Around the globe, they number about 600,000 who can never disobey her. Also, to establish ties and friendship with Abdi Agha Sharafani, a man of courage and status; you may need him and men like him as friends and followers. May God grant your political objectives and oppressed Kurdistan freedom and deliverance.

My personal wish
I wish very much to visit you, hoping to attain some of my goals and desires that are far from being personal. They are just patriotic desires that I have had for years and been infatuated with for a long time. Therefore, please let me know if the British policy would permit educated people such as myself to visit my revered lord.

Translation from Arabic of Document No. 10

Imadia

July 12, 1945

[to] His Eminence Mulla Mustafa, Esq.

Greetings and regards,
Here, we are fine, and my case has ended. I'm now in Imadia. I am thinking of going to Barwari and wait for your orders, because I've heard that you will come to our area. I do not want to write everything, since you may visit the Mizzori region. Let me know so I can be in attendance. Unlike others, I am dependable, and God willing, the future will prove my loyalty and honesty. I am unlike my miserable rival, I mean Saeed Agha; or others.

In closing, I am waiting for an answer soon. I bow to His Excellency Sheikh Ahmad and send my regards to all the brothers.

Ahmad Haji Rashid Beg al-Barwari

Translation from Arabic of Document No. 11

To Mulla Mustafa Barzani, Esq.

I received your Memorandum and the government approved it because of the powers vested in it by law to keep peace, law and order, and to resolve discord among individuals. Because the case of the Mizzoris and Brivkanis impinged on common rights [rights of the state] in addition to the rights of individuals, the government deemed it important to take the necessary measures to resolve it. However, because Abd al-Aziz Haji Malo has escaped, it is necessary to pursue him. Therefore, your duty requires you to advise him to surrender to the government. Then the government will exercise its authority, which it does not relin-quish for anyone. It will deal with the case according to the system of tribal cases through a council of arbiters selected by both sides.

Other attempts are useless and will not bring any results. The government, more than anybody else, does not wish to harm the poor, women and children. Thus I ask you to pay attention to the above, and advise the fugitives to surrender to the government. In this manner, justice will prevail in each case. Therefore, you are asked to return to your area and return the armed men to their homes. In this manner you will prove your love of good and your loyalty to the government. Peace be upon you.

[signed]
Governor of Mosul
Mosul, August 2, 1945

Translation from Arabic of Document No. 12

Office of the Political Commissioner of the British Forces in the Northern Region of Iraq, Mosul

Number: M/15/528

Date: August 3, 1945

Respectfully, to Mulla Mustafa

Greetings,
I am in receipt of your letter of August 1, 1945 in response to my letter dated July 29, 1945. I see that you refuse to come to Mosul to meet His Excellency the Governor and myself.

His Excellency the British Ambassador has ordered me to inform you that your behav-ior has become a burden. And if as you say you are not to do anything that worries Britain, you must hold true to your promise to me personally and quit your moves that will even-tually lead the Iraqi government to take action against you.

I want to let you know clearly and unequivocally that this is the last time the British Embassy will warn you. If you insist on breaking your promise, then you must not expect any assistance or sympathy from us. You will bear full responsibility for the consequences.

I was hoping to give you this message personally, but since you refuse to meet with His Excellency the Governor and myself, I am writing to you accordingly, with our highest regards.

Lt. Col. R. Mead
Political Commissioner in Mosul

Translation from Arabic of Document No. 13

(WARNING)

To: Mulla Mustafa Barzani

Because of the crimes you and your followers have committed in the Barzan region, disturbing the peace and security of the citizens, the government has decided to bring peace to this area and eradicate crime therefrom. It has thus became necessary to warn you to surrender with other Barzani criminals to the government within three days of receiving this warning. Otherwise the government will take necessary measures, and you will bear responsibility for all cost in lives and possessions.

Sa'id Qazzaz
Governor of Arbil
August 12, 1945

Translation from Kurdish of Document No. 14

Sheikh Abdullah Afandi, son of the martyr Sheikh Abd al-Qadir Nahri, a well-known Kurdish dignitary from a deep-rooted family, resided in the village of Diza in the Mergavar region near Urmia. He was well-respected and trusted by the masses of Kurdistan. He sent this open letter to the Kurdish intelligentsia and tribal chiefs, coaxing and encouraging them to support the Barzan revolution, and not to be lured by enemy temptations.

Massoud Barzani

In the Name of Allah, the Merciful, the Compassionate

[To] His Excellency, dear Champion of the Kurds
Long live the Kurds and Greater Kurdistan in freedom
In HIS grace, I hope that you will always be strong and sublime. As you know, all nations of the world are using this historic opportunity to work for self-determination and honored sovereignty in the field of international politics; all except the Kurdish people, whose voice is not heard anywhere. It appears that they have decided on slavery and capitulation to foreign countries, meaning the decision to renew the rights of slavery to their old masters without privilege.

Dear friend, you know the extent of the oppression borne by Kurds, and their great sacrifices to free themselves from slavery. Undoubtedly, the souls of Kurdish martyrs and worthy people are looking down on us with shame and discontent. Strange! aren't we humans? Don't we have the right to live in freedom, like the other nations of the world? Or at least, like the Arabs, the Persians and the Jews? It has been decided that these shall achieve their goals in their days. Odd! don't we have the right to life? If we do have (such a right), why don't we proclaim it? Why don't we fight for our freedom? Why don't we pluck out selfishness and corruption from our ranks to truly become sincere brothers and struggle hand in hand for an honorable death on the road of eternal freedom and joy? Today Mulla Mustafa, a Kurdish young man, is in the trenches of struggle, sincerely with a new nationalist spirit, and against the occupiers. How astonishing! Will we remain spectators and not help him in any way, and concur with his enemies? let him be expunged? How astonishing! the flame of freedom is not extinguished in the hearts of the Kurdish people. The misery and torment we suffer at the hands of the usurping enemy will not occur again.

Your Excellency, as you know that the revolt of the Turkish Kurdistan continued from 1925 to 1928, and because of Kurdish discord and of accord with enemies to kill our own people, because of our selfishness and corruption, because of all that, Turkish Kurdistan was brought to its knees and a great number of Kurds were killed. Chiefs, Sheikhs, learned men and dignitaries were executed, and suffering touched all Kurds. As a result, Kurdistan fell at the hands of the occupying enemy.

Please, to save the happiness of the Kurdish people and Kurdistan, wake up from this lethargy, and appreciate our duties in this period of history when the fates of all the nations of the world are being decided.

I implore Almighty God to fulfill our aspirations; with our sincere wishes,

Sheikh Abdullah Sheikh Abd al-Qadir
October 4, 1945/Shawwal 27, 1364 [A.H.]
[Sealed with his seal]

Translation from Kurdish of Document No. 15

No.:

Date: 16/12/24 Solar Hijri

KURDISTAN DEMOCRATIC PARTY
Local Committee of Shino (Oshnoviyeh)

An order issued by dear brother Hussein Froher
Transmitted via telephone from Naghadeh

Upon instructions from the president of the Republic of Kurdistan, please inform those who are hosting our Barzani brothers to provide all possible assistance at all levels. They must not be estranged or let down. Inform the leadership of anyone who delays execution of this order.

Hussein Froher

The above was Brother Hussein Froher's telegram issued to all residents of the Shino (Ashnawiya) region. We stress that all are to obey and willingly carry out the blessed instructions of our leader.

[Signed]
Officer in Charge
Local Committee of Shino [Oshnoviyeh]
al-Qazi Khafari
[Committee Stamp]

Translation from Russian of Document No. 16

Barzani's Memorandum to Baqirov[1]

1947

(To) Comrade Baqirov, the Secretary of the Communist (Bolshevik) Party of Azerbaijan and Leader of the Peoples of the East

It is a high honor for me to introduce myself for the first time to a noble person like you. For many years, the peoples of the East have been oppressed. The Kurdish nation is among

---

1. Elena Andreeva of New York University translated this document from Russian into English.

them. It has suffered enormously from the reactionary regimes of Turkey, Iran, Iraq, and from the exploitative policies of England and America.

Since the time when the Kurdish nation was honored with your attention and became close to you, it has recognized this as the only symbol of its freedom and independence. That is why we, as a group of Kurdish democrats, officers, and fighters, have asked for your protection and sympathy.

The reactionary government of Iran with the support of the Anglo-American exploiters, directed its armed force against the Kurdish Republic, destroyed the democratic Kurdish government and the Shah's army occupied the Kurdish land.

The fascist government of Turkey seized a large part of Kurdistan and turned it into a prison, where Kurds live in extremely severe and difficult conditions. At present, thousands of Kurdish democrats and freedom-loving Kurds are arrested and thrown into Iranian prisons.

Initially, it seemed that there was no such force that could change the destiny of the Kurds and redeem them from misfortune. However, the coalescence of the Kurdish nation under the banner of democracy and hope for the Great Teacher and Leader, Stalin has destroyed all the obstacles in our path. The attention given to us by Comrade Baqirov, the father and leader of the Peoples of the East, has become a great hope for the Kurdish nation.

The days of reaction, oppression, and exploitation are almost gone. They are living their last days.

The Barzani tribe, for which I am responsible, is one of the largest Kurdish tribes. Its struggle for liberation started under the leadership of my late brother, Sheikh Abd al-Salam in 1894. During the Turkish Sultan Abd al-Hamid's reign, Sheikh Abd al-Salam founded a clandestine organization in the city of Istanbul, and led the struggle for the national independence of the Kurdish people. Owing to the activities of this organization, and with the participation of the other Kurdish tribes, the liberation movement pervaded Iraq in 1904. The movement continued until 1914, when, during opposition to Sultan Rashad, it pursued its desperate struggle against the Ottoman Empire. This movement did not bring about the desired results and it eventually ended in our defeat. My brother was arrested and executed by Turkish butchers in the town of Mosul, while my family and I immigrated to Iran.

After that, my brother, Sheikh Ahmad, was chosen head of the tribe and in 1920 the ceaseless struggle against the increasingly exploitative policies of the British started.

During the years 1942–1945, the struggle was going on against the Iraqi government which was supported by the exploitative policies of the British. In 1945, as a result of the onset of the enemy, we had to immigrate to Iran along with our families and tribe.

There, in Iranian Kurdistan, the red star brightened our lives. Since that time, we have participated in organizing of the democratic government of Kurdistan and, together with our Azerbaijani brothers, we combated against the Iranian army in Rezaye and elsewhere. Thousands of fighters from the Barzani tribe were fighting there, defending the borders of Azerbaijan and free Kurdistan. Also, they were defeating the enemy in the areas of Saqiz, Sardasht, and other mountain regions.

The heroic struggle of the freedom-loving Azerbaijanis and Kurds led to the triumph of freedom and to strengthening democracy in Azerbaijan and Kurdistan.

On December 11, 1946, the political situation compelled the Azerbaijani army to retreat, and the Kurdish government to surrender. However, we, the Barzani tribe, refused to capitulate to the enemy and organized our struggle under the title of the Liberation of Kurdistan Front. For six months we stood firm against our enemies, conquerors and aggressors in Iran.

After arduous battles, we moved to Iraq in order to organize a guerrilla movement. We led a partisan war in Iraq for one month, then went to Soviet territory along the Irano-Turkish border. On the border, armies of both countries [Iran and Turkey] tried to block our way in order to annihilate us. They chased us all the time.

Our past struggle for liberation is known to our neighbors. Despite the violent reaction, the leftist media and organs of the democratic parties explained our struggle and popularized it among their peoples. These organs of the press are the following: Iraqi Tribes and Peoples magazine; S. al-Beirutiya;[2] al-Ahram, the Egyptian magazine [sic]; Kurdistan newspaper, organ of the Kurdistan Democratic Party published in Mahabad; Nishtiman [Homeland] magazine; The Iraqi Kurd, communist newspaper; Rizgari [Deliverance]; and Nidhal al-Akrad [The Struggle of the Kurds], an independent Egyptian publication (in this book our struggle has been described).

Our tribe consists of 50.000 people. There are no landlords among us; each person owns some land, cattle, and sheep. In 1914, my brother Sheikh Abd al-Salam divided our land among the peasants equitably and fairly. This division has remained in effect to this day in our villages, whose number of plots reaches 400. This is how the land problem has been solved in the villages of the Barzani tribe, whereby every person has his individual farm; and in this way the social relationships between peasants and landowners have been regulated.

Among our tribes and social relations, the ultimate goal consists of achieving freedom and independence. In order to achieve them, we rebelled many times because they were our want and primary goal.

We chose to tie our destiny with the Soviets, because this power supports the freedom and hope of peoples.

These bonds were established in May 1944. At that time, the Freedom Front already existed among the Barzani tribe. Since then, I have kept in touch with military and political representatives of the Soviet State.

After December 11, 1946, namely after the seizure of Kurdish and Azerbaijani lands by the Iranian army, the situation changed. My relationship with soviet politicians was no longer on the basis of the truth which had been tested in practice for years and proved to me.

Undoubtedly, soviet politicians had expected the forthcoming events in Kurdistan and Azerbaijan. When the events started the situation of the Barzanis was more difficult in comparison to the others. Firstly, the Barzanis had immigrated to Iran and other countries, secondly, the men were in the battle on the front, and their wives and children were left without heads of their families.

The soviet politicians should have warned us before the events started so that we could have prepared ourselves. We would not have scattered our forces and would not have died in the mountains. Despite that, we resisted the Iranian army for five months. All famous radio stations spoke about our struggle, and spread the information about us through the whole world. The thunder of the aerial bombardments which we were undergoing near Rezaye could be heard on Soviet territory. However, it attracted no sympathy from the Soviet government. Neither Azerbaijani nor Moscow radio stations mentioned our movement even once.

The Soviet press did not give us enough attention. Nobody from the Soviet government came to us, inspired us or showed us the way.

If politics prevented talking about us or providing us with weapons, you cannot entirely forget about us and leave us to fate's mercy.

---

2. A possible reference to the Lebanese newspaper al-Safir.

After we had recognized the futility of our guerrilla movement, we decided to come to the Soviet land in order to save what was left of our forces.

Aided by our faith and devotion, we broke fearlessly and resolutely through the lines and trenches of the Turkish, Iranian, and Iraqi armies, which blocked our way and attempted to annihilate us, and headed for the Soviet borders.

We arrived at the Soviet border and wanted to cross to the USSR, but Soviet officials did not help us or show us a place where we could ford the river. They kept us on the [other] bank of the river. Finally, in order to save ourselves, we had to abandon most of our weapons to the enemy and crossed the river into the USSR with a little load.

In the city of Nakhichevan, I was separated from my brethren for 40 days. During that time, I lived in a room which was more of a prison than anything else. I considered this to be unsuitable for me for I had not anticipated this in the Soviet territory. In the town of Shusha, the treatment was the same.

My people's conditions were no better than my own. I love them like the apple of my eye. To date, opportunities have not been created for them. They live on collective farms and do masonry and earthwork. They do not deserve this life and work. They cannot work on an equal footing with the experienced, educated Soviet collective farmers as they are not familiar with this type of work. Many of them are nearly without clothing, and some of them are living in conditions which are not suitable even for cattle.

These people represent Kurdish people; they lost their lands, families and everything they had in the struggle for democracy and freedom. In order to prepare themselves for the new struggle, they have sought refuge in the Soviet land. They have not come here for commerce or in search of other economic benefits. They are one of the peoples of the East and, as representatives of Kurdish people, they are guided by the Soviet Union. You, being a dear and close friend of the peoples of the East, ought to know about their misery, needs and deeds.

I consider it to be my duty to inform you of the situation of the Barzani immigrants and ask you to assist them in their needs and wishes:

My first request is a meeting with you. Of course your time is precious, but we also have a right to take some of your time and inform you about our necessary questions in person.

We believe that everything is in the state of permanent evolution, and conditions change with change in the material being. Depending on these circumstances, political opportunities change, too. Therefore, time creates new opportunities for the victory of democracy every day. We await the time when we shall return home, with the help of the Soviet and other democratic peoples.

I regret that, despite my people's and my own residence in the Soviet territory, we have not had any access to the new knowledge yet. We certainly should make use of scientific, cultural, and political knowledge. There is no doubt that work is a sacred duty, but education and knowledge take precedence.

In the Soviet Union, there are 496 of my fellow Kurds. I ask that they be moved to one location. Taking into consideration the future needs, they should study political and military sciences, be trained in using heavy weapons and learn military rules. Ten people should be selected and sent to an air-force school. In special courses they should learn the theory of military tactics and the use of the modern weapons. They should be instructed in history, mathematics, geography, medicine, military science and other subjects if necessary. They should be taught how to conduct themselves in public, taught rules and new culture.

It is easy to find instructors for them. For example, among the Soviet officers, there are Captain Jafarov and others who know Kurdish. In addition, the officers and some of the Barzanis speak Azerbaijani. Those who do not know it can learn it gradually while in the process of studying. This way, we could educate cadres for the future of the Kurds and for democracy.

It is not my goal to be the head of this tribe. No, this depends on the will and desire of the Kurds. Every Barzani officer has 100 subordinate people who are devoted to him. Some of them are heads of separate Kurdish *ta'ifes* [sects/clans] and posses a lot of authority and influence. They participated in many battles and a number of freedom-loving Kurds gathered around each of them and took part in the struggle together with them. These officers practically demonstrated that they deserve their military rank.

I ask you to treat them generously. It is clear to me and to all people that supporting 469 people is not difficult for the great and strong Soviet State at a time when its government is known to be the defender of all the freedom-loving peoples.

When I suggest to gather all of them in one location, my motives are the following: their training and provision could be regulated by one organization and in this way it would be easy to watch them and be informed about their situation. After they are gathered together, I ask that a plane or any other means of transportation be put at my disposal to enable me to visit them often. They have a rich experience in fighting and I highly value them. I am unable to do anything without them.

As comrade Stalin has said, "Men are the most valued of living beings." These are the words of the Great Leader. In addition to the fact that Barzanis are human beings, they are also revolutionaries.

A Kurdish youth, Abdullah Oglu Aziz Shamzini is currently studying here in Baku, at Azerbaijan University. This young man joined our forces during the battles of 1942–1945. He had served in the Iraqi army at the rank of captain. He later deserted and together with some other Kurdish officers joined the Barzani forces. He fought on our side with exceptional enthusiasm and faith and demonstrated prowess in the battle. In Iran, too, he proved himself in the struggle against the Iranian government.

Aziz comes from a respected, efficient, and freedom-loving Kurdish family. His *Nahri* tribe enjoys high respect and authority in Kurdistan. His cousins on his father's side opposed him and went to the camp of the reactionaries but Aziz remained unshaken on the path to his goal.

As a result of the recent events, some of the Iraqi Kurdish officers who had joined us together with Aziz were arrested and executed by the Iraqi government. Now Aziz remains a valued living memory of these officers to us. I implore you to be kind to him, treat him well and, if feasible, send him to the Barzanis who are here. I think that Aziz will agree to be in the ranks of his fellow fighters.

In addition to Aziz, there are some Kurdish youths who are studying in political and other schools here. They are exemplary of the sons of the Kurdish people. In particular, your fatherly attention to Rahim Kazi-zadeh gives us hope and we are very grateful to you for that.

I have one more favor to ask of you. I ask that you instruct the Azerbaijani radio station to reserve some time every day for broadcasting in Kurdish. Our voice will give confidence and hope to the Kurdish people. This voice from the radio will reach our enemies like thunder and at the same time inspire the Kurdish people of new heroic deeds. This will pave the way to defend the rights of the Kurdish people in international organizations and the United Nations.

When the power of the Kurdish people is officially enhanced by the Soviet State, this power will certainly grow around the world and this will impact the prestige of our enemy.

A monthly magazine should be published in Kurdish to promote the cultural, political, and economic situation in Kurdistan on its pages. Through this magazine, we will address the way to liberate the Kurdish people, compile a history of the revolutionary movement in Kurdistan and demonstrate the current oppression of Kurds and their lack of rights there. We will demonstrate that the Kurdish people is one of the viable and progressive peoples of the East but their name has recently been erased from [the pages of] history and dictionaries. Nevertheless, this people will live and prosper.

We ask for your help to bring our voice to the United Nations and protest the suppression of the Kurds by the four reactionary governments: Turkey, Iran, Iraq, and Syria.

When the masks are torn and truth uncovered, it will become clear what sort of oppression the Kurdish people have been subjected to. Even the peoples of South Africa have not endured such treatment. We deem it necessary to apprise you, leader of the Peoples of the East, of all this.

I hope to be able to visit the Leader of the working people of the world, Comrade Stalin, and to tell him about the misfortunes of the Kurdish people. Your attention to the peoples of the East, including the Kurds, gives us hope. That is why I strive for a meeting with you. If I were able to meet Comrade Stalin, it would be to my delight and that of the Kurdish people. I am trying to achieve this and I ask you, Comrade Baqirov, as a close companion of Comrade Stalin to assist me in realizing my wish. I would thus see Moscow, the hope of the working people all over the world, and Stalingrad, where the Red Army had defeated the enemy and laid down the foundation for victory.

I reiterate my desire to meet Comrade Stalin, and wait for my dream to come true. This depends on your kindness. I will need political and party education and ask you to provide me with it.

I have one more request: My nephew, Sheikh Sulayman Barzani, is living with me now. He has taken part in all the military and political battles and demonstrated practical abilities which have made him a close aide and comrade to me. In my absence, be it temporary or for longer periods, Sheikh Sulayman can deservedly replace me and you may benefit from his abilities.

I hope that you will allow me to meet you and then I will have an opportunity to explain our circumstances in a more precise manner.

Son and servant of the Kurds,
Signed
Mustafa Barzani
November 15, 1947
Baku

Translation from Persian of Document No. 17

The Government of Iran
Center for Documents and Statistics
Document No. 12/3
14 Behman 1326

[Stamp of the Ministry of Foreign Affairs]

... [I]f it happened, the government does not allow even its own non-Iranian employees to do such work. Also, no Iranian plane did or does conduct any reconnaissance on the border points. Therefore, how could it take such photographs? I find myself obliged to point out few clear facts, and to bring them to the attention of the government of the Soviet Union.

Soviet forces in Iranian Azerbaijan settled according to the Tripartite Treaty concluded on 9 Behman, 1320, without harassing the treasonous anarchist group which appeared in that province and defied the central government under the direction of Soviet officials who did not cease to provide moral and material support to the group. Even after Soviet authorities ended their protection inside Iran of these treacherous and anarchist elements that chose to flee on the 19th day of the month Azar, 1325, instead of facing the rage of the people of Azerbaijan and the wrath of Iranian public opinion, the government of the Soviet Union opened its borders and allowed them to enter its territory. According to information confirmed, the Soviet government continues to support these elements and works to prop them up, as well as the tone of the broadcasts of Radio Moscow, Radio Baku, and the underground radio which unmistakably is beamed from some point in the Caucasus in the name of the Azerbaijan Democratic Party. In addition, the continued Soviet troop movements between border posts and exercises that are conducted at border points, which the government of Iran has strongly protested, all fully confirm this ongoing Soviet policy while the friendly ties between the governments of Iran and the Soviet Union require the Soviet government to receive the Iranian request appropriately in accordance with Memorandum No. 4865 dated 27/9/1325 concerning the return of these perfidious and anarchist elements to Iran, and to refrain from conducting border exercises which cause turmoil and concern to all Iranians especially those living in the border areas.

In addition to what has been stated above, the Soviet government did not heed the Iranian request to turn over the group of robbers and looters commanded by Mulla Mustafa Barzani, the person who killed and pillaged during the Soviet army's presence in Azerbaijan. He was backed by Soviet officials and their army of occupation. He held the rank of general and led his group confidently under Soviet protection in Iran. When they were pursued and sought to escape, the government of Iran informed the Soviet government beforehand and insistently [Soviet] demanded rejection of this looting group's request for asylum and sanctuary. Sad to say, the Soviet government did not respond to this legitimate Iranian request. In fact, the above-mentioned looters crossed the border at the Araxes River [point] with the help of Soviet border officials on the 21st day of the month of Khurdad, 1326, in the border region of Qaraqoyoon.

Undoubtedly you will agree that the way the Soviet government dealt with the fugitives on the 19th day of the month of Azar, 1325, or (Bishawari) and his comrades, and the fugitives the 21st day of the month of Khurdad, 1326, or the looting Barzanis, the provision of actual protection and allowing them to regroup inside Soviet territories for the purpose of violating Iranian territorial sovereignty and providing the necessary means, as well as publishing and broadcasting equipment, to create ideological confusion and [to cause a] rift in Soviet–Iranian relations. This is in outright violation of Chapter Five of the Friendship Treaty signed on February 21, 1921 between the Soviet and Iranian governments.

In informing Your Excellency of all the above facts, I find it necessary to bring to your attention the point that by using some American officers who have been employed since the war to run the affairs of the Iranian military and police, we do not see any contradiction or breach of the February 21, 1921 Treaty and it cannot at all be considered an anomaly or linked to the said Treaty because it is an internal issue only. Discussion of the subject will be considered an open interference in the internal affairs of a sovereign nation. In return, the Iranian government wishes to strengthen friendship and neighborly ties between the two countries. The Soviet government ought to pay attention to the issue of hostile acts from within its borders by looting and anarchist elements against the security of Iran, and to respond favorably to the requests of the government of the Shah in this regard. We take this opportunity to renew our utmost regards.

Translation from Kurdish of Document No. 18

Barzani's speech on January 19, 1948 at momentous Kurdish meeting in Baku

Introduction

We are meeting here today, on this occasion in the name of our Kurdish people. In opening our third session, I first congratulate you and our striving Kurdish people.

In the partisan movements we conducted in Iran, Turkey, and Iraq, the Kurdish nation openly showed us their feelings, sentiments, and sincerity. In the spirit of brotherhood, Kurdish villagers and patriotic leaders, then expressed their deep loyalty in our reception and farewell. The tears of Kurdish women and children in farewell, clearly reaffirmed the nation's loyalty and love to us.

Despite mountainous roads and difficult terrain, and without regard to fear, oppression and enemy crimes, thousands of Kurdish villagers, leaders and notable patriots with their families and children carried food, clothes and other necessities; carried all they could. They would usually line up on those difficult roadsides we passed through. They gave us their loads of food, bread and clothes, and more importantly, they welcomed, and gave us the greetings and love of the Kurdish nation. They would loudly cry out, "Be safe! may God protect you!, we wish you victory! for we are waiting for you to return shortly, our deliverance." My brothers, these are the words, sincere but repressed sentiments of the Kurdish nation for us.

Experience gained from our past revolts clearly demonstrated the backing of our heroic Kurdish nation, the iron Kurdish will, the spirit to revolt, and eagerness to be free. Eagerness to be free of oppression, injustice, tyrants and reactionaries; eagerness to break the doors of the greater prison. Our nation sees us and our Democratic Party as a liberation force; it demands and awaits deliverance. Led by our Democratic Party, if our struggle is guided and organized by a modern ideology, certainly, no reactionary force can defeat us, and with all our struggle, we will definitely reach our goal of freedom.

My brothers, despite our enemies' endless attempts to extinguish the flame of struggle and the spirit of freedom in Kurdistan, again we find in the heart of every Kurd, in contrast to our vicious and bloodthirsty enemies, the spirit of liberty and the flame of revolt are growing and becoming stronger day after day. Consistent with proven natural laws, our current struggle is inspired by and embodies new ideology to lead the Kurdish nation to true freedom. Our striving brothers trusted us in electing us to the Central Committee of the Democratic Party. They have entrusted us with their destiny. With our long and hard struggle, we earned the confidence of our nation; and I can say with pride, that this trust is the utmost of our pleasure and joy. Our resolve has been affirmed a hundred fold to continue our struggle. We and the comrades who elected us have proven through experience that we form the most progressive and revolutionary elements of the Kurdish nations, and that we defend Kurdish interests.

Of those progressive and literate comrades, villagers, chiefs and great Kurdish patriots and revolutionaries who since 1913 have, with their struggle, courage, and the sacrifice of their bothers and relatives, earned the support, love and deep loyalty of the Kurdish nation. The Kurdish nation deeply trusted them. Having participated in many Kurdish liberation movements, they have etched it in our collective memory that they truly are the continuation of Kurdish history. They have truly represented our people.

This Committee of ours, in essence their extension, truly represents and can lead the Kurdish nation in all aspects. Therefore, upon us rests a great historic task. We expect to face much difficulty. Despite adversity, we must go on firm and steadfast. Upon the activities of our Committee rests the future and destiny of eleven million Kurds. Hopeful, now they are awaiting our efforts.

My brothers, I am most confident that our talk will be effective and the cause for clasping our hands in brotherhood, friendship and untiring, and devoted labor day and night for our goals of liberty and democracy.

Kurdish History

As you all well know, in the history of the east, the Kurdish rule and civilization began 3,000 years before Christ. Our enemies have always wanted to deny [the existence of the] Kurdish civilization, but they have failed. Undeniable, our people inhabited the Zagros mountains. They were known as Kardo, or Kurdo. Populating a part of Iran and eastern Anatolia, they established a vast empire between 800 and 400 B.C. the Medes, who formed most of Iran's ancient history and civilization.

Like all Middle Eastern peoples, the Kurds came under the Islamic rule. Intermingled with and participating in the Islamic empire, our people played a significant role in building Islamic civilization. [One great exemplar is] the Kurdish hero Saladin Ayobi, whose role in defense of the Islamic world against the crusaders in the middle of the twelfth century is well established.

Then, as the Islamic rule declined, a new struggle and renaissance of the eastern peoples began to take root. Among the first were the Kurds, who established their free and independent states. The following are some of those states:

(1) In the 18th Century, in Iranian Kurdistan, the State of Karim Khan Zand was founded.
(2) In 1790 in Iraq, the Baban State was founded.
(3) In 1812, in Turkey, the Badrkhan State was founded.
(4) In 1826, in Iraq, the princes of Rewanduz and Khanzadeh founded their own government.
(5) In 1880, the Barzan rulers in Iraq and the Shamzinan rulers in Turkey founded their governments under the name of self-rule ("khod Mukhatari").

These are examples that prove to us and to the peoples of the world that the Kurdish people have expressed at every opportunity their outrage and wrath against occupying enemies. They have never submitted, and have always been proud of their nationality, language and culture. For their freedom, they have sacrificed thousands of their heroes. That's why our forefathers preferred freedom on mountaintops they climbed in tough times of struggle to city life. I would like to take this opportunity to present glimpses of the modern Kurdish struggle, inspired by its past and continuing on this road of no regrets.

Kurdish Revolutions

1. The beloved leader and Kurdish hero Sheikh Abaidullah Shamzini who in 1880 led his revolt against Ottoman imperialism to liberate Kurdistan. In a short time, his revolution spread to include eastern Anatolia and much of Iranian Kurdistan. In a battle, he was captured and exiled to Arabia and Hijaz. He died during his exile in 1893.

2. The second beloved leader and Kurdish hero Sheikh Abd al-Salam Barzani, who began his struggle in 1914 to liberate Kurdistan from Ottoman oppression and injustice. He led the struggle for a whole year until he was captured through a cowardly plot in Iran. He was taken to Mosul, where he was executed in 1915.

3. The beloved Kurdish hero Sheikh Abd al-Qadir Shamzini led a bloody revolt against the oppression and injustice by the Turkish state in 1924. In a short time period, a bloody struggle swept eastern Anatolia. The flames of his revolution continued until 1930. In this great and bloody revolt, the Kurdish people offered up half a million martyrs, among them, leaders and heroes such as Sheikh Saeed of Khinis in the Darsim region, whose sacrifice was unmatched. He was executed like his many colleagues, the great leaders Sheikh Abd al-Qadir Shamzini, Sayyed Mohammed Shamzini, Dr. Fuad, Khaled Beg, and hundreds of other leaders who were executed between 1924 and 1930 in Diyarbekr.

This long struggle ended in 1930 as the Ararat Movement, a guerrilla against the tyrant Riza Shah Pahlavi, led by the Kurdish hero, Farzandeh, began to take root, and the struggle moved to Iran. He was martyred, and with him the Kurds gave another half million martyrs.

4. In 1918, as the British army of occupation advanced to take over Kurdistan, the Kurdish hero Sheikh Ahmad Barzani resisted, keeping his region free until 1932, when a much larger British army attacked the free region of Barzan. Led by Sheikh Ahmad Barzani, the Kurdish people struggled in a bloody fight until 1935, when he and other Barzan leaders were exiled until 1943, and the flames of this revolt were only temporarily extinguished.

5. In 1919, in the region of Suleimaniyya, in Iraq, the Kurdish people led by Sheikh Mahmud Hafeed revolted against Britain. Sheikh Mahmud was captured during a battle and remained in exile until 1941.

6. Led by the hero, Ismail Agha (Simko) Shikak, the Kurdish people revolted in 1921 against the tyranny and oppression of Riza Shah. With his organized army, Simko was successful in controlling all of Iranian Kurdistan. In a cowardly ploy by the Iranian state, he was assassinated in Shino. Unchecked, Iranian tyrants committed atrocities in Kurdistan until 1941, when the Soviet Red Army liberated those areas from the fascist rule of Riza Khan.

7. In 1943, we began our liberation struggle in Barzan to establish an organized, democratic and free administration. Successful, we continued autonomous until 1945 when the governments of Britain and Iraq amassed a large army. With our comrades and families, we withdrew to free Kurdistan in Iran, after fierce battles and bloody struggle. We participated in the liberation movement in Iranian Kurdistan. With the Iranian Kurds, our struggle culminated the founding of a democratic state in Iran.

8. After the hated rule of Riza Shah was destroyed in 1941, a free Kurdish democratic state was founded under the leadership of Qazi Mohammed in 1945. And in [Dikaber—December?] of 1945, Kurdish leaders and nobles, along with the Barzani Militia, rid parts of Iranian Kurdistan of the fascist elements and the agents of Riza Shah and established the democratic government of Qazi Mohammed. With their Azerbaijani brothers, our army struggled in a year-long fight against the reactionaries of Tehran.

9. On December 12, 1946, the traitor Qawam al-Saltaneh violated his pledge and broke his word of honor to Azerbaijan and Kurdistan. With his large army of reactionaries, he attacked Azerbaijan and Kurdistan. For six long months of fierce and bloody fighting, our courageous forces had the upper hand in every battle. However, with active American and British support, and coordination with the Iraqi and Turkish armies, the reactionary forces of Iran, using information from American and Iranian agents, attacked us at our weak point, that is the presence of our families with us on the front. Thus, under heavy aerial and artillery bombardment, some of our units, after long resistance, were caught between the

Turkish and Iraqi armies. After much killing, they were captured. After this tragedy, we changed our mode of organized resistance to that of a guerilla warfare on which we continue to rely to this day.

The victorious, Tehran reactionaries committed barbaric crimes, unmatched even in the middle ages, which continue to this day. As you knew, our beloved leader Qazi Mohammed and his brothers had met on December 14, 1946 with the vengeful Iranian general Hamayoni, who had given them his word of honor and pledged their safety. They believed him and surrendered. However, like other Iranian criminals, this most shameless man has no honor. He treacherously executed our beloved leader and his brothers in Mahabad.

10. Over the past half century, the Kurdish people have given a million progressive fighters, courageous heroes and brilliant leaders. All were martyred defending the freedom of the Kurds and Kurdistan. In addition, more than two million Kurds have been deported, exiled and made homeless. Five thousand Kurdish villages and towns have been destroyed and ransacked. Our Kurdish people continue today to give ample sacrifices in their struggle on the path of freedom.

11. In short, our continuous struggle in Kurdistan was neither random nor casual. It involved daily thinking and planning. Guided and directed by Kurdish political parties, participants in these uprisings have helped to shape ideas and to define national political and democratic goals.

As you and the world know, the revolution of Sheikh Abd al-Qadir Shamzini was directed and organized by the Kurdish Party Peshkawtin o Sarkawtini Kurd—Ascendance and Advancement which was established in Istanbul by a group of conscientious educated Kurds. This same party organized and directed the struggle of Sheikh Abd al-Salam Barzani in Iraq, and the uprising of Sheikh Saeed Khinisi in Darsim. Ismail Agha (Simko) Shikak's struggle was directed by the Kurdistan Independence Committee, which was founded by a group of Kurdish leaders and patriotic notables.

The Peshtiwani [Support] Party, founded in Iraq, organized and directed the revolts of Sheikh Mahmud. Sheikh Ahmad Barzani's revolt of 1918 was organized and directed by the [Unity of National Front Party]. Our revolt of 1945 was organized and led by the Azadi [Freedom] Party, which was founded in Barzan, in cooperation with the Hiwa [Hope] Party, founded in Baghdad by a group of students and educated Kurds, and the Iraqi Communist Party. A party representative was sent to Mahabad. The Kurdish Resurrection Party (Jianaway Kurd), founded by a group of Mahabad youth, was behind the awakening in Mahabad, while the KDP organized and led the revolution until December 12, 1946. And our current struggle continues to be under the leadership of the KDP.

Imperialism and the Kurdish Struggle

1. The Kurdish struggle for freedom and independence is unparalleled. More than any other Middle Eastern nation, the Kurds, have resisted injustice and occupation. For their homeland and liberty, the Kurds have sacrificed the lives of thousands of their heroic sons. Our spiteful enemies, the enemies of mankind and freedom, countered and suppressed our struggle with aerial and artillery firepower, with mass slaughters, mass deportations and exiles, and the packing of prisons with our freedom fighters.

2. After World War I, in 1920 independence and freedom granted to the Kurds in the Treaty of Sèvres. Then in 1921, with the Treaty of Lousanne, British imperialism, in accordance with its criminal and hideous policy, sold the destiny of the Kurdish nation to Kamal Ataturk in exchange for the oil of Kirkuk and Mosul. Thus, in the next twenty years,

Kurdish revolts flared up in Turkey, Iran and Iraq, in bloody armed struggles. British imperialism guided and taught our enemies, supported all the barbaric crimes they committed against us, and prevented our voice from reaching the world. Their reactionary propaganda depicted our national struggle as religious and feudalist movements and often as acts of banditry, denying the Kurdish struggle for freedom.

3. Furthermore, from 1918 until 1947, the modern British army of occupa-tion in Iraq suppressed the Kurdish liberation movement in Suleimaniyya and Barzan mercilessly and unconscionably, and destroyed centers of revolutionary leadership.

4. The Sa'd Abad Accord of 1937 was aimed first and foremost at the Kurdish liberation movement. It is another hideous side of the British policy to drive a wedge between the Soviet Union and peoples of the Middle East, including our Kurdish people, and to prevent their pleas from reaching the Soviet Union. Despite the bankruptcy of this Treaty, after World War II, Britain worked to revive it once again in the month of [Reforal?] in 1947. Nuri al-Sa'id, the British special agent and then Iraqi Premier, suggested the formation of regular joint Iraqi, Iranian and Turkish army, under one command, to wipe out all Kurdish liberation movements.

5. World War II introduced another imperialistic country into the Middle East; that is American imperialism, to replace the aging British [power]. Unable to sustain world leadership, British policies of old imperialism no longer fit the new variables in the Middle East. First, American imperialism intervened in the affairs of the democratic government of Kurdistan by supporting the government of Qavam al-Saltana on December 12, 1946, and worked to topple the government of Azerbaijan. They succeeded in toppling both free governments. Had it not been for Anglo-American support and guidance, Qavam al-Saltaneh would have never dared to violate his pledges to both republics of Azerbaijan and Kurdistan, suddenly and without hesitation. These facts are public and acknowledged by American and Iranian officials.

Again, had it not been for the Anglo-American cooperation in free Kurdistan, and their agents, recruited with American dollars, and benefiting from their services on the war fronts of Mahabad and Raza'ia (Urmia) against the Kurdish democratic army, the drug-infested army of the Shah would never have been able to resist our heroes. They did so with American arms, spies, and agents' acts of treason and terrorism.

6. Heroic Barzani forces badly defeated the Iranian reactionaries in March 1947 on three fronts. As their Anglo-American masters realized the extent of Iranian losses, they brought in their puppets from Turkey and Iraq. Their units actually crossed into Iranian territory without regard to international laws and codes of ethics. Their barbaric bombardment resulted in great losses in Barzani women and children. At the same time, they enforced an economic and political blockade on the fledgling Republic of Mahabad. They also used traitors, who sold their homeland, to further their objectives and disseminate their propaganda.

7. These are some examples of the activities and plots of imperialism against our revolutionary movement.

8. The world knows that there is historical strife and animosity between the Turks, Iranians and Arabs, some of which are religious and sectarian, and some of which are territorial and border disputes. Among them, deep-rooted antipathy and complex unresolved problems remain. However, as soon as the issue of Kurds and free Kurdistan comes into play, they set aside their differences and cooperate as brothers to conclude criminal agreements against Kurdish liberation.

Why is it that these three nations, enemies throughout history, in various circumstances and at various times become friends and conclude agreements to preserve each other's peace and stability against the Kurdish people?

Despite the existence of other motives and reasons, I believe the single most important reason that comes into play behind closed doors is the criminal and hideous policy of imperialism. The subversive imperialistic policy, whatever guise or form it may take, is the only reason for peoples' enslavement and loss of freedoms; the same imperialism which we have known and seen for some time. Therefore, it is our duty and that of the KDP to expose and foil imperialistic plots.

9. My brothers, one of the examples that will advance our goals is to observe the emerging democratic nations in the East and in the West after World War II. New and democratic countries have emerged. They have introduced their unity, progress and civilization to peoples of the world, and that has attracted world attention.

Imperialist forces are in decline and moving swiftly to their end. British imperialism is now moribund and moving toward its grave. The same can be said of American imperialism, which is poised to replace British imperialism. Despite its dollar power, American imperialist policies remain weak, backward, and lacking in strategy. Behold, countries receiving American aid are gradually enslaved by the dollar. Soon economic corruption and starvation set in. The law of natural selection shows that imperialistic policy is weakening and will soon end. For solving the question of our freedom, this is absolute and without a doubt.

A Brief Statement of the Social, Economic and Political Conditions of Our Present-Day Kurdistan

1. The Kurds of Turkey live under brutal suppression and injustice by the fascist Turkish ruling class, under unparalleled fear and threat. We can consider them kept in a dark prison by the brute beast of fascism with no lights whatsoever.

They have neither public nor clandestine organizations. However, those young Kurds who once migrated from Turkey to Syria, where they founded the Kurdish Democratic Party, were able to disseminate some of their own political thought in Turkish Kurdistan among literate Kurds and leaders, especially in the Diyarbakr area.

Both the Azadi (Freedom) Party, founded in Barzan, and the KDP, founded in Iran, were successful in raising awareness and spreading modern political ideas across the borders in Turkish Kurdistan near to Barzan and the Iranian borders.

As a result of the suppressive policies and crimes of the Turkish fascist regime against the Kurds, including transporting thousands of Kurds deep into Turkey, groups of workers and educated Kurds have now emerged. They are preparing for and anxiously awaiting an opportunity to establish a democratic patriotic party to lead the Kurdish ascent.

2. To some degree, the conditions of Iraqi Kurds are better than those of their brethren in Turkish and Iranian Kurdistan because of Iraq's fear of our parties which have always struggled against the government, and because of the support we get from democratic, communist and patriotic organizations in Iraq and the Arab world, in addition to the Kurdish progressive awareness against foreign imperialism. Of supportive parties we mention are the Iraqi Communist Party, the National Democratic Party, the People's Party, and the Workers Union [Yekeity Kargaran].

For these reasons, Iraqi rulers and their British masters have used a policy of appeasement at the popular level, [to appeal to] the simpleminded and to pacify our people. In Iraq, there are a number of political parties. Some are legal and others are underground. The People's Party, the National Democratic Party and the Workers' Union, which were formed in the cities, are legal. Clandestine parties include our KDP, which lately joined ranks with the Kurdish Communist Party, in addition to the Rizgari Kurd Party (Kurdish Deliverance Party). All these parties struggled initially for a single goal, that is, the awakening of the Kurdish nation, and the struggle against imperialism.

3. As for the conditions of the Kurds in Iran, after our latest battle with the criminals and the heinous crimes perpetrated on our Kurdish people there by the reactionary government of Iran, silence pervaded Kurdistan. We know well that crimes, executions, assassinations, imprisonment, deportation, looting and terror committed in Kurdistan, the reactionary government of Iran, and its malicious propaganda campaign through its agents and American dollars have further solidified the resolve of the Iranian Kurds to continue the struggle a hundred fold.

Villagers and peasants, clerics and learned men, leaders and great patriots of the Iranian Kurds have hidden their weapons in the mountains. They are eager to resist Iranian tyranny and oppression, and eager for the rise and progress of the Kurds. They are waiting for an opportunity, for a final confrontation and a just recompense. This time, no courtesy or mercy is needed in dealing with imperialists and reactionaries.

Naturally and obviously, there is no nation without a few traitors who sell their homeland. In Kurdistan, there are also traitors and opportunists such as Omer Khan Shikak, Nuri Beg, Mam Aziz, Ali Ilkhani and Mohammed Agha Abbas. They have no significance whatsoever against all the toilers, villagers, peasants, leaders and great patriots.

As you all know, the Kurdistan society today consists of the following classes:

1. Kurdish peasants and villagers constitute the largest class of the Kurdish society.
2. The intelligentsia, including teachers, students, clerics and low ranking government employees, also constitute a class.
3. Kurdish workers who live in Kurdistan's large cities such as Karmanshah, Diyarbakr, Van and Mosul constitute a small class.
4. Owners of small artisan shops constitute a very small class.
5. Aghas and tribal chiefs constitute another class.
6. Merchants and small grocery-shop owners constitute a class as well.

Hence, a large segment of Kurdistan is still at the stage of feudalism and fiefdoms. The other segment is at the bourgeois stage. Generally, Kurds remain devoted to their way of life and traditions, and remain respectful and loyal to their leaders who sacrifice for Kurdistan. They have not submitted to enemies; they respect and honor their women; they protect the honors of their families and tribes.

Genuine Kurdish traditions and traits are, in fact, [characterized by their desire] to live in dignity and freedom. And if they feel that they are right, they will not back down. They honor their promises and steadfastly defend their word, even unto death. Death will not stop them from resisting those who betrayed them and their homeland for personal gain. We must acknowledge that they are the bearers of the spirit and ethics of the Kurdish nation. Generally, the Kurdish nation, by nature, tends to uphold law and democracy.

Political Objectives

1. With the liberation of Iranian Kurdistan, a democratic republic is to be established and run by a freely elected national council through secret ballot.

2. We extend the hand of friendship and fraternal unity to the Azerbaijani democratic group, and together we struggle against foreign imperialism and Iranian reactionaries, and for the Iranian peoples to gain their true freedom and legal rights through continuous common struggle.

3. A Kurdish republic in Iranian Kurdistan will be the nucleus for a liberated Greater Kurdistan through the establishing of a Kurdish republic in Iraqi Kurdistan, and another in a part of Turkey, and help establish democratic movements in other parts where they will augment liberation movements until all Kurdistan is free of the chains of slavery and foreign influence.

4. Our Party seeks to establish fraternal ties with all democratic and progressive parties and organizations, to cooperate with them on the basis of brotherhood and friendship especially the Democratic Party of Azerbaijan, the Tudeh Party of Iran, Arabic and Turkish democratic parties to stand together in the face of the imperialists and reactionaries, and to put an end to them and to Fascism.

5. To frame a political and economic pact with the Iranian and Azerbaijani national governments, and to establish a united front to defend this pact against foreign pressures.

6. To frame pacts of political and economic friendship with democratic governments beginning with the government of the Soviet Union.

7. To establish absolute democracy in Kurdistan. Based on current conditions, it is necessary that all Kurdish classes and those who live in Kurdistan, participate in the government through free elections, without discrimination or prejudice.

Economic Objectives

8. It is necessary to raise the economic level of the Kurdish people, especially villagers and peasants; to improve and enrich their living conditions.

9. Grazing fields and pastures, rivers, roads, unexploited mineral resources and forests belong to the people and to the public sector.

10. Government-purchased or occupied land must be redistributed among the impoverished villagers and peasants.

11. To create a working class in Kurdistan, so it moves quickly from feudalism into the bourgeoisie stage, it is necessary to exploit the raw material of Kurdistan and to encourage industries, especially to encourage the manufacturing of tools and agricultural machinery.

12. To protect the rights of peasants and villagers, it is necessary to make and enact a law governing the relationship between peasants and landowners. Accordingly, villagers and peasants can retain some of their crops in return for their labor. It is also necessary to enact a similar law to protect the rights of workers and to regulate working hours.

13. It is absolutely necessary to ban foreign exploitative companies and eradicate exploitative tycoons and capitalists in Kurdistan. In their stead, cooperative companies, based on national interests and under the supervision of the national government, are to be established.

14. To establish a Central Bank as well as an Agricultural Bank, in order to free Kurdish peasants from interests and loans.

15. To promote cooperative work, national industries, domestic trade, and increase commercial exchange with friendly democratic nations.

16. To establish policies for the drilling and use of oil and other natural resources.

17. To improve agriculture and protect forestry, and to further develop tobacco farming through scientific means to benefit the people.

18. To crossbreed and improve cattle and sheep resources in Kurdistan.

19. The cost of running the government must be just and correspond to the national revenues and standard of living.

Social Objectives

20. It is necessary to foster education and literacy, in Kurdistan. Education through the sixth grade must be compulsory, and attention must be paid to kindergartens for children. To increase women's participation in the life of society, girls' schools ought to be opened to increase their literacy rate. Establish universities and higher education institutions, increase scholarships for study abroad, and promote the Kurdish language.

21. Combat the spirit of feudalism, tribalism, and hegemony to end harmful contentions such as sectarian, ethnic and religious conflicts.

22. Pay attention to public health, increase free hospital services at all levels, with the focus on ending epidemic and transmitted diseases such as malaria.

23. Establish and foster youth organizations under our Party's supervision.

24. Establish labor unions guided by the KDP, in addition to social organizations and village unions.

25. Promote modern civilization for example, by building modern villages in Kurdistan, as in developed societies.

26. Guarantee the freedom of religious beliefs and practices, the freedom of language and publishing, as well as freedom for all ideologies except that of fascism.

27. Promote and establish physical education centers, theater and cinema houses; and encourage such activities.

28. Eradicate corrupt elements in the society such as hypocrites, bribe-takers, and those who unfairly defend the interests of their relatives. Fight prostitution, narcotics and gambling. On the other hand, respect responsible people, reward and provide opportunities for those who sincerely serve their country and protect its interests.

General Objectives

29. In order for Kurdistan to lead a free and independent life, it is imperative that all good citizens serve their homeland, receive military training, and serve in the armed forces for a specified period.

30. Our Party and its Platform must adhere to the principles of democracy and take into account the current social, economic and political conditions of Kurdistan with the ability to make amendments in accordance with changing times and circumstances.

31. Our Party defends the interests of every class among the Kurds, including chieftains, merchants, workers, small landowners, skilled workers, peasants, and intelligentsia. It brings all of them together under the banner of national liberation of the homeland and defending the joint interests of all classes. Under the banner of this Party, class struggle in Kurdistan is not appropriate. Our Party is progressive in essence, as it is clear in its program and tactics.

32. As a result of our tireless struggle, it behooves our Party to adhere to its progressive and democratic platform. By so doing, we will secure the real wishes and interests as well as the freedom of the Kurdish people. Other than that, any organization founded in Kurdistan, under the guise of democracy and in the name of liberty that is born of the

sinister minds and imagination of the imperialists will run counter to the interests of the Kurds and seek to crush them in the shackles of servitude. Therefore, any organization or government not inspired by our Party or not founded on a democratic basis, is the fabrication of the sinister imperialists and goes counter to Kurdish interests. It follows that we must fight such hollow organizations, and all the schemes of the imperialists.

In summary, this speech was about Kurdish history and those significant factors that have impeded the Kurdish progress and civilization and led to our current situation in Kurdistan. I have presented you with information that I have learned through my personal experience and from various sources that I remember from the long struggle of my life of which I spoke today.

Of course I have no doubt that each one of you has a lot of knowledge based on his personal experience. Therefore, I ask you here to express any opinion you may have, which we will consider in our discussion in accordance with the interests and the good of the Kurds in order to reach specific and clear conclusions. This will determine our Party's fundamental policy. In our next session, we will vote on this and after reaching a decision, the form and bylaws of the Platform will take shape and be put into effect. May Almighty Allah grant us success in reaching our goals.

Our motto is: We Fight for a Free Homeland and a Prosperous People. The secret lies in the fact that our struggle is a just one, for the good of our people and for humanity.

Our Pledge to the Kurdish Nation

Sacrificing and oppressed Kurdish people, we assure you of our democratic principles and the purity of our patriotic intentions. We promise that we will never rest until we restore your usurped rights, rescue you from injustice, captivity and deportation and rid you of the domination with everything in our power.

We promise to sacrifice our personal interests for your public interest, to relinquish our desires and wishes for the public good, to strengthen the ties of unity among us and raise public awareness in order to realize the goals and advance the progress of the Kurdish people.

We have proved all this on the field of struggle, far from empty words and theoretical propagandas.

Our bitter experiences full of sacrifice under the worst of circumstances are known to the Kurdish masses. The result is renewed and deep-rooted national awareness, and the rekindled flame of freedom among all sectors of the Kurdish nation. You find the signposts of our revolution for freedom in every mountain, plateau, valley and forest. Is there any stronger evidence than the trenches and the graves of the martyrs that stand as witnesses to our offerings? That is our duty and we do not expect anything in return. Our motto is: A Free Homeland and a Prosperous People.

To the worthy souls of our martyrs, we pledge to continue on their heroic path and to realize the goals for which they sacrificed their lives; we promise to justly avenge your spilled blood on the bloodthirsty fascists and occupiers, to prove to the world that your exceptional heroism and high morale instilled in us the spirit of revolution and luminous sentiments so that we can proudly say among the nations of the world that we are of the nation of those prominent heroes. If your sacred blood was not a high enough price for the liberty of Kurdistan, we are ready and proud to add our own to secure happiness and freedom for our nation. We cite the heroism of our martyrs and their struggle for our just cause.

O people, we promise to establish social justice on democratic foundations in Kurdistan. Without prejudice, we will respect and defend the rights of all citizens, sects, tribes and non-Kurdish ethnic minorities. Aggression and all acts of personal revenge or any other oppressive measure against any group or tribe undoubtedly contradicts the basic tenets of our Party and must be fought by all means. Our Party has one constant and uncompromising enemy; foreign imperialism.

We pledge to recognize the rights of all classes, tribes and ethnic groups, to assist them to unite and fight on one front against imperialism. Triumphant, all will participate in the national government, provided all are united.

1. As you all know, our Party does not begin today. It was founded in Mahabad two years ago, and its program and bylaws are known to you. But you know that after the attack by the forces of the traitor Qawam al-Saltana moved in on December 12, 1946 (Adhan 21, 1325), the Central Committee and most of the organization of the KDP broke down as a result of the surrender of the majority of Central Committee members and the reinstatement of government administration in the Mahabad region. Despite the harshest of conditions, we were able to establish the Liberation Force of Democratic Kurdistan. For six months, we fought a force larger and many times better equipped than ours.

Because of the shift in international politics and the breakdown of the internal Party organization, we held our first Congress in a liberated region of Kurdistan. The Congress was held in Shino on January 15, 1947 (26/10/[1]325) and attended by representatives of the liberated areas of Sardasht, Lahijan, Naghadeh, Doli, Barandizi, Margawar, Targawar and Shino. The Congress adopted several resolutions and approved the new program to deal with the new circumstances and to draw up new political, economic and general social policies. These show the amendments to the original Party Platform.

Resolutions of the Shino Congress were translated into Persian and copies were sent to our comrades in Iran. Presented for your information, your review and consideration on this 20 day of January, 1947.

Our goals: From all the subjects I went over in detail, I pointed out a number of goals that I find it necessary that our Party works for in the early phases of our struggle.

Translation from Arabic of Document No. 19

Lausanne, Switzerland

18 June 1958

[To] His Eminence, the Great Patriotic Leader Barzani,
Hero of the Kurds and of Kurdistan

After tendering our regards, please allow me, in a few words, to express my feelings of love, glory and greatness for you, sentiments that have touched the heart of every sincere Kurd.

Regardless of class, all Kurds are proud of your heroism which will remain luminous in our heart-wrenching history. While continuing the struggle, we look forward to the day of freedom in which to meet you again with your brave officers, brothers and men, in our homeland, Kurdistan, free and liberated from oppression and imperialism.

Please accept the first issue of 'Kurdistan,' a publication of the Cultural Organization of Kurdish Students in Europe.

I wish you personally and all those with you good health and the best of times in the generous Soviet country. We look forward to the day of freedom. Live long for Kurdish hopes, and stand steadfast for Kurdish national liberation.

Live long and ever happy, my dear. With my highest regards,

Sincerely,

Ismet Cherif

Translation from Arabic of Document No. 20

To the Great Kurdish Leader Mustafa Barzani, Moscow

We, the Kurdish students meeting in London on January 2, 1958, take this opportunity to express our heartfelt appreciation and gratitude to you personally for your work and sacrifices for Kurdistan, for your leadership of the Kurdish national struggle in Iraqi Kurdistan, and to the armed Kurdish forces in the Republic of Kurdistan in Iran, as well as for your view of the Kurdish cause and the causes of other neighboring peoples. All bring pride and glory to all of us Kurds.

We, and honorable Kurds, will never forget you. As always, we will support Kurdistan. Please allow us to mention a few modest activities of the Kurdish youth here. Certainly you will be pleased. Kurdish youth are organized in a 'Cultural Society of Kurdish Students in Europe' which works to strengthen ties among Kurdish students, promote Kurdish literature and culture, and introduce Kurdistan and the Kurdish national heritage to the peoples of the world. The Society publishes a magazine called Kurdistan and held a cultural conference earlier this year in London. About 95 Kurdish students from various European colleges and universities, majoring in various sciences, engineering, the arts and literature, attended the conference.

In the political realm, we elected a "Kurdish Committee" to organize our political activities, which our Cultural Society cannot do. The Committee issued a call to all Kurds to hold a general Kurdish conference, representing all Kurdish ideological and patriotic trends and organizations, as well as cultural societies and their branches, to study the Kurdish question and define a unified policy to achieve the just Kurdish national demands. The call has gained much support among the Kurds. The Committee is now preparing to establish a Preparatory Committee to organize the General Kurdish Conference which in our view will help liberate Kurdistan and free our Kurdish nation.

The Committee sent a Kurdish delegation to the Congress of Afro-Asian peoples in Cairo and collected the necessary funds for it. It also informs the world of conditions in Kurdistan through the press, publications and lectures. Currently a signature-collection campaign is underway. A memorandum will be signed by as many Kurds as possible to be presented to Soviet authorities to establish a Kurdish broadcasting station in the Soviet Union. In addition to our studies, we carry out these activities because we believe it is our duty to serve our beloved Kurdish nation. In service to our people, you will be happy to know that we do not oppose the cause of peace and other peoples' causes; we cooperate with them so as to serve the joint Kurdish interests and theirs. With our highest regards and warmest wishes.

The Kurdish Committee in Europe

Translation from Arabic of Document No. 21

Kurdistan Democratic Party of Iraq

Peking, 5 October, 1955

To [Comrade] Leader General Mustafa Barzani and Dear Comrade Mir Haj

Honorable Comrades, please allow me to greet you warmly on behalf of the Central Committee and all affiliates of our Party, on behalf of all decent Kurds who love their cherished Kurdistan, and on behalf of those who find you sincere leaders and great comrades on the road of the struggle to liberate Kurdistan and to establish a People's Democratic Republic.

For a while, the Party could not send you reports about its circumstances and those of the Kurdish liberation movement in Iraq and Iraqi Kurdistan in general. Despite difficulties in contacting you, the Party bears responsibility to some degree. Covering this long period of communication problems, I will write briefly, as my position and circumstances permit. If you would like more details, let me know of a way to contact you. The Party wants to provide details and answer all your questions. Left with short notice, I was unable to prepare a more detailed report. I will divide this report, which the Party has asked me to write, into the following sections:

State of the Party

Despite the shortcomings (in its leadership and secondary cadres, and internal conditions and bylaws) that date back to its foundation, our Party has made fair strides and enjoyed the support of masses in villages and towns, some big and small landowners, patriotic merchants as well as the intelligentsia regardless of the vicious attacks on it by right-wingers disguised as leftists, especially those of the Fahd Core, which carried the name of the Iraqi Communist Party (ICP), which Martyr Fahd founded. As our Party grew in numbers, well-organized activities were carried out by most branches and by the Center.

One of our serious mistakes was our inability to effectively embrace this huge increase of members and supporters, and turn them into a conscientious revolutionary cadre.

After the free Barzanis returned home in 1947, our Party led the campaign, to defend them, including protests and collecting signatures, and demanded that the government pardon and resettle them in their original areas. As the government prepared to execute the four officers, Mustafa Khoshnaw, Khairullah, Izzat and Mohammed Mahmud, the Party led a strong protest to stop their executions; later, the Party protested their executions, issued communiqués and publicized their speeches and last wishes before execution, which were obtained quickly. Mass protests were organized in many parts of Iraqi Kurdistan especially in Suleimaniyya, as the city went on strike and into mourning for three days.

During the January 1948 Uprising, our Party, led popular battles against imperialism, in cooperation with the People's Party, the progressive wing of the National Democratic Party, and ICP's Core Group. Our Party played a significant role in all battles while a Coordination Committee was being formed. We erred on some issues during the Uprising, such as our position in regard to elections. We entered the elections without imposing any condition on the enemy, i.e., direct elections, and without preparing the populace to lead them in battles against the reactionaries, and without patriotic slogans exposing the reactionary imperialistic plans. Our party entered the elections as if we only wanted seats in the

Parliament. However, we were successful among all groups in analyzing the situation after the Uprising. We called all parties and organizations to cooperate and unite in one anti-imperialist front. We exposed the Cabinet of Mohammed Hadid which came in to let things quiet down and prepare for the return of the top reactionaries; and we exposed the danger of the Palestine Plot. After that, only our Party took the correct line in the Arab East and Iraqi Kurdistan concerning the Palestine question, and denounced the sending of armies to Palestine, because our Party knew the truth about the imperialist conspiracy through the infamous war in Palestine. Our Party exposed the treason of King Abdullah of Jordan and the ruling Iraqi cliques. We organized delegations and set memoranda to resolve the Barzani question and demanded our people's rights. The period of calm and preparation was over after orchestrating elections which clearly distorted the will of the people scandalously; even government Ministers acknowledged this deception.

Having cooked up the dirty conspiracy of the Palestine war and declared martial law, the government, furthered by the treason of the ICP's Core Group, played an abhorrent terrorist role against the nationalist government. No sooner were they released than many of the Core Group's top officials confessed and in the wink of an eye became spies, and testified against them in court, against the patriots. Many Iraqi and Kurdish patriots fell victims to their treason. Our Party received its share of this new wave of oppression. Of our comrades, Dr. Jafar Mohammed Karim, a top KDP leader inside [Iraq], was stripped of his citizenship. He filled in for the President in running the day-to-day Party business. Sentenced to two years in prison were [Comrade] Attorney Ibrahim Ahmad, current General Secretary (and then Chairman of the regional committee of Suleimaniyya Province), Comrade Attorney Omer Mustafa, current Politburo member (and then organizer of the Regional Committee in Baghdad). Two members of the first Central Committee were also sentenced to prison terms. First, attorney Rashid Abd al-Qadir was sentenced to 3 years because of his role as the Party's representative in the Coordination Committee during the Uprising, and because leaders of ICP's Core Group testified against him; second, attorney Awni Yousif was sentenced to a year and a half. (Both were expelled from the Party but continue to support it. The first was expelled because he signed an appeal for clemency and a statement of regret; the second because of his anarchic behavior and ideological deviation.) Many others were sentenced to varying periods in jail.... Other leading members fled, among them Salih Yousifi, attorney Rashid Bajelan, Sheikh Latif who left the Party because of differences with Hamza during the Uprising. (Because of this wave of terrorism and arrests, the activities of some Party chapters were curtailed, as in Arbil and Mosul, and especially because Party cadres were not formed to carry on activities under adverse conditions.) The only active Central Committee members who remained were attorney, Comrade Hamza Abdullah [the highest ranking in the chain of Party command], engineer, Comrade Ali Abdullah, who was in Koy Sanjaq, attorney, Comrade Karim Tawfiq, who was employed in Koy Sanjaq, and Mr. Mohammed Ziyad. Hamza Abdullah effectively ran the Politburo alone. During that time, negligence prevailed among the leadership especially Comrade Hamza himself. The central organ of the Party was not published regularly. Leadership made no new and well-thought out attempts to rebuild the shattered pieces of Party organization, despite opportunities that could have been used.

Our Party's influence is growing in spite of terrorism, because of others' bankruptcies especially the ICP's Core Group, whose leaders' treachery has become the high fashion of the season. In Iraqi Kurdistan, they are almost bankrupt as well. However, our Party was unable to take advantage of the situation because of negligence on the part of the leadership.... In late 1949 or early 1950, Hamza Abdullah was arrested in Suleimaniyya and sent under guard to Baghdad. After his arrest, a number of comrades in Koy Sanjaq, i.e.,

Ali Abdullah (current Politburo member), Comrade Bakr Ismail (a Party member) and (then) Comrade Abd al-Karim Tawfiq, Mr. Mohammed Amin Maroof and attorney Omer Habib were assisted by Comrade Mohammed Ziyad to reorganize the center temporarily and prepare for a Party Congress. This Committee failed to accomplish the objectives it had set for itself, and Abd al-Karim Tawfiq quickly resigned. The Local Committee in Baghdad was active and it asked to hold a Party Congress. Instead, they held a Conference with representatives from Suleimaniyya, Baghdad, Fayli Kurds, Halabja, Kirkuk, Mosul and Koy Sanjaq attending. This Conference was also attended by Comrade Ali Abdullah, and Mr. Awni Yousif who had just been released from prison. This Conference, a weak leadership committee was elected, with most members illiterate in Marxism-Leninism such as Salih Rushdi, Mustafa Karim (who deserted Party ranks later), Mohammed Musa Sadiq (high school student), Awni Yousif, Ali Hamdi (who despite his loyalty and drive, could not discharge his duties at the Center), Nuri Mohammed Amin, who deserted later (now he is an engineer; he's in the money and without a care!). However, among them was Comrade Ali Abdullah, a mature and discerning man who knows Marxism-Leninism well. . . . Shortly thereafter, strangely, Hamza Abdullah was released from prison although terrorism had lessened and martial law was lifted. There were no tangible evidence against him. His release and the permission to stay to regain his citizenship were unusual. After his release, he asked the new Central Committee (of which he was a member according to the first Charter) to freeze his membership and permit him to freely contact government officials in regards to his citizenship. He declined his charge as first in command. Instead, he asked to write articles for *Rizgari* and cultural publications. The new Central Committee found Hamza's request peculiar and rejected it. He was upset and resigned from the Party. His resignation was hastily accepted. Earlier, an important event had occurred, which was briefly that Hamza had once told Comrade Ali Abdullah that an official in the British embassy had asked to meet Hamza (through the attorney Zayd Amad Othman, the son of Othman Afandi of Arbil who was a Senator), and Awni and Hamza had told him (Zayd) that it was not necessary to bring Awni and that he was enough. This official had met Hamza with Zayd by chance. The three went to Abdullah's Cabaret in Baghdad. During that time, the following conversation took place: The British official who was called al-Haj had asked why Hamza was so loved by the Kurds. Hamza replied: Because he was oppressed by the government. Then al-Haj asked if it was possible to return Barzani and his group to Iraq by acquitting them, and for Barzani to become anti-Soviet. Hamza had replied that the return of the general and his men was tied to his citizenship, and that the general would not become anti-Soviet because the Kurds do not deny anyone who does them a favor. Then the question of Kurdish autonomy in Iraq came up. . . . Hamza asked Ali not to tell anyone, but Ali insisted he would only tell Awni, to which Hamza agreed. Besides Ali, Mr. Massoud, (Saeed) the Party messenger, knew about this. Messenger Saeed had informed Ali after a while that Hamza had met with the British again, and had not told Ali. Massoud asked Ali not to tell Hamza that he (Massoud) told him (Ali) . . .

The Local Committees of Koy Sanjaq (I was in charge then) and Suleimaniyya objected to Hamza's resignation. With a weak Center unable to issue publications and newspapers, discord developed between myself and the Koy Sanjaq Local Committee. This Committee asked the Center to reconsider Hamza's decision and return him to the Party immediately. After awhile, the Central Committee was compelled to return Hamza, a new Center was established, as was a new Politburo comprised of Hamza, Ali Abdullah, Awni Yousif (this was strange because each was in a city), with Hamza being first in charge (he was free in Suleimaniyya by then). In a subsequent Central Committee meeting, it was decided to hand over to Hamza all Party press and to authorize him to call for a Congress. However Salih Rushdi and Mustafa Karim refused to turn in the press which the Faylis held in

Baghdad. Their action resulted in the Party's loss of that press.... Both were considered break-aways, and they led a propaganda campaign divulging Party secrets in Baghdad and elsewhere. During the time of the second Central Committee, the Party organization in Arbil City was rebuilt, the party base among the Balak peasants was re-established by Comrade Hayder Mohammed Amin (currently: Local Committee member in Baghdad; completed college, majoring in secondary education but was never appointed). Then (a slightly amended) typed Party program was issued and a press release written by Hamza regarding the international and domestic political line was also issued.

Then, the Second Congress was called to session in 1950. In addition to Party chapters, Comrade Ibrahim Ahmad and Mr. Jalil Hoshyar, both lawyers who have [————]. The Second Congress was held in Baghdad with delegates from Arbil, Balak, Koy Sanjaq, Suleimaniyya, Halabja and Baghdad in attendance. Salih Rushdi and his friend Mustafa Karim refused to participate despite Comrade Ibrahim Ahmad's attempts to persuade them. In the congress, Hamza had the majority; however, he agreed, with Ibrahim [Ahmad] and Ali Abdullah to form a Central Committee, neither from the quarrelling parties nor from the previous Central Committee members, to reorganize Party ranks, issue publications, and prepare for the Third Congress. As I was a staunch supporter of Hamza, he asked me to persuade the rest. Hamza and I did persuade them, and when I was elected to the Central Committee, I gave up my position for Jalil Hoshyar, provided the Central Committee was kept neutral.... During this time, Salih Rushdi and Mustafa Karim founded a new party and called it the 'Kurdish Democratic Party of Iraq'. In other words, these naive people thought merely replacing the Kurdish word 'party' with its Arabic 'Hizb' [party] changed the essence of the Party!! Their clique dissipated after about a year.

Most members returned to Party ranks but Salih himself joined the ICP's Core Group and was imprisoned for two years. In prison, their differences surfaced. He was expelled and brutally beaten by Hamid Othman's group, the current secretary of the Core Group. He currently works with the Unity Party of Communists.

The new Committee, headed by Comrade Ibrahim Ahmad (the current Party secretary), immediately issued Congress's typed final Communiqué. Three press releases to prepare the rank and file, collect funds to purchase a press, and regarding the call for neutrality (by the National Democratic Party and an independent group of Iraqi politicians) were issued respectively. The Central Committee denounced the call for neutrality, asked the masses to actively defend peace and oppose war plans, and proclaimed that our Party and the masses of Kurdistan would never be neutral in the struggle between the forces of good and evil, between peace and war, that they would stand fast with the great Soviet Union, if imperialist countries attacked, that we would bear arms under the leadership of the Soviet Union. This release reflected well on our Party. This leading role, despite some negligence, was characterized by the correct Marxist analysis of events. Comrade Ibrahim Ahmad defined the correct position regarding elections and debunked the continued call for a boycott, a stance of the petite bourgeoisie when they failed to send representatives to the Parliament. He added that our position was not so much to elect representatives, as to shape the election battle against imperialism and reactionaries; to expose the aggressive war plans; to shape the national mottos for the masses and prepare them to struggle against imperialism and reactionaries; to let them realize that elections will not change much, only revolutionary means will ensure change. He clearly exposed government and reactionary interference in elections. He proclaimed to the Party that boycotting is correct only when the national movement is in the van, and revolution or armed revolt is about to mature. Then, keeping the Party busy with elections would be a step backward. A correct and revolutionary position regarding elections did not exist in Iraq. Leftist and bourgeois groups considered our position a move to the right. However, we stood firm, and, our Party proved our position correct. Later, all recognized our correct position. Against this background, our Party entered elections in 1952 and its candidate Masoud Mohammed Jali, a lawyer, won in Koy Sanjag.

This period was characterized by a strong campaign against Kurdish traitors such as Ali Kamal Majid and other supporters of the Constitutional Unity and the Socialist Nation [Umma] parties, old agents of imperialism. The Party organization was rebuilt in many areas; central publications in Kurdish, and the *Nida' Kurdistan* [Kurdistan Call] in Arabic were issued. After Hamza was expelled from the Party, there was a split during this period.

To sum up, Hamza was suddenly arrested and sent to Turkey in the summer of 1951. A wave of arrests of suspected Party members followed. Among them, Comrade Ibrahim Ahmad, Ali Abdullah, lawyers Omer Mustafa and Omer Habib, Awni Yousif and myself (Jalal Husam ad-Din Talabani-Pirot) and tens of others from Arbil, Suleimaniyya, Koy Sanjaq and Kirkuk. We were summarily tried in Arbil and sentenced to exile and deportation. Comrade Ibrahim was deported to Kirkuk, Comrades Ali Abdullah, Omer Mustafa, Salih Shams (a worker) and I were deported to Mosul. Others were deported to Imarah and Ramadi. Our sentences were revoked on appeal and we were released. While in Mosul, I received a letter from Hamza informing me that he had bribed the Turks and escaped, that he was in Zakho and wanted to find a place in Mosul. I immediately contacted our comrades in Mosul and they prepared a place for him. I informed the Center and they agreed to ask him to come. He did. The Party's condition was that Hamza write articles and the Center would select the appropriate ones for publication provided the Party guaranteed his living. The Center further suspected Hamza this time when he returned, since Governor Saeed Qazzaz of Mosul and the Chief of Police, Sana, were aware of his escape!! Furthermore, Saeed Qazzaz employed Hamza's nephew based on his recommendation!! Still he demanded to be in charge of Party publications, member education and communications. In other words, he was to be the Party's dictator! Furthermore, his family was relocated to join him, while the Center insisted on his family remaining away from him. Comrade Ibrahim promised to personally support them.

Hamza violated all conditions, and he was expelled from the Party. He must pledge to follow the Party Charter and Resolutions (according to Congress's Resolution that all members must obey the Center and the Party during the preparation period for the next Congress). Violators would be expelled immediately. Expelled, he tried to form a splinter group. He wrote letters to many people including myself. I advised him not to and went to him, asking him to cease these activities. Meanwhile, the Suleimaniyya Local Committee backed him up, since this Committee had already violated Party resolutions by issuing a press release charging the Central Committee with treason for delaying publications, despite the Central Committee's attempts to convey the fact that the Party did not own the necessary equipment and was trying to purchase it. Incognizant, they clung to their views. Once expelled, they went over to Hamza's malicious group. This is how Hamza's splinter group came about. They called themselves the 'Progressive Wing of the Kurdish Democratic Party, Iraq.'

In the winter of 1951–52, the Party succeeded in acquiring, and operating a press. In September 1952, the first issue of *Rizgari* in Kurdish was published after a long absence of about two years during which Hamza, Salih Rushdi and Awni Yousif were unable to publish it despite owning the equipment.

Once again, the Party reorganized and rebuilt its decimated parts. In the first half of 1952, the Party successfully rebuilt Party organization in Suleimaniyya, Halabja, Panjawin, Qala Diza, Rania, Baghdad, Aqra, Kirkuk, Arbil, Balak, and their dependencies. The Koy Sanjaq Chapter was intact. In the second half, we destroyed Salih Rushdi's splinter group and persuaded most members to return to Party ranks. Shortly thereafter, Salih Rushdi dissolved his group. In an attempt to persuade Hamza's group to return to Party ranks, we accepted those who had been expelled including Hamza, and permitted their delegates to attend the next Congress. I negotiated with this group, then called Region 2 of the KDP, Iraq. Persuaded by Hamza, their representatives did not attend the Third Congress in January 1953.

Meanwhile, the Party had successfully formulated our motto of the right to self deter-mination for the Kurdish people, and the Kurdish-Arab brotherhood in Iraq. Even ICP's Core Group which in 1945–1948 denied the existence of Kurds and Kurdistan, was com-pelled in 1952 to adopt the same motto including the right to secede (which they retracted later). Saturated with cosmopolitanism, Core Group's Kurdish members strongly opposed liberation movements, i.e., the Barzan revolution and democratic government of Kurdistan which they described as an American imperialist conspiracy. We also established contacts with Comrade Dr. Jafar Mohammed Karim and our brothers of the KDP [Iran]. At this time, the Party called for an anti-imperialism anti-war national front. We worked hard to unify the peace movement in Iraqi Kurdistan and to enlighten people the truth about this movement, since support ebbed as ICP's leftist Core Group split off.

In January of 1953, the Party's Third Congress was held with all Party Chapters repre-sented according to our Charter, and all Central Committee members. Comrade Ibrahim Ahmad's report, about international and domestic circumstances, the importance of devel-oping leadership and local Party cadres, and our ties to other parties, was adopted. The Congress amended the Party's program and Charter, and unanimously approved changing our name to 'KDP, Iraq'. It only outlined program and charter changes and left the details to be worked out by the new Central Committee. Once elected, the new Central Committee members pledged to uphold all Party responsibilities to the best of their abilities. They were:

The attorney, Comrade Ibrahim Ahmad, General Secretary; the attorney, Comrade Omer Mustafa, Politburo Member; (then) the attorney, Comrade Jalil Hoshyar, Politburo Member; Comrades Ali Abdullah, Nuri Saddique Shawais, Jalal Talabani. After the hero, Comrade Nuri Ahmad Taha was released from prison, the Central Committee appointed him, an alternate member of the Central Committee in accordance with the Party Charter and charged him with reorganizing the Party around the new Central Committee.

The Congress also drew up a policy concerning patriotic parties and groups. It recog-nized attorney Aziz Sharif, current Secretary of the Unity of the Iraqi Communist Party and the former president of the People's Party, for his honorable stand and scientific book about the Kurdish question in Iraq. In his book, he defended the Kurdish right to self-determination, including independence. He examined the significance of the Kurdish lib-eration movement in relation to the liberation of Iraq and the Middle East. The Congress called upon all patriotic parties, groups and individuals to unite in one national front against imperialism and war alliances, and for the democratic rights of Iraqi peoples. In regard to Hamza and his group, the Congress approved his expulsion, considering his actions divisive and a rightist split, his defeatist position toward the Iraqi government, his breach of Party policy in making contact with the British on his own. As for members of his circle, the Congress decided to re-admit them individually but never as a group.

In the light of instructions from the Congress, the Central Committee formulated the Party program. Most importantly, it defined the relationship between the struggle of the masses of Kurdistan and Iraq, clearly adopted popular democracy, scientifically resolved the issues of agriculture, recognized that the Kurdish nationalism and its liberation move-ment are part of the universal cause of international socialism, proclaimed the Party ready to sacrifice its Kurdish national interest if it conflicted with the interests of international socialism, and included the interim demands for Kurdistan and Iraq.

We presented our program to Comrade Dr. Jafar Mohammed Karim who was in Tehran and asked for his views and those of the Tudeh comrades. We also sent a copy of our program to our comrades in the KDP [Iran] asking for their opinion. Comrade Dr. Jafar objected on three points:

1. He said that we sacrifice our Kurdish national interest for the sake of inter-national socialism if conflicted. He said that this formulation was correct and necessary, but, stated outright it gave the enemy a weapon with which to attack us.

2. Listing the struggle for Kurdish to be the official language as a note in our program was weak. He asked that it be written into a main Article.

3. He asked that we correct a typographical error which if uncorrected would mean that the leader of the peoples' camp is the Soviet Union and all popular democratic nations, while the Soviet Union is the leader of the peace and democracy camp. After reading Comrade Jafar's report, the Central Committee unanimously approved it and justified it to party Comrades. Excluding the above, no one else objected to anything in our program. In addition, the Central Committee accomplished the following:

1. Our Party and Unity of Communists Party called for a unified national front.

2. We participated in peace-movement activities, and our Party had the honor to correct the Iraqi peace movement anomalies spawned by the ICP's Core Group. Our participation expanded the movement especially in Iraqi Kurdistan. Dignitaries who participated included Mr. Anwar Jaff (former Representative of Halabja), Mohammed Ziyad Agha (former Representative of Koy Sanjaq), Massoud Mohammed (Koy Sanjaq's Representative to the Parliament when it existed), Qasim al-Mulla (son of Mulla Afandi of Arbil), Ahmad Mohammed Amin Dizayee (a young landlord and member of the Party) and tens of other religious and social notables in Kurdistan. Prominent in the peace movement, were our comrades, i.e., Comrade Ibrahim Ahmad, who received the award of Iraqi peace supporters, Comrades Nuri Ahmad Taha and Massoud Mohammed. With our many members in the National Committee for the Supporters of Peace in Iraq, our Party established and supervised Peace Committees in Suleimaniyya, Halabja, Qala Diza, Koy Sanjaq, Rania, Kirkuk and Arbil, etc. Committees included all social strata.

3. The Democratic Union of Kurdistan Youth in Iraq was founded, (which I represented when I went to China); the Student Union of Kurdistan, Iraq, and a peasants' newspaper was issued called the "Peasants' Cry", in addition to the "Youth Struggle" for the Youth Union and the "Kurdistan Students Union" for the students.

4. We established peasant organizations in the regions of Dizaye, Shahrazur, Makhmur, Pishdar (and Merga), and Aqra. (Our Party is now working to establish Peasants' Union of Kurdistan, Iraq.) Party activities were expanded among the farmers and peasants of Koy Sanjaq, Rania, and Balak and now we operate farm Party Chapters. We reorganized our Chapters in the Province of Mosul (Mosul, Aqra, Imadia, Bamerni, and when I left, work was underway to include Zakho). These were in addition to Shaqlawa, Habbania and the Faylis. Currently, Khanaqin (where there are many Party supporters), and Kifri (where the Party has some members) are being reorganized. In Sharbajer and Suleimaniyya, the Party enjoys much support, especially among the peasants, small landowners and some tribes (some tribes support us and played a role in the previous elections; organized a great reception for Comrade Ibrahim Ahmad and other comrades in 1954. Thousands attended and hundreds of their horsemen). The Party is now working to organize chapters among the peasants and tribes.

Party chapters were established in Altin Kopru-Pirdi, Makhmur, Panjaween and Ain Zaleh; also a labor union to organize the railroad employees of Arbil and Kirkuk.

5. The subsidiary newsletter, *Nida' Kurdistan* is published again and an educational periodical called *Regay Niwé* has come out. The Party currently publishes *Rizgari* [Deliverance], the central organ of the party, in Kurdish, *Nida' Kurdistan* [Kurdistan Call] in Arabic, *Nirkay Jutyar* [Peasants' Cry] in Kurdish, and the educational *Regay Niwé* [New Path]. Youth and student organizations publish their own journals.

6. The Party adopted the correct mottos for national liberation, elections, popular democracy and ethno-nationalism among other issues to rally the masses of Kurdistan and, to a large extent, Arab progressives.

7. The Party works to unify the Iraqi Communist movement. We established contacts with Communist organizations, groups and individuals in Iraq. About a year ago, our Party called on all Communists to hold a conference with our participation to resolve their differences in light of Marxism-Leninism, and to be supervised by Tudeh or the Communist Party of Syria. All but the ICP's Core Group agreed. We are serious about unifying the Iraqi Communist movement and establishing ties similar to those of the KDP [Iran] with Tudeh, between our Party and the united Iraqi Communist movement, or with the proper track if unification is not achieved soon.

8. The Party published two volumes of the book *'Anti Du Kring'* [sic] which was translated into Arabic by attorney Dawood al-Sayigh, former leader of the Communist Action Group. He is now our friend and [our] Party helps him a great deal. He is interested in translating Marxist books for the Party.

9. The Party strengthened ties with the KDP [Iran] and contacted the Tudeh Party through Comrade Jafar.

10. The Party entered elections during the time of Arshad al-Omeri in Suleimaniyya, Halabja, Koy Sanjaq, Rania, Arbil, Makhmur, and our friend, Rashid Bajelan ran in Khanaqin. He is a strong supporter and a former Party member. During Arshad's time, the Party's candidate won in Koy Sanjaq (Massoud Mohammed) unopposed. In Suleimaniyya, Comrade Ibrahim Ahmad's win would have been certain if it were not for government intervention and the wave of arrests just before elections. Hundreds of people were arrested, Comrade Ibrahim was kidnapped and sent to an unknown destination until arrangements were made. Despite his arrest, Comrade Ibrahim won about 90 percent of the total votes in Suleimaniyya City. With minimum electoral freedom, our candidates and those we supported would have certainly won in Makhmur, Arbil and Halabja. The Party entered elections under patriotic slogans, i.e., 'Defend Peace and Against War Alliances,' 'Support Friendship with the Soviet Union,' 'Iraq: Recognize People's Republic of China and other peoples democratic republics,' 'Abolish imperialistic pacts such as the Anglo-Iraqi and Turco-Iraqi pacts,' 'Support nationalization of oil and annul imperialistic oil deals,' 'Secure democratic freedoms and the Barzanis' demands,' 'Release and compensate prisoners,' 'Improve the conditions of workers and peasants,' and 'Land reform and rent reduction now.' During elections, the Party organized mass meetings and demonstrations. Our Party entered elections during the time of Nuri a-Sa'id as well. The Party strongly resisted and exposed government interference, especially in Suleimaniyya and Koy Sanjaq. In these election battles, the Party formulated many appropriate slogans, exposed war conspiracies successfully, and thus gained much popularity.

11. The Party organized the Newroz Celebrations of 1954 in Arbil, Suleimaniyya, Halabja, Koy Sanjaq where mass gatherings were held with tens of thousands of workers, peasants, intelligentsia and laborers in attendance. Patriotic slogans, speeches outlining

Kurdish demands, and patriotic songs were presented. Furthermore, tens of white pigeons, symbolizing peace, were released into the air. Peace and strengthening ties with the Soviet Union and other popular democracies were among the important popular mottos raised in these meetings.

12. The Party translated some Marxist books into Kurdish and Arabic (perhaps they are being printed now). We published a small booklet in Kurdish about peace.

13. Preparing for the Warsaw Festival, we sent a delegation of seven members from the Youth Union and its supporters (excluding our students in Europe). Others could not attend because of delays in their paperwork.

14. The Party established contacts with the Kurds of Syria and Turkish Kurdistan.

15. The Congress considered our leader General Barzani president of the Party and re-elected him, and Comrade Mir Haj.

The Party's Foreign Contacts

Based on recommendations of the third Congress, the Central Committee sent a letter to the KDP [Iran] requesting a meeting to expand cooperation, exchange information and publications, etc. Later, comrades of the KDP [Iran] visited us and brought some press releases and other publications. During this time [...] a report from Party members in Baghdad stating that [...] through Party channels letters and publications asking to be collected by the Central Committee, but were not received because, of delays in Karmanshah, as we learned later. In another letter, Comrade Jafar sent a reply to our letter explaining his activities in London and Iran. He suggested we send a representative to Iran to contact the Tudeh Party and ask for their assistance to resolve our differences with the Communists in Iraq. This was the report and publications that we did not receive. The Party decided to send a representative to Iran while we sent our publications to the KDP [Iran]. Some of them came to Iran to contact us, among them Comrade Ghani Ballouriyan. He and others were hosted by the KDP [Iran] and contacted Comrade Ibrahim who wrote a report about the situation in Iraq and sent it to him in Iran. Ballouriyan contacted Iraqi Communist organizations through us. Our relationship with the KDP [Iran] grew stronger and we assisted them with 300 dinars and a press machine (five or six months ago). During their stay in Iranian Kurdistan, they tried to resolve our differences with Hamza's group. In their presence, we agreed on certain things to bring them back. However, Hamza's splinter later evaded a group return to Party ranks. We have continued to communicate with the KDP [Iran], and our ties are now much stronger.

With regard to sending a comrades to Iran, it was postponed because of Zahidi's imperialistic reactionary coup d'état and the deteriorating conditions in Iran. Last winter, a Tudeh comrade stopped in Baghdad on his way to Europe. Through an address obtained in Tehran, he contacted our party branch in Baghdad. A few comrades and I read the KDP [Iran]'s draft program which he had brought along. We helped him financially and otherwise. Comrades, I was to send you a report via the Tudeh comrade. I got the finished report to relay to him, as he had promised to send it to you. Unfortunately, I was arrested the following morning as he left Baghdad. The letter was never delivered.

In addition, the Party sent a memorandum to the British Communist Party explaining in brief the situation of the Iraqi Communist movement.

Our Party has weak links to the Kurds in Syria and Turkish Kurdistan. We hope that our links will expand soon.

Current Status of Our Party

We can summarize the Party situation as follows:

1. Our Party relatively enjoys high popular support among the people of Iraqi Kurdistan. Our movement has begun moving into the countryside as more attention is given to peasants. Our Central Leadership especially the current Politburo is very strong. Comrade Ibrahim Ahmad is well- educated, broad-minded, with a good grasp of Marxism-Leninism. Comrade engineer Ali Abdullah is also well-educated, mature and possesses fine organizational skills. Comrade Umar Mustafa is a revolutionary and his education is fair.

Our party mottos, as well as our plans of struggle are scientific and correct. However, our shortcomings continue to be leaders' neglecting to publish regularly, creating party cadres, and establishing strong links with the outside world. Having discussed them at its latest meeting during Eid al-Adha [Muslim Feast], the Central Committee decided to work to remedy these shortcomings.

2. Our appropriate mottos have gradually dominated the activities of other groups as well.

Our Relations with the Communist Movement in Iraq

Groups that act as organizations, and have publications and activities are three in number:

1. The ICP's Core Group, the most numerous among organizations (when I mentioned numbers, I mean among the educated and petite bourgeoisie, for these Communist organizations did not even partially take root among the workers and peasants). (The labor movement is very weak because of the Core Group's damaging deviations that devastated the labor movement.)

The Core Group's dicta are unsound and shaky at any point in time. At this time, their position regarding the fundamental issues of popular democracy, the peasants and ethnonationalism is unclear. Their tactical mottos are mostly leftist; they played a major role in giving the peace movement the tinge of Communism and dragged it into left wing extremism. The same is true of their roles in the student, youth and labor movements. Strategically, they assert that Martyr Fahd's Accord is their guide, which is a rightist Accord when dealing with the issues of ethnicity and authority during the national liberation phase. It strives for a bourgeois (not popular) democracy, and regarding nationalism, it considers the Kurds an ethnic minority, not a nation. Therefore, it demands equality between Arabs and Kurds, not the international Leninist watchword of right to self-determination . . . the same is true of his [Fahd's] position regarding the Iraqi Constitution, seeking amendments!! and other issues.

Their position regarding unity of the Communist movement is blind hostility . . . and as regards other groups, they attack, defame with cheap accusations, and derision. Anyone who is not with them they accuse of spying and treason as they did attorneys Aziz Sharif, Hamza Abdullah and Jamal al-Hayderi . . . etc.

The Core Group almost went bankrupt and would have accepted the unity motto if it were not for the recognition given by the British Communist Party which saluted and invited them to their Congress. Undoubtedly, it was unstudied, impromptu and incorrect. For the Core Group, it was a shot in the arm, especially among the ranks of the unaware, and that's what most of their anomalous ranks are.

Currently among the Core Group, there is a group that works under the command of Mr. Najad Ahmad and Mr. Adib. They have studied in Czechoslovakia for two years. This internal group works closely with us to unify the Communist movement. In their ranks are many of the conscientious members of the Core Group in Baghdad. They support the existence and position of our party in creating linkage with the 'correct' ICP, similar to that of the KDP [Iran] and the glorious Tudeh Party. Generally speaking, the Core Group is weak in the north but influential among Baghdad students. Hameed Othman leads this group.

2. The second group is the ICP's Workers' Pennant (Rayat al-Shagheela), led by Jamal al-Hayderi. They represent Martyr Fahd's tract best, a rightist regarding the Kurdish question and the issues of peasants and popular democracy. It is strong in Najaf and Karbala. Among their prominent leaders are Hamza Salman, and Jamal al-Hayderi.

3. The third group is the Communists' Unity Party headed by Mr. Aziz Sharif and their central publication is "An-Nidhal" [The Struggle]. This group is well-organized and its core mottos, stressing the issues of popular democracy, peasants and Kurds, are correct. Their motto regarding elections was incorrect. They have limited their efforts to workers, with strong chapters among the workers of Mosul, Kadhimiya and Basra. They are weak among students and the intelligentsia. They are the remaining elements of the Peoples' Party which lasted (others of the Core Group joined them, . . . etc). Our Party has strong ties to this organization, and we work together for the unity of the Iraqi Communist movement. As we know, this group has established ties to the Communist Parties of Syria and Lebanon.

Our relationship with the ICP's Workers' Pennant is not bad despite our profound differences with regard to fundamental issues. We want to attend them to the issue of unity. Our relations with the ICP's Core Group deteriorated lately, despite our Party's efforts. We were in agreement regarding elections in Suleimaniyya and the Peace Movement and tried to attract them to the issue of unity. However, as usual, they are attacking us unfairly and incorrectly from time to time for no reason, which has forced our Party to respond openly and without childish fracas. Practically speaking, this group serves neither the Iraqi people nor the Iraqi working class. Their subversive position has deviated from the political and syndicalist movements of the working class, as well as the peace, student and youth movements. They have undermined the interest of workers and the masses in general. There are many spies among them, especially in Kirkuk, Suleimaniyya, Koy Sanjaq and Baghdad where our party is secure.

The Iraqi government always tries to create a din around this group and the Bureau of Investigations attributes the activities of others to this group . . . !

To unify the Communist movement, our Party's practical steps are strengthening ties with the Communists' Unity Party, the bloc inside the Core Group, and independent Communists such as Dawood al-Sayigh and the like. About a year ago, our Party sent a memorandum to all three splinter groups (Core, Pennant, and Struggle) asking them to hold a conference to resolve differences among them and with us in light of Marxism-Leninism, and end all splinter groups that divide the Communist movement. The Pennant and Struggle groups responded favorably, but not the Core Group.

This is a brief description of the situation of the Party and its ties to groups from 1949 until now. The Party has charged me to ask the following of you, dear Comrade:

1. It is necessary to maintain contact with us through finding means to communicate with you so we can send you the news, information and reports.
2. Assist the Party in translating Marxist books into Kurdish, strengthening the Party's contacts with the outside, creating a Party leadership cadre abroad (in popular democratic countries and the Soviet Union).

3. To issue statements, calls and articles by the Comrade leader Mustafa Barzani. His words will affirm the will of the masses and push the movement forward especially under these circumstances when the imperialist propaganda is active among the Kurds, and I will write some to you. Again, I hope that you will fulfill the above-mentioned requests.

Imperialistic Propaganda among Iraqi Kurds

For a while, American intelligence circles have worked to gain active support among Iraqi Kurds and to inject damaging anti-Soviet propaganda through the infamous "Payam" magazine published by the Department of Educational Relations in the American Embassy in Baghdad. It is also directed against the peace movement and our comrades such as Comrade Ibrahim Ahmad who was viciously attacked in this anti-peace magazine...

About two years ago, an official from the American Embassy contacted one of the Kurdish tribal chiefs (details available at the Politburo because I do not know all details, thus, I just point it out) offering American assistance to the Kurds to enact Kurdish-only operations. They asked the Embassy to contact Comrade Ibrahim but the Party rejected it. This year, the American Consulate in Kirkuk repeatedly tried to contact Mr. Ibrahim [Ahmad] but he rejected it with Party approval... However, the American government continues to send its Embassy staff to Kurdistan to rally supporters and lovers! The American Ambassador personally visited Kurdistan more than once. The said Embassy has ties to Sheikh Baba Ali [...] with Zayd Ahmad Othman of Arbil. In their tours they attacked our Party, and described it as Communist. Once, when the American Ambassador was in Shaqlawa at Saddique Miran's house and a few members of the Parliament and Kurdish dignitaries (!!) were present, the American Ambassador in his conversation asked them to demand the teaching of Kurdish language and literature in the schools. A simple-minded representative responded, "This is the KDP's task, not ours." The Ambassador answered that the KDP was a Communist party, and dangerous and that it was not in the best interests of America and Britain to comment here!! Our Party responded with a sustained attack on American imperialism in meetings, demonstrations, articles, newspapers, gatherings, festivals, elections, and other occasions, exposing hostile American plans, its war and brutal policy in Korea and other parts of the world, and its policy against Kurds and Kurdistan. Thus, Americans began suppressing the democratic liberation movement in Iranian Kurdistan.

Our Party continuously attacks the aggressive American policy and shows the luminous peaceful policy of the glorious Soviet Union, a policy which works to ensure peoples' liberty and happiness. We point out the role of the Soviet Union in destroying fascism, and in liberating peoples, in the defense of peace and assisting peoples of the world, the Kurds and Kurdistan. Our Party will never be casual or delay in defending the Soviet Union. Our Party is doing as much as possible to strengthen ties between the Soviet Union and Iraq. The motto of strengthening friendship and ties with the Soviet Union and recognizing the People's Republic of China and other popular democracies was one of the most obvious ones in elections, mass meetings and memorandums.

The British imperialism is also publishing a newspaper through Guiw Mukiryani in Arbil called "*Hataw*" [Sunshine]. It is temporarily weekly. This was a magazine supposed to be published by the British Consulate in Mosul with attorney Sa'id Kani Marani as its executive director and it was to be called "Dangi Rasti" [Voice of Truth]. Our Party recognized and exposed the project early on. Then, the director of the Kirkuk Oil Company contacted Qasim Mulla Effendi in order that he oversee the publication of a newspaper in Arbil and said the company and the Embassy would assist him, provided he would publish certain articles for them. He declined. Lastly, by means of Abdulla Scot, the English spy, the project of 'Hataw' magazine was arranged by Guiw to propagate its venom. The American government now thinks of designating parts of the programs of Voice of America (Voice of Satan—as *Rizgari* called it) to broadcast in Kurdish. They have increased the programs of the Kurdish Division in Baghdad [Radio]. We feel it is imperative to have Kurdish broadcasting from Moscow or to establish a station such as the Azerbaijani one.

This my glorious comrades, is what I could write in a hurry as the Party requested. We would like to have more contact with you to send you more detailed reports about our activities. We would like to hear your views and observations, which we desperately need.

"Forward under the leadership of the hero of the liberation of Kurdistan, General Mustafa Barzani" (the official closing phrase for all Party communications).

Jalal Husam ad-Din Talabani "Pirot"
Member of the Central Committee, in charge of Student Affairs
Moscow, October 8, 1952

Some brief news about the Barzanis

Sheikh Ahmad, Sheikh Mohammed Siddique, Sheikh Ahmad's son, and the older son of the leader Barzani are still in Basra prison, and their families are there. The other son of the leader (Luqman) is now with his mother in Mosul. The government pays them a nice monthly stipend. One family is in Baghdad and another in Imarah. The total number of those remaining in prison or exile are (102). [...] is now in Koy Sanjaq area.

In closing, I wish, glorious comrades, to assure you that the banner of revolutionary struggle for liberating Kurdistan and its happiness, for free independent, people's democratic Kurdistan which is a friend of the great Soviet Union, impenetrable fort of peace and a friend of our pure, great and sincere people, is still high above our masses.... We will never leave the battlefield until victory is achieved. Day after day, our skills and experiences are accumulating, and we do benefit from the previous struggle. Let us all vociferate:

Long live independent people's democratic Kurdistan
Long live the great USSR, leader of people's camp and peace, the friend of our people and
    all peoples.
Long live our struggling Party and its greatest leader General Mustafa Barzani
Long live world peace, and death to the Anglo-American warmongers.

Pirot

Translation from Arabic of Document No. 22

Honorable Comrade Leader Mustafa Barzani,

Please allow me to greet you on behalf of the Central Committee and all affiliates of our Party, The Unified Democratic Party of Kurdistan. I wish you a long and happy life.

No doubt, you know of the Party's attempts to contact you, as you are our Party's President. You have been repeatedly elected in the Party Congresses since you founded it in 1946. The Kurdish movement has been united by establishing a vanguard new Kurdistan party, namely the Unified Democratic Party of Kurdistan (Parti Democrati Yakgirtoi Kurdistan). Again, you were unanimously re-elected President of the Party. It is truly unfortunate that we are not allowed to communicate with you while we are going through very sensitive and difficult times. Daily imperialistic schemes and conspiracies are being drawn up against Kurdistan by Anglo-American imperialism. We are in dire need of your guidance and the views of Soviet comrades. As you know, our contacts with Soviet comrades ended in 1949, and you know that our Party was established with their knowledge and approval. It is annoying not to have their advice and guidance as the Kurdish liberation movement advances as never before. Party influence among the masses and all segments of our society had increased dramatically despite hard times and an atmosphere saturated with imperialistic plots and abundant propaganda in Kurdistan against the great Soviet Union. Americans publish a Kurdish magazine and pamphlets in Kurdish, and broadcast in Kurdish from Baghdad, Tehran, Tabriz and Sanandaj, in addition to a wide range of activities by their spies and agents and other means of communication.

Our Party considers communication with you and the Soviet comrades essential, beneficial, and necessary to safeguard the interests of the Kurdish liberation movement and the great socialist camp, headed by the Soviet Union. Because of the vast achievements since its Twentieth Party Congress, we had hoped, the grand Soviet Communist Party, would ease communication with you and Soviet comrades, especially in light of assurances by the Central Committee of the Communist Party of the Soviet Union to further ties with fraternal and progressive parties of the world.

If I, an authorized member of the Central Committee of our Party, could not contact you, as it appears to me, then it is imperative that I write this letter. Before writing about the general conditions of the Party and the movement, I wish to inform you of the Central Committee's resolution and pressing desire to send a high-level delegation which you are to lead in discourse with the Soviet comrades regarding Kurdistan, the growing anti-imperialist movement in Iraq and the entire Middle East, and American plots and spying activities in Kurdistan that compel us to press for answers. The Party is asking you to contact Soviet officials to facilitate the visit and the tasks of the delegation. I repeat that we are in dire need of your guidance and the advice of Soviet comrades. Therefore, please do all you can to expedite this visit.

1. Party Situation

After unifying the Kurdish liberation movement in the Unified Democratic Party of Kurdistan resulting from the agreement of the KDP, Hamza Abdullah's group which had split off as I mentioned in my first letter in 1950, a group of Communist Kurds, and a number of independent individuals, a provisional Central Committee was formed with the following members:

1. Comrade Leader Mustafa Barzani, President
2. Comrade attorney Ibrahim Ahmad, member
3. Comrade engineer Ali Abdullah, member
4. Comrade Nuri Ahmad Taha, member
5. Comrade attorney Omer Mustafa Dabbabeh, member
6. Comrade attorney Hamza Abdullah, member
7. Comrade Jalal Talabani (law), member
8. Comrade Habib Mohammed Karim (senior law student but expelled from school), member
9. Comrade Najad Ahmad Aziz (graduate of party school in Czechoslovakia), member
10. Comrade Khasro Tawfiq (graduate of the School of Economy and Commerce), member

Immediately, the Central Committee proclaimed the founding of the Party in a press release, and began expressing its views in it official organ "Khabati Kurdistan"— "Kurdistan Struggle." The Central Committee went on to issue a provisional charter, organize branches, appoint Party cadres, renew ties with the ICP and other patriotic organizations about which I will be talking later. The permanent bureau consisted of comrades Ibrahim Ahmad, Omer Mustafa, Hamza Abdullah, and Jalal Talabani.

Our Party has strong chapters in Suleimaniyya, Kirkuk, Arbil, Koy Sanjaq, Pishdar, Halabja, Panjawin, Rewanduz, the Dizayee farming communities, Shahrazur, Merga, Aqra, and the Bahdinan region, notably Zakho.

Our Party is also strong in the army, including Kurdish officers and comprising chapters for all ranks and soldiers. Party chapters are also strong among the peasants, the Kurdistan Student Union, and the Democratic Union of Kurdistan Youth. A committee was formed to accommodate tribal leaders of Pishdar, Rania, Rewanduz, Jaff, Suleimaniyya and Koy Sanjaq areas, and Yazidi tribes. This Committee is supervised and led by our Party.

Many Kurdish notables endorse our party, including Sheikh Latif Sheikh Mahmud al-Hafeed, as well as Mohammed Ziyad and Massoud Mohammed; both former Representatives and known patriots.

In sum, our Party is a force to be reckoned with and can accomplish many mass and revolutionary tasks. We control military barracks and complete brigades in Arbil, Kirkuk and Mosul. We can mobilize peasants, laborers and city workers. The Party continues to make great strides organizationally and educationally, and to prepare party cadres.

2. Party Relations with the Iraqi Communist Party

Once established, our leaders immediately contacted ICP leaders. On our team were comrades Hamza, Jalal, Khasro and Habib. On their team were comrades Hussain Radhi (first in charge), Jamal al-Hayderi, Aziz al-Sheikh and Yousif Matti. We agreed to promote an atmosphere for friendship and brotherhood, provided the ICP's propaganda attacks ceased. Furthermore, the following points were agreed upon:

1. It is a historical necessity to have a vanguard democratic party in Kurdistan, accepted in form and reality by the masses to lead their struggle.
2. Strengthen ties, exchange views and cooperate.
3. Work together on revolutionary projects.
4. Back the Kurdish liberation movement, because it is glorious, revolutionary and anti-imperialist. Encourage and revive Kurdish nationalism, and jointly introduce the Kurdish cause abroad.

However, we differed on the following: the ICP maintained their view of having their branch operate in Kurdistan. Members would affiliate with both parties, that is, the ICP and the vanguard party of Kurdistan. Our Party's view is that it is wrong and unjustified to have their chapter function exactly as the existing leading party which is also guided by Marxism-Leninism. I have sent you a copy of our Party's letter concerning this to Communist organizations before unification. It is worth mentioning that ICP chapters in Kurdistan support our view. They are now debating their leaders that the only correct way to work in Kurdistan is to have a party, democratic in form and Marxist-Leninist in essence, that can rally the masses and lead the Kurdish national movement, without being exploited by imperialistic, chauvinistic and reactionary elements, and seriously considering the ethnic, historical, political and economic realities of Kurdistan (ICP chapters are very weak in Kurdistan).

Currently, leaders of both parties are negotiating this point. We hope to unify all parts of the revolutionary movement in Kurdistan under the banner of one leading party (ours).

3. The Kurdish National Movement

In addition to the oppressive Baghdad Pact and the activities and publications of our party, the inflamed Arab nationalism indirectly abetted the awakening and augmenting the national spirit of the Kurdish masses through its triumphs, and cultivating anti-imperialist sentiments. The masses are now strongly moving to realize our national goals led by our Party to unify struggle with Arab masses. The masses are genuinely moved and guided by leader Mustafa Barzani's immortal call of 1946, in which he said "I call equally on both Kurdish and Arab peoples to cooperate [with each other] and unify their struggle against a common enemy, imperialism and its agents, a call for each people to live on his land happy and independent."

However, the lack of enthusiasm on the part of the Arab nationalist movement to back the Kurdish movement along with imperialist intrigues and plots affected, at least partially, the innocent masses, the Kurdish bourgeoisie and sometimes even nationalists. Still, we have worked tirelessly to buttress the unity of struggle and to foil imperialist intrigues. Frankly, I should say that we need statements by the leader Barzani who enjoys great popularity, and influence and is loved by the masses of Kurdistan. Barzani has truly become a legendary figure, beloved as the Egyptian magazine al-Tahrir put it. With his public statements and guidance, he can contribute greatly to the foiling of imperialists' intrigues, strengthen and guide the Kurdish national movement properly, and inspire hope in many people. In this regard, we also need the assistance and guidance of the Soviet Union, and we wish a Kurdish radio station would broadcast from the Soviet Union which will contribute to raising awareness, awaken and alert the masses of Kurdistan, foil imperialist plots, defeat anti-peace and anti-Soviet propaganda.

The Kurdish national movement is a logical result of the Kurds' enslavement, division and oppression; in other words, it is an historical phenomenon beyond people's control. Therefore, it can and should be led and directed to serve, generally speaking, Kurdistan and the international proletariat movement (notably the socialist camp). To be neglected and left alone, the Kurdish national movement will clearly be exploited by reactionaries and the nationalist bourgeoisie to serve imperialism against the eastern peoples' anti-imperialist liberation movements, especially the erupting Arab liberation movement. Therefore, our party embraces it, adopts activities and tactics to ensure steering the Kurdish national movement under its direction and leadership, to prevent nationalist bourgeois and imperialist elements from taking over. Thus, we must adopt a realistic and scientific approach, and avoid falling into leftist and rightist childish aberrations.

4. Party Contact with parts of Kurdistan annexed to Iran, Turkey and Syrian Kurds

Our Party maintains regular contacts with the KDP [Iran] in the part of our homeland annexed to Iran. These are strong and effective contacts, inclusive of all forms of cooperation, exchanging views, assistance and joining efforts.

We have contacts with the Kurds of Turkey and currently work is underway to help them establish a vanguard party. There are hundreds of nationalist Kurds who have contacts with our Party and wish to be organized and advised, and our Party is moving in this direction. As regards the Syrian Kurds, our Party's view is that they should not do anything that will offend and annoy the Arab nationalist bourgeoisie; they should assist the Arab nationalist movement as best as they can, join their struggle under the leadership of the Syrian Communist Party, and protect Syria from imperialist conspiracies. If they worked in the Kurdish national movement, they should channel their work into Turkey and the part of Kurdistan annexed to it. Our Party will work with the KDP [Iran] to establish organizational links among all Kurdish parties, if not unifying them in a single party, because the Kurdish movement in each part of Kurdistan is an integral part of the general Kurdish national movement attested to by history and historical conditions. Our Party is making delightful strides in this respect.

5. We and the Soviet Union

As you know, the attitude of our leading party, guided by Marxism-Leninism, towards the Soviet Union is fraternal and friendly. Our Party expressed, the utmost deference, respect and gratitude to the glorious Soviet Communist Party, and we are delighted at its achievements since its Twentieth Party Congress. Our Party has been and will remain loyal to its principles and ideological ties with the Soviet Communist Party. Steadfast, we remain supportive of the Soviet Union, mighty leader of the socialist camp, defend and explain their policies to the Kurdish people in particular and the Iraqi people in general. We have been successful in our efforts and will continue on this path.

Eager, our Party wishes to commence direct relations with the glorious Soviet Communist party as they may see it suffice. Thus, the Central Committee authorized me to ask you, the president of our party and leader of our people, to inform the comrades of our desire to send a delegation provided that you and other comrades that you recommend such as Sayyed Aziz and Mir Haj will join the delegation. You head the delegation in meetings with the Soviet comrades. I stress this request and ask you on behalf of the Party, to put forth your best possible efforts to reach this objective for establishing such ties that serve the interests of the Soviet Union and Kurdistan, the general anti-imperialist movement, and in the interest of international peace as well.

I also wish to inform you that the enormous imperialist propaganda against the Soviet Union in Kurdistan, the absence of a Soviet broadcast in Kurdish, the lack of clarity in the Soviet policy toward Kurdistan, and the Soviets' stating nothing about the Kurds and Kurdistan put us in a difficult position and negatively affect the credulous masses and the educated bourgeois Kurds negatively, who have begun to ask, "Why the Soviets do not help the Kurds as they do the Arabs? Why is there not a Kurdish broadcast while they broadcast in all other languages? Why…? Why…?… etc."

Therefore, establishing ties between our party and the Soviet Communist Party, even undeclared, to provide guidance and direction, and establishing a Kurdish broadcast in the Soviet Union are necessary to frustrate imperialist plots and end skepticism among the Kurds. Thus, on behalf of the Party I ask you to present this issue to the Soviet comrades.

Imperialist Plots in Kurdistan

With the increasing power of the Arab liberation movement, and the increasing influence of our Party within the Kurdish national movement in Kurdistan, imperialist circles and

Americans in particular began broad and continuous activities among Kurdish notables, tribal chiefs, educated bourgeoisie, promising to serve the Kurds and Kurdistan if they become realists and distance themselves from the Soviet Union. They contacted Sheikh Baba Ali Sheikh Mahmud (former Minister) and invited him to America. When he went, they explained to him at the US State Department that Americans favor Kurdish autonomy and liberation, provided the Kurds remain American friends and reject Soviet friendship!! Baba Ali told them that the Kurdish national movement and the forces of the Kurdish people are now led by the Party (ours), which is the only one that can speak for the Kurds. The Americans told him that the Party is pro-Soviet and refuses even to negotiate with America or its officials. How could he win their friendship of America? Baba Ali returned, and our Party contacted him and warned him of the consequences of being deceived by the Americans. He promised to do his best. I suggest that you write him a letter on the occasion of his father's death, and alert him to the imperialist propaganda, and ask him to help and cooperate with the nationalist movement led by our Party.

American newspapers publicized an American project carried out by Turkey stating that Turkey would grant autonomy to the part of Kurdistan annexed to it, and use it as a nucleus to unify Kurdistan under Turkey. Furthermore, American officials and spies in Kurdistan are calling for Kurdish–American friendship so they will help us gain our freedom!!

I am sure that you know that Americans are publishing a Kurdish magazine in their embassy in Baghdad. Thousands of copies are distributed free of charge. Many pamphlets are also being published, all of which attack the Soviet Union, glorify America and war. These are in addition to Kurdish broadcasts from Tehran, Baghdad, Tabriz and Sanandaj. Thus, I repeat, to frustrate these American and other plots, we need the help of the Soviet Union, and to strengthen leader Barzani's contacts with his party and people, and to establish a Kurdish broadcasting in the Soviet Union.

British officials have said that their biggest political mistake in Iraq was not pardoning leader Barzani and letting him go to the Soviet Union. They have said it repeatedly (as the chief of Staff said in the presence of the leader's oldest son Sheikh Obeid, and in the presence of Sheikh Mohammed Sadiq). They are prepared to give the leader whatever he wants in money, status and a position no less than that of Abul Ilah in the Iraqi state, if he returns, becomes their friend and rejects Soviet friendship!! They would also give the Kurds autonomy...etc. I did at the time write to you the details of your son and Sheikh Sadiq's meeting with the chief of staff.

The propaganda apparaturs of the British and their accomplices have become active lately. Saeed Qazzaz and Ali Kamal have visited Kurdistan repeatedly to unite the Kurds under their leadership (as they say) and serve Kurdistan through Britain. They say in their propaganda that Russians are not doing and will not do anything for the Kurds, and that they only want to exploit the Kurds for their own ends, and that wise Kurds should befriend Britain to gain our rights.

Our Party did not remain silent. We exposed them and alerted people to their dangers. We expanded and intensified our patriotic activities and contacts with all segments of the Kurdistan society, especially with tribal chiefs, and educated patriotic bourgeoisie to prevent them from falling into the imperi-alist trap.

Dear honorable President, this is a summary of Party activities and I look forward to seeing you, or to your receiving the Party delegation which we intend to send to you. We will provide detailed information about the Party and in general. Before closing, I repeat my wish that you contact me as soon as possible, and that you put forth your best efforts to persuade the Soviet comrades of the necessity of my contacting you and of receiving our Party delegation, and to inform high officials of the comrades in order to accomplish this.

Finally, I salute you once again on behalf of our Party and people. You are the esteemed leader, and all the comrades with you and under your command. Honored and acclaimed, live long for us and for our people.

Sincerely,

Member of the Permanent Bureau of the Leadership Board of the Unified Democratic Party of Kurdistan
Jalal Talabani

[Signed]
July 30, 1957

> I may tell the holder of this letter details of news from your family. They are all well, and anxious to hear your news, and read your letters. I am also sending pictures of the male members of your family.

Translation from Kurdish of Document No. 23

LEADER OF THE KURDS: BARZANI

Towering... Barzani,
In the struggle for homeland
In the battlefield,
He is a Knight, a hero...
     Mighty, Elegant, and
     The elixir of Kurdistan

He is the essence of Kurdistan
So, no match for
     Barzani's ...
     Barzani's elegance

* * *

Barzani... Barzani...
Who hasn't Known
     This name?
Whoever saw, or
     Heard
In the east
The Middle East
In winter and summer
Who is to speak out?
Who is to struggle?
     With many countries, and
     The enemy of nations,
     Many imperialists
Who has become a legend
Who has become a sway.

* * *

The armies of Nuri Sa'id[3]
With the Georges[4] combined
Mightily, they fight
But can never run this prince
      This lion
Into their trap...

Armies of the Turks and Iran,
With Truman's airforce, combined
Unshaken, he remained...
They never win a thing...

On mountain peaks
In the Battlefield,
Again, who roars
who fights, but Barzani
      ...Barzani

* * *

Camps and garrisons, he broke
A thousand chambers, he tore
As sparks, as clouds
Whatever and wherever,
Lightening and thunder
      As he goes to dance,
      He goes to fight
Borders, he pierced...
Camps, he penetrated

...

...

Strikes at the heart of Turks
Goes to the Kurdish north
Becomes an arrow and bow...
He extends to Iran

...

With their pipes
Opium, they smoke,
To their death, they succumb
And they say:

...

...

* * *

---

3. A prominent Iraqi politician and Prime Minister before the 1958 Revolution.
4. Georges, the plural of George, an English name, in reference to the British. Perhaps George Sykes, the British Prime Minister then.

O Persian brother
O proud Arab brother
O democratic Turk
We are all brothers
We are friends and neighbors
Our enemies are the Americans
Britons... Britons
From now on do not be
     Their golden money

Our leader, Barzani
All should know him,
     The freedom leader...
Renowned among people...
Wake up, and move the globe
Rally around him...
Cry out: long live Barzani!
Savior of humanity!

Qadri Jan

Translation from Kurdish of Document No. 24

THE KURDISH RENAISSANCE LEAGUE

Long live the Kurds and Greater Kurdistan

Your honor, Leader of Liberation Mulla Mustafa Barzani

Having heard the news of your blessed liberation revolt, we send you this letter on behalf of the Kurdish Renaissance League (KJK) A. Kh., hoping that you will respond in detail.

1. First we congratulate the leader and the victorious Kurdistan Liberation Army.

2. The reason to express this overwhelming sentiment for you is our feeling of Kurdish brotherhood in struggle. To be of practical and effective assistance to you, and because we appreciate your position regarding international political responsibility, we must know the following information:

3. What are the determinants of your revolution? Do you demand the liberation of Iraqi Kurdistan or all of Kurdistan, including the Turkish part?

4. What is your position regarding foreigners' policies in Iraq? If you were threatened or persuaded, will you stop it [revolution] or continue?

5. Our view is that your blessed revolution should adopt an all-encompassing name, that is, to demand the liberation of all Kurdistan. Thus, all Kurds in the world will have to consult and cooperate with you, and to establish a Kurdish army of all Kurds in the world under your leadership. To accomplish this, they must prepare to hold a conference, and you should organize it in cooperation with your and our consultative committees. A date should be set, and it should be held either in Iraqi or Iranian Kurdistan. This conference should define comprehensive national Kurdish demands, and all of us should sign it. This conference should also establish a Kurdish military system, and define the responsibilities of all sides in the national revolution.

6. You ought to explain to us your combat position along with the enemy's war position in fine and precise detail, explaining the attitude of the Iraqi Kurdish tribes toward you.

7. For liberating the Kurds, of course the policy of one of the great powers should support us. In our opinion this power is the Soviet State, because we cannot be neutral with all countries. What are your views in this regard?

8. Most important of all is that you explain to us as soon as possible your views regarding the British view of your revolution, and what is your discourse with them? We know clearly that it is unthinkable that the British were neutral about this revolution.

9. You are a freedom-loving leader. At the very least, you are fighting for justice for your tribe. In the spirit of Kurdish brotherhood in struggle, the Iranian Kurds are eager to see you victorious. They are prepared to assist you as much as political circumstances permit in our country. When we present these questions, our goal is to make available much assistance and make your blessed movement a total national movement, and to record your honor in history by the A.Kh. City Council.

Translation from Kurdish of Document No. 25

Letter from Qadri Jan, the Great Kurdish Poet

Barzani was scheduled to stop in Damascus on his way from Cairo to Baghdad to visit Kurdish brothers there but his agenda changed and he returned to Baghdad non-stop.

Our great leader:

First, I am honored to bow in respect and welcome you. I salute your return. I do not know why you did not stop in Syria. Many of our Kurdish brothers wish to see their leader to ease the troubles of long years. Your return boosted the morale of the Kurdish masses. Regardless of tendency and belief, the Kurds are brothers, ... accept and are proud of your leadership. Undoubtedly, your presence will strengthen the beloved Republic of Iraq and solidify Kurdish-Arab fraternity.

In addition to the Kurds, I am certain that Arab, Iranian and Turkish patriots are also pleased to see you return [home]. Of course, you value and esteem the achievements of the Kurdish struggle with the support and cooperation of free peoples. Delighted to see you come home, Khalid Begdash trusts that all Kurds ought to rally behind their only leader, Barzani, and to follow his wise policies. He sends you his greetings ... our comrades are thrilled and send their warmest regards. If I can, I will visit you. My best regards to brothers As'ad and Mir Haj. My regards go to brothers Sadiq and Ubaidullah as well.

Sincerely,

Qadri Jan
Damascus, October 14, 1958

Translation from Kurdish of Document No. 26

Letter from the Late Ismail Haqqi Shawais, a Loyal Friend of [Mustafa] Barzani's
Massoud Barzani

Dokan, Dumazbalu
November 8, 1958

To: Our great and beloved President Mustafa Barzani, foe of feudalism and imperialism.

...In your oblation, I stand. We thank the leader of Iraq, defeater of imperialism and reactionaries, Abd al-Karim Qasim for the amnesty and order to allow your return to Iraq. Your Eminence's return has had a great effect on Iraqi, Turkish and Iranian Kurdistan. We thank you for carrying the torch of liberty in Iraq... especially for your statement, "We, the Iraqi Kurds, will be sincere, loyal and sacrificing soldiers of the Republic." Such teaching and guidance worried the Turco-Iranian reactionaries and imperialist circles, and led the enemy to despair. Under Abd al-Karim Qasim's leadership, the morale of imperialists and reactionaries, God willing, will collapse, not only in Iraq, but in the whole Middle East. No matter how long and difficult the road is, no matter what the problems and obstacles are, God willing, we will all be free because of your efforts and heroism. Your return home is a great omen for defeating imperialism, reactionary and feudalism.

Live long, and I stand ready in your command and oblation.

Your loyal follower
Ismail Haqqi Shawais, Liaison Officer
Dumazbalu Company, Dokan

Translation from Arabic of Document No. 27

Long Live Kurdish-Arab Fraternity under Our Sole Leader Abd al-Karim Qasim
A Salute to the First Patriot, His Eminence Mustafa Barzani

Astounding the world, He marched	at a dawn in July, justice reigned
We said, our leader has revolted	chains destroyed and injustice blind
Razed the palace of prostitution	and nest of treason, combined
Triumphant, backed by God and people	led us to victory, not to be confined
Qasim, we have a leader in you	to the sun of glory we're to climb
Listen to his clarion call,	for a republic so so refined
On the ruins of corruption, all	loyal and mighty hands intertwined
Blessed be our people, inspired	by brotherhood united and kind
Allies, we will remain in time	sunny and sweet, in an everlasting bond
Brothers are Kurds and Arabs	their call to victory is forever fine
A traitor among us will meet	his fate at the righteous one's hand

* * *

O Mustafa, beacon of our struggle	A salute from those who strove and defied
A salute from those who backed our defiance	comrades, a people who for virtue vied
Home again, I salute you, dear, beloved	our camp is now fortified
Your struggle is proof of heroism	the sly you slew; the evil you denied
You raised the banner above the shooting start;	Injustice you bound till it died
We will defend you, victory for our people	for our fight, the appeal you rectified
Steadfast, we advance, the will of 'Karim'	We plot our peace, an era dignified
To live in harmony, to exhume	a shining peace, and goodness is deified
All rally behind our leader	an invincible army when justified

seeking justice, not disappointed   adversaries will not be satisfied
When the going gets tough, we are lions;   the land we walk shakes and is terrified

Sincerely,

The Iraqi Patriot
Ibrahim al-Haj Sa'id
Karantina, Baghdad, June 16

Translation from Kurdish of Document No. 28

A Congratulatory Letter from Tahsin Mohammed Amin Jwanroyi to Barzani

Kurdish Student Society in Europe
England Branch
c/o 37 King Street
London, W.C.2.

Leader of the Kurds, General Mustafa Barzani

On behalf of all members of the England Branch, I salute you, your comrades and the rest of the Barzani heroes. You served well and contributed greatly to the struggle of the Kurdish people and all anti-imperialists, and for liberation movements of all oppressed peoples. With Arab brothers, you brought down the rule of agents of imperialism such as the traitor Nuri al-Sa'id and his supporters.

Your return after the July 14 Revolution with the rest of the Barzani brothers is a source of pride and dignity for all. Kurdish students warmly welcome you home and hope for the Kurdish-Arab fraternity, because of your and your comrades' struggle, continued success and cooperation. We wish democratic Iraq great strides, happiness, and triumph under the leadership of Staff Brigadier Abd al-Karim Qasim.

Tahsin Mohammed Amin, Secretary
England Branch
London, April 24, 1959

Translation from Kurdish of Document No. 29

A Letter from Kamal Fuad, Secretary General of the Kurdish Students Society in Europe, to Barzani

KURDISH STUDENTS SOCIETY IN EUROPE
Berlin
Reference: B11
Date: August 11, 1959

To: The valiant Kurdish patriotic leader,
Mustafa Barzani, Respectfully

Warm Revolutionary Greetings

Your worthy letter to the Fourth Congress of our Society was affably and proudly received by participants. It delighted us all, and it was hailed by long and solid rounds of applause.

Unanimously decided upon, the Congress sends you this letter of appreciation to express our gratitude. We strongly believe that you, a sincere Kurdish leader, will continue to serve the Kurdish liberation movement for the goals and rights of the Kurdish people and Kurdistan, to safeguard the beloved Republic of Iraq, a democratic republic of Arabs and Kurds alike, to tirelessly carry on your glorious struggle, and resolutely work to unify the Kurdish liberation movement in all parts of our beloved and partitioned Kurdistan, the hope of every sincere and honorable Kurd.

—Live long in happiness on the road to achieve a unified and liberated Kurdistan under the standard of democracy and peace.

—Long live the democratic Republic of Iraq, the beloved republic of Arabs and Kurds.

Fuad Kamal, Secretary General
Kurdish Student Society in Europe

Translation from Arabic of Document No. 30

Date: November 27, 1958
To: Our sincere Comrade Mustafa Barzani

Warm greetings of camaraderie

Our motivation is utmost sincerity to party principles. The revolutionary Kurdish liberation movement is a tributary of the international democratic and socialist movement led by socialist countries and guided by the USSR with the aim of ending imperialism and ridding humanity forever of exploitation, oppression, reactionism and war, and to achieve sovereignty, prosperity, progress and peace for mankind.

Over the past ten years, a salient fact in the history of the Kurdish revolutionary liberation movement which cannot be denied under any circumstance is our Party. Our Party, with the revolutionary vanguards which eventually formed our Party, has effectively guided the liberation movement to free our Kurdish people. With revolutionary steadfastness and adaptability, our Party has inspired the striving masses to pursue a Marxist path in wisely and consciously espousing developmental phases of the Kurdish movement as circumstances and 'soviet' traits in Kurdistan permit. Our Party's correct policies greatly abated the impact of isolationism and extreme leftist tendencies in the movement of the Kurdish people. Our Party has played its full role in leading and linking together the struggle of the Kurdish and Arabic peoples.

The revolutionary watchwords and objectives that the Party upheld and fought for under the most difficult conditions best demonstrate the realism and legitimacy of Kurdish needs and aspirations in a free and dignified life. In its long and hard struggle on the path of struggle to achieve its long-term goals, the Party has committed errors and deviations that not only do not serve the correct path of development of the Kurdish movement, but harm the Marxist-Leninist theory which guides the Party struggle. However, the history of the world revolutionary movements in general and the experiences of Communist parties in particular teach us that mistakes and deviations can occur in any Marxist party regardless of its level of consciousness or richness of experience. It teaches us that correcting errors and deviations and providing safeguards to prevent repeating them is the only way to move the party forward.

The purpose of this report is to deal with the shortcomings of our Party and to get rid of its mistakes and deviations during this sensitive period in the history of our liberation movement, so we can carry out its tremendous responsibilities for our people and the revolutionary movement in general.

This report is designated to outline party errors and deviation caused by individual positions and views which the Politburo upheld. These positions in fact represented Shorishgeir and other current Politburo members, Tishk, Bakhtiyar and Shorishgeir's clique: in other words, those who control the Party leadership.

Misunderstanding the Revolution, and its Marxist and Scientific Analysis

Party leaders did not understand the nature of the July 14 Revolution, and failed to analyze it correctly in light of Marxist-Leninist theory and Iraq's special circumstances, which in fact is a democratic patriotic revolution (bourgeois democracy in this case) caused by the struggle of all revolutionary classes and brought a patriotic government to power representing the will of the people in its democratic orientation on a revolutionary path expressed in ending reactionaries and feudalism on the domestic front and siding with peoples striving against imperialism and war on the international front. The revolution belonged to the people, Arabs and Kurds, while the masses played a leading role. Yet, it was, in appearance and form, a military coup d'état. The challenge came from the army, which is a part of the people. Leader Abd al-Karim Qasim and his sincere comrades expressed the will of workers, peasants and various petty and patriotic bourgeoisie. Also, representatives of the large Arab bourgeoisie with chauvinistic orientation came to power, seeking to expand its reign of the larger market in the name of Arab unity and the unified Arab country from the gulf to the ocean. This course was expressed by the Baath and Independence Parties as well as by the conspirator Abd al-Salam Arif and his group. These are fundamentally anti-democracy forces.

In the first few hours after the triumph of the July 14 Revolution, its democratic orientation was clear, notably in its leader Abd al-Karim Qasim who relied heavily on the coalition of the democratic forces. In response, liberation forces stood united against reactionaries and imperialists supporting, with all their power and capabilities the sincere leaders of the Revolution.

Unable to recognize these issues and arrive at rational conclusions in light of correct analysis, Party leadership, therefore, failed to recognize the democratic forces to adjoin within the Revolution. They analyzed the Revolution erroneously, deeming it a movement by a few members of the Armed Forces. Against this background, Party leaders pursued a reactionary and chauvinistic path which led to a series of errors and deviations. Therefore:

First, certain elements rallied around Party leaders who defied the Party core. Our sincere comrades in the Baath and the IP initiated ties with their representative and with Abd al-Salam Arif while the ICP and the NDP were in an intense struggle against the reactionary front represented by Abd al-Salam Arif, the Baath and the IP. The ICP's wrong position and the special orientation of the NDP (stemming from being a patriotic bourgeois participant in the Revolution) were used to continue on this dangerous path, contrary to democracy and the interests of our people and party.

Recognizing the nature of the revolution, many of our comrades demanded that Party leadership take correct stance in regard to events and political tendencies in Iraq. This was expressed in a number of Central Committee Resolutions in mid-November to correct

Party orientation, which current Politburo members failed to comprehend and implement as necessary. The policy of collaboration and rapprochement with representatives of the expansionist Arab bourgeoisie, which clearly stood against the Kurdish people and the July 14 Revolution, has harmed the Party and the Kurdish liberation movement. Within democratic circles, it created suspicions vis-à-vis the Kurdish cause which our Party represents, and isolated our Party from the masses and from the democratic front in Iraq.

Second, Party leaders did not stop there. They opposed the public's demand for cooperation between the two main parties in Kurdistan. They continued a policy of cooperation and reconciliation with the Baath and the IP, and a clearly hostile policy toward the ICP, representing the toiling Arab masses who clearly and naturally adopted a policy of supporting the Republic, confirming and augmenting its democratic orientation. The same is true regarding the NDP, representing the free Iraqi Arab bourgeoisie acting to keep its holdings in the Iraqi market and Iraqi economy. And at this important juncture, their interests clashed with those of the expansionist Arab haute bourgeoisie and were counter to the credo of comprehensive unity—against the expansionist haute bourgeoisie (with anti-democracy orientation). Thus, to control the largest possible market, they adopted the watch-word "A single Arab country from the gulf to the ocean"; and when they feel their interests are in danger, they readily throw themselves on the imperialist bosom.

At first sight, one can recognize that the Baath and the IP are less democratic than the NDP. In fact as soon as they assume power, they tend to be publicly and clearly antagonistic. Therefore, Shorishgeir, Tishk and their clique succumbed to such political thought that they repeatedly stated that there are two parties which in Iraq represent the people: the Baath and our Party, which represent the Arab and Kurdish nations, respectively. What a scientific Marxist-Leninist view!!

The policy of cooperation with representatives of the Baath and the IP and antagonism vis-à-vis the ICP and the NDP, in addition to obvious negativism regarding Abd al-Karim Qasim early on has marred our Party and will not be easily erased because of the single handed behaviors of these comrades who control the Party but do not understand its interests. Abd al-Karim Qasim represented the democratic trend in the Revolution for his reliance on people's forces and belief in democracy. Despite cautions and advice from friendly circles, they slept on rings of fire and distanced themselves from the Party base and the people. They did not learn their lesson which led to the isolation of the Party from the democratic front, and thus fell into the rightist front, and widened the gap between the Party and the leader Abd al-Karim Qasim. Therefore, the Party was unable to reach its objectives of Kurdish demands and goals, including those in the Provisional Constitution. The government feared Party orientation and adopted a position marked by suspicion and caution, believing that the Party holds a separatist tendency. This policy led to breakdown in the Kurdish liberation movement and distorted the bright revolutionary face of the Party's struggle.

Third, this narrow interpretation of the Revolution, the erroneous single-mindedness deeply rooted in the past, the widening gap between the comrades in charge and the masses without consideration for their views, all led to leadership's self-containment and distortion of the Party's revolutionary struggle. They neglected their leadership role and their political, pedagogical, ideological, and organizational responsibilities, while concentration of all leadership responsibilities in their own hands limited their activities to their personal contacts with government circles (unfortunately the reactionary ones) and made it appear as if they were leaders of the inner circles. They ignored the criticism and observations of comrade members and supporters of the Party. Valuable criticism and worthy observations were met with hostility. They followed their own wishes and views. They isolated themselves from the Party and the people and isolated the Party from the masses and the Democratic Front.

It may be assigned that the Party solidified ranks and put down roots. True, but not because of their efforts. It is because of the efforts and resistance of members and other leaders who stood fast and guided the Party and the masses correctly toward democracy and worked to circumvent the blunders of the comrades in charge. If it had not been for their mistakes, the Party's consolidation [of power] would have been many times over. They did not solve organizational problems and did not study circumstances, Party circles and forces. They neglected regions such as Bahdinan completely and drowned the Party in discouraging, grotesque ideas. They incurred a strong reaction from members and supporters. But they neglected criticism and self-criticism and acted beyond the principle of democratic centralism, creating a clique from members of the Leadership Committee to solidify their absolutism. They prevented capable members from exercising their leadership, guidance and political responsibilities in the Party.

Comrade Shorishgeir did not and does not refrain from humiliating and cursing Party and Central Committee members who criticize him. Politburo members are accepting his mistakes without opposition. Absolutism is destroying the free spirit of the Central Committee members; thus the Party is losing its efforts and activities. They have violated the principle of internationalism in their thinking, organizational and political practices. Examples are numerous. Shorishgeir scolded Comrade Kaweh because he expressed a correct opinion regarding the truth of the Baath and its reactionaries among the Jadirites. He banned him from participating in a delegation meeting Mahdawi on a decisive night for the Party to express the truth about the Party's position and policy regarding the leader Abd al-Karim Qasim and his democratic government. Shorishgeir repeatedly chastened Coms. Hiwa, Nabaz, Lazguin and others of the Central Committee. Furthermore, Shorishgeir has gone so far to scold and curse Comrade Kaweh as he was compelled to disagree with him. In addition to cursing other comrades in Central Committee meetings, he has fought with them, and moved to expel them from the Central Committee and the Party altogether on trumped-up charges.

We and many Party comrades and chapters recognized these mistakes at the time, but we were unable to correct them because of their single mindedness and dictatorial style in imposing their views, circumventing decisive action to correct these mistakes or to effectively table them for discussion. Your return greatly eased this task since you confronted those in control of the leadership with these mistakes; notably the fundamental ones. Your correct position solidified the correct orientation crystallized in the last Central Committee meeting which could discuss those wrong positions, and decided to inform the Party base. Although the Central Committee could not elect a new Politburo which could implement the new orientation, its resolutions were an important step for the Party to move in the right direction. The Party concluded the Cooperation Accord with ICP and joined NUF. Other successes are that the party solidified its position, the democratic orientation of the Republic, and support for its president, eased tensions with the ICP, improved the views of the democratic circles regarding our Party and our people's liberation movement to protect the Republic.

Unable to implement the new plan, those in control of Party leadership in the Politburo moved in the opposite direction, blocked by their old mentality. They issued Central Committee Resolutions after the conclusion of the Cooperation Accord. The Resolutions did not mention Party criticism and mistakes regarding the Baath, Abd al-Salam Arif, the ICP, the Democratic Front and others. Furthermore, they included the views of Comrade Shorishgeir, the dominant Politburo member, but not the views and resolutions of the Central Committee; for example:

1. Resolutions attacked the ICP in pursuit of the wrong policy which the Central Committee criticized and decided to end.

2. Did not define the Party position and policy since the July 14 Revolution as regards political events and important issues according to a Central Committee Resolution which stated that the Politburo was to define and announce the correct Party position regarding each significant political event. The Politburo proceeded with its wrong plan contrary to Party policy. For example, the Politburo did not denounce Abd al-Salam Arif's plot of assassination, and despite suggestions by two members of the Central Committee (Kaweh and Hiwa), nothing was said about US Secretary of State's visit to Tehran and later, the conclusion of a military accord between Iran and the USA.

3. The Party has not exercised self-criticism with regard to antagonizing the ICP in the past and sympathizing with the Baath. This attitude is clear in a statement by a KSU chapter which was written by Party comrades in that region and finalized by Comrade Shorishgeir. The statement's tone antagonized the democratic front led by the ICP within the General Student Union of Iraq. Shorishgeir supported the Baath students; the Politburo member, Bakhtiyar signed a statement by the Baathist students supporting their view of allowing foreign Arab students to vote in student elections while the government banned foreign students from voting in the Charter it published for the General Student Union of Iraq. This position led to Baathist students issuing a statement attacking the government and appreciating solidarity by Kurdistan students which marred the Party reputation.

Material and Ideological Roots of Errors and Deviations

The question which poses itself after all that has been said is: Why could a few members of the Central Committee dominate the Party while sincere Party comrades could not put an end to their behavior and reckon with Party interests during all this time? In fact, to correctly understand these mistakes and deviations, we must understand the real reasons before and after the Revolution. A brief description follows:

1. The Party's total isolation from the national democratic movement in Iraq caused by the narrow vision of comrades in charge.

2. Our absence in the NUF caused by the Baath's rejection and the ICP's indifference, in fact opposition to us, suspicions it created, as well as our comrades' lack of enthusiasm to join the NUF.

3. The strong grip of nationalist elements on the leadership, e.g. Shorishgeir, because of Party's special circumstances, including the indecisiveness of Marxist comrades with correct tendencies.

4. A Conference or Congress to elect a new Central Committee to lead a vanguard party such as ours was never held.

5. Shorishgeir and his clique fought sincere comrades by all means possible, regardless of ethics and camaraderie, including cursing, humiliating, and false accusations...etc. This led to despair, although it does not justify the passivity of such comrades as Kaweh in particular.

6. Contrary to Marxist ideology, the ICP waged an unfair, unjustified total campaign in Kurdistan against our revolutionary vanguard Party, including our sincere leaders and members. A long campaign relied solely on lies, distortions, accusations and untrue characterizations. These were in fact against the goals and policies pursued by the sincere members of our Party who always worked selflessly for the just and legitimate rights of the Kurdish liberation movement. This led to the weakening of the Kurdish liberation movement and our revolutionary leading Party. In fact it weakened the whole revolutionary liberation movement in Iraq. This directly contradicted the principles of Marxism-Leninism which from the ICP should not have departed in deciding their policy toward our Party and our people's revolutionary movement.

The ICP's erroneous views and its stand against our Party and our people's liberation movement were a corollary of expressing the interests of the Arab bourgeoisie in Iraq, not the interests of the workers. Indeed, the interests of the working class and the Arab people in Iraq do not contradict the interest of our Kurdish people in self-determination and in achieving its educational, political and economic goals.

Animosity toward our Party and the movement of our people only serves the interests of the avaricious bourgeoisie seeking to selfishly exploit Kurdistan and control its markets. The ICP's misdirected antagonistic position toward our Party, which represents the Kurdish liberation movement, had created isolationism, narrow nationalist and at times bigoted views, in general with our Party, as a reaction to the ICP's unfair campaigns and especially led to mistakes and temptations within our Party Leadership.

7. Reactionary and imperialist propaganda, which goes back as far as the era of the monarchy, has played a role against our Party and our People's Liberation Movement, which they described as separatist in order to isolate it from the Arab movement and to create a hostile front.

This view continues to be seen with many government officials, including politicians, administrators, military commanders and others. All the negative publicity and propaganda created an atmosphere of doubt and caution within the Republic's government and leaders vis-à-vis our Party and the Kurdish liberation movement, despite our Party and people's loyalty and struggle to preserve the Republic, enhance the Kurdish-Arab brotherhood, and to foil reactionary and imperialist plots. Our Party was compelled to establish contacts with all sides, including representatives of the rightist wing in the government which is demanding [Arab] unity, in order to negate the accusation of separatism, which in turn facilitated distancing Party leadership from the democratic front influenced by comrades who conducted these contacts.

Our dear comrade:
The immense responsibility we are faced with at this critical juncture in the history of our Party made it necessary to be very frank in pointing out our mistakes and deviations so as to put an end to them. We believe that our sincere and unbiased recognition of our own mistakes is the best guarantor of our Party's progress to play its historic role in leading our people's struggle for peace, liberation and democracy. We ask you to contribute with us to measures dealing with any errors, shortcomings and deviations, identifying those responsible and punishing them.

We trust that the efforts of our sincere comrades will succeed.

Salih Rushdi (Hiwa)	Nijad (Kaweh)	Khasro Tawfiq (Nabaz)
Central Comm. Member	Central Comm. Member	Central Comm. Member

Translation from Arabic of Document No. 31

Dear Mr. President
Comrade Members of the Central Committee

Revolutionary Greetings:

In its meeting on December 22, 1958, the Politburo decided to call for a regular Central Committee meeting on January 5, 1959 at the Politburo Headquarters which will require your presence earlier than the designated time. The Politburo is preparing an agenda that includes the following:

1. Reading and discussing the Politburo's report.
2. Determining the possibility of and need for a Party Congress.
3. Deliberating a resolution to establish a party for all Kurdistan.
4. Studying the circumstances of our Revolution, and the means to enhance its correct democratic orientation and NUF role in this regard.
5. Taking necessary measures to augment party unity; how to rally the masses and prepare cadres.
6. Mending Party prestige and organization based on past experience including youth, student and other mass and social organizations.

Kurdistan Democratic Party
The Politburo

[stamped]
No.: 42
Date: December 23, 1958

Translation of Document No. 32

Bakhtiyar and Majeed are the noms de guerre for Salih al-Hayderi and Hameed Othman, respectively.

Massoud Barzani

To: The Honorable President of the Party,
Honored Comrades of the Central Committee

Revolutionary greetings

As you know, our Kurdistan Democratic Party suffers from ideological, political and organizational difficulties. These are not new. They date as far back as its founding in 1946. They stem from the fact that the Party has not succeeded in gaining maturity or securing the wherewithal needed to become a vanguard party despite its constant claims to be one. Changing the party's name, adopting Marxism-Leninism before 1956, and forming a new (united) party did not change party essence. It remains a national democratic one. Changing its leading members did not change its class nature. Since the July 14 Revolution, the dilemma of leadership has become more salient and party responsibilities have become more diversified and complex. The KDP failed to play a leading role despite its successes in areas of cooperation with the national front and other forces.

As days passed, it became more urgent to solve differences with the ICP on an ideological basis, because no problem can be solved in Kurdistan or in Iraq as a whole without the ICP. The National Cooperation Accord was a great introductory step to resolving the unity issue which our Central Committee considered the main issue to be achieved after attaining cooperation.

Obviously, in our Party there are varied views about the unity issue. The prevalent idea until now has been to achieve unity by dissolving the ICP organizations in

Kurdistan. Another view is to proclaim Communism and change the name of our party to the Communist Party of Kurdistan. Based on our experience and after analyzing circumstances in light of our expertise within the KDP, we find it necessary to offer our view to the Central Committee to discuss in its first meeting and to present to the next Congress, so that the Party will have the final say in this regard.

Just by changing Party name from "Democratic" to "Communist" or by just adopting Marxist ideology in Party literature, the state of Party leadership, organization and ideology will not change. Such a change will hinder the solving of the issue of unity with the ICP. Our Party is solidly fixed in a national democratic and patriotic frame and will not be affected by changing persons or names. The KDP was founded as a historical and national necessity and will preserve its national democratic and patriotic character. Therefore, our best course is full solidarity with the ICP and strong ties to the Kurdish masses. These traits are two sides of the same coin, inseparable because enhancing ties to the masses requires strong ties of struggle with the ICP and vice versa. Therefore, in our view, neither changing the Party's name nor proclaiming Marxism will serve the Kurdish cause and the joint struggle against imperialism. A correct and bold solution applicable to the conditions of democratic and patriotic revolution in Iraq and the common cause of the Kurdish people is to preserve the ICP's local chapters and integrate them in a dual organization inside our Democratic Party, provided that the main mass activities are under the name of the Democratic Party. Later, a more mature study can be conducted regarding the best form of social organizations in Kurdistan. With our highest regards.

January 28, 1959

Bakhtiyar
Politburo Member

Majeed
Politburo Member

Translation from Kurdish of Document No. 33

Shorish is the nom de guerre of Nuri Ahmad Taha. Other noms de guerre mentioned in the letter are Lazgin for Hamza Abdullah, Tishk for Ibrahim Ahmad, Nabaz for Khasro Tawfiq, Salih for Salih al-Hayderi and Mulla Majeed for Hameed Othman.
Massoud Barzani

Baghdad, January 29, 1959

Comrade President of the United Democratic Party of Kurdistan, respectfully:

Revolutionary Greetings. Because I consider myself truly loyal to my Party, President and people, I find it necessary to not hold back from reporting mistakes I see. I report them so you can deal with them before it is too late, for our Party is near collapse.

1. The prestige of our Party and of a number of our comrades has been damaged, which deterred you from approaching the Party after you returned. However, with your wisdom, sincerity and knowledge, you continued the struggle to rid the Party of its damaged reputation.

2. The negative statements attributed to us were mainly untrue. A very few were true, but did not include all Central Committee members.

3. A Party decision to return Comrade Najat to work in Suleimaniyya angered Comrade Lazgin. He insisted that unless Najat remained in Baghdad, he would resign. We were coerced into agreeing that Comrade Kaweh remains to avoid the Boss's wrath, for we thought he might influence you to oppose us. Thus, Kaweh remained here with Comrade Nabaz and the defeated opportunist Comrade Salih Rushdi. They sent you a report which led to anarchy and almost destroyed our Party. In addition, he led a propaganda campaign among the masses and encouraged Party members to visit and speak against some Central Committee members. They swayed you into suspecting Tishk and Jalal, and requesting their suspension. To preserve our Party's unity, we suspended both comrades, who did not object. Furthermore, both worked with more enthusiasm than before. However, instead of expelling Comrade Nabaz, he was brought to the Politburo based on your view, contrary to organizational principles of a revolutionary Party. He and the other two cowardly and defeated opportunist comrades risked splitting and destroying the Party. At any rate, he reached the Politburo.

4. It had been decided that the Politburo would meet on the 25th. However at the first meeting, Mr. Hamza Abdullah had said that Khasro would stay here permanently. I asked why? He said because this has been decided. I asked who decided it? He replied, Mulla Mustafa. I said, "I disagree. This is a Politburo decision." He said, "The majority of the Politburo has agreed, and the majority is, Mulla Mustafa, Khasro and myself." I told him I would go to the President and inform him that we are in disagreement. Let's move to the conversation on the 28th of the month. We were to report to the President's house at 8 o'clock. I arrived at ten minutes to seven. As I arrived at the gate, there was a jeep leaving your house and I waved to it to stop. I saw Khasro in the jeep, and I asked him, where he was going. He said, Comrade Mulla Mustafa has been out since this morning. If he returns, he will not be able to meet with us, so we are leaving." I told him, "You are leaving but we will meet without him." He replied that he was very tired and he had a headache and was unable to stay. He was going to rest. I told him, "Well, go but Mulla Majeed will not be able to leave Kirkuk again." They left. At 8 o'clock, both Mulla Majeed and Comrade Salih arrived. I told them what had happened, and both were very upset. Mulla Majeed wanted to meet you to complain but you were very busy in the north. We had to leave. On the way back, I told my comrades that I could no longer deal with it since the clique, Hamza, Khasro, Najat and others, continue to work together. They said that they also felt the clique's work but not as critically as I did. After much debate, I told them, "Well, what if we go to Najat's house and find the three comrades there! Would you be convinced of what is being done secretly, and that they consider themselves the Politburo?" They said, "Let's go." We went to Najat's house. I entered first unexpectedly. All three comrades were seated. Before Mr. Lazgin, was a written letter. They were disturbed, and Lazgin hastily tried to hide it so I would not see it. Immediately, I returned and called Majeed and Salih. We went in and sat down without gripe or complaint.

Dear respected Comrade, is this party loyalty?! These three and Salih Rushdi need to be taught a good lesson. You ought to know that these comrades are driving the Party to extinction. They work for their goals and to test old intentions. Otherwise, I swear you to Your Honor, what does it mean for the Ross and Khasro not to meet with the Politburo, but they go to Najat's house to meet. Like other Party comrades, I have been hurt because of my Party work. I ignored it, and continued to obey Party orders under all circumstances. However, after this, I do not want to put my fate in their hands. Regardless of their intentions, they are driving the party to destruction. Therefore, I suggest the following:

(1) Expel Comrade Khasro from the Politburo and ban him from coming to Baghdad. Let him go to Mosul. (2) Expel Comrade Hamza from the Politburo, and have him work

for you here. (3) Return Comrade Najat to Suleimaniyya: a. to quit his bad attitude, and b. Suleimaniyya needs him for his knowledge of Youth affairs. (4) The Politburo should temporarily go to Kirkuk until other comrades return and Congress is held, provided the Politburo consists of comrades Hameed, Salih and Hilmi.

My respected Comrade, if these measures are not taken, the Party will face the risk of extinction.

Note: The Central Committee decided not to announce the suspension of Tishk and Jalal.

Therefore, please check how Shawkat Aqrawi learned about the expulsion of these two comrades.

—Long live the KDP, the people and the president's loyalists.

—Down with the selfish opportunists.

Shorish

Translation from Kurdish of Document No. 34

A Report by a Group of Advanced Party Cadre

To: The Honorable Central Committee,

Revolutionary Greetings:

After a careful reading of the Central Committee Resolutions, and the regular publication regarding membership fees, rumors spread among Party members. All members and cells were unhappy. Rumor had it that certain members of the Central Committee were expelled as the Statement No. 16 said that membership dues from Rizgar are not to be sent to Jalal, and are to be sent to the authorized (S) instead. Here, rumors and chaos prevailed, because the Politburo and the Central Committee could have solved the problem easily, correctly and conscientiously, if they had wanted to; without the members' knowledge and without spreading rumors among Party ranks. It is not a difficult problem to solve. Unlike the problem of convincing our dear friend, the ICP, that 'the Kurds are a nation'. This has taken so much time to realize that Party confidentiality was breached, and the names of all Central Committee and Politburo members were made public. Such an act smells of sabotage, not reform. Central Committee Resolutions (page 3, distribution) point out confession and skepticism within the Party spread. In our view, this is incorrect. Members and the masses did not feel deviation from the Party line, even if it existed. It should not have been spread as such because it led to many rumors in Party ranks. True, we do not claim that our Party never erred, because no one is perfect. Only those who do not work and remain constant will not err, just as their teacher says, "Who does not work, does not err."

Page 6 of the Central Committee Resolutions makes it clear that we must work well with the ICP and that we must remain silent even when they err against us. Frankly, it appears that the Politburo and the Central Committee are not aware of the reality and of the ICP chapter in Kurdistan. Comrades, you must realize that the ICP considers us a bourgeois nationalist democratic party as they explained in their pamphlet "In Response to Nationalist Bourgeois Ideas" which stated "The KDP is not a Marxist-Leninist but a nationalist bourgeois, organization." Hence, we were described for a while as American, separatist, the party of Saeed Qazzaz and Tawfiq Wahbi, mercenaries and at times they called our Comrade patriot Hameed demented. While Tarique al-Sha'ab [People's Path] waged its daily campaigns, our comrades generally responded rationally and correctly, and acted in conformity with the Cooperation Accord. Furthermore, they spread rumors against the hero of the Kurdish people, Mustafa Barzani, chewing as beasts the words of Mukarram Talabani by saying that if Mulla Mustafa Barzani had lived in a village, he would have learned more than what he learned in Russia. In addition, they described him as a tribal chief, a feudalist, and say that Mulla Mustafa's revolt was a tribal revolt as Comrade Justa heard from Comrade Hameed that he said that they did not allow him to write an article about the Revolution. Central Committee comrades; why should we be silent any more?! At any rate, an objective response to these accusations is necessary, because silence means weakness. As we try to approach them, they move away.

On page 7 of the Central Committee Resolutions, it is clear that there has been a special leap to the left lately. But it is said that it has not been felt. If it existed, why has it not been made public? Let's suppose that it is true, then, was it the conduct of the whole Party or only one member? If it was of only one member, why is the whole Party accused, if it is not to destroy the Party! The ICP is exploiting this situation to further its own interests and to split party ranks.

Based on the Resolutions and the internal newsletter, much discord is obvious. Differences will ultimately drag our Party onto dangerous slopes. These rumors and chaos are to be dealt with by holding a Conference according to the Charter as soon as possible, if it is not possible now. It is imperative to bring all comrades together without delay in a Conference to strike mercilessly at devious elements. But break Party unity. Any delay at a time in which our Party is taking root amongst the masses will be a serious crime. History enjoins our courageous and experienced President, Mustafa Barzani to end these rumors and chaos, to remove all obstacles before our Party that destroy its unity. Regardless of who they are, these elements who want to destroy our Party are to be struck mercilessly, especially during this critical time during which our Party is deepening its roots among the masses of Kurdistan. Therefore, holding this Conference is extremely necessary, for animosity and rumors are plentiful, and the names of all Central Committee and Politburo members are known.

Among the Central Committee Resolutions on page 9, a Congress must be held to elect a legitimate and responsible Central Committee. This means that the current Central Committee is not legitimate and must be replaced by a legitimate one. It is worth mentioning that the internal newsletter dated February 18, stated that the Central Committee Resolutions must be followed . . . well, when the Central Committee is not legitimate, why are its Resolutions legitimate then? Again, it states that the Politburo has asked to implement these Resolutions. We do not know why the Central Committee is not legitimate whilst its Resolutions are legitimate! And everyone knows that the Central Committee is the one that elects the Politburo.

It is unfortunate for the Central Committee to make such errors in our Party publications. We all demand a Conference be held as soon as possible to strike at all elements working to confuse the Party program and to destroy it.

[signed] Posta, Shakh, Azad, Shirzad, Safeen, Das Comrade Pishko did not attend this meeting.

Please submit this report to President M. Barzani.

Translation from Arabic of Document No. 35

Manifesto of the United Democratic Party of Kurdistan (UPDK)

On the 14th of this month, six months will have passed since the July 14 Revolution culminated in the founding of the Republic. To inform and properly guide the Kurdish masses, we wish to briefly express KDP views and attitude regarding social and political developments as well as current policies and what ought to be done in the best interest of the people and the Republic in light of President Abd al-Karim Qasim's speech on the National Day of our heroic army.

A great fact proven by reality is that the July 14 Revolution was and will forever remain the people's Revolution, regardless of class, in which the army was the vanguard. Loyal sons, the army had responded to the spirit of the people. Together, the army and people moved to crush tyranny and injustice, to liberate the Iraqi people from despotism, corruption and to break the chains that as the country's veteran leader said for so long enslaved them and hindered their progress. By nature, the Revolution was not a military coup d'état as imperialistic propaganda tries to cast doubts about its popular support among our people.

In Kurdistan and in Basra alike, the Iraqi people took part in the revolution. As the army controlled strategic points in Baghdad, the masses inhibited forces of suppression in the provincial, district and subdistrict centers forcing administrators and many army officers to either submit to the Republic or be dismissed. The Kurdish masses in Suleimaniyya, for example, firmly controlled government functions and kept law and order for three days, ensuring the loyalty of government officials, military commanders and police chiefs to the Republic, after which they turned all responsibility over to representatives of the Republic while remaining on guard ready to sacrifice for the Revolution. Furthermore, the populace has taken a more active role in preserving the progressive, democratic and patriotic path of the July 14 Revolution over the past six months.

This will not inhibit our people's active role in the future to attain the goals of the revolution. No enemy barrier is too great to break through now or in the future. Looking into the future through these wonderful examples, we find that the July 14 Revolution is a people's revolution, a revolution of Arabs, Kurds, and all honorable people of Iraq. It is the revolution of the masses of workers, peasants, soldiers, officers and patriots. This is the view of our United Democratic Party of Kurdistan, and it is a realistic view.

Another principle of the glorious Revolution, boldly proclaimed by the President, the revolutionary son of Iraq, in his speech, is the principle of the people's sovereignty, as he said, "I proclaim to you all that people are the force to dictate their will anywhere, anytime, and we in the Republic of Iraq, are guarded by this force." Naturally, people cannot dictate their will unless they have authority. The people's authority is their control over their destiny and homeland. The Iraqi people are comprised of two main nations, Arab and Kurdish. The government then belongs to both main nations. Since it was founded on the remains of the imperialistic reactionary monarchy, it is a new authority signifying the will of the vast majority of the people of Iraq. It signifies the will of both main nations. Hence, the national sovereignty belongs to the masses of both nations. This is exactly the patriotic content of the July 14 Revolution.

The masses of Kurdistan have all the right to exercise power and authority along with their Arab brothers in Iraq according to the principles affirmed by the Revolution and proclaimed by leader Abd al-Karim Qasim. Vital issues need quick solutions from the Republic's government. Bordering Iran and Turkey, Iraqi Kurdistan does not enjoy PRM protection, specifically the Barzanis, of whom every honorable free patriot will testify to their sacrifices defending the Republic, leader of Iraq Abd al-Karim Qasim, and patriot Mustafa Barzani. The administrative system needs radical reform to bring in sincere local patriots to respond to the needs and reforms demanded by the Kurdish masses.

Our Provisional Constitution stated that Arabs and Kurds are associates in Iraq. It authorized the Kurds to exercise their national rights within the framework of Iraqi unity. The simplest of their association and rights is enjoying their educational rights in their language, and the use of Kurdish in courts in their cities.

Strangely, the simplest people observe that censorship bars the Kurds from using the word Kurdistan to refer to their beloved homeland in the press and publications. It has been said in many government and political circles that the name of Kurdistan is barred because it implies the separation of Iraqi Kurdistan from the rest of Iraq. Sincerely and frankly, we tell our government and the leader of Iraq Abd al-Karim Qasim that such skepticism opens a reach in the unity and solidarity of the two bravely and sincerely fraternal nations. Among the fruits of our popular revolution is the Republic's policy to defend peace. "Our army will be factored in for stability, and will defend peace in this country and this region." As the President proclaimed, peace is the cause of the people in Iraq, in the Middle East and in the world. It is the primary cause for all peoples of the world, and our policy is to avoid war and defend peace. This is a policy dictated by the principles of a popular revolution in the second half of the twentieth century. It is dictated by the interests of our people and the interests of all peoples in the world.

As a policy, our Republic follows the principle of non-allied positive neutralism, a policy to break away from the aggressive war oriented alliances of imperialism, to stop capitalists from exploiting our natural resources and our wealth. With this policy, the Republic has expanded peace and ended one of the forts of war and aggression in the "free world" of which Iraq was previously a part. The path chosen by the Republic does not mean severing cooperative and friendly ties based on mutual interests with other countries. Non-alliance, in our Revolution's view, means indifference, refraining from all bias against a socio-political system in any country. Positive neutralism and non-alliance do not preclude political, educational and economic cooperation with the USSR, the People's Republic of China and all socialist countries. On the contrary, cooperation as such augments Iraq's independence, economy and progress. The USSR and socialist countries wish Iraq progress and prosperity. Without their support, the Republic of Iraq will be a weak prey to imperialist countries.

One of the Revolution's achievements is the agrarian reform which aims to end feudalism, and transfer land ownerships to peasants. This is sufficient to show the democratic content of the Revolution. It has allowed the democratic forces to organize in a unified patriotic front to defend the interests of the people, preserve the revolutionary achievements and defend the Republic against internal and external enemies. The more progressive democratic forces are making great strides in the Republic led by hero Abd al-Karim Qasim, toward better cooperation.

In Iraqi Kurdistan, where only our UDPK and ICP really exist, both parties are collaborating under the banner of the National Cooperation Accord, which is inseparable from the NUF. Despite the fact that Iraqi masses have rallied around the NUF, with the vast majority tending to parties with a progressive and democratic orientation, there still are residues of monarchists, remains of reactionaries, fake nationalists, students of dictatorship under the pretext of Arab unity, and Turanis, who continue to find fertile grounds in Iraq to implement their conspiracies with help from spies of imperialism. All because the government and leader of Iraq avoid using necessary decisiveness against their destructive and hostile designs against the Republic, the independence of Iraq and people's national interests.

We trust that the leader of the July 14 Revolution and his government will in the end respond to the people's demands to purge the state system of those who exploit the Republic's democratic protection guaranteed by the constitution. Constitution's harmony with the national and patriotic aspirations is the hope of all Kurds, in Iraq as well as in Syria, Iran and Turkey. They consider the birth of our beloved Republic the birth of their national and patriotic sovereignty, which they have not enjoyed for generations.

Many have concluded that barring the name Kurdistan means, barring the Kurds from establishing their special social organizations such as the Kurdistan Student Union, the Youth Union of Kurdistan and others. Such preclusions contradict the spirit of the Revolution, the Revolution of Kurds and Arabs, the spirit of our Constitution which is based on the will of the people, the will of Kurds and Arabs alike.

—Life and glory to our Iraqi Republic, the Republic of Kurds and Arabs.
—Long live the able guide of our Republic, leader Abd al-Karim Qasim.
—Long live fraternity and solidarity of the Arab and Kurdish nations.

Politburo of the
United Democratic Party of Kurdistan
January 17, 1959

Translation from Kurdish of Document No. 36

A Report Submitted by KDP's Suleimaniyya Local Committee

February 16, 1959

To: Comrade Mustafa Barzani, President of the United Democratic Party of Kurdistan, Respectfully

We are delighted for the United Democratic Party of Kurdistan's (UDPK) embrace of Marxism-Leninism, a glorious achievement, a step which the majority of our comrades deem important in our Party's life. We, at the Suleimaniyya Local Committee, clearly assert that this glorious act will advance and enable our party to fully lead the vast majority of the masses of Kurdistan, to advance our revolutionary struggle, and prevent any deviation from the Marxist-Leninist path.

The UPDK can lead workers, peasants and citizens of Kurdistan effectively to preserve our beloved Democratic Republic and for peace and cooperation with all peoples of the world especially the socialist camp led by the great friend of he Kurdish nation and peoples of the world, the USSR. Because of this belief, we beg to intensify the struggle to cultivate Marxism-Leninism in UDPK ranks. Anyone who tries, for any reason, to block our Marxist-Leninist path and does not understand the gist of ideas held by members and supporters of our Democratic Party, is to be isolated with no link to the vast majority of the masses of Kurdistan. By proclaiming Marxism-Leninism, we trust that our party will play a major political role in Kurdistan and Iraq. It will guide workers, peasants and all citizens in Kurdistan to the correct path.

However, to suppress Marxism in any way is to mean that the UPDK will rally the white collars. Isolated from the people, our Party's leading role of 15 years will go in vain, and will deal a powerful blow to all forces of democracy and Communism in Kurdistan and Iraq. A case in point is the move of more than 200 ICP members to the UDPK as a direct result of espousing Marxism.

Therefore, on behalf of the hundreds of members and thousands of supporters of the UDPK in Suleimaniyya City, we implore you to personally represent us to affirm Marxist-Leninist ideas, and not to allow anyone to lead our Party off this path. We believe that Communism is desirable in Kurdistan, and no organization has challenged it. Brutally and with all its might, imperialism suppressed all Kurdish revolts for independence after World War I. Therefore, the Kurdish people have seen the ugly face of international imperialism and learned at first hand that it alone is our enemy. During World War II, the revolts in Kurdistan came face to face with international imperialism and came to trust that the socialist camp led by the great bastion of peace, the USSR, is the only historic friend we have. Based on these significant political provisos and the current class changes in Kurdistan, the Kurds need their own leading Marxist-Leninist party. Until now, it has been true that the people of Kurdistan could not play their historic role without a vanguard party because our Party has greatly affected ICP ideas and beliefs and prevented its deviation from Marxism-Leninism in Kurdistan since for more than seven years the ICP did not recognize the very existence of Kurdistan, its unique circumstances, and its different mode of struggle. For a long time, the ICP vehemently refused to recognize the Kurdish national traits. But because of the UDPK, the leading party of the struggle of the masses in Kurdistan, the ICP came to recognize that Kurdistan is partitioned and that the Kurdish nation has all its national traits such as language, psychological make-up, and a homeland . . . and as our respected guide stated, "Each nation has its own path to reach socialism." He explained that, "The struggle of Eastern peoples is extremely complex in comparison to the struggle of European peoples." Therefore, in light of the mentioned provisos, Kurdistan has its special circumstances and the existence of our Party is a dire necessity for the people of Kurdistan in order to reach the socialist stage.

In the name of the UDPK's Local Committee of Suleimaniyya, we appeal to our dear President to work with party masses to always enhance and advance the Party, and seek assistance from the socialist countries and the democracy front so our Party can play its historic role. We call [on you] not to deviate now from the Party path, to augment the Marxist-Leninist orientation day after day, to destroy those who have worked for decades to suppress the struggle of the people of Kurdistan.

We have affirmed that the UDPK's problems are caused by disharmony and the ongoing conflict among Central Committee members, including the Politburo. It has risked division and the loss of our long years of struggle. It only serves those who try to impose their views on the Party. Our Party is not for one or two peoples; it is not the party of individuals. It is the party of the masses of Kurdistan. This Party has sacrificed much, and many among its rank and file were arrested and executed in defense of our principles and because of a few individuals.

On these grounds, our Party is the vanguard of the workers and peasants. The condition of the Committee above is not in the interest of the people of Kurdistan. The struggle and discord among Central Committee members is hurting our party. Therefore, we ask our beloved President, and on behalf of thousands of workers and peasants, to objectively and wisely put an end to this problem to preserve Party unity and lead it out of this grave danger.

To deal with the current struggle within the Central Committee and Politburo and to avoid destroying Party unity, we recommend a Party Congress as soon as possible to expel elements responsible for slowing Party progress and planting seeds of division and betraying Marxism-Leninism, and to bring new loyal believers to the Central Committee and Politburo.

Note: To our dear President, we affirm the following:

The best course of action for members is to preserve the UDPK's unity at any cost and circumvent anyone who erroneously wants to destroy our Party. You personally represent all those who have wholeheartedly struggled for long years in order for our Party to fully lead the poor, the toilers and patriots in Kurdistan. Never allow any one to divide this bastion, because we trust that you will play an important role in accomplishing what has been said in this letter. We have been deeply wounded because of the chaos in the Central Committee which forced us to inform our President of our views and that of thousands of members and supporters of our Democratic Party. We implore you to personally send a committee of sincere and able comrades to learn members' problems in more detail. We at the Suleimaniyya Local Committee will continue to inform you of all significant problems.

Let the banner of Marxism-Leninism rise high on the peaks of Kurdistan.
Long live the UDPK under the leadership of Mustafa Barzani
Long live all Marxist-Leninist parties in the world.
... Forward

The United Democratic Party of Kurdistan
Local Committee of Suleimaniyya
Baghdad

February 16, 1959

Translation from Arabic of Document No. 37

Zal was the nom de guerre of the late Hayder Mohammed Amin, head of the KDP's Local Committee in Arbil.

Massoud Barzani

UNITED DEMOCRATIC PARTY OF KURDISTAN

To: The Politburo

Comrade patriots, greetings of national struggle. In expression of my faith and trust in our vanguard party of our beloved Kurdistan, I present this report to you.

Comrades, I am pleased that you are aware of malicious groups leveling accusations at our Party and comrades. First they accused us of separatism, second of chauvinism, yet again of being agents of imperialism. We are constantly accused of collaborating with this party or that person. The source is obvious. I want to inform you that recently accusations have surfaced in Party ranks and perhaps in the leadership against sincere comrades who struggled and faithfully sacrificed for the Party, people and homeland. Charges clearly indicate that there are in our ranks saboteurs and impressionable individuals whose conduct serves only the enemies of our striving people.

They are as bats, which menace at night and vanish in the day, to hide their conduct. They work behind the scenes, provoke Party members, accuse sincere comrades of sympathizing with tribal chieftains, and antagonizing the such-and-such party. These charges were circulated and attributed to comrades A, C, 'A, 'A and others. Furthermore, they were involved in subversive activities, created cliques within the Party, and provoked members to rebel against our leadership. I have learned from credible sources that on the night of December 21, 1958 a group of them met with our leader Mulla Mustafa Barzani at his house. They falsely accused Party leaders of founding a new party and leadership. The meeting was tense, and the President guided them to the right path, that is, to rally around our leading party until a number of our patriots abroad return home. Then this problem can be dealt with. But they refused and insisted that the President should agree. After 15 days, they responded to the President in a Memorandum.

Comrades, we know that the Party Charter is clear to the leading Party members. All members have the right to criticize and self-criticize. Have they ever criticized before and the leadership did not respond?! Or is it that the Party does not apply the principle of democratic centralism, criticism and self-criticism? Or is it that they violated the Party Charter regardless? Violators must be punished as soon as possible, because their conduct serves the enemies of our people. Remember that our Party is based on democratic centralism. It is a party of ironclad loyalty based on criticism and self-criticism. It does not and will not allow splitters and anarchists in the Party. It must purge its ranks of such individuals without mercy. Forward, comrades, under the leadership of our leader Mulla Mustafa Barzani.

Zal
December 22, 1959

Translation from Arabic of Document No. 38

Zal was the nom de guerre of the late Hayder Mohammed Amin, head of the KDP's Local Committee in Arbil.

Massoud Barzani

United Democratic Party of Kurdistan

To: the Central Committee

Comrades, revolutionary greetings

According to Article 2, Chapter C, Paragraph 1, [on] the right to criticize and offer explanations, I am submitting this report to clarify, inform and criticize, as all members of our Party have the right to.

Comrades, through the Committee Chairman, I received the Politburo decision revoking my membership in the Local Committee on March 2, 1959. While I was happy and proud to receive it from higher Party authorities and glad to abide by it, I found it unfair because of the reason cited at this specific time. The Politburo may believe me wrong as I object, calling the decision unfair. If I am wrong I apologize.

Comrades, for your information, the Politburo decision describes me as incompetent. I wish to state that I carried out my duties as a loyal soldier at the worst hours for our Party masses. I am and will remain loyal to the end. I defended Party unity, secrets and literature as I continued our struggle during the worst era of terror. I faithfully upheld Party principles during my tenure at the Local Committee. Other responsible comrades fled and abandoned their Party duties. I mean those who were and still are members of the Central Committee. Alone I shouldered Local Committee obligations. After the glorious July 14 Revolution, the same comrades became competent, valiant and heroes leading our Revolutionary Party.

Comrades, who was competent in times of terror? Was it I or the comrades! Or did they become patriots after the July 14 Revolution? In the era of our beloved

Republic, the era of peace, stability and freedom, I am called incompetent! Is this the reason for the Politburo's decision?

If competence is only after the July 14 Revolution, in the era of peace and freedom, not when terror reigned, then I neither agree nor trust the comrades who fled only to return today as heroes and patriots leading our Party and raising banners high as if they were heroes of the Free Algiers Revolution, proud and competent! Therefore, I consider the Politburo's decision unfair and irresponsible. And if this is how the Politburo defines competency, then I conclude that the reason was not competency, but that untold reasons led to this decision. Furthermore, I can cite the names of Local Committee members who are not competent to be Party members, let alone members of the Local Committee. They are unable to discharge their responsibilities, or even attend meetings! In addition to their poor reputation inside and outside Party ranks, they spend their nights drinking in bars. Is this competency? Or is it that the Politburo is unaware of divulging Party secrets in such places!

While the Politburo issued its decision to expel me for incompetency, another decision was issued to the contrary. That is to replace me with two comrades. Who are they? They are Comrades Mohammed Karim and Dawood. I wish to ask your Committee, does the Politburo wish to raise the adequacy level of Local Committee members based on education, prestige or competency? Or does it do the opposite?!

I have learned that Comrade Mohammed Karim's reputation is not so good in Suleimaniyya and that his transfer from there is directly related to it. Our Party Charter bans the membership of the disreputable according to Article 2 of Chapter 2. How did the Politburo promote him to member of a local Committee? Isn't this a violation? Comrades, if education was everything, then it is wrong and neither serves Party interests nor raises the adequacy level of local Committees.

As to our second comrade, Dawood, he joined the Party a short time before the Revolution. I ask your Committee to decide. I find it strange for the Politburo to decide without examining either his reputation among the Fayli Kurds or his understanding of Marxism-Leninism. Furthermore, the two comrades of the Local Committee, Mohammed and Abd al-Hussein, know much about their issues, if they really want Party interests, and not their personal interests. Only a month ago, both objected to accepting him as a Party member. How did the Politburo promoted him to the Local Committee? They know his bad reputation and history, and his Party loyalty is questionable. They called him an opportunist, said that he worked for the ICP and us at the same time. Nominated by the ICP, indeed, he ran opposing our candidate at the Fayli School. This was their view of him. Is it possible that in only two months he changed his character, reputation, history and struggle as well as his nightly drinking circles? I do not believe it!

Comrades, I wish to inform you that the Politburo often commits organizational and political errors, issues repressive measure and others. As their impact is easily not seen, we all pay in consequence. Eventually the facts will emerge. I trust that the truth about competent, sincere members loyal to the principles and unity of our Party will unfold, as well as the truth about incompetents and opportunists in our Party. Then, it is imperative to side with the truth and fight mistakes. This is hard for some Party comrades to do.

We must be bold in educating and criticizing comrades and ourselves when blunders and deviations are committed. This is the way to become a pure, sincere, progressive and revolutionary Party. We must examine our ideology and correct our errors. We must view issues and comrades according to Marxist-Leninist theory and a consistent Party attitude. We must adopt correct positions and a suitable mode for our revolutionary struggle. We must not work for our narrow personal interests even if it delays our march.

Comrades, Politburo members, in my view, are working for their own narrow personal interests, which is wrong. Personal frictions should be fought and uprooted from the Party. We must determine who is right and who is wrong; who is competent and who is not, to return to our principles, and to prevent the Politburo from committing mistakes and harming Party prestige. This is the way.

Comrades, before I close this letter, I wish to reiterate that I will remain a loyal soldier in the vanguard of Party masses, ready to sacrifice for our Party principles to liberate our beloved Kurdistan, and to struggle according to Marxist-Leninist principles, which are the true path of out Party for fruitful revolutionary action.

Always forward, in the vanguard of our party masses, and under the leadership of our heroic leader, Mulla Mustafa Barzani.

Zal
March 7, 1959

Translation from Arabic of Document No. 39

A Call From the KDP's Local Committee In Arbil

United Democratic Party of Kurdistan

A call from the Arbil Local Committee

Striving compatriots,

Revolutionary Greetings:
In its January session, the Central Committee and Politburo issued a Resolution which this Local Committee finds it necessary to analyze and explain to all Party members and supporters.

After in-depth, objective and scientific analysis to assess the Central Committee resolution in light of Party activities and its meager achievements in the favorable period that followed the abiding July 14 Revolution, and after careful evaluation of the factors that hindered Party progress, obstructed the broadening and deepening of its popular base among the masses of Kurdistan as they contributed to its isolation, accusation of chauvinism, rightism and separatism, we concluded that two conflicting tendencies emerged after the July 14 Revolution. One tendency is the nationalist bourgeoisie and the other is democratic. Our Party has drifted along with the nationalist bourgeois as it moved away from eleven democratic forces. An obvious sign of this move toward the extreme right is the failure to join the National Front, since participation would have advanced the interest of Kurdistan and the Kurdish cause.

For narrow gains, our Party gave up fundamental demands of the citizens of Iraqi Kurdistan, demands that are strongly tied to the triumph of democracy. It failed to mobilize and lead the masses, failed to disseminate its ideas and principles to take root among the people. Party failure is attributed to our lethargic leaders instead of vigorous work, to opposing the ICP, and to drifting away from the Republic's leaders.

After careful evaluation of these facts, the Local Committee in Arbil has decided to support the Party's latest steps, and sees them to be correct, worthy and valuable means to correct past errors and return our party to its genuine path. Our Local Committee salutes these bold and decisive steps, will pursue them precisely, and stand fast against anyone who tries to oppose them, to subvert or divide the Party under the pretext that these Resolutions will lead to assimilation and ICP control. These assumptions are baseless. In fact, our

Committee believes these revolutionary steps by the Politburo will solidify and deepen our Party roots among the masses of Kurdistan, in cooperation with a friendly ICP. They serve the best interests of the Kurds', Kurdistan and the Republic.

Our Committee calls upon all comrades to defend Party unity and discipline, to strike subversive and anarchist activities with an iron fist, to persistently struggle to crush the rightist degenerates, to cultivate correct ideas among workers, peasants, toilers intelligentsia, and all the masses of Kurdistan, and all who genuinely struggle to preserve the Republic of Iraq, the Republic of Arabs and Kurds, to enrich its democratic content, and to realize the national rights of the freedom-loving Kurdish people.

Comrades, we struggle to eradicate subversive anti-Republic and anti-people gangs, to ensure liberty and democracy, to give land to the peasants, to found heavy industries in all parts of Iraq, to improve the standard of living for Iraqi workers, to befriend and cooperate with the international democratic camp against imperialism and war, A victory achieved by the Revolution against imperialism is a splendid victory for the Kurds and Kurdistan.

Comrades, fight alongside your ICP comrades, and other democratic forces for the common goals of all the masses of Iraq. Forward under the leadership of our Party.

The Local Committee in Arbil
March 2, 1959

Translation from Kurdish of Document No. 40

A Report Submitted by a Number of Party Cadres in Koy Sanjaq

To: UDPK Central Committee and President

Warm revolutionary regards:
We, members of cells meeting with our officers, wish to covey our view regarding Party Resolutions and the Internal Communiqué of the Local Committee in Arbil.

This meeting, discussion and report come after our several verbal and written communications with the Local Committee of Arbil were totally ignored. Therefore, it is imperative to inform a higher committee and the beloved President of our Party of the issue so it is not repeated. Our criticisms are the following:

1. As we read the Resolutions, frankly we sensed contradictions regarding the Politburo's discernment of a rightist drift. We never felt such a move before. We were led to democracy and Marxism. Mistakes should have been dealt with internally without informing ordinary Party members and the unaffiliated public. Falsely, it charged that our Party failed to attract the masses of Kurdistan. The masses of Kurdistan remain attached to us regardless of ICP rumors. Behaving in a friendly manner, we did not argue with them, despite charges of Americanism and separatism. Our Party treated them appropriately, peacefully, and proved our innocence to masses of Kurdistan and their propaganda lies... then, we were branded troublemakers in the Committee. If true, then all of them are responsible. Sad for what they hoped to achieve, instead of reforming the Central Committee, they exposed themselves! This is not dealing with a problem. It is destructive to our party at this critical time in which all reactionary factions are fighting us.

Brothers, you have charged the Party with rightist deviation. Further flexibility is a crime and means giving in to the ICP. We are of Marxism, guided by true Marxism. To the hero claiming deviation and nationalist bourgeoisie, why did you leave your cherished ICP and join our beloved party? Why did you join before knowing that our Party is a bourgeois one? Why did you come to us? Was our Party different then than now? And why did the brothers of H and S do what they did to these two compatriots who travelled the world to introduce the Kurdish liberation movement? They participated in all Congresses. You have personal vendettas against them. Wasn't it brother Ibrahim who shot him? Wasn't it brother Jalal who took the voice of the Kurdish liberation movement around the world? You forgot all that because their enemies wanted to humiliate them and now you are doing the same. Yes, I can prove that there are many contradictions in many places; in Koyé[5] for example, they sympathize with tribal chiefs. Discipline must be through warnings, not paralyzing the Party because of a simple error.... Don't you realize that you are responsible for our people?

2. Later, a statement issued in Arbil under the name of the Local Committee there. It sounded like the Central Committee. I can say that it exposed itself and failed to reach the masses of workers and peasants. It stated that the bourgeois tendency exploited the democratic one. Where were you, patriots of the Arbil Local Committee? I can confidently say that they will vanish after the chaos. Negligent, the Local Committee is now a tool in ICP hands, while they have accused us of everything in the book. They expelled all who had Kurdish nationalist blood in their veins and continue to fight all active elements. Now, they want to convince us that Arbil needs special attention because of its special circumstances! Where is the end? We are almost finished in the city. But, because of the peasants' activism, we continue to be strong. We have learned that they do not want our active presence in the city. This is not only our criticism, but it is the criticism of the masses of Arbil.

3. We find ourselves as tools in their hands. Yes, I agree to friendly cooperation with them but we must not efface ourselves lest this justify the stabbing of the Kurdish movement. Yes, mostly we did our part and believed that it was in the interest of our Party but never to harm anyone.... They told us that as we worked endlessly, they would suspend us for a month.

Cell Officer	Cell member	Cell member	Cell member
Bakhtiyar	Khoshnaw	Drakht	Shakhawan
Cell member	Cell member	Cell member	Cell member
Pasawan	Kaka Khosh	Nabard	Dilsouz-3

Translation from Kurdish of Document No. 41

Ziring is the nom de guerre of Jalil Hoshyar.

Massoud Barzani

To: The President of the UDPK, respectfully:

Warm revolutionary regards:
Since the Politburo began attacking our Party in its publications, like many others, I sensed subversion which over time became clear and salient. As I mentioned in my previous report, the [Polit]bureau had sent its envoy to Arbil on February 26, 1959. After a brief discussion, I was unfairly suspended. A day later, it was revealed to Party and non-Party members alike, including ICP members. In Shaqlawa, a senior and active *peshmerga* comrade who rallied villagers and peasants in the whole region faced the same fate as mine. Now people are quitting our party.

---

5. Most likely he means Koy Sanjaq.

The Arbil Local Committee is pursuing a similar policy. They neglected two very important committees, namely Kandinawa and Qaraj, with affiliates over 500 when I was their contact. They have not been contacted since. They are showing aloofness and quitting. Then, I had asked verbally and in writing to deal with both Committees. They have neglected the villages around Arbil that were never neglected before. They are now. In Arbil city, they continue to expel comrades. For example, one night ten young comrades came to the Center with their weapons during the Mosul conspiracy to guard and they asked Comrade Asim to appoint them. He told them, "We are a political party and have nothing to do with jobs. We do not need those who ask for jobs." He let them go away! This while the Communists scoured the city to employ their supporters especially workers. Ten of these went away angry.

After I was suspended, the Arbil Local Committee added two more members. Not only evading their Party duties, they have suspended the activities of the Peasants' Cooperative purely out of negligence. Both statements issued by our Committee clearly point out subversion. If criticized, they claim that anarchists are plotting. These issues clearly show the risks to our Party, and undoubtedly threaten its very existence. Obviously, any harm or damage to the Party is also harmful to the masses of Kurdistan. Therefore, I ask you to act as soon as possible in a way to preserve our Party unity and advance Party interests.

Sincerely

Ziring

Copy to:

(1) The Politburo, FYI   (2) The Central Committee, FYI as well.

Translation from Kurdish of Document No. 42

A Report Submitted by Ziring, A Central Committee Member; Ziring is the nom de guerre of Jalil Hoshyar.

Massoud Barzani

To: The President of the UDPK, respectfully
      The Politburo of the UDPK
      The Central Committee of the UDPK

Warm revolutionary regards:
Because of our internal problems which threaten the existence of our Party, I, a loyal member, find it necessary to present the following criticism and facts:

My Criticism Regarding Party Publications: The Politburo's disclaimer regarding the published introduction to the Central Committee Resolution in its January session directly contradicts Central Committee Resolutions. Only one day after the meetings, Comrade Shorishgeir said: "I was expelled from the Bureau for no reason requiring such action. I left upon the President's request to preserve Party unity. If you think that I did something illegal, you ought to tell me before the Central Committee so I can defend myself. Otherwise, I will not let the Politburo issue anything unfair in this regard." Comrade Tishk said the same thing. Comrade Lazgin responded "No. No, there is no such thing. We are not issuing anything about either one of you. If we want to issue an 'explanation' we will say: 'based on Party interest, only organizational changes were made.'" Then I asked: "What if Party members asked what the changes are?" Comrade Majeed responded: "We will say, 'These are issues known by and pertaining to leadership only. All questions should go through the chain of command to be answered…'" Since the Politburo has issued such a disclaimer, I wish to go on record with the following criticism:

— "The Party fell short in accommodating the public flow…" This is untrue. The masses are with the Party from Sarbani to the borders of Kurdistan forcibly annexed to Iran; from the Arbil plain to the Gardi region, as well as Molgya, Shemamik, Pisht Zei, Kandinawa, and Qaraj. This can be proven by the reports of the Arbil Peasants' Committee which I chaired.
— "Party leadership fell short in leading the masses of Kurdistan." This is also untrue since our party established 8 farm cooperatives in the Arbil plain only. They have applied for permits that are under consideration now.
— "Blunders and deviations of Party leadership led to skepticism regarding Party policies as a whole." I affirm that even if deviations did occur, it was not the entire Party.
— "Doubts leaked to the broadest masses in Iraqi Kurdistan." This is absolutely untrue, because the steps taken according to paragraphs A, B, and C of the first Article of this report clearly negate the existence of such doubts. I should state here that our Party suffered distortions in some areas not because of deviations as the Politburo asserts, but because of the ICP's relentless campaigns that described us as Americans, feudalists, and separatists…. In addition, perhaps the conduct of certain individuals worked as a catalyst to spread their propaganda. This could have been corrected through criticism. There was no need for this legal blow to the Party from the Politburo.
— On page 7 under 'General Party Congress', it says "Disturbance in the Party's ideological unity and irregularity in its policies and orientation, and its recent move to the right." This statement was not approved in its entirety by the Central Committee, as the Politburo asserted and published it under Central Committees name, noting the word "recent" during which Comrades Lazgin, Bakhtiyar, and Majeed formed the majority in the Politburo. Therefore, they are more responsible than Comrades Tishk and Shorishgeir.
— On page 9, it says "to elect its permanent and legitimate leadership." In other words, the current leadership is not legitimate; and as the internal pamphlet stated, "against Politburo's legitimate authority." Apparently, the Politburo does not remember that the current "legitimate" Politburo was elected by the "legitimate leadership!" How could it be legitimate then? Didn't the Kurdish proverb say that "Kashk and whey are siblings?"[6]
— Of the internal pamphlet, the paragraph begins with "any initiative to form blocks and splinters." Isn't it a legitimate right of the majority to request a Central Committee meeting according to paragraph 13 of Article 5 of the Party Charter? Is this what you called 'splitting'?

My Criticism of the Politburo: The internal pamphlet says "any tendency to liberalism"…Liberalism is what Comrade Majeed did. He encouraged the democratic women, youth and students of Kurdistan to affiliate with the 'League' and the 'Iraqi Democratic Youth,' which contravenes Central Committee Resolutions.

Comrade Bakhtiyar spoke to two students in Baghdad, namely Siddique and Mahmud, about suspending comrades from the Central Committee. He told them, "we will destroy them publicly.'" This is in fact a breach of Party confidentiality and a disservice to the national movement.

---

6. Kashk is a Kurdish food made from fermented bulgur and yogurt. The Kurdish proverb, 'Kashkish bray dowya,' denotes that the two are inextricably intertwined.

My Criticism of Politburo Comrades Lazgin and Majeed: When I learned of Comrade Lazgin's return to Arbil, I went to welcome him and speak to him regarding Party activities. I joined most Arbil Local Committee members who were visiting him at the time. Here, I record the following criticisms:

— They spoke to me regarding the Central Committee which made it known to all present that I was a member of the Central Committee with them. This is in contravention of the Party charter, and it is a breach of Party confidentiality.
— Because I and seven other Central Committee members constituted the majority, we requested a Central Committee meeting to deal with the problems and the struggle inside the Leadership Committee. Hence, I was considered a break-a-way and out to form a bloc. Comrade Lazgin decided to suspend me and stated in his decision "I was authorized and sent by the Politburo, thus I decided to suspend you." I felt that these comrades came only to suspend comrades who are active and refuse to haphazardly follow in order to serve our Party better.

I do not oppose the purging of party ranks and I do not object to correcting deviations because I know that such steps strengthen the Party and I consider them as precautions taken by the Party of the future. However, these steps are to be taken at the right time and place and are to be for building the Party in order to avoid unwarranted consequences. I believe if the Politburo wanted to carry out such a purge as a sincere step, they should have not done it in such a manner.

The Politburo should have presented a detailed report to the Congress explaining all deviations and treasons. The Politburo should have put it before the Congress to investigate and take decisive but fair measures against those elements that the betrayed the Party. Then it would have been right to disseminate as widely as possible, not only to Party members but to all the masses of Kurdistan. Then, all would have congratulated them.

Based on what I have mentioned above, and in light of the recommendations submitted on January 28, 1959 by two members of the Politburo, Majeed and Bakhtiyar, to the President and Central Committee, I believe that there is a subversive hand in the Politburo assigned to destroy our Party, especially as I see Ittihad al-Sha'ab [*People's Union*, the ICP's official paper] waging war on our Party and its democratic organizations. Instead of responding, the Politburo issued what has been discussed. It is nothing but a way to trouble and destroy our Party. Therefore, I recommend the following:

— To immediately suspend all Politburo activities,
— To swiftly call for a Central Committee meeting, and
— To hold a conference as soon as possible to deal with the problems and to hold them responsible for deviation, subversion and other negative conduct.

Remaining silent will continue the internal struggle until it becomes a crisis. It is clear that our Party is moving on a destructive path. Forward under the leadership of our Party, the true representative of the masses of Kurdistan.

Ziring

Member of the Central Committee
February 27, 1959

Translation from Arabic of Document No. 43

The KDP'S Press Release
On the First Anniversary of the July 14 Revolution

THE UNITED DEMOCRATIC PARTY OF KURDISTAN

Press Release
On the Occasion of the First Anniversary of the
Glorious July 14 Revolution

Led by Abd al-Karim Qasim, the July 14 Revolution was a great historic event. It is a total social transformation, the peak of all uprisings, armed revolts and the unremitting patriotic struggle of all Iraqi people including our Kurdish people against imperialism, monarchy and reactionaries since the imperialists occupied Iraq. In a few hours, it crowned the revolutionary struggle of our people with a magnificent victory. It ended the hated rule of the despotic monarchs, and the tyranny, corruption and oppression of the triad, Nuri al-Sa'id, Abd al-Ilah, and Faisal. It founded a democratic republic and a revolutionary patriotic rule. Indeed, it destroyed the main link in the chain of imperialist schemes for the Middle East. It replaced the Iraqi monarchy, a strong bastion of imperialism, war and hostility with a fortified castle for peace, freedom and democracy in the Middle East.

The Revolutionary republic continued to break the chains of foreign domination and war plans, one after another consistently and successfully as it continued its democratic and liberating path by renouncing the Baghdad Pact, the Eisenhower Doctrine, Mutual Security and Military Aid Accords with the USA, the bilateral agreement with Britain concluded in April and the return of both the Shu'aiba and Habbania bases, and escaping the British economic sphere of influence. The Republic now pursues an independent foreign policy which serves peace according to the resolutions and principles of the Bandung Conference, the policy of peaceful co-existence, positive neutralism and anti-imperialism. Iraq is resuming relations with all countries on the bases of equality and mutual interests, concluding educational and trade accords with friendly nations, the USSR and the socialist camp, and defending our independence.

Led by the sincere son of Iraq Abd al-Karim Qasim, domestically our Republic has pursued a democratic policy, issued the Provisional Constitution which guarantees democratic freedoms for all Iraq's fraternal nationalities and religious minorities, legislated the Law of Agrarian Reform and guaranteed to control the lands of larger feudalists to emancipate the peasants. It passed a number of laws to ensure the people's exercise of their freedoms of assembly, education and thought. Popular organizations, guilds and agricultural cooperatives were founded as soon as these laws were enacted. It is implementing a policy of economic revival to improve the standard of living for the working class and all the people of Iraq, and planning to establish an industrial base and equip the army with modern weaponry to defend the country. Iraq, the Republic of Arabs and Kurds, has achieved significant victories in all these fields in the first year of the Republic. In our Republic, our Kurdish people are free after much suffering and dual oppression before the Revolution, that of imperialism and ugly racism. Our Party, in its thirteen years of glorious struggle, had led, along with other revolutionary parties and democratic and patriotic forces of Iraq, the struggle of our people against imperialism, monarchy and reactionaries, has contributed much to the struggle for peace, liberty and democracy, and given magnificent examples of courage, sacrifice, and heroism.

Our Kurdish people is the people of the revolts of Barzan, Sueiymaniyya, Sinjar revolts and the armed insurgencies throughout Kurdistan against imperialism, reactionaries, and the past monarchist regimes. Our Party never laid down the arms of revolutionary struggle even for a moment. It never retreated from the theater of struggle against imperialism and feudalism before or after the [July 14] Revolution, which it defended to safeguard the Republic and its democratic course within the NUF. Our Party rallied behind the leader Abd al-Karim Qasim firmly and it will remain steadfast on the path of freedom, democracy and peace.

From the very first moments, our Party answered the call of the revolution and its victorious leader Abd al-Karim Qasim. Masses of the Party and the Kurdish people stood ready throughout Kurdistan to crush any reactionary force opposing the Revolution. They, in fact, controlled and guarded all government centers and strategic points and thus dealt the death blow to the old regime and prevented any counter-revolutionary attacks. Indeed, our party unconditionally put all its capabilities under the command of the Revolution and its leader to defend the July 14 Revolution and preserve its democratic orientation. In so doing, it played an active and significant role in crushing all attempts to challenge the Revolution and its leader Abd al-Karim Qasim. In cooperation with other patriotic forces and the Arab masses, our Party boldly led the Kurdish masses to crush the traitor Shawwaf's plot in Mosul. In this patriotic and honorable battle, our party sacrificed many of its members and supporters. It played the main role in crushing the reactionary rebellion in Baradost, and the courageous Barzanis were in the forefront of the struggle under the leadership of the prominent patriot Mustafa Barzani.

Our Party will continue to strive to unify national ranks and forces of the national front to defend the Revolution, its democratic path, and to protect the revolutionary accomplishments under the leadership of Abd al-Karim Qasim. Our Party will continue to struggle to enhance the Arab-Kurdish brotherhood, the solidarity of the people, military and government to crush enemy attempts to bring back imperialism, divide national ranks, isolate the President from the people, and reverse the achievements of the Revolution and replace them with imperialist domination and reactionary privileges.

Our people rejoice on this sacred occasion as they embrace their heroic Barzanis whom the Revolution brought home after thirteen years of exile. As our Party participated in public ceremonies of this great occasion, the first anniversary of the July 14 Revolution, we call upon all patriotic forces to solidify the unity of all democratic forces for all fraternal peoples of Iraq, to remain alert to thwart all enemy conspiracies against the immortal republic, and to achieve more victories, for a better future of all Iraqis, and for our Kurdish people to exercise their national rights recognized by the glorious July 14 Revolution.

— The July 14 Revolution will continue despite imperialists and reactionaries.
— Forward under the banner of the victorious July 14 Revolution.
— Long live the Republic of Iraq, the Republic of Arabs and Kurds, free and democratic under the leadership of Abd al-Karim Qasim.
— Long live the unity of democratic forces, the strong shield of our eternal Republic.

Central Committee
United Democratic Party of Kurdistan
July 14, 1959

Translation from Arabic of Document No. 44

A Handwritten Report By Jalal Talabani Regarding the Position and Conduct of Feudalists.

Massoud Barzani

CONCERNING ANTI-REPUBLIC INCIDENTS IN THE KURDISH REGION ORGANIZED BY AGENTS OF IMPERIALISM AND FEUDALIST TRAITORS

No.: 1
Date: November 16, 1958

For some time, elements loyal to imperialism and some feudalist traitors known for their loyalty to monarchy have been provoking the dark reactionary forces against the Republic of Iraq in order to cause chaos, confusion and trouble for the country. These traitors have worked hard to provoke the people, divide ranks and falsely accuse Kurdish patriots of separatism and destruction in order to drive a wedge between Kurdish citizens and the government of their beloved Republic, a wedge that will allow them to destroy from within. The People's awareness and leaders of the Republic, notably the savior and champion of the people, foiled their plots. Then, attempts were expanded to criminal acts. They moved from propaganda against patriots to criminal activities such as killing citizens and looting their possessions. These traitors are committing their crimes in the following areas:

A. The Pishdar region: Feudalist elements known for their reactionary tendencies and loyalty to imperialism are forming armed gangs and committing heinous crimes. Bayiz Babakr Salim Agha (a member of the Parliament under the monarchy) of the Babakr al-A'war's group, the son of Bapir Babakr Salim Agha, Hama Abbas Agha and a few of his followers fled to Iran some time ago. They were welcomed and officially received by royal guards, music and salutation! Agents of imperialism, Ali Agha Mangoor and his two brothers, are actively working for the Iranian and imperialist intelligence circles. To form a joint front against Iraq, Iranian border officers arranged to settle their differences with Pishdar chieftains. They have contacted and bribed chieftains. Undoubtedly, many are waiting to harvest their tobacco crops and then join the traitors in Iran. Recently, they contacted the villagers of Betwain whose plots were flooded with Dokan water. They are enticing them to resist authorities and remain in their areas to create chaos and bloodshed.

November 25, 1958:

Feudalist gangs committed a number of crimes, many of which the following list clarifies:

1. Feudalist groups enticed several soldiers to escape to Iran and form armed gangs to raid, rob, and loot the area. Mahmud Hama Agha confessed to the Commander of the army depot that he had gone to Iran after being contacted by feudalists, specifically Bayiz Babakr Agha.
2. Feudalist gangs burned the house of Abdullah Mam Rasoul because he met with the patriots of Qala Diza.
3. Another feudalist armed band attacked the house of Ali Mam Riza and shot him four times.
4. An armed band robbed and looted the house of Haji Rasoul.
5. They raided the house of Ali Haj Ahmad for receiving Sheikh Khalid in his house.
6. They assassinated the student Hamza for playing the role of a peasant in 'Uncle Omer'. They threatened to kill him before committing the crime.

7. Feudalist gangs burned the house of Abdullah Mamesh in the village of Gird Mayta, and attempted to assassinate him.
8. Rostam Majar was assassinated after he left a feudalist band and refused to obey their orders.
9. Feudalist gangs carried out a repulsive attack on a woman in the village of Shoran.
10. Feudalist gangsters assaulted and threatened Husam ad-Din Tayib, a detention petty officer because he did not heed their wishes.
11. Haji Ahmad Pour Rihan was assassinated between Qala Diza and Sangasar.
12. A feudalist gang carried out a three-hour-long armed attacked on the Hairo police station.
13. They stole three herds of sheep from the villages of Hairo, Mirayin and Badmazi, and sent them to Iran.
14. Feudalists cut the nose of a man named Abdullah in Hairo to teach the rest a lesson.
15. They destroyed a tobacco farm and shot at Sulayman Hasna Jol in the village of Omerkakok.
16. During an armed assault by Bayiz Babakr Agha and his gang on the village of Sayyed Ahmadan, they burned the house of the village chief, Mohammed Agha.
17. Armed attack on the house of Hama Soor, supervisor of the village of Sayyed Ahmad.
18. They shot at Jihangeer Mahmud in the village of Bimoush and threatened to kill him.
19. Expulsion of four farming families from the village of Gird Maytar by Babakr Agha and his gang. They threatened to kill the following peasants, Mohammed Abdullah Mamesh, Abdullah Mamesh, Maroof Saeed and Hama Rash Khidhir.
20. Feudalist groups are in constant contact, [with one another], including adversaries, to unify their efforts against the Republic.

B. The Rewanduz and Zebar Region: The old imperialist agent Sheikh Rashid of Lolan is intensifying efforts to contact Iran and Turkey, and has repeatedly visited Turkish and Iranian officers dressed in Kurdish clothes. They provide him with money and arms to instigate trouble and unrest through organizing armed gangs against Barzan and the government.

Ahmad Agha Zebari and other feudalist traitors and reactionaries in the Aqra area are also in contact with Turkey and its loyal Turanis in Kirkuk. They receive money, weapons, threaten citizens, instigate domestic troubles, and are waging a propaganda campaign against the patriots in Aqra and Barzan.

C. Incidents in the Aqra Region: A block of reactionary forces have been organized against the Republic and President Abd al-Karim Qasim. The former Garrison Commander helped them clearly and openly. Under their command, he arrested patriots under the pretext of separatism. He told them that soon Abd al-Salam would take over, and that he would personally execute Aqra patriots to avenge the feudalists. Through Turani employees, reactionary groups are in touch with the Turani Association in Kirkuk. A number of incidents have occurred there; among them:

1. Khorshid Arab Agha killed three peasants and wounded five others in the village of Sheikh Khalik in the Ashayir al-Sab'a subdistrict.
2. Ahmad Zebari led an assault on the village of Harn in the Nahla subdistrict and rained bullets on the village for seven hours.
3. Ahmad Zebari's gang assassinated Abdullah Tanoos of Sayan village.

D. The Kirkuk Region: The Turani Association is accumulating explosives and locally-made bombs. Their members are being trained on the use of firearms. They are openly threatening to make Kirkuk another Cyprus. They are plotting, contacting imperialists, reactionaries, the hateful, and supporters of the monarchy to unify them and incite them against the Republic. We still remember the hideous attempt they plotted on the life of Mulla Mustafa Barzani and his colleagues!

Turanis have penetrated the ranks of Police, the Department of Education, and government offices. They are organizing spy cells for America, Britain and Turkey. They openly work for the Baghdad Pact, and recently, they controlled post and telegraph offices. They steal letters and send them to their masters.

Recommendations to Correct the Situation and End These Crimes:

1. Organize the government system after purging and appoint competent and loyal individuals as provincial, district and subdistrict governors as well as the commanders of army and police.
2. Deport the traitors among the tribal chieftains, and impose a stricter surveillance.
3. Fight the Turani Movement and all reactionary feudalist groups.
4. Detain conspiring chieftains and pursue gangsters and those who fled.
5. Carry out necessary economic, administrative, educational and health reforms in the area.

Translation from Arabic of Document No. 45

Report by the [Iraqi Army] Commander of the Third Squadron of the Suleimaniyya Training Depot Regarding the Position of Pishdar (Qala Diza) Chieftains

The Position in Qala Diza

1. Chieftains who leave Qala Diza for Iran have ongoing solid contact with the Republic's enemies such as Americans, Britons, and Iranians, because their escape is more political than just being chased by simple peasants or peasants being provoked against them by a small group.
2. I heard from several people, including Ali Agha Merga (No. 21091) and soldier Hussein Ahmad of the Second Detachment, that chieftains remaining in Qala Diza because of their personal interests are enticing people into escaping to Iran. He has visited Babakr Agha in his village, since he was his follower for some time. Unlike previous visits, he was treated particularly well, asked to sit next to him, and offered tea and asked about the following issues:
   a. How they are treated by their officers.
   b. How do they like the Republic and their training.
   c. Number of night guards and their weapons.
   d. Guard and officer sleeping quarters and warehouses.
   e. If he is satisfied or wishes to join his son in Iran.
   f. He was encouraged to join them, and asked to call his colleagues to be patient and wait until the time comes to receive their weapons and munitions.
3. Peasants unanimously want the Republic but are intimidated by the armed chieftains and their men who raid their villages, loot their possessions and herds and even burn their villages. They do not have even a single gun. Villages near the Iranian border where there are no police stations are especially vulnerable.
4. Soldiers and police in Qala Diza are not reliable because they are from Qala Diza and have interests vested in the region. Soldiers may change sides and take their weapons in a critical time. Also, the police in some stations are reluctant to enforce the laws against those who cross the borders.

5. Most employees take the position of an outsider and do not enforce the laws concerning important issues.

I recommend:

1. Replace the Qala Diza police and trained soldiers who have ties with feudalists. They are unreliable because of shared interests with their chieftains. Bring in soldiers and police from outside Qala Diza.
2. Build a high, strong wall around the army camp to protect it.
3. To ensure the safety of peasants and their possessions, those who support the Republic, it is necessary to do the following:
   a. arm a number of peasants to guard the villages at night.
   b. establish police stations in the villages near the border.
   c. establish PRM centers in Qala Diza.
4. Send for a new mobile police force.
5. To improve the standard of living, the following must be done:
   a. Restore the road between Qala Diza and Suleimaniyya through Rania because of the unavailability of the road through Dokan.
   b. Secure clean drinking water.
   c. Increase Qala Diza's share of flour because of the presence of police and army and because of crop shortage this year.

Major Mustafa Abdullah
Deputy Commander of the Third Company
At the Training Depot in Suleimaniyya
Abd al-Rahman Khalid
December 1, 1958

Translation from Kurdish of Document No. 46

A Report by the KDP's Rania Local Committee Regarding Conditions in that Region

KURDISTAN DEMOCRATIC PARTY, IRAQ

Local Committee of Rania

November 20, 1959
A Statement for Members and Supporters

Led by the defeater of imperialism, Abd al-Karim Qasim, the rising sun of the July 14 Revolution shone on mountain tops of Kurdistan and marked the day of liberation for the people of Kurdistan. Since the Revolution's first communiqúe, the Republic has moved consistently on a defined path. The military, and all Iraqi Arabs, Kurds and other nationalities have contributed to the founding of our Republic. Our vanguard KDP continues to be ready today, supported by all honorable Kurds, to sacrifice for our democratic Republic and President Abd al-Karim Qasim.

Sometimes we hear odd voices of the agents of imperialism, governments in Tehran, Ankara and 'Free Iraq' hostile to our Party constantly attempting to steer our party off the democratic path, to project our Party as Republic's and President hero Abd al-Karim Qasim's enemy. Let frustrated dogs bark forever. The people of Iraqi Kurdistan and the other three occupied parts are prepared to sacrifice for peace, democracy, freedom, to defend our Republic and President Qasim. Do these voices come from abroad only!?

No, they come from within as well. At times, we hear that "the KDP is American, again, the KDP is feudalist, and still again, the KDP is separatist—wants to separate from Iraq, or the KDP refuses to distribute land among the peasants!!!" How long will these voices continue, agents of Imperialism?!

Our Party, vanguard of the honorable masses of Kurdistan, will not honor you with a response. You are to die in shame. The people and the President know you well as servants of imperialism. Rejoice, our Iraqi Republic, the Republic of Arabs, Kurds and other nationalities. Rejoice, our people, and let democracy triumph.

Comrades, Do you hear these ugly and odd voices in your areas? Get to know them. They are either naive, or tricked into working for imperialism. You ought to struggle hard within the ranks of our KDP to end these voices. Struggle with your Arab brothers to eradicate the remains of imperialism, feudalism and reactionary rule. Forward Under the Leadership of the Kurdistan Democratic Party, Iraq.

Translation from Kurdish of Document No. 47

A Hand-written Letter from Dr. Abd al-Rahman Qasimlu to Barzani Regarding the State of the Kurdistan Democratic Party, Iran

It is obvious from the contents of this letter that Abdullah Ishaqi, better known as Ahmad Tawfiq, played a significant role in running Party affairs at a critical time. This refutes what some of the KDPI leaders unfortunately now assert to distort and omit the role of a prominent patriot who served the KDPI more than anybody else did.

Massoud Barzani

Some Information About The Kurdistan Democratic Party, Iran (KDPI)

KDPI activities have advanced notably after the 1953 coup d'état since the Party decided to work independently and run the affairs of Kurdistan alone.

Areas where KDPI enjoys much support are: Shapour, Selmas, Urmia (Reza'ia) and vicinities, Mahabad, Sardasht, Shino, Sundus and all areas surrounding these towns, Saquiz, Baneh and surrounding villages, the city of Sanandaj and vicinities, and the city of Kermanshah, in which KDPI has recently begun an intense struggle.

Areas where the national movement enjoys support and influence are: the regions of Jalalis, Shikaks, Margaver and Targaver, the region of Mangor, Piran and Lajan, the villages surrounding Shino, Mahabad, and the region of Pishdariyan to the Iraqi border, Baneh and its vicinities, the region of Jwanro and Hawraman. The national movement is very strong along the Iran–Iraq borders, from Shino all the way to Kermanshah.

The KDPI has chapters, in all these villages. Several chapters form a Subdistrict Committee, and a number of these form a Local Committee. There are City Committees in the cities that are then tied to the Central Committee which guides the struggle.

Three people of the Central Committee run the affairs of the Party, namely Abdullah Ishaqi, Aziz Yousifi, and Rahmatullah Shari'ati.

I am not certain of the exact number of Party members, since we rarely keep count because of our underground work. I have been away from Kurdistan for a year, and many changes have occurred on the political life in Kurdistan since then. The changes were mainly in the interest of the Movement and the Party. What I can say is that members of KDPI are now numbered in the thousands.

Translation from Kurdish of Document No. 48

Number and Names of the KDPI's Central Committee Members as Presented by Abdullah Ishaqi, Known as Ahmad Tawfiq, in a Hand-Written Letter to Barzani.

Massoud Barzani

Names of the Central Committee (CC) Members of the Kurdistan Democratic Party, Iran

1. Aziz Yousifi, CC member on death row.
2. Rahmatullah Shari'ati, CC member on death row.
3. Sayyed Abdullah Ishaqi, CC member and an undercover cadre.
4. Ghani Ballouriyan, CC consultant on death row.
5. Hashim Amal at-Tullab, CC consultant and an undercover cadre.
6. Hashim Hussien Zadeh, CC consultant and an undercover cadre.
7. Dr. Ali Mawlawi, CC consultant, imprisoned for life.
8. Qasim Sultaniyan, CC consultant and an undercover cadre.

Total membership and those recommended is 7000 (seven thousand).

Translation from Kurdish of Document No. 49

Bekr is another nom de guerre of Abdullah Ishaqi's.

Massoud Barzani

Comrade Mustafa Barzani, Commander in chief of the struggle of the Kurdish nation

With my highest regards, I submit a copy of the letter I wrote to members of the Central Committee of Kurdistan Democratic Party, Iran (KDPI) for your personal information and knowledge.

Comrades of the Central Committee of the KDPI

With my highest regards and hope for your triumph and success, especially your recent achievement in strengthening the Party among the masses and the steps you have taken to hold a Party Congress.

A. To provide information and shed light on the persons who recently escaped to Iraq, and of course, I hope this information will remain within the Central Committee. Over the past year, the negative conduct of some has created difficulties for Party comrades here. Thus, I find it necessary to inform you in writing the following:

1. Comrade "Karim-Anwari," the Leadership Committee decided unanimously in its meeting in the summer of 1956 on his suspension for reasons known to Leadership Committee comrades, and the decision has not been reconsidered yet.
2. The aforementioned Comrade "Salih-Tawfiq"—his organizational status is unknown because he refused his duties as a Branch Committee member for a year, during which he stayed away. But after the July 14 Revolution, he began to assume responsibility, and before long he left for Iraq without the approval of the Local Committee and the Committee of the Mahabad region under the pretext of escaping the Iranian government. Comrades had advised him to remain in the area undercover and designated a place for him. However, as soon as he was informed of the decision not to enter Iraq, he

violated the article of Party discipline and crossed into Iraq. Thus, he no longer abides by Party discipline.

3. Comrade 'Jalal-Ahmad' has been suspended since the fall of 1954 following a unanimous Central Committee decision in full meeting for several ethical and political reasons. The decision has not been reconsidered since.

4. Comrade 'Jamal Tawfiq' submitted his resignation from the Party to the Local Committee in his town, in 1955 and verbally confirmed his request to a Central Committee member who tried to persuade him otherwise. However, persuading him proved to be difficult because it was not a political decision, but concerned with love and establishing a family. Therefore, the Committee of the Mahabad Region approved his resignation. Contact with him has been personal and not organizational since then. Comrades will issue the Party's official decisions regarding them in the near future.

In conclusion, comrades, I wish, to hear from you, in response to this letter regarding the bad conduct of these comrades, because their fates will be decided as was the case with their friends Najad and others. A Party meeting will reach a final decision and will officially be submitted to you and to our dear Comrade Mustafa Barzani. Within the Party framework, please inform us in advance regarding any contact or representation established with comrades or supporters of the KDP so we can respond to their requests in a more efficient manner and prevent problems and regrets on both sides.

B. It is necessary that I ask you to inform me several days before the opening of the Congress so I can prepare a congratulatory letter expressing the ideological policy of the KDP to present it to the Congress together with the official congratulatory letter of the KDP Leadership Committee.

I wish you victory, with my highest regards.
Bekr, Representative
Leadership Committee
Kurdistan Democratic Party
September 26, 1959

Translation from Kurdish of Document No. 50

Ahmad Tawfiq is the nom de guerre of Abdullah Ishaqi, General Secretary of the KDPI (1959–1965).

Massoud Barzani

Steadfast comrade Mustafa Barzani, Esq.

With my warmest regards, I wish you and the great Sheikh good health and honor. I learned that you are comfortable in Barzan and am delighted. But I believe that enemies of our nation will undoubtedly try to disturb this repose. Last night I heard that brothers Sadiq, Abbas, and Ubaidullah returned. I do not know how. But it was said that their return was satisfactory.

A few days ago, they gathered tribal chiefs. I heard some negative statements from affiliates of the Jaff Tribe which contradict what brother Abbas said. He had told you that the Jaff tribe had proclaimed its position and was moving on a slippery slope. Their talks here in Baghdad indicate that these pathetic people still live in the dark and that they have been deceived.

Dear sir, I believe that you have decided not to return until they improve conditions of the region . . . in fact, it is a very acceptable idea. I will also take a position in light of this idea. These dull messrs are useless to our country and our oppressed people. Strange and ignorant, they do not know the conditions in the Barzan region and its surroundings. Let's leave them alone. The idea of you not returning to Baghdad is well thought out, and very acceptable especially now that you have taken major steps under the guidance of our great hope (the greater Sheikh) to end the troubles and chaos. Today, I will go to Bapir Agha Noor ad-Din who is in Baghdad for medical treatment. I've heard that he will meet the President next Sunday and I am supposed to meet 'Fattah' at Rashid Arif's residence. We will tell him that if he is to take the wrong path he will be ashamed before God, the Kurdish people and his homeland, Kurdistan. With Kaka Ziyad, we are also to meet with two or three groups regarding the conditions of our refugee brothers.

In fact, their conditions have deteriorated and disgraced us on both political and humanitarian levels. We are sad and depressed, and those who smoke also have handfuls of free Aspirin from the Sarchinar Pharmacy to treat their headaches.

Personally, I have closed all doors. Now, I owe more than 1500 dinars in Suleimaniyya, and 600 dinars in Baghdad. We do not really know what to do! They do not allow me to assign them to the villages and towns surrounding Suleimaniyya to work and farm. Now, there are only twenty days left for peasants to begin farming in the countryside because only tobacco and beans can be farmed, or to work on farms. Here, no one asks about us. I have gone to Iskan and waited all day to meet brother Awni to no avail, let alone brothers in the Party.

Dear sir, I present this situation to you, not out of self-love, but as a national and party duty. I am aware of the problems in your area, but I still wish you to guide us to take the next required step, because if this continues, a situation will occur that will humiliate every sincere Kurd. Now, it is late, so I have given brother Mustafa few verbal suggestions. Again, may God grant you and the great Sheikh good health and honor. With my highest regards.

Ahmad Tawfiq
May 5, 1960

Translation from Kurdish of Document No. 51

A Report Sent by Ahmad Tawfiq

Respectfully, Mr. Barzani

Warmest regards. After three days of waiting to meet Party comrades, I am sorry to report that they did not have the time to meet me! During these three days, I received two telephone calls asking me to return without delay since they have been suffering and humiliated. It seems that they think others are responsible for their plight, but I feel I am. If I were to behave like others who dominate the theater today, if I would change my color and form, and beg the influential and powerful, I would have been able, under their wing of course, to change my standing and that of my comrades, the refugees. Now, I am returning to my comrades and we will die but will never waver. We do not fear hunger or homelessness. Eight years have passed and we continue in worse-than-ever conditions. I trust that our standing with the masses grows stronger every day. Despite our miserable conditions, we will go on with pride and dignity without submitting to the enemies of the Kurds. Our worst pain is because of the attitude of our Party brothers vis-à-vis 200–250 patriots who left their homes and possessions to struggle for the Kurds and Kurdistan. This attitude creates "Iraqi" and "Iranian" proclivities, as ugly and scorching to our hearts as they can be.

The more important issue than the refugees is the relationship between the KDP and the KDPI. Not only is this relationship unclear, no one speaks of it or holds a meeting to discuss it. Why? No one knows except the Party's Central Committee. Perhaps I should say the Politburo for more clarity. ... Well, the Almighty is the most powerful. For a long time, the destiny of the Kurdish people has been left to fate and luck. ... Do you see what enemies have done to us, we the indigent Kurds? ... Our necks are thinner than a thread!! This is why you see us in this condition!

My dear friend, today at five o'clock I will be going to our comrades in Suleimaniyya. However, when brothers in the Party reconsider their position vis-à-vis the struggle in Iraqi Kurdistan and the relationship with the movements of other parts of Kurdistan, if you wish to order [me to do so], I will return, despite all that I have endured over the past two years traveling back and forth. A strong relationship between Iranian Kurdistan and here is our national and historic responsibility. It is our pride and patriotism as well. May God grant you good health and honor, with my kindest regards.

Ahmad Tawfiq
May 26, 1960

Translation from Persian of Document No. 52

Zagros is the symbolic name for the Central Committee of the Kurdistan Democratic Party, Iran.

Massoud Barzani

Central Committee of the USSR Communist Party

Dear Comrades,

Our sincere regards. Pursuant to our previous communication via your comrades here ( ) [sic] regarding our representatives' trip to the Soviet Union, we find it necessary to explain the following points:

A. After consultation and deliberation, it has been decided that the members of our delegation would be as follows:

1. Qasim Sultaniyan, known in Iraq as Kamal Ahmad,
2. Sulayman Mu'ini, and
3. Abdullah Ishaqi, Known in Iraq as Ahmad Tawfiq.

Please register their names as such when you grant visas and prepare for their reception.
B. It is preferred, and we find it as a good opportunity, to arrange for the trip of our delegation with Comrade leader Mustafa Barzani in the Soviet Union.
C. Because of the limited financial ability of the Party, we need your assistance at least to cover the trip and meetings.
With our highest regards and appreciation.

For the Central Committee of the
Kurdistan Democratic Party

Zagros
92 S/November 1, 1960

Translation from Persian of Document No. 53

A Congratulatory Letter from the Central Committee of the Kurdistan Democratic Party, Iran to the Central Committee of the Soviet Communist Party

Central Committee of the USSR Communist Party

Dear Comrades,

After presenting comradely greetings on the occasion of the great October Revolution, the beginning of a new chapter of the lives of world toilers, the founding of Soviet authority and victory over the decayed Czarist bourgeois establishments, the Central Committee of the KDP sends its best wishes to you and through you to all peoples of the USSR.

The Kurds, an oppressed and persecuted people, recognize the greatness and significance of the Revolution of freedom which liberated the brave Soviet peoples. On this occasion, we feel that it is our duty to express the joy and happiness of our Kurdish people in Iranian Kurdistan, especially members of the KDP, on the anniversary of the great October Revolution.

We are delighted that the leader of the Kurdish people Mustafa Barzani is participating on behalf of the Kurdish people in the great festivities of the Soviet peoples.

We salute all Socialist Republics of the Soviet Union, the strong and mighty bastion. A salute from the Kurdish people to the peoples of the Soviet Union, the genuine friend of all peoples.

Long live the splendid peace.

For the Central Committee of the
Kurdistan Democratic Party

Zagros
91 S/November 10, 1960

Translation from Kurdish of Document No. 54

Sharif is the nom de guerre of Barzani, and Ahmad Kwestani is the nom de guerre of Abdullah Ishaqi.

Massoud Barzani

Dear brother Sharif,

It has been five months since I saw you. I take this opportunity to send you a warm Kurdish greeting, and I ask God to grant good health and honor for the great Sheikh. In this regard I am not alone; all honorable and sincere Kurds wish you good health and dominion.

Since I will be returning from Baghdad with my comrades to visit you, I will be brief. "Our friend" asked to meet with me on short notice through brothers Ubaidullah and Sayyed Aziz. I met with him. He said a lot, and I will tell you what when I see you in person. After a year, he gave us 350 dinars, a repayment of the debt he owed you. I am returning it to you with the carrier of this letter. It appeared that he gave me the sum to give to my colleagues. However, I prefer to visit you with my colleagues and you may lend us the money then. I will tell you the reasons later.

I wish to let you know that I will visit you with my colleagues because of ideological differences regarding the Party, and of course many other reasons. It is better to receive them well. They are motivated young men and I am sure you will boost their morale. To let you know in brief what are the issues? Qadir is deviating and is close to the Communists. He has written to them and tried hard until he was able to pull in Comrade Kamal, who is becoming a left-wing extremist. It will be appropriate to respect Comrade Kamal because of his glorious and honorable past. I wish to let you know that we have suspended Qadir. We will not allow him to interfere, and he will not accompany us to visit you. I hope that you will not use that sum to replace the sum you have already decided to grant us.

I believe it is better not to speak of the contents of this letter when we visit you, especially in regards to the money, because I will tell the brothers that "that friend" explained that they have to meet Mr. Sharif.

Finally, I bow in respect to the great Sheikh. May God grant him good health and honor. With my highest regards.

Ahmad Kwestani
May 31, 1961

Translation from Kurdish of Document No. 55

A List Showing the Subsidy that Barzani was Providing to the Kurdistan Democratic Party, Iran.

Monthly stipends paid to professional cadres		*January 7, 1959*
1. Jwanmir		7 dinars
2. Siyamend	Baneh and Sardasht	7 dinars
3. Mamand	Mangor, Gork, Mahal Dibokri	7 dinars
4. Pirot	Mangor	7 dinars
5. Gulawi	Miyandoab, Sayin Qala	7 dinars
6. Sharif		7 dinars
7. Asos	Qasiya, Pik	7 dinars
8. Gamo		7 dinars
9. Sa'doon, family and children	Mashlola, Mahabad	14 dinars
10. Kirmanj, family and children	Karmanshah	10 dinars
11. Awat, family and children	Baneh vicinity	10 dinars
12. Yolo, family and children	Mahabad vicinity	10 dinars
13. Zhin, family and children	Khaneh (Piranshehr)	10 dinars
14. Nishtiman, family and children	Naghadeh	10 dinars
15. Shirwani, family and children	Mahabad	10 dinars
16. Kawa, family and children	Naghadeh and Ashnawiya	10 dinars
17. Nasser, family and children	Raza'ia	10 dinars
18. Sahand, family and children	Miyandoab	10 dinars
19. Blaiseh, family and children	Sanandaj	10 dinars
20. Kurd Pour	Sanandaj	7 dinars
21. Bakhawani, with family	Tehran	14 dinars
22. Piroz, with family	Tehran	14 dinars
23. Umaid	Tehran	10 dinars

24. Jamshid	Karmanshah	10 dinars
25. Hiwa	Sanandaj	10 dinars
26. Ararat	Shahpour (Salami)	10 dinars
27. Zirang, with family	Baneh	10 dinars
28. Bibak, with family	Baneh	10 dinars
Total		265 dinars

Arms provided to guard Party roads and locations and the traveling of undercover cadres:

1. (10) infantry rifles (long Birnos) at 90 dinars each	900 dinars
2. (15) small and large revolvers, price range 23–36 dinars each	473 dinars
Total	1373 dinars

Minimum:

1. (6) Birno rifles	540 dinars
2. (10) revolvers	520 dinars
Total	1060 dinars

Emergency Aid: Housing expenses of Party members in the cities

1. House in Tehran	21 dinars
2. House in Mahabad	13 dinars
3. House in Naghadeh	13 dinars
4. House in Urmia (Raza'ia)	13 dinars
5. House in Baghdad	30 dinars
6. House in Suleimaniyya	23 dinars
Total	113 dinars

Monthly transportation and travels:

1. (4) mules	180 dinars
2. (10) horses with saddles	360 dinars
3. (2) Jeeps	900 dinars
4. (2) trucks	1700 dinars
Total	2140 dinars

Annual rent for Party members in the villages:

1. Saloak village	Baneh	180 dinars
2. Rafta village	Mahabad, Mangor	90 dinars
3. Kani Zard village	Khaneh Lajan	225 dinars
4. Dimlini village	Khaneh, Piran	270 dinars
Total		765 dinars

January 7, 1959

1. (9) individual cadres at 7 dinars each 63 dinars	
2. (3) individual cadres at 10 dinars each 30 dinars	
3. (3) cadres with their families at 14 dinars each	42 dinars
4. (13) cadres with small and medium families at 10 each	130 dinars
Total: 28 cadres	265 dinars

A. Our immediate financial needs:

1. Monthly stipends for 28 cadres	265 dinars
2. Traditional armaments	1373 dinars

3. Cost of protecting Party houses in the cities	113 dinars
4. Emergency aid in 1959	100 dinars
5. Transportation and travel	2140 dinars
6. Rent for Party members in the villages	765 dinars
Total	4756 dinars

B. *Monthly stipends:*

1. Salaries of 28 cadres	265 dinars
2. Party houses in the cities	113 dinars
3. Set monthly stipends for 1959	100 dinars
Total	478 dinars

C. *Emergency aid in 1959:*

1. 10 infantry Birno rifles and 15 revolvers	1373 dinars
2. 2 old jeeps and 2 old trucks	2140 dinars
3. Rent for Party members in the villages	765 dinars
Total	4278 dinars

Translation from Arabic of Document No. 56

Text of the agreement between the two fraternal parties of Iran and Syria. The Central Committee of the Kurdistan Democratic Party, Iraq did not then believe that circumstances were suitable for such an agreement to be signed.

Massoud Barzani

Regarding the views of the Kurdistan Democratic Party, Iran (KDPI) and the Kurdistan Democratic Party, Syria (KDP-Syria) at the meeting held by their representatives in Iraqi Kurdistan on June 25, 1961

In response to a call by the KDPI to all Kurdistan Parties regarding its proposal to form a Kurdistan-wide Committee consisting of representatives of Kurdistan parties to unify efforts and coordinate plans throughout Kurdistan, the Central Committee of the KDP-Syria in its meeting in early May of 1961 decided to send a representative member of its Politburo to Iraqi Kurdistan to establish contacts with representatives of both sister parties to reach a consensus regarding the founding of the proposed Committee.

At the meeting, representatives of both Parties exchanged information about political conditions in Kurdistan in general and the parts in Iran and Syria in particular. In an atmosphere of mutual understanding of their political and organizational difficulties, they arrived at a consensus regarding the following points that concerned both parties:

1. The supreme goal of the Kurdish liberation movement is to liberate and unify Kurdistan. Hence, the struggle in each part of Kurdistan must be geared to achieve this goal, and the tactics of any one Party must be adjusted to realize this goal.
2. Both Parties regard the formation of a Kurdistan-wide committee as a national duty, considering that the imposed borders partitioning Kurdistan are not recognized by the Kurdish people, and that the struggle in Kurdistan is an indivisible whole.

3. Both Parties decided to form a Committee as the first step and a nucleus to form a joint Committee. They find it necessary to postpone such a step until KDP [Iraq] clarifies its position regarding this Committee.
4. Both Parties agree that Party activities are not in the best Kurdish national interests in Turkish Kurdistan because, first and foremost, of the Kurdistan parties' lack of collaborative struggle in Kurdistan in general and Turkish Kurdistan in particular. Therefore, they call upon all those sincerely pledged to the Kurdish cause to unify efforts as soon as possible and establish the proposed Committee so the Kurdish revolutionary movement will play its full role.
5. Representatives of both Parties welcome the leadership of the brave patriot Mustafa Barzani in any Committee or General Command to direct the struggle throughout Kurdistan or in the parts in Iran and Syria.
6. Regarding the location and how to form the Committee, its status and the nature of its decisions, the nature of the struggle in each part of Kurdistan will be agreed upon by representatives of parties joining the Committee.
7. Representatives of both parties will provide a copy of these Resolutions to Comrade Mustafa Barzani, so as President of the KDP, he will attempt, to deal with his Party's unenthusiastic attitude regarding the founding of the Committee, because the KDPI and KDP-Syria will implement these Resolutions three months from this date and form the Committee.

Note 1: Three copies were made; a copy for each Party and a copy for Comrade Mustafa Barzani.
Note 2: These resolutions were to be written in Kurdish, but because of urgency, they were written in Arabic.

Abdullah Ishaqi, Representative
Secretariat of
Kurdistan Democratic Party, Iran
[signed] June 30, 1961

Abd al-Hamid Sulayman Darwish, Representative
The Politburo of
Kurdistan Democratic Party, Syria
[signed and sealed]

Translation from Arabic of Document No. 57

The KDP's memorandum to the Iraqi Communist Party (ICP) regarding their strained relationship

To: The Central Committee of ICP

Greetings,

Because of the UDPK's interest in the genuine orientation of the patriotic movement in Iraq, its success in the struggle against imperialism and the reactionary regime, we find it necessary to ask that parties coalesced in the NUF cooperate with us on the same general basis that has been agreed upon by the NUF parties. In this regard, our Party's efforts have met with resistance by some, and with a campaign of vilification distorting the truth about our Party by other members in the Front. This situation has resulted in creating a charged atmosphere against our Party to mar the friendly ties between our two peoples, and cultivates doubts in the Kurdish struggle and legitimate rights within the framework of Iraqi unity, the general and clear path of struggle to strengthen the Republic and expand its democracy. Despite this unconstructive attitude by some members of the NUF (especially the ICP), our Party has played a role in attracting the broadest segment of the masses in Kurdistan and rallied them behind our fledgling Republic, never troubled by the malicious propaganda campaign, and has focused the struggle against imperialist propaganda trying to make Kurdistan into a conduct for discord and feuding.

Based on understanding the common interests of the two peoples of our Republic, our Party has properly assessed its leading role in Kurdistan to augment the ties of brotherhood and joint struggle. Obviously, the existence of multiple parties demonstrates the multiplicity of tendencies. However, this does not necessarily mean the lack of joint goals or call for discord among parties. Our Party did not carry the banner of Kurdish struggle for freedom in isolation from the Arab struggle for freedom. In fact, it has always unified the army of struggle for common goals against common enemies. Under the monarchy, our Party carried on the front page of its newspaper the motto of "establishing a patriotic democratic government in Iraq", a goal all patriotic for which parties struggled and which was accomplished by the July 14 Revolution under the leadership of the Free Officers in our national army.

Despite isolation and NUF rejection, the UDPK played its patriotic role before and after the July 14 Revolution. However, being outside the NUF has created many difficulties. Furthermore, our Party represents the just ambitions of the Kurdish people recognized by the Republic's Provisional Constitution. It is not an ignoble patriotic force in the liberation movement in Iraq. Therefore, isolating it reflects skepticism in the struggle of the Kurdish people for their legitimate rights recognized by the July 14 Revolution. This means allowing the opportunity for imperialistic enemies and their agents inside and outside Iraq to use this phenomenon, that is, our Party's remaining outside the NUF, to sabotage the deep brotherly ties between our two peoples, to stir up trouble in the national movement, to encourage isolationism among the Kurds, and above all, to insist on keeping our Party out of the Iraqi National Front under the rule of a patriotic Republic brought about by the long and bloody joint struggle of our peoples. It also means following the same hated imperialistic discriminatory policy that has appeared in the form of segregation against anything that is Kurdish even if this 'Kurdish thing' is purely democratic and patriotic.

Based on this understanding, in our view, our Party's joining the NUF is a great patriotic necessity dictated by the interests of our Republic and the continued brotherhood of our peoples and the triumph of genuine democracy in the country. It cannot be postponed any longer, because, under current conditions, imperialists are plotting against the Kurds and Kurdistan.

Of course, a responsive revolution to the Kurdish rights should reflect the same in the conduct of all patriotic circles. The cause is not as much Kurdish concern as it is the cause of joint Iraqi achievement in particular and international peace in general. We hold your party, the ICP, directly responsible for keeping our Party out of the NUF because you did not reflect the facts about our Party honestly and without Party bias. On the contrary, you have created a strife and chaos as bad as could be. You helped divisionists to create a fake uproar regarding our Party and its leaders under the pretext of separatism at times, and cooperation with this Party and that Minister at other times until these lies and descriptions turned into a weapon in the hands of organizations hostile to Communism. You tore the ICP and the liberation movement apart, causing a rift in the unity of our people and to cause the national movement to swerve from the right path while we are in dire need of unifying our ranks and of being alert to foil the malicious imperialistic plots aiming to thwart our Revolution.

Earlier we asked to cooperate if the ICP publicly admits, in some form, errors in accusing our Party. It was not a consent to work among the masses as you have announced. It was to normalize the atmosphere to cooperate since agreements have been violated for the most trivial or personal behavior. Instead of heeding our suggestion, you published the "Front's Charter" in Kurdistan with intent to enter bilateral agreements without regard for our absence from the NUF. UDPK membership [in the NUF] is urgent and realistic to give all patriotic forces a more unified outlook.

We believe that bilateral agreements in the new era must be in accordance with general principles that are approved by the NUF in order to keep the national unity strong and solid.

Other forces mentioned in your program, which approve in principle the same specific goals regarding Kurdistan, are NUF members. Thus, there is no reason to isolate other democratic forces and disregard their efforts to achieve the same goals. Furthermore, we ought not to list goals for propaganda purposes only. Goals are to be realized. Therefore, significant forces ought to be presented as they are, not to the contrary. Why does the NUF program limit the work of our Party to Kurdistan? Meanwhile, we consider our Party the vanguard of struggle in Kurdistan, and we will not deal with the problems of Kurdistan in isolation from the general circumstances of Iraq. Our Party considers the cause of Iraqi Kurdistan part of the Iraqi cause. It is the responsibility of the Iraqi state and the policy of the patriotic parties to solve the issues concerning Kurdistan.

Accordingly, we believe, in principle, that both Parties must collaborate and cooperate. In other words, cooperation in party mottos, positions and solidarity between party forces anywhere they may be, after normalizing relations with the NUF. Differences between our Parties are not because of a motto or a position. We believe that your insistence on keeping your Party Chapters in Kurdistan is the main reason for discord. The solution our Party presented, to dissolve our and your Party organizations in Kurdistan and found a new democratic party, is a solution that is increasingly recognized by the cognizant elements who understand the circumstances in Kurdistan and the masses who are tired of divisions. Despite the fact that we are faced with the task of unifying the movement in Kurdistan as we explained, we believe that our cooperation is a step in this direction. Furthermore, our serious cooperation at the national level in Iraq will make Kurdistan a strong bastion for our beloved Republic and against the joint enemies of our country and republic. Therefore, in accordance with the principle of cooperation on which our Party has resolved to move, we have appointed a representative to contact your representative to conduct the initial negotiations to set up a program of cooperation as soon as possible.

Naturally, you should end the wave of attacks and charges against our Party to prepare an atmosphere conducive to such cooperation and in the spirit of sincere brotherhood. With our highest regards.

The Permanent Bureau
of the Central Leadership of the
Unified Democratic Party in Kurdistan
October 18, 1958

Translation from Arabic of Document No. 58

A Hand-Written Report by Jalal Talabani about the Conduct of the Communists

No sage in Iraq can deny the negative consequences of the ICP's wrong policy, a policy of leaders who greatly damaged the prestige of the Communist movement, USSR. It weakened the unity of the whole national movement and brought about an atmosphere of discord and division for all its parties. Below, I will list some shameful events that led to the destruction of the NUF and of the KDP–ICP Cooperation Accord.

1. The ICP leadership waged a large-scale attack on the KDP, asserting that the KDP is American and receives US dollars. They publicized their lies among Arabs and Kurds, and informed the government and President Abd al-Karim Qasim.

2. The ICP leadership widely accused the KDP of separatism and hostility toward the Republic. They exploited legitimate Kurdish demands as evidence of KDP separatism. When the KDP demanded our cultural rights and a Kurdish directorate of cultural and educational affairs, they sarcastically called it the directorate of 'Qiliyasan' after an ill-famed village, and presented it to the government as evidence of KDP separatism.

3. The ICP led a strong campaign accusing the KDP of serving feudalism, and provoked landowners, including those patriots who were in the peace movement. Indeed, they turned all landowners against the Republic and led many loyalists to join the traitors in Iran. Among those who fled to Iran were men who were considered Communists under the monarchy, such as Sheikh Mohammed Salih of Kleesa, near Kirkuk.

4. In effect, the Communists opposed all Kurdish rights including the recognition of Kurds and Kurdistan. Many of them in Suleimaniyya, Halabja, Koy Sanjaq and Rewanduz chanted Death to the Kurds and Kurdistan. Perhaps the incident of aggression against fifty young people of the Democratic Union of Kurdistan Youth a few months after the Revolution is a good example. As these youth went to visit their brothers in the Union's chapter in Halabja, Communists met them with pistols, daggers and clubs. They badly beat the youths and wounded sixteen of them. They would put their weapons to their heads and tell them "Dog, say I am from Kurdistan to kill you!" or "Say, Down with the Kurds and Kurdistan before I kill you!"

5. When the Minister of State, Fuad Arif visited Koy Sanjaq, the Communists gathered their forces, attacked KDP supporters, tore up their signs and loudly chanted "Death to the Kurds and Kurdistan," and officially requested the government to arrest all KDP affiliates.

6. In Koy Sanjaq, the ICP chief Fatih Rasoul told the District Governor that the KDP was plotting a U.S. conspiracy against the Republic. When our Party Representative criticized him at a NUF meeting, he insisted it was his patriotic task.

7. In Rewanduz, at a public meeting of Party members to commemorate the anniversary of four Kurdish martyrs on June 19, a Communist girl cried out "Death to the Kurds and Kurdistan" in response to calls by Party members "Glory for the martyrs of the Kurds and Kurdistan." Her colleagues chanted her call time and again.

8. In Zakho, Communists falsely informed the government that KDP members there were plotting an American conspiracy.

9. In Arbil in the presence of Arab nationalist officers who later supported the reactionary Shawwaf movement, the Communist in charge, Nafi' Younis, and others went to the Intelligence Officer Dawood al-Sayyed Khalil and told him that the KDP was plotting a separatist conspiracy and persuaded him to take measures against KDP a wide-spread campaign of arrests of Party members in Arbil, Koy Sanjaq, Shaqlawa and Rewanduz. Everywhere, they collaborated with nationalist officers among the Arab chauvinists who hated Kurdish nationalism, against the KDP and the democratic Kurdish movement.

10. In the presence of the PRM and Dawood aj-Janabi as Commander of the Second Division of the Iraqi army, they barred Party members from joining the PRM and committed the worst of terrorist activities against KDP members.

11. In Suleimaniyya, Rania and Qala Diza, the Communist PRM officer, accompanied by a well-known Communist, Karim Ahmad, member of the ICP's Central Committee and in his presence, gave [a speech] in all three cities asserting that the KDP and its Youth chapters are American agents and receive US dollars.

12. In Qala Diza, they arrested seven KDP members and drove them to Kirkuk. They demanded that they curse the KDP, Mulla Mustafa and Ibrahim Ahmad in order to release them. This is exactly how the Communists were pressured to curse Stalin, Fahd and the Communist Party under the monarchy. Our affiliates remained in jail for almost a month because they refused cursing and were tortured by Communists in a way rarely matched even under the monarchy.

13. In Rania, they arrested (8) KDP members who were asked to renounce their Party membership and goals. Severely tortured, they were released only after intervention from Baghdad at the highest level.

14. In Koy Sanjaq, they arrested (18) Party peasants. After two months of imprisonment, they were released, as Communist influence receded. The only reason [they were arrested] was that they were KDP members who refused to renounce Party membership and principles as well as refusing to affiliate with the ICP.

15. The PRM searched several houses of Party members in Gorashin village and stole everything useful. They were arrested and their guns and daggers were confiscated for their personal use, not for the State.

16. In the village of Gardi Azaban, near Arbil, a gang of PRM arrested senior KDP comrades, tied one with a rope to a pick-up truck [and dragged him] until his ribs were smashed and [he was] unconscious...

17. Using army units under their control, they waged a campaign against peasants loyal to our Party. Tens were arrested and the possessions of a similar number were looted. Their officers gave public speeches claiming that KDP members are American agents and receive American dollars, and they must be crushed and removed from contact with the masses.

18. In Koy Sanjaq, a group of Communists attacked a mud worker who was selling Khabat, the KDP newspaper. He was fired from his job, beaten, tied with a rope and dragged all the way to che governmental complex. He was hospitalized for two months, after which they tried to deport him, claiming that he was an Iranian Kurd. After two months of being moved from jail to jail, Communist influence had receded and this Kurdish worker was finally released.

19. In Khanaqin Communists (PRM) organized an armed attack on KDP members and assaulted their notables; they tried to drag Aziz Pishitiwan, a teacher who had lost his job 15 years earlier because of the Kurdish revolt in Barzan. Several others were beaten and arrested for 4 days.

20. In Imadia, they repeatedly assaulted Party members and wrote in their newspaper that they clashed with agents of imperialism and feudalism, meaning the KDP.

21. In Shaqlawa, they collaborated with feudalists Siddique Beg Miran, Othman Beg and Omer Beg against Party members to inform on them to the government and have them arrested.

22. They spread propaganda among the people especially in their demonstrations and meetings repeating in Kurdish "KDP is the party of dogs, the party of tribal chiefs and feudalists" in sarcasm aimed at our party slogan of "Our Party is the Party of the people, the Party of workers and peasants." In a similar manner, in Arbil they spread the following: "Our party is a dry battery, the party of Nasser and Shawwaf."

23. At the festivities of May 1, 1959, Communists barred KDP workers in many cities from participating in the celebrations, and in Arbil, Mr. Nafi' Younis said in response to a request from our Representative in the NUF committee and the Cooperation Accord, "The masses do not accept you. Therefor, we bar you from participation by force."

24. They arrested our Party chief in Arbil, attorney Shams ad-Din Mufti, after his return with a Party force from suppressing the rebel Lolan, under the pretext that he was heading the assumed American plot.

25. When a Czechoslovakian delegation visited Arbil, they held a mass meeting in the clubhouse. Representatives of ICP organizations were allowed to give speeches. No KDP representative or KDP affiliated popular organizations were allowed to give as much as a welcoming speech. When they were asked by Minister Faisal al-Samir, who was then director general, about the absence of the KDP, the ICP's senior cadre Francis Abd al-Ahad said, "KDP members are conspirators and were arrested yesterday." Faisal al-Samir, and Karim Shakir, the current director of the Baghdad radio station, both testify to this.

26. In Kirkuk Communists collaborated with the Turanis and tried to create a group in Arbil to oppose Kurdish nationalism. Mr. Mokarram Talabani stated in the presence of the Governor of Kirkuk and a group of Kurds and Turcomans that the government erred when entering Article Two in the Constitution. It should have entered Turcomans as equals to Arabs and Kurds. When one of our Party leaders explained that Arabs and Kurds are the main nationalities and the rest are ethnic minorities and even the Czech Constitution does not mention ethnic minorities as equals to their main nationalities, the Czechs and Slovaks, he said that this was chauvinism and an imperialist idea!

Attitude of Iraqi Communists Regarding Kurdish National Rights

Since 1951 the Communists have considered the Kurdish people an ethnic minority like the Turcomans, Assyrians and Armenians. They have denied the existence of the Kurdish nation. They have argued with our Party members that the Kurds are not a nation and that Kurdistan is an imperialist illusion.

In 1951 when Baha ad-Din assumed leadership, they amended their old Charter known as the Charter of Fahd, and recognized the Kurds as a nation with the right to self-determination, and described the Charter of Fahd as opportunistic. When Baha ad-Din was arrested in 1952, the Communists retracted their position on the Kurdish question which was [criticized] by Mr. Aziz Sharif in his book *The Kurdish Question in Iraq*, an underground publication. Since then, they have not adopted a correct position. In reality, their position borders on Arab bourgeois ideology and chauvinism, and they have suppressed the right to self-determination, even the right of autonomy, where the Kurdish people are concerned. They do, in fact, fight all Kurdistan democratic organizations inside Iraq and abroad.

Translation from Kurdish of Document No. 59

Part of a Report by the Kurdistan Student Union

b. Obviously, college students boycotted the elections. Elected committees have been established unopposed. In other words, they do not represent a segment of the student population which decided to keep their Union since they do not believe in the one mentioned. In addition, they decided to withdraw their winning students in high schools from the Conference. High school withdrawals and college boycotts mean that a fair segment of students do not believe in that Union and will maintain their own. If we withdraw from the Conference, it will mean continuation of the status quo, since there were three Unions and each operates on its own. Therefore, our assessment of the situation is the following:

— For the new Union to gain legitimacy and represent at least the majority of Iraqi students including Kurdistan, the Iraqis do not want us to withdraw, hoping to legitimize their Union.

— We will contact the ministry during our withdrawal and before the conference in order to recognize the existence of the Kurdistan Student Union, along with issuing memoranda and publications to underscore our principles and bring the majority of Kurdistan students back to this idea. We will attempt to make Iraqi students understand this point as well.

5. If nothing is achieved, we will continue our work as before and keep our Union.

These are our ideas. We hope that you will study them carefully and let us know your impressions.
Forward always...

High Committee of the
Kurdistan Student Union, Iraq
November 17, 1948

Translation from Arabic of Document No. 60

Memorandum of the Kurdistan Student Union

The Student Union of Kurdistan, Iraq (KSU) finds it necessary to shed some light on the following facts:

1. The KSU of Iraq was founded in 1953 to express the reality of our student movement and its patriotic, social and educational goals, thus, realizing the necessity to unify, lead and coordinate the struggle and activities of students for a better future, free and democratic academia to learning sciences, education and a bright future. Our people need educated experts in various arts and science specialties.

The special circumstances, nationalist issues and the historic phase which our people and students are undergoing provides all the necessary conditions to organize our students in union of their own which does not contradict the unity of the democratic student movement in Iraq to realize our common goals, especially as our union has expressed its full readiness to unify efforts and struggle with the rest of Iraqi students, to serve the interests of the people, the country and the Republic, the interests of Arab, Kurdish and other national minorities alike.

The KSU has relentlessly struggled and sacrificed in the battle of honor, the national student battle against imperialism, the hated monarchy and their treasonous agents until the immortal July 14 Revolution broke out, a Revolution led by our patriotic army and backed by the proud Iraqi people, including all classes and ranks thus realizing the greatest goal of our union in establishing a patriotic government and moving on the road to democracy. The KSU continues the struggle to buttress our beloved Iraqi Republic led by Abd al-Karim Qasim to realize the rest of our goals of peace, democracy, friendship and education.

Undoubtedly, we play our role in the struggle for international peace, fighting cosmopolitan and chauvinist, war, racial and national discrimination ideas. We contribute as well to buttressing the eternal fraternity and friendship between Arab and Kurdish peoples and all ethnic minorities of Turcomans, Armenians, Assyrians, and our Kurdish and Arab brother students in other parts of the Arab and Kurdish homelands. We struggle to unify the struggle of the student of Iraqi Kurdistan with the Arab and world students, to realize our national and student goals, to revive our national heritage and revolutionary glories, to raise the democratic awareness. This role of ours will strengthen the struggle of all Arab and other students in the world, and will bring them closer to their noble goals. Therefore, naturally our union will expect support and assistance from Arab and other students in the world.

2. The existence of the KSU does not mean division and discord among Iraqi students. Obviously, a student organization is not a political party and is formed on the bases that students are "a group of people living in similar circumstances and comparable conditions," since student problems and goals cannot be solved and realized respectively but through organized struggle which can be done only through organization and mobilization of forces in a rational manner and according to correct and scientific principles. Therefore, wherever there are common problems and demands under specific circumstances, there is a necessity to struggle and solve them, hence, the necessity to found an organization to lead the struggle. Accordingly, Kurdistan students face specific problems, specific circumstances, and have specific demands that necessitate the existence of our union, the KSU. Our willingness to join as a member in the General Student Union of Iraq (GSU) negates all charges of separatism and division ... etc. This proves that the KSU can rally and unify all student forces with their Iraqi counterparts. It can defend and preserve our national Kurdish heritage and culture, render the necessary efforts to solve their educational problems while no other organization, preoccupied by general struggle, can exert such necessary efforts. Furthermore, the Students of Iraqi Kurdistan know better than others their own problems and bear the responsibility to solve them, to realize their demands, and aspirations and to struggle for their own rights.

3. The KSU strives to unify struggle with the rest of Iraqi students. Since its founding, the KSU has worked to strengthen and buttress the common struggle with their Arab brothers and other Iraqi students on correct scientific bases. The KSU asked the GSU to collaborate and join the struggle according to agreed upon terms.

After long deliberations and after the KSU exerted great efforts on both domestic and international levels, we reached an agreement with the GSU in 1956 on the day of the conference of the International Student Union (IUS) which was attended by a KSU observer representative within the Iraqi delegation. This Prague agreement was concluded in the presence of the guide Sadiq Babek, in charge of the Middle East Section of the IUS. He advised the necessity of the existence of an organization for the students of Iraqi Kurdistan under the name of the Kurdistan Student Union, Iraq. Later, the KSU and the GSU agreed to combine the chapters of both unions in Iraqi Kurdistan into a single organization called the Student Union of Iraqi Kurdistan, and a high Committee of both sides was formed. Both organizations in Kurdistan were indeed combined into one union which joined the GSU as a member. This agreement was carried out for about two years. . . . On July 14, the day of the immortal Revolution, GSU members proclaimed that this agreement was wrong. The KSU upheld it and insisted on implementing its terms, and demanded the GSU uphold and implement its terms as well. Despite rejecting our demand, we continued to cooperate in service of the best interests of the student movement and its joint struggle.

The KSU continues to view its own existence as a student, patriotic and historical necessity. It realizes that neither the Iraqi union nor any other can defend and struggle for all our patriotic and student goals. Despite some of the best progressive Arab members, the GSU does not uphold a single goal of ours, while it wholeheartedly upholds and supports Arab goals from the ocean to the gulf. The GSU does not work for any of our national goals in the Iranian and Turkish parts of Kurdistan despite atrocities committed against our people there. In international circles, Iraqi delegations are purely Arabic and no Kurdish delegation is allowed to express the just demands, goals, and aspirations of the Kurdish people. These facts are common knowledge.

Furthermore, the KSU's existence is a constitutional right according to Article 3 of the Provisional Constitution of our Republic. It recognized the Kurdish national rights in Iraq. Naturally, national rights include, first of all, the rights of Kurdish organizations, the simplest of which are the educational, social and other organizations. Therefore, our union insists on having an organization for the students of Kurdistan.

It is worth mentioning that our students' and people's exercise of their national rights will strengthen the unity of the two fraternal peoples and buttress Iraqi unity. History has made it amply clear that in multi-ethnic states, brotherhood among peoples cannot be sustained unless people's national rights are granted and exercised equally and freely by all. Czechoslovakia is a splendid example. On the contrary, to deny national rights and bar their free exercise will undoubtedly destroy unity and mar fraternity among peoples. Therefore, we who struggle for the exercise of our national rights are serving our republic and the cause of Iraqi brotherhood and unity of our two fraternal peoples. In practice, we end the role of imperialist propaganda and that broadcasted by Tehran radio asserting that the Kurds are beguiled and will get no national rights. Those who bar us from exercising our rights under the pretext of Iraqi unity, joint struggle and other excuses are indeed, consciously or unconsciously, harming our common cause, our fraternal unity, and genuine Iraqi unity.

4. Having said all this, it is our belief and right that the new Iraqi student union recognizes the KSU's necessity to exist as a member in the new union. Otherwise, the KSU will continue its glorious struggle. Our victory is inevitable because our cause is just, and justice will always prevail.

Translation from Kurdish of Document No. 61

A Report by the KDP Chapter in Rewanduz Regarding the Conduct of Communists

Important and Very Urgent

To: President of the Unified Kurdistan Democratic Party (UDPK), Baghdad Respectfully submitted.

Copy to: Arbil Local Committee of the UDPK.

Revolutionary greetings:

Precisely after Newroz Day, [there occurred] a recent and significant change in ICP policy in the Rewanduz region threatening our Party and the national movement in general. Careful analysis and evaluation clearly revealed that it was neither a hasty and spontaneous development nor a transitional measure... UDPK hostile, it is based on belief and for tactical gains and power... that is clearing parties and isolating ours from the masses by falsely accusing us of treason and collaboration with feudalism and reactionaries. The ICP aim is to exclusively dominate the political theater. We never thought of weakening ICP or questioned the glorious Marxist-Leninist principles. We have led the masses on this path and according to this ideology.... Unhappy with our move adopting Marxism-Leninism as our ideology or guide, they fear our move will weaken and lead to their diminishing. Their propaganda is focussed on [conveying the message that the KDP cannot lead workers, peasants and the poor to realize their hopes and goals. Against our will, they want us to be the party of tribal chiefs, feudalists and the bourgeoisie. Of course, by bourgeoisie they mean the dark bourgeoisie. Cursing and provoking, they are openly fighting us.... They are teaching the students of Iraq, especially girls and women, to curse us in the stores and market places... (Death to KDP)... in the cities, they teach villagers... and some nefarious individuals to curse us and spread it about that the KDP is like the Baath... and it will face a fate like those in Mosul, dragged in the streets. The ICP claims that the KDP is against the beloved Republic, supports its enemies and imperialism. They shamelessly watch UDPK activities. They are creating a deep rift between the two Parties, undermining the patriotic movement and turning the masses away from it. Below are some illegitimate ICP practices in Rewanduz for your information and to take immediate measures to end this deteriorating situation.

1. Since Newroz, they have ignored the Cooperation Accord and the UDPK altogether.

2. They established a Workers' Union without informing us. They gathered a number of workers and gave a speech on the basis that "today is our day", and there are no others. They requested their Union permit in Rewanduz despite knowing that more than 70% of Rewanduz workers are with us. Despite our explanation that there should be only one union, our workers pressed us to establish our own. Having two unions in the Rewanduz area contradicts the Cooperation Accord and the interests of the working class. We told them that when a permit is granted they may join as well. As we keep faith, the ICP ignores us.

3. The ICP's Hussein Haji Tahir, while in the Cooperation Committee, said to two of our workers, "Why are you to tie your fates to the KDP! You'll suffer and become unemployed if you stay with the UDPK, since it will not be permitted to work. Just like the Baathists, the day will come when we will make a second Mosul here." They were advised to stay away from the KDP and to join the ICP.

4. A few days ago, someone carried a letter from one of the villages to a member of our local Committee. A stranger in Rewanduz, he asked where so and so's shop was. Hussein Haji Tahir, an ICP member, answered, "What do you want from him?" He told him that he had a letter for him. Hussein Haji Tahir told him, "So and so is my brother. Give me the letter." The man handed him the letter. Eventually we learned of the incident and retrieved the letter... but after Hussein Haji Tahir got what he wanted. This is how they humiliate us and check our secrets.

5. In the market places and in front of shops, they come in groups armed with clubs and sticks, curse and abuse our comrades in order to provoke, exploit and ignite conflicts. Our comrades have been boiling as well. We fear an eruption of hostilities.

6. In cars and in demonstrations, they go into bazaars, attack our Party and as they pass in cars, they shout to provoke our comrades.

7. If a tribal chief or a spy comes to town, they spread it about that he is a UDPK member, and attach all negatives to the UDPK.

8. They curse our comrades and mar their reputations. Lately, they have became so brazen they attack Mustafa Barzani in cafés and before the masses in an attempt to defame and tarnish his struggle and prestige... Ibrahim Ahmad and others are denigrated constantly.

9. The Communists waged a propaganda campaign against our chapter in Diyana, asserting that the UDPK is discriminating against Assyrians and informed the government that the UDPK went to Diyana to drive a wedge between the Kurds and Assyrians. They lashed out at our Chapter and pleaded for the Assyrians, claiming that there is no need for two parties in Diyana. Sheikh Najim and Hayder Qadir, two ICP functionaries, openly spread this odious propaganda. Avoiding unwarranted consequences, we 'froze' our activities and remained silent.... I believe that brother Hamid Othman of Rewanduz is well aware of the situation in Diyana with the Assyrians.

10. As requested by the Minister of Guidance, a joint committee from the ICP and UDPK visited him to end this discord. However, the ICP official, Sheikh Sulayman Mustafa, attacked our superior and accused him of suspicious contacts with conspirators and corrupt elements. When he was asked to clarify that and to provide one single name of those in contact with our superior, the ICP envoy was speechless and lowered his eyes. Even the Minister was angry with him and said to him "Hush, hush. Don't turn this place into your market." He hushed and the episode was over. After the meeting, they stayed with the lieutenant colonel who was with the Minister, the Police Chief and their staff. They must have spoken negatively and lied about the KDP, and members of our local Committee especially our Committee Chair. If this is ignored by our leadership, it will certainly have adverse consequences.

11. On the evening of April 4, 1959 Kurdistan Democratic Youth, Rewanduz chapter, produced a play and brothers from Kawkolan were invited. They came to Rewanduz and attended the play. As our comrades came from Kawkolan, ICP members stopped them in the city and assaulted them under the pretext that "You must be searched ... we do not trust you." This is how they treat us.

12. Within Rewanduz again, they fight our educated members and accuse them of treason, spying, terrorism and separatism to taint their reputation and humiliate them in public. The ugliest thing they did in this regard is their assault on our Chairman. They believe that he is everything, and our party activities depend solely on him. They believe if he is removed, the KDP is destroyed then and there. Therefore, they are fighting our Chairman at all levels. ... For three months and until yesterday April 9, 1959, they could not affect him because he is well known, admirable and trustworthy. He is a true patriot and loyal. All their plots failed until April 9.

On April 9, 1959 Fuad Arif, Minister of Guidance, came to Rewanduz. In the evening, the Military Governor issued an order to arrest two individuals from Rewanduz, and forced them into exile in the south. Both had no contact with the KDP at all. This is a fact of which the ICP is well aware. But because their children are in college and some of them are government employees, and some of their relatives are KDP members, just as other relatives are ICP members, the ICP exploited the issue and their members went into the streets chanting "KDP members are under arrest ... all are traitors ... all are being exiled." Thus, they created a tense atmosphere and spread it about that our Committee Chairman "the senior traitor KDP secretary" was also arrested and that he was exiled to Samawa.

Another local ICP Committee member, [and the] head of the Student Union Committee, also an ICP member, gathered people in their café and spoke "Brothers, I want to give you the good news that the head of the UDPK was a traitor and he was arrested; the day will come for the rest." (This proved that the KDP is a traitor and [its members] must be dragged through the streets!) He had told one of the comrades earlier that he ought to go into hiding before they arrested him, and told another, to run away before being arrested. They applauded and danced in the café, delighted at the arrest of KDP members. Almost in hysteria, they moved northward through the town singing and shouting. In this manner, they try to induce hysteria in the public and fight our Party in the streets. They attacked our members with daggers in full view of the public. This is unbearable and dangerous. It must be resolved immediately. We are prepared to provide names and witnesses for investigation. The UDPK comrade who was assaulted in public, accused of treason and other crimes decided to take his case to the court against Hussein Haji Tahir, Taqi ad-Din and Zrar Abdullah, all prominent ICP members; but in accordance with the Committee resolution, he is awaiting leadership measures. So, please let us know quickly. Should he go to court or not? How will the case impact the National Front and the High Committee of

Cooperation? To date, Communists have not stopped attacking us. In fact, they are becoming more severe, to get him out of here regardless of the cost. We are afraid that they will assault him. Then we will have to respond and take revenge for ourselves. We believe that the government is involved against us. Please let the leadership know immediately to protect our comrades, and not to permit these schemes.

Translation from Arabic of Document No. 62

A Report from the KDP's Local Committee in Zakho to Barzani

The great patriot Mustafa Barzani, Esq.

With our utmost allegiance and loyalty, we wish you good health and success. Trustworthy hero and loyal soldier, we all have and will sacrifice our lives and possessions for our eternal Republic and glorious leader Abd al-Karim Qasim. We have and will continue to prove our sincerity over time. Thus, our utmost loyalty to our Republic and leader demands that we present the ongoing events in our district (Zakho). We hope that you will decisively present them to the officials to avoid what might happen in the future.

Early on we called for and demanded the establishment of the PRM in Zakho. This was done. Unfortunately, the PRM Commander, First Lt. Adnan, asserts exclusive reservation for the Communists. To avoid the citizens' aversion and animosity, we have repeatedly discussed with him a halt to limiting PRM to Communists. Furthermore, he should, as an army officer, be above proclivities and orientations according to the principle set forth by leader Abd al-Karim Qasim. His conduct has remained unchanged, until now. Below is a list summarizing his violations and suspicions regarding his Comrade, Second Lt. Sinharib, Commander of the PRM in Pesh Khabur, whose conduct is the same.

1. First Lt. PRM Commander Adnan's participation, with the district governor of Zakho, Mr. Salim Abd al-Razzaq and other ICP affiliates in the town of Zakho, to form Farm Cooperatives. For the past two months, he has been sending armed PRM to villages threatening and pressuring peasants to sign up.

2. In First Lt. Adnan's presence, PRM members said that anyone not affiliated with the ICP will not be accepted in the PRM. Other PRM members harassed a minority of democratic PRM members: if they do not chant 'the party of comrades is a great party' they should leave the PRM.

3. Just before the past Eid al-Adha (Muslim Holiday), the PRM and the District Governor talked about organizing Communist-only border guard units. Zakho's Army Induction Officer is also involved.

4. Before the al-Adha Holiday, a delegation went to Mosul to complain to the Division Commander against the district governor and PRM Commander for their pro-ICP conduct excluding all other sincere citizens despite that we are many times more than they, and loyal to the immortal Republic and president Abd al-Karim Qasim. Incidentally, they met the Mosul Intelligence Officer, an army major, who insulted them by saying "You are complaining about the Communists while you are the culprits... etc." The delegation verbally informed the Division Commander of what they heard from the Chief of Intelligence. It was humiliating to a patriotic delegation which had actually come to complain regarding the conduct of the District Governor and the PRM commander.

5. Again just before the Grand Feast, Second Lt. Mohammed Rashid al-Haj Badri, a ranking officer in Mosul known for his pro-ICP conduct, came to Zakho and visited the

village of Aspindarok of the Sindi Subdistrict. Later we learned that a vehicle carrying a coffin went to this and other nearby villages, namely Livo, Nav Kendal, and Mirgasur. This coffin was one of those seen on the Mosul-Zakho road and suspected to be full of weapons. It was confiscated.

6. Late afternoon of June 25, 1959, a dispatch indicated confiscation of a coffin full of weapons from a PRM member traveling from Mosul to Zakho. At the same time, a delegation of the Defense League of Women's Rights travelled from Mosul to Zakho. Threats of dragging in the streets, their known slogans as well as slogans from those who received them were: "Tonight 'proxies' will be trimmed/People, execute your pledge tonight." At night, a PRM group was seen on the outskirts of Zakho on the road to Mosul, waiting, we think, to receive munitions.

7. Despite the Military Governor-General's cable requesting that all PRM weapons and munitions be stored in depots and should not be carried, Lt. Adnan, PRM commander in Zakho, did not lay down his arms. When he was informed, he said that he would act according to his own interpretation of the order because the situation in Zakho was different from other places. Later, he had to turn arms in. However, on the night of June 27, 1959, the PRM retrieved their weapons and munitions from the depot by an order from Lt. Adnan who disappeared all night and day, raising anxiety and rumors in Zakho. At the time, we informed the District Governor and Police Chief of our readiness to sacrifice for our eternal Republic and leader Abd al-Karim Qasim, and that we awaited their orders to crush any plot against our Republic and champion Abd al-Karim Qasim. They told us to stay alert without causing any provocation. We are ready to meet any suspicious move.

8. Second Lt. Sinharib, commander of the PRM in Pesh Khabur is a copycat of Lt. Adnan. Disobeying the Military Governor-General, his PRM are still armed, and threaten villagers that they will be arrested if they do not join the ICP.

9. The PRM commander and his militia continue to hold suspicious secret meetings. After midnight they went out in a car to some Sindi villages and returned just before dawn. They were seen by the guards, the police and some of our loyal citizens. They were heard talking about the leader because he did not go along with them. They do not dare talk in our comrades' presence because they know that we are loyal soldiers, ready to sacrifice, and we have wide popular support inside and outside the town. Didn't we happily march on Mosul and quell Shawwaf's ugly plot? They had only two unarmed out of a 200 strong force, and Zakho citizens are well aware of that.

10. The PRM commander distributed the arms he received among his special group, and they still have them.

11. Lt. Col. Mohammed Ali, who used to come from Kirkuk to search and arrest the indicted with a feudalist from Zakho, now visits in the company of Communists. He walks behind Communist representatives from Mosul. Once he visited the Worker's Union in Zakho and threatened to arrest anyone who refuses to join the Communists.

12. We suspect that the PRM are bringing weapons from Mosul to Zakho. Their women have indicated this. We are seriously looking for evidence, and ready to crush any dirty plot against the republic and its president.

13. We sent someone to Mosul to inform the Division Commander of the situation described above. He had gone to Baghdad. Excluding the named 'Sha'ban,' a telephone directory attendant, no one can be depended on at the Telephone and Post office. The corporal in charge of the communications in Zakho Intelligence is not reliable either. This is what we thought Your Eminence should know. We have promised to remain loyal soldiers and alert guards ready to sacrifice at a moment's notice to defend our beloved Republic and leader Abd al-Karim Qasim. We are under your command and await your advice on this path and sacred sacrifice. May Allah protect you, a loyal defender of our immortal Republic and our only leader Abd al-Karim Qasim.

P.S.: You may learn more detail from the bearer of this letter.

P.P.S.: We have send two of our members to see you. They have important information regarding the foundations of a conspiracy against our immortal Republic and leader Abd al-Karim Qasim, and against our Eminence. Please see them in private, and you may trust and depend on them because they are very loyal to the Republic, the leader, you and the people.

Local Committee of Zakho

[Seal—No. 15, Date: July, 3, 1959]

Translation from Arabic of Document No. 63

A Report from the Khanaqin Area Regarding Problems with the ICP

1. On the night of June 18, 1959, a group of UDPK members and supporters, on their way from Khanquin to Kifri, stopped here for an hour to rest. Immediately after they left, ICP affiliates, led by Hama Ahmad Rustam, Ahmad Fattah Rustam and Ali Muhyeddin, organized an armed demonstration attacking our homes and chanting "Your party is pure, half vile, half evil." In this raid, they fired their guns in the presence of all 22 village police.

2. On the night of June 21, 1959, another armed demonstration including guns, was led by some of those mentioned in paragraph 1 on the anniversary of the martyrdom of the five peasants in Nasiriyya. As usual, they chanted slogans against us. Furthermore, they attacked the homes of Sheikh and his son Ali Sheikh. Both were dragged out into the street and beaten for no fault of theirs. In this demonstration, Ahmad Fattah Rustam, Hama Ahmad Rustam, Mahmud Amin, Amin Sameen, Khola Pikha, Mohammed Qaleh Mizgard, Bakr Abd al-Karim, Shilair, and Hamad Pira who are ICP affiliates attacked Mohammed Wali, Wali Ali, Jairan Akbar, Saeed Sheikh, Ali Sheikh, Mohammed Chatri, Badee'a Sheikh, Lamima Sheikh, all UDPK affiliates, with clubs, daggers and stones that resulted in stabbing both Mohammed Wali and Mohammed Chatri with daggers and Jairan Akbar receiving a gun shot wound. Both Mohammed Wali and Jairan Akbar are hospitalized in the al-Jamhori Hospital. Both are in critical condition. Mohammed Chatri and Saeed Sheikh are in jail at the Kifri Police Station, despite their multiple injuries. All Kalar police testify to the truth of these incidents.

3. On June 14, 1959, while we were sitting in the café of Shirwaneh Police Station with Hama Khan, corporal in charge of the station, Ahmad Fattah Rustam stated that "Leader Abd al-Karim Qasim committed a mistake and if he had not recanted, we would have completely destroyed him." The corporal objected by saying that it is not appropriate for any loyal person to say this about the popular and only leader Abd al-Karim Qasim. Rustam insisted and repeated his statement.

4. Ahmad Fattah Rustam, Hama Ahmad Rustam, Mahmud al-Haj Pidra Muhyeddin, Khola Pikha, Rahim Khaza, Othman Khidir, Ali Muhyeddin, Omer Khidir, Hama Saeed Qadir Aghamir, Qadir Nadir, Hama Sabir, Shafiq al-Haj Majeed, Mahmud Hayder Ahmad Jaff and many other ICP affiliates openly carry various types of arms. They provoke and attack us constantly. We are not allowed to carry even sticks and daggers. We are still silent and suffering!

5. On June 21, 1959, a demonstration was organized in Tuz Khormato on the anniversary of the martyrdom of the five peasants in Nasiriyya. There was an ICP group led by Salih Felamerz, Sheikh Tayyib, Shahbaz, and Zayn al-Abideen. In the demonstration Salih Felamerz attacked a number of UDPK affiliates. Because they were armed, the UDPK

group registered a complaint with the government office. As a result, Commander of the Military Police in Kirkuk, Fakhri Abd al-Karim, came to investigate. Instead of objective investigation, he snubbed and abused the democrats despite the fact they were assaulted. He said "All Kurds are traitors and conspirators. I curse the dead of those who admitted you into the PRM . . . Pimps . . . Kurds are all sh—" Then he turned to an ICP group there, pointing to the democrats. "By God, were not these agents of Nuri al-Sa'id?" They responded "Yes, by God, they were worse than spies."

After all this cursing and humiliation, they took Salih Felamerz to Kirkuk. The next day, he returned carrying an automatic gun of the Sten type. He walked the streets cursing and assaulting any democrat who came his way. We were forced to send a telegram to His Eminence the Military Governor-General letting him know of the results. Then, we heard that he sent a military vehicle from Kirkuk. We do not know what measure he will take against him. Despite all this, we are still patiently waiting and loyal to our Republic, and we will remain steadfast to sacrifice all we have for our Republic and our one and only President, the Staff Colonel.

Mohammed Qadir Amin   Ali Saleem
[Signed]   [Signed]

Translation from Arabic of Document No. 64

A Report submitted by a Kurdish Sergeant to KDP leadership about what befell Kurdish officers and soldiers during the Shawwaf Movement.
Massoud Barzani

A Report by Sergeant Siddique Abd al-Aziz of the Lesser Mobilization Wing About the al-Shawwaf Conspiracy

On March 5, 1959 the Brigade issued a directive to all units of the Mosul camp to remain on alert because of Peace Supporters' arrival on March 6, 1959 in Mosul. On March 7, 1959 at 3:00 P.M., the alert was lifted and I went to the town and saw a demonstration repeating "Long Live Abd al-Karim Qasim." I went home. At 6.00 P.M., a camp Corp. came and asked me to return to the Stone Barrack in half an hour. I dressed and went to a bus stop near the Textile Factory at about 7:00 P.M. I found that buses were not running. I asked the guard and he told me that a curfew was in effect. Since the camp was very far, I called Lt. Col. Mikhael Abd al-Karim and told him that I was stranded. He told me to stay home. The next morning, March 8, 1959, I arrived at the camp in a military vehicle at 7:15 A.M. As I reached the camp shop, I found that the Stone Barracks were surrounded by guards from the Fifth Brigade. I was astounded. I asked a soldier and he told me that a number of patriotic officers had been under arrest since midnight. He added that they were looking for me. I knew that a plot against the government of Iraq was underway. I tried to escape by the back door. As I reached the stone staircase, I found guards who told me that leaving the camp has forbidden. I returned and tried to leave through the door leading to the riverside. I found it closed and guarded. I returned to the main gate and a Lance Corp. told me that the Commander was looking for me. We went together but did not find him. The traitor Lt. Kamil Ismail spotted us. He told me that I was under arrest. At this time, first Lt. Yousif Miran and Col. Salim of the Engineering Battalion entered the citadel. The traitor Lt. Kamil and his soldiers aimed their automatic rifles and ordered the two officers to drop their weapons and that they were under arrest. As Lt. Yousif Miran pulled his handgun, the traitor Corp. Mal Allah struck him on the hand with his pistol and led them to the jail. I found an opportunity to escape through the long tunnel leading to the south gate of the citadel. At the end of that tunnel, I found guards carrying automatic rifles. I went toward the river and I found the banks guarded by automatic fire from the top of the castle. Trapped, I returned, only to meet the traitor Lt. Kamil Ismail who directed his automatic rifle at me and yelled, "Didn't I tell you to wait here?" I told him that I had not moved. He ordered me to the jail. I asked, "why am I arrested? Is there an order to arrest me?" He said, "go to jail or I will shoot you." He added that "You are under arrest by the order of the Brigade Commander." I found the jail was full of patriots. Of them I remember Corps Ayyob Khalid, Khalid Taha and Hatim Ubaid, Lance Corps, the late Mustafa Taili, privates Jafar Abd al-Karim and Zuhair Yasin, and finally, myself of the Lesser Mobilization Wing. From the Engineering Battalion were Head Corp. Salih, sergeants Mustafa, Ahmad, Mohammed Siddique, Salah, and some others whose names I do not recall.

As I entered, they welcomed me and I greeted them all and reassured them. They said the plot is underway and here we are all in jail. Reassuringly, I told them that they were not alone and the conspiracy would not succeed, that I had seen in the adjacent room many arrested civilians, and in the next room another group of civilians, that I had heard the radio moments earlier that President Abd al-Karim Qasim is alive and well and would deal with it forcefully and decisively. They asked "Are you certain that the president is alive?" I replied, "Of course I am sure." They were somewhat reassured. Half an hour later, the door opened and the traitor Lt. Kamil Ismail was standing in the door with his automatic rifle in his hand and soldiers were lined up in two rows; each was carrying an automatic rifle. The Lt. called us to get out. As we did, we were standing between two rows of soldiers. He ordered us to move. We walked toward the gate leading to the river. We told each other that the game is about over and it was time for farewell comrades. However, before reaching the outer gate, guards climbed the stone staircase leading to the second floor and ordered us to follow them up. We took deep breaths and climbed up the stairs. They took us to a room on the second floor, overlooking the street leading to the river and the forest of the southern side of the citadel.

About 25 of us were crammed in a small room which holds only two beds. In the next room, there were about 35 people. The majority of us were Kurds. Among us were only 3 or 4 of our Arab comrades. Our total was about 65, food and water were forbidden, lavatories were replaced with metal containers. We would ask the head guard, Lance Corp. Abd al-Jabbar of our wing, about the events. He would bring us the latest correct news. At about 4:00 P.M. of March 8, 1959, the traitor Lt. Khairullah Askr entered our room, ordered us to stand in one row and said that they were not Abd al-Karim Qasim and that they would shoot us dead. With his mouth he produced sounds imitating automatic guns. Pointing to Head Corp. Salih of the Engineering Battalion, he said, "And you, of course chief of the cell here." Salih replied, "I do not know what you mean?" The traitor said to him, "By Stalin, do you not know about the cell? Tell me how many do you command? He did not answer him. Corp. Hatim Ubaid of the Mobilization Wing asked him, "Sir what did I do?" As the traitor Lt. turned to him, I said, "Sir, only two days ago you were with us at the Mobilization seminar and we served and taught you. Are you going to shoot us for our efforts?" He lowered his rifle and said, "no, you rank officers of the Mobilization Wing do not have to worry. You are arrested for security and to control any move you might do. We will release you tomorrow at 12:00 noon, so do not worry..." Then the traitor left after he almost killed us. Ten minutes later, the head guard came in and gave us the good news by saying that Baghdad had learned of the conspiracy, and Shawwaf had been dismissed. We were delighted and began clapping, singing Long Live Leader Abd al-Karim Qasim until 6:30 P.M. when a car from the Engineering Battalion brought us food. Under the rice in the huge container, there were thin but strong cords and an iron saw to cut the iron bars if we needed to. Later, we agreed to cut the iron window grilles and use the ropes to go down the windows. At least 30 feet high, it would be impossible to escape without the cords. At about 9:00 P.M., I looked out the window and I found that they had put an armed guard for each window. Then, we began discussing the situation and the means that would ensure our escape and obtaining arms. In the end, we did not find any other way but to break the door and take over the rifles and lances. At 9:30 P.M., the head guard, a loyalist, was replaced by a corp. of the traitors. We realized that the game was dangerous. At 10:05 P.M., the officer on call, Major Abd al-Jabbar Abd al-Rahman of the Lesser Mobilization Wing, stopped by the guard near the windows and asked him about his duty. The guard replied, "I am guarding the windows." He told him, "Be alert and if any prisoner tries to escape through the window, you are to shoot him or stab him with your lance." The guard replied, "Yes sir." Then, Corp. Khalid Taha told me, "Did you hear what the Major said?" I said, "Yes, and God willing he will be punished for this statement." We feared they would banish us at night to a faraway place. Therefore, we decided to have four of us guard the door. If traitors attacked us, then the four guards would respond by a suicide attack. Thus, we would overpower them by sheer numbers; but nothing happened that night.

On the morning of March 9, 1959, we learned that the patriotic officers were still in their cell, unharmed. At 7:00 we heard the sound of machine-gun fire from the al-Ghuzlani Garrison. Then we saw two airplanes of the Fury type in the sky of Mosul. We feared that the Furies were those under the control of al-Shawwal and his clique in Mosul. The shooting intensified and then stopped after a short while. At about 8:30 we saw four airplanes of the Villi type in the sky. We were delighted to see them, gave them a standing ovation and sang Long Live Abd al-Karim Qasim. We saw them swoop toward the headquarters of the traitor Shawwaf. There was a loud explosion, and dark smoke billowed. We knew that bold pilots scored direct hits. Shooting intensified and the noise got close to our jail (Stone Barracks). A few of us tried to break open the door, but we decided that it was too dangerous to go out since traitors were everywhere. After only fifteen minutes, we saw a mixed civilian and military demonstration marching from Dawwaseh toward the castle. They shouted, "Long Live Abd al-Karim Qasim, and no leader but him, down with renegade traitors." As they approached the Works Office, guards on top of the building opened fire and killed three of them. The demonstrators moved into the Works Plaza and behind the walls. We heard a voice shouting "Do not fire, you will not escape, traitors. The dirty Shawwaf has been killed and they are dragging him through the streets. If you do not believe us, we will bring him here for you to see with your own eyes." The traitors responded with more fire. A civilian wearing a dark coat proceeded until he approached the citadel and yelled, "Soldiers do not fire at your brothers. They are from you and for you. You traitor officers, why do you insist on rebellion? You know that the conspiracy has failed, and your commander, al-Shawwaf is being dragged through the streets." They kept firing but the man continued to advance. Suddenly, the shooting stopped for about fifteen minutes, then we heard intensified shooting in the airport camp, and the noise became closer and we heard soldiers in the southern forest of the citadel. Under intense fire, many demonstrators fell in the forest near the wall and the rest retreated and moved to the east of the castle on the riverside. At this time Lt. Col. Abd al-Majeed Abd al-Hakim al-Radhwani came to the prison door and asked, "Who is there?" We replied "Non-coms, should we break the door?" He said "No, just wait." At this very moment private first class Hussein Ahmad Abdullah of the Mobilization Wing came in carrying a picture of Abd al-Karim Qasim and said, "Brothers break the door, the Engineering Battalion is here." The Lt. Col. responded, "Under whose order?" The private told him, "My order." We did not wait. We destroyed the door and window in the blink of an eye and took the weapons from the guards; only three rifles. I asked the guard, "Where are the guns and the munitions?" He said that the Corp. took them, and he left only five bullets per rifle.

Three rank officers armed with rifles and the rest of us with pieces of wood from the broken door, we quickly moved through the space between the soldiers loyal to us and the traitors without being hit despite heavy firing. We reached a corner where soldiers had arrived before us and each of us took an automatic gun or a rifle. Six of us climbed to the top of the citadel. They were petty officer trainees late Hazim, Corp. Ayyob Khalid, and Lance Corp. late Mustafa Taili and another non com—whose name I don't call, and myself. We took shelter behind the wall, and I was beside the late Lance Corp. Mustafa Taili. We saw someone firing from his 'Bern' machine gun into the street at the approaching demonstrators. I told the late Mustafa Taili of the fire behind him so as to warn him. Then, I fired a round and signaled to him to stop. He looked at us and turned his gun on us as if to shoot. I did not give him a second chance and opened fire until my gun was empty. I returned to get more munitions and before me were the first private Hussein Abdullah and Corp. Ayyob Khalid. On the stone stairs, two fell and rolled down. They were petty officer trainee Hazim and Lance Corp. Mustafa Taili. A riot swept us, all wanting to go back up, but some rank officers stopped us saying that it was suicide to go back up. Some of us went to release the Free Officers from prison. I was behind Corp. Khalid Taha, protecting his back as he advanced. As we approached Wing headquarters, we came under fire, and Corp. Khalid Taha stopped suddenly and turned to me, I saw him bleeding. I asked him, Brother are you O.K.?" He said slight injury and continued toward the officers' prison. I left him and moved down to the civilians' prison. I found the door broken and prisoners leaving. I greeted them and I saw Lt. Col. Majeed al-Radhwani sitting at the door of the weapons depot, his pistol still in his hand. He stood up and greeted me and said that he broke the door of the civilian prison and that he did so and so. I replied that he did it after knowing that they failed, and he would see how we would finish them. I kept watching him until a Free Officer took him to jail.

Then, we cleared all the rooms of the stone garrison. The roof of the castle remained [to be taken] because of the intense resistance. Each rank officer occupied a section of the castle and began throwing explosives and hand grenades onto the roof to kill their resistance. We tried several times to climb to the top but failed. At about 7:30 P.M. on the evening of March 9, 1959, we saw a few persons walking on the roof toward the stairs leading down, Head Corp. Salih of the Engineering Battalion called to them, "Turn yourselves in and we guarantee your safety." They stopped at the top of the stairs. It was very dark and we could not turn on lights for fear of being seen. They said, "We are afraid if we give up, you will kill us." We said, "No not at all." Lt. Yousif Miran came and they brought a portable light. He ordered them to drop their weapons down the stairs. They did. Then we ordered them to come down. They did and they were eight rank officers, one first private, and six privates. We asked them if there was anyone remaining on the roof. They said only one; they were not certain if killed or wounded. They said that the traitor officers had left at dusk. We did not believe them and did not go up for fear of being tricked. We took them to jail and all their weapons were automatic of 'Port Saeed' type. We armed ourselves with their weapons and a private had only 20 bullets left because he did not know how to use his gun, and the bullets were in his pocket. We left the staircase under heavy guard. Rank officers split up, each controlling one section of the castle. The shooting continued until the morning of March 10, 1959. Then, we completely controlled the castle including the roof which was empty except for one killed. Having secured the citadel, some of us went to the city to command the soldiers and each cleared a section with the help of an armored vehicle and rank officers of various units. In two days, the city was well cleared.

Officers and rank officers who participated in the conspiracy at Stone Garrison were:

1. Lt. Col. Abd al-Majeed al-Radhwani, armed and active participant; he was a member of the plot from the Lesser Mobilization Wing.

2. Major Adnan Shams ad-Din, armed and very active in the conspiracy (Mobilization Wing).
3. Major Mohammed Rajab Mohammed, armed at Mosul police headquarter (Mobilization Wing).
4. Major Ali Hussein al-Khaffaf, very active and head of the conspiracy in the Lesser Mobilization Wing. Away from the Wing, he was at the Shawwaf Radio station.
5. Major Abd al-Jabbar Abd al-Rahman, armed but not very active (Lesser Mobilization Wing).
6. Major Khair ad-Din Ali, much like a woman, a coward and could not kill a bird.
7. First Lt. Kamil Ismail, very active and did several tasks simultaneously (Fifth Brigade).
8. First Lt. Khairullah Askar, very dangerous and active; he was killing patriots in cold blood. He shot Lt. Col. Abdullah al-Shawi (Armored Vehicles Battalion).
9. First Lt. Ismail, a member of the Armored Vehicles Battalion.
10. First Lt. Sheikh Salih, commander of the occupying detachment of the stone barracks (Fifth Brigade).
11. Corp. Abdullah Mohammed Abboush, very enthusiastic, as if he was the leader of the movement (Mobilization Wing).
12. Corp. Khalaf Hussein, a conspirator and commander of the guards of the rank officers' prison (Mobilization Wing).
13. Corp. Mal Allah, a mad dog who controlled the prisoners (Detachment of the Military Police).
14. Corp. Ghazi, always accompanied the traitor officers as if he was one (Fifth Brigade).
15. Corp. Ibrahim Mohammed, inactive (Mobilization Wing).
16. Second Corp. Sahir Farhood, commander of the guards of the main gate in the conspiracy and told the guard, "Now we got rid of the infidels" (Lesser Mobilization Wing).

Martyrs who were killed in or near the Stone Barracks:

1. Lt. Col. Abdullah al-Shawi, martyred at the main gate by the traitor Khairullah Askar.
2. Patriot Kamil al-Qazanchi, martyred in the hall leading to the lavatories by traitors Mahmud Aziz and Mal Allah and was lying in the middle of the hall at the lavatory door. Assisted by a soldier, I moved him to a clean corner of the room he was killed in.
3. Petty officer trainee Hazim, martyred on the roof of the castle, and I was with him only a few moments before he was martyred.
4. Lance Corp. Mustafa Taili, also martyred on the roof of the castle, and I was beside him a moment before.
5. Head Corp. Haraz, martyred inside the small door leading to the Wing's shop.
6. Private Ahmad Abd al-Qadir, martyred in the Wing's field as he held the picture of leader Abd al-Karim Qasim.

I saw others killed and wounded; I could not recognize them because they were far off and I could not reach them.

Translation from Arabic of Document No. 65

A Report Submitted by a KDP Cadre in Kirkuk

1. Coming from Baghdad with attorney Nur ad-Din al-Wa'idh, Abd al-Wahab al-Mzairi visited Kirkuk October 1–4. Upon their arrival, they contacted Vice Mayor of Kirkuk, his accountant, Salih Ishaq, Jalal Sofi, a retired officer and owner of the Aphrodite

Store, Kamel at-Tikriti, and retired pilot Major Yaha Jawad (whose wife is British), retired Major Abbadi, and retired pilot Major Abd al-Rahman al-Afghani. They met at the Oil Company Club with the knowledge of its director and his assistant Taha Mahjool, and Security Adjutant Sabah Bayati.

2. Accompanied by Wa'idh, Oil Company's Police Adjutant Taha Mahjool, Azizi held his meeting at the Oil Company Club in the presence of a butler named Mirza.

3. Azizi and Wa'idh met with the Transit Police Adjutant and officers of the Second Division. It was also attended by Police Petty Officer Ibrahim al-Zawi. Then they met with Mr. O'Dell and Mr. Paulman, Director of Employment, Mr. Greg, Assistant to the Director General of the Oil Company, a British Jew. After the meeting, he returned to Baghdad on an Oil Company plane. All accompanied him to the airport, witnessed by Abdullah Agha, the company's Fire and Rescue worker who went to the airport as required by his job, and Abd Musa, an airport fuel station worker.

4. A British spy named V. Rainter arrived in Kirkuk five days ago from abroad through Lebanon. He is still in Kirkuk.

5. Meetings continue at the Kirkuk Oil Company attended by Col. Adil Amin Khaki, Mr. Over Tall, Public Works, Mr. O'Dell, Intelligence, Mr. Vandi Foul 'Accident', Mr. Linki, Mr. Latik, Oil Industry, Mr. Edmonds, Politician, Mr. Hodgix, Politician, Mr. Poulman, Employment, Mr. Fraizer, Politician, Staff Col. Ibrahim Faisal, and Staff Major Abd al-Ghani of the Second Division. Adil was appointed in the place of Mansoor al-Khayyat, Lt. Pilot Muhsin Subghatullah who meets Britons at Butrus's Residence, an employee of the company.

6. Chieftains of Dulaim tribes are in contact with assistant director general of the company Mr. Greg, a British Jew, and Staff Brigadier General Ibrahim Faisal, retired Lt. Col. Fadhil Abbad al-Mikradi.

7. Adam, an Assyrian, accountant at the Dairalak Office, meets with Na'il al-Yaqoobi, some Englishmen and retired officers in his house, and sometimes in a house on the Kirkuk-Baghdad Highway. Adam is in contact with the US Embassy in Baghdad.

8. Nahidh al-Chadiri (Khalifa Hilmi Samareh, a Palestinian), Abd al-Wahid Fahmi, Isa Nariman, Baha ad-Din Wali, retired Col. Sham ad-Din At-Tayyar, Mr. Bern Eid, former British Minister of Post and Telegraph, and a 'Mister' in K-3. These are the middlemen between the UAR and traitors in Iraq, the reactionaries who smuggle weapons from the UAR to Iraq for conspirators and to smuggle those Iraqis who want to escape to the UAR, with their direct and ongoing contacts with the tribal chiefs in Kirkuk 'Haweeja' al-Asi, Mudhir al-Asi, chieftains of Sammarra, Tikrit and Dulaim. Nahidh has contacts in the Foreign Ministry in Baghdad and through them, he gets important and secret information about the Iraqi government. He also has contact with Col. doctor Ramzi Khayyat in Habbaniya, and this doctor is Hilmi Samareh's brother-in-law.

9. Waleed, inspector of the Company's stores, the middleman between the reactionaries in Mosul and Kirkuk, Mr. Langley and Mr. Cape of the IPC [Iraqi Petroleum Company].

10. al-Thawra Hotel (the source of conspiracies). Guests at this hotel are 65 men of the traitors' clique. No one else is allowed in this hotel unless known to be a supporter of the traitors and all are paid by a reactionary named Ali Mustafa Agha. It is designated for their meetings only. A few days ago, a meeting was held there and was attended by Khalaf al-Iqabi, Ali Mustafa Agha, and Staff Col. Ibrahim Faisal of the Second Division. They planned to disturb the peaceful march to be held in Kirkuk on the occasion of the leader leaving the hospital. Every ten days, a meeting is held and is attended by Mulla Sabir Mulla Ahmad as well. Six days ago, a meeting was held and attended by Police Adjutant Mohammed Bashar Ali who came from Diwaniya, Mulla Sabir, Younis Omer, retired Col. Shakir Sabir, retired Lt. Col. Abd al-Azal Shakir, Kamal Beg, a resident of al-Qal'a, and

his son Sabah Kamal. After the meeting, Adjutant Mohammed Bashar, Mulla Sabir, Col. Shakir Sabir, and Younis Omer travelled to Baghdad, with the owner of the hotel, Haji Ghafoor.

11. Middlemen between the Company in Kirkuk and reactionaries in Baghdad, Mousl, Kirkuk, Tikrit and the Dulaim are Kamil at-Tikriti, Hamad Mulla Majeed, a Company employee, Majeed Dara, a dismissed Petty Police Officer who is currently employed by the Company, and Edward al-Warith, Sami, and John of the Company.

12. The district Governor of Aneh Abd al-Rahman Abd al-Razzaq known as Abakh, is the middleman between the reactionaries in Aneh region, T-1, K-3, and the reactionary traitors in Kirkuk and the Company, and the contact between the Governor and the reactionaries is the Governor's relative, Ramzi Khonkar, who returned from there only three days ago.

13. To serve imperialist interests, the Company pays the salaries of Najad Awchi who at times hosts meetings in his house in Kirkuk, Baha ad-Din Fojudeh, attorney Ata Tarzi Bashi, and Sati' Katib al-Shagra. The first two have put their vehicles at the company's service as needed not to be suspected when they send their messengers to Ramadi, Baghdad and Mosul to meet with their groups or exchange information. They are allowed to go anywhere day and night despite the curfew.

14. Also, meetings are alternated between the residences of Fuad Ali and Rif'at al-Yaqoobi, Lt. Ismail Khalil, Assistant to the Commander of Military Police of Kirkuk, and Abdullah Koar, the Police contractor, and Head Corp. of the Military Police Unit Hameed, Jamal al-Khayyat, Musheer Haj Hussein, president of Dibs Power Company, and Amin al-Hallaq.

15. 1. Noor ad-Din al-Wa'idh
2. Mulla Siddique
3. Omer Siddique, Driver of the Geological Company to transport Ahmad Najim ad-Din.
4. Sheikh Abdullah Sheikh, Oil Liaison Clerk, a cousin of the broadcaster.
5. Ali Hussein, Company's firetruck driver, Dibs.
6. Ibrahim Hussein, Company's firetruck nurse, Dibs.
7. Abd al-Sattar Faisal, firetruck driver.
8. Izz ad-Din, Director of Company's Fire Department. The Company usually sends him to Europe and Turkey (Mr. Van de [Wohl], director of Accident, a former British Army Intelligence Officer in Khanaqin).

Notes:

— Confidentiality Special Clerk of Mr. Langly's office is Abbas Fathullah in APC, Kirkuk.
— Individuals from Tikrit with ongoing contacts with the Company are Sayyed Bakr Tikriti and Asi Tikriti, a former prisoner.
— Witnesses from Kirkuk's Security Police are:

1. Mohammed Abdullah
2. Latif Mohammed Salih
3. Ahmad Sharif
4. Ali Ridha

An army Major, Commander of the Kirkuk Airport, called on October 9, 1959 on the airport's secure telephone which is directly connected to Baghdad, and spoke to an employee of the Baghdad airport asking him, "How is the situation there? Too bad they did not catch the group. Tell me how is Midhat?" This conversation was witnessed by Lance Corp. of Communications Ibrahim Mulla Mohammed, Communications Private Mohammed.

Translation from Arabic of Document No. 66

KDP's Call Which Most Likely Dated Back to Late 1958

A Call from the United Democratic Party of Kurdistan

Strugglers for peace and democracy in the world!

The triumph of the July 14 Revolution and founding of the beloved Republic of Iraq not only broke the backbone of imperialism in the Middle East and uprooted the warmonger and hostile Baghdad Pact, it made Iraq a castle of peace and democracy in the region. It was a fatal blow that astounded imperialism and their agents. But soon recovered, they began conspiring to regain control and put us back between the jaws of servility, poverty and imperialistic oppression, and back in the prison of the Baghdad Pact.

In Iraqi Kurdistan they are disseminating poisonous propaganda against the fledgling Republic of Iraq, the Republic of Arabs and Kurds. They lie regarding charges of separatism and accuse Kurdish patriots and their vanguard Party. Many fraudulent and misleading reports were submitted to the government of Iraq. They did all they could to incite the government against our patriots and Party. Their vicious goal was to drive a wedge between the republican government and the Kurdish liberation movement, and the vanguard of Kurdish masses, our Party, only to find a way to fight our Republic and destroy it from within. The struggle of our Party and wisdom of the heroic leader Abd al-Karim Qasim have thwarted the imperialistic conspiracy and prevented them from reaching their goal.

While patriotic forces are at each other's throats, and concealed by all the propaganda fog and lies, imperialism was able to incite the reactionary forces of Turanis loyal to them, and loyal to fascist Turkey more than to their country, and treasonous Kurdish feudalists against the security and sovereignty of the Republic. The following crimes, committed by imperialists and their agents in full view of reactionary employees, prove beyond the shadow of a doubt the truth of our statement above:

First, the conspiracy Turanis plotted on October 25, 1958 as the great patriot Mustafa Barzani visited Kirkuk. This blind conspiracy in which the criminal Turani Mustafa Raghib, an old imperialist agent, played a large role, the American Vice Consul and Oil Company spies openly provoked, directed and supervised. Furthermore, Turanis continue to buy and store large quantities of weapons, and train their affiliates to fight and use various weapons. They assert they will turn Kirkuk into a second Cyprus! It is well known that these Turanis are always ready to carry out orders from Turkey and the Baghdad Pact to realize the wishes of imperialism.

Second, in Zebar and Aqra, a spiteful gang of treasonous reactionaries, former spies and criminal feudalists, such as Ahmad Agha Zebari, Mohammed Faris Agha, Simko Faris Agha in the Zibar region and Othman Mustafa, Fa'iq Mustafa, Mulla Mustafa, Jawad Ali, Haji Khandan, Khorshid Arab Agha, and the Surchi chieftains Sabir Raqeeb and Sadroak Bade' in the Aqra region continue to spy for Turkey, and imperialistic circles continue killing and battering peasants, as happened in the village of Heren where 3 peasants were murdered and another five wounded. Abdullah Tato was suffocated on his way by the same criminal gang which maintains close ties with American and British spies in Mosul and with Turanis in Kirkuk. They are serious about rallying reactionary forces ready for treason under any banner in order to ignite riots, and plots from within.

Third, in the Baradost and Balak region surrounding Barzan, the vile spy Sheikh Rashid of Lolan and Sheikh Ala'd Din continue to conspire against the Republic in addition to their hosting Turkish and Iranian officers and assisting foreign spies.

Fourth, in the Pishdar region, many treasonous chieftains such as Baiz Bapir Salim Agha, Bapir Babekr Salim Agha's son, Hama Abbas Agha have fled to eastern Kurdistan, which is forcibly annexed to Iran. They continue to conspire with the traitor Ali Agha, his two brothers, and other treasonous chieftains to disturb the peace, commit murders, robberies, destruction, provoking soldiers of the Pishdar garrison to flee to Iran as the soldier Mahmud Hama Agha confessed to the Commander of the depot that Baiz Babekr Agha had incited him to flee to Iran. These agents of imperialism have committed numerous crimes in this important region, including but not limited to the following:

1. Murdering Hamza, member of the Kurdistan Student Union of Iraq, Rostam Hajar, and Haji Ahmad Boriman.
2. Shooting at the patriot Ali Mam Ridha, the house of Ali Haji Ahmad in Qala Diza, the house of Hama Soor, village supervisor of Sayyed Ahmadan, and Jihangeer in Bimoush village.
3. Burning the houses of Abullah Mam Rasoul and Abdullah Mamesh in the village of Girdamayta, and mounting an armed attack on the village of Sayyed Ahmadan and burning the house of its chieftain Mohammed Agha, and the armed attack on the Hero police station.
4. The grotesque assault on a woman in Shoran, the assault on Husam ad-Din Tayyib, confiscation petty officer of Qala Diza.
5. Raiding Hero, Mirbi and Bawazi villages, and stealing three herds of sheep.

Fifth, in the Khanaqin region, gangs armed by Iran are violating Iraqi sovereignty and often steal herds of sheep and loot possessions. Iranian government has armed loyal tribes in occupied Kurdistan and enticed them to attack Iraqi border civilians.

Sixth, in the Imadia region, Turkish gangs and bandits steal sheep and cattle, assault civilians in border areas, and often assault villages near the border.

Seventh, Turkish and Iranian amassment of troops along the Iraqi–Iranian–Turkish borders under the supervision of numerous American officers in Sardasht and Diyarbakr. They organize plots against the Republic of Iraq. Furthermore, Tehran Radio broadcasting in Persian, Kurdish and Arabic, and radio stations in Karmanshah, Sinna, Mahabad and Tabriz broadcasting in Kurdish continue to attack the Republic of Iraq and call upon the Kurds to rebel and disobey Baghdad and to take refuge in the Aryan Iran!

Eighth, British and American spies are becoming noticeably more active in Iraqi Kurdistan against the Republic of Iraq. They conspire and plot internal disturbances.

Honorable Masses of Iraqi Kurdistan, the aforementioned facts clearly demonstrate that American and British imperialism and Turkish and Persian fascists are trying to provoke unrest and riots in Iraqi Kurdistan. Undoubtedly, you are aware that these criminal attempts are against your national interests, and they are a continuation of their criminal policy vis-à-vis the Kurds and Kurdistan, a policy to eradicate the Kurdish nation, to divide and occupy Kurdistan, to exploit its tremendous wealth and resources, a policy to keep our people politically, economically, socially and educationally backward. These fierce enemies of the Kurdish people want today to deceive the people of Kurdistan, and entice them against the Republic of Iraq, our beloved Republic.

Certainly, you will not allow their hellish programs to pass, and you understand well the extent of the danger these imperialistic conspiracies pose to your beloved Republic, and to our life of liberty, happiness and democracy which you enjoy, and to your bright future and good reputation. Be alert, and be careful of these games, unite your forces and be prepared to foil all imperialistic plots against our beloved Republic led by its champion Abd al-Karim Qasim.

All sincere Iraqi patriots, our Party is putting before you these tangible facts and calls upon you all to hurry and unite your forces in NUF to defend the Republic and its democratic orientation, and to resist all imperialistic conspiracies. Our Party promises you to continue the struggle, as an NUF member, with all it has against imperialism and its wicked plots.

—Long live the beloved Republic of Iraq led by its hero Abd al-Karim Qasim.
—Long live Arab-Kurdish fraternity, the cornerstone of our victories.
—Death and shame to the agents of imperialism, reactionaries and traitors.
—Long live the Iraqi NUF.

Politburo of the United Democratic Party of Kurdistan

Translation from Arabic of Document No. 67

Turcoman's Response to the KDP's Call

DEMOCRATIC TURCOMANS

In response to the KDP's Assertions:

Leaders of democracy and peace . . . Free Iraqis!

The triumph of our glorious Revolution, the Revolution of the Army and the people on the eternal July 14, and the alertness of Iraqi people have prevented some of the extremist Kurds from realizing their separatist aims, which are no secret. Knowing this fact has driven some to list accusations against Iraqi Turcoman patriots who struggle for peace, democracy, free and dignified life, and Iraqi integrity. The stand of Iraqi Turcoman patriots is the best deterrence to these accusations. The Gawerbaghi massacre in which Kirkuk gave up 27 martyrs and more than fifty wounded of its best young patriots in oblation on freedom's gallows in June, 1946, is the best example of their struggle; and Turcomans' participation in the mighty peoples uprising in 1948 in protest against the unjust Portsmouth Treaty is another example of their fighting spirit.

The entire Kirkuk citizenry's staging a huge demonstration in support of the Army's Revolution and its bold leaders on July 14, and the outpouring of their supportive cables is a third example of their patriotism. We are proud that our delegation, which travelled to Baghdad to tender allegiance and loyalty to our beloved Republic and to demonstrate our support of the sacred Revolution and of our only leader Abd al-Karim Qasim, was the greatest of delegations.

All these are defenses against the charge of Turanism, an accusation for cheap consumption rendered now and then by a band of extremist Kurds. Turanism is a known movement which aims to incorporate all the Turks in the world into one country, and our innocence of this accusation is obvious to the Revolutionary government and the Iraqi people. We will refrain from further detail.

The events of Kirkuk, as known by our government, can be summarized as follows:

On October 25, 1958, the patriot Barzani returned from Suleimaniyya to Kirkuk on his way to Baghdad. Extremist Kurds who came from outside Kirkuk exploited this occasion and provoked the residents of Kirkuk by their banners and outcries against Iraqi unity in general and Turcomans' in particular. One of these outcries was "Kirkuk is the city of the Kurds, and let foreigners leave" and Kirkuk being a Turcoman city is an indisputable fact.

They marched in the streets of Kirkuk raising hostile banners and chanting "Down with imperialism and its agents," pointing at passers-by and those in cafés. Later, they attacked cafés and stores, destroying glasses, furniture and pictures. To this point, the registry of damage is available with the Government; look it up if you want the truth, KDP!

Mustafa Raghib being leader of the riot in Kirkuk is a lie, unacceptable because he was not in Kirkuk at the time. He has been living in Baghdad for a long time. About the accusation of him being an agent of imperialism, we remind you of his role in the Palestine war. If he were an agent of imperialism, he would not have thrown his resignation in the face of Aduw al-Ilah[7] in that critical time and pulled out of the game of the war in Palestine. In regard to Kirkuk's residents purchasing weapons and training, we only refer you to the military intelligence in Kirkuk to show you the weapons they confiscated in al-Rafidain Hotel from those feudalist Kurdish extremists.

All these facts protect us against lies and unjust assertions. If what the KDP asserts about Kirkuk residents' storing weapons and training with them is true, why do not they inform concerned authorities to take necessary measure against them? We are ready to cooperate with the KDP or any other party or organization in Iraq to uncover such acts if they exist. Finally, we call upon you, patriots, defenders of the Republic and all who struggle to preserve the unity of Iraq and for peace, to work together and support each other, Arabs, Kurds, Turcomans and all minorities. We call upon you all to be alert and not to listen to the assertions of extremists, fascists and chauvinists. We call upon you to work hand in hand to end them and to rally behind our only champion, he whom we know, and no other leader, Abd al-Karim Qasim.

—Long live the Republic of Iraq, free and democratic led by our great President Abd al-Karim Qasim.
—Long live Arab-Kurd-Turcoman fraternity
—Long live the National Front
—Death to imperialism, its reactionary agents, dividers of ranks

For democratic Iraqi Turcomans

Translation from Kurdish of Document No. 68

An Urgent Dispatch by a KDP Cadre in Kirkuk

To: Committee of the great UDPK in Kirkuk

Yesterday, a number of Turanis left Kirkuk for Baghdad to assassinate the great patriot of Kurdistan and Iraq Mulla Mustafa Barzani. From their sources, I learned that most of these Turanis are staying at the "New Kirkuk Hotel" near the Defense Gate, while a few of them are staying at the "Express Hotel of the North" near Maidan . . . I heard this from the Security Police Corp.

Bateen
January 22, 1959

---

7. Aduw al-Ilah (enemy of God) is reference to Abd al-Ilah (servant of God), Regent of the Iraqi monarchy.

Translation from Arabic of Document No. 69

Two News Bulletins Reports from a Party Source

Comrade Bradost reported the following:

1. Chief of Security Police, Adjutants Khairi and Ilyas who both work in the clerical section of the Kirkuk Security Police, Jamal Ilyas Fargholi of the Kirkuk Transit Tax Office who is being transferred to Basra now, Petty Officers Sabah of Kirkuk Security and Ibrahim al-Azzawi of the Oil Companies Police, retired Major Abbadi who works in the Power Department of Dubiza [Dibs], retired pilot Yahya Jawad of the Kirkuk Oil Company Number 8, Kamil Ali Beg al-Tikriti, Nadir Jadir of the Kirkuk Oil Company, Hussein Ali, a retired army man known as "the German," Kalil Fattah, a second car, Adnan Hassan who was a clerk at the American Consulate in Kirkuk, Rif'at Yaqoobi, the clerk in the Kirkuk Security Directorate, Nawzad, owner of the al-Alamain Cinema, Khalaf Janabi, a contractor for the Oil Company, Ali Agha, a resident of al-Qal'a, Awni Fuad, owner of a Maintenance Garage, Rahman Mustafa Nuri, Karim Awchi known as Karim Koar, Baqir who is currently unemployed, Dhia' Talib, a pharmacist at the Kirkuk Pharmacy, and Mahdi, an employee of the Oil Company who is a nephew of Atta Khairullah. These are corrupt men and traitors, in close collaboration with each other, especially the Chief of Security, Adjutants Ilyas, and Khairi, who meet regularly at Khairi's house, as well as the Commander of the Military Police, Ismail Khalil.

2. The Secret Police operative code-named '1' sent us a letter signed with his name, the original with Comrade Bradost, in which he states, "One day I was standing by the door of Chief of Security, and both Adjutants Ilyas and Mohammed Jawad were in his office. Ilyas told M. J., 'You're wrong to rely on Ramzi Khonkar. He is a Turani and does not work for Arabism.'"

3. This man Ramzi Khonkar is a Turani traitor. He is the man who forged the Census records of 1957 and was tried for replacing Kurds with Turcomans in the Census. He is the one who set up the Yelden Café from which they attacked those who were in the Great Patriot Mulla Mustafa Barzani's Farewell ... Now, we are certain, it is also No. 1's report that Ramzi Khonkar often travels to Syria and maintains strong ties to the corrupt traitors active against our patriotic government in Kirkuk and Turanis currently residing in Baghdad, in al-A'dhamiyya such as the Yaqoobites and Awchis.

4. No. 1 mentioned above stated in his report that No. 2 has detailed information of these critical contacts. Because of fear of the Kirkuk Security Chief, he could not reveal such information. If he is transferred anywhere else, he will reveal all secrets of this menacing network ...

5. Nos. 3, 4, 5, and 6 were transferred because they wrote reports regarding these traitors and they cabled Baghdad on November 14, 1959, requesting the arrest of Ramzi Khonkar.

6. No. 7 informed us that they brought weapons several times from Marina, near a point where the Tigris and Great Zab meet; about 14 kilometers. They cross the river on boats to Hawija and distribute the weapons among the al-Ubaid tribe through their chieftains, Mudhir al-Asi and al-Asi. Both have visited the Kirkuk Chief of Security and his Adjutant under the pretext of banquets and repast. ... To date, we know of three "batches" of weapons, each about 10–20 rifles and automatic guns, which they have brought.

7. There is an undercover policeman, a Baathist and trustee whom the director of the Kirkuk Security sends now and then on official tasks to Baghdad to secure his ongoing contacts with Baathists there.

8. First Lt. pilot Muhsin Sibghatullah al-Omeri is constantly contacting politicians at the Oil Company and treasonous Tashnaq Armenians.

9. Every 10–15 days, the traitors come from Hawija with the Commander of the Military Police and others of their followers, meet at the residence of Mudhir al-Tikriti and renew their contacts until they return.

10. Often they bring weapons from Hawija in vehicles belonging to the Office of Irrigation to the house of Mudhir al-Tikriti's cousin. These weapons are brought in for Mudhir himself but unloaded there as a coverup since Mudhir is a suspect. We have learned that vehicles are used to transport weapons without the knowledge of any engineer or responsible official in the Irrigation Office.

11. Besides Company and Land Bureau employees, there is another man at Hussein Jum'a's house. He claims that his visitor is the Director General of Prisons. On investigation, we have learned that the Director General of Prisons has visited Kirkuk recently. This person is questionable.

12. Police Petty Officer Faiq al-Bayati of the Kirkuk Security Office is in contact with the Turanis. Always he encourages them to be bold and take revenge on the Kurds.

13. Thunoun, the Palestinian surgeon, who owns a poultry farm about 12 miles beyond K-1 Station on the road to Hawija, met on January 8, 1960 with Mr. Ibrahim, Director of Roads, Ali Mustafa, Director of Communications of the Company, retired pilot Col. Shamsuddin, at his farm, from about 7:00 P.M.–9:30 P.M. He never cared about anything but his chickens! Now, he has moved there and turned his house into a meeting place for treasonous Arab sheikhs, English-men and corrupt treasonous Turanis. These traitors meet at this place far from the eyes of citizens.

14. Baathists have begun transferring their known members, changing their vehicles to mislead citizens and hide their wicked actions.

15. As mentioned, 8 have been transferred in 3 batches, and they are ready to expose all Baathist cells and conspirators. They say that they will help if there is a place for weapons. If desired, all 8 will be under our supervision. They will have to give up their identifications because they are useless in their current suits...

From Kirkuk
January 14, 1960

News:

1. Abbadi Hussein, director of the National Power Company of the Northern region in Dibs, is a very active member of the Arab Baath Party and mostly meets with the following individuals:
   a. Younis Mohammed, employee of the said company.
   b. Sabi' Khammas, employee of the said company.
   c. Rajab, employee of the said company.
   d. Salih Hammoudi, employee of the said company.
   e. Mujbil Mohammed, employee of the said company.
   f. Salih Mutlag, employee of the said company.
   g. The son of Sheikh Binyan, an Arab sheikh in Hawija. We have not learned his name yet. They meet in secret, especially during times that are highly suspicious, for example, at the time of the odious plot on the life of the leader and injuring him with a bullet of treason and injustice...Despite the curfew, one night at about 9:00 P.M. they met with more than 40 people at the Drilling Camp in Dibs.

2. Khairi, a physical education and social sciences teacher at the Imam Qasim High School, is very active in plotting and causing unrest. He has contacts with the reactionary treacherous officers...a Lt. Col. at the airport named Mun'im calls and talks on the

telephone. Khairi's tie to the Deputy Commander is stronger than Mun'im's. Often, a car (Toren: tag # 13050) asks for him at the school, waits and picks him up after class. It belongs to the Deputy Commander.

On June 17, 1960, as Khairi returned from Baghdad... the same car picked him up at 4:00 P.M. He was in class. The car waited until 4:30 P.M. and took him toward Qourna.

3. Sabir, owner of "Amraz Electronics" on al-Awqaf street, secretly meets with Major Ihsan Abdullah and Shakir Shukri, employee of the local Administration, in his own store. They panic if they are seen or someone enters the store while together....

4. Col. Ibrahim Khidhayyer visits the Oil Company every day under the pretext of needing something. One day he goes to get chicken, another to get plants, turkey, and so on...

5. Dr. Khalil Taha, Dr. Rif'at Qutub, Lt. Col. Abdul Latif Abd al-Ghani, the Intelligence Officer, the Rations Officer, and the Deputy Commander meet in Sayyed Ahmad Sa'ati's shop. To date, the Deputy Commander has visited Sa'ati's residence twice...

6. Sayyed Haseeb Sayyed Najib, Director of Endowments, Sabir Mohammed al-Hanith, Cleric of the Musalla Mosque meet secretly, often at Sayyed Haseeb's house. Sayyed Hadi Sayyed Najib, a retired teacher, and Sayyed Ra'uf, Sayyed Haseeb's nephew, are also known to be with them.

This is what we have today. We have many other places under surveillance. We will provide you with information as it becomes available.

From Kirkuk
January 28, 1960

Translation from Arabic of Document No. 70

A letter from Sheikh Ahmad Barzani to his brother Mustafa Barzani regarding Zebari and Surchi raids on Barzan villages. They were enticed by the Police Chief of Mosul Ismail al-Abbawi.

Massoud Barzani

To: His Excellency, my dear brother Mustafa Barzani

Sincere greetings. May God grant you health, happiness and success. Enticed by Ismail Abbawi and his like, betrayers of the Republic and its loyal citizens, it is lamentable that Zebaris and Surchis attacked our village of Zaiwa. To reach his goal, God forbid, he works to detach every loyal citizen from our only leader Abd al-Karim Qasim, who rescued and purged the country of the sins of imperialism and its agents. I still uphold my pledge in the presence of our only leader to be his and the fledgling Republic's loyal soldier. The traitors are trying with all their might and vengeance against Barzan to drive a wedge between us. Ferocious against us, they will not reach their goal. Now, we only want to be loyal to our Republic. May Allah perpetuate its reign.

We are all well, and do not worry about us. No tragedy will befall us but by the might of God. Brother, isn't this our bad luck and lack of fortune? Otherwise, why would this happen to us despite our loyalty and sincere intentions. For those, rely on Allah, He is their guardian and their defense. May success be with you.

Your Brother
[signed]
Ahmad Barzani
May 28, 1960

Translation from Arabic of Document No. 71

A Letter from Sadiq Babo Barzani to His Uncle Mustafa Barzani Regarding A Plan to Disarm the Barzanis

His Excellency, Uncle Mustafa Barzani, respectfully

Greetings and honor. I hope that all is well for you. I wish to inform you that I learned from a trustworthy source that the Governor of Arbil Province made the suggestion in a secret Memorandum to disarm Barzanis and Zebaris. The Commander of the Second Division in Kirkuk supported him, and both were backed by the Director General of Security. Uncle, you realize the danger of this Memorandum by the Governor of Arbil, supported by the Commander and the Director General, one of the Army and the other of the Security! Undoubtedly, this is a planned scheme, an ugly plot against the Republic and against the beloved leader Abd al-Karim Qasim. They are trying to divide us and detach Barzanis from the leader, but they will never succeed. Barzanis are loyal and strong guards of the leader and the Republic. Despite this, I hope that you will pay close attention and inform the leader of this matter. Please note that their objective is to disarm Barzanis alone because most of the Zebaris' weapons are not registered, so how can they be disarmed? Please accept my highest regards.

Sincerely,

[signed]
Sadiq Barzani
December 23, 1959

Translation from Kurdish of Document No. 72

A Letter from Jalal Talabani to Barzani, Who was on Vacation in the Barzan Region

Baghdad   April 20, 1960

To: His Excellency, very dear and respected President, Mustafa Barzani

After tendering my respects and very warm greetings, I wish you continued health and happiness. If you wish to learn about your junior [himself], thank God and you, I am very well. I found it necessary to send you this letter via brother Asaad regarding the following issues:

1. Legally, time for the Party Congress is approaching. It must be held in the next 5–6 months. Obviously, your presence is necessary for the Congress and the Party to succeed and to plan the appropriate and correct course of action.
2. Your absence from Makokian's reception is spoken of very negatively by the Communists and the vile group (Hamza and Najad) as well.
3. Your stay in Barzan all this time might not be interpreted as normal by the government, especially by enemies of the Kurdish people and the leader.

Respected President, your return at this time carries great significance... let it be as you wish. Whatever you see appropriate, I will accept. Finally, I kiss the hands of our great Sheikh in due respect, and many greetings to brother Sadiq.
    Long live for the Republic and for the Kurds and Kurdistan; and for

Your Sincere Junior
Jalal Talabani
[signed]

Translation from Kurdish of Document No. 73

A letter from the late martyr Salih Yousifi to Barzani. He was asked to survey the views of some tribal chiefs with patriotic tendencies and cooperation with the Party.

To: Beloved of the people, great President Mustafa Barzani

With heartfelt love and loyalty, I salute you. The instructions you sent with our brother Zaki Kamil will be observed and implemented rationally and wisely. Our brothers have committed some errors despite some positive [things]. We must be careful and cautious just as we should be bold in tough times. Our hope and faith are very strong in the victory of our people. Yes, we must go for the long haul.

Although it is correct that we cannot openly work against them, our brothers are ready as well as our brothers abroad to end reactionism.

All are loyal to you and the people. Haji Sadiq Barro with his tribe send their regards. Brother Saadullah, the bearer of this letter is honest, sacrificing and trustworthy. He is to visit you regarding our brothers of Imadia. Please help him and let us know, verbally or in writing, of any service your wish us to provide.

Live long, a luminous torch for the country.

Sincerely,

Salih Yousifi
[signed]
May 25, 1960

Translation from Arabic of Document No. 74

A report from Mosul regarding the hostile conduct of the Police Chief of Mosul, Ismail Abbawi, against the Kurds.

Massoud Barzani

The situation in Mosul is as follows:

1. The investigating Judge Salim al-Sha'ar releases Baathist detainees and returns all seized documents without delay or postponement. He is in agreement with the Security Adjutant Fadhil Sayyed who is a Turani and Baathist, the Governor of the province and Ismail Abbawi.
2. Members of the treasonous Baathist Party are continuing their conspiratorial activities in the open against the Iraqi Republic. They are supported in their conspiratorial pernicious activities by the Governor of the Province, Director of Border Police Rifat Sayyed Nafi' al-Omeri, Director of Records, Security Adjutant Fadhil Sayyed Hussein, the known conspirator chief of the an-Nu'maniya Quarter Mulla Isa, and Mahmud al-Mukhtar of Nabi Sheit, a known conspirator. The Iraqi-Syrian border is open for smugglers. On January 20, 1960, two employees of the Mosul Rations were arrested for smuggling food to fugitives (from Baghdad to Syria). They are Ghazi Mohammed Musa and Ghanim Abdullah Saeed. Both are active members of the treasonous Baath Party in Mosul.
3. Reactionaries in the province have revived and begun their overt conspiratorial activities.
4. The Police Chief of the Province recently transferred all loyal police from city stations away to remote districts. This is intended to carry out his hostile activities against patriots. Perhaps there are anti-Republic groups who wish to get rid of loyalists.

From Mosul

Translation from Arabic of Document No. 75

A list of Ahmad Zebari's assaults on peasants in Aqra region which the government took no action to prevent.

1. Stealing 260 sheep from the village of Davarey.
2. Robbing 60 sheep from the village of Gribish and wounding a villager.
3. Expelling Younis Kadani from the village of Gissey, and wounding his son, Ismail.
4. Burning the village of Dissey, stealing its 50 sheep, and wounding a villager, Bilal.
5. Stealing 60 sheep from the village of Shahey.
6. Taking a rifle from the son of Mohammed Tahir, chief of the village of Bakurman.
7. Stealing 150 sheep and expelling Shisho, chief of village of Chami Shurta.
8. Stealing 360 sheep and expelling Haji from the village of Chami Shirin.
9. Stealing 558 sheep from the village of Chami belonging to Ismail Chami.
10. Firing at Ali Mustafa Abdullah in Aqra.
11. Stealing 80 sheep from the village of Aspindar.
12. Robbing and looting the village of Chami Sinney. Mohammed Salim, a villager, was wounded. He is the son of Haji Agha and nephew of Ahmad Agha Zebari.
13. Stealing 200 head of cattle from Salaira Bakr, an 'English' rifle, a hunting rifle, a sewing machine, a radio and the furniture from his other house in the village of Mirzik.
14. Murdering Qumsir's daughter. He is a cousin of Tiari chief, Oudish, of Davarey village.
15. Wounding the son-in-law of Oudish, a policeman, in the village of Davarey in the prepense of Aqra police Adjutant, station chief, and 25 policemen.
16. Murdering Darwish Hussein in the village of Heren.
17. Stealing the loads of (16) mules from the village of Davarey on their way to Aqra.
18. Deporting the residents of Gozkey, Shahey and Gisey village in the Nahla subdistrict, and taking over these villages.
19. Nu'man Agha and his followers of Shahey, left their village and moved to Arbil in fear of the Zebaris.
20. Confiscating commercial merchandise from Tawfiq Mamer of Bilah while transporting it from Aqra to Bilah.
21. Stealing 400 sheep from Habib Yousif, Rashid Abdullah and others of Qudish village. The village is in Imadia [district].

Translation from Arabic of Document No. 76

An ICP statement clearly outlining government provocations.

A Statement from the Iraqi Communist Party

Struggle to end oppression, threatening of Barzani citizens, and defend the democratic rights of the Kurdish people

Citizens and sons of our great nation:

For months the reactionary feudalist and imperialistic activities have noticeably increased in Kurdistan with participation by official and non-official individuals in the security apparatus and other governmental systems. Behind these activities are the exploiting oil companies, the CENTO Pact and other Anglo-American imperialistic circles. It appears in some respects that they are encouraged by the government and its offices in hopes of directing it against the democratic movement, peaceful Barzani citizens and those loyal to the Republic.

Assassinations, assaults, throwing explosives orchestrated by security gangs and provocation by feudalists have intensified to a new level which seriously threatens to provoke strife and infighting among our people. Not long ago, large scale fighting broke out in Kirkuk in which Security and Military Police offices played a major role and a number of Kurdish, Turcoman and other citizens were lost to infighting, which damaged the economic life and spread insecurity. At the same time, there was propaganda indicating that the Shoresh [Revolution] Party, known for its ties to imperialism, would launch a 'revolution' in Suleimaniyya to establish a Kurdish government! Then, those remaining of Nuri al-Sa'id's feudalist [Parliament] Representatives returned from the laps of their Iranian and CENTO pact masters disguised as defenders of the Kurds and Kurdistan! Feudalists are provoked against the democratic peasants movement in all Kurdistan, especially against the Barzanis.

Matching this debunking reactionary imperialistic activism, some of Baghdad's treasonous press try, hopelessly, to invoke racist tendencies and call for the national liquidation [of Kurds] ignoring the distinct Kurdish national character, to retract the basic rights realized by the July 14 Revolution. Obviously, what these questionable papers published has directly echoed the official policies fighting the Kurdish press and national political movement in Kurdistan, and condemning Kurdish educational and democratic conferences including activities of the Directorate of the Kurdish Education, rendering Articles of the Provisional Constitution and official positive statements mere ink on paper. Pressured by feudalist delegations sent by oil companies and CENTO alliance, the government retreated in its appeasement measures of monetary assistance and weapons, and increasing the pressure on the Communist and democratic parties and forces in Kurdistan, replacing administrators and other citizens with those who hate democracy, especially Kurdish rights and national character.

As an extension to this damaging policy, the government is relying on vengeful feudalist gangs to expand its current provocations and direct it to be an armed tribal aggression against citizens of Barzan who were displaced for more than a decade as a result of the imperialistic monarchy's oppression, to be followed by armed government intervention to once again oppress these courageous citizens. Feudalist gangs left over from the monarchy as well as some tribal chiefs of Zebaris, Harkis and Baradostis relying on government encouragement and openly stating their dirty intentions against the Barzanis are promoting their support by the government authorities. Security, intelligence and administrative apparatuses of the government in the areas where provocations occur themselves actively promote tribal, racist and party conflicts, and use them to justify the continuing blatant dictatorship, harming the peace and security of the country, and deny the most basic of people's rights and liberties. They jeopardize our national independence.

Unfortunately, the conduct of the government and its apparatuses in many ways meets the desires of imperialistic exploiting oil companies. They are spending millions of dollars, have activated their spy networks and agents to break down the unity of our people and patriotic forces and confiscate their liberties, isolate the national teacher and weaken the Iraqi position in the oil maneuvers.

Patriotic forces and masses of our people in Kurdistan and elsewhere in the country are quite correct when they worry about the schemes plotted against our Barzani citizens whose long history is decorated with patriotism, pride and sacrifice. They are convinced of provocations and bad intentions that are a part of a policy of oppression and terrorizing the democratic forces. Our country is moving to continue to suppress the Kurdish national rights, and to rejuvenate the feudalist gangs and retreat and appease them and the Anglo-American imperialistic circles that stand behind them.

Our Iraqi Communist Party calls upon the masses of the people in Kurdistan and elsewhere in Iraq of Arabs, Kurds, Turcomans and others, and calls upon patriotic and democratic forces and the government to be alert and aware of the plots of imperialists, their associates and agents of feudalists and others, to unite in the struggle against imperialism, feudalism and reactionary rule, and demands that the government end its policy of organized provocation against citizens and the sincere forces, end its policy designed against people's rights, end its policy aimed at dividing the people and the patriotic forces on the grounds that this policy has nothing in common with the interests of the people and seriously threatens the future of the nation and the accomplishments of the Revolution.

Our Iraqi Communist Party calls upon the people and the patriotic forces to strengthen solidarity and unify ranks to stop provocations against the courageous Barzanis, to defend the rights and liberties of the Kurdish people and ethnic minorities. These rights are indivisible parts of the democratic rights and liberties that all invincible Iraqi people are struggling for.

The popular masses and patriotic forces are more convinced day after day that what is called the "exceptional period" and the continuation of the single-handed dictatorship are bringing more tragedies and atrocities to our people, confiscate their democratic rights and threaten national independence which was brought about by tens of long years of hard struggle. Therefore, a popular revolution is taking root day after day demanding and struggling for the end of the policy of single-handed military dictatorship, and the establishment of a national reality on new democratic foundations.

The Iraqi Communist Party
Baghdad, May 30, 1961

Appendix I

Players of Major Roles in the 1943–1945 Battles

Once he returned to the Barzan region, Barzani studied the experiences and skills of his friends and supporters. He knew some of them well, since they had lived together. Many had been martyred, others had died, and many more had been exiled to the cities. Among them, were Ahmad Nadir, Khalil Khoshavi, Salim Khoshavi, Abdullah Kirkamoyi and Awla Beg. Only few were left, such as Hassan Mohammed Amin Birsiyavi, Rasho Khal Hamza and Omer Abdullah Khalanayi.

Therefore, Barzani was not all sure as to how the revolutionary forces would be organized and who would be able to take command. Therefore, he took time during the battles of 1943–1945 to identify those who would be able to play important leadership roles in battles and in handling logistics and management otherwise. Many of the young people whom Barzani identified in those battles indeed assumed leadership roles later either during 1945–1957, in Mahabad, or on their historic march to the Soviet Union, or even in the September Revolution.

It is important for the Kurds to know and remember that there are many unknown soldiers who sacrificed their lives for the Kurds and Kurdistan. Unknown, even by name, many are either permanently disabled or old age has caught up with them. In their last years, they still continue the March of Struggle to their last breath.

To all those martyrs who gave their lives for their people and homeland, we bow with admiration and honor as we remember them. To all those who gave their best years to the Kurds and Kurdistan, we bow in reverence and respect. To all those who struggled during the worst of times so that we could be where we are today, many of whom we unable to mention, may we [ask] them to accept our heartfelt apology.

The following lists are of only a few of those heroes who played glorious roles in the battles of 1943–1945:

1. Mohammed Amin Mirkhan Mergasuri: A comrade of Barzani, who accompanied him to the Soviet Union. He led a large force in the September Revolution in 1961 and liberated many of the areas of Dohuk Province. He was critically wounded in the Battle of Miraiba on March 7, 1962. Lacking medical treatment, he was turned in to the government. He was transported to a hospital in Mosul. In a cowardly plot orchestrated by the government in cooperation with mercenaries, he was shot to death while on his hospital bed. He was martyred on the evening of March 18, 1962. His body was sent to Mergasur, his birthplace, for burial.
2. Shaikhomer Shanadari: A Barzani comrade who accompanied Barzani to the Soviet Union. He was martyred on Mount Peris in the spring of 1961.

3. Hassan Mohammed Amin Birsiyavi: Participated in the first Barzan uprising. He was martyred on Mount Qalandar in 1945.

4. As'ad Khoshavi: A comrade of Barzani, who accompanied him to the Soviet Union. He was the younger brother of Khalil Khoshavi. Because of his abilities and after the liberation of most of Dohuk Province, Barzani appointed him commander of the revolutionary forces there. When the Kurdistan Revolutionary Army was organized, he was appointed Commander of the First Corps. Despite his serious illness in Iran, the Shah did not allow him to seek treatment abroad. He died in May of 1978.

5. Milo Liri: He was martyred in the Mako area in June of 1947 by the Iranian aerial bombardment.

6. Aziz Agha Zrari: A bold and courageous commander, he was martyred at the battle of Nahla on September 12, 1945.

7. Mirza Agha Rasho: A Barzani comrade, who accompanied Barzani to the Soviet Union. He was martyred late in September of 1961 at a fierce battle in the Nahla lowlands against the government forces and mercenaries.

8. Aziz Mohammed Dolamari: A Barzani comrade who accompanied Barzani to the Soviet Union. He was Barzani's personal companion and in charge of his guards. He was martyred on September 6, 1981.

9. Nuri Shirwani: He died of typhoid in 1946 and was buried near the village of Safwan in Iranian Kurdistan.

10. Nabi Hassan [Sar Asin—Iron Head]: A Barzani comrade who accompanied him to the Soviet Union. He was nicknamed "Iron Head" for having received several shots in the head and survived. He was martyred in May of 1962.

11. Kako Mulla Ali: After Mohammed Amin Mirkhan was martyred, he was appointed Commander of his force. Paralyzed from his injuries at the fierce battle of Mount Piran, old age is catching up with him.

12. Mohammed Kooch: He was martyred at the 1945 Battle of Nahla.

13. Hassan Sulayman Kakshar: He was martyred in 1947 somewhere between Naghadeh and Ashnawiya in Iranian Kurdistan.

14. Aris Khano: A Barzani comrade in the Soviet Union. He played an important role in the struggle. Sadly, old age has caught up with him.

15. Salim Abudullah: He was martyred in 1943.

16. Hussein Jerjis Bindori: A Barzani comrade who accompanied Barzani to the Soviet Union. He died in 1966.

17. Hajji Birokhi: A hero of the September Revolution. He was wounded several times, and unfortunately he remains paralyzed.

18. Mulla Shini Qurtas Bidaroni: A Barzani comrade in the Soviet Union. After Aziz Agha Zrari was martyred, Barzani appointed him to command the Aqra front during the September Revolution. He was martyred on June 27, 1963.

19. Ibrahim Yousif Dolamari: Died of typhoid in Mahabad in 1946. This epidemic spread among the Barzanis and killed more than two thousand of them.

20. Ahmad Goran: A comrade of Ahmad Nadir, the well-known commander. He was martyred at some point during the Nahla battles of 1945.

21. Yassin Bindori: He was martyred at some point during the Nahla battles of 1945.

Appendix 2

List of Armed Men Who Accompanied Barzani in the Historic March to the Soviet Union

	Name	Place of Birth	Notes
1	Mulla Ibrahim Babakr	Hasnaka, Barozhi	
2	Ibrahim Jalal	Shikak	[Arrested by Iraq; fate unknown][1]
3	Ibrahim Hassan	Bibile, Dolamari	Martyred early in the September Revolution in 1961
4	Ibrahim Hussein Khardini	Khardin, Dolamari	Martyred in the Battle of Ba'uthra in the spring of 1963
5	Ibrahim Shaikho Ibrahim	Shanadar, Shirwani	[Died in 1982]
6	Ibrahim Qurtas Ahmad	Safti, Nizari	[Died in 1974]
7	Ibrahim Mirali	Korkayi, Shirwani	[Deceased]
8	Ibrahim Khoshavi Rashid Navkhosh	Palani, Mizori	[Arrested by Iraq on 31 July 1983; fate unknown]
9	Ahmad Brindar Chicho	Shifki, Mizori	[Arrested by Iraq on 31 July 1983; fate unknown]
10	Ahmad Paidawi	Paidawi, Mizori	Died in the USSR
11	Ahmad Hado Ahmad	Shanader, Shirwani	Died in Iraq
12	Mulla Ahmad Hado	Laira Bir, Shirwani	[Martyred]
13	Ahmad Hassan Lashkiri	Bistrei, Shirwani	[Still alive]
14	Ahmad Jaseem	Pindor, Mizori	[Still alive]
15	Ahmad Taha Younis	Isomar, Nizari	[Arrested by Iraq, fate unkown]
16	Ahmad Ali	Kani Gelan, Mizori	[Still alive]
17	Ahmad Ali Mahmud	Argosh, Mizori	[Still alive]
18	Ahmad Ali Jam	Argosh, Mizori	[Still alive]

---

1. Data in brackets are taken from Shawkat Sheikh Yazdin's 1996 Kurdish translation *Ji Mehabada Xwini Heta Keviyen Arasé* (From Bloody Mahabad to the Banks of the Araxes) of Najaf Quli Pisyan's (1949) book.

19	Mulla Ahmad Hassan Lashkiri	Bistir, Shirwani	[Still alive]
20	Ahmad Muhammed Soot	Hostan, Barozhi	[Died in 1984]
21	Ahmad Miro Anter	Biri, Doski Zhori	Remained in the USSR [living in Zawita, Iraq]
22	Ahmad Hawar Salim	Shanader, Shirwani	Died in 1972
23	Ahmad Mulla Yahya	Kaklei, Shirwani	[Deceased]
24	Ahmad Yousif Abdullah	Safti, Nizari	[Still alive]
25	Asa'd Ham [Mohammed Khalid]	Bazi-Barozhi	[Arrested by Iraqi government on 31 July, 1983; fate unknown]
26	As'ad Khoshavi	Seilki-Mizori	Died in Iran in 1977
27	As'ad Rasho Mulla	Mergasur-Shirwani	Martyred in the Battle of Mareiba in Spring 1963
28	As'ad Sulaiman Qadir	Deizo-Mizori	Martyred in summer, 1961
29	Iskandar Mulla Salam	Biri-Doski Zhori	Died in the USSR
30	Ismail Mulla Ahmad Ali	Baban-Barozhi	[Arrested by Iraq on 31 July 1983; fate unknown]
31	Ismail Mulla Ahya Mohammed	Liri-Shirwani	[Still alive]
32	Ismail Sulaiman	Teili-Mizori	[Arrested by Iraq on 31 July 1983; fate unknown]
33	Ismail Abdullah Hamira	Pindro-Mizori	Died in 1985
34	Sayyed Ismail Sayyed Ghafoor	Irwan-Nizari	Died in Zaiwa, Iran
35	Ismail Taha Ali	Bazi-Barozhi	[Arrested by Iraq on 31 July 1983; fate unknown]
36	Ismail Mohammed	Hostani-Barozhi	[Still alive]
37	Agha Ali Mirkhan	Navdari-Nizari	Died in 1972
38	Avdal Mustafa Omer	Bawa, Mergasuri	[Still alive]
39	Avdal Mikail	Bijyan-Mizori	Died in the USSR
40	Al Ali Al	Hafniki-Barozhi	[Arrested by Iraq on 31 July 1983, fate unknown]
41	Al Shaikomer	Bidarin-Shirwani	Died
42	Alyas Othman Othman	Risha-Barozhi	[Still alive]
43	Omer Hado Omer	Shanader-Shirwani	[Died in 1995]
44	Ino Dawood Shakr	Toli-Gardi	Died in the USSR
45	Babakr Sheikh Yasin	Karkamo-Shirwani	[Still alive]
46	Babakr Mohammed Zubeir	Hasini-Barozhi	[Still alive]
47	Badin Qadir Badin	Dizo-Mizori	Martyred in the summer of 1963
48	Bidro Lashiri	Bistri-Shirwani	[Still alive]
49	Bahjat Abul Qadir [Abdul Khaliq]	Aqra	Deceased
50	Bijan Jundo Ali	Shikak	Died in Iran
51	Piro Chicho Aziz	Guizi-Mizori	Martyred at the Battle of Mako, Iran in 1947
52	Piro Haso Ibrahim	Kaliti-Gardi	[Arrested by Iraq. Fate unkown]
53	Piro Yousif Hirori	Hiror-Barwari	[Still alive]
54	Tajdin Agha Tajdin	Kiloki-Shirwani	[Still alive]
55	Tajdin Mulla Hassan	Biyi-Shirwani	[Still alive]

56	Tawfiq Khawaja Mir	Miroz-Mizori	Stayed in the USSR, [returned to Kurdistan before the uprising]
57	Tailo Baqi Mohammed	Raizani-Shirwani	[Arrested by Iraq on 31 July 1983; fate unknown]
58	Taili Abdul Karim	Kiliti-Gardi	Martyred in Zait, on the Iraqi–Turkish border in 1947
59	Taimiz Arab Qatran	Seilki-Mizori	[Still alive]
60	Taimor Musa Jafar	Shikak	[Still alive]
61	Jadir Jangeer Jadir	Miroz-Mizori	Died in the USSR in 1953
62	Jadir Aziz	Argosh-Mizori	[Arrested by Iraq on 31 July 1983; fate unknown]
63	Jibrail Yahya	Biri-Doski Zhori	[Deceased]
64	Jam Ali Jam	Argosh-Mizori	[Deceased. Did not go to USSR; returned]
65	Jum'ah Mustafa Yousif	Teili-Mizori	[Arrested by Iraq on 31 July 1983; fate unknown]
66	Jamil Tawfiq 'Soor	Bamerni	Martyred at the battle of Mount Matin, Iraq, in 1963
67	Jamil Abdullah Hassan	Avdur-Mizor	[Arrested by Iraq on 31 July 1983; fate unknown]
68	Jawhar Hussein Mohammed	Seilki Mizori	Martyred at the battle of Mount Matin, Iraq, in 1963
69	Chato Mohammed Abdul Karim	Babeisiv-Mizori	[Arrested by Iraq; fate unknown]
70	Chich Hatam Shamdin	Shangil-Mizori	[Died in 1988]
71	Chicho Ahmad Had	Sarderi-Shirwani	[Deceased]
72	Haji Ali Jibrail	Dori-Shirwani	Died in Iraq in 1981
73	Haji Sheikh Amir	Zrari-Shirwani	[Still alive]
74	Haji Isa Goran	Miroz-Mizori	[Martyred in Barwari Bala]
75	Haji Malo Chawshin	Lairabir-Shirwani	[Still alive]
76	Hachik Mohammed Hachik	Chami-Shirwani	[Still alive]
77	Hadi Hasko	Vazhi-Shirwani	Martyred on May 6, 1966
78	Hali Ahmad Khoshkali	Khoshkali-Dolamari	Martyred in 1965 near the Jamhuri Hospital in Mosul, Iraq
79	Hali Ahmad Hali	Binibiya-Shirwani	Deceased
80	Hali Agha Tajdin	Kiloki-Shirwani	Died in Iraq
81	Hali Hussein	Kiloki-Shirwani	Died in Iraq
82	Hali Mohammed Qadir	Khalani-Dolamari	[Martyred in Rewanduz battle in 1995]
83	Hali Mam Hado	Sardari-Shirwani	[Arrested in Iraq; fate unknown]
84	Hajji Ahmad Omer	Rizyan-Barozhi	[Martyred]
85	Hajji Ahmad	Shila Dizi	[Deceased]
86	Hajji Abu Bakr Sheikh	Palana-Mizori	Died in Iraq
87	Hajji Haidar Sulaiman	Argosh-Mizori	[Deceased]
88	Hajji Aziz Mirza	Guizi-Mizor	[Died on his way to the USSR at the village of Diri]

89 Hajji Omer Abdullah	Kiliti-Gardi	[Martyred]
90 Hajji Mulla Ali Sulayman	Avdur-Mizori	[Arrested by Iraq on 31 July 1983; fate unknown]
91 Hado Ahmad Hado	Sarderi-Shirwani	[Still alive]
92 Hado Hassan Ahmad	Liri-Shirwani	Died in the USSR in 1954
93 Hado Fattah Mir Hamad	Gorato-Shirwani	Martyred in the summer of 1961, early in the September Revolution
94 Hado Qadir Qadir	Bawi	[Still alive]
95 Hado Hamad Mishk (Pirya)	Raizani-Shirwani	[Arrested by Iraq on 31 July 1983; fate unknown]
96 Hasko Ibrahim Abdullah	Khoshkan-Shirwani	[Still alive]
97 Hasko Chicho Abdullah	Barzan-Barozhi	Died in the USSR, 1951
98 Hasko Miro	Zrari-Shirwani	Martyred in the summer of 1961
99 Hassan Ahmad	Zhazhoki-Shirwani	[Still alive]
100 Hassan Ahmad Khan [Naz]	Shitni-Dolamari	Died in 1973
101 Mulla Hassan Bayazdin	Barzan-Barozhi	Executed in Baghdad in 1975
102 Hassan Khal Hamza	Mergasur	[Still alive]
103 Hassan Sulaiman Mulla	Zhazhok-Shirwan	[Arrested in Iraq; fate unknown]
104 Hassan Simail	Shanader-Shirwani	Stayed in the USSR
105 Hassan Swar Omer	Liri-Shirwani	Died in Iraq
106 Hassan Shamdin Hatim	Shangil-Mizori	Died in the USSR
107 Hassan Abdullah Ahmad	Seilki-Mizori	[Died in Iran]
108 Hassan Ali Hassan	Aspindal-Shirwani	[Still alive]
109 Hassan Mohammed	Gran-Gardi	Died in 1973
110 Hassan Mohammed Gardi	Raizan-Shirwani	Died in 1973
111 Hassan Mulla Mohammed Tajdin	Mergasur	[Still alive]
112 Hassan Mustafa Othman	Binibiya-Shirwani	[Deceased]
113 Hassan Mulla	Rezani-Shirwani	
114 Hassan Mulla Yahya Hassan	Dizo-Mizori	[Still alive]
115 Haso Salih Nadir	Sidan-Mizori	[Martyred]
116 Haso Faqih Ahmad	Babki-Shirwani	[Returned to USSR and stayed there]
117 Haso Mohammed Kakshar	Mergasur	[Still alive]
118 Haso Mulla	Vazhi-Shirwani	[Still alive]
119 Haso Mirkhan Ahmad	Khardin, Dolamari	[Still alive]
120 Haso Mirkhan Ghazali	Zhazhok, Shirwani	Martyred at Qandil in 1983
121 Husain Ahmad Shar	Korki-Shirwani	[Deceased]
122 Husain Bakr Beg	Bapishti	[Deceased]
123 Husain Jerjis Saeed	Pindro, Mizori	Died in Barwari Bala in 1964
124 Husain Khal Mullah Ibrahim	Babki, Shirwani	Died in January of 1981
125 Husain Rashid Shamdin	Argosh, Mizori	[Still alive]
126 Husain Sulaiman Mulla	Bazi, Barozhi	[Arrested by Iraq on 31 July 1983; fate unknown]
127 Husain Ali Horamari	Hostan, Barozhi	Died in Iran in 1983

128	Husain Faqi Hasik	Bardari, Shirwani	Martyred in 1983
129	Husain Mohammed Husain	Hopa, Gardi	[Deceased]
130	Husain Mohammed Salim	Argosh, Mizori	[Arrested by Iraq; fate unknown]
131	Husain Mir Shukr	Birokh, Gardi [Mizori]	Died in 1969
132	Hakim Mam Omer Mulla Shin	Hostan, Barozhi	[Died in Iran]
133	Hakim Yasin Taha	Pindro, Mizori	[Deceased]
134	Ham Ahmad Ham (Mami Sinami)	Argosh, Mizori	[Deceased]
135	Hamd ad-Din Abdullah	Shitni, Dolamari	Died in 1961
136	Hamo [Ahmad] Rash	Safti, Nizari	[Died in Iran]
137	Khano Joj Khan	Zhazhok, Shirwani	[Still alive]
138	Khalid Mohammed Zubeir	Hasin, Barozhi	Died in 1973
139	Khalid Mulla Ali	Raizan, Shirwani	[Deceased]
140	Khidir Khano Sheikhomer	Bidod, Shirwani	[Still alive]
141	Khidir Hassan Abbas	Khalakan, Balek	[Martyred]
142	Khidir Ramazan Ramo	Silivani	Died in Iraq
143	Khidir Isa Omer	Goski, Dolamari	[Still alive]
144	Khidir Mulla Sulaiman Othman	Banibiya, Shirwani	[Still alive]
145	Khalil Ibrahim Othman	Argosh, Mizori	[Deceased]
146	Khalil Shaikho Moho	Aspindar, Mizori	Martyred in 1963
147	Khalil Ali Sulayman	Avdur, Mizori	[Arrested by Iraq; fate unknown]
148	Khamo Shamdin Bayazdin	Moka, Mizori	[Arrested by Iraq on 31 July 1983; fate unknown]
149	Khawaja Haji Mawlud	Hopa, Gardi	[Deceased]
150	Khodadad Hassan Khan Begzadeh	Solki	[Died in Arbil]
151	Khwasti Sinjo Khwasti	Argosh, Mizori	[Didn't reach the USSR; returned]
152	Khorshid Teili	Teili, Mizori	[Martyred]
153	Khorshid Nabo	Horamari, Doski	Died in the USSR [in 1949]
154	Khorshid Yousif Sulayman	Argosh, Mizori	[Martyred]
155	Khoshawi Sofi Mohammed	Zrari, Shirwani	[Arrested in Iraq; fate unknown]
156	Khoshawi Mohammed Hassan	Bikhshash, Shirwani	Martyred in 1963
157	Khoshavi Mulla Mohammed	Kani Lanj, Shirwani	[Still alive]
158	Dawood Ali Ham [Jamil]	Argosh, Mizori	[Arrested by Iraq on 31 July 1983; fate unknown]
159	Dawood Yohanna (Lawoko)	Urmia, Raza'ia	[Died in Karaj, Iran]
160	Darwish Omer Aziz	Argoshi, Mizori	[Died in Iran]
161	Darwish Kako Qurtas	Laira Bir, Shirwani	[Still alive]
162	Darwish Miro Mohammed Amin	Birsiyav, Shirwani	[Still alive]
163	Rahman Mahmud Soor	Dargala	Stayed in the USSR
164	Mulla Rasool Mohammed	Mirgasur	Died in the USSR [in 1950]
165	Rashid Karim Sulayman	Mawat, Mizori	[Died on October 1, 1976]
166	Rashid Baqi Mohammed	Korki, Shirwani	[Still alive]

167 Rashid Hamo Haji	Shangeel, Mizori	[Still alive]
168 Rashid Rasool Qurtas	Laira Bir, Shirwani	[Still alive]
169 Rashid Aziz Rashid	Bira Kapra, Zebari	[Martyred]
170 Rashid Aziz	Argosh, Mizori	[Didn't reach the USSR; returned]
171 Rashid Nabi Abd al-Rahman	Argosh, Mizori	[Still alive]
172 Ridha Warmayi	Urmia (Raza'ia)	[Deceased]
173 Ramadhan Haji Omer	[Korran], Mizori	[Deceased]
174 Rihana Shlaymoon Khanano	Bediyal, Shirwani	[Died in Tehran, Iran]
175 Zuber Faquo Hassan	Isomari, Nizari	Martyred at the Battle of Miraiba in 1963
176 Zrar Sulayman Beg Sulayman	Dargala, Balek	[Still alive]
177 Ziyab Dar	Barzan, Barozhi	Died in Iraqi Kurdistan in 1976
178 Ziyab Ziyab Ali	Hasini, Barozhi	Died in Iraq
179 Zairo Aziz	Argosh, Mizori	Deceased, [did not go to the USSR; returned]
180 Sako Ali Mohammed	Kani Lanj, Shirwani	[Still alive]
181 Sado Qadir	Kiliti, Gardi	[Still alive]
182 Sa'di Qasim Shin	Palana, Mizori	[Died in 1993]
183 Saeed Ahmad Nadir	Bidod, Shirwani	[Still alive]
184 Saeed Abu bakr Sheikh	Palana, Mizori	[Martyred]
185 Saeed Abdul Karim	Kiliti, Gardi	[Still alive]
186 Saeed Mulla Abdullah Qasim	Shingeel, Mizori	[Arrested by Iraq on 31 July 1983; fate unknown]
187 Saeed Abdul Wahab Sheikhomer	Argosh, Mizori	[Still alive]
188 Mulla Saeed Ali	Mariwan, Iran	Died in Iran in 1981
189 Saeed Omer Jamil	Argoshi, Mizori	[Arrested by Iraq on 31 July 1983; fate unknown]
190 Saeed Mulla Omer Saeed	Biye, Shirwani	[Died in 1981]
191 Saeed Wali Beg	Raizan, Shirwani	[Still alive]
192 Salim Husain Murad	Shivi [Gwizi], Mizori	Died on 28 March 1988
193 Salim Khan Mar'an	Bidod, Shirwani	[Martyred]
194 Salim Rash	Argosh, Mizori	[Deceased]
195 Salim Rashid Salam	Babsiv, Mizori	[Still alive]
196 Salim Zubeir Mulla	Barzan, Barozhi	Victim of Sept. 29, 1971 conspiracy on Barzani's life
197 Salim Shaikhomer	Bidod, Shirwani	[Deceased]
198 Salim Saeed Faqih Abd al-Rahman	Barzan, Barozhi	[Arrested by Iraq on 31 July 1983; fate unknown]
199 Salim Aziz	Korki, Shirwani	[Still alive]
200 Salim Isa Yasin	Pindro, Mizori	[Deceased]
201 Sulaiman Beg Bakr Beg	Dargala, Balek	Died in 1974
202 Sulaiman Hado Shino	Zrari, Shirwani	[Still alive]
203 Sulaiman Hakim Yasin	Pindro, Mizori	[Still alive]
204 Sulaiman Khal Al	Bardari, Shirwani	[Deceased]
205 Sulaiman Shawali	Shanader, Shirwani	Martyred in the summer of 1963

206	Sulaiman Sharif Mulla Hassan	Barzan, Barozhi	[Deceased]
207	Sulaiman [Yasin Ali] Shivi	Shivi, Mizori	Died in the USSR
208	Sulayman Soora (Mulla)	Aqra	[Still alive]
209	Sulayman Sheikh Abd al-Salam	Barzan, Barozhi	Died in Iraqi Kurdistan in 1979
210	Sulaiman Ali Yasin	Safti, Nizari	Died in Iraq in 1984
211	Sulaiman Omer Abdullah	Khalan, Dolamari	Martyred in Lolan battle in 1959
212	Sulaiman Faquo Hassan	Isomari, Nizari	[Still alive]
213	Sulaiman Laj Husain	Aspindari, Mizori	Martyred in 1963
214	Sulaiman Mirkhan Arab	Kani Dairi, Shirwani	[Still alive]
215	Sulaiman Mirkhan Ahmad	Khardin, Dolamari	Martyred in Ba'thra's 1963 battle
216	Siyamand Aziz Aris	Mergasur	Martyred in 1966
217	Sayyed Salim Sayyed Hamid	Arbil	Martyred in 1975
218	Sayyed Faqih Sakwayi	Sakwa, Shirwani	[Arrested by Iraq on 31 July 1983; fate unknown]
219	Sayyed Mohammed Amin Sayyed	Bazi, Barozhi	Died in 1982
220	Sin Hassan Tajdin	Laira Bir, Shirwani	Died in Iran in 1981
221	Sin Ali	Safti, Nizari	Died in the USSR
222	Shakir Beg Oghez Beg	Safti, Nizari	Died in the USSR
223	Shahin Ibrahim Shahin	Zarini, Gardi	[Arrested by Iraq; fate unknown]
224	Shahin Ali	Mamiski, Shirwani	
225	Sharaf Mulla Salam	Biri, Doski Zhori	Died in 1971
226	Mulla Sharif Tajdin	Kani Dairi, Shirwani	[Martyred]
227	Sharif Qurtas	Mulla	Zrari, Shirwani [Still alive]
228	Sharif Lashkiri Husain	Bistir, Shirwani	Died in 1967
229	Shafiq Mulla Abdullah Qasim	Shangeel, Mizori	[Arrested by Iraq on 31 July 1983; fate unknown]
230	Shukr Dawood Abdi	Argosh, Mizori	[Deceased]
231	Shukr Muhammed Ahmad	Sinki, Mizori	Died in 1973
232	Mulla Shini Qurtas	Bidaron, Shirwani	Martyred on 27 June 1963 [at Peires]
233	Sheikh Yazdin Mohammed	Dawitk, Mizori	[Still alive]
234	Shaikho Babok Qurtas	Mergasur	[Still alive]
235	Shaikho Omer Agha	Boli, Balek	[Still alive]
236	Shaikho Omer Zubeir	Raziyan, Barozhi	
237	Shaikho Omer Aziz	Kani Dairi, Shirwani	[Still alive]
238	Shaikhomer [Mar'an Hassan]	Dizo, Mizori	Died in Iraq
239	Shaikhomer Ahmad Had	Sardari, Shirwani	[Deceased]
240	Shaikhomer Shinik	Dairishki, Shirwani	[Arrested by Iraq on 31 July 1983; fate unknown]
241	Shaikhomer Murad Khan	Vazhi, Shirwani	[Arrested in Iraq; fate unknown]
242	Shaikhomer Mohammed Ahmad	Zait, Gardi	[Arrested in Iraq, fate unknown]
243	Shaikhomer Mulla Younis	Shanader, Shirwani	Martyred [fighting Zebaris] in 1961

244 Sadiq Sulayman	Barzani, Barozhi	Died in Iraq
245 Salih Ahmad Husain	Vazhi, Shirwani	[Arrested in Iraq; fate unknown]
246 Salih Ahmad	Koramarki, Doski	
247 Salih Hassan	Shivi, Mizori	
248 Salih Khano Othman	Zaiwi, Nizari	[Still alive]
249 Mulla Salih Ali	Shanader, Shirwani	[Still alive]
250 Salih Tahir Khiziran	Seilki, Mizori	[Arrested by Iraq on 31 July 1983; fate unknown]
251 Salih Abdullah Faqih	Biban, Barozhi	[Still alive]
252 Salih Ali Agha Mahmud	Khairozok, Shirwani	[Arrested by Iraq on 31 July 1983; fate unknown]
253 Salih Ali Ziyab	Halinka, Barozhi	[Arrested by Iraq on 31 July 1983; fate unknown]
254 Salih Omer Haji	Palana, Mizori	[Deceased]
255 Salih Mohammed Moho	Aspindari, Mizori	[Deceased]
256 Salih Mohammed Liri	Lira, Shirwani	[Martyred]
257 Salih Mohammed Qurtas	Laira Biri, Shirwani	[Still alive]
258 Saddiq Bakhshi	Dashtazei, Shirwani	[Still alive]
259 Saddiq Khalil Yahya	Kaniyata, Shirwani	[Still alive]
260 Soorkan Mulla Bas	Mergasur, Barozhi	
261 Tahir Sharif Ali	Hamdila, Barozhi	[Arrested by Iraq on 31 July 1983; fate unknown]
262 Tahir Azo	Birsyal, Shirwani	Martyred in 1967
263 Mulla Taha	Kolaka, Nizari	Died in Iraq [Died in Zaiwa, Iran]
264 Taha Askander	Risha, Barozhi	[Arrested by Iraq on 31 July 1983; fate unknown]
265 Taha Haji Taha	Miroz, Mizori	[Died at Goratu]
266 Taha Hado Chicho (Taha Rashk)	Birokh, Gardi	Died in Zaiwa, Iran in 1981
267 Taha Yasin Shukr	Miroz, Mizori	[Deceased]
268 Taha Qadir Zahir	Hostani, Barozhi	Fate: Unknown
269 Aris Khano	Bidaron, Shirwani	[Died in Naghade, Iran]
270 Aris Mohammed Khan	Hostan, Barozhi	[Still alive]
271 Abd al-Rahman Mustafa Chalabi	Goma Shin	[Deceased]
272 Abd al-Rahma Mulla Habib	Birsyal, Shirwani	
273 Abd al-Rahman Ali Younis	Zaiwa, Nizari	Died in Iraq in 1973
274 Abd al-Rahman Mufti	Imadia	[Deceased]
275 Abd al-Rahman Yahya	Biye, Shirwani	[Still alive]
276 Abd al-Rahman Abdullah	Babke, Shirwani	[Still alive]
277 Abd al-Rahim Jaseem	Bindro, Mizori	Martyred in 1983 at Qandeel
278 Abul Karim Ibrahim	Kiliti, Gardi	[Martyred]
279 Abul Karim Ahmad	Bazi, Gardi	Died in the USSR
280 Abdullah Ahmad Aris	Mergasur	[Still alive]
281 Abdullah Hassan Abdullah	Avadur, Mizori	Died in Iraq
282 Abdullah Jasim Beg Tahir	Khairozok, Shirwani	Died in 1961 at Kakli
283 Abdullah Husain Jerjis	Bindro, Mizori	[Still alive]
284 Abdullah Hamo Osman	Gozi, Mizori	[Deceased]

285 Abdullah Dawood	Barzan, Barozhi	[Still alive]
286 Mulla Abdullah Ziyab	Zaiwa, Nizari	
287 Abdullah Saeed Ahmad	Khalan, Dolameri	[Died in Iran]
288 Abdullah Sulaiman Abd al-Rahman	Barzan, Barozhi	[Died in Iraq in 1976]
289 Abdullah Salih Abdullah	Bikoli, Mizori	[Arrested by Iraq on 31 July 1983; fate unknown]
290 Abdullah Isa Isa	Shitna, Dolamari	[Deceased]
291 Abdullah Mahmud Ismail	Hasin, Barozhi	Died in Iraq in 1973
292 Abdullah Mulla Hassan	Barzan, Barozhi	[Deceased]
293 Abdish Omer Abdish	Aspindar, Mizori	Died in Iraq
294 Othman Bayazdin	Barzan, Barozhi	Died in the USSR in 1950
295 Othman Hassan Mahmud	Baban, Barozhi	[Arrested by Iraq on 31 July 1983; fate unknown]
296 Othman Miro	Dor, Shirwani	Died in the snow on the Iranian border
297 Azo Hamo	Bidaron, Shirwani	[Still alive]
298 Azo Shaikhomer	Shanader, Shirwani	[Died in 1988]
299 Azo Qasim	Babki, Shirwani	[Still alive]
300 Azo Mulla Habib	Birsyal, Shirwani	Martyred in the summer of 1969
301 Aziz Mustafa Chalabi	Goma Shin	[Martyred]
302 Aziz Salih Aziz	Liri, Shirwani	[Still alive]
303 Aziz Aziz	Kani Lanj, Shirwani	Died in 1982
304 Aziz Qadir Miran	Kaloki, Shirwani	[Deceased]
305 Aziz Qazi Mohammed	Harir, Doski Zhori	[Alive in the USA]
306 Aziz Mamil Aziz	Laira Bir, Shirwani	Died in 1980
307 Aziz Mohammed Qadir	Khalan, Dolamari	Martyred in [Zaiwa], Iran, in 1981
308 Aziz Mohammed Jibrail	Bindro, Mizori	Died in Iraq
309 Avdal Husain Mir Shukr	Birokh, Gardi	Died in the USSR in 1953
310 Ali Agha Mahmud	Khirozok, Shirwani	Died in Iraq
311 Ali Jangeer	Miroz, Mizori	Died in the USSR
312 Ali Hasain [Shin]	Toyi, Gardi	[Still alive]
313 Ali Khan Avdal	Kanyata, Shirwani	Died in 1978
314 Mulla Ali Khido	Zhazhoki, Shirwani	Died in 1978
315 Ali Khalil Khoshavi	Seilke, Mizori	[Still alive]
316 Ali Zairo Ali	Muke, Mizori	[Still alive]
317 Ali Sulayman Fatah	Sulaymania	Died in the USSR
318 Ali Sha'ban Ismail	Hasnika, Barozhi	[Martyred in Arbil in 1995]
319 Ali Omer Mohammed	Risha, Barozhi	Died in Iraq [arrested; fate unknown]
320 Ali Ghazi Ismail	Teili, Mizori	[Deceased]
321 Ali Lachin	Karkamo, Shirwani	Died in Iraq in 1975
322 Ali Mohammed Qurtas	Laira Bir, Shirwani	[Still alive]
323 Sheikh Ali Sheikh Mohammed Siddiq	Barzan, Barozhi	[Deceased]
324 Ali Mohammed Goch	Mergasuri	Died in 1986
325 Ali Mustafa Omer	Lilok, Dolamari	[Still alive]
326 Ali Mirozi	Mirozi, Mizori	

327 Ali Younis	Bindro, Mizori	Died in the USSR
328 Amar Mulla Shini	Hostan, Barozhi	[Deceased]
329 Omer Agha Mohammed	Lilok, Dolamari	[Martyred at Ziyarat on 11 May 1995]
330 Omer Oghez	Koran, Mizori	[Deceased]
331 Omer Bapir Nabi	Zhazhok, Shirwani	[Arrested by Iraq on 31 July 1983; fate unknown]
332 Omer Bazidin Qadir	Banan, Mizori	Died in Iraq
333 Omer Othman Chimcho	Bindro, Mizori	[Arrested by Iraq on 31 July 1983; fate unknown]
334 Omer Hassan Ali	Hostan, Barozhi	[Arrested by Iraq on 31 July 1983; fate unknown]
335 Omer Husain Mohammed	Shikak	[Deceased]
336 Omer Shaikha Mir	Zrara, Shirwani	Died in the USSR in 1949
337 Omer Shaikho Abd al-Rahman	Safte, Nizari	[Arrested by Iraq on 31 July 1983; fate unknown]
338 Omer Abdullah Aziz	Hostan, Barozhi	Died in the USSR
339 Omer Faqih	Bidaron, Shirwani	[Still alive]
340 Omer Mustafa Baso	Isomar, Nizari	Died in the USSR
341 Omer Mohammed Jibrail	Bindro, Mizori	[Deceased]
342 Omer Mohammed Amin	Liri, Shirwani	[Deceased]
343 Omer Mohammed Sharif	Shikak	
344 Isa Hakim Yasin	Bindro, Mizori	[Still alive]
345 Isa Khalid Husain	Bazi, Barozhi	[Arrested by Iraq on 31 July 1983; fate unknown]
346 Isa Swar Isa	Seilki, Mizori	Martyred on 19 March 1975
347 Isa Ali Sheikh	Balana, Mizori	[Still alive]
348 Isa Mohammed Malko	Kani Lanj, Shirwani	[Arrest by Iraq; fate unknown]
349 Ghazali Ibrahim Agha	Chami, Shirwani	[Still alive]
350 Ghazali Mirkhan Ghazali	Zhazhok, Shirwani	[Martyred]
351 Faris Nu'man Shaikomer	Rezi, Gardi	[Martyred]
352 Faris Mustafa Abdullah	Hostan, Barozhi	Died in 1969
353 Faffah Beg Ahmad Khan	Shitna, Dolamari	[Martyred]
354 Fattah Omer Jamil	Argosh, Mizori	Martyred in the battle of Shirwan in 1963
355 Fayzi Othman Hamira	Bindro, Mizori	[Still alive]
356 Fayzi Malko Abdullah	Barzan, Barozhi	Died in 1971
357 Firya Malo Khaja Chawshin	Laira Biri, Shirwani	[Died in 1994]
358 Faz Hado	Bidaron, Shirwani	[Deceased]
359 Faqih Salih Bakhsh	Dashtazei	Remained in the USSR
360 Faqih Hassan Miro	Eidlib, Mizori	[Martyred]
361 Faqih Mohammed Husain	Zaiwayi, Nizari	Died in 1962
362 Qadir Ibrahim Shahin	Mamisk, Shirwani	[Arrested by Iraq on 31 July 1983; fate unknown]
363 Qadir Darwish Musa	Aqra	Died in Iraq
364 Qadir Mohammed Omer	Safti, Nizari	[Still alive]
365 Qadir Ahmad	Gora Tu, Shirwani	Died in Iraq
366 Qasim Sa'di Abdi	Argosh, Mizori	[Arrested by Iraq; fate unknown]
367 Qasim Salim Yasin	Birsiyav	[Still alive]

368 Qapo Khalid Zubeir	Barzan, Barozhi	[Arrested by Iraq on 31 July 1983; fate unknown]
369 Khadhim Mustafa Omer	Shanader, Shirwani	[Still alive]
370 Kadhim Dhulumat	Bal, Shikak	[Still alive]
371 Karim Abdullah Khidir	Shino, Iran	Died in 1965
372 Karim Malko	Barzan, Barozhi	Died in Iraq
373 Kazho Abdullah Mulla Piramir	Zhazhok, Shirwani	[Still alive]
374 Kako Husain	Kilok, Shirwani	
375 Kakshar Ahmad Aris	Mergasur	[Died in Iran]
376 Goran Isa Goran	Miroz, Mizori	[Deceased]
377 Gurgo Mahmud	Babka, Shirwani	Died in 1975 in Zaiwa, Iran
378 Laviko Mamand Maseeh	Saro Kani, Shirwani	[Still alive]
379 Malikho Mahmud Omer	Shanader, Shirwani	Died in 1967 [or in 1972]
380 Malikho Mirali Salim	Korkei, Shirwani	[Deceased]
381 Mam Husain Abdul Qadir	Koyi (Koy Sanjaq)	Died in 1969 [or 1961]
382 Mamis Rashid	Mamisk, Shirwani	[Still alive]
383 Mam Mirza Alandi	Shikak	Died in the USSR
384 Mamand Maseeh Hali	Saro Kani, Shirwani	[Deceased]
385 Majeed Avdal Nabi	Bosi, Mizori	[Still alive]
386 Majeed Haji Taha	Miroz, Mizori	[Still alive]
387 Majeed Mikaeel Haji	Bijiyan, Mizori	[Deceased]
388 Maseeh Abdullah Husain	Havnika, Barozhi	[Arrested by Iraq on 31 July 1983; fate unknown]
389 Mohammed Ahmad Rash Agha	Safti, Nizari	
390 Mohammed Agha Babakr (Bo Bakr)	Shitna, Dolamari	[Deceased]
391 Mohammed Agha Rash Shamdin	Argosh, Mizori	[Still alive]
392 Mohammed Agha Abdullah Husain	Khalan, Dolamari	[Died in Iran]
393 Mohammed Amin Hassan	Khalan, Dolamari	[Still alive]
394 Mohammed Amin Saeed Othman	Zaiwa, Nizari	[Still alive]
395 Mohammed Amin Shamdin Khalid	Argosh, Mizori	[Still alive]
396 Mohammed Amin Faqih Hassan	Dargala, Zebari	[Still alive]
397 Mohammed Amin Tahir Mahmud	Biye, Shirwani	[Still alive]
398 Mohammed Amin Faqih Othman	Bistre, Shirwani	[Still alive]
399 Mohammed Amin Krait	Biri, Doski Zhori	[Martyred]
400 Mohammed Amin Mirkhan	Mergasur, Shirwani	Martyred at the battle of Mireiba in 1962
401 Mohammed Amin Mikaeel	Mirozi, Mizori	[Deceased]
402 Mohammed Bako Babakr	Miroz, Mizori	[Deceased]
403 Mohammed Tajdin	Liri, Shirwani	Died in 1967
404 Mohammed Jundi Jibrail	Shangeel, Mizori	[Died in 1994]

405 Mohammed Hama [Jamil Ali]	Argosh, Mizori	Died in 1967
406 Mohammed Chawshin Shaikho	Argosh, Mizori	[Martyred]
407 Mohammed Cheecho Amin	Bindro, Mizori	[Still alive]
408 Mohammed Hado (Tonyar)	Zenan, Dolamari	[Still alive]
409 Mohammed Hassan Khidir	Bani, Shirwani	[Still alive]
410 Mulla Mohammed Hassan	Vazhi, Shirwani	Martyred in 1961
411 Mohammed Mohu [Hamo Osman]	Gozi, Mizori	[Martyred on 11 March 1991 in the take over of the (Ba'th) HQ in Arbil]
412 Mohammed Khal Mulla	Babka, Shirwani	Died in the USSR in 1949
413 Mohammed Rashid Mohammed	Baseiv, Mizori	[Still alive]
414 Mohammed Swar Mohammed	Miroz, Mizori	[Still alive]
415 Mohammed Sharif Bakr Mustafa	Badila	Martyred in Iraq in 1963
416 Mohammed Shukr	Barzan, Barozhi	Died in 1977
417 Mohammed Shiro Darwish	Havnika, Barozhi	Died in Iraq
418 Mohammed Taha Hassan	Safti, Nizari	[Deceased]
419 Mohammed Abdullah Husain	Bazi, Barozhi	[Arrested by Iraq; fate unknown]
420 Mohammed Abdullah Hassan	Isomar	[Still alive]
421 Mohammed Othman Mustafa	Aspindar, Mizori	[Martyred]
422 Mohammed Aziz Mohammed	Aspindar, Mizori	[Arrested by Iraq; fate unknown]
423 Mohammed Aziz	Mergasur, Shirwani	[Deceased]
424 Mohammed Ali Al	Havnika, Barozhi	[Died in Iran]
425 Mohammed Isa Mohammed	Mergasur, Shirwani	[Still alive]
426 Mohammed Faqih Yazdin	Gozi, Mizori	[Deceased]
427 Mohammed Najib	Mayi, Barwari	[Still alive]
428 Mohammed Nooh Mohammed	Aspindar, Mizori	[Still alive]
429 Mohammed Mam Rash Shamdin	Shangeel, Mizori	[Arrested by Iraq on 31 July 1983; fate unknown]
430 Mohammed Mahmud Zubeir	Barzan, Barozhi	[Died in Naghadeh, Iran]
431 Mohammed Mustafa Mulla Ham	Kani Lanj, Shirwani	Died in Iraq
432 Mohammed Mulla Mohammed	Barzan, Barozhi	Martyred in Mako battle, Iran, 1947
433 Mohammed Yasin Mohammed	Bindro, Mizori	[Deceased]
434 Mohammed Hali	Havdiyan, Diyana	[Deceased]
435 Mahmud Abd al-Rahman (Mahmud Qoola)	Babka, Shirwani	Martyred in Zawita battle in early 1962
436 Sayyed Mahmud Ajam	Urmia (Raza'ia)	[Deceased]
437 Mahmud Faqih Ahmad	Babka, Shirwani	Died in 1963
438 Mahmud Wasman	Laira Biri, Shirwani	[Arrested by Iraq; fate unknown]
439 Muho Hassan Shukr	Shangeel, Mizori	[Still alive]
440 Mamo Shivan Agha	Shanader, Shirwani	[Still alive]
441 Muho Ali Shiro	Havniki, Barozhi	[Arrested by Iraq; fate unknown]
442 Muhyeddin Babazadeh	Balanish	Died in the USSR

443 Murad Agha Shaikho	Biri, Doski Zhori	Died in 1984
444 Murad Mikaeel Haji	Bizhyan, Mizori	[Deceased]
445 Mar'an Mohammed	Kilit, Gardi	[Still alive in Turkey]
446 Mustafa Ayyob Chicho	Shivke, Mizori	[Deceased]
447 Mustafa Jangeer	Safi, Doski Zhori	[Miroz, Mizori], Died in 1986
448 Mustafa Rasho	Liloki, Dolamari	
449 Mustafa Saeed Chicho	Dawitka	[Arrested by Iraq; fate unknown]
450 Mustafa Sharif Mustafa	Alqosh, Barwari	[Deceased]
451 Corp. Mustafa Sharif	Doski	Died in the USSR
452 Mustafa Jadir Aris	Miroz, Mizori	[Martyred]
453 Mustafa Mulla Shini Hakim	Hostan, Barozhi	Died in the USSR
454 Mustafa Salih Mulla Bas	Zaiwa, Nizari	[Still alive]
455 Mustafa Abdullah Faqih Nabi	Karkamo, Shirwani	[Still alive]
456 Mustafa Abdullah Hadi	Hezan, Dolamari	[Still alive]
457 Mustafa Omer Yasin	Safti, Nizari	[Died in 1968]
458 Mustafa Gohar Mohammed	Barzan, Barozhi	[Arrested by Iraq on 31 July 1983; fate unknown]
459 Mustafa Mohammed [Haj Mamek]	Barzan, Barozhi	[Arrested by Iraq; on 31 July 1983; fate unknown]
460 Mustafa Darwish Sheikh Nirgis	Teili, Mizori	[Martyred]
461 Mufradi Khano Hado	Kani Lanj, Shirwani	[Arrested by Iraq; fate unknown]
462 Mal Sofi Ham	Hasin, Barozhi	[Deceased]
463 Mil Mohammed Amin	Liri, Shirwani	Martyred in Mako battle, Iran, 1947
464 Mulla Rash Ahmad	Mazina, Dolamari	[Still alive]
465 Malak Abdullah Sulayman	Argosh, Mizori	[Deceased]
466 Mulla Goch Khidir	Baban, Barozhi	[Arrested by Iraq; fate unknown]
467 Mulla Mirkhan Bayasdin	Dor, Shirwani	[Died in Karaj, Iran]
468 Malham Ibrahim Khan	Teili, Mizori	Died in 1965
469 Malko Zairo	Saro Kani, Shirwani	Martyred in the spring of 1966
470 Malko Abbas Mohammed Amin	Birsiyav, Shirwani	[Still alive]
471 Malo Piro Ahmad	Bistri, Shirwani	[Still alive]
472 Malo Hassan Malo	Baweh	[Still alive]
473 Malo Qurtas Saeed	Babka, Shirwani	Died in 1984
474 Musa Beg Oghez Beg	Riza, Gardi	Martyred early in September 1961
475 Musa Navkhosh	Banan, Mizori	[Deceased]
476 Miran Mirkhan	Saro Kani, Shirwani	Remained in the USSR
477 Mir Haj Ahmad	Aqra	[Died in Baghdad]
478 Mirkhan Mamand Tajdin	Kani Dairi, Shirwani	Died in March of 1963
479 Mirkhan Nabi Othman	Zrara, Shirwani	[Alive—returned half-way from USSR]
480 Mirza Agha Rasho	Mergasur, Shirwani	Martyred in September of 1961
481 Mirza Agha Abdullah Mirkhan	Mergasur, Shirwani	[Arrested by Iraq; fate unknown]

482 Miro Jooj	Bidaron, Shirwani	[Still alive]
483 Miro Hayder Karim	Toyi, Gardi	[Remained in USSR, deceased]
484 Miro Mahmud Sharwini	Sharwini, Gardi	[Deceased]
485 Miro Mohammed Ismail	Shirwan	[Still alive]
486 Miro Mirali Salim	Korkei, Shirwani	Died in 1974
487 Mikaeel Mohammed Jibrail	Bindro, Mizori	[Arrested by Iraq; fate unknown]
488 Navkhosh Husain	Laira Bir, Shirwani	Died in the USSR
489 Navkhosh Hado Qurtas	Laira Bir, Shirwani	[Still alive]
490 Nabi Hassan Abdullah	Khalan, Dolamari	Martyred in May of 1963
491 Mulla Nabi Yasin	Bindro, Mizori	Martyred in 1975
492 Nu'man Abd al-Rahman Younis	Barzan, Barozhi	Died in 1975
493 Humaira Qasim Bajo	Mamisk, Shirwani	[Arrested by Iraq; fate unknown]
494 Wasman Shaikho	Zhazhok, Shirwani	[Still alive]
495 Sheikh Wasman Mohammed Amin	Mergasuri	
496 Ways Ali Hado	Shanader, Shirwani	[Died on 1 May 1992 in Iran]
497 Yasin Rashid (Rash)	Miroz, Mizori	Martyred in 1963
498 Yasin Mikaeel Omer	Seilki, Mizori	[Still alive]
499 Yousif Abd al-Rahman Mohammed	Safti, Nizari	[Deceased]
500 Mulla Yousif Mustafa	Shanader, Shirwani	[Died in 1995]
501 Ibrahim Shaikho	Liri, Shirwani	Died in 1986
502 Qadir Abdullah	Bindro, Mizori	Died in 1985
503 [Ahmad Ali Sablaghi	Sablagh]	
504 [Jawhar Mohammed Ali	Teili	Deceased]
505 [Husain Ahmad Tahir	Isho Kor	Martyred]
506 [Husain Ibrahim Saltih	Dawitka	Martyred]
507 [Hamid Khosrowi	Iranian Kurdistan	Alive in Iraqi Kurdistan]
508 [Sa'id Aziz Abdullah	Urmia]	
509 [Hassan Mohammed	Rezan, Shirwani]	
510 [Anbar Jibrail	Bindro	Martyred]
511 [Mohammed Ali Alijan	Bazi	Martyred]
512 [Mustafa Lawe	Dur	Remained in the USSR]
513 [Hamo Sulayman Rashid	Hiran, Mizori	Martyred]
514 [Tamr Mustafa Hassan	Binave	Martyred]
515 [Husain Mulla Taha	Bidaron	Deceased]
516 [Mohammed Ali Sheikh Mamud	Argosh]	
517 [Mohammed Ali Yousif	Argosh	Arrested by Iraq; fate unknown]

Notes

General Introduction

1. Randal, Jonathan. *After Such Knowledge What Forgiveness?* Farrar, Straus and Giroux, New York, 1997 (p. 111).
2. Hamilton, Archibald M. *Road Through Kurdistan.* Faber, London, 1937.
3. The retired army commander, Al-Uqaili, characterized President Arif's visit to Kurdistan to meet Mustafa Barzani as one of 'capitulation.'
4. Exclusive interview with Mr. Massoud Barzani in the Washington D.C. area on September 26, 1998, shortly after he and Mr. Jalal Talabani had been received by Secretary of State, Ms. M. Albright, at the U.S. Department of State, where they signed the Washington Accord for furthering peace in Iraqi Kurdistan.
5. Reflecting on that, Massoud Barzani said, "I was born under the Kurdish flag. I am proud of it and ready to die for it," while addressing the Kurdish Parliament in Arbil, in August 1999.
6. Laizer, Sheri. *Martyrs, Traitors, and Patriots: Kurdistan after the Gulf War.* Zed Books, London, 1996 (pp. 167–168).
7. *Ibid.* (p. 166).
8. The New Encyclopaedia Britannica. Encyclopaedia Britannica Inc. Chicago. 1987, p. 378
9. McDowall, David. *Modern History of the Kurds.* I.B. Tauris, London, 1997 (p. 6).
10. Chaliand, Gerard. *People without a Country.* Zed Press, London, 1980 (p. 11).
11. The term *Kurdistan* has apparently become a metaphor for divisiveness. See, for instance, what this writer has to say about the difficulties of transcending disciplinary boundaries: "The field of inquiry lies at the intersection of linguistics and anthropology, sociology and hermeneutics, folklore and political science, speech and social psychology and, like Kurdistan, remains a *terra incognita* divided among competing states." See Saville-Troike, M. *The Ethnography of Communication: An Introduction.* Basil Blackwell. New York, 1982 (p. 249).
12. McDowall, David. *The Kurds* (Report no. 23) Minority Rights Group, London, 1989 (p. 15).
13. See page 157 in Vanly, Ismet. *Kurdistan in Iraq.* In G. Chaliand. *People without a Country.* Zed Press, London, 1980 (pp. 153–210).
14. "Unity, freedom, and socialism" is the motto of the Socialist Arab Ba'th Party.
15. This bloody purge occurred soon after then Vice President Saddam Hussein replaced Ahmed Hassan al-Bakr as president in 1979.
16. This is in fact fewer than one-quarter of the student body at New York University.
17. Kurdistan is 4/5 the size of France, according to Reclus, Elisée. *Novelle Geographie Universalle.* Hatchett, Paris, 1876–1894. Lucien Rambout states that the land mass of Kurdistan is 530,000 km². See his *Les Kurds et les Droit.* Les editions du Cerf, Paris, 1947.

18. Watts, Nicole. *Expanding Kurdish Studies: A Review Essay*, Bulletin of the Middle East Studies Association, MESA Press. Tucson. Arizona. 1998 (p. 19, no. 1, Vol. 32)

Chapter One

1. The Treaty of Sèvres, signed by Turkey and the Allied powers on August 10, 1920, laid out the following terms with regard to the Kurds:

Article 62:
A Commission sitting at Constantinople and composed of three members appointed by the British, French, and Italian Governments, respectively, shall draft within six months from the coming into force of the present Treaty a scheme of local autonomy for the predominantly Kurdish areas lying east of the Euphrates, south of the southern boundary of Armenia as it may be hereafter determined, and north of the frontier of Turkey with Syria and Mesopotamia,... [as defined in Article 27, II. (2) and (3). If unanimity cannot be secured on any question, it will be referred by the members of the Commission to their respective Governments. The scheme shall contain full safeguards for the protection of the Assyro-Chaldeans and other racial or religious minorities within these areas, and with this object a Commission composed of British, French, Italian, Persian and Kurdish representatives shall visit the spot to examine and decide what rectifications, if any, should be made to the Turkish frontier where, under the provisions of the present Treaty, that frontier coincides with that of Persia."]

Article 63:
The Turkish Government hereby agrees to accept and execute the decisions of both the Commissions mentioned in Article 62 within three months from their communication to the said Government.

Article 64:
If within one year from the coming into force of the present Treaty the Kurdish peoples within the areas defined in Article 62 shall address themselves to the Council of the League of Nations in such a manner as to show that a majority of the population of these areas desires independence from Turkey, and if the Council then considers that these peoples are capable of such independence and recommends that it should be granted to them, Turkey hereby agrees to execute such a recommendation, and to renounce all rights and title over these areas.

The detailed provisions for such renunciation will form the subject of a separate agreement between the Principal Allied Powers and Turkey.

If and when such renunciation takes place, no objection will be raised by the Principle Allied Powers to the voluntary adhesion to such an independent Kurdish State of the Kurds inhabiting that part of Kurdistan which has been hitherto been [sic] included in the Mosul Vilayet.

This treaty was ratified with the participation of Great Britain, France, Greece, Italy, Romania, Yugoslavia, Poland, Czechoslovakia, Belgium, Japan, the Hijaz (later to become Saudi Arabia) and the Turkish Empire, as well as a Kurdish–Armenian delegation, which had presented a joint memorandum listing the Kurdish and Armenian demands.

2. On July 24, 1923, the parties at the Lausanne Conference signed a peace treaty that annulled the Treaty of Sèvres; Kemalist Turkey kept most of Kurdish territories. The treaty made no mention whatsoever of the Kurds' national rights. It included a few

stipulations regarding the protection of minorities in Section 3, Articles 37–44. Articles 37 and 39 are as follows:

Article 37:
Turkey commits itself to recognize the stipulations contained in Articles 38–44 as fundamental laws and to ensure that no law, no regulation and no official action will stand in contradiction or opposition to these stipulations, and that no law, regulation, or official action shall prevail against them.

Article 39:
There will be no official restriction on any Turkish citizen's right to use any language he wishes, whether in private, in commercial dealings, in matters of religion, in print, or at a public gathering.

Regardless of the existence of an official language, appropriate facilities will be provided for any non-Turkish-speaking citizen of Turkey to use his own language before the courts.

3. Britain, France, and the United States of America convened in San Remo in March 1920 to decide on the affairs of Arab countries in what is known today as the San Remo Pact. The Mosul Vilayet was placed under French mandate according to secret treaties between Britain and France. At this conference, France ceded the Vilayet of Mosul to Britain. Iraq and Palestine were put under British mandate, provided that the Balfour Declaration would be fulfilled; Syria and Lebanon were put under French mandate.

[The discovery of oil in the Vilayet of Mosul was a major consideration in reapportioning the area between Britain and France, which also brought the United States into the picture. Of the San Remo Pact, Kendal Nezan writes:

> The (San Remo) Pact soon became the subject of a virulent press campaign in the U.S. The American government protested that its interests had been slighted by this "iniquitous carving-up." After laborious negotiations, the Americans obtained a 20 percent share in Turkish Petroleum, the company which held exclusive rights to the exploitation of the Mosul and Mesopotamian oil fields. The main shareholder in this company was none other than Lord Curzon, the head of the British delegation to the Lausanne Conference. The American, French, and British governments finally settled the distribution of shares in Turkish Petroleum in May 1923 (Chaliand 1980, p. 59).]

4. After the Treaty of Lausanne was signed, the League of Nations appointed a technical committee in Brussels to draw up the border between Turkey and Iraq. Later, the Council of the League formed a three-man committee (The Hungarian Teleki [a former prime minister], the Swedish [Charge d'affaires] Fersen, and the Belgian [Colonel] Paulus) to study the border problem. The committee visited both the governments of Britain and Turkey, where a Turkish member joined them. They arrived in Baghdad on January 16, 1925, and an Iraqi member was added to the committee. They traveled extensively in all areas of the Mosul Vilayet. Eventually they presented a report to the League of Nations on July 16, 1925. In it, they affirmed the suitability of the Brussels Line as a border between Turkey and Iraq. Consequently the Mosul Vilayet was annexed to Iraq.

The committee also recommended the protection of Kurdish rights, which the countries in question completely ignored. In his book *Kurds, Turks and Arabs*, Edmonds (1957) stated that, "Teleki strongly opposed any suggestion to cut a 'child in halves to satisfy two 'mothers.'"

In short, the Brussels Line is the current frontier between Turkey and Iraq.

5. [The signatories of CENTO, which was known as the Baghdad Pact, were Britain, Iran, Iraq, Pakistan, and Turkey.]

6. Actually Sheikh Mahmud was only appointed governor of Suleimaniyya Province. Later he proclaimed himself king of Kurdistan. However, he could not extend his authority much beyond the borders of Suleimaniyya Province.

Chapter Two

1. [Dervish house of the Sufi order; from the Turkish word *tekke* (dervish).]
2. [The spelling of the word Mulla reflects its Arabic pronunciation. In Kurdish it sounds like Mala (with the second vowel being long and accented). It means (Muslim) cleric.]
3. [The September Revolution lasted from September 11, 1961 (hence the name) until March 11, 1970, when Mustafa Barzani concluded the March Accord of peace with Baghdad. Then KDP Politburo member Massoud Barzani played a major role in the preceding negotiations.]
4. [The Kurdish term Binajé (sedentary) refers to the settled segment of the Harki tribe that comprised the nomadic and the sedentary.]
5. The Kurdish word for 'hope' is *hevi* in the Kurmanji dialect and *hiwa* in Sorani.
6. [Sum paid to the government to be exempt from conscription.]
7. The Assyrian stronghold located in the province of Hakkari in Turkish Kurdistan.
8. Walati Zheri is the southern part of the Mizuri tribal land—the area behind Mount Shirin, north of Barzan. Among its important villages are Shangail, Teel, Daweedaka, Babsiva, and Hizan.
9. Gangachin is a village between Urmiya and Siro, close to the Turkish border.

Chapter Three

1. The Piyaw Valley is in the Surchi region, east of Barzan. The Barzan–Khileifan Road passes through this region.
2. The Balek region is located to the north of Rewanduz and stretches across the Hamilton Road all the way up to Rayat.
3. Bira Kapra is a village in the Zebar region, located on the northern side of Mount Peris and across the Great Zab from Bilah.
4. Sa'id Wali Beg, a renowned military commander from the Shirwani tribe, was the father of Wali Beg, who was also martyred in August 1945.
5. Bilah, a village to the south of Barzan and on the bank of the Great Zab, was the district center of Zebar when administrative units were drawn for the first time. The district center was later moved to Mergasur.
6. Bradost is a tribe that resides in the area east of the Barzan region. This tribe was headed by Mahmud Beg, whereas the religious authority was in the hands of Sheikh Rasheed of Lolan. Sidakan, in the Rewanduz District, was the center of this tribe.
7. Girkal, Kolak, and Babiki are the outermost Shirwani villages, near the frontiers of the Bradost tribe.

Chapter Four

1. Hostan Village is located about ten kilometers [six miles] northeast of Barzan in the territory of the Barozhi tribe.
2. Wali Beg is the son of Sa'id. He was martyred in August 1945, when he went to the police station in Mergasur to inquire about some business on behalf of the local

citizens. He was shot and killed inside the police station. The Barzanis considered him to be one of their important leaders.

3. Ahmad Nadir is the father of Dr. Sa'id, who was elected to the Central Committee of the KDP at the Ninth Congress.
4. The Zeit Valley is the narrow gorge stretching all the way to the border behind the village of Zeit, which is west of Shirwan and near the Turkish border.

Chapter Five

1. Gavar is a Kurdish district center in the state of Hakkari in Turkish Kurdistan. Van is the center of the state of Van, known for its beautiful Lake Van and towering Mount Sipan.
2. Shamdinan is a Kurdish district in the province of Hakkari in Turkish Kurdistan. The villages of Nahri and Gardi are within its jurisdiction.
3. Samad Granaee was a peasant from Grana and an acquaintance of Barzani. He lived in Barzan between 1920 and 1926.

Chapter Six

1. See Chapter 3, on the Battle of Barqi Beg.
2. Doski Zhuri is a segment of the Doski tribe, northwest of Barzan. They were often assailed by Rekanis.
3. [al-Imam Muhammad bin Idris al-Shafi'i (768–820) was a scholar of Isamic jurisprudence.]
4. Contemporaries of Barzani from childhood, both Mustafa Abdullah and Sulayman Soorah were from the Aqra area. Both died before him. They were exemplary in their sincerity and discipline, particularly Mustafa, who was Barzani's trusted personal aide.
5. Qarani Agha Mamesh, chief of the Mamesh tribe in Iranian Kurdistan, resided in the village of Pisooh. His reputation was tarnished because of his ties to reactionary regimes.
6. Regent Abd al-Ilah, a maternal uncle of King Faisal II, was the guardian of Iraq's royal crown. He was a friend of Mahmud Beg Khalifa Samad. Because of their strong ties, the regent spent most of his summer vacations in Mergasur. He enjoyed the scenery and the fresh mountain waters.
7. Khalifah Samad was chief of the Bradost tribe. He resided in the village of Majaiser, near Sidakan. He died in 1965.
8. Kele Shin—or the Blue Stone—is a point on the Iraq–Iran border in the Shino (Oshnoviyeh) area, where the Kaila Shin was set, as legend has it, some time before Christ.

Chapter Seven

1. Haji Baba Sheikh was from a well-known religious family in the Bokan area. He was the prime minister of the Republic of Mahabad.
2. Koolij is located between Khaneh and Jildiyan, on the side of Mount Sipi-raize, it is where Mamand Agha lived.
3. Qarani Agha Mamesh was one of the influential chiefs of the Mamesh tribe. He resided in the village of Pisooh, on the Jildiyan–Mahabad Road, and he was known for his perfidious role vis-à-vis the Kurdish cause.

4. Mamek Khailani was a chief of the Khailani tribe. The Khailanis were nomads who raised sheep. In the summer, they moved to the mountains, where water and pastures were available, and return to their villages on the Harir plain in the winter.
5. Mergamir is south of Kele Shin and it is a beautiful summer resort north of Birkam Village.
6. J.K. are the initials of *Jhianaway Kurd* (Kurds' Revival). This Society was founded in Mahabad on September 16, 1943. It actively organized the Kurdish masses in Iran and established links to other parts of Kurdistan. In August 1945, this society evolved to become the KDP.

Chapter Eight

1. [The Kurdish word *peshmerga* is used to refer to a Kurdish freedom fighter. It means "the one who confronts death."]

Chapter Nine

1. Of a noble and patriotic family, Wahab Mohammed Ali Agha Jundiyan joined Barzani in Mahabad. He returned to Iraq with some others and was imprisoned for several years. He joined the September Revolution and was elected to the Revolutionary Command Council in 1964. He died of cardiac arrest on February 6, 1972.
2. Pisho Sayyed Taha was the son of Sayyed Taha bin Sheikh Mohammed Siddique Nahri, who died in 1969.
3. With the initiative of a group of Kurdish progressive officers and intelligentsia, the clandestine Hiwa Party was founded in 1939. The nationalist progressive program of the HP called for full recognition of legitimate Kurdish national rights and opposed Fascism during World War II. [The Kurdish word *hiwa* means "hope"; and thus, *Parti Hiwa* translates to Party of Hope.]

   The HP attracted a great number of erudite Kurds, including students, teachers, physicians, and lawyers and was not limited to Iraqi Kurds. In fact, the HP established good relations with the Kurds of Iran, Turkey, and Syria to organize the Kurdish liberation movement.
4. *Jash* is a term [meaning "burro" in Kurdish, disparagingly] used to describe collaborators who have betrayed their national cause and cooperated with the government against the partisans.
5. These officers were members of the HP, and they rendered great services to the revolution. They were in contact with Barzani.

Chapter Ten

1. Ahmad Shabaz was the chief of a large segment of the Baleki tribe, who resided in the village of Sarshima. He was a close associate of Barzani and well-trusted. He died in 1972.
2. Kalhi Rekani, chief of the Rekan tribe, continued to serve enemies of the Kurdish people to his death. Rashid of Lolan, religious leader of the Bradost tribe, resided in his tribal center in Lolan. Both died in the 1960s.
3. A chief of the Khoshnaw tribe, Salih Beg Miran resided in Shaqlawa. He played an important role in promoting and supporting the Barzan Revolt of 1945 and thereafter.

4. Mulla Afandi was a religious, learned, and wealthy man of Arbil.
5. Chief of the Harki tribe, Fattah Agha Harki played a positive role in 1943–1945. He died in the mid-1960s.

Chapter Eleven

1. I believe that KHK are the initials of *Komalay Hiwai Kurdistan*—the Kurdistan Hope Society.
2. D was the *nom de guerre* of an emissary. I could not find a key list or a letter among Barzani's documents.
3. B denotes Baghdad.
4. S denotes Suleimaniyya.
5. *Pileng* is the *nom de guerre* of a courier.
6. K is the symbol denoting Kirkuk.

Chapter Twelve

1. The dispute between the two families began because a son of Haji Malo kidnapped the daughter of a Birivkan sheikh. It escalated into armed clashes that killed many on both sides, including Haji Malo himself.
2. Hassan Arab Agha was the chief of the settled Shamkan tribe in the Sheikan (Ein Sifni) District.
3. *Ba'udreh* was the Yazidis' religious center in the Sheikhan District.

Chapter Thirteen

1. Hori is located north of Mount Shirin, where Sheikh Ahmad Barzani spent his summers.
2. Mohammed Siddique Barzani was the second brother of Sheikh Ahmad Barzani and older than Mulla Mustafa Barzani.
3. Sari Bardi is a strategic point between Diyana and Sidakan.
4. Located on the Rewanduz–Mergasur Road, Maidan Morik is between Mazna and Hawidyan. In this battle, the government forces were seriously defeated, and two 75-mm artillery guns were captured by the partisans. First Lieutenant Mohammed Nuri Khalil, commander of the artillery battery, was the only one who escaped, taking the breeches of both guns with him. For this action, he was awarded the Medal for Courage. In the 1960s, he was commander of the Fifth Army Division. He was known for his hatred of the Kurdish people.

Chapter Fourteen

1. *Jhianaway Kurd* (Kurds' Revival).
2. Dalanpar is a towering mountain; the borders of Iraq, Iran, and Turkey meet at its peak.
3. Sulayman Beg Dargala joined Barzani in Mahabad, accompanied him to the Soviet Union and remained loyal to the day he died in May 1974.

Chapter Fifteen

1. [On March 21, Kurds celebrate their new year. *Nawroz* means New Day.]

Chapter Sixteen

1. [*Toman* is an Iranian monetary unit.]
2. Not Khalil Khoshavi as stated by Eagleton in *The Republic of Mahabad of 1946* (Arabic translation, p. 171).
3. [*Qur'an* (*The Koran*), Chapter II ("The Cow"), verse 286.]

Chapter Seventeen

1. [The *Kurdistan Democratic Party of Iran* (KDPI) was founded on August 16, 1945. On its first anniversary, the *Kurdistan Democratic Party* (KDP) of Iraq was founded in Mahabad, seat of the nascent Kurdish Republic, on August 16, 1946.]
2. For more information about the history of the first Party Congress, see Abdullah (*Tarikh al-Hizb al-Dimuqrati al-Kurdistani, al-Iraq min Mu'tamarihi al-Ta'sisi hatta Mu'tamarihi al-Talith*, 1984).

Chapter Eighteen

1. [Eagleton is the author of *The Republic of Mahabad of 1946* (1972, Arabic Translation), which is the only full-length work dealing with the ephemeral Kurdish Republic in Iranian Kurdistan.]

Chapter Twenty

1. Barandiz Valley is between the city of Urmia and the Margavar region.
2. Qasimlu Valley is between Oshnoviyeh and Urmia.
3. General Hamayoni was the commander of the Iranian army that marched on Kurdistan.
4. Quoli Khan Qarapapagh was one of the influential chiefs of the Turkoman Qarapapagh tribe in the region of Naghadeh.

Chapter Twenty-One

1. Silweh is a village near Piranshahr, once the center of the Mamesh tribe.
2. Bisweh is a village of the Mamesh tribe.
3. [The Somay route is located] in the Shikak region, on the Iranian–Turkish border.

Chapter Twenty-Two

1. An Iranian officer, Tafrashiyan participated in the Khurasan uprising and served in the Azerbaijani Army. After the collapse of the Republic of Azerbaijan, he stayed with Barzani and participated in several battles against the Iranians. He was an artillery officer and sought refuge in Iraq in 1947. The Iraqi government handed him over to Iran in 1950. He was released from prison in 1963.
2. Nalos is a village near Oshnoviyeh.
3. Gojar is a village of the Begzadeh tribe.

4. Hoirko was one of the feudal lords of the Begzadeh region.
5. All are located in the Margavar region.
6. [The sentence is written in Arabic, but the Kurdish word *Peshawa*, which literally means pioneer or vanguard, is used to refer to Qazi Mohammed.]
7. [*Qur'an* (*The Koran*), Chapter II ("The Cow"), verse 156.]

Chapter Twenty-Four

1. As military operations began, martial law was declared for the Barzan region, its surrounding areas, and all areas where military operations were conducted.
2. Sa'id Agha Garmavi, chief of the Upper Doski tribe.
3. By others, perhaps he meant the British.
4. Royi Shin is a river separating the Barzan and Rekan regions.

Chapter Twenty-Five

1. Sarachilo was a Soviet police post in Soviet Armenia.
2. The Araxes River formed the official border between Iran and the Soviet Union.
3. Alas, ye people! Alas, ye people!
   Fallen am I into the Araxes;
   The waters are not fordable.
   I know no way to follow them.
   So old, if I take one step, I will fall down.
   Even here, grief has struck me down,
   And the agony of separation, and chill sighs.
   Doctor, I don't want your medicine; leave me alone;
   Perhaps with my sighs Fate will turn upside down
   Or overturn and turn my age with it,
   Or be struck with an atomic bomb.
   Then will my prayers be answered.
   In my earthen home I will have no wish.
   Then, preach over me in Kurdish
   And say, "You died, your wish fulfilled."

Chapter Twenty-Six

1. Given a choice between Azerbaijan and Armenia, the Barzanis opted to stay in Azerbaijan, thinking the Azeri *modus vivendi* and culture closer to their own. It became clear later that this was wrong. With all due respect to the Azeri people, Baqirov was not any different from other enemies of the Kurds.
2. [Lavrenti Pavlovich Beria (1899–1953) was head of the Soviet Secret Police (NKVD). He became the chief of the security police in Georgia in 1921 and took part in Stalin's purges and controlled labor camps in 1938 as the NKVD head. After Stalin's death in 1953, he was arrested and executed for treason.]

Chapter Twenty-Seven

1. These were some of the principal leaders.

Chapter Thirty

1. In addition to committing countless crimes against Soviet citizens and repeatedly breaking the laws of the land, this gang was also accused of having ties to the United States.

Chapter Thirty-Two

1. Mr. Voloshin was a Khrushchev aide and relative.
2. [His name is also spelled Gamal Abdel Nasser.]

Introduction to Part IV

1. [Kamil Chadirchi (1897–1968) of the Al-Ahali group and subsequently cofounder of the National Democratic Party (NDP).]
2. [CENTO comprised Britain, Iran, (monarchic) Iraq, Pakistan, and Turkey.]
3. [This occurred soon after then Vice President Saddam Hussein replaced Ahmed Hassan al-Bakr as president.]
4. ["Unity, freedom, and socialism" is the motto of the Arab Socialist Ba'th Party.]
5. [a.k.a. Lawrence of Arabia, the famous British army officer.]

Chapter Thirty-Three

1. [Born in Ta'if in Hijaz (today's Saudi Arabia), the Hashemite *Faisal I* (1883–1933), was made king of Syria by the British in 1920. When the French Army entered Syria, Faisal I withdrew to Iraq as its first king (1921–1933). He died of a heart attack in Switzerland and was buried in Baghdad. He was succeeded by his son *Ghazi*, who was born in Mecca, Hijaz, in 1912. Ghazi reigned until he was killed in a car accident in 1939. His four-year old son, *Faisal II*, the crown prince, was not crowned until May 2, 1953. In the interim, his maternal uncle, Prince Abd al-Ilah was regent. After bachelor Faisal II's coronation, Abd al-Ilah became the crown prince. Both were killed along with other members of the royal family, on the first day of the July 14 Revolution of 1958, which ended the monarchy in Iraq.]
2. [Edmonds has spelled the word the way it is pronounced in Kurdish. It is also spelled Suleimaniyya.]
3. The current Turko–Iraqi border, as it was drawn by the League of Nations' technical committee.
4. [There are three main Christian communities in Iraq: The Assyrians, the Chaldeans, and the Armenians. The affinity of the first two was the subject of discussion in 1999 in terms of representation in the parliament of Iraqi Kurdistan. The followers of Nestorious, patriarch of Constantinople in 428, are known as Assyrians or Nestorians, whereas the Nestorians who later accepted the Vatican's authority are called Chaldeans. The Iraqi Armenians have a separate church.]
5. [The countries of CENTO, which was known as the Baghdad Pact, were Britain, Iran, Iraq, Pakistan, and Turkey.]

Chapter Thirty-Four

1. Personal interview with Mr. Ali Abdullah.
2. [The United Arab Republic (UAR) comprised Egypt and Syria under the leadership of President Nasser.]

Chapter Thirty-Five

1. [The Conference was held from April 18 to 24, 1955, in Bandung, Indonesia, and was attended by the country's President Sukarno and other founders of the Movement of the Non-Aligned Countries: Nasser of Egypt and Josip Broz Tito of Yugoslavia.]
2. Returning from a special visit to Moscow to secure the Soviet backing for the July 14 Revolution, President Nasser stopped in Damascus, the capital of the northern [Syrian] region of the UAR.
3. [From the archives of the British Foreign Office—wording and formatting verbatim.]
4. [The reaction of the other CENTO (Baghdad Pact) member country, Pakistan, is contained in the document below from the archives of the British Foreign Office:

SECRET
UNITED KINGDOM HIGH COMMISSION,
KARACHI.
5th August, 1958.
EXT.358/I1.

Dear Gilberts

I have just been reading James Bowker's Dispatch No. 85 of 25th July about the recent deliberations between the Turkish President and Government with the Shah of Iran and the President of Pakistan.
2. In paragraph 3 or his Dispatch Bowker refers to a reported Turkish Intention to invade Iraq and ends his paragraph by saying that he does not know to what extent, if at all, the proposed intention had the backing of the Shah or President Mirza.
3. I can add a little to this in the light of my talk with President Iskander Mirza last Saturday. He told me that [Turkish Prime Minister] Menderes had put forward the suggestion that Turkey should invade Iraq with four divisions which could be made available at short notice. The President said he had been completely horrified at the suggestion and had spoken very forcibly to Mr. Menderes who had at last been persuaded to see the folly of such action.
4. I am sending copies of this letter to the recipients of Bowker's dispatch.

Yours sincerely,
A. C. B. Symon.]
5. It is not clear to me how the writer of the report could make such a colossal mistake which might have been willful. [These provinces have been predominantly Kurdish.]
6. [From the archives of the British Foreign Office—wording and formatting verbatim.]
7. [From the archives of the British Foreign Office—wording and formatting verbatim.]

Chapter Thirty-Six

1. [Coincidentally, the author, Massoud Barzani, was born on this day.]
2. Hamza Abdullah, Mir Haj Ahmad, Izzat Abdul Aziz, Khairullah Abdul Karim, Mustafa Khoshnaw, Mohammed Mahmud Qudsi, and Nuri Ahmad Taha.
3. Ali Abdullah told me that the Istiqlal [Independence] Party, especially its leader, Siddique Shanshal, graciously provided much assistance that day to arrange the meeting between the Kurdish delegation and the leaders of the revolution.
4. Sheikh Ahmad was supposed to have been executed under a 1947 court verdict. Iraq commuted the death sentence, but the Sheikh refused to appeal to the regent or to Nuri Sa'id for clemency, despite Britain's many promises. He remained in prison until the July 14 Revolution.
5. [He used the Kurdish expression, "*Kaka, biro biro.*"]
6. KDP archives.
7. KDP archives.
8. *Rizgari* magazine [in Kurdish], issues 2 and 3, April 1, 1959.
9. KDP archives.

Chapter Thirty-Eight

1. They were Khasrow Tawfiq, Salih al-Haidari, Hamid Othman, Nijad Ahmad, and Kamal Fuad.
2. KDP archives.
3. [A donum (from Ottoman Turkish *dönüm*) is a measure of land that is equal to 2,472 square meters or 0.618 of an acre.]
4. See [AUTHOR PLEASE PROVIDE CORRECT REF].
5. KDP archives.

Chapter Thirty-Nine

1. [*New York Times* correspondent and author of a book on the Kurds, *Journey among Brave Men* (1964).]
2. KDP archives.

Chapter Forty

1. ICP Central Committee's report as approved by the party conference in September of 1956.
2. See Document no. 57.
3. KDP archives.
4. KDP archives.

Chapter Forty-One

1. In his book, *al-Iraq al-Jumhuri* (Republican Iraq, 1974), Majid Khadduri wrote, "In January, 1960, Mulla Mustafa Barzani and Ibrahim Ahmad, supported by others mostly of the Barzan tribe, submitted their application for a party permit to the Minister of the

Interior..." I do not know how Majid Khadduri, a well-known researcher, historian, and academic, made this error, and I am not sure from what source he obtained his data. In the interests of accuracy, and to correct his information, I am providing the names of those who submitted the application to show that only [Mustafa] Barzani was from the Barzan tribe but the rest were from other areas of Kurdistan: Mustafa Barzani, Barzan; Ibrahim Ahmad, Suleimaniyya; Nuri S. Shaways, Suleimaniyya; Omer Mustafa, Koy Sanjaq; Ali Abdullah, Koy Sanjaq; Salih Abdullah Yousifi, Zakho; Mulla Abdullah Ismail, Arbil; Hilmi Ali Sharif, Khanaquin; Ismail Arif, Suleimaniyya; and Shams al-Din Mufti, Arbil.

Chapter Forty-Two

1. [The Bandung Conference of the Non-Aligned Movement countries was held from April 18 to 24, 1955, in Bandung, Indonesia.]

Chapter Forty-Three

1. KDP archives.
2. [The Ba'th Party came to power in a bloody military coup in February 1963, was over-thrown in a military coup led by Abd al-Salam Arif nine months later in November, and returned to power in another coup in 1968.]
3. KDP archives.
4. [Aziz Sharif was an Iraqi politician, prominent in the Partisans of Peace movement in the 1950s and was minister of justice in the early 1970s.]

Chapter Forty-Four

1. KDP archives.

Chapter Forty-Five

1. [Zoroastrian Kurds professed Islam circa 18 Hijrah (A.D. 640) when the Islamic conquest led by Khalid bin al-Walid and 'Ayyadh bin Ghanam reached Kurdistan.]
2. [Dr. Shakir Khasbak is a scholar and former Baghdad University professor.]
3. [Aziz Sharif was the non-Ba'thist minister of justice in the cabinet when he played a sig-nificant role in the negotiations that led to the signing of the March 11, 1970 Accord, known as the March Manifesto, between the Kurds and the Central Government in Iraq.]
4. [A career diplomat, Abd al-Rahman al-Bazzaz became prime minister under President Abd al-Rahman Arif before the Ba'th Party came to power in the coup of 1968, after which he was imprisoned and reportedly tortured to death.]

Chapter Forty-Six

1. [Mikhail Suslov (1902–1982) was a prominent figure in the Communist Party of the Soviet Union and member of its politbureau.]

Bibliography

Unpublished Sources

What I have personally heard from [Mustafa] Barzani and his compatriots.
[Mustafa] Barzani's personal notes and the documents he kept.
Archives of the Kurdistan Democratic Party (KDP), Iraq.

Published Sources[1]

In Arabic[2]

Abdullah, Ali. *Tarikh al-Hizb al-Dimuqrati al-Kurdistani, al-Iraq min Mu'tamarihi al-Ta'sisi hatta Mu'tamarihi al-Thalith* (History of the Kurdistan Democratic Party, Iraq from its Founding Congress to its Third Congress), Khabat Press,[3] 1984.

al-A'dhami, Walid Mohammed Sa'id. *Thawrat 14 Tammuz wa Abdul Karim Qasim fil Watha'iq al-Britaniyya* (The July 14 Revolution and Abdul Karim Qasim in the British Documents), first ed., al-Dar al-'Arabiyya Press, Baghdad, 1989.

al-Alawi, Hassan. *Abdul Karim Qasim, Ru'ya Ba'd al-Ishrin* (abd al-Karim Qasim: Profile after Twenty Years), al-Zawra' Press, London, 1983.

al-Bazzaz, Abd al-Rahman. *al-Iraq min al-Ihtilal Hatta al-Istiqlal* (Iraq from Occupation to Independence), 3rd ed., al-'Ani Press, Baghdad, 1967.

al-Durrah, Mahmud. *al-Qadhiyya al-Kurdiyya* (The Kurdish Cause), 2nd ed., Beirut, 1966.

—— *Thawrat al-Mawsil al-Qawmiyya: 1959* (The Nationalist Revolution of Mosul: 1958), first ed., Baghdad, 1987.

al-Hassani, Abd al-Razzaq. *Tarikh al-Wizarat al-Iraqiyya* (The History of Iraqi Cabinets), (10 vols.) Sidon, 1953–1961.

Ali, Mohammad Kazim. *al-Iraq fi 'Ahd Abd al-Karim Qasim: 1958–1963* (Iraq Under Abd al-Karim Qasim: 1958–1963), Maktabat al-Yaqzah al-'Arabiyya. Baghdad [1989].

al-Masira al-Tarikhiya ila al-Ittihad al-Suviati (The Historic March to the Soviet Union), Khabat Press, 1982.

---

1. These are sources used by Massoud Barzani. Every effort has been made to provide any missing information regarding publishers, dates, and/or page numbers but success has not always been the result.
2. Well-versed in Kurdish, Arabic, and Persian, the author, Massoud Barzani, has used references in these languages in addition to works translated into them from other languages. For the convenience of the English reader, when the original work is in English or when there is either an English translation of an entry or an English version of it, the information has been provided in the category of English references.
3. Khabat Press belongs to the KDP of Iraq.

al-Uqaili, Staff Colonel Abd al-Aziz. *Harakat Barzan al-Ula: 1932* (The First Revolts of Barzan in 1932), al-Shabab Press, Baghdad, September 17, 1955.

al-Zubaidi, Laith Abd al-Hassan. *Thawrat 14 Tammuz 1958 fil Iraq* (The Revolution of July 14, 1958 in Iraq), first ed., al-Hurriyya Press, Baghdad, 1979.

Ardalan, Ismail. *Asrar Barzan* (The Secrets of Barzan), trans. by Maruf al-Karadaghi, Baghdad, 1958.

Ashirian, S. J. *al-Haraka al-Wataniyya al-Dimuqratiyya fi Kurdistan al-Iraq: 1961–1968* (The Patriotic Democratic Movements in Iraqi Kurdistan: 1961–1968), trans. by Walato, first ed., al-Katib Press, Beirut, June 1978.

Bell, Miss [Gertrude]. *Fusul min Tarikh al-Iraq al-Hadith* (Chapters from Iraq's Recent History), trans. from English by Jafar al-Khayyat, 2nd ed., Baghdad, 1971.

Bullard, Sir Reader. *Baritanya wa al-Sharq al-Awsat* (Britain and The Middle East), trans. by Hassan Ahmad al-Salman, Baghdad, 1956.

Chiawuk, Maruf. *Ma'sat Barzan al-Mazluma* (The Tragedy of Oppressed Barzan), Baghdad, 1954.

Damalouji, Siddique. *Imarat Bahdinan al-Kurdiyya Aw Imarat al-Imadiyya* (The Kurdish Bahdinan Principality or the Imadiyya Principality), New al-Ittihad Press, Mosul, 1952.

Dimchenko, Pavel Ivanovich. *The Blazing Iraqi Kurdistan*, trans. by Dr. Jerjis Hassan, Khabat Press.

Dirasat Kurdiyya (Kurdish Studies). Issues 1 and 2, a publication of the Kurdish Institute in Paris, January, 1985.

Eagleton, William. *Jumhuriyyat Mahabad: 1946* (The Republic of Mahabad of 1946), trans. by Jerjis Fathullah, Dar al-Tali'a, Beirut, 1972.

Edmonds, C. G. *Kurd wa Turk wa Arab* (Kurds, Turks and Arabs), trans. by Jerjis Fathullah, Times Press, Baghdad, 1971.

Fathullah, Jerjis. *al-Iraq fi A'hd Qasim; Ara' wa Khawatir: 1958–1988* (Iraq Under Qasim; Views and Reflections: 1958–1988), Nabaz Press, Sweden, 1989.

Fawzi, Ahmad. *Abdussalam Mohamed Arif* (Abd al-Salam Mohammed Arif), first ed., al-Diwani Press, Baghdad, 1989.

Ghareeb, Edmond. *al-Haraka al-Qawmiyya al-Kurdiyya* (The Kurdish National Movement), al-Nahar Press, Beirut, 1973.

Hamilton, A. M. *Tariq fi Kurdistan* (Road through Kurdistan), trans. by Jerjis Fathullah, al-Jahiz Press, Baghdad, 1973.

Hay, W. R. *Sanatan fi Kurdistan* (Two Years in Kurdistan), trans. by Fuad Jamil, first ed., Baghdad, 1973.

Heikal, Mohamed Hasaneyn. *Sanawat al-Ghalayan* (The Years of Simmering), first ed., Ahram Press, Cairo, 1988.

Husayn, Khalil Ibrahim. *Mawsu'at 14 Tammuz* (The Encyclopedia of July 14), vols. 1, 2, 4, 6. Dar al-Hurriyyah Press, Baghdad, 1988–1989.

Khadduri, Majid. *al-Iraq al-Jumhuri* (Republican Iraq), first ed., United Press, Beirut, 1974.

Khairi, Su'ad, *Thawrat 14 Tammuz* (The July 14 Revolution), first ed., Ibn Khaldun Press, Beirut, October 1, 1981.

Khasbak, Shakir. *al-Kurd wa al-Mas'ala al-Kurdiyya fil Iraq* (Kurds and the Kurdish Question in Iraq), Baghdad, 1959.[4]

—— *al-Akrad* (The Kurds), Baghdad, 1972.

—— *Shimal al-Iraq* (Northern Iraq), Baghdad, 1973.

---

4. A second and more widely circulated edition appeared in Beirut in 1989.

Mustafa, Staff Colonel Hassan. *al-Barzaniyyun* (The Barzanis), Dar al-Tali'a, Beirut, 1963.
Nikitine, Basil. *al-Akrad* (The Kurds), Dar al-Rawa'i', Beirut, 1976.[5]
Sako, Fuad. *al-Usus al-Qanuniyya li Haq al-Sha'b al-Kurdi fi Taqrir al-Masir* (Legal Foundations for the right of the Kurdish People in Self Determination), al-Hadaf Press, Detroit, April 1987.
Schmidt, Dana Adams. *Rihla Bayna Rijal Shuj'an* (Journey among Brave Men), trans. by Jerjis Fathullah, Dar al-Tali'a, Beirut, 1972.
Shaways, Nuri. *Muthakkarat Nuri Shawais* (Memoirs of Nuri Shawais).
Shirko, Bela J. *al-Mas'ala al-Kurdiyya* (The Kurdish Question), Cairo, 1930.[6]
Tafrishian. *Intifadhat Khurasan* (The Khurasan Uprising).
Talabani, Jalal. *Kurdistan wa al-Haraka al-Qawmiyya al-Kurdiyya* (Kurdistan and the Kurdish National Movement), 2nd ed., al-Tali'a Press, Beirut, March 1981.
Zaki, Mohammed Amin. *Tarikh al-Kurd wa Kurdistan* (The History of Kurds and Kurdistan). Baghdad, 1961.[7]

In English
Bell, Gertrude. *The Letters of Gertrude Bell*, Boni and Liveright, New York, 1927.
Bullard, Sir William Reeder. *Britain and the Middle East from Earliest Times to 1963*, Hutchinson, London, ca. 1964.
Eagleton, William, Jr. *The Kurdish Republic of Mahabad of 1946*, Oxford University Press, Oxford, 1963.
Edmonds, C. J. *Kurds, Turks and Arabs: Politics, Travel and Research in Northern Iraq, 1919–1925*, Oxford University Press, Oxford, 1957.
Hamilton, Archibald M. *Road through Kurdistan*, Faber, London, 1937.
Hay, W. R. *Two Years in Kurdistan: Experiences of a Political Officer 1918–1920*, London, 1921.
Khadduri, Majid. *Republican Iraq: A Study in Iraqi Politics since the Revolution of 1958*, Oxford University Press, London, 1969.
Nikitine, Basil. *Les Kurdes: Etude Sociologique et historique*, Paris, 1956.
Schmidt, Dana Adams. *Journey among Brave Men*, Little, Brown & Co., Boston, 1964.

In Kurdish
Hilmi, Rafique. *Yaddasht* (Memoirs), Baghdad, 1957.
Piramerd. *Diwani Piramerd* (Anthology of [Kurdish poet and philosopher] Piramerd).
Sajjadi, Ala'uddin. *Shorishakani Kurd* (Kurds' Revolts), Baghdad, 1959.
Pisyan, Najaf Quli. *Ji Mehabada Xwini Heta Keviyen Arasé* (From Bloody Mahabad to the Banks of the Araxes), trans. into Kurdish by Shawkat Sheikh Yazdin, Arbil 1996.

5. Translated from French. Nikitine was the Russian Consul in Persia.
6. According to the Egyptian author and journalist, Durriyya 'Awni, *Bela J. Shirko* is the pseudonym of her Kurdish father Mohammed Ali 'Awni, who has also published under his real name.
7. Mohammed Amin Zaki Beg's *Khulasat Tarikh al-Kurd wa Kurdistan* (A Brief History of the Kurds and Kurdistan) was translated from Kurdish into Arabic by Mohammed Ali 'Awni and published by al-Sa'ada Press in Cairo in 1936.

In Persian

Arfa, Hassan. *Kurdha va Yak Barrasi-i Tarikhi va Siyasi* (Kurds and a Historical and Political Examination), [Tehran!] 1966.

Pisyan, Najaf Quli. *Az Mahabad-i Khonin Ta Karanahay-i Aras* (From Bloody Mahabad to the Banks of the Araxes), Tehran, 1328 [1949 A.D.].

Taraqqi Magazine, issue no. 831, Tehran, December 15, 1958.